W9-CZI-862

WITHDRAWN

Carleton College
*Laurence McKinley Gould
Library*

Gift of

Ronald Hubbs

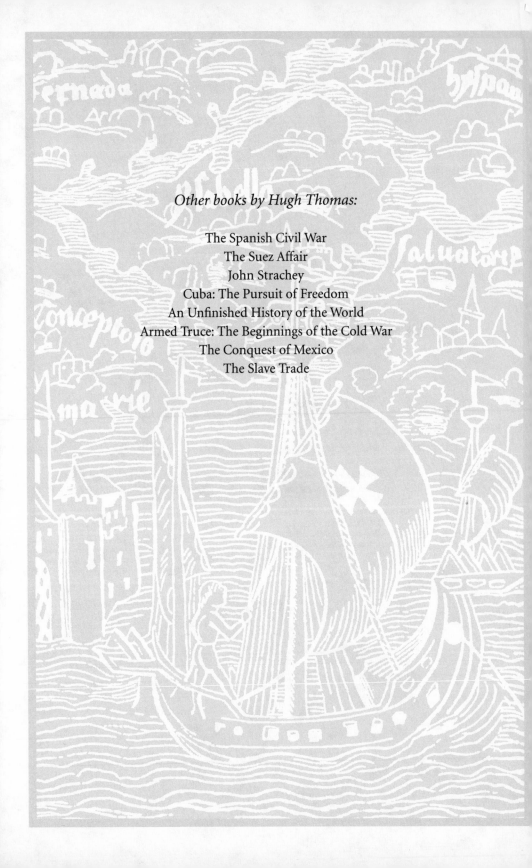

Other books by Hugh Thomas:

The Spanish Civil War
The Suez Affair
John Strachey
Cuba: The Pursuit of Freedom
An Unfinished History of the World
Armed Truce: The Beginnings of the Cold War
The Conquest of Mexico
The Slave Trade

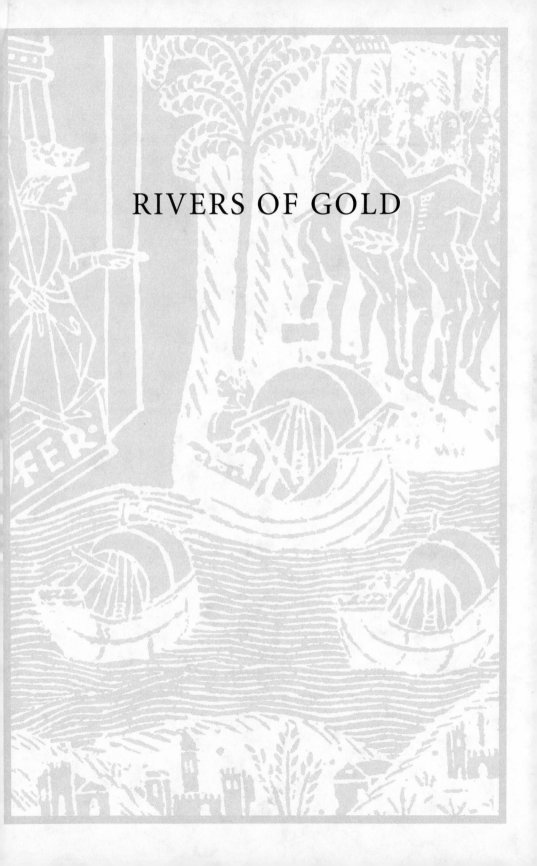

RIVERS OF GOLD

RIVERS OF GOLD

The Rise of the Spanish Empire,
from Columbus to Magellan

Hugh Thomas

Random House
New York

Copyright © 2003 by Hugh Thomas

All rights reserved under International and Pan-American
Copyright Conventions. Published in the United States by
Random House, an imprint of The Random House Publishing
Group, a division of Random House, Inc., New York.

RANDOM HOUSE and colophon are registered trademarks
of Random House, Inc.

Originally published in 2003 by Weidenfeld & Nicolson, London.

Library of Congress Cataloging-in-Publication Data

Thomas, Hugh.
Rivers of gold : the rise of the Spanish Empire, from Columbus
to Magellan / Hugh Thomas.—1st ed.
p.   cm.
Includes bibliographical references and index.
ISBN 0-375-50204-1 (hardcover)
1. Latin America—History—To 1600.   2. Latin America—
Discovery and exploration—Spanish.   3. Latin America—
Discovery and exploration—Religious aspects.   4. Spain—
History—Ferdinand and Isabella, 1479–1516.   5. Spain—
History—Charles I, 1516–1556.   6. Spain—Colonies—
America—History—16th century.   I. Title.

F1411.T36   2004

980'.01—dc22   2003069316

Printed in the United States of America on acid-free paper

Random House website address: www.atrandom.com

4 6 8 9 7 5

Book Design by Mercedes Everett

E
123
.T56
2003

011705 - 3080 X10

To carry out the conquest of so many countries, to cross so many seas and so many rivers, valleys, forests and mountains, to travel down the Amazon from its headwaters in Peru to the Atlantic, as the astonishing Orellana did, to challenge Moctezuma and Atahualpa in their own countries, as Cortés and Pizarro did, to survive the march along the banks of the wonderful river Magdalena, some great idea was needed as well as human will ("human will not calm calculation"), something which focused the mind was necessary—just as some idea was necessary to sustain the Spaniards in their seven hundred years' struggle against Islam.

AMÉRICO CASTRO,
The Structure of Spanish History

How many valleys and how many flowers, simple and delicious! How many sea coasts with very long beaches and most excellent ports! How many and what vast lakes! How many fountains both hot and cold, very close, some of them, and others farther away . . . !

GONZALO FERNÁNDEZ DE OVIEDO,
Historia general y natural de las Indias

Here I cannot forbear to commend the patient virtue of the Spaniards: we seldom or never find any nation hath endured so many misadventures and miseries as the Spaniards have done in their Indian discoveries; yet persisting in their enterprises, with invincible constancy, they have annexed to their kingdom so many goodly provinces, as bury the remembrance of all dangers past. Tempests and shipwrecks, famine, overthrows, mutinies, heat and cold, pestilence and all manner of diseases, both old and new, together with extreme poverty and want of all things needful, have been the enemies wherewith every one of their most noble discoverers, at one time or another, hath encountered.

SIR WALTER RALEIGH,
The History of the World

Contents

Book Nine

MAGELLAN AND ELCANO

Book Ten

THE NEW EMPIRE

Illustrations

Between pages 170 and 171:

Our Lady of the Catholic Monarchs, Anon., c. 1490 (Museum of the Prado, Madrid: Bridgeman Art Library).

King Fernando. Detail from *Our Lady of the Catholic Monarchs*, Anon., c. 1490 (Museum of the Prado, Madrid: Bridgeman Art Library).

Queen Isabel. Detail from *Our Lady of the Catholic Monarchs*, Anon., c. 1490 (Museum of the Prado, Madrid: Bridgeman Art Library).

King Fernando. *The Master of the Legend of the Magdalena* (Kunsthistorisches Museum, Vienna: Erich Lessing/Album).

Queen Isabel, Anon., c. 1500 (Royal Palace, Madrid: Oronoz).

Portrait of Germaine de Foix, Anon. (Museo Provincial, Valencia: Oronoz).

The tomb of the Infante Juan, sculpted by Domenico Fancelli (Church of St. Thomas, Ávila: Oronoz).

Philip the Fair by Juan de Flandes, c. 1500 (Kunsthistorisches Museum, Vienna: Erich Lessing/Album).

Princess Juana "la Loca" by Juan de Flandes, c. 1500 (Kunsthistorisches Museum, Vienna: Erich Lessing/Album).

The Archduchess Margaret by Bernaert van Orley (Royal Monastery, Brou).

Jacob Fugger by Albrecht Dürer, 1518 (Staatsgalerie, Augsburg: Erich Lessing/Album).

Bust of Charles I of Spain by Konrad Meit (Gruuthusmuseum, Bruges: Erich Lessing/Album).

Two panels, showing the meeting at Remesal between Philip the Fair and King Fernando, and a festival held in honor of Philip the Fair (Château de la Follie, Ecaussinnes).

The conquest of Oran. Photograph of a fresco by Juan de Borgoña (Mozarab Chapel, Toledo Cathedral: Oronoz).

The arms of conquest: sword for horsemen, pike, and crossbow (Museo de Ejercito, Madrid).

The Spanish Kings and Cardinal Mendoza enter Granada in 1492. Photograph of an altar carving (in the Capilla Grande, Granada: Oronoz).

Fadrique Álvarez de Toledo, Duke of Alba, by Christophe Amberger (Palacio de Liria, Madrid: Oronoz).

Íñigo López de Mendoza by Jorge Inglés (Palacio del Infantado, Guadalajara: Oronoz).

Our Lady of Granada, Cristi II, c. 1500 (Museo del Castillo, Gerona: AISA).

Between pages 298 and 299:

An *auto-de-fe* by Pedro Berruguete, c. 1490 (Museum of the Prado, Madrid: Gianni Dagli Orti/Corbis).

Pope Adrian VI by Cristofano dell 'Altissimo (Uffizi Gallery, Florence: Scala Picture Library).

Bust of Cardinal Cisneros by Bigarny (University of Madrid: Erich Lessing/Album).

Portrait of Guillaume de Croÿ, Anon. (Musée des Beaux Arts, Brussels: Erich Lessing/Album).

Mercurino de Gattinara by Jan Vermeyer (Musée des Beaux Arts, Brussels: AISA).

Paolo Toscanelli's Map, a planisphere of 1474 (National Library, Florence: Scala Picture Library).

Our Lady of La Antigua (Seville Cathedral).

Portrait of a man believed to be Christopher Columbus, c. 1446–1506, by Sebastiano del Piombo (Metropolitan Museum of Art, New York: Bettmann/Corbis).

Amerigo Vespucci, in the *Madonna della Misericordia* by Domenico Ghirlandaio (Church of Ognissanti, Florence: Archivi Alinari).

Cardinal Fonseca. Detail from Retablo in Palencia Cathedral by Jan Joest de Calcar (Palencia Cathedral: Institut Amatller d'Art Hispànic).

Portrait of Fernando Magellan, Anon. (Kunsthistorisches Museum, Vienna: Scala Picture Library).

Medal showing Hernán Cortés by Christoph Weiditz, c. 1528 (British Museum), and a drawing of Cortés by Weiditz, c. 1528 (Biblioteca Nacional, Madrid).

Preparations for the voyage, in the *Trachtenbuch* of Christoph Weiditz, c. 1528 (Biblioteca Nacional, Madrid).

Arms of conquest: sword of the Gran Capitán (Real Armería, Madrid); falconet, lombard (Museo del Ejercito, Madrid); armor of Charles V (Real Armería, Madrid).

The Wheel of Fortune in a tapestry in the Honores series, from the workshop of Pieter van Aelst, after a cartoon by Bernaert van Orley (La Granja, Segovia).

Golden objects from the Americas (Museo del Banco Central de Costa Rica, San José).

Between pages 426 and 427:

Indigenous peoples, in the *Trachtenbuch* of Christoph Weiditz, c. 1528 (Biblioteca Nacional, Madrid).

Engraving of Francisco de los Cobos, Anon., 1537, in *Catálogo de Barcía* (Biblioteca Nacional, Madrid).

Sancho de Matienzo. Photograph from the *Retablo del Convento de San Jerónimo,* Villasana de Mena, Burgos, destroyed in the civil war, 1936 (Institut Amatller d'Art Hispànic).

Laurent de Gorrevod, window of the church at Brou.

Bartolomé de las Casas (Archivo de Indias, Seville).

Scenes from Castile, in the *Trachtenbuch* of Christoph Weiditz, c. 1528 (Biblioteca Nacional, Madrid).

Scenes from the Florentine Codex, Fray Bernardino de Sahagún (Biblioteca Laurenziana, Florence).

Gold from New Spain (Museum of National History, New York).

Maps

Introduction

Vasco Núñez de Balboa wrote to the Spanish King, Fernando, in 1513 that in the settlement of Darien, in the Gulf of Urabá, now in Colombia, there were rivers of gold. They had more gold, he added, than health, and indeed were more short of food than of gold. The letter led to a gold rush to Central America from Castile. But both there and elsewhere in the Americas the search for gold was combined with the pursuit of souls for Christianity, a thirst for knowledge about the New World, and the desire for glory.

This book considers the first two generations of explorers, colonizers, governors, and missionaries who opened the way to Spain's vast American empire, which lasted over three hundred years, more than the British, the French, the Dutch, or the Russian equivalents. Many countries have later had moments of colossal energy: France in the eighteenth century, Britain in the nineteenth, Germany in the early twentieth, the United States in the late twentieth. The late fifteenth and early sixteenth centuries constituted Spain's extraordinary era (though Italians and Portuguese played a part in the story).

Each of the chapters in *Rivers of Gold* concerns itself with epoch-making events: the fall of Granada, the establishment of a united Spain, the expulsion of the Spanish Jews, Columbus's discovery of the New World, the Spanish conquests of the main Caribbean islands, the beginning of the colonization of the South American mainland at Darien, the early protests by Dominicans against the ill-treatment of the Indians, the inception of the tireless work of Father Bartolomé de las Casas on behalf of the indigenous peoples, the coming of the black slave trade, the election of Charles V as Holy Roman Emperor, the conquest of Cuba by Diego Velázquez and of Mexico by Hernán Cortés, and the journey of Magellan around the world.

I have traveled to many of the places mentioned in the book. Thus I have been to wild Madrigal de las Altas Torres, where Queen Isabel was born, and to the church of San Miguel, in Segovia, where she was proclaimed queen. I have passed many happy times in Seville and in Sanlúcar de Barrameda, from where most ships bound for the empire set off, and I have walked from Moguer to Palos, whence Columbus sailed for the first time. I know the monastery of La Rábida, where he was welcomed. I have been to Sos, where Fernando el Católico was born, and to Madrigalejo, where he died, and to Molins de Rey, where Bartolomé de las Casas talked so eloquently to Charles V. I know the bridge where Columbus was overtaken in January 1492 by a royal messenger on his way from Granada, and Santa Fe, where Columbus signed his contract with the Catholic Kings. I have seen the house where Diego Velázquez was born in Cuéllar and the site of his tertulias in Santiago de Cuba. I have visited the house where Juan Ponce de León lived in what is now the Dominican Republic and the bay where he first set foot in Puerto Rico. I know Cozumel, Isla Mujeres, and Vera Cruz, where Cortés and his predecessors landed, and I have traveled the road from there to Mexico/Tenochtitlan, the path taken by Cortés and his men in 1519. I have visited the Pearl Coast and Cartagena de Indias, on the north coast of South America. I have seen the Cabo Gracias a Dios, where Columbus met the Maya merchants in 1502, and I know St. Ann's Bay (New Seville), where he spent a sad year in Jamaica in 1503. The chief exception to my journeys to the places concerned in this book is the first Spanish mainland colony of Darien, in the Gulf of Urabá, in the north of Colombia near the Panamanian border. That territory is in the hands of guerrillas whose interests do not, it would seem, include the need to assist the visiting historian. To compensate for this lacuna, though, I have held in my own hands the first edition of *Amadís de Gaula* (Saragossa, 1508) in the British Library.

I wish to add a few words about the illustrations. The line drawings at the opening of each section are contemporary. In general that is also true of the illustrations proper, though one or two are just a little later than the subject (for example, the reproduction of the statue on the tomb of the Infante Juan by the Florentine Domenico Fancelli). The same is true of the two portraits of Cortés by Weiditz c. 1528 but from life, for Cortés was in Spain in that year and made friends with the painter. I also included a famous but much later portrait of Bartolomé de las Casas.

Chapters 33, 34, and 35 presented a serious difficulty, for I have already written a book about the conquest of Mexico. I can only hope that these three chapters will seem distilled and abbreviated wisdom. I have tried to summarize, not to repeat.

I want here to recognize the help given by numerous friends in the writing of this book. These include Homero and Betty Aridjis (Mexico), Rafael Atienza (Seville), Guillermo Baralt (Puerto Rico), Mariluz Barreiros (Tenerife), Niccoló Capponi (Florentine archives), Anthony Cheetham, Professor Edward Cooper (families of fifteenth-century Spain), Jonathan Doria (Rome), John Elliott, David Jones (librarian of the House of Lords), Felipe Fernández-Armesto, Antonia Fraser (religious questions), Carlos and Silvia Fuentes (Mexico), Manuel Antonio García Arévalo (Santo Domingo), Ian Gibson (Granada), Juan Gil (Seville), Mauricio González (Jerez de la Frontera), John and Sukie Hemming (Brazil), David Henige (problems of population), Eusebio Leal (Cuba), Vicente Lleó (Seville), Carmen Mena (Seville), Francisco Morales Padrón (Seville), Benzion Netanyahu (the Inquisition), the late Mauricio Obregón (the Caribbean), Gerarda de Orleans (Sanlúcar de Barrameda), Juan Pérez de Tudela (Madrid), Richard and Irene Pipes (the Virgin Islands), Marita Martínez del Río de Redo (Mexico), Oscar and Annette de la Renta (Santo Domingo), Arthur Ross (Jamaica), Fray Vicente Rubio (Santo Domingo), Ignacio and María Gloría Segorbe (Seville), Santiago and Isabelle Tamarón, Gina Thomas (German texts), Consuelo Varela (Seville), and En-riqueta Vila Villar (Seville).

I should like to thank the directors and librarians of the British Library in London, the London Library, the Bibliothèque Nationale in Paris, the Biblioteca Nacional in Madrid, the Archivo Histórico Nacional in Simancas, the Archivo General de Indias in Seville, the Archivo de Protocolos of Seville, and the Archivo Histórico Nacional in Madrid.

I am also most grateful to Gloria Gutiérrez of the Agencia Balcells, and Andrew Wylie, my agent in New York. I should particularly like to thank Scott Moyers, once of Random House, New York, for his meticulous work on an early version of the book, and his successor, David Ebershoff, for his support. My wife, Vanessa, kindly read the book in manuscript and also in proof. My dear friend Anthony Grigg also read the proofs. I am very grateful to Teresa Velasco for carefully typing and retyping the manuscript and to Douglas Matthews for making the index so well and so quickly.

I pay tribute to the endeavors of two scholars of the past whose work has assisted so many: Ernst Schäfer, a man in the great tradition of German scholarship, for his index to the two series of collected, previously unpublished official documents taken from the Archivo de Indias (see *CDI* and *CDIU* in the Bibliography); and Antonio Muro Orejón for his comparable work on the catalogue of American documents in the Archivo de Protocolos de Sevilla (see also the Bibliography).

Hugh Thomas, March 17, 2003

Notes

1. I have usually anglicized Spanish place-names where English versions exist: Havana, not La Habana; Seville, not Sevilla. But I have generally left Christian names as they are in Spanish: Juana, not Joanna; Fernando, not Ferdinand. I have translated titles: Duke, not Duque.

2. In Spain in the sixteenth century, people chose their surnames from any of those of their four grandparents. Thus two brothers might have quite different names: a Las Casas might be a brother of a Peñalosa.

3. I have sought to standardize all money references so that all is expressed in maravedís.

4. The large number of quotations that I take from the writings of Bartolomé de las Casas, Gonzalo Fernández de Oviedo, Columbus himself, and Peter Martyr de Anglería, as well as from the collected documents of Martín Fernández de Navarrete and the *Colección de documentos inéditos* relative to the discovery of and conquests in the New World, are my own work. The many hours that I have spent on this wonderful task have been among the most delightful of my life.

Book One

SPAIN AT THE CROSSROADS

The frontispiece of *Amadís de Gaula,* the most
popular novel of the sixteenth century.

Spain in 1492

FRANCE

Atlantic Ocean

Corunna
Santiago de Compostela
Tuy
Orense
Oviedo
Léon
Remesal
Benavente
Palencia
Valladolid
Salamanca
El Burgo de Osma
Sepúlveda
Béjar
Ávila
Santander
Laredo
Bilbao
Burgos
Calahorra
Aranda de Duero
Soria
Sigüenza
Madrid
San Sebastián
Pamplona
Sos
Saragossa
Calatayud
Barcelona

PORTUGAL

Cáceres
Trujillo
Medellín
Jerez de los Caballeros
Guadalupe
Córdoba
Écija
Seville
Huelva
Baeza
Jaén
Granada
Ronda
Malaga
Almería
Murcia
Valencia
Gandía
Palma [de Mallorca]

MINORCA
MAJORCA
IBIZA

Cadiz

Mediterranean Sea

kingdom of Castille	kingdom of Aragon
kingdom of Navarre	emirate of Granada
border	boundary of a realm or region within a kingdom

I

"This city is a wife, whose husband is the hill"

Stay awhile here on the terrace of the Alhambra and look about you.
This city is a wife, whose husband is the hill.
Girt she is by water and by flowers
Which glisten at her throat,
Ringed with streams; and, behold the groves of trees which are the
    wedding guests,
Whose thirst is assuaged by the water-channels.
The Alhambra sits like a garland on Granada's brow,
On which the stars are entwined,
And the Alhambra (may God preserve it!)
Is the ruby set above that garland.
Granada is the bride whose headdress is the Alhambra
And whose jewels and adornments are its flowers.

Ibn Zamrak, c. 1450[1]

The Spanish army and the court lay in Andalusia, at Santa Fe, a new white-painted town that King Fernando and Queen Isabel had built to serve their siege of Granada, the last Islamic city in Spain to resist the Christians. It was the autumn of 1491. Those who know the fertile plain, the *vega,* in which Granada stands, at that season of the year will recall the slight chill on the fine mornings, the blue sky at noon, and the sparkle from the high sierra to the south, with its near-perpetual snow.

Santa Fe had been constructed by soldiers, quickly, in eighty days, in the shape of a gridiron within a cross, four hundred paces long by three hundred broad. Coincidentally, and after Fernando's decision to build, a fire had destroyed the old Spanish camp nearby.[2] The Queen had narrowly escaped being burned in her tent and had had to borrow clothes from a friend. Several villages had been razed by soldiers to provide material for the new town. But Santa Fe now had a mayor, a courtier who had been among the heroes

of an earlier stage of the war against Granada: Francisco de Bobadilla, a
comendador (commander) of the military Order of Calatrava, one of the
semireligious brotherhoods that had played such a part in the Christian reconquest of Spain. Bobadilla was also *maestresala* (steward) of the monarchs
and brother of the Queen's best friend, Beatriz de Bobadilla.[3] There were
now stables for a thousand horses. The intimation of permanence, combined with the speed with which Santa Fe had been built, constituted a good
psychological weapon against the Muslims.[4]

Santa Fe is still today a small, shining, white town. One can stand in the
square before the church of Santa María de la Encarnación, built in the sixteenth century, and gaze, in four directions, down whitewashed streets.
Gates surmounted by chapels stand at the center of each of four old external
walls, which, in their gleaming paint, seem at once new and immortal. Over
the entrance to the church a lance has been sculpted, accompanying the
words "*¡Ave María!,*" to recall a Christian knight, Hernán Pérez de Pulgar,
"he of the doughty deeds,"[5] who, one night the previous winter, had gone to
Granada by a secret tunnel in order to pin, with his dagger, a parchment
bearing those same words over the entrance to the main mosque.[6]

Pulgar's action recalled that the conflict against the Muslims in which
the Christians were engaged was for many a noble war in which men wanted
to be seen to be brave. Most of the aristocracy of Spain had taken part, and
many were competing not only for the conquest of the Muslim city, but also
for fame.

Granada, 2,500 feet above sea level, is six miles to the east of Santa Fe.
From the Spanish camp, the city looked to be a congeries of palaces and
small houses, provided with water from the nearby Sierra Nevada by the two
rivers, the Xenil and the Darro, which were said to wed, as well as meet, just
short of the city. "What has Cairo to boast of, with her Nile, when Granada
has her thousand Niles?" Muslim poets asked. From tall minarets, above
mosques that the Christians believed would soon be converted into
churches, the muezzin called the faithful to prayer; but the Spanish monarchs, eight years before, had obtained from the tolerant Genoese Pope, Innocent VIII, the right of patronage to all the churches and convents
established in conquered territory.[7] Spanish soldiers on reconnaissance
could look into the besieged city: rest their eyes on the Arch of the Ears, and
on the Plaza del Arenal, not to speak of the Bibarrambla, a quarter of artisans, and a densely built residential district, El Albaicín.

The city was more like those of Muslim North Africa than of Christian
Spain, as one or two experienced Spanish soldiers would have been able to
recall. The beauty of Granada's blue tiles could not be seen from afar; nor

could the Christians see such mottoes in Arabic as "Be not the indolent one" or "There is no conqueror but God," nor even "Blessed be He who gave to the Imam Mohammed a mansion which exceeds all others in beauty." But the rumor of the wealth in Granada was diffused in the Christian camp. Some Castilians thought that there was gold in the River Darro; while the more hardheaded Spanish commanders knew that Granada's principal product was silk, sometimes brought raw from Italy but usually deriving from the mulberries of the valley of the Alpujarras to the south, beyond the Sierra Nevada, and sold in many colors in the market of *la alcaicería.*

Higher up, there was the Moorish kings' lovely, rambling palace of the Alhambra, mostly built in the thirteenth and fourteenth centuries, much of the work performed by Christian slaves. Again, from the Spanish camp, one could not see the multitude of arches leading there from one magnificent room to another. But one could glimpse the strong towers and the wooden galleries that linked them. Higher still, at the end of a path bordered by myrtle and bay, there were the beautiful gardens of the Generalife, full of remarkable fruits, where splendid fountains flowed, or so the spies said.[8]

In the town, the besiegers could observe too the strange apparel of a multitude of men and women in Muslim dress, since the latter, in burkas, appeared to be wearing shrouds, these covering not just their bodies but most of their faces. At night, they resembled ghosts.[9] Here, too, were refugees who had fled from the Christians after earlier battles, from other cities, but also people who had refused to live as subject Muslims (*mudéjares*), under the peace terms offered in such places as Huéscar, Zahara, Malaga, Alcalá de los Gazules, and Antequera.[10]

At that time, only a few of their counterparts, Christians who had survived through the generations of Mohammedan rule, *mozárabes,* lived in Granada; most of those who once had lived there had been deported, being perceived by the rulers as a potential military threat. There were some Jews in Granada, but their customs, like their food and official language, were largely Muslim. They fitted better into the life of the city than the Christians.

Granada was the capital of an emirate that had come into being in the thirteenth century, in the shadow of the fall of other Muslim monarchies in Córdoba, Valencia, Jaén, and Seville. The emirs were from a family, the Nasrids, which had emerged in the 1240s when a clever general from the little town of Arjona, in central Andalusia, seven miles south of Andújar, made himself a monarch, as Muhammad I. He made peace with the Christians, sent five hundred men to help King Fernando capture Seville, and paid a tribute to the Castilians. That relation continued indefinitely: Granada sent gold to Castile until 1480 in order to be allowed to continue her separate being, though whether that constituted what the Christians called "vassal-dom" is open to argument.

The city under siege in 1491 was the last stronghold of a Muslim empire that had once stretched to the Pyrenees and beyond, and had included such northern Spanish lands as Galicia and, for a time, Asturias. Once the Muslim civilization in Spain had been rich, sophisticated, and scholarly, and Castilians, like other Christians, had learned much from it. But European civilization no longer looked to the Muslim world for inspiration. Instead, Granada had been chosen as a redoubt, both religious and military, by the Nasrids. Though its politics had been scandalous, murder and treachery being normal in the ruling family, its mullahs had been austere.[11] Muslims elsewhere had been enjoined to flee there by their leaders: "By God, O Muslims, Granada has no equal, and there is nothing like service on the frontier during the Holy War. . . . Al-Andalus . . . where in the words of the Prophet, the living are happy and the dead are martyrs, is a city to which, as long as it endures, Christians will be led as prisoners. . . ."[12]

Despite such advice, however, many Muslims lived in cities in Christian Spain in *morerías* (Muslim ghettoes): 30,000, say, in Aragon, chiefly in the valley of the Ebro; perhaps 75,000 in Valencia; and 15,000 to 25,000 in Castile.[13] Their condition was the same, whether they were the victims of recent conquests or whether their ancestors had surrendered to Christian Spain in the thirteenth century or even before. If the Christians captured a Muslim town after a battle, the citizens would be driven out; but when a city surrendered without a fight, they would often settle to become *mudéjares*.[14] The latter decision seemed a danger for Islam. A Muslim lawyer wrote: "One has to beware of the pervasive effect of their [Christian] way of life, their language, their dress, their objectionable habits and their influence on people living with them over a long period of time, as has occurred in the case of the [Muslim] inhabitants of Ávila and other places, for they have lost their Arabic and, when the Arabic language dies out, so does devotion."[15] But then it was also contrary to Islamic law for a state to pay tribute to a Christian king, as Granada had done for most of her existence.

Christian practices varied. Navarre, an independent kingdom in the north, astride the Pyrenees, was particularly tolerant of Islam, the south of Spain less so. The use of Arabic was accepted in Valencia longer than anywhere else. Most Christian authorities in Castile, however, permitted Muslim customs. The prevailing legal code, of Alfonso X, *Las Siete Partidas,* had specified that "the Moors should live among the Christians in the same manner as . . . the Jews, observing their own laws and causing no offense to ours. . . . They ought not to have their property stolen from them."[16]

Many Christian leaders of the Spanish army at Santa Fe knew the Arab world well. Some had divided loyalties. A few knights in the Christian army were of Muslim descent, while converts or traitors had played a part in these wars for many years. The conflicts during the last generation had ensured contacts, many of doubtful respectability; and one famous Muslim family, the Abencerrajes, much spoken of in ballads, had taken refuge with the Duke of Medina Sidonia in the 1460s.[17]

In Granada, a recent monarch, Abú el-Hassan, had made a beautiful Christian prisoner, Isabel de Solís, into his favorite bride under the name of Zoraya. Hence, naturally, there was hatred between the two families of Abú el-Hassan's wives.

The war against Granada had sometimes looked a well-matched one; the Spaniards had suffered defeats. But it now seemed certain that the emirate would soon yield, and the war end with a Christian triumph. After nearly eight hundred years, the entire peninsula would be free from Muslim rule. The victory would, if it came, derive from many things: the Muslims' farming in the *vega* had been ruined by repeated Spanish raids, *talas,* carried out after 1482 from the newly conquered city of Alhama. These had destroyed wheat and olives. Other Castilian pressure had also been effective. City after city had fallen, even high-walled Ronda, which had been reputed impregnable; while, in 1487, the surrender to Castile of the port of Malaga seemed to have decided the war. Thousands were captured, hundreds enslaved.[18]

Granada still had an outlet to the sea over the mountains of the south, through the fishing village of Adra, and so, in theory, reinforcements from North Africa could be obtained. But that help did not come. The Muslim emirates in the Maghreb were friendly to the Nasrids but were at that time ineffective. Only one village outside Granada now provided fruit and vegetables, that of Alfacar, four miles away to the east on the slopes of the Sierra de Huétor. The ambivalent Emir, Boabdil, had once been a prisoner of the Christians, and though he had broken the terms of his family's agreement with the Spaniards at least once, his loyalty to his own people was now questionable. Similar divisions within Granada had played a part in the Christian victories, especially after 1485, when the Spanish armies had cut the emirate into two parts.

It was not immediately obvious why the Christian campaign against Granada had been embarked upon in the early 1480s. Here were about half a million Muslims, whose rulers surely could have been bullied into reviving the payment of tribute, which they had paid fairly consistently for 250 years. There might be a need to wipe out the memory of 1481, when Mullay Hassan, uncle of King Boabdil, had seized the Christian town of Zahara (while its governor, Gonzalo Saavedra, had been carousing in Seville) and put much of the town to the sword. But revenge had surely been accomplished by Christian victories such as those in Alhama, Lucena, and Ronda.

At all events, a decision to absorb Granada into Castile had been taken at the Cortes (parliament) of Toledo in 1480. The chronicler Alonso de Palencia, who knew Queen Isabel well, believed that she and her husband, King Fernando, had been determined to bring to an end the independence of Granada from the very beginning of their reign. They had made truces with the emirate in the 1470s when they had domestic problems to settle, but when these were resolved, they instructed Diego Merlo, a bureaucrat of Seville, to embark on an offensive against Granada.[19]

The truth is that that emirate had in the thirteenth and most of the fourteenth centuries been seen by the Christians as just a lordship for Muslims within Castile. The rulers of Granada would sometimes send soldiers to fight for the king of Castile. But it seemed recently that they had taken advantage of the civil wars in Castile and, during one of Isabel's truces, had broken the old links. Now was the time to prevent such things recurring (this was Fernando's explanation to the Mamelukes of Egypt).[20] The wealth of Granada, though overestimated, was also attractive to the Christians, even if much of it depended on Genoese merchants (the Centurioni, the Palavicini, the Vivaldi) as well as the Datini of Prato, whose trading had linked Muslim Spain to North Africa and thence to Italy, and who might not remain there after the military defeat of the last Nasrids. The Genoese were, of course, Christian, but their entrepreneurs wore that faith lightly.

Fernando and Isabel were certainly anxious to please the Pope, and the nuncio of Pope Sixtus IV, Niccoló Franco, had talked in the 1470s of the danger of the survival of a Muslim enclave in Spain, at the same time as he had spoken adversely of the Jews in Castile. That Pope had issued a crusading bull calling for war against Granada in 1479 and repeated it in another such document, Orthodoxae Fidei, of 1482. The swift conversion of mosques to churches, with a lavish ornament of crosses and bells, had been a mark of all towns captured by Christians. Christianity had always played a central role in the Castilian army. The soldiers in battle were preceded by a silver cross that had been a present from the same Pope Sixtus IV. It was carried ahead of the ensign of Santiago, the patron of the country. The army was also accompanied by the sword of San Fernando, the king who had conquered Seville in the thirteenth century, as well as by the banner of San Isidore, the

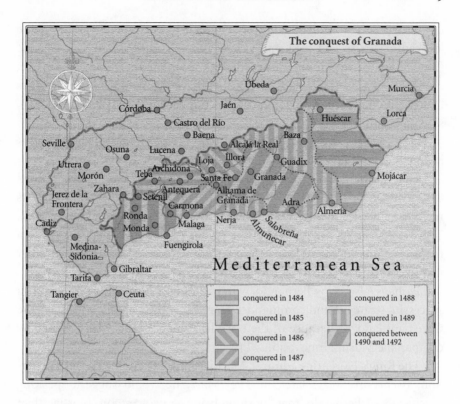

The conquest of Granada

Úbeda
Murcia
Córdoba
Jaén
Lorca
Huéscar
Castro del Río
Baena
Baza
Seville
Osuna
Lucena
Alcalá la Real
Utrera
Loja
Illora
Guadix
Morón
Teba
Archidona
Santa Fe
Granada
Mojácar
Jerez de la
Frontera
Zahara
Setenil
Antequera
Alhama de
Granada
Adra
Almería
Cadiz
Ronda
Carmona
Monda
Malaga
Nerja
Salobreña
Almuñecar
Medina-
Sidonia
Fuengirola
Mediterranean Sea
Gibraltar
Tarifa
Tangier
Ceuta

conquered in 1484	conquered in 1488
conquered in 1485	conquered in 1489
conquered in 1486	conquered between 1490 and 1492
conquered in 1487	

learned Archbishop of Seville in the seventh. Priests were always available to sing a Te Deum, and archbishops and bishops were often present in battles.

Those were days when popes and cardinals expected to win their own combats. Bishops surrounded themselves with households of armed retainers. They vied with one another in the splendor of their troops. When necessary, churchmen could fight, and fight they did, their forces being sometimes augmented by mercenaries. They had many political roles. Luis Ortega, Bishop of Jaén, had been a good governor of Alhama after its conquest in 1482, while Archbishop Carrillo had led troops (against King Fernando) at the Battle of Toro in 1475. The bishops of Palencia, Ávila, and Salamanca had respectively led 200, 150, and 120 lancers, paid by themselves, in that same civil war.[21]

One purpose of the war with Granada was probably strategic: to wrest the southeast coast of Spain from a power that had links with the feared, aggressive international menace of the Turks.[22] At least twice in the past, a king of Navarre had sought an alliance with Granada, and so to face Castile with the prospect of a war on two fronts.[23] In those circumstances, it could seem, as it had to the nuncio Franco, an outrage that there should still be an Islamic monarchy on the Spanish mainland. The Muslims of the Maghreb might one

day recover their confidence and help Granada in the future. In addition, the
last century or so had seen much skirmishing along the Christian-Islamic
frontier. Foolhardy raiding disturbed every truce and threatened commerce,
even if it inspired fine ballads concerning brave commanders on both sides
lightly mounted on splendid horses (each riding Moorish style, *"a la jineta"*),
serving beautiful ladies with style or cunning, leading at least to the capture
of a herd of cattle. In these ballads, Christians and Muslims were presented as
having the same admirable qualities, and villains were absent.

That undisciplined frontier life seemed dangerous to monarchs imbued
with a desire for efficiency, and who anyway disliked the idea of aristocrats
making names for themselves in conflicts that the Crown could not control.
There was always a risk, too, that minor raids might by accident grow into a
major war at what might turn out to be an inconvenient moment for other
reasons.

Perhaps, also, King Fernando, who had proved himself in earlier wars a
successful strategist and commander, feared that the military advantage the
Christians enjoyed because of their artillery might one day be matched by
comparable Muslim innovations.[24]

The King's Florentine admirer, Machiavelli, had a more cynical explanation: twenty-five years later, in *The Prince*, he would suggest, speaking
specifically of Fernando, that "nothing brings a prince more prestige than
great campaigns and striking demonstrations of personal abilities." So perhaps the campaign in Granada was the final settlement of a national challenge, an endeavor in which feuding noblemen might come together in loyal
agreement. Machiavelli thought that Fernando had used the conflict "to en-
gage the energies of the barons of Castile who, as they were giving their
minds to the war, had no mind for causing trouble at home. In this way,
without their realizing what was happening, he increased his standing and
his control over them."[25]

The Duke of Medina Sidonia, head of the Guzmán family, had thus become reconciled with his old enemy, the Count of Arios, the leader of the
Ponce de León family, when he brought his reinforcements to save the latter
before the walls of Alhama. Joint service to a common, national cause was
drawing these aristocrats together in a way that they had never contemplated in the days of peace. Then Juan López de Pacheco, Marquis of Villena,
an old antagonist of the Queen, had been active against the Muslims in the
Alpujarras, the fertile mountains to the south of the city, only the previous
year. Rodrígo Téllez Girón, Master of the Order of Calatrava, had opposed
Isabel in the civil war in the 1470s; but he died in her cause at Loja in 1482. A
national nobility with patriotic loyalties was thus being born.

2

"The only happy country"

Spain is the only happy country . . .

Peter Martyr, LETTERS, 1490

The court of Spain that had organized the war against Granada was peripatetic. Its annual progress had for generations resembled that of the flocks of merino sheep that were taken from summer to winter grazing grounds and back again. Recently, the royal peregrinations had been mostly in the southeast, for the needs of war had dictated royal movements. But before the hostilities, the center of Spanish power, law, and administration had been nomadic.[1] In one year, for example, the monarchs stopped in twenty separate cities, as well as in many villages where they and their suites passed uncomfortable nights between larger towns. They had been to the grain-producing territories in the south and west, as well as the basin of the Ebro, but they had not neglected the less fertile regions, such as Galicia and the Basque country. They went to wine-making areas, such as the rich land around Seville but also the central Duero valley and lower Galicia. They knew as much about seigneurial property as they did about ecclesiastical and royal holdings—those being then the three great divisions of ownership.

In 1488, the court had spent January in time-honored Saragossa, moved through Aragon to the enlightened port of Valencia at the end of April, and in May gone down to Murcia, a city whose impressive walls guarded little of interest. The monarchs then separated, the King going to a military camp near the sea, at Vera, the Queen remaining in Murcia. But in August, the court, reunited, had returned to Castile, passing a few days at Ocaña, near Toledo, which, with its abundant waters, was a favorite resort of the Queen's, before reaching austere Valladolid in September, where Isabel spent the rest of the year, while Fernando went to the rich ecclesiastical towns of Plasencia and Tordesillas, on the Duero.[2]

Such journeys had marked the fifteen years of the reign of these monarchs. They had characterized, too, the rule of their ancestors.[3] Governance

for all these rulers implied thousands of hours on horseback: the saddle constituted the real throne of Spain.[4] At each stop, cabinets and cases containing
papers and registries, chests full of Flemish tapestries and pictures, luxurious dresses and jackets from the Low Countries, files and wax for seals, all
carried on mules, would be unpacked.[5] Every Friday, whether they were in
Seville or Segovia, in Murcia or in Madrid, the monarchs would set aside
time for public audiences in which they personally dispensed justice.[6]

The palaces, monasteries, or castles where the court stayed were much
alike: usually constructed around open courtyards, the exteriors designed
for defense, not decoration, any attempt at which was, as a rule, confined to
the wall above the entrance. Little outside these edifices betrayed how many
floors there were within. Most of them had circular towers at each corner
that contrasted with the rectangular design of the place, while square-hewn
ashlars gave a finish to those corners. The Spanish monarchs thus saw much
rough construction in these houses of the noblemen where they passed so
much time.

At that time, Valladolid, the largest city of Castile after Seville, was visited
by the monarchs and the court more than anywhere else. Indeed, it was almost
a capital, and it had benefited: the new chancellery, or supreme court, of
Castile sat there permanently after 1480, and that city's elaborate College of
San Gregorio, founded by the Queen's late confessor, the erudite Alonso de
Burgos, afterwards Bishop of Palencia, was among the architectural jewels of
the time; though, like its more elaborate neighbor, the College of Santa Cruz,
commissioned by Cardinal Mendoza from the outstanding Spanish architect
Enrique de Egas, it was still being built. These new colleges seemed to the new
generation of bishops and professors to be the keys to learning. Yet it did not
occur to Spanish kings to envy, much less copy, the fixed capitals that their
sedentary neighbors in Portugal, France, and England—indeed, in Granada—
had long ago established. Had not emperors also been itinerant in Rome?[7]
These royal journeys were hard on both court and advisers, as well as monarchs (especially those who suffered from gout). The wise procuress, Celestina, was caused by Fernando de Rojas, in the great novel of that name, to
remark: "He who lives in many places rests in none"; and to quote Seneca:
"Wanderers have many dwelling places but few friends."

It is true that Isabel, then pregnant, had lingered in 1478 in Seville, while
her husband, Fernando, repaired to Barcelona and to Saragossa to face what
were perceived as threats from Islam and from France. Sometimes, too, the
King would choose a place to stay a few days where the hunting was good;
and both monarchs would often be found in Jeronymite monasteries,[8] such
as that fine agricultural enterprise, La Mejorada, near Medina del Campo, or

the Franciscan foundation of El Abrojo, near Valladolid, in order temporarily to escape the world.[9]

These stately travels had benefits: Fernando and Isabel had visited nearly every part of Spain and delivered justice there to plaintiffs. English monarchs sometimes stayed all their days in the home counties, French ones rarely left the Île de France. But Spanish rulers knew their own realms better than those others did theirs. When they sought to establish a balance between conflicting demands for land, they knew the practical effects of their own judgments. They also met provincial men who, they noted, might become good public servants.[10] It was all the more important to carry out these journeys because the kingdoms were fragmented. Fernando and Isabel had, whenever necessary, met their four Cortes (parliaments), of Cataluña and Aragon, of Valencia as well as of Castile. In 1486 they had even been in remote Galicia, primarily to repress the insurrection of a count of Lemos. Once there, however, they had not only supervised the destruction of twenty castles of potentially rebellious noblemen but had visited Santiago to pray before the tomb of the apostle St. James, and they commissioned the great Egas to build the hospice next to the late Bishop Diego Gemírez's cathedral—an edifice that, it was hoped, might constitute a school for doctors as well as a refuge for pilgrims.[11]

The monarchs had also been twice to Bilbao, while Fernando had been to Guernica in 1476, and sworn there to respect the *fueros* (rights) of Vizcaya. The only part of Spain they had not visited was Asturias, cradle of their kingdom though it was. Oviedo, the ancient capital, remained cut off behind high mountains, which a distant ancestor of Fernando and Isabel, King García of Asturias, had crossed in 912, never to return.[12]

The journeys of the monarchs were echoed, if not matched, by those of their grandest noblemen. For they, too, often had property in several parts of the kingdom and moved between these possessions regularly.[13]

The cities of Castile where the monarchs stayed can be seen in the drawings of the Flemish painter Anton van den Wyngaerde. True, the artist was active two generations later, and some of the cities that he carefully sketched grew in the interval; in the light of this increase, in the mid-sixteenth century, Fray Ignacio de Buendía wrote his curious play *El Triunfo de Llaneza*, protesting against the migration of peasants to the towns in search of money. While Barcelona boasted about 25,000 people in 1512, there were over 40,000 there in Wyngaerde's time.[14] In Buendía's day, depopulation was marked in the countryside. The character, too, of some cities changed; the new cathedral in Seville was only finished in 1506. After 1492 Granada built churches. But there is no guide so detailed as that of this Fleming, and many

of the towers, palaces, streets, and walls in 1490 must have been much as they
appear in his elegant representations.

The German painter Christoph Weiditz, of Strasbourg, recorded how
the people of Spain looked. Again, his skillful "costume book" was also compiled later, but fashion did not change quickly and Weiditz's knights, ladies,
sea captains, and black and Muslim slaves of 1528 would have been recognizable to the traveling monarchs of 1490. Are they caricatures, his laughing
merchants, his buxom countesses, his pensive sea captains, his hardworking
servants and slaves, and his bumptious horsemen?[15] Even a superficial reading of the one Spanish masterpiece of the time that retains its savor today, *La
Celestina,* suggests that the men and women of 1490 were much as Weiditz
depicted them.

The court implied, first and foremost, the presence of the Queen and the
King, placed in that order, for Queen Isabel was the more powerful of the
two. Her collaboration with King Fernando was thought a marvel at the time,
and it is difficult to think of another example of two married sovereigns acting so successfully together. William and Mary in England? The power of the
former was far greater than that of the Queen. There had been two kings in
Sparta and two consuls in Rome, but such precedents are inadequate. Perhaps surprisingly, the success of this matrimonial collaboration has never led
to a repetition of their example.

These monarchs were much seen about in Santa Fe in 1491, usually on
horseback. We can glimpse Isabel's purposeful character from looking at
her statue, praying intelligently in the Chapel Royal of the cathedral of
Granada, as designed by Felipe de Bigarny.[16] Fair-haired, blue-eyed, and
white-skinned like most of her family, the Trastámara, we see her, too, in
many portraits.[17]

In 1491, Isabel was forty years old, having been born in 1451 in a palace of
her father, King Juan II of Castile, in the small but many-towered town of
Madrigal de las Altas Torres in Castile, a day's ride south of the market city
of Medina del Campo. It was not a monumental building, merely one for
occasional residence on a royal journey. When King Juan died in 1454 and
was succeeded by Isabel's older half-brother, Enrique IV, she removed to
Arévalo, twenty miles to the east, where she lived for seven years with her increasingly senile mother. There were many *mudéjar* buildings there and
other reminders of what the Christians had conquered, *mudéjares* among
them. In Arévalo, they and the Jews were tolerated minorities, and the rabbi
and his son were well known there for their eloquence. As a child, Isabel

often visited the Franciscan monastery outside the town, founded, it is said, by St. Francis in person; she became fond of that order, and would even ask to be buried in a Franciscan habit. The Castilian childhood of Isabel marked her: the heat in summer, the cold in winter, the wild winds, the isolation of the towns.

Her education and that of her brother Alfonso were, first, entrusted to Lope de Barrientos, a Dominican who became a tolerant bishop of Segovia. Later, in her schoolroom, there was the learned Rodrigo Sánchez de Arévalo, bishop of Palencia, who had been his monarch's representative in Rome. He was a theorist who had expounded the idea of the supremacy of the Castilian monarchy in Europe; his *Historia Hispánica* claimed that, in classical times, Castile had been not only preponderant over Portugal, Navarre, and Granada, but also over France and England. His high-flown assertions about the role of his country, as well as of the monarchy, must have influenced his pupil.

From the words of one or the other of these tutors, Isabel came to admire, too, the memory of Joan of Arc. When she married, she was presented with a chronicle about the famous maid of Orléans by an anonymous poet, which encouraged Isabel to dream that she, too, might one day recover her ancestors' lost kingdoms—in her case, Granada.

Soon she and her brother Alfonso went to court to live in the suite of Queen Juana at Segovia (the Queen Mother, Queen Isabel, now scarcely coherent, remained another forty years at Arévalo).[18] Despite the charms of Segovia, then being reconstructed by royal patronage, that must have been a difficult time for her; for the Queen, if beautiful, was undisciplined and unpredictable.[19] The King, Enrique, pretended to adopt Moorish customs, Christianity was mocked, the war against Islam discounted. The memory of that wild court surely influenced Isabel's later austerity. Various marriages were suggested for her, all with political consequences: the Duke of Guyenne, brother of the King of France, an association that would have been helpful in respect of policy toward Navarre; the elderly King Afonso of Portugal, which would have removed any risk of war in the west; perhaps Richard, Duke of York, Shakespeare's future murderous monarch Richard III; the powerful nobleman Pedro Girón, brother of the Marquis of Villena, who had the authority to bring much of the landed aristocracy into submission to the Crown. But what about the promising heir to the throne of Aragon, Isabel's second cousin, Fernando, who himself had a good claim to the throne of Castile and with whom a marriage might mean a union of Spanish crowns?

In the meantime, Isabel's cause as queen-to-be was propagated by the enemies of her half-brother, the King. Civil war between two groups of

Castilian noblemen began on a low level, and in 1468, after Isabel's full brother Alfonso died in her presence at Cardeñosa, near Ávila, she became the candidate of King Enrique's enemies to the throne. They chose her because they thought they could dictate to her. She, on the other hand, seems to have been determined to win the Castilian crown at all costs and would make whatever compromise was necessary to ensure that.

The next few years in Isabel's life are complex, comprehensible perhaps only to a genealogist, a notary, or a gossip. Yet we must make an effort to understand what transpired, since these events explain the rest of Isabel's life. It was a story played out in Old Castile, in towns such as Segovia, Madrigal de las Altas Torres, with its high winds, in Arévalo, Ocaña, and, to some extent, Madrid, city of the future.

King Enrique was a singular individual, perhaps homosexual, periodically impotent (his first marriage to Blanca of Navarre had been annulled for that reason). He was impulsive, procrastinatory, occasionally creative, often lazy. But he was no fool.[20] By the aristocrats he was thought to be manageable. The dominant churchman of the realm, the turbulent Archbishop of Toledo, Alfonso Carrillo de Acuña, wanted Isabel proclaimed queen there and then, while the friend of the King since their childhood and the most powerful nobleman, Juan Pacheco, the Marquis of Villena and "majordomo" of the country, merely wanted her named heiress. Carrillo hoped that Isabel would eventually marry Fernando of Aragon. But Pacheco's candidate for her hand was Afonso of Portugal, and he and Enrique worked out an elaborate scheme to that end.[21] In the end, Isabel accepted being named the heiress, not the queen; and hesitated further about her marriage—as well she might, since she was barely seventeen years old.

King Enrique accepted Isabel as his heiress, being persuaded for a time that, though young, she was a more convincing candidate for a throne than his own daughter Juana, then aged five, nicknamed "La Beltraneja" after Beltrán, Duke of Alburquerque, "the good knight" (*el buen caballero*), for there were grounds for thinking that he might have been her true father.[22] There followed a ceremony of reconciliation of all parties at the Jeronymite monastery of Guisando, in the foothills of the Gredos Mountains. Isabel, now formally Princess of Asturias, went to live at the spa of Ocaña, near Toledo, with its delicious waters, a stronghold of Pacheco, where the King, too, had spent much of his time.

The Infanta already had that essential mechanism for political power, a well-chosen household. This was headed by her lady-in-waiting's husband, Gonzalo Chacón, once a steward to Álvaro de Luna, the longtime first minister of King Juan I; and his cousin, Gutierre de Cárdenas,[23] the court major-

domo, who had skillfully emerged from the household of Archbishop Carrillo. Ocaña was the headquarters of Cárdenas, for his palace was there, its
columns surmounted by representations of shells and coats of arms, still vis-
ible today, and it was there that Isabel lodged. Both Cárdenas and Chacón
were in 1469 young men, determined to achieve the glittering prizes of success in public life.

The learned Alonso de Palencia,[24] historian and humanist, an excellent
Latinist, already fifty, was Isabel's secretary. His treatise on how to win military victories was much read by would-be soldiers. He had worked for the
equally erudite *converso* Bishop of Burgos, Alonso de Cartagena, and, when
in Italy, had met the brightest and best of his generation. One historian hails
him as the "nearest to a full Italian humanist that Spain produced" at that
time.[25] The distinction of Isabel's advisers was an explanation for her success
as a queen. Beatriz de Bobadilla, later Marquesa of Moya, and Mencía de la
Torre were her chief ladies.

King Enrique gave Isabel the market city of Medina del Campo to provide her with an income, and authority over the mint at Ávila as well.[26]

Isabel decided on Fernando of Aragon as a husband. He was the only
male member of the royal house of Trastámara, to which she herself belonged, and was, by most judgments, her heir. He was both brave and per-
sonable. She had not met him, but she saw the benefits for Castile of such a
match. Probably a marriage with him would at least ensure her own control
of the kingdom. Union with Aragon-Cataluña would also strengthen Castile
rather than commit her to support adventures in the Atlantic, as would
surely have occurred had Isabel married the King of Portugal.

The court of Aragon had worked for this solution. Indeed, the betrothal
was a triumph for them, above all, despite the fact that the union depended
for its legality on a document forged by Antonio Veneris, the papal representative in Spain, allowing Fernando to marry someone who was within
the third degree of cousinage with him. A secret document preliminary to
the wedding was signed in January 1469. Isabel was less than eighteen, Fernando only sixteen.[27]

Aragon meant much more than the inland region of that name. It implied
also Cataluña, Valencia, and the Balearic Islands, as well as Sicily and Sardinia. Aragon had a constitutional system in which order and liberty were
remarkably well balanced and in whose elaboration merchants had played a
part. Barcelona had a good postal service, and there were important professional organizations. The parliament, or Cortes, of the Aragonese territories

was powerful, while the chief justice in Aragon was an independent magistrate who played an important part in maintaining the law. The parliamentarians of Cataluña were concerned with political liberty. King Alfonso the Magnanimous, the uncle of Fernando, who had reigned before Fernando's father, had ensured Aragonese control of southern Italy, though his long absences from Spain had weakened his standing there.[28]

At first sight the kingdom of Aragon thus seemed more dynamic as well as more diverse than Castile. But Cataluña was in economic decline. The prosperous days when she had dominated the eastern Mediterranean were over, even if Valencia's developing commerce partly compensated for the change. Further, Castile had markets in northern Europe, such as Flanders and England, through successful wool exports. These brought prosperity to the Cantabrian coast, especially to ports such as Corunna, Santander, Laredo, and San Sebastián, whose merchants had, in the late thirteenth century, devised a society, "the Brotherhood of the Marshes,"[29] to protect their interests. The fairs at Medina del Campo, the merchants of Burgos, the sea captains and traders in Seville were every year more well known outside Spain.[30] The Cortes in Castile was certainly less powerful than that in Aragon; the Crown depended less on it, for it had alternative sources of money. That Cortes was inadequate as a legislative power,[31] yet despite that Castile was growing richer.

The King, hearing of the marriage plans of his half-sister Isabel, said he would detain her if she did not leave such a decision to him. It was a reasonable reaction. But her reply was to arrange for Archbishop Carrillo to send troops to escort her to Valladolid, where she knew herself to be safe in the palace of Juan de Vivero, who was married to a cousin of Fernando and was a nephew of the Archbishop, and had himself once been royal treasurer. From there she sent Fray (Friar) Alonso de Palencia and Gutierre de Cárdenas to seek out Fernando of Aragon. The prince required no persuading to return with them to Castile, which he did romantically and without guards, though bruised by a stone thrown at him and his party in Burgo de Osma.[32]

In Dueñas, a town belonging to Pedro de Acuña, Count of Buendía, a brother of Archbishop Carrillo, between the cities of Valladolid and Palencia on the frontier of Old and New Castile, Cárdenas presented Fernando to Isabel on October 14, 1469, with the words "This is he, this is he" (Ese es, ese es), a phrase that figured thereafter on his coat of arms, in the form of linked S's. The two were mutually impressed, a notary recorded their pledges, and Isabel wrote to her brother, King Enrique: "By my letters and messengers, I now notify your highness of my determined will concerning my marriage."

She was devoted to Fernando thereafter, and resented his continual infidelities.[33] He, too, seemed enthusiastic: "I beg your ladyship that your letters
come more often because, on my life, they are very late in arriving."[34] The
Archbishop presided at the wedding in Vivero's palace in Valladolid. Few national figures were present except for Fadrique Enríquez, the Admiral of
Castile, Fernando's uncle. Two of Fernando's illegitimate children, Alonso
and Juana de Aragón, were also there.[35] Fray Pero López de Alcalá read out
the questionable bull of Pope Pius II excluding any sin of consanguinity; another, genuine, document eventually came from Rome.

The fact that Castile accounted for, say, 4 million people and Aragon
probably less than a million gave Isabel an advantage in dealing with Fernando.[36] But all the same this was a marriage warmly supported by King
Juan II of Aragon and his friends among the aristocrats and churchmen of
his country.[37]

Fernando of Aragon had been born in 1452, a year after Isabel, in a house of
the family of Sada at Sos, in the high Pyrenees in Aragon, where his mother,
Juana Enríquez, his father's second wife, had gone for the birth because of
the air. Noblemen of Aragon would in those days often travel for the summer to that valley, and the remains of their palaces can still be seen. The historian Hernando del Pulgar said of the young Fernando: "He had so singular
a grace that everyone who talked to him wanted to serve him."[38] A modern
historian wrote that he was "the most genial of the political rulers of the Renaissance."[39] He seemed affable, deft, and gallant. But his motto was: "Like
an anvil, I keep silent because of the times." In comparison to his father, he
was frugal, and so some thought him mean. He liked hunting, gambling,
and jousting, and above all, women.[40]

As with Isabel, we can see from portraits what he looked like: in the Real
Monasterio de las Huelgas in Burgos, he appears rather dark in complexion.
In the Prado, in the picture known as *Our Lady of the Catholic Monarchs*, we
see him praying, and in the Colegiata de Santa María Daroca, we observe
him with his son, the precocious Infante Juan.[41]

Fernando was a second cousin of Isabel's, on the paternal side, for
Aragon had been ruled for nearly a hundred years by a junior branch of the
Castilian Trastámaras, and he and his family still owned large Castilian
properties. All his life had been spent in the zones of power. He had been his
father's deputy in Cataluña when aged only nine, and he became lieutenant
of that realm at sixteen. These were years of civil war. Fernando became used
to making decisions in conjunction with his strong-minded mother, Juana

Enríquez, sister of the Admiral of Castile.[42] But that lady died of cancer, and the young prince, in tears, told the notables of Valencia: "Lords, you all know with what hardships my lady mother has sustained the war to keep Catalonia within the house of Aragón. I see my father old, and myself very young. Therefore, I commend myself to you and place myself in your hands, and ask you to consider me your son."

This prince knew that his marriage might lead to the union of the realms of Aragon (with Valencia and Cataluña) and Castile, and he relished the thought of it. His grandfather on his paternal side, King Fernando, called "of Antequera" because of his victory against the Moors there, had predicted and desired it.

Fernando gave much thought as to how innovations effective in Aragon or Cataluña might be introduced into Castile. But he undertook, with regard to any authority that he might exercise in Castile, to respect traditional arrangements and to sign everything jointly with Isabel.

After her wise marriage, Isabel sent a conciliatory embassy to her brother, King Enrique, assuring him of her and Fernando's loyalty. But they were suspect and the royal couple had to withdraw from Valladolid, for that city was soon besieged by a noble loyal to the Crown, the Count of Benavente. In 1470, it seemed that they held only Medina del Campo and Ávila, and even there they seemed insecure. Enrique disinherited Isabel and again declared his daughter, Juana, his heir. He tore up the compromise of Guisando. Moving to Medina del Río Seco, the seat of the Enríquez family, Isabel wrote a denunciation of the King in March 1471. Riots broke out in many cities, both sides seeming for a time to lose control of their territories to rebellious noblemen.

These troubles were repaired in 1473 after discussions in which one agent of Isabel's, her treasurer, the painstaking Alonso de Quintanilla,[43] is said to have paid thirty-six visits to the court of King Enrique at Alcalá. Others who distinguished themselves by their prudence included Andrés de Cabrera,[44] the commander of the Alcázar (fortress) in Segovia, who was now married to Isabel's friend Beatriz de Bobadilla. Another peacemaker was Pedro González de Mendoza, the young cardinal bishop of Calahorra, who (under papal pressure) changed sides, with the rest of the Mendoza family, to begin twenty years of service to Isabel.[45] At all events, the King and his half-sister spent Epiphany together in 1474 in the remodeled Alcázar of Segovia. Enrique sang, Isabel danced.[46] But it was their last celebration, for less than a year later, in December, King Enrique died suddenly in the then small town of Madrid.

When Isabel received the news, still at Segovia, she audaciously went first in mourning (white serge) to Mass at the church of San Martín. She left for the Alcázar and then repaired the next morning to the smaller, closer church of San Miguel, dazzlingly dressed in gold and, on a platform, was proclaimed Queen of Castile.[47] She took an oath; her little court (Andrés de Cabrera, Gonzalo Chacón, Gutierre de Cárdenas, and Alonso de Palencia) knelt, as did the municipal council of Segovia, which then formed the only guarantee of her grasp on national power. Cárdenas rode in front of a procession with a naked sword to recall that royal authority could punish evil-doers.[48]

The young historian Hernán Pulgar, who had been taught in the school for royal secretaries, meantime busied himself by listing queens who had come to the throne in Castile since the eighth century (he could not have done the same for Aragon since the Salic Law there deprived women of any right to rule). The Queen could also congratulate herself that the royal treasury was still in the Alcázar in Segovia and was therefore in the hands of her close friends the Cabreras. Fernando, who was in Aragon at the time of Enrique's death, hastened to Segovia, and after some apparent disagreements, his advisers and Isabel's worked out an understanding between the two of them, which was signed on January 15, 1475.

By this, the Crown of Castile was vested in the Queen. But it was agreed that Fernando and Isabel could jointly issue decrees, and approve coins and sign papers. Fernando's name was to precede that of the Queen in state documents, but her coat of arms would come first. Homage would be sworn to her, castles would be obedient to her, she alone would appoint officials in Castile, and though Fernando could, like her, apportion revenues, she alone would concede grants. The Queen would name commanders of fortresses, though her husband, because of his apparent prowess in war, would name those to command armies. All orders of Fernando in relation to war would automatically be valid, but not otherwise. The two would administer justice jointly when they were together but could do so separately when apart for both kingdoms, though they would always take care to be mindful of the Council of the Realm, the influential committee then composed of noble-men, clergy, and a few educated laymen, or *letrados*. The two would be jointly considered kings of Castile, León, and Sicily and princes of Aragon. Should Fernando die, Isabel would inherit the Crown of Aragon, despite the fact that women never as a rule reigned there. It was also understood that should Isabel die, her eldest son (or daughter) would succeed, not Fernando.

Fernando accepted these arrangements, though he disliked some of the concessions that Isabel's advisers had persuaded him to accept, and he made plans to abandon Segovia. Archbishop Carrillo, angry at not having been consulted, berated both Isabel and Fernando, and announced that he, too, was leaving. Isabel ignored the Archbishop, but begged Fernando to remain. He did stay, and Isabel accepted some small changes in the agreed declarations; for example, they would have a joint coat of arms, one seal only would be used, and both their portraits would appear on coinage. They would also have a joint household.[49] These institutional arrangements, with Castile as the dominant partner in a unique union, endured.

Isabel was thereafter guided by two men, apart from her astute husband: first, Mendoza, the Cardinal, now Archbishop of Seville; and second, Hernando de Talavera, the Jeronymite prior of Our Lady of the Prado in Valladolid, her confessor after 1475.

The able, subtle, and handsome Cardinal Pedro González de Mendoza, the aristocrat of the Spanish Church, the "third King of Spain," as he would soon be known, in his red hat and cloak, presided over the Council of the Realm, just as he would ride by the Queen's side in battle. Aged sixty-two in 1491, he was the ninth and youngest son of the enlightened Íñigo Hurtado de Mendoza, Marquis of Santillana, a poet and humane aristocrat, a man cultivated enough to rival any prince in Italy. Las Casas, in his history, wrote of the Cardinal's "great virtue, prudence, and fidelity to the monarchs," as well as "his generosity of spirit and lineage."[50] Few would dwell on his private virtues but his other qualities were difficult to contest. The Mendoza family was the most powerful in Castile, with members of it in influential positions everywhere. The brothers, sisters, nephews, and nieces of the Cardinal were the masters of church and state.

The young Mendoza had been sent as a boy to live with a cousin, Gutierre Gómez de Toledo, Bishop of Palencia, though he lived in Toledo. After reading law at the university of Salamanca, the future cardinal became, first, parish priest of Hita, fifteen miles north of Guadalajara, of which city he then was named archdeacon. He learned both Greek and Latin so well that his magnificent father asked him to translate the *Iliad* for him, as well as the *Aeneid* and some poems of Ovid's. In 1454, Mendoza became Bishop of Calahorra, in effect a family see. He moved to the court, negotiated an understanding between his family and the King, now that his father, who had once been a rebel, was dead, and he baptized King Enrique's presumed daughter, the unfortunate Juana.

Mendoza sought a compromise in the feud between the nobles and Enrique, warning that those who did not obey even a bad king were schismatics. Thanks to the friendship of a clever, if self-indulgent, visitor from the Vatican, Rodrigo Borgia, already a cardinal, who was in Castile in 1472, Mendoza became "Cardinal of Spain." From 1474, Mendoza was the Queen's right-hand man, a more modern minister than the formidable Archbishop Carrillo, though the latter had greatly helped Isabel ten years before. He also fought at Toro, where he was wounded. In 1485, he became Archbishop of Toledo and Primate of All Spain.

Mendoza was assiduous in ensuring offices for his protégés who were, however, usually the best men for the work concerned. He was active in the war against Granada, at one time holding field command; and, after the surrender of Guadix and Almería, he commissioned the carving of depictions of the surrender of fifty-four Moorish cities for the choir of Toledo Cathedral. This work, by many hands, but much of it by the imaginative Rodrigo Alemán, was unfinished in 1491, as was the campaign that inspired it. The Cardinal is to be seen, in a bas-relief by Felipe de Borgoña, riding next to the monarchs, a most determined warrior-bishop, a coat of mail over his surplice. We can see him depicted, too, in stone before the high altar of Granada, mounted on a mule, in gloves, his "pinched, aquiline face," as Richard Ford had it, contrasting with the chubbier features of the monarchs.[51] Even more warlike is his portrait on the ceiling of his own College of San Gregorio in Valladolid.[52]

Mendoza was selective in his loyalty to religious doctrine. He maintained the most succulent table in Spain. He had illegitimate sons by Mencía de Lemos, one of the wild maids of honor of the libertine Queen Juana, conceived while he was Bishop of Sigüenza; and Queen Isabel, though straitlaced, once asked her confessor if "the sins of the cardinal do not seem very pretty."[53] Mendoza arranged the legitimation of these children, and the eldest, Rodrigo, became Count of Cid and Marquis of Cenete.

Close to Mendoza in those days, and constantly available, was Fray Hernando de Talavera, the Queen's confessor. Like that of most royal confessors, his influence was immense if mysterious. He had Jewish blood and one day would suffer a little in consequence.

But earlier, he, a protégé of Mendoza, wrote his sermon on the theme "How all loyal Christians should renew their spirits during Advent" as a "mirror of princes" for Isabel, binding royal power to virtue, arguing that

if you are a Queen, you ought to be a model and inspiration to your subjects. . . . Rise, rise in the air and contemplate the crown of glory . . . for, through these works and considerations, you will preserve, like the eagle [the symbol of St. John the Evangelist, whom Isabel had adopted as an inspiration], the strength and vigor of your youth. Renew your noble spirit through God, and gain perfection, for you have the condition of a

mistress and lady so perfect and are as full of virtue and goodness as is
the eagle among birds.[54]

Talavera entered the Council of the Realm on Mendoza's suggestion and
remained a powerful influence both there and on Isabel for twenty-five
years, doing all he could for her, even drawing up a schedule of the best way
of organizing her time. It was widely said that whereas confessors usually
knelt to hear confessions of royal personages, Talavera stood while Isabel
was on her knees. In 1475, he wrote a guide for the spiritual life of friars; Isabel asked him to explain the same to her. He demurred, saying that what
was good for religious people did not apply to the secular world. She insisted
that Fray Hernando write nine chapters for her spiritual guidance.[55]

Isabel herself was serious, decisive, unbending, resolute. She was also
straightforward. She did not smile readily, though she had a taste for irony.
She admired learning and could read Latin; she loved music, often traveling
with a choir of twenty-five or more. She listened often to the music of *vi-
huelas,* old guitars, and, later, to the *Cancionero del palacio* of the delightful
Juan del Encina, sung, like most of his poems, either to the six-stringed viol
or the lute. What, one wonders, would she have made of his:

> *Más vale penar,*
> *sufriendo dolores*
> *que estar sin amores.*[56]

> Better to suffer pain
> To live in grief
> Than to be without love.

Isabel saw ceremony and music as useful in assisting government and
increased the luxury of the royal style of living accordingly. For that reason,
she spent liberally on clothes, although by the time of the siege of Granada,
she usually wore a gloomy black.[57] But she also was said to have liked fancy-
dress balls. She admired Flemish painters and bought at least one Memling
(now in the royal chapel in Granada). She loved dogs and parrots, and
would often be accompanied by civets. She could be vengeful, but was almost always pious. She was more cultivated than Fernando, her husband,
and had four hundred books in her library, a great number for that day. She
also encouraged the new art of printing. Her Italian chaplain, Lucio Marineo Sículo, said that in the 1490s she would hear Mass daily and would pray
the canonical hours as if she were a nun. She remembered the adage: "Those

monarchs who do not fear God fear their subjects." It is possible that she became a tertiary Franciscan in the Convento of San Juan Pablo of Valladolid.
Another Italian, Peter Martyr de Anglería, wrote: "Even the Queen herself,
whom the whole world in part respects, in part fears, and in part admires,
when you have been permitted free access to her, you find her closed off in
sadness." Was it, he wondered, that she thought that with so many deaths in
her immediate family (three of her children would die before her), God had
abandoned her?[58]

The work of Isabel in the first ten years of her time as both heiress and
Queen of Castile was, however, remarkable by any standard. No woman in
history has exceeded her achievement.

A popular song ran:

> *Flores de Aragón, flores de Aragón,*
> *Dentro de Castilla son*
> *Flores de Aragón en Castilla son.*

> Flowers of Aragon, flowers of Aragon,
> Inside Castile
> The flowers of Aragon are growing.

Fernando, when he became a knight of the Burgundian Order of the
Golden Fleece, adopted as an emblem the Yoke and Arrows, the yoke indi-
cating the union of the realms, the F signifying Fernando, the Y standing for
Ysabel.

These two monarchs launched their kingdoms on a collaboration that,
if not always happy, was immensely important and profitable for both
realms. Yet the troubles of Spain were not over with the seizure of authority
by Isabel. If most of the north of Spain supported her by celebrations, much
of the south was equivocal. A new Marquis of Villena, Pacheco's son, was
firmly for the twelve-year-old Juana, the dead King Enrique's daughter, who
was in his control and who was referred to by Isabel's friends with the ambiguous designation "the Queen's daughter." Pacheco's lands in the south
and east were themselves able to provide an army. He was now supported by
a disgruntled Archbishop Carrillo; the Count of Benavente, a power in
northwestern Castile; Rodrigo Ponce de León in Seville; and Álvaro de
Stúñiga, Duke of Béjar, in Extremadura. King Afonso of Portugal announced his intention to marry Juana, and war broke out, many more towns
declaring for her. A Portuguese army entered northwestern Castile. Some
have suggested that this was a frivolous war.[59] But had the Portuguese and La

Beltraneja won, the future of the peninsula would have been quite different for there would have been a Portuguese-Castilian union in place of an Aragonese-Castilian one. The benefits of the first consummation would not have been worthless. But they would have changed history.

After much skirmishing and maneuvering, some incursions into Portugal, and efforts by Isabel and Fernando to negotiate peace, the latter met Afonso in battle in March 1476 at Peleagonzalo, outside Toro, the walled frontier city on the River Duero. Though his men were tired and his artillery did not arrive in time to be used, Fernando's victory was overwhelming. The war continued for a time off the coast of Africa, and fighting in Extremadura persisted. But Juana's cause was lost.[60] Afonso, who had already given up the throne of Portugal to his son, attempted to persuade France to help him, without success.

Next year, Fernando succeeded his father on the throne of Aragon. He was as tireless in pursuing the interests of that realm as he was in serving those of his wife.

As a man of Castilian blood, but brought up in Aragon, Fernando was ideal for his complex role. He brought knowledge of successful Aragonese and Catalan practice to serve Castile. He was more easygoing than the Queen, but was also more ruthless, more calculating, and more cynical. These qualities fitted well with the prophecies by some friars that he would be the king who would win back the Holy Land for Christendom.[61] He was hardworking and efficient, though with a sense of humor that his wife did not seem to share. His wise instinct was to seek moderate solutions to problems, in the expectation that they would thereby last longer.[62]

Fernando could be sententious if it seemed necessary: "In all my realms, I am always accustomed to look at the public good rather than my private interest," he once wrote to his best general, Gonzalo Fernández de Córdoba, "El Gran Capitán," who had suggested special concessions in relation to the provision of wheat in Sicily.[63] Despite his frequent affectionate words to his wife, his instincts were those of a calculating machine rather than of a man of passion. The German traveler Munzer, however, recalled him as always hovering "between gravity and laughter."[64] In his and Isabel's time, Spain was starting to look outward, not toward the Mediterranean where Aragon had been active for generations, but at the Atlantic. The conquest of the Canary Islands seems a minor matter. Yet just as in winter a shaft of sunlight suggests the approach of spring, so did the Spanish concern with the Canary archipelago promise a genuinely international vocation. The Italian courtier Peter Martyr thought that as a result of the achievements of the two monarchs, Spain was "the only happy country."[65]

3

"Great tranquility and order"

The Catholic monarchs were very celebrated in those days for their
wisdom and for having brought great tranquility and order into
their realms.

Guicciardini, HISTORY OF ITALY

In their years of joint power, Fernando and Isabel achieved singular success.
It is hard to distinguish important matters on which they differed. Their
motto *"Tanto monta, monta tanto, Isabel como Fernando"* ("It comes to the
same thing, Isabel is the same as Fernando") indicated their equality: that
both monarchs could rule in both their realms and also in that of the other.
But it was, to begin with, a personal device of Fernando's, suggesting that if
something was complicated, it was better to cut through it, as Alexander cut
the Gordian knot.[1]

Both Isabel and Fernando inherited from their ancestors a belief in royal
justice that sought to protect the weak without ceasing to reward the successful. They had as serious a sense of their obligations as of their glory. They
also had a gift for inspiring confidence even among their poorer subjects.
They brought to an end the chronic civil wars that had characterized the relations of monarchs and noblemen in both their realms. Every chronicler of
the time testified to the violence of the old days, even if their accounts
should sometimes be discounted because of their desire to please the new
régime.[2] Their achievements have been compared to those of their contemporaries in France and England, in both of which countries monarchs restored civil order after years of civil war. But in neither of those two other
realms was there a new unification such as that which now existed between
Castile and Aragon.

By traveling continually, by harsh suppression of revolts, and by the judicious use of rewards and titles, the two monarchs were reducing the nobility to an estate of the realm when it had previously been a rival to the
Crown. Castilian noblemen might still dominate local politics, but they no

longer dictated national affairs. For example, they had in the past constituted a majority in the Council of the Realm. But after the Cortes of 1480, of
Toledo, that body had a prelate (Cardinal Mendoza, to begin with) as its
chairman, with eight or nine learned civil servants (letrados) as members,
together with three knights. Nobles and senior churchmen could continue
to attend, but without voting. It was a committee that, having once been judicial, was to become the directing element in administration.[3] More and
more legal work was meanwhile performed by the supreme court (audiencia
real) whose judges (oidores) met at Valladolid.

The appointment of the corregidor (co-councillor)[4] already to be found
in most large cities, strengthened royal power, for this representative of the
Crown, often a member of the lesser nobility, presided over meetings of the
town councils. A typical corregidor (that of Toledo) was a poet, Gómez Manrique, whose brother was the Master of the Order of Santiago.[5] There were
in 1490 about fifty corregidores dotted throughout the realm, spokesmen for
centralizing power—in often unpromising territory such as the marquisate
of Villena.

The Florentine historian Francesco Guicciardini, a diplomat in Spain in
1512, wrote that the two sovereigns were "very celebrated in those days"—his
days, he meant—"for their wisdom and for having brought great tranquility
and order into their realms that had formerly been most turbulent."[6]

Until the days of Fernando and Isabel, most of the royal income had
come from taxes on sales (alcabala) or customs duties (almojarifazgo). Although the united monarchy did not neglect those, new men now devised
new ways of raising money, in theory for the war against Islam, but which
they expected to maintain afterwards (a tax known as the cruzada, the crusade; a share of tithes and subsidies from ecclesiastical assemblies; and direct
levies both on bishops and on towns). The Crown also devised profitable
arrangements with the Mesta, the board that controlled the two and a half
million or so merino sheep of Castile.[7] In 1488, the Crown tried to regularize
the diverse methods of weighing produce, with many variations between different ounces, by decreeing that all weights should conform to recently established national standards.[8] Fernando was also seeking to make himself the
Grand Master of all three of the important military orders (Santiago, Alcántara, and Calatrava), bringing him wealth as well as power, for those undertakings held much land and, in the past, had constituted the reason for the
power of the greatest noblemen, such as Álvaro de Luna and Juan Pacheco.

The Crown in Castile was thus able to dispense with the Cortes for long
periods, for it had less need to seek grants than was the case in Aragon. No
Cortes in Castile was summoned between 1480 and 1498. That assembly was

anyway, as mentioned earlier, less influential than the similar bodies in Fernando's realms. Attendance of clergy and nobles was not required and was therefore rare. The cities that sent *procuradores* (representatives) to the Cortes were only seventeen,[9] and for much of the fifteenth century, these men had been limited to two per city. That meant that when the Queen felt she should call a Cortes because she needed money for war, she had merely to face and persuade thirty-four men, of whom a few were her friends, and others might be persuaded to be so.

Internationally, the King of Portugal was restrained after his defeat in the 1470s and no longer constituted a threat to Castile—or, for that matter, to the Canary Islands, which were now largely under Spanish direction (as was that part of the coastline of Africa opposite)—even if of those isles, Tenerife and La Palma still remained to be conquered. Peace reigned, too, with France, though the future of Perpignan and Roussillon (conquered by France in the 1460s) was uncertain. England was tied to Castile by a treaty of mutual protection against France, signed in Medina del Campo in 1489. These diplomatic successes were partly the consequence of Fernando's establishment of regular ambassadors in five European capitals. That enabled him to be better informed than his fellow monarchs. The success was also a consequence of the fact that Castile and Aragon, however separate domestically, already counted as one power internationally.

The development, on the suggestion of Isabel's adviser Quintanilla, at the Cortes of Madrigal of 1476, of a national version of the armed brotherhoods (*hermandades*), which had been set up to ensure order locally, created the semblance of a Castilian police, also with judicial functions: every town had to provide a horseman for every one hundred householders. The first commander was Fernando's illegitimate brother, Alfonso de Aragón, Duke of Villahermosa.[10]

As usual, when monarchs seem to be responsible for great changes, some insist that the transformation began long before the reigns of those particular kings. The historian Tarsicio de Azcona, for example, speaks of the entire family of Trastámara and their supporters as revolutionaries.[11] But the feats of these last two members of the family, Isabel and Fernando, were quite special.

Exactly how many soldiers were assembled at Santa Fe in 1491 for the final battle against Islam in Spain is difficult to say: perhaps there were six thousand to ten thousand knights and ten thousand to sixteen thousand infantrymen, in an army possibly totaling some eighty thousand.[12]

Fernando had shown himself prudent as commander in chief, a characteristic he had demonstrated before, in the campaigns against Portugal and the rebellious Castilians. The destruction of Tájara, the siege of Malaga, the capture of the supposedly impregnable Ronda, and the seizures of smaller places such as Setenil (where the King's grandfather, another Fernando, had been defeated) and Alora ("thou well-walled city, astride the stream") had been triumphs for him; and he had learned to improvise in adverse circumstances.[13]

The Queen, too, in her preparations in Córdoba in 1484, as much as at the siege of Burgos, had shown herself a skillful commissary, a founder of military hospitals, and an efficient provider of artillery, food, horses, and men. Engineers, builders of roads, blacksmiths, and oxen were all required. To organize these was no ordinary task: the army of Castile needed thirty thousand pounds of wheat and barley every day.[14]

Outstanding among the leading Spanish commanders was the impetuous Rodrigo Ponce de León, Count of Arcos, red-haired and tall, the hero of both the contemporary chronicler Andrés de Bernáldez and the nineteenth-century American historian William Prescott. Don Rodrigo embodied the idea of a love of chivalry, worshiping honor, valor, loyalty to the monarch, courtesy, and generosity. The Scottish philosopher David Hume correctly reflected that in "the fifteenth century in Spain, chivalry and knighthood were raised by the overflowing imagination of the people to a cult."[15] Ponce de León best embodies that mood.

Though Don Rodrigo had once supported Juana la Beltraneja and the Portuguese, and broken the royal truce with Granada in 1477 to seize two small Islamic towns the next year, he had also saved the life of Fernando in battle.[16] He was an accomplished commander: he had, in 1482, gathered 2,500 horsemen and 3,000 foot soldiers at Marchena and taken them undetected across difficult country to capture the rich city of Alhama—the most remarkable single feat of the war. He had also imaginatively built a wooden fortress capable of harboring 14,000 infantry and 2,500 horsemen to serve the besieging forces outside Malaga in 1487.

A more cosmopolitan knight was Íñigo López de Mendoza, the sumptuous Count of Tendilla, a nephew of Cardinal Mendoza who became the first governor of Alhama after its fall. He had then been ambassador to Rome and had astounded even the Vatican by his extravagant conduct.[17] Neither should we forget the hereditary Constable of Castile, Pedro Fernández de Velasco, Count of Haro, who had been wounded in the face at Loja (the constabulary had been made hereditary in his family in 1472, just as the admiralty of Castile had been given over to the family of Enríquez, a good way of ensuring loyalty). The Duke of Medina Sidonia, the uncrowned monarch of Seville, had meanwhile offered a hundred galleys full of supplies to the royal army for the siege of Malaga.

These and many other noblemen rode into war as if they had at least glanced at such works as *A Treatise on the Perfection of Military Triumph* (*Tratado de la Perfección del Triunfo Militar*) by the Queen's secretary, Alonso de Palencia, or *The Catechism of Knights* (*Doctrinal de los Caballeros*) by the late Bishop of Burgos, Alonso de Cartagena.

Historians used once to dwell on the clothes used in this perambulatory, bellicose court—rightly, since both men and women dressed to impress. Thus we hear how the English knight Sir Edward Woodville was "sheathed in complete mail" over which he wore a "French surcoat of dark silk brocade." Horses also often wore silk, and the mules on which the Queen's ladies rode were, we hear, "richly caparisoned." The Queen on occasion wore a skirt of brocade. Her friend Felipa de Portugal had such heavy ornamentation on her dress that it diverted the dagger of a would-be assassin at Malaga.[18] War thus stimulated every kind of commerce as it always inspires technological innovation. The captains of Castile were living between several worlds.

Serving these captains were men from all parts of Spain. They were divided roughly into eight groups. First, there were the municipal forces, both cavalry and infantry, the former dominating. All regions of Spain, including remote Galicia and Vizcaya, sent some men. Second, there were the three main military orders, Santiago, Alcántara, and Calatrava, which had played such a part in earlier wars against Islam. They were mobilized for the last time in this war against Granada. The Order of Santiago furnished about 1,500 knights and perhaps 5,000 infantrymen, the other two a little fewer.[19] They did not always perform well: the commander of the Order of Santiago, Alonso de Cárdenas, in 1483 led an attack toward Malaga from Antequera, but lost his way in the Sierra de Ajarquía and was heavily defeated, though he himself escaped with his life.

Third, the monarchs had a royal guard of one thousand mounted lancers. These were commanded in 1490 by Gonzalo Fernández de Córdoba, a younger son of one of the great families of the city from which he took his name. In his youth a page of Archbishop Carrillo, he fought continuously in the war against Granada from Alhama onward, being wounded in battle and being particularly effective in the unromantic business of the *tala,* the destruction of agriculture in the *vega* of Granada. He was already held to be a "mirror of courtesy": lordly with lords, soldierly with soldiers, at ease in palaces with courtiers, adept at maintaining his equilibrium in all circum-

stances, especially in combat. His mastery of Arabic made him a good negotiator as well as a warrior. The most feared of Castilian leaders, Fernández de
Córdoba was an Achilles without his sulky vanity; indeed, without his heel.[20]

Every monarch of Castile had also about fifty bodyguards, the so-called
monteros de Espinosa, armed with crossbows, traditionally from the pic-
turesque Castilian town of that name, in a pretty valley in the southern
foothills of the Cantabrian mountains. Their task was to preserve the king
by night as well as by day.[21]

Then, fourth, there were troops deriving from the Hermandad, the police force that had been founded on a national level in 1476 but that was diverted by the war into making a military contribution of about 1,500 lancers
and fifty handgunners divided into captaincies. These troops were often
commanded by noblemen and used to man garrisons in captured towns.

It would be foolish, too, to forget the army of servants and slaves who attended the monarchs and all other distinguished members of the court, including churchmen. Perhaps there were a thousand people in the royal
service altogether.[22] The slaves included Canary Islanders, Muslims captured
in earlier wars, and blacks from Africa.

Members of the Spanish court, the Spanish nobility and the tradespeo-
ple, the clergymen and the bakers all usually owned one or two slaves each,
and in the case of great men, many more. The Duke of Medina Sidonia in
1492, for example, had ninety-five slaves, many of them Muslim and nearly
forty black.[23] There may have been about 100,000 slaves in Spain in 1490,
Seville having the largest such population. Some slaves could have been the
descendants of the many eastern European slaves who had been sold in
western Europe during the Middle Ages, giving indeed the word *slav* to this
status of service in place of the old Latin *servus.*

The diversity of Spanish medieval slaves was extraordinary: there were
Circassians, Bosnians, Poles, and Russians. Some would have been captured
in battles against Granada and might themselves be Muslims. Others would
have been bought in the thriving slave markets of the western Mediterranean, perhaps in Barcelona or in Valencia, in Genoa or in Naples. Some
slaves were men or women seized in the Canary Islands, even in the still unconquered Tenerife or in the already subdued La Palma or Gomera. Yet others, principally Berbers, came from Spain's little outpost in northwest Africa,
Sahara, on the coast almost in sight of the Canary island of Lanzarote. A few
black slaves were bought from merchants in Lisbon who, for the last two
generations, had been trading people whom they had acquired on the west
coast of Africa, anywhere between Senegal and the Congo, perhaps from

Guinea; many were sold by Florentine or Genoese merchants in Portugal, or by their agents in Seville.

The number of slaves was not surprising. Slavery had never died since the days of antiquity in the Mediterranean and, if anything, had been given a boost by the wars in Spain between the Christians and the Muslims. Christians customarily made slaves of their Muslim captives; and Muslims did the same with Christian prisoners, sometimes taking them to North Africa to work on public undertakings, just as Christians employed their Muslim slaves for building. Many slaves were employed as domestic servants, but others worked in the sugar mills in the Atlantic islands (the Azores, Madeira, or the Canary Islands). Some were hired out by their masters for wages. Christian law, as seen in the medieval King Alfonso's *Siete Partidas,* and Muslim law, as enshrined in the Koran, carefully indicated the place a slave should occupy in society. Sometimes slaves could hold property, and sometimes they could buy their liberty. Sometimes they were treated better than servants by their masters. Masters had complete power over their slaves except that they could neither kill nor mutilate them; and no Jew or Muslim in the Christian kingdoms could have Christians as slaves. These slaves were taken for granted, and no protest of any sort was contemplated. It was obligatory to treat slaves humanely. But no one thought that the institution should be abolished.

Slavery had come to seem uneconomic, it is true, in northern Europe. The English, the northern Franks, and the Flemings already found it better to pay for labor when feudal bonds declined. But the Muslim world, above all the Ottoman Empire, depended absolutely on slavery for its smooth running; and, at this time, the slave trade across the Sahara still exceeded in volume and value the coastal commerce managed by the Portuguese.[24]

The Crown of Castile also had its own version of the feudal system, for next among the combatants outside Granada were the vassals who received either land or an income in return for their service. About one thousand of these men were usually paid daily wages. To them should be added both cavalry and infantry from towns in the royal domains.

Many noblemen also contributed substantial forces. The lords concerned did not wish their men to be fitted into any national command structure. All the same, the monarchs often gave such nobles a specific rank to encourage them to provide men. Thus the Duke of Alba had the designation of captain-general. The nobles of Castile were unenthusiastic about the war, but those of Andalusia were more committed and often rode at the head of several hundred men.

A few soldiers, too, had been attracted to the army by the chance offered of purging their guilt for some crime on condition that they served.

The soldiers developed some national spirit. Peter Martyr de Anglería, the Italian courtier, wrote to the Archbishop of Milan asking: "Who would have believed that the Asturians, Gallegos, Basques, and the inhabitants of the Cantabrian mountains, men accustomed to deeds of atrocious violence, and to brawl on the slightest occasions at home, should mingle amicably not only with one another, but with the Toledans and the wily and jealous Andalusians; all living together in harmonious subordination to authority, like members in one family, speaking one tongue, and nurtured under a common discipline?"[25] Much the same reflection would occur to the historian Fernández de Oviedo in Panama a generation later.[26] It was the need to present a common front against an enemy that brought the Spaniards together. Even in the thirteenth century, Catalans had fought at the Battle of Las Navas de Tolosa against the Muslims under the command of a king of Castile.

There were, finally, in the Spanish army many foreigners. Was this not a crusade? One Portuguese captain who fought was Francisco de Almeida, who within fifteen years would become the first viceroy of the Portuguese possessions in India. One can explain his presence by the fact that earlier in the century, Isabel's great-uncle Henry the Navigator, before he began to sponsor expeditions to West Africa, had wanted to take part in the conquest of Granada. The Duke of Gandia, son of Cardinal Rodrigo Borgia, had also made an *acte de présence* in the war in the 1480s. A few Swiss mercenaries were there, led by Gaspar de Frey, and earlier in the war, at the siege of Loja, there had been Sir Edward Woodville, brother of the Queen of England,[27] who had brought three hundred men, some from that northern land itself, others from Scotland, Ireland, Brittany, and Burgundy, mostly armed with battle-axes and longbows. Some men from Bruges came, too—of whom one, Pierre Alimané, captured by the enemy, escaped from Fez by winning the heart of one of the Muslim princesses. Genoese ships belonging to Giuliano Grimaldi and Pascual Lomellini, in the service of Castile, guarded the Straits of Gibraltar.

The army was organized in groups known as *batallas;* the vanguard being as a rule headed by the Grand Master of the Order of Santiago, the rearguard either by the Constable of Castile (Pedro Fernández de Velasco) or Diego Fernández de Córdoba, marshal of the royal pages (the elder brother of Gonzalo, the "Gran Capitán"). The King would expect to ride just before the rearguard, flanked by two companies of soldiers recruited by the authorities in Seville and Córdoba. A thousand or so artillery wagons would travel behind him.[28]

Mention of artillery recalls that the Christians fought this war as if in two eras; the knightly orders, with their religious sense of brotherhood, recalled the high Middle Ages, as did the heavy lances, spears, halberds, and pikes as well as longbows and crossbows. The Castilians also had medieval siege inventions such as *bastidas*, which enabled attackers to rise to the tops of walls; "royal stairways" by which infantry could be hauled by pulley to the battlements of the defenders; leather-covered tents enabling the Castilians to approach walls at ground level; as well as large catapults. Miners from Asturias might be asked to dig a hole beneath the walls of besieged towns.

But the artillery wagons seemed to be of a new age. New weapons included the arquebus, invented about 1470, which for the first time enabled a single soldier to have a powder-fired weapon.[29] Lombards (or mortars)[30] were even more innovatory, being cannons twelve feet in length, made of iron or bronze, two inches thick, and held together by iron rings; they threw balls of stone, sometimes a foot in diameter, as many as 140 a day, sometimes weighing 175 pounds; or they might fire globe-shaped masses of inflammable ingredients mixed with gunpowder. Would Ronda have fallen without the lombards, Alcalá el Real? The war had thus been a modern one in which sieges were carried to success by artillery. The latter had enabled the Castilians to mount attacks on city after city, capturing, as it were, "one by one" the grains of the "pomegranate" ("Granada" is the Spanish word for that fruit).[31]

Many of these new weapons, such as the two hundred pieces of artillery, mostly made in Écija, between Córdoba and Seville, needed not only explosive gunpowder but expensive Burgundians, Germans, or Frenchmen to service them. Still, Francisco Ramírez, one of the best new soldiers who had done much damage in blowing up the walls of Malaga, came from Madrid, while many of the cannonballs came from the Sierra Morena, especially from the town of Constantina.

There was one more sign of modernity among the leaders in the Castilian-Aragonese army, one thing that distinguished the men and women at the court of Ferdinand and Isabel from all their predecessors: many of them were readers, some of them owned books, those new "golden objects" made possible for the first time in 1450 by Gutenberg in Germany and, after about 1470, by printers in Spain, principally in Seville, Valencia, and Segovia (the first press seems to have been that set up in Segovia in 1471 by John Parix of Heidelberg). Many printers were Germans—the result of a growing commerce with Germany in which the printing capital, Nuremberg, figured substantially, though Castile also imported German metal objects, linen, and fustian.[32]

As yet, few books contrived to entertain. But there were learned publications, soon there would be engravings, and there were editions of the classics. The letters of Cicero to his friends were available, as were the works of Ovid and Pliny. There was Ptolemy's *Geography;* there was St. Augustine's *City of God;* and, shortly, there would be novels. Indeed, one of the finest of these, Joanot Martorell's *Tirant lo Blanc,* appeared in 1490 in over seven hundred copies in Valencia.[33] It would be considered by Cervantes the "best book in the world . . ." because "the *caballeros* in it are human beings, not dummies. . . ." It is a lascivious volume, especially the last chapters. It also well reflects the blend of savagery and chivalry in war at that time; its cosmopolitan component can be seen from the brief appearance in it of Sir Anthony Woodville (an elder brother of Edward) as the "Senyor d'Escala Rompuda," while the first part of the book treats of a Muslim invasion of England that is defeated by the Earl of Warwick.

Tirant lo Blanc was among the first of many "chivalrous" works whose great sale marked the next hundred years. Reading soon became for the first time less a scholarly ritual than a habit, even though books might still be conceived as to be read aloud. Long accounts of extraordinary exploits by knightly heroes in strange lands presented an ideal in which courage, virtue, strength, and passion all played a part.[34] Queen Isabel, we know, had *The Ballad of Merlin* and *The Quest for the Holy Grail* in her library. All were foretastes of Spanish adventures in the New World.

These "chivalrous" novels reflect a world in which frontiers of states were loose; and while readers were carried away by adventures in "Great Britain" or Constantinople, numerous foreigners were to be seen in the courts of both king and noblemen. From Flanders came architects: for example, Juan de Guas, who designed the church of San Juan de los Reyes in Toledo, a Franciscan monastery that was the supreme artistic achievement of the time, as well as the Duke of Infantado's palace at Guadalajara. One Spanish court painter, Michael Littow, was an Estonian. Italian writers such as Peter Martyr or Marineo Siculo gave lessons to noblemen, and soon the Florentine sculptor Domenico Fancelli would begin work on his remarkable tombs.[35] Ballads and romantic stories also ignored the boundaries of states. Thus most knights in Spain thought of "the paladin Roland" and the King of France as their own heroes, though their geographical knowledge was faulty and they seem to have imagined that the French capital was on a Spanish river:

Cata Francia, cata Paris la ciudad,
Cata las aguas del Duero, do van a dar en el mar!

Look at France, look at Paris the city,
Look at the waters of the Douro which run down to the sea.

Most of the monarchs' counselors were at Santa Fe in 1491, for the place was a court as well as a headquarters. Those present included all the experienced advisers of Isabel (for instance the Chacóns, Alonso de Quintanilla, Gutierre de Cárdenas, Andrés Cabrera, and Beatriz de Bobadilla). Fernando also had his staff with him; in addition to the skillful treasurer of Aragon, Alonso de la Caballería, there were about sixteen "fernandine" secretaries.[36] Of first importance was the international secretary, Miguel Pérez de Almazán. There were, too, Juan Cabrero, the King's steward and inseparable companion, who slept in his room and was his closest confidant, and Gabriel Sánchez, his personal treasurer, a *converso* like Caballería. There was Juan de Coloma, a competent private secretary who had been working for Fernando since 1469, a man of rural origin who had married a granddaughter of the chief magistrate of Aragon, Martín Díaz de Aux. There was, too, in Santa Fe, Luís Santangel, who arranged the income of the Hermandad, another *converso* and an astute businessman who was related to both Sánchez and Caballería.

Besides these mature statesmen of the back rooms, there were numerous younger persons, some of whom we know only by their names at the bottom of royal documents, while some were men of the future, already seeing how, with hard work and a reputation for reliability, they might ultimately climb to destinations of importance. We should imagine all these men dining together daily, developing a collegiate understanding over chickpeas, biscuits, stews, and fortified wine from, say, Cazalla de la Sierra in the Sierra Morena.

These civil servants were occasionally churchmen, sometimes bishops, sometimes monks or priors, but they were often educated men, *letrados,* who, ten or twenty years before, had merely been promising students of law at the University of Salamanca. A few were judges. A typical public servant was Lorenzo Galíndez de Carvajal, a young Extremeño who was just beginning his impressive progress upward through the committees that surrounded the monarchs. Even if crowded in small rooms, inconveniently placed, often sleeping on rough floors and in great heat, these bureaucrats must have welcomed the establishment of the court at Santa Fe, a rest from perpetual travel.

Many of these were men whose ancestors, a hundred years before, had converted rapidly, after the brutal pogroms of the late fourteenth century, from Judaism. Most of them—and that was also true of the merchants with whom they associated, by cousinly connection or friendship—were by 1490 serious Christians and had forgotten the Jewish faith of their forebears. A few, however, through family tradition or perhaps from indolence, maintained some Jewish customs, such as washing the dead before burial, eating garlic fried with oil, or turning to the wall when they died; and a still smaller number were true secret Jews, privately keeping the Sabbath, clandestinely eating meat on Fridays, and even cherishing the intoxicating hope that the Messiah would soon reveal Himself, perhaps in Seville, where the Queen, during her long stay in 1478, had noticed what she judged to be a disgraceful liturgical laxity.[37] The prior of the Dominican convent, Fray Alonso de Hojeda, had told her that many *conversos* in Seville were returning to their Jewish faith and were threatening the survival of Christianity. His order then mounted a campaign of propaganda against the *conversos.*

So the Spanish monarchs, in 1478, had asked Pope Sixtus IV to set up a Holy Office, or Inquisition, to root out these dangers. The procedure of such an organized inquiry had a long history in the Middle Ages. Indeed, a rather ineffective body had been established with the same purpose in the reign of Isabel's brother, King Enrique. So Spain slid into accepting what turned out to be an iniquity without any sense of it seeming a radical innovation.

Jews had constituted an important minority in Spain since Roman days. Many had played a major part in administration in the fourteenth century. In 1391, there had been frequent popular attacks against them, above all in the large cities. At that same time thousands of Jews, perhaps two-thirds of the total, had themselves christened in order to avoid further persecution. The Crown encouraged such baptisms. Many of these *conversos* entered the government or went effectively into the Church as well as remaining dominant in commerce. One rabbi in Castile, the learned ha-Levi, even became Bishop of Burgos under the name of Alonso de Santa María.

The *conversos* prospered. They were prominent among those who sought to introduce Italian humanism into Spain, but they remained an endogamous sect within society and within the Church, and so they attracted attention, envy, and hostility—at least after 1449 when there were riots against "new Christians" in Toledo, where rivalries between old Christians and *conversos* were intense.[38] In other places such hatreds blended with traditional enmities between two groups of families. A special case was that in Córdoba where there had even been a massacre of *conversos* in 1473.[39] Still, *conversos* continued to be bishops, royal secretaries, bankers, changers of money, and priors in monasteries, and they married into the nobility.

Was the purpose of the new Inquisition to find a way of deciding who among the *conversos* were false Christians?[40] For it seems obvious that the principal charge of secret heresy was believed absolutely by the monarchs and by the public.[41] Was the aim of the Inquisition to "destroy the *converso* community"? Did the two rulers, traditional protectors of the Jews as well as of the *conversos*, come "to realize that to continue protecting them could cost them too much in terms of their relations with the majority of the people and that the presence of the Jews, despite the advantages which it offered, was more of a liability than an asset?"[42] The first historian of the Inquisition, Llorente, a Marxist before Marx, thought that the motive for setting up the Inquisition was largely financial, while the great German historian von Ranke thought it a further means of securing absolute authority for the monarchs. The Spanish medievalist Menéndez Pelayo thought that the aim was the extirpation of a heresy that really did threaten Christianity, while the mercurial Américo Castro thought that the Inquisition was a typically Jewish idea actually devised by *conversos* to protect themselves, which was out of keeping with Spanish traditions!

Was the aim of the Crown in establishing the Holy Office on the contrary to stifle the growing popular movement against the *conversos*? Many old Christians thought that most, or even all, *conversos* and their descendants were secret Jews or, at least, were falling back into Jewish ways because of the excessive tolerance of the Church; and certainly some Jews, in the days of popular persecution in the late fourteenth century, had converted out of fear. Rabbis thought that all Jews forcibly converted to Christendom had always to be seen as Jews, and their children, too.

Whatever the royal motives, Pope Sixtus IV announced a bull (*Exigit Sincere Devotionis*) establishing an Inquisition. Two Inquisitors, both Dominicans, were appointed in Seville in 1480. They were guided by medieval texts that had been in use against, for example, the Cathars. They went about their business with energy and established their headquarters and their jail in the castle of San Jorge in Triana, just across the Guadalquivir from Seville. Investigations were secret, and the accused might be held in prison for months, even years, while the case against them was prepared. The accused did have the right to defense lawyers, but these were chosen by the Inquisition itself. Those found to be secret Jews were burned ("relaxed to the secular arm" was the expression used) just outside the city after a public and ceremonial denunciation at an *auto-de-fe*, while those who fled in time were burned in effigy. Others were fined (*reconciliado*) and caused to march barefoot through the streets wearing the famous *sambenito* modeled on the chasuble and a long pointed hat. There were other punishments: house arrest or forced attendance at Mass on such and such a number of days.

Many *conversos* did flee Seville, some to Rome, where Sixtus IV helped
them, even writing in 1482 to Fernando and Isabel about the excesses of the
Inquisitors. He also quashed sentences against *conversos* who could sustain
their claim to have been unfairly accused.

All the same, the Inquisition was soon to be found in almost all the big
cities of Castile. The establishment of the Holy Office in the kingdom of
Aragon was more difficult, since it was necessary to bring to an end some existing institutions that had the same purpose. There was special hostility,
too, to the idea that Castilian Inquisitors should play a part. There were
protests from traditionalists as well as "new Christians," and it seems reasonably certain that the murder of the Inquisitor Pedro Arbués in 1485 in the
cathedral of Saragossa, which caused a scandal in Christian Aragon, was the
responsibility of the latter.

Those who died because of the denunciations of the Inquisition, followed by the secret trials and imprisonments, and then the "relaxation" of
the "guilty" to the civil power, may have exceeded two thousand in number
by the year of the siege of Granada.[43] In addition, most of those accused who
managed to establish innocence never recovered the property confiscated at
the beginning of their investigation. The Inquisition was acting against *conversos*, not Jews, but, of course, there was a connection, as events were to
show.

A number of important Jews as well as *conversos* were present in Santa
Fe; for example, Abraham Señor, a financier with many official roles. There
was Isaac Abravanel, a famous tax collector who had fled from Portugal after
an alleged plot in 1485.[44] There was also the Queen's doctor, Lorenzo Badoz,
and the King's, David Abenacaya of Ytarrega.[45]

The Church in Spain then boasted forty-eight bishops,[46] of whom many
were often at court, as they were at Santa Fe. Many managed, ex officio, vast
properties, especially the Archbishop of Toledo, and all were free of taxes.
Ten Castilian cathedrals, including the primatial see of Toledo, had, between
them, control over thirty towns and over 2,300 vassals.[47] The bishops were
headed by Mendoza, both Cardinal and Archbishop, but others were nearly
as warlike, and almost as active, if not as rich. In the past, the rule had been:
if a bishop died in Rome, his see would be filled by the Pope; in all other
cases, the cathedral chapter (*cabildo*) would propose a name, though they
had to consider any suggestion made by the monarch; the latter's wishes
now gradually became decisive.

There were also, outside the walls of Granada, members of the contemplative orders, the Benedictines and the Jeronymites, as well as the active brotherhoods, such as Dominicans and Franciscans, the latter including the sect known as the Observants, who were reforming members in search of a more spiritual life. Among these, the Jeronymites, only a century old, with their marvelous headquarters at Guadalupe, had a special place in the heart of the Queen.[48]

In Santa Fe, there were, too, younger members of the royal family, especially Don Juan, the thirteen-year-old heir of the monarchs, their pride and their expectation. With him was his household—an unusual mixture of mature advisers, playmates, and fellow students of writing, arithmetic, geometry, and Latin. The Infante Juan's court at Almazán on the border of Aragon and Castile would later be composed of a brilliant combination of people, some of whom (Nicolás de Ovando, Cristóbal de Cuéllar, Gonzalo Fernández de Oviedo) would later be seen in posts of significance throughout what became the Spanish Empire.[49]

Also in the ranks of Castile before the siege of Granada were the aristocrats of the realm, mostly rich dukes and counts, noblemen of a few generations at the most, for, as in England, civil wars had destroyed nearly all the families that had dominated the high Middle Ages.[50] The powerful chief minister of Juan II, Álvaro de Luna, who really ruled Spain from 1420 till 1453, had created a new hierarchy of noblemen, beginning in 1438 with the Count of Alba de Tormes, the ancestor of the Albas. These new titles were hereditary and were now given to men who were not members of the royal family. The grant of a hereditary title—"to you and your descendants forevermore"—also gave to the nobleman concerned permanent rights to the estate from which he took his name. Thus the grant of the first hereditary marquisate (of Santillana, in 1445) assured the Mendozas the city and lands of Santillana, in Cantabria. At Santa Fe, the noblemen would be easily recognized, for they would customarily wear spurs of silver or gold and shining breastplates.

A modern historian has written that the Spanish nobility at the end of the fifteenth century constituted one large family headed by the King.[51] It would have been better to say that that large family, with about twenty branches, was headed by the Mendozas, of which the Duke of Infantado was the senior member. But even his title was less than twenty years old, while the Duke of Medina Sidonia's title dated from 1444, Alba (as a duke) from only 1472, and Nájera from 1482. The Duke of Medinaceli was of royal blood, but his dukedom dated only from 1479.

These personages were present outside Granada because, being who they were, they were obliged by ancient custom to attend the monarch in crisis. Kings throughout the Middle Ages had given land to nobles in return for provision of men in war or, to lesser nobles, in return for their own services. In 1491, great nobles were still expected to contribute to the King's wars—men, money, or their own valor. They anticipated, too, benefits from their service, especially in the form of land. Noble families had their lands guaranteed them by a royal grant of an entailment (*mayorazgo*), by which an estate was guaranteed not to diminish but by which the head of the family was obliged to concern himself with his younger brothers and their descendants, as well as to find dowries for his sisters. These families were often attended by private courts that might include poets and scholars, as well as librarians and musicians.

Alongside the great noblemen there were knights, some of whom owned lordships, which gave them status but scarcely a livelihood. An ambitious knight would therefore work at court, perhaps, to begin with, as a *continuo*, a courtier in attendance, one of about a hundred, and he might be paid a few thousand maravedís; or he might find himself at a lord's court, where his income would be smaller. In war, these knights would often be grouped in companies of between 150 and 350 men, some of them being so-called armed knights (*caballeros armados*) or sometimes simply squires (*escuderos*).

Another class attached to the court were the hidalgos—poor gentlemen, that is, good at fighting, and usually as loyal to their lords as to the King; some of them were concerned with administration, too, and were often held to be creative (*ingenioso*) as well as brave. *Hidalguismo*, we are told, was, "as well as a class division, a frame of mind, but it was not enough just to be valiant, one had to show oneself as such."[52] An impertinent act of courage, such as that of Hernán de Pulgar before the mosque of Granada, was the action of a true hidalgo.

The pursuit of fame was not yet in Spain what it was in Italy. Few Spaniards had read Plutarch, Suetonius, or Petrarch. But for a hundred years there had been a cult of ballads written in Castilian that talked of historical heroes such as Caesar, Alexander, and Charlemagne as if they were contemporaries; and well-brought-up men were accustomed to lace their conversation with allusions to antiquity.

The war had not been continuously gentlemanly: the Muslims often tipped their arrows with poison from aconites or wolfbane, which grew wild in the Sierra Nevada. When a Muslim seer, Ibrahim al-Jarbi from Tunisia, attacked Álvaro de Portugal and his wife at the siege of Malaga, believing them to be Fernando and Isabel, he was torn to pieces, and his remains were thrown back into the city by a siege catapult. His body was sewn together again there with silk and given a fine funeral before a Christian prisoner was executed and his dead body mounted on an ass and sent to wander off into the Christian camp.[53]

Last but certainly not least, the war was expensive. The total cost was perhaps 800 million maravedís, raised in a multitude of ways. This had led, among other things, to a special tax on the Jewish community of Spain of no less than 50 million maravedís.[54]

The court of Christian Spain under Fernando and Isabel, like all courts, was also attended, wherever it was, in Santa Fe or in Santiago de Compostela, by a host of expectant plaintiffs; some of them were scholars of distinction, some near-beggars, all hopeful for a nod or even a smile of recognition from a secretary. There were those who hoped to gain enough money to afford a plate of chickpeas by singing or playing the *vihuela*.

Among these individuals in Santa Fe was a tall, purposeful, prematurely white-haired man—it had once been red—his eyes blue, his nose aquiline, and his high cheeks often turning scarlet, on a long face. He would tell anyone who cared to listen curious geographical things. He had been at court for about five years and was astounded that people did not listen to him more. But with the war coming to its conclusion, what, really, could he have expected? He seemed to have a sense neither of judgment nor of humor, and never joked about himself. He was pious and on Sundays did nothing except pray. Indeed, in respect of fasting, saying prayers, and condemning blasphemy, he might have been a member of a religious order. Yet he was affable and friendly. His favorite oath was "By San Fernando," and his only rebuke, "God take you." He spoke Spanish fluently, but with an accent that no one could place. He never explained exactly whence he came, but most people thought that he was from Genoa. He had been to Guinea and the Cape Verde Islands and so knew of the astonishing achievements of captains from Lisbon on the west coast of Africa since the days of Henry the Navigator. People also said that this individual had sold sugar in the Canaries, on behalf of Florentine merchants. He had powerful friends: the Duke of Medinaceli liked him and even the great Cardinal Mendoza interested himself in him from time to time. He was an exotic figure in a court that, for all its foreign alliances and marriages, was somewhat peninsular in its attitudes. (In 1488,

Peter Martyr had written that Spain was the last attic of a vast palace in which Italy was the main salon, the emporium of the world.)[55] This stranger was a well-known sight, for he had long been waiting for some royal sign of encouragement. Yet familiarity bred respect for him. He wanted support from the Crown for a journey that he wished to make to the West, across what was thought of as the "Ocean Sea." His name was Columbus.[56]

Book Two

COLUMBUS

Insula hyspana

Columbus makes landfall, and Indians flee.
An illustration from Columbus's first letter
describing his discoveries, published in 1493.

4

"Only by monarchs"

Such an enterprise could only be undertaken by monarchs.

Queen Isabel to the Duke of
Medinaceli, 1491[1]

Columbus was a citizen of Genoa, and that port seemed then the center of the world:

> So many are the Genoese,
> And so sure-footed everywhere,
> They go to any place they please,
> And re-create their city there.[2]

Genoese merchants dominated Mediterranean commerce. The Pope, Innocent VIII, was Genoese, having been born Giovanni Battista Cibo, in a family renowned for shipping grain from Tunis to Europe. One Cibo had been a governor of Chios in the fourteenth century. Giovanni Battista Cibo had been the protégé of an austere cardinal, Calandrini, half-brother of Pope Nicholas V, founder of the Vatican Library, who came from the pretty Genoese frontier town of Sarzana. After another Genoese, Francesco della Rovere, had been elected Pope, as Sixtus IV, Cibo rose effortlessly to become the favored candidate for the throne of St. Peter in 1484. In that place of honor, he was rather unsuccessful: the historian Guicciardini described him as useless so far as improvement in public welfare was concerned.[3] The magisterial place that the head of the Church had in the minds of all Christians, kings as well as laborers, archbishops as well as priests and monks, found in Cibo an unworthy representative. Yet it is to his credit that he built a beautiful double fountain in St. Peter's Square, in addition to a shrine for the Holy Spear; and it was at least said that no one left a conversation with him without feeling consoled.[4]

Roman aristocrats referred to Pope Innocent as "the Genoese sailor."

That was an insult in the Holy City, but it would have been so in few other places. The Genoese might be disliked, but they were respected; in the novel *Tirant lo Blanc* we read how the hero is adjured to "rout those wicked Genoese, since the crueler their deaths, the more glorious your name will resound."[5] Petrarch, at that time the cynosure of all affections, had thought Genoa "a truly regal city."[6]

St. Ferdinand had given the Genoese a special quarter in Seville with their own chapel, a quay, and a public bath. The Genoese family of Centurione (Centurión in Spain) were the most important businessmen of Malaga, both before and after its fall to the Christians; and Malaga had been the northern center of the African gold trade. Another Centurión bought sugar in Madeira, while a brother of his was busy selling silk in Granada. The Dorias sold olive oil from the valley of the Guadalquivir, while Francesco Pinelli of Genoa (Piñelo to his Spanish friends) was among those who financed the conquest of Gran Canaria in the Canary Islands, where he had built the first sugar mill. He also became the joint treasurer of the Santa Hermandad, the embryonic national Castilian police, with Luis Santangel. Francesco Ripparolo (Riberol in Spain) traded in dye stuffs, especially orchil, in the Canaries; afterwards, he sold soap in Seville, in respect of which commodity he later obtained a valuable monopoly.

The Grimaldi of Genoa were interested in wheat, while their relations, the Castiglione, dealt in wool. Other Genoese mercantile families who made the best of opportunities in Spain included the Vivaldi, of whom two brothers had sailed the Atlantic in 1291 to search for "the regions of India by way of the Ocean" (and were never heard of again), and the large Fornari family, who had been concerned in selling slaves in Chios. A Genoese, Lanzarotto Malocello, had discovered (or rediscovered) the Canary Islands about 1330 and raised there a Castilian flag on the island of Lanzarote, which name derives from his own. Another Genoese, Antonio Usodimare, also of a mercantile family in the Portuguese service, had been the first European to sail up the Rivers Senegal and Gambia. Yet one more citizen of Genoa, Antonio Noli, first established on Portugal's behalf an effective settlement in the Cape Verde Islands. The Portuguese navy had been founded by a Genoese and had been commanded by his descendants, who took the title of admiral for several generations.

Genoese entrepreneurs had also taken the initiative in growing sugarcane in the Algarve. The Lomellini controlled the Portuguese gold trade, and relations of theirs dominated not only the salt and silver commerce of Sardinia, but the mastic in Chios.[7] Genoese were dominant in commerce at Ceuta after its capture by Portugal in 1415, and most of the gold brought from black Africa by caravan ended up there.[8] Sovereignty of the Atlantic islands had been divided between the kings of Castile and Portugal by treaty—Madeira, the Azores, and the Cape Verde Islands remaining with the Portuguese, the Canaries with the Spaniards; but the Genoese were to be found on all the islands, whether under a Spanish or a Portuguese flag.

The Genoese were specialists in trading slaves. Unlike the Portuguese, whose captains usually were exercised by the need to go through at least the motions of conversion of captives, they were not troubled by such concerns. The Genoese enslaved and sold, in the Crimea as in Chios, in Tunis as in Ceuta, in Malaga as in Granada, men, women, and children of all hues and races: Circassians and Ethiopians, Slavs and Bosnians, Berbers and black Africans, Canary Islanders and Greeks all found a market.[9]

These families usually retained establishments in their home city, and one can still see their palaces—some of them, like those of the Doria, standing triumphant above the ruins of the twentieth century; others, like those of the Centurioni, barely distinguishable among the decayed buildings near the port. These sumptuous establishments were often embellished by treasures made possible by Spanish adventures in which the Genoese had outmaneuvered their rivals, such as the once preeminent Catalans, though Genoa itself was not an imperial-minded city, as was Venice. For Genoese merchants acted on their own, without consideration of interests at home. That they played such a part in European enterprise in the Atlantic was neither a collective nor a state decision; it derived from the hardheaded calculation of financial advantages by about fifty dynamic families or associations.[10]

The Genoese were not the only Italians to be established in southern Spain and Portugal. Bartolomeo Marchionni, for example, from Florence, was the most important slave merchant of Lisbon; he sold black slaves so successfully there that he was thought of as an honorary Portuguese. His partners in Seville included Juanotto Berardi and Amerigo Vespucci, also Florentines, trading not only African slaves bought from Lisbon but captives from the Canary Islands; and it had been a Venetian, the ingenious Alvise Ca' da Mosto, who had discovered the Cape Verde Islands for the King of Portugal in the 1450s.

In those days the Church of Rome was not yet represented in Spain by a permanent nuncio. But many churchmen came and went, while other Italians made up for the absence of a permanent ambassador, even in the Spanish camp of Santa Fe before Granada. Among these was Peter Martyr de Anglería, a brilliant and learned man born in a village on Lake Maggiore who had come to Spain with the Count of Tendilla, ex-ambassador in Rome.

Martyr had then been asked to educate the sons of Spanish noblemen. He wrote vivid letters in rough Latin to his Italian benefactors, such as Cardinal Ascanio Sforza, brother of Ludovico il Moro, the artful Duke of Milan, and to successive popes. He would be among the most valuable witnesses of the next twenty extraordinary years in Castile. A humanist chaplain and professor of linguistics from Sicily, Lucius Marineo Sículo, was also at the Spanish court, having been inspired to come to Spain by Fadrique Enríquez, the son of the Admiral of Castile.[11] Artists from Italy, such as Nicolás Pisano, were busy reviving the character and color of the tiles of Seville.

Nor was the interchange exclusively one way: Castilians were to be found in Bologna and other Italian universities while Catalan consuls were established in the cities of the kingdom of Naples, as in Venice, Florence, Pisa, and Genoa. Lorenzo Vázquez of Segovia, "the Spanish Brunelleschi," trained as an architect in Rome and Bologna, was in the 1490s remodeling the Colegio de Santa Cruz in Valladolid and was also at work on the Duke of Medinaceli's palace at Cogolludo, near Guadalajara, as well as a new archiepiscopal residence in the latter city for Cardinal Mendoza.[12]

These men stood for a growing Spanish connection with the center of culture in Europe. The time had not quite come when, thanks to the influence of printing, the revered Florentine Petrarch would dictate the rhythms, even the subject matter, of most Spanish poems. Yet most ambitious writers in Spain were in the 1490s already arranging to spend time in Italy, just as enlightened Englishmen would do in the eighteenth century. Soon, Fernando and Isabel would send armies there in support of their own claim to Naples, led by the best of their generals, Gonzalo Fernández de Córdoba, El Gran Capitán. He would benignly reflect *¡España, las armas! ¡Italia, la pluma!*[13]

Spain appreciated Italy for things other than literature: when Queen Isabel at Seville was offered a luxurious cloak for her favorite Virgin, she requested a fine cape of brocade, made by her own preferred designer from Venice, Francesco del Nero.[14]

Despite the role of Venice, Florence, and Rome in the Spain of Fernando and Isabel, it was fitting that the Pope in those days should have been a Genoese on both sides of his family. It was also appropriate that that eternal supplicant at court, the white-haired mariner Christopher Columbus, or Cristóbal Colón, to use his Spanish name, should have been born in Genoa.

Columbus, as he is known in the English-speaking world, did not seem quite at home in the company of the forementioned great Genoese merchants. But then he was not at ease in any circle. That is why some have sought to establish him as a Gallego, a Jew, or a Majorcan.[15] One writer thought that Columbus spoke Castilian since, though "his half-Jewish family" (as the author insisted) emigrated from Galicia after 1391, they always talked Castilian at home. But Genoa was not very welcoming to Jews, and it seems a tall tale. Columbus often appeared hostile to both Jews and *conversos* in conversation and letters,[16] but that proves nothing, for some of the most virulent anti-Semites were *conversos*. He was certainly a serious Christian who preferred not to work on Sundays.[17]

Columbus himself recalled that he was from Genoa when seeking to establish a feudal entail (*mayorazgo*) in Spain for his family in 1497. He explained then, too, that he had always desired to have a house in Genoa.[18] In a codicil to his will, just before his death in 1506, he mentioned only Genoese friends, except for "the Jew who guards the gate of the Jewish district in Lisbon."[19]

Such mystery as Columbus created about his birth may be explained by shame about his origins, for his father, Domenico Colombo, from Moconesi, in the valley of Fontanabuona, above the city of Genoa, seems to have been merely a weaver, as was his mother, Susanna Fontanarossa. Domenico was probably later the landlord of an inn in Savona, thirty-five miles west of Genoa, the birthplace of Pope Sixtus IV. But that did not constitute much of a social rise. Columbus never afterwards talked of his parents or, indeed, of his sister, Binachinetta, who married a cheese merchant, or of his brother Giovanni Pelegrino, who stayed at home. However, two other brothers, Bartolomeo and Diego, were constantly with him in Spain and in the New World, and two of his nephews joined him there also. Columbus once said that he "was not the first admiral" in his family, but perhaps he was referring to his wife's ancestors, who, as will be seen, were active in a thousand ways.

As mentioned earlier, the accent and speech of Columbus have excited attention. Las Casas, who knew him, thought that he certainly spoke as if his native language had been something other than Castilian.[20] He always had Portuguese words in his vocabulary, a sign, it has been thought, that he learned Spanish in his years in Lisbon between 1474 and 1485. He never composed letters in Italian. Probably that was because he knew the Genoese dialect, which was only rarely written.

Columbus's early life can be re-created from his own later comments and from those of his son Fernando, who wrote a biography that has many merits. Thus he told the King and Queen of Spain in 1501 that he had been to sea at an early age.[21] Fernando Colón (so we shall call him, for he was fully Hispanized) said that his father had studied at the University of Pavia.[22] Las Casas also said that Columbus studied the rudiments of letters, especially grammar, and Latin at Pavia.[23] But the historian Father Andrés Bernáldez,

with whom Columbus once stayed in his house outside Seville, said that
Columbus was "a man of great intellect but little education."[24] The stay at
Pavia seems doubtful.

Columbus's first maritime exploit was in 1472, when he was twenty-one.
He seems to have been a simple mariner on a ship belonging jointly to Paolo
di Negro and Nicoloso Spinola, both of well-known mercantile families in
Genoa. They apparently went to the Aragonese dependency of Tunis, where
the Cibo family was powerful, and captured a ship belonging to merchants
from Barcelona. Columbus then went, in the *Roxana*, a ship whose owner
was that same Paolo di Negro, to the Genoese colony of Chios, off Smyrna,
in the Aegean, an island port concerned with the sale not only of slaves but
of Atlantic sugar as well as mastic, a gum used to make varnish. He seems to
have been to Lisbon for the first time in 1476, where he was shipwrecked
after a battle at sea, presumably with Castilians, while on board the *Bechalla*,
a ship belonging to another Genoese, Ludovico Centurión. Then in 1477,
Columbus sailed to Ireland, and perhaps to Iceland, on another of Paolo di
Negro's and Spinola's boats, again presumably as a sailor.[25]

The next year, Centurión suggested that Columbus should work for him
selling sugar in Madeira, "a land of many canes," as the Venetian Alvise Ca'
da Mosto put it, about 1460; and this he seems to have done, so learning of a
plantation colony that already employed black African slaves as well as enslaved Canary Islanders (the first sugar mill in Madeira had been built in
1452). Columbus would have learned of the elaborate network of channels
and tunnels, some of mortar and some carved from the rock, known as *le-
vadas,* that brought water to the terraced plots. Much of the sugar that
Columbus sold must have gone to the Low Countries, where it was often exchanged for luxurious clothes. But how and where did he make these sales?
The record is silent.

Before he went to Madeira, perhaps in 1477, Columbus married Felipa
Palastrelli (Perestrelo in Portuguese), a sister of the hereditary governor of
Porto Santo, the smaller of the two islands of the Madeira archipelago but
the first one to be colonized.

Felipa's father, Bartolomeo, by then dead, himself governor of Porto
Santo before his son, came from Piacenza, in northern Italy. Felipa's mother,
Isabel Muñiz, was descended from a captain who helped in 1147 to capture
the castle of São Jorge from the Moors. A part of Lisbon is still called the
Puerta de Martím Muñiz. Isabel's father, Gil Ayres Muñiz, had a fine property in the Algarve and had been with the Portuguese expedition at the successful siege of Ceuta in 1420. So Columbus had married into a family with
useful connections.

After the fall of Ceuta, Portugal embarked upon a half century of astounding maritime activity. Columbus would have become aware of it even before he arrived in Lisbon, if only because of the role of the Genoese. The expansion was inspired by Prince Henry the Navigator, brother of King João, and one of the commanders at Ceuta.[26] His first venture was the occupation, beginning about 1425, of the previously uninhabited islands of Madeira (so-called from the timber-bearing forest, *madeira* being the Portuguese for "wood") and, about 1431, of the Azores (a word meaning "the hawks"). Both these groups of islands were colonized by Portuguese, but Flemings as well as Italians also played a part. Both places yielded wax, honey, and dye, from resins of "dragon's blood" of the dragon tree, and of the lichen orchil, increasingly sought after by those who wanted violet cloth. Columbus would have been impressed by how far out both these archipelagos were in the ocean: one thousand miles and six hundred miles, respectively, from Lisbon. Porto Santo, twenty-eight miles from the main island, was the most easily cultivated of the two islands of the Madeiras: it had been easy to colonize for it was treeless and flat, and the sea nearby teemed with fish. The mountainous main island of Madeira was covered by trees till a fierce fire destroyed most of that forest.

Henry next sent expeditions down the West African coast. His primary purpose was to find a sea route to the sources of African gold on the headwaters of the Rivers Niger and Volta. In 1434, one of his captains, Gil Eannes, sailed around Cape Bojador, a headland that had been seen as impassable (though one of the French conquerors of the Canaries had probably sailed past it earlier). It had been put out, probably by Muslims to discourage adventures there, that sailors turned black if they rounded Cape Bojador and that any ship that sailed there would be consumed by the heat.

In the next few years, most of western Africa was discovered by Portuguese captains: Mauretania, the River Senegal, the River Gambia, the Cape Verde Islands (in 1455), the Pepper, Ivory, Gold, and Slave Coasts, and then the kingdom of Benin, the mouth of the Niger, and the Cameroons had all been visited before Columbus arrived in Lisbon.

A second motive for these African adventures was both a strategic and a religious one: the Portuguese royal family, as good Christian soldiers, sought a way of attacking Islam from its rear.

By 1470, the pursuit of black slaves had also come to be an important part of these adventures, Lisbon becoming a center for the sale and further shipment of slaves to Mediterranean markets, both Christian and Muslim. Many Italians had again been engaged in these undertakings; there was, for example, a Genoese, Luca Cassano, who had set himself up as a slave trader in Terceira in the Azores, and the Venetian Alvise Ca' da Mosto had brought back slaves from the River Gambia. The Lomellini family continued their wide-ranging banking activities in Lisbon. The Florentine Marchionni, from a family known in Genoese Crimea as slavers, was beginning in 1470 to establish his position as the master slave trader in that capital.

These Portuguese voyages have seemed, in the eye of history, less important than those of Columbus. But as a Dutch traveler remarked in the eighteenth century, the Portuguese served for "setting the dogs to spring the game" in the era of European expansion.[27] The journeys initiated the age of discovery of which Columbus would become the supreme hero; and they have a wonderful innovative audacity, remarkable in a small nation that had never before made a mark on history.

For a time, Columbus and Felipa, his wife, lived in Lisbon in the house of her mother, Isabel Muñiz. They went, too, to Porto Santo and then to Funchal, in Madeira. When, in Funchal, Felipa died giving birth to a son, Diego Columbus returned to Lisbon and worked partly as a bookseller, partly as a cartographer. His devoted brother Bartolomeo joined him from Genoa. Columbus must then have met mariners and merchants who knew the Ocean Sea, as the Atlantic was then known, for it was still believed by most educated people, following the Greek geographer Ptolemy, that that great expanse of water surrounded a single global landmass.

There were many curious stories abroad in those years about sailing west to find more Atlantic islands, "Antilla" and "Brasil," for example, or St. Ursula's island or St. Brendan's. The sea then seemed a magical place, full of extraordinary possibilities, while interest in the idea of the "Antipodes" had been excited by the publication in 1469 in Spanish of the geography of the Greek Strabo; that first-century geographer had even talked of the possibility of "sailing direct from Spain to the Indies."[28] About a dozen Portuguese voyages were dispatched westward between 1430 and 1490. Perhaps some sailors of that nation had heard of the medieval Norse expeditions to Greenland, Vinland, and North America. After all, the last Greenlander of Norse origin died only in the fifteenth century.[29]

That the earth was round had been realized for many generations. The Greek astronomers of Miletus had even thought, about 500 B.C., that the world was a sphere. That view had been advanced by the geometer Pythagoras. Though much of Greek learning was later lost, the Catholic Church had accepted this hypothesis by about A.D. 750, and in the fifteenth century, the "sphericity" of the planet was generally agreed. Only a few ignorant people still tried to maintain that it was flat.

Columbus sailed with a Portuguese expedition down the coast of West Africa as far as the new fortress of El Mina, on the Gold Coast, touching at the Cape Verde Islands, which were even more of a plantation colony than Madeira, drawing heavily on slaves from mainland Africa nearby. Again, it seems evident that he was just a sailor, if perhaps now one with some authority. He apparently stopped on the Pepper (Malaguetta) Coast, where he later claimed to have seen sirens. That was either in 1481, when the trading fortress of El Mina was being built, or in 1485, when the cartographer José Vizinho was also there, having been sent by "the perfect prince," King João, to calculate the height of the sun on the Equator. Columbus is said to have been accompanied by his brother Bartolomeo.[30] On these journeys he must have become fully acquainted with the vessel that had already enabled the Portuguese to do so much, the caravel: a small, "lateen"-rigged ship with the speed, maneuverability, and shallow draft that allowed it to beat against contrary winds much better than older, square-rigged ships.[31]

Columbus read as well as traveled. He probably came across Seneca's surprising statement that one could sail from Spain to the Indies in only a few days.[32] He certainly examined Marco Polo's summary of information that had been posted up on the Bridge of the Rialto in Venice for the benefit of other travelers to the East, and also his memoir, dictated to a fellow prisoner when in a Genoese jail. The latter book was full of engaging stories, including tales of Amazons and men with dog's heads. Marco Polo had reported Cipangu (Japan) to be 1,500 miles east of China and that there were no less than 1,378 islands lying off Asia.[33]

Another work that Columbus read (at this time or later) was the *Imago Mundi* by Pierre d'Ailly, a cosmographer of the early fifteenth century who had been also Bishop of Cambrai, cardinal and confessor to the King of France. In this the clever Frenchman discussed not only astronomy but the size of the world. He suggested that the Atlantic was narrow, that Seneca had been right to say that with a favorable wind one could cross it in a few days, and that the Antipodes existed. Alongside the first of these propositions Columbus annotated in his copy: "There is no reason to believe that the ocean covers half the earth."[34] Columbus also studied *The Description of Asia* by the Sienese Pope Pius II (Aeneas Silvius Piccolomini), who had insisted that all seas were navigable and all lands habitable. That pontiff also believed that one could travel from Europe to Asia via the West.

Columbus naturally looked, too, at a new edition of Ptolemy's *Geogra-*

phy, the most famous book on the subject, known in a Latin translation from 1406, published in Vicenza in 1475, and later printed in edition after edition. This work had been written by an Alexandrine scholar about A.D. 150. It named eight thousand places and included maps and tables. The most important idea in it was that geography meant the accurate fixing of positions by latitude and longitude, astronomically determined. Much of the information in Ptolemy derived from gossip, but the book was believed at the time to have a scientific basis. Columbus probably saw the second edition, published in Bologna in 1477, which included twenty-six maps of Asia, Africa, and Europe. He read, too, the curious but successful work of the armchair traveler "Sir John Mandeville," invented tales of adventures of which several editions were soon also available.[35] He may have seen maps belonging to his father-in-law, for Perestrelli seems to have been one of Henry the Navigator's advisers on oceanic exploration.[36]

Finally, Columbus was given several letters by an elderly, erudite, and humane Florentine, Paolo del Pozzo Toscanelli, who had insisted in a letter of 1474 to a Portuguese canon, Fernão Martins, one of King Afonso V's chaplains, that a western route to China was possible: "I sent to His Majesty this map which I have designed . . . and on which I have marked the coasts and islands which may serve as a starting point when you undertake this navigation in steering always westward."[37] Toscanelli, head of a family business in Florence dealing in skins and spices, also said that in letters he had discussed with the King of Portugal "the shortest route from here to the islands of the Indies where the spices grow, a route shorter than that via Guinea." The journey might be broken in "Antilla" or Japan. Columbus transcribed this letter in his own copy of Pope Pius II's book. Toscanelli added in another letter that the Emperor of China thought that this western route from Europe to his country might be about 3,900 nautical miles but that he himself considered that a sensible figure might be 6,500 miles. He sent Columbus a copy of this last letter, perhaps in 1481.[38] Later still, he told Columbus: "I am persuaded that this voyage is not as difficult as is thought."[39]

In consequence, Columbus drew his own conclusions. He accepted Pierre d'Ailly's view that the Atlantic was not so broad as it seemed,[40] and Toscanelli's that it could be crossed. Fernando Colón wrote that his father also began to think that "just as some Portuguese were sailing so far to the south, in the same way one could navigate to the west, and it was logical that one would meet land in that direction."[41] He noted, Fernando Colón added, any useful ideas that sailors or merchants might have, becoming "convinced that to the west of the Canary and the Cape Verde Islands lay many islands and lands."

Toscanelli was the decisive influence on Columbus, who mentions him again and again in his own letters. In his diary of his first voyage, he speaks of "Paolo Físico" more often than of his Spanish companions. Toscanelli was imaginative, however, and he was quite wrong in his estimate of the distance from the Canary Islands to Japan.[42]

From the fifteenth century onward there has been a story that Columbus was inspired to reach his conclusions by an "unknown pilot," perhaps a Portuguese or an Andalusian, who on his deathbed said that he had been swept by a storm to the West Indies while on his way from Portugal to England. This pilot was said to have spoken of naked people living amiably in the sun of what seems to have been the Caribbean. Most historians of the sixteenth century (Fernández de Oviedo, López de Gómara, Fernando Colón, for example) dismissed this tale, which ran quite against the expectations of Columbus, who never anticipated finding primitive people in his New World. On the contrary, he expected to meet the sophisticated Ashikaga shogun of Japan or the Ming emperor of China. But the story has survived; and, in the twentieth century, several distinguished writers vehemently supported the theory of the "unknown pilot."[43] For example, one historian has written that Columbus learned "not only thereby the existence of oceanic lands in the West belonging, as he believed, to the East Indies, but the precise distance from the Old World, as well as their exact place in the immense sea."[44] But actually the "unknown pilot" is unnecessary to explain Columbus's frame of mind; with the help of Pierre d'Ailly and Toscanelli alone, a Frenchman and a Florentine, his plan was virtually made.

In 1484, Columbus put a scheme of sailing west to Cipangu (Japan) and China to King João of Portugal, who had devoted more attention than any other monarch to the idea of discovery. Portuguese explorers had already discovered sophisticated principalities, such as Benin, and observed colossal African rivers, such as the Senegal, the Gambia, the Niger, even the Congo. In the early 1480s, Diogo Cão nearly reached the Cape of Good Hope. It was therefore difficult to interest the King in any plan for a western route to China. João, however, put Columbus's scheme to a committee of inquiry— the first of several that the Genoese would encounter in the next ten years. It was standard practice in those days, as in our times, for governments to ask experts to give advice on anything untoward.

This committee in Lisbon, the Junta dos Matemáticos, included the cartographer José Vizinho, with whom Columbus had perhaps traveled to West Africa; the Bishop of Ceuta, Diogo Ortiz de Vilhegas (a Castilian from Calzadilla, near Coria, Cáceres);[45] and the eccentric astronomer Maestre Rodrigo, with whom Columbus had already discussed the delicate matter of the height of the sun on the Equator.

The Junta decided that Cipangu must be much farther away than Columbus (and Toscanelli) thought—on which matter they were right—and that no expedition could be fitted out with food and water to travel across so enormous an expanse of sea. No crew could be disciplined for so long. But as soon as King João rejected Columbus, he is said, on Bishop Ortiz's advice, to have sent a caravel west from the Cape Verde Islands to investigate the Atlantic; it returned after many days with no news.[46]

Rebuffed in Portugal, Columbus decided to approach the monarchs in Spain, to which he had not previously been. But that country, like Portugal, had her outposts in the Atlantic, in her case, the Canary Islands; and, in the colonization of those, Genoese were playing a part. Columbus would have been aware of that and would have realized from Toscanelli's letter that the Canaries were the best place from which to embark upon any transatlantic journey.

The Canaries comprise many islands, a few large and many small, of which the closest was fifty miles off northwest Africa and 750 from southwest Spain, being then thirteen days' normal sail from Cadiz. The archipelago, probably known to the ancients as "the Fortunate Islands," was, as earlier shown, first visited in the fourteenth century by a Castilian fleet led by a Genoese, Lanzarotto Malocello. Another Castilian expedition in 1402 was that of French adventurers Jean de Béthencourt, Lord of Grainville in Normandy, and Gadifer de la Salle, of Poitou. Béthencourt eventually established a principality of his own on Lanzarote and two other smaller islands, Fuerteventura and Hierro, the indigenous opposition being less strong there than on Gran Canaria and Tenerife. He divided up the land that he seized among his followers, chiefly Castilians but also some Normans. Quarrels followed; the Portuguese made claims, and Henry the Navigator coveted the islands and fought unsuccessfully for them. Eventually, the dominant authorities became the Medina Sidonias, the noblemen of Seville, and the Peraza family, also Sevillano in origin. Missionaries sought to convert the indigenous population, including those on the unconquered islands, while sea captains captured others to be sold as slaves in Spain.[47]

The Portuguese in the end accepted Castilian control of the Canary Islands by the Treaty of Alcaçovas in 1479, as well as of a stretch of territory opposite, the modern territory of Sahara, so enclosing "the Little Sea" (El Mar Pequeño), one of the best fishing grounds. In return, Castile accepted the Portuguese possession of the Azores and Madeira, and her monopoly of trade with the rest of West Africa.[48] Soon the Castilians, led by Pedro de Vera, from Jerez de la Frontera, managed after considerable fighting to master

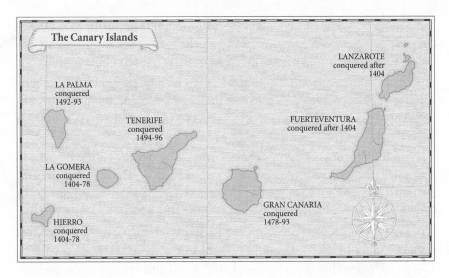

The Canary Islands

LANZAROTE
conquered after
1404

LA PALMA
conquered
1492-93

TENERIFE
conquered
1494-96

FUERTEVENTURA
conquered after 1404

LA GOMERA
conquered
1404-78

HIERRO
conquered
1404-78

GRAN CANARIA
conquered
1478-93

most of Gran Canaria in 1487. La Palma was also conquered early in the 1490s. That left only Tenerife in the hands of indigenous people.

Those "Canarians" are mysterious. Were they Berber, African, or even European in origin? Probably the first, though no one can say for certain, or even what they looked like. Columbus reported them, unhelpfully, to be neither light nor dark, and the records of the sales of slaves speak of them as both.[49] The French in the early fifteenth century thought them "tall and formidable." The Canary Islanders do not seem to have known anything of navigation (or had forgotten it) and so never left their archipelago, and did not even travel from one island to another. They knew nothing of bread. They had no horses, and Castilian cavalry terrified them. They had many languages and were ruled by numerous independent kinglets. They fought well with stones and sticks, but their numbers were already falling because of contact with European diseases. The Spaniards had been able to conduct themselves much as they wished in these islands since the native population was so few, perhaps 14,000 in Tenerife, 6,000 in Gran Canaria, and 1,500 elsewhere.[50]

The Canary Islands became a source of wealth for Castile. Numerous Canary Islanders had been kidnapped since the 1450s and sold as slaves in Andalusia. Since they had been untouched by Islam, they were considered more reliable than Berbers (Muslims were notoriously troublesome, being usually faithful to their religion). Several influential men at the Spanish court, such as the senior adviser Gutierre de Cárdenas, drew good incomes from the sale of products from the islands such as orchil, of which Cárdenas had a monopoly. His colleague Alonso de Quintanilla had gained the help of Genoese Sevillanos to assist in financing these conquests. Ludovico Centurión built a sugar mill in 1484 on Gran Canaria, even though the subjugation of the island was still incomplete; and a bishop, of Rubicon, had been appointed (Juan de Frías). These conquests by Castile in the fifteenth century constituted a step toward the New World, even though it was not known then to exist.

Columbus does not seem to have visited the Canaries before he went to Spain. He would have mentioned it had that been so. The fact that Columbus was believed to have had a love affair with a later governor of La Gomera, Beatriz de Bobadilla, implies nothing since he met her in Córdoba. But, as suggested earlier, he knew before going to Spain that any Castilian captain sailing to the West would do well to use the Canaries as a base; as Toscanelli had said, such a journey should start from as far south as possible in order to take advantage of the prevailing winds. The winds of the Atlantic drive clockwise in what seems to be a large wheel. The latitudinal character of the system was to be the key to sailing to the New World for generations, and Columbus would have known it from talking to sailors in Lisbon.

Columbus arrived in Andalusia in the second half of 1485 and made his way to the Franciscan monastery of La Rábida, near where the mud-red Rio Tinto enters the Atlantic. The monks at the *convento* were not only interested in the needs of sailors but could offer information. They knew useful things—that, for example, the sight of a flock of birds must suggest that land was close. Among those at La Rábida were Fray Francisco (Alfonso) de Bolaños, who had been concerned in the evangelization of the Canary Islands and of Guinea, and had even secured a benign papal statement in favor of slaves and a criticism of the slave trade.[51] Fray Juan Pérez talked of astronomy to Columbus, who also established a friendship with Fray Antonio de Marchena.

La Rábida was then a kind of maritime university.[52] A lay brother there, Pedro de Velasco, had been, in his youth, pilot to Diogo de Teive, who had served Prince Henry the Navigator and had been among the first to plant sugar in Madeira. Velasco himself had looked for Atlantis as a young man, and still might be persuaded to talk of the banks of clouds at sea in the evening that suggested to mariners that they might be about to reach land, for the sea, like the desert, had its mirages. Even now "so often a capricious cloud covers everything and frequently one is confused by low clouds which seem to have the shape of mountains, hills, and valleys."[53]

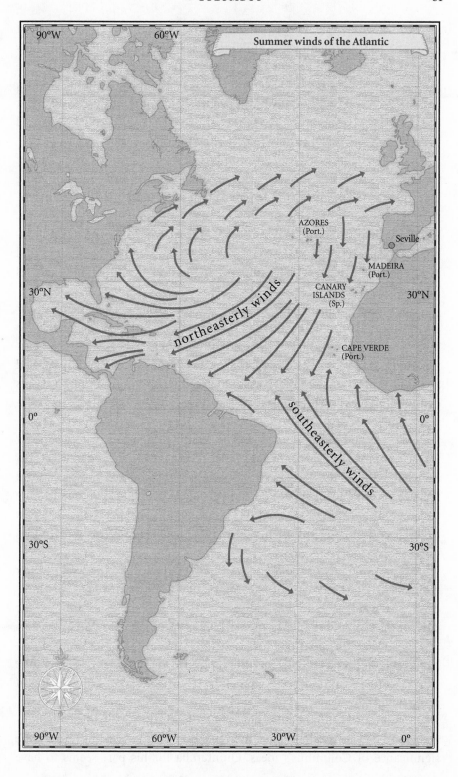

Summer winds of the Atlantic

90°W   60°W

AZORES
(Port.)

Seville

MADEIRA
(Port.)

30°N   30°N

CANARY
ISLANDS
(Sp.)

northeasterly winds

CAPE VERDE
(Port.)

0°   0°

southeasterly winds

30°S   30°S

90°W   60°W   30°W   0°

Years later, people would remember how Columbus arrived on foot at the monastery, a brilliant white building under a sparkling blue sky, and how he begged water and bread for his son Diego, then about six years old.[54] The garden is doubtless more lovely today than it was then; the bougainvillea and the cypresses that now give such beauty were not there in the 1480s. But the rich yellow stone in the patio, the white walls, and the tiled roofs and towers are surely much as they were in the fifteenth century.

Marchena and Pérez urged Columbus to make his way to the court of Castile. They were well connected, for Pérez had once been a confessor to the Queen herself. They gave him letters so that he could establish his credentials. So, no doubt praying first before the beautiful Christ of La Rábida, Columbus left for Seville and then for Córdoba, where the court was, leaving Diego, his son, with his sister-in-law, Briolanja Muñiz, who had married an Aragonese, Miguel Muliart, and was living near Huelva at San Juan del Puerto.[55]

Columbus reached Córdoba in the summer of 1485. There he met Beatriz Enríquez de Araña, a girl from Santa María de Trasierra, a few miles to the north of the city. She was the ward of her uncle, a locally powerful citizen, Rodrigo Hernández de Araña. Columbus lived with her and by her had a second, if illegitimate, child, Fernando. He also met long-standing advisers of the monarchs, such as Talavera, Isabel's confessor; Santangel, the treasurer; Quintanilla, the most effective of the Queen's courtiers; Juan Cabrero, the closest friend of the King; and even Cardinal Mendoza, whose support was so desirable.[56] Probably he made these acquaintanceships thanks to Fray Marchena and Pérez. But though Columbus encountered these powerful men, they could not ensure that he saw the Queen, and he had to follow the court, in the autumn of 1485, across Castile, on its usual peregrinations past Andújar and Linares, and then Valdepeñas, Ocaña, and Alcalá de Henares, outside Madrid.

Alcalá was a city of the Mendozas, half a day's ride to the west of their main palace in Guadalajara. There, on the site of the destroyed Moorish Alcázar, in the substantial episcopal palace, which still stands gigantic on the edge of the city, and thanks to the backing of the great cardinal, Columbus saw the Queen. Mendoza had told Isabel that the Genoese was astute, intelligent, able, and well versed in cosmography. He therefore suggested that the Crown should assist him with a few ships. They would cost little and might bring many benefits.[57]

Mendoza was still the most powerful individual in Spain after the monarchs, and he was the first public man in either Spain or Portugal to see the significance of Columbus's ideas. Quintanilla for his part seems to have thought that it would be wise for Spain to explore beyond Cape Bojador so as not to leave Portugal alone in the task of exploring the ocean. His foresight should not be forgotten.

The first discussion between Columbus and the monarchs, on January 20, 1486, in the cardinal's palace, did not prosper.[58] Fernando had provided himself with a copy of Ptolemy's *Geography* beforehand, and it did not seem to support Columbus's case. The King was interested in the Canary Islands, but only as a possible stepping-stone on the route to the African gold mines.[59] True, the monarchs seemed curious about the route of which Columbus spoke, and they were interested in the map of the world that he showed them and that perhaps had been drawn by his brother Bartolomeo ("the map put them in the mood to see what he had described").[60] But Columbus allowed his imagination a free run[61] and, most unwisely, he must have made it clear that he wanted to be admiral of the Ocean Sea, viceroy, and governor, too. (Probably he had made the same demands in Portugal.)[62] These titles all had implications for the Spanish Crown. Though the designation "admiral" may, in Columbus's mind, have had connections with the Genoese Pessagho family's use of the title in the Portuguese navy, it invited comparison in Spain with the "admiral of Castile," an office recently named hereditary in the family of the Enríquez, cousins of Fernando.[63] There was only one precedent for a viceroy in Castile, namely that of Galicia—even if there had been several such officials in the service of the King of Aragon. Probably Fernando was specially irritated by these demands. Governor? It, too, was a title recently used in connection with Galicia, the marquisate of Villena, and the Canary Islands, but was not otherwise known.

Both Fernando and Isabel were the heirs of kings who, in their time, had promoted much foreign activity. The civilized royal house of Aragon had always been interested in the outside world, and Fernando's uncle, King Alfonso the Magnanimous, had spent more time in Naples than he had in Spain. Tunis had been an Aragonese dependency in the thirteenth century, and African conquests were still coveted. Columbus was not dealing with isolationists.

But Columbus's self-assertions ignored the royal preoccupations with the war against Granada. As Las Casas put it, "When monarchs have a war to deal with, they understand little, and wish to understand little, of other matters."[64]

The Catholic Kings' relations with the Republic of Genoa were also at the time poor. Thus it seemed as if the ideas of Columbus would be laid aside. About thirty years later, a lawyer, Tristán de León, wrote that the difficulty was that "the only certainty was what Columbus said."[65] Then Columbus told the monarchs that he would present to them a person who believed in him. He sent for Fray Antonio de Marchena of La Rábida, who agreed that what Columbus had claimed was largely true. Marchena wrote to suggest that at least an inquiry should be made, as had happened in Lisbon.[66] His monastery had supported the conquest of the Canary Islands so as to add to the total of Christian souls. Columbus seemed to be offering the opportunity for even more evangelization.

The monarchs agreed to an inquiry. The most important member of the committee, the "chairman," was the Queen's confessor, Talavera, who was told to assemble "people who were most versed in that matter of cosmography, of whom there were, however, few in Castile."[67] While the specialists were at work, it was agreed that Columbus should remain at court, wherever that was, and be paid a small pension of 12,000 maravedís.[68]

But the work of Talavera and his friends was delayed because of setbacks in the war in Granada. Columbus had to wait. He used his time well. He earned some money making maps, and he met more influential people. These included his fellow Genoese, the two rich Francescos, Piñelo and Rivarolo, who had helped to finance the conquest of the Canaries, and the even more powerful Gutierre de Cárdenas, he of the naked sword in Segovia in 1474. Perhaps these men thought that at least Columbus might give Castile some new islands, like the Canaries. Most important, Columbus made friends with the Dominican theologian Diego Deza, till recently professor of theology at Salamanca and now prior of the college of San Sebastian there, as well as tutor-in-chief to the heir to the throne, the Infante Juan, to whom he gave daily Latin lessons. Why Deza and Columbus should have become so friendly is unclear, but they did so, elective affinities obviously playing their customary part. It was a friendship that stood Columbus in good stead.[69]

Deza found Columbus lodgings in the Dominican convent in Salamanca and introduced him to his friends, including the nurse of the Infante, Juana Velázquez de la Torre, and her cousin, Juan Velázquez de Cuéllar, the prince's treasurer. The Infante was fond of Juana and once, still under ten, said to her, "You must have me for a husband and nobody else." Columbus also became attached to Juana, and she became his confidante.[70] Cardinal Mendoza maintained his interest and sometimes had Columbus to dine, as did the *contador* Quintanilla. Talavera continued to give Columbus small regular payments, as decided by the monarchs.

The committee of inquiry, in which Talavera was the dominant influence, met during the winter of 1486–87, in Salamanca. Its conclusions were as negative as those of the similar body in Lisbon. These good and great men, like their Portuguese equivalents, thought that what Columbus claimed about the distance of China and the ease of travel there could not be true. They considered that the Crown could gain nothing from supporting Columbus and that, if it did give such backing, the royal authority would be diminished.[71]

This depressing decision was communicated to Columbus in August 1487. The committee reduced the brutality of their conclusion by saying that they did not exclude the possibility that one day, when the Crown's war with Granada had been won, their judgment might be reconsidered; perhaps the agreeable Dr. Deza had insisted on that qualification to the committee's reply. All the same, Columbus was naturally disheartened. He decided to re- turn to Portugal. Bartolomeo, his brother, had written recently of a new op- timism there while the explorer Bartolomeu Díaz was setting out that same August, to make another attempt to reach the southernmost point of Africa (Las Casas thought that Bartolomeo Colón took part in that heroic voy- age).[72] That was the year, too, that another remarkable Portuguese traveler, Pero de Covilhan, reached Calicut, in India, in a Muslim pilgrim boat from the Red Sea.

Early in 1488, King João sent Columbus a safe-conduct to Lisbon, which Columbus showed to King Fernando and Queen Isabel in Murcia.[73] But at that time the Spanish monarchs were still preoccupied by the war against Granada, and the document had no effect one way or the other.

Back in Lisbon by October 1488, Columbus was once again thwarted. King João had half-changed his mind about the value of an Atlantic route to China, but had sent westward a small expedition under a Fleming, Ferdi- nand van Olmen, with two caravels (at his own cost) to discover "a great is- land or islands where it is said that there might be the site of seven cities." But no one heard any more of that journey. Van Olmen, presumed lost, had had to start from the Azores, which was a less helpful point of embarkation, as Columbus knew, than the Canaries.

Columbus was probably in Lisbon, though, in December 1488 when Bartolomeu Díaz returned, perhaps accompanied by Bartolomeo Colón, from rounding the southern promontory of Africa, which he had optimisti- cally named the Cape of Good Hope.[74] Having found a southern route to India, the King of Portugal had no interest in a new western way.

Failing yet again to find the backing that he needed, Columbus contem- plated an approach to the kings of France and England. After all, Spain and Portugal were not the only seafaring states. So he dispatched his brother

Bartolomeo to London.[75] But his ill luck held: Bartolomeo was captured at sea by pirates and spent two years in a private prison. Columbus, who did not hear of this new setback immediately, returned to the monastery of La Rábida, which then seemed the only place that had time for him and his ideas. Fray Antonio de Marchena maintained his enthusiasm, as did Fray Juan Pérez. Marchena suggested that Columbus might approach with advantage the Duke of Medina Sidonia, whose ships dominated the Straits of Gibraltar and who, from his white palace that overlooked Sanlúcar de Barrameda, at the mouth of the River Guadalquivir, controlled local fishing. The Duke was popularly known as the king of tuna fish ("El Rey de los Atunes"). He had invested heavily in sugar in the Canary Islands and would soon have substantial property in Tenerife. Surely he had ships to spare. But Medina Sidonia had committed his ships to the war against Granada and did not expose himself to Columbus's charm.[76]

Columbus's next activity is mysterious, for we find the monarchs sending letters to the municipal councils of Andalusia telling them to be sure to provide food and lodging for Columbus because he was engaged in various services for them.[77] Perhaps he was providing intelligence about the war, though what it might have been is difficult to imagine. Whatever it was, it must have helped to make possible another discussion with the Queen. On this occasion, he saw Isabel alone, in the castle at Jaén, for Fernando was in the military camp at Baza.

Isabel seems to have talked to Columbus at length and to have left the clear impression that she might help him once Granada had fallen. She had at that time a copy of the wild stories of "Sir John Mandeville" and, though usually hardheaded, she always had a weakness for plausible dreamers. Her first ally, Archbishop Carrillo, for example, had introduced her in the 1470s to a certain Fernando Alarcón, who had promised to turn all her iron to gold. Perhaps in this new conversation, Isabel learned of Columbus's journey to Africa in the 1480s, and perhaps he discussed with her his conviction that he had divine support, and how Jerusalem and its liberation were always on his mind. At the end of their talk, Isabel gave Columbus more money for his expenses and invited him to be present in her train at the expected surrender of the Moorish city of Baza at the end of 1490.

Having heard nothing from his brother Bartolomeo, though presumably knowing that he had encountered difficulties, Columbus determined to go himself to France. He was dissuaded by the theologian Dr. Deza.[78] But then he had some good luck: he met the Duke of Medinaceli.

The Duke of Medinaceli, Luis de la Cerda, was then nearly fifty. He was the first duke. He might have been king, but his ancestors had abandoned their excellent claim. Still, King Fernando had recognized that if the royal family were to die out—and it could—the Duke might succeed to the throne.[79] Like most other noblemen, the Duke was a grandson of the celebrated Marqués de Santillana, and thus was a nephew of Cardinal Mendoza and a cousin of the Duke of Alba. Medinaceli shared jurisdiction over Puerto de Santa María, and he controlled Huelva. Though not a warrior, he took part in most of the wars of Granada. He once refused to detach any of his own troops from his white standard and place them under the Count of Benavente, saying, "Tell your master that I came here at the head of my household to serve him, and they go nowhere without me as leader."[80]

Medinaceli had his main residence now in Puerto de Santa María, and there, by a servant, Catalina del Puerto, he had several children, one of whom, Juan, would succeed him. His butler, a certain Romero, possibly a Jew, talked to him of Columbus, and the Duke summoned the Genoese to see him.[81] He was impressed. Indeed, he was convinced. He gave him food, money, and lodging. Columbus talked extensively not only with the Duke but with his sailors and probably also with the *corregidor* of El Puerto, the historian Diego de Valera, then in his seventies. Valera had written several histories of Castile in which he had taken a monarchist position. "Remember, you reign in God's stead on earth," he had told the King after the capture of Ronda. "It is clear that Our Lord intends to carry out what has been proposed for centuries, to wit, you shall not only put all the realms of Spain under your royal scepter, but you will subjugate regions beyond the sea." He had also informed King Fernando in 1482 of his ideas of how to gain victory in Granada.[82] He was just the kind of man with whom Columbus would have liked to have talked extensively. He and his son Charles had performed well in the naval war against Portugal of the 1470s and gained the royal confidence. No doubt, too, Columbus talked to Charles, who had commanded a fleet off Africa.

Medinaceli wanted to help Columbus. But as a loyal duke, not too far from the throne, he did not feel able to act without royal approval.[83] He wrote to the Queen telling of his willingness to support Columbus.[84] The Queen wrote to thank Medinaceli for his suggestions, saying what a pleasure it was to have in her realm such wonderful people as he, disposed to act with such public spirit. But an enterprise such as Columbus proposed "could only be one for monarchs."[85] She did not want noblemen carving out independent domains for themselves in the Indies or anywhere else. She asked, too, that Columbus be asked to go to the court again without delay.

The Duke was annoyed, but he accepted that the will of the Queen constituted the will of God. A year or two later, he wrote to his uncle, Cardinal Mendoza:[86]

I don't know if your eminence knows that I had in my house for a long time Christopher Columbus who came from Portugal and wished to go to see the King of France to seek his support. I myself wanted to send him from El Puerto with three or four caravels with a good infrastructure. But, as I saw that this was something for the Queen, I wrote to her, and she asked me to send him to her because, if anyone had to support him, it had to be her.[87]

So the weary Genoese prepared to return once more to the court, by now outside Granada. All the same, he lingered with Medinaceli and did not reach the valley of Granada till midsummer 1491. He reached his destination, as so often, at the wrong moment. The camp burned down just after he arrived. No one was interested in his ideas. Columbus decided once and for all to go to France. Before setting off, though, he decided to return to the monastery of La Rábida; and on the way, in Córdoba, he also said goodbye, probably for the last time, to his mistress, Beatriz Enríquez, and his son Fernando.

He reached La Rábida in October. The monks realized that Columbus was now going to seek French backing and beseeched him to remain with them for a few more weeks, while they communicated again with the Queen; and Fray Juan Pérez, Isabel's onetime confessor, the "guardian of the monastery," wrote to tell her that if she did not change her mind about Columbus, it would be too late. His letter was taken to Santa Fe by a pilot of Lepe, Sebastián Rodríguez. The Queen replied that she would see Columbus immediately, and sent 20,000 maravedís for clothes to be worn at court and for a mule for him to ride in her presence. Once more he set off optimistically across Andalusia.

The role of Fray Juan Pérez was significant: he belonged to that branch of the Franciscan order that had been influenced by the millenarian Cistercian Joaquín de Fiore, abbot in two monasteries of Calabria in the twelfth century. Fray Juan wanted to secure royal support for Columbus on the supposition that what Abbot Joaquín had fancifully called "the last age of humanity" might be about to begin.

Once more, however, Pérez's and Columbus's hopes were thwarted. First, Columbus had again to make his case to a committee of "men most eminent in rank." Again, we do not know exactly who these were, but probably as ever Talavera was the president of the committee. Perhaps Medinaceli participated, as well as Alessandro Geraldini, a recently arrived humanist from Genoa, one of the teachers of the Infante Juan. We can imagine how Columbus produced his maps again, his letters from Toscanelli, his interpretation of d'Ailly, his notes on Ptolemy, his well-remembered quotations from Mandeville and from Pope Pius II, his own memories of the Atlantic. Perhaps he mentioned again the possibility of being able to finance a campaign to recover Jerusalem: "I protested to Your Highnesses that everything gained as a result of this voyage would be spent in the conquest of Jerusalem, and your Highnesses laughed and said that the idea pleased them."[88]

But in these weeks, Granada was about to surrender, and the minds of the monarchs, their courtiers, and their learned advisers were on the Old World. The committee made no immediate decision, and Columbus waited all that autumn of 1491, with nothing else to do save observe how the Muslims in Granada were considering surrender without fighting.

5

"For God's sake, tell me
what song you are singing"

For God's sake, sailor, tell me what song you are singing!
—I shall not tell you unless you agree to sail with me.

BALLAD OF COUNT ARNALDOS, 1492

Within Granada in November 1491 there was discussion of a possible sur-render to the Christians. An Arab account tells how there came together, in a consultative assembly, the leading men, nobles and common folk alike, with Islamic lawyers, guild wardens, elders, learned men, such courageous knights as were still alive—indeed, anybody in Granada with some insight into affairs.[1] They all went to see the Emir (Boabdil) and told him of the condition of the people and in what a sorry state they were. Their city was a large one, they said, for which supplies of food were inadequate even in times of peace. So how could they manage when almost nothing was com-ing in? The route to bring food from the rich villages in the Alpujarras to the south had been cut. The best of the Muslim knights were dead; those who remained were weakened by wounds. The people were unable to go out to seek food or to cultivate the land.

Few of the Muslim brethren in North Africa across the sea had come to help, though they had been asked to. The Christian enemy was becoming ever stronger and was building elaborate siege works. Yet the winter had begun, much of the enemy's army had dispersed, and military operations had been suspended. If the Muslims were now to open talks with the Chris-tians, their approach would surely be well received. The Christians would probably agree to what was asked of them. If, however, they were to wait till spring, the Christian armies would attack, the Muslims would be weaker, the famine worse. The Christians might not be ready to accept the tolerant terms that they, the Muslims, were seeking, and they and their city might not be saved from a brutal conquest. Some of the Muslims who had fled to the Christian camp would be ready to point out to their new friends the vulnerable places in the defenses. An honorable surrender now seemed more appropriate than a brutal military defeat in a few months' time.

So it was agreed by all in Granada that "they should send an emissary for a talk to the Christian king. Some [Muslims] thought that secretly Boabdil and his ministers had already agreed to hand over the city to Fernando but, fearing the reaction of the common people, kept them duped. At all events, when the leaders sent word to Fernando, they found that he was happy to grant their requests. . . ."[2]

The details of the surrender were worked out by El Gran Capitán, Gonzalo Fernández de Córdoba, an Arab speaker and the rising star in the Spanish army, and al-Mulih, the Arab governor of the city, who asked, "What certainty can Boabdil have that the King and Queen will let my lord have the Alpujarras [the valleys between the city and the sea that the Muslims insisted remain theirs] which is the first clause in our negotiations, and that they will really treat him as a relative?" "The obligation will last, señor governor," replied Fernández de Córdoba, "for as long as his excellency Boabdil remains in the service of their Highnesses."[3]

On November 28, 1491, terms of surrender, the *"Capitulaciones,"* were ratified by both sides.[4] They were liberal. They were signed by the two Spanish monarchs and witnessed by the experienced secretary Hernando de Zafra. The main item was that, within forty days, the Moorish King would surrender to Isabel and Fernando the fortress of the Alhambra and the gate of the Albaicín, "so that their Highnesses may occupy them with their troops." The Christian monarchs would accept all those who lived in Granada as their vassals "and natural subjects." The Muslims would be able to remain in their houses and farms forever. Boabdil and all his people would "live in their own religion and not permit their mosques to be taken from them." The conquered people would also continue to be "judged by their own laws." Those among them who wanted to go and live in Barbary, North Africa, would be allowed to sell their property and make such profits as they could. They could have free transport to where they wanted, in large ships, for up to three years. Muslims who stayed behind would not have to wear distinctive clothing and would pay the same taxes as they had paid before. Christians would not enter mosques without permission. Jews would not be able to be nominated as tax collectors over any Muslim, or have any command over them. Muslim rites would be preserved. Lawsuits between Muslims would be judged by their own law, and any suit between people of the two religions would have both a Christian and a Muslim judge. Any Muslim captive who succeeded in fleeing to Granada would be declared free.

No Muslim would be forced to be a Christian against his or her will. No one would be asked to return goods seized during the war. The judges, mayors, and governors appointed by Fernando and Isabel would be persons who would honor the Muslims and treat them kindly (*amorosamente*). No one would be called to account for anything that had happened before the surrender. All prisoners were to be released, those in Andalusia within five months, those in Castile within eight. Muslim inheritance law would be respected, as would all donations to mosques. Muslims would not be conscripted for military service on behalf of Castile against their will, and Christian and Muslim slaughterhouses would remain separate.

These terms resembled those that Fernando's Aragonese predecessors had negotiated generations before at the surrender of Valencia. In the novel *Amadís de Gaula,* this new submission is spoken of as "the saintly conquest."[5] Certainly it was, in the face of it, benign. It recalls the Chinese dictum that the greatest victory is one in which a city gives in without a fight. It was an anticipation, too, of innumerable capitulations by non-Christian people to Spaniards in America.

When the prisoners in Granada were handed over, there was much excitement, and a holy man began to shout that the Muslims were still certain to win if only they exalted Muhammad. There was uproar, and Boabdil was detained against his will for a time in the Alhambra. He wrote to Fernando saying he thought that the city should be handed over there and then, not waiting, as had been planned, for Epiphany, in order to avoid further protests of that nature.[6]

So on January 1, 1492, Gutierre de Cárdenas, the same *mayordomo* who had proclaimed Isabel queen eighteen years before in Segovia, now escorted by al-Mulih and Ibn Kumasha, rode into the palace of the Alhambra to accept the surrender of the last Muslim city of western Europe. He received the keys of the city and gave a written receipt for them. On January 2, he and his men took over the strongpoints of Granada, and bells were placed in the mosques. Columbus recalled later seeing the flags of Castile and Aragon being raised on the towers of the Alhambra. Boabdil, meantime, formally handed the keys of the city to Fernando. Fernando gave them to the Queen, who in turn presented them to the Infante Juan, who left them with the Count of Tendilla, who was, of course, a Mendoza and would be the new Christian governor.[7] Thus it was that the pomegranate emblem of Granada passed to join the royal arms of Castile.[8]

Tendilla and Talavera, the new Governor and newly appointed Archbishop of Granada, went into the city with Cárdenas. On January 6, the monarchs solemnly entered the city, though they remained living at Santa Fe.[9] The Alhambra seemed a marvel to all: Peter Martyr wrote to Cardinal

Arcimboldo in Rome: "O immortal Gods, what a palace! It is unique in the world."[10]

There were celebrations throughout Europe. In Rome, Cardinal Rafaelo Riano staged a dramatic representation of the events in Granada and, on February 1, the Spanish Cardinal Borgia, dean of the college of cardinals, offered a bullfight in Rome (such a thing had never been seen there before)[11] and presided over a procession between the Church of Santiago de los Españoles to the Palazzo Navona, where Pope Innocent celebrated Mass in the open air in honor of the victory. The fall of Granada was an event that seemed in Rome almost to make up for the loss of Constantinople in 1453. It certainly compensated for the loss of Otranto in 1480, when twelve thousand of the inhabitants were allegedly put to death by Muslims with horrible tortures, many thrown off a cliff to be eaten by dogs, while the aged Archbishop, who had remained at his altar to the last, was sawn in two.[12]

The work of the incorporation of Granada into Castile was placed in the hands of Governor Tendilla and Archbishop Talavera, assisted by the royal secretary Hernando de Zafra. A descendant of Jews, Talavera was tolerant of Muslims. He learned Arabic and prepared a simple Catechism that would enable all new Christians to know the new faith. He hired special preachers to explain Christianity. His enthusiasm was contagious, and he became known as the *afaquí santo* (the beloved leader). Thousands of Muslims converted in consequence. Tendilla, equally tolerant, allowed the mosques generally to continue, even if he had the main one converted into a Christian cathedral, later rebuilt in the style of the Renaissance by the great architects Egas and Silöe.[13] Altogether about 200,000 to 300,000 Muslims thereby joined Castile (including those who had surrendered since 1481 in places other than the city of Granada). Most of the land in the valley had already been divided up among the conquerors, and now the rest, and much of the city, followed. We see memories of these partitions in place-names; thus the foothills of the Sierra Nevada, south of Guadix, are still known as the "Marquesado de Cenete," even if the Marqués has long since left.[14]

In these dramatic new circumstances, the committee designated to consider Columbus's plans anew met in Santa Fe and reached the usual negative decision about them. Isabel and Fernando advised Columbus to leave Granada quickly; and, indeed, he left in dudgeon for Córdoba, not for La Rábida, determined to head for France.[15] He may have heard from his brother Bartolomeo, now free and in England, that captains in Bristol had recently sent out caravels in search of "the island of Brazil," which signified a territory where brazilwood might be found, as the Spanish ambassador to London, Pedro de Ayala, would report some years later.[16]

But the Aragonese *converso* treasurer, Luis Santangel, intervened and, according to Fernando Colón, persuaded the Queen to change her mind.[17] Deza and the secretary Cabrero are said to have acted similarly with Fernando.[18] Santangel told Isabel that if she supported Columbus, she would be taking a small risk for an opportunity of glory. If another king sponsored Columbus, and the journey turned out a success, she would be criticized in Spain. Columbus, Santangel thought, was a "wise and prudent man and of an excellent intelligence." He appealed to her often expressed desire to appear preeminent among monarchs, and to try to seek out "the grandeurs and secrets of this universe."[19] Santangel added that he knew his action exceeded "the limits or rules of his office as treasurer, but he was in mind to say what his heart told him."[20] Quintanilla, the chief accountant of Castile, had always liked Columbus and again spoke accordingly, while Beatriz de Bobadilla, also still the chief lady-in-waiting of the Queen, the most influential woman at court after the Queen herself, is said to have talked to Isabel, too, in favor of Columbus.[21] Piñelo, Santangel's Genoese partner, also gave his support.

Thus the Queen was persuaded. Isabel suggested that she should wait until reparations from the war permitted funding, though if Santangel thought it necessary, she "was ready to pledge her jewels for the cost of the expedition."[22] Santangel drily said that that would not be necessary; he would easily find the sum necessary. After all, that was surely little in comparison with what might be forthcoming.[23] In practice, the money came partly from Santangel and partly from Piñelo.[24] Perhaps they cynically thought that, despite Columbus's talk of China and the Indies, at least some more Canary Islands would be found. Some of Isabel's jewels were already at Santangel's bank in Valencia, including her ruby and gold necklace, as surety for 25,000 florins borrowed for the campaign of 1490 that captured the city of Baza. A crown had also been pledged to Santangel in return for 35,000 florins and another, with more jewels, for 50,000 florins that had been placed in the cathedral in Barcelona.

So in early April 1492 a messenger, in the form of a court constable, went from the monarchs to fetch Columbus. But the furious Genoese had by then already left Santa Fe and had reached Pinos, about five miles to the north. He was making for France. It is said that the messenger caught up with him on the ancient bridge.[25] The messenger must have made very clear that the royal mood had changed absolutely since Columbus would not have returned yet again had he not been guaranteed success.

In Santa Fe, Santangel and then the monarchs received Columbus and instructed the experienced Aragonese secretary Juan de Coloma to draw up warrants by which Columbus was charged to carry out the discoveries that he had always desired.

There is a ballad in Spain that tells of Count Arnaldos, who, one St. John's Day, June 25, at the height of summer, went hawking. He saw from the top of a cliff a ship with a silk sail. A sailor was singing a song that calmed the sea, soothed the winds, caused the fish to come to the surface and the marine birds to perch on the mast. "For God's sake," called the Count, "tell me what are you singing?" But it was a magic song, and the sailor replied: "I shall not tell you unless you agree to sail with me." The sailor was the incarnation of Columbus. Unlike the monarchs, the nobles, and the secretaries, who had spent their lives in Castile or Aragon, Columbus had traveled far: Africa, the Atlantic islands, the Aegean, Algiers, even Ireland. He had gone everywhere looking for help; his life resembled that in a novel of chivalry, for the heroes in such works were always seeing kings and flattering queens and asking for their assistance. But his real journeys were only just beginning.

The King and Queen of Aragon and Castile founded the Spanish Empire in the Americas when, on April 17, 1492, at Santa Fe, they committed themselves to support the expedition of Columbus on his own extraordinary terms. Both monarchs, and both secretariats at their disposal, were parties to the arrangements for the so-called *Capitulaciones* with the Genoese.[26] Possibly the secretary Juan de Coloma used a draft of Columbus's, itself perhaps written by Fray Juan Pérez, as his text to begin with; that would explain the emphasis given to matters affecting Columbus's status.[27]

The document of April 17 had five items. First, it named Columbus "Admiral of the Ocean Sea"[28] and any "islands and mainlands"[29] that he had already discovered,[30] just as the King's uncle, Fadrique Enríquez, "was Admiral of Castile." As with Enríquez (since 1472 only), the title would be hereditary. Columbus would also be nominated viceroy and governor-general in all the islands and mainlands that he would discover in the future. These titles would also be considered hereditary, in contrast to all precedents.

Columbus would be named "Don," at the time a specific title: a hidalgo with privileges (a right not to be taxed, for example). For all important public offices in any newly discovered lands, Columbus would have the right to nominate three candidates (a *terna*), of which the King would choose one. That was an ancient Castilian usage. Columbus would also have a right to a tenth of everything—pearls, gold, silver, other precious metals, spices—

found in any new territories. On all ships taking part in commerce with those new territories, Columbus would be able to load an eighth of all goods. Finally, he was to be informed of any lawsuit that might take place as a result of commerce in or to those territories.[31]

The expedition planned by Columbus would not cost much: only 2 million maravedís in all. In comparison, the cost of the wedding of the Infanta Catalina in London to Prince Arthur was 60 million maravedís, and the annual income of the Duke of Medinaceli from El Puerto de Santa María alone was over 4 million.[32] The monarchs would have spent far more than what they needed for Columbus's journey on the spectacular wedding that they had organized in 1490 when their daughter Isabel married Prince Afonso of Portugal. "Who could recount the triumph, the celebrations, the jousts, the bands . . ." wrote the chronicler Bernáldez, who would afterwards receive Columbus as his guest at his curacy, of that occasion.[33]

Columbus's 2 million were, all the same, raised in a roundabout way. Thus the two senior treasurers of Aragon (Santangel) and Castile (Piñelo), a *converso* and a Genoese, respectively, would raise just over half of what was necessary, 1,140,000 maravedís, from profits from the sale of indulgences in the province of Extremadura.[34] Then the small port of Palos on the Río Tinto, north of Huelva, owed the Crown the service of two ships for a year, for Diego Rodríguez Prieto, of that place, had robbed some Portuguese ships. It was agreed that Palos should settle this debt that had been assumed by the Crown of Castile by providing two ships to serve with Columbus. The town council of Palos and even most sailors there opposed the idea, but they were soothed by a well-known captain of the town, Martín Alonso Pinzón, who argued that there would be benefits for them.

The rest of the sum required for the journey was raised by Columbus himself, who borrowed some of it from his Florentine friend Juanotto Berardi, a dealer in many goods, including slaves, in Seville. He was an associate of the rich Florentine of Lisbon Bartolomeo Marchionni, who had interests in so many undertakings. Berardi had also, since 1489, been the leading representative of the younger branch of the Medici in Seville. Perhaps some other Italian merchants invested something, as probably did the Duke of Medinaceli.[35]

The agreement with Columbus was refined, in another document of April 30, a "letter of privileges" that was signed by the monarchs, the faithful Juan de Coloma, and another group of secretaries.[36] Columbus was henceforth referred to as "Admiral, Viceroy, and Governor," not "Governor-General." It is unclear if that was a demotion, but if so, it was a modest one.

It is true that in yet another document of April 30, asking the municipalities of Andalusia to assist Columbus by providing wine, meat, wood, fish, and gunpowder, the monarchs spoke of him as merely their "captain."[37] But that was a more informal note. More important was the fact that the first document was cast—deliberately, one must assume—in the form of a royal grant and was therefore revocable. It included the provision that Columbus could hear all suits, civil or criminal. He could punish those found guilty and even impose a death penalty, though for abuses in that regard he could himself be punished. He could judge cases even in Castile if they concerned commerce in territories that he had discovered.

All these concessions granted to Columbus were extraordinary. The titles were especially curious. No doubt they were accepted because the monarchs had known since 1487 that the supplicant before them had demanded no less. That had probably delayed agreement. The civil servants would have known that they were giving an authority to Columbus that contrasted with the monarchs' desire to assert their own authority in all departments. Perhaps that discrepancy, if such it was, can be explained since the powers that Columbus was being given were over territory which was still a figment of the imagination. Still, Viceroy, Governor, Admiral! What titles were these! Far grander, it seemed, than *adelantado,* the impressive title that had recently been granted to Alfonso Fernández de Lugo in Tenerife, in the Canaries.

What territories did Columbus expect that he might conquer for Spain? He anticipated finding various islands, but these included Cipangu (Japan) and a mainland (*tierra firme*), that is, China (Cathay). Yet there was no mention in the *Capitulaciones* of the Indies, nor of Cathay, though Columbus would take with him letters to the Great Khan and an interpreter who knew some Eastern languages. Perhaps he expected to find a backward territory off China or Japan that he could seize without difficulty? It is unclear. Nor is it obvious what the Crown thought.

Obviously, there was a mixture of motives. An economic purpose is certain. The monarchs knew that, after the conquest of Granada, they would lose money in the short term. The patrimonial lands of the Nasrids, which were the chief items of booty for the Crown from the conquest of Granada, were small in size and had been ravaged. So it would be silly to neglect what might be another source of income. Cabrero, Santangel, Piñelo, and other Genoese bankers would have taken up this position with the King and Queen.

A second motive was a desire to outmaneuver the King of Portugal. That may have seemed less necessary in the 1490s than it had been ten years before, but, all the same, Isabel did not want Columbus to escape to serve another court. In the fifteenth century as in the twentieth, rulers allowed their imperial claims to be affected by what their neighbors were thinking.

The Portuguese had imagined that one benefit of their own expeditions in West Africa would be that they might succeed in outflanking Islam from the rear. That motive could play no part in respect of the westward journeys from Spain. Columbus always insisted that one of his goals was to liberate Jerusalem from the East. But there was at first no other stipulated missionary purpose.[38]

Perhaps Fernando and Isabel wanted to support Columbus because of a new Castilian mood of confidence, amounting to what seems to have been a sense of destiny. The monarchs did have a desire "to unlock geography's closed doors," as Las Casas would dramatically put the matter.[39] Remember the superior education of Isabel. That new mood was expressed that summer by the famous grammarian Antonio de Nebrija, who, in his introduction to his Spanish grammar, dated August 18, 1492, wrote, remembering Rome, that "language was always the companion of empire" (*siempre la lengua fue compañera del imperio*).[40] Nebrija, at that time about fifty and a professor at Salamanca University, was the great scholar of the time and was at the height of his influence—a power he did not mind flaunting.

But also important in explaining the newfound enthusiasm shown by the monarchs for Columbus was perhaps their preoccupation, that spring of 1492, with a different matter: their decision, also reached in the aftermath of victory in Granada, to place a harsh choice before Castilian Jews: to convert to Christianity or to leave the country. The decision on these measures had been made sometime in March, and the decrees on the matter, one for Castile, one for Aragon, were composed by March 31, though they were not communicated to the Jews, nor indeed to anyone, till the end of April. Thus the timing of a new policy toward the Castilian Jews was interwoven with that toward Columbus, though the first seemed much more significant to the monarchs. Columbus was intercepted at Pinos a few days after the decree about Jewry had been written. The *Capitulaciones* with Columbus were dated April 17, Tuesday of Holy Week, in fact, and the decree naming the choices facing the Jews was published on April 29, Quasimodo (or Low) Sunday.

The decree, written by the Inquisitor Torquemada, provided that "the holy evangelical and the Catholic faith" had to be preached to all the Jews of Castile, and gave them till the end of July to be baptized or to leave the country.[41] If, unwisely, as the monarchs judged, they decided to go, they were to be allowed to take most of their movable property with them, but no money, gold, silver, arms nor, indeed, horses. Those who decided to convert to Christianity would be fully accepted in the Catholic community. The decree explained that the last few years in Spain had shown that there were, in the country, many bad Christians—a euphemism for incompletely converted Jews—and that that had been the consequence of the continued possibility of communication with Jewry.[42] Peter Martyr commented that the Jews, being generally richer than the Christians, were well placed to corrupt and seduce *conversos*.[43] Remember that the rabbis did not accept that Jews forcibly converted could be considered real Christians.

The decree must be seen against the background of the establishment of the Holy Office, the Inquisition, in 1480. Since then, about thirteen thousand people had been found guilty of carrying on secret Jewish practices and, as mentioned before, perhaps two thousand had in consequence died. These spiritual deviations had been, so the authorities thought or affected to think, partly because of the continued temptations offered by the presence of Jews with their synagogues, libraries, and often eloquent rabbis. The Crown had tried at the Cortes of Toledo in 1480 to segregate the Jews by a policy of separation, but it seemed obvious that they had continued to hold meetings, to teach, to circumcise *conversos* as well as Jews, and perhaps to give books of Hebrew prayers to the former; they slaughtered cattle in the traditional Jewish way and ate unleavened bread. The Crown thought that one reason some—many, they believed—*conversos* maintained Jewish rites and customs was their continuing contact with practicing Jews.

The monarchs and their advisers apparently thought that because of the weakness of humanity, the "devilish tricks and seductions" of the Jews might conquer Christendom unless "the main cause of the danger," the Jews themselves, were removed.[44] In 1483, the Inquisitors had sought to expel all Jews living in the dioceses of Seville and Córdoba, and indeed many had fled elsewhere, though they had usually remained in Spain. That meant the hitherto Jewish suburb of Triana was empty, ready to lodge sailors, it might have been said. Then there had been various scandalous cases in which Jews and *conversos* had seemed to be detected in agreement, but in one of the most notorious instances, that of Benito García and the "Holy Child of La Guardia" in 1490 (culminating in an *auto-de-fe* in Ávila in November 1491), the evidence seems fraudulent.[45]

The purpose of the new decree of 1492, as far as the monarchs were concerned (especially Fernando), was to finish with Judaism, but not with the persons of the Jews, who both monarchs hoped would mostly convert to Christianity. Had not the pious Majorcan mystic Ramón Llull, in the thirteenth century, proposed a great catechism to liberate the Jews from the influence of rabbis, and suggested the expulsion of those who were recalcitrant?[46] The monarchs were also determined to save from "popular wrath" their *converso* advisers: Talavera, for example, the Queen's confessor until that same spring; Cabrera, the Marquis of Moya; the treasurer, Alonso de la Caballería; the rising young Miguel Pérez de Almazán, their secretary for international affairs; Hernando de Pulgar, the royal chronicler, who had written a letter of protest to Cardinal Mendoza against the actions of the Holy Office;[47] even Luis Santangel, the treasurer of the Hermandad, who had taken the initiative in backing Columbus.

The decline of the influence of Talavera after the victory in Granada probably explains much. Of course, he had been appointed archbishop of Granada, which, in the circumstances of 1492, was no sinecure. He had been appointed as a man capable of carrying out a difficult task. But he was no longer in daily contact with the Queen. On the recommendation of Cardinal Mendoza, he was succeeded by a formidable Franciscan, Francisco (Gonzalo) Jiménez de Cisneros.

Cisneros belonged to a noble family without money. He had been born in Torrelaguna, a town near Madrid and close to the pass of Somosierra, controlled by the Mendozas as long ago as 1436. So he was already nearly sixty. His father had been a receiver of tithes for the Crown. Dry, tall, bony, with a long face, a protruding upper lip, a large nose, and bushy eyebrows, looking a little like a greyhound, always enveloped in a cloak of rough cloth, he had small, black, lively eyes and a rather strident voice, corrected by a careful pronunciation. He ate much but drank little. Selfless, austere, modest, devout, a lover of culture, he was physically strong and single-minded. He hated corruption. He worked eighteen hours a day, effectively, often reducing his advisers to exhaustion. Peter Martyr said, with his customary exaggeration, no doubt, that Cisneros had the acuity of Augustine, the abstinence of Jerome, and the severity of Ambrose.[48] He wore a hair shirt, it was said, he frequently scourged himself, he experienced ecstasies, and he conversed with long-dead saints.

Cisneros had studied at the University of Salamanca, lived in Rome, been archpriest of Uceda, to the north of Madrid, and was for a time in the clerical prison of Santorcaz because of a quarrel over the nomination to that benefice, for which he was punished by Archbishop Carrillo. He then worked in Sigüenza for Cardinal Mendoza, who saw in him a man of the future, since he showed himself an exemplary administrator. He became a Franciscan in 1484, in the new monastery of San Juan de los Reyes, Toledo, changing his Christian name from Gonzalo to Francisco. He joined the Observants, the most austere of the Franciscan sections, in the monastery of La

Salceda, Segovia, founded by Fray Juan de Villacreces. He soon became the superior there. Fearing (Martyr said) "the inconstancy of the world and the snares of the devil, he abandoned everything in order not to become caught up in pernicious gratifications and delights."[49] He sought to carry through the Observants' reform in the Franciscan order, destroying the easygoing subdivisions with zeal. But though he belonged to a mendicant order, he was born to command, not to beg.[50]

Mendoza ordered his protégé Cisneros to accept nomination as the Queen's confessor, fearing that otherwise he might refuse. Isabel took to him; indeed, she found in Cisneros, Martyr wrote to his old patron, the Count of Tendilla, what "she most ardently desired, a man to whom she can disclose in tranquility her innermost secrets . . . this was the cause of her extraordinary content."[51] Cisneros was a determined reformer who gave the Spanish Church as much strength as he gave the Queen. He would soon found a new university in Alcalá, the Complutense, concentrating on theology, based on an Observant Franciscan study house established twenty years before. He republished the rules of his own order. He was much concerned with improving the music and liturgy of the Church and was also anxious to preserve the Mozarabic ritual, which had survived the long period of Muslim domination. Though the decree of 1492 expelling the Jews was probably written by the Inquisitor Torquemada, Cisneros may have influenced its wording, its ruthlessness, and its simplicity. Surely it was he who insisted to the monarchs after the fall of Granada that in their realms there should be no more infidels.[52]

This decree of March 1492 astonished the Jews of Spain. There had been, as we have seen, increasingly strict regulation of Jewish life: the Cortes of Toledo had insisted on the establishment of ghettos, a physical separation between Jews and Christians.[53] Then there had been the expulsion of the Jews in Andalusia. They had virtually ceased living in cities and were more to be found in minor towns and villages. But nobody had had any expectation that anything like full expulsion was likely, for they had always been defended by the Crown. The Jews realized that the decree was aimed primarily at conversion, not at exclusion; but they also knew that the monarchs had miscalculated.

Three of the most prominent Jews are said to have gone to the King. These were Isaac Abravanel, Abraham Señor, and Meir Mehamed. Abravanel came from a family of Castilian Jews that had fled to Portugal after the persecutions of 1391. He had been the treasurer of King Afonso V of Portugal and had been the chief tax collector and financial adviser of the Duke of Viseu, who was said to have tried to overthrow the Portuguese monarchy in

1484 and had then been executed. Abravanel, like the Duke's descendants, the Braganza family, had gone to Spain, where he had prospered, collecting taxes for the leader of the Mendozas, the Duke of Infantado, as he had earlier done in Portugal. He lent the monarchs substantial sums for the war against Granada. He had often expressed himself strongly about the *conversos* and had declared that they as a class were being falsely accused of secret Judaizing, as he, a Jew, should know.[54] He himself had strong Hebraic views and believed that the Messiah had already been born and would manifest himself soon, probably in 1503.[55] As for Abraham Señor, he had been the treasurer of the Santa Hermandad before Luis de Santangel and had raised much money at the time of the siege of Malaga to ransom the Jews of that city. He had been judge of the Jewish communities, too. Meir Mehamed was his son-in-law, and was a rabbi as well as a tax collector.

The three begged the King to abandon the decree. Fernando apparently said that he would consider the matter. Encouraged, the three Jews offered him 300,000 ducats if he canceled the decree altogether; that is, 112 million maravedís, fifty times more than the projected cost of the expedition of Columbus. Fernando was tempted but finally refused, saying that his decision had been a joint one with Isabel.

Abravanel says that he spoke to the King three times—to no avail. He and Señor then went to the Queen and said that if she thought the Jews could be brought to surrender by this kind of measure, she was mistaken. Jews had existed since the beginning of the world, they had always outlived those who had tried to do away with them, and it was beyond human capacity to destroy them. Those who tried to do so always brought divine castigation on themselves. Abravanel asked Isabel to influence Fernando to withdraw the decree. She replied that she could not think of such a thing even if she had wished it: "The King's heart was in the hand of the Lord as water in the rivers. He turns it whithersoever he wills." She begged them to convert.[56]

The two Jewish leaders decided that the Queen—or was it Cisneros?—was more responsible than the King for the decree. In that, they were wrong. No evidence suggests that the two monarchs differed on this or on any other important matter. Yet the long stay that Isabel had had in Seville in 1477–78 had been a bitter experience for her, since she had seen such laxity that she supposed radical measures were necessary if the Church was to be saved. Hence the Inquisition, hence the attempted segregation of Jewry, and hence now the tragic decree imposing the sad choice.

Abravanel and his companions then separated. Abraham Señor converted to Christianity, as did his son-in-law, Meir Mehamed, along with the most prominent rabbi, Rabbi Abraham. The ceremony of baptism was performed in June in the church of the Jeronymite monastery of Guadalupe, and the monarchs were the godparents. Señor became Fernan Núñez Coronel and Mehamed, Fernan Pérez Coronel. But Abravanel went to Naples. There he wrote continuously, his house was ransacked by the French army in 1495, and later he went to Venice, where he died. He remained an inspiration long after his death.[57]

The reluctance of the Jews to convert was much greater than the monarchs had supposed would be the case, for many remained "pertinacious and unbelieving"; and many rabbis did "whatever they could to strengthen them in their faith." Thousands decided to leave Spain. Some *conversos* left, too. Still, friars were everywhere to be seen trying to persuade Jews to convert, and some were successful. For example, a famous preacher, Fray Luís de Sepúlveda, went to the towns of Maqueda and Torrijos, and secured the conversion of almost all the Jews there. Nearly all the Jewish population of a hundred people in Teruel is said to have converted. But the upheaval was all the same considerable. Emigration meant the hasty sale of houses and furniture, of heirlooms and cattle, of vineyards and property. The Jews mostly went to Morocco or to Portugal, and the accounts of their ill treatment in the first supposed haven are distressing.

The figures are disputed. Thus one historian considers that, out of 80,000 Spanish Jews in 1492, 40,000 left.[58] Another, writing at much the same time, thought that there were 200,000 Jews in 1492, of whom again half converted. The most learned Spanish sociologist of Jewry also thought that there were 200,000 Jews in 1490, of whom 50,000 converted.[59] We are in a world of inspired guesses. There were 216 Jewish districts in Castile in 1474, in which perhaps 15,000 families lived. For Aragon there is no figure. But certainly something over 50,000 Jews left, probably over 70,000.

Thus ended the Sephardim, a brilliant Spanish culture, at the very same moment that Spain was about to embark on innumerable new conquests in the New World. Henceforward there would, in theory and in law, be no Spanish Jews, only converted Jews, *conversos,* some being the descendants of converts of the era of persecution in the late fourteenth century, others of those who converted, like Rabbi Abraham Señor, in 1492. Many of these, despairing of Castile, played a part in the New World. Their journeys there might sometimes have been illegal, but they went all the same. Other Jews, themselves well received in the Ottoman Empire and in Italy, lived on to adorn the lives of their new countries, though often experiencing profound nostalgia for the quarters they had to abandon so suddenly.[60]

This expulsion was not a holocaust. It was a deliberate export of intransigent Jews whose numbers the monarchs hoped, and supposed, would be few. They were surprised. But their actions should be compared with similar ones undertaken in England, say, in the thirteenth century, not that of brutal Germany in the 1940s.

At the same time, another emigration began. In 1492, all those who spoke Spanish lived on the peninsula that Castile and Aragon shared with Portugal. It would never be so again. Men and women from those lands were soon to find themselves in tropical or subtropical America, and there they would establish a new and ingenious society whose time may still be to come.

6

"A white stretch of land"

Juan Rodríguez Bermejo saw a white stretch of land and shouted, "Land! Land!" and he fired a lombard.

> *Columbus and his men approaching San Salvador,*
> *October 1492*

So it was against a background of intolerance that Columbus, in the early summer of 1492, made his way from Granada to Palos de la Frontera, near Huelva. Palos today is a small, sleepy town some miles inland from the Río Tinto. There are strawberry fields in what was the harbor in the fifteenth century, for the river silted up and then dried out. But in 1492, Palos was a busy small port with perhaps three thousand inhabitants, playing a part in trade with Portugal, the Canary Islands, and the Spanish section of the African coast. It was close to the monastery of La Rábida, and Columbus could use that establishment as a base.[1]

Before he reached there, Columbus had secured one more honor: Diego Colón, his son by Felipa Muñiz, now twelve years old, became a page to the Infante Juan, shortly joining a famous kindergarten at Almazán where he would make friendships that would last him the rest of his life.[2] Columbus surely owed this honor to the backing of Fray Diego de Deza.

The royal decree requiring the services of the port of Palos was read out there on May 23 in the new church of San Jorge, overlooking the harbor, by the notary Francisco Fernández: "Know ye that, whereas for certain things done and committed by you to our disservice, you were condemned, and obliged by our council to provide us for a year with two equipped vessels at your charge." In the congregation were Columbus, his mentor Fray Juan Pérez, the mayor and magistrates of the town as well as the councillors (*regidores*), and the *procurador*.[3] There were also present the brothers Martín Alonso Quintero Pinzón and Vicente Yáñez Pinzón, prominent citizens of Palos and well known in the world of mariners. Their task was to arrange the proposed voyage; their expectation, Las Casas says, was that they would be rich and powerful in consequence.[4]

The ships provided by Palos, the *Pinta* (painted lady) and the *Niña* (girl), were small, fifty-five- to sixty-ton caravels, each about seventy feet long by twenty-five feet wide, and eleven feet in depth. Both had three masts. The *Pinta* belonged to Gómez Rascón, from a *converso* family that had already suffered from the Inquisition, and Cristóbal Quintero, from another seafaring family of the town. The former sailed with Columbus. The *Niña* was owned by Juan Niño, after whom it was named, who came from the slightly larger port of Moguer, a few miles higher up the red Río Tinto—now, like Palos, some distance from it.[5] These two ships would be captained by the two brothers. A third ship was hired by Columbus himself: the *Santa María,* also known as the *María Galante.*[6] About one hundred tons, with a round hull, built in Galicia, and square-rigged, she was hired from Juan de la Cosa, a captain who came from near Santoña, in Cantabria, but had lived most of his life in El Puerto de Santa María. He had belonged to the household of the Duke of Medinaceli, where Columbus probably first met him.

Having found his ships, Columbus went ahead to seek crews, and in this he was helped decisively by the Pinzóns, who found most of the eighty or so men who sailed. Many of these had had experience of voyages to the Canaries or Lisbon.

The Pinzóns' help had been assured by either Fray Antonio Marchena or Fray Juán Pérez, Columbus's friends at La Rábida. Fernán Pérez Camacho, a sailor, later reported that Fray Antonio had told Martín Pinzón that it would please God if much land was found.

The majority of the crews came from other ports of the Río Tinto, Moguer, and Huelva, as well as Palos, but there were also a few from Seville. Moguer had had a Jewish district until 1486. Palos had some difficulties on that score with a recent commander of its fort.[7] In consequence, some of the crews with Columbus may have been Jewish. There were several Basques on board the ships; they could probably recall to advantage their experience of fishing in the Atlantic. About ten sailors came from Cantabria. There were two Portuguese, a small number considering the constant interchange of Castilian and Portuguese sailors in Atlantic ports in those days.[8] Four or five men were criminals allowed to escape justice by their enlistment; among these was Bartolomé de Torre, who had killed a rival in a brawl. Another Torre, Luis, a *converso* who knew both Arabic and Hebrew but of course not the indigenous languages, sailed as an interpreter.

There were some royal officials on the expedition; for example, Diego de Araña, a cousin of Columbus's mistress in Córdoba, was chief constable, while Pedro Gutiérrez, once chief butler of the King, was a royal supervisor. There was also Juan de Peñalosa, another *converso* and a courtier, whose main task was to persuade the crews to unite under Columbus—a difficult task because the Admiral, as he was now always known, was Genoese. The curiosity of this voyage was that no priest sailed.[9]

Martín Alonso Pinzón, an experienced captain then in his late forties, a little older than Columbus, was the decisive personality in all the preparations. After his death, his friends and relations made extravagant claims on his behalf. For example, Arias Pérez, his son, wrote that when in Rome on business in 1491, Pinzón had convinced himself, by a study of "charts in the Library of the Vatican," that there was some sense in Columbus's ideas. Pinzón was said, too, to have found in that library a document written in Solomon's time that argued that if one traveled west from the Mediterranean, one would soon find oneself in Japan. A citizen of Moguer, Francisco García Vallejo, argued that had it not been for Pinzón, Columbus would never have set out. A cousin of Pinzón's, Juan de Umbria, said much the same.[10] All these stories may be inventions: we hear nothing about the Vatican Library in any document contemporary with the expedition. But it would seem obvious, from his subsequent actions as well as his conduct before the expedition set out, that Pinzón had hopes of seizing control of the voyage. He was a powerful captain and had been often to Lisbon and the Canary Islands. He was connected by blood with most of the shipbuilders and other captains of the ports in the Rio Tinto. He seems to have made decisions quickly and to have been ruthless. He gave Columbus a great deal of trouble and could have given him much more had events turned out differently.

We examine the list of those who first set off to what became the Spanish Empire in the Indies with little sense of surprise. There is a Vélez de Mendoza, two other Mendozas, one from Guadalajara, the heart of Mendoza power, and so perhaps an illegitimate member of the famous family. We see a Godoy and a Patiño. There is a Foronda and a Vergara, a Baraona and a Talavera. These are names that might have filled any Castilian ship in those days or, indeed, a modern Spanish cabinet. There were also a few foreign names, a characteristic, despite prohibitions, of Spain's empire for many generations.

Before he left, Columbus was conceded a pension of 10,000 maravedís a year, deriving from the royal income in Córdoba; and it was there that, in this first year, Columbus's mistress, Beatriz Enríquez de Arana, received the money.[11]

The voyage started "half an hour before sunrise" on August 3, 1492.

Twenty-six men were on the *Pinta,* twenty-four on the *Niña,* forty on the *Santa María.* These were paid 1,000 maravedís a month if they were experienced sailors, 600 if they were novices. None in fact would be paid anything until 1513, when gold from the Indies was more available to the Crown.[12] They had on board typical objects for this kind of journey such as would have been known to Columbus from his expedition with the Portuguese to the west coast of Africa: hawks' bells, glass beads from Venice, and other glass objects for trading, as well as food expected to last: salted cod, bacon, and biscuits. There was also flour, wine, olive oil, and, of course, water— enough for a year. Perhaps the wine was manzanilla from Sanlúcar de Barrameda or port from Cazalla de la Sierra, or some similar wine fortified with brandy, that great Benedictine medieval invention without which none of the ensuing expeditions could have been carried through so well.[13] Despite many complaints on other scores during the voyage, there seems never to have been any shortage of food.

Columbus also took with him a number of hourglasses, probably made in Venice.[14] They only lasted a quarter of an hour or half an hour at most, giving a heavy responsibility to those whose task was to note the time that had passed. Columbus had, of course, a compass, as did the other two captains, of a type that measured in *cuartas* (angles of eleven degrees). This ingenious twelfth-century Chinese invention had been in use in Italy since about 1400 and had been shown by the Portuguese off the coast of Africa to be an essential instrument of discovery. All the pilots had with them stones that enabled them to magnetize faulty needles. Columbus also had an astrolabe, inaccurate though such things then were; it enabled him to calculate his approximate latitude by finding meridian altitudes of the sun. His was probably a version of the one devised by the brilliant Nuremberger Martin Behaim.[15] He also had a map, perhaps based on that given to him by Toscanelli. He kept all these objects in his small cabin on the *Santa María* where he wrote his daily record, which was itself a radical change, for such diaries were unknown before.[16]

These three caravels are ships of legend: we see them always in our imagination, each with its three masts, its white sails with their red crosses slightly billowing in the wind. A caravel, it is perhaps necessary to add, was a small ship of often less than one hundred tons. The galleys of, say, Venice or Florence in the past might have been of three hundred tons, those of Barcelona or Marseilles four hundred, while the vast merchant ships of Genoa, which Columbus would have known as a boy, were one thousand tons. Caravels were intended, however, for long voyages or for piracy, rather than for carrying heavy products. They were light and almost spherical.[17]

The journey of Columbus between August and October 1492 has been so often described that it may seem superfluous to say anything more. Yet some new light may yet be cast. The first stage, from the Río Tinto, lasted a week. This was always an easy journey because of the favorable currents and the winds; it was the return from the Canaries that, in the days of sail, necessitated tacking, often for many days. This voyage took Columbus to Gran Canaria, where he remained with his three ships almost a month. For the *Pinta*'s rudder needed attention, the rigging of the *Niña* left much to be desired, and it also seemed necessary to procure more supplies—some of the well-known goat cheese from the westernmost Canary Island of La Gomera, which had an excellent deepwater harbor. Columbus chose the Canaries as his final point of departure because he knew how the winds blew in the Atlantic and because, as we know, Toscanelli recommended it. He had to sail from a Spanish port, anyway, which ruled out the Portuguese archipelagoes of the Azores or Madeira.

At that time, all the Canary Islands except Tenerife, the biggest, were under direct Spanish rule. La Palma, for example, had been occupied in 1491. The monarchs had recently also approved a plan of Alonso Fernández de Lugo's, a Castilian entrepreneur and commander, to capture Tenerife, with its magical volcano, El Teide, so often hidden by cloud. He would take with him twelve hundred men and twenty thousand goats and sheep. He knew the Canary Islands well, for he had founded the first sugar mill, Agaete, in Gran Canaria, but had sold it to finance his conquest of Tenerife. He was much assisted by the brilliant missionary work beforehand of the indigenous Christian Francisca de Gazmira. Meanwhile, the Treaty of Alcáçovas of 1479 had enabled the Castilians under Jofre Tenorio to build a tower, Santa Cruz de la Mar Pequeña, on the African coast opposite Lanzarote. It was to be a starting point for trade with Africa, including, of course, trade in slaves.

The de facto Spanish Governor of La Gomera at that time was Beatriz de Bobadilla (not to be confused with her cousin, the Queen's friend of the same name, the Marquesa of Moya). This Beatriz was known as "the huntress" (*la cazadora*), "as cruel as she was beautiful," legend says, who had accompanied her husband, Hernán Peraza, to the island and then, when he was murdered in 1488, herself fought back, reestablishing Spanish control with much bloodshed.[18] As has been intimated, rumor said that she had had an affair with the King and, in Córdoba, with Columbus.[19] But those delicate matters have never been clarified. At all events, Beatriz was in no way helpful to the expedition of 1492.

Yet it was appropriate for Columbus to spend so long in this archipelago, for in the islands he could observe for himself an interesting combina-

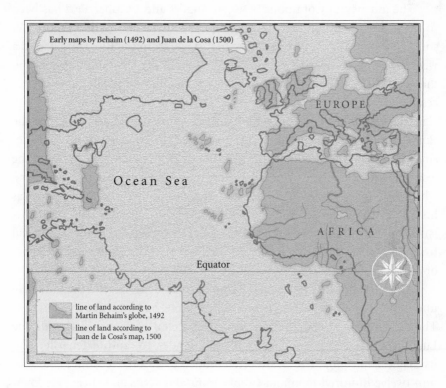

Early maps by Behaim (1492) and Juan de la Cosa (1500)

EUROPE

Ocean Sea

AFRICA

Equator

line of land according to
Martin Behaim's globe, 1492
line of land according to
Juan de la Cosa's map, 1500

tion of private enterprise and state control. That combination had also occurred and worked in the Balearic Islands in the fourteenth century. It is
true that Majorca had been a royal conquest, as Minorca had been. But Ibiza
and Formentera had been conquered by private crusaders, acting with royal
approval. In the Canaries, also, men who were half generals, half entrepreneurs financed journeys of their own, having received overall royal approval.
That arrangement must have interested Columbus. In its harking back to
the Reconquista, as in its anticipation of what would happen in the New
World, the conquests in the Canaries can be seen as a "laboratory" for
Spain's colonial foundations.[20] A visit to the Canary Islands even now gives
the traveler a whiff of what he can expect to encounter in Spanish America:
the light, the architecture, the color, even the accented, undoubtedly maritime Spanish.

    The Canaries were still productive. The lichen orchil was as ever being
strenuously sought by the royal adviser Gutierre de Cárdenas and his wife,
Teresa, who sold it to Genoese merchants for its use as a dye. Sugar mills,
served by black slaves imported from Africa, were being built, often with
Genoese money behind them (there would be about thirty by 1515, and

probably their produce exceeded that of Madeira by then). The first denunciations of ill-treatment of indigenous people had also already been made in the Canaries, for example, by Father Juan Alfonso de Idularen and Father Miguel López de la Serna, in a report to the Queen. In this, Pedro de Vera, the conqueror of Gran Canaria, would figure as the villain, a slave dealer and brutal commander. That, too, anticipated similar accusations soon to be made in the New World. So did the decline of the native population as a consequence of contact with Spanish disease, not to speak of divisions among the conquered peoples, so that some men from Gran Canaria helped in the conquest of Tenerife—something that conquistadors on the American mainland would also soon inspire, to their advantage.

Columbus and his three ships finally left La Gomera on September 6 after praying at its large new parish church, San Sebastián, which still today looks out over the ocean. Columbus set off westward, with a deviation to the southwest. The trade winds, *las brisas,* as the Spaniards would call them, filled his sails. That was the best way to sail to the West Indies, and the sea there soon became known as the Ladies' Gulf, El Golfo de Damas. Before he set off, Columbus heard from the captain of a ship that had come from the Canary Island of El Hierro that Portuguese caravels were in the eastern Atlantic, hoping to obstruct his voyage. Perhaps the King of Portugal was anxious to wreak revenge on him for transferring his loyalty to Spain. But Columbus maneuvered around this danger, if it existed. He anyway believed from the beginning that his real enemies would be more likely to be on board his own ships. Thus, from his fourth day out, he kept two sets of logs: one accurate, the other in which he deliberately underestimated the miles that he had covered, in order not to distress his crew. Perhaps his intention was also to keep the route a secret from colleagues who might later be rivals. The last sight of the Old World for the expedition, as it was for so many others in the future, was that of the volcano, El Teide, on Tenerife.

On September 22, Columbus showed Pinzón his map "in which the Admiral seemed to have painted certain islands in the sea." Las Casas reported that this was Toscanelli's map. But Columbus did not sail by that. It must have been a different one.[21]

Two days later, there was unrest on the ships. None of the sailors had ever been so long away from the sight of land. Some thought it "great madness and self-inflicted homicide to risk their lives in order to follow the folly of a foreigner who was ready to die to make himself a *gran señor.*"[22] Others believed that they should murder Columbus by throwing him overboard. This crisis was overcome, and the little fleet sailed on fairly calmly for an-

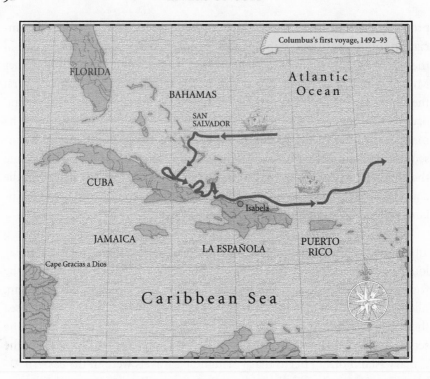

other two weeks. They still saw nothing. Columbus did not strengthen his
position by beginning to compare himself with Moses.[23]

On October 5, Pinzón and Columbus quarreled. The former suggested
making a sharp turn to the south and so, he assumed, heading directly for
Cipangu (Japan). Columbus thought that they should go ahead as fast as
possible to China. Their knowledge of the Far East was, as can be seen, modest. Friends of Pinzón afterwards alleged that this was when Columbus
asked the former what to do.[24] The sailor Francisco García Vallejo later commented that Columbus summoned his two fellow captains—and perhaps
the pilots, too—and asked their advice about his crew, who seemed to be
suffering so much.

> Vincente Yáñez, the captain of the *Niña,* said: "Let's go on for two thou-
> sand leagues and then, if we don't find what we are looking for, we must
> turn round." But his brother, Martín Alonso Pinzón, said: "How is this,
> *señor?* We set off from Palos and now you are distressed! Onward, *señor,*
> and God give us a victory so that we find land. God would never like us
> so shamefully to turn around." Columbus then said, "May you be
> blessed." And it was because of the said Martín Alonso Pinzón that they
> went ahead. . . .[25]

Next day, there were other complaints, this time from among the Basque sailors on the *Santa María*. Apparently Columbus persuaded Martín Alonso to quiet them down. But after a few more days "the men seemed to be able to endure no more."[26] In a conversation in Columbus's cabin on the *Santa María*, the brothers Pinzón, with Peralonso Niño, gave Columbus three more days to discover land. If he did not do so, they said that they would make for home. At least one historian says that Columbus now told Martín Alonso Pinzón his story of the "unknown pilot" in the hope that that would calm him.[27]

On October 10, Columbus announced that he would give a coat of silk to the man who first saw land. The idea was received in silence. What use would such a thing be in the ocean? But that day Columbus and Martín Alonso both noticed birds. The latter wisely said, "Those birds do not fly like that with no reason." The same night, Columbus, Pedro Gutiérrez, and the *veedor* Rodrigo Sánchez thought that they saw light ahead that they believed must be land. The next night, two hours after midnight, with a full moon, Juan Rodríguez Bermejo, also known as Rodrigo de Triana, a sailor from Seville on the *Pinta*, saw "a white stretch of land" (*una cabeza blanca de tierra*) and shouted, "Land! Land!" and he fired a lombard.[28] The next day, October 12, Columbus made landfall.[29]

We can easily imagine the excitement of the ninety members of Columbus's expedition as they anchored offshore in the calm, blue waters, the sea lapping at the ships' gunwales—the first time in history that a European boat stopped in what we must now consider "American" waters.

Columbus had probably arrived at Long Bay, on what is now known as Watling Island, then known to its indigenous inhabitants as Guanahaní. Columbus named the place "San Salvador," the first of innumerable islands to which he gave names, usually those of saints.[30] He saw inhabitants whom he called "Indians" from the beginning. They seemed simple people, though their presents to him, of parrots, javelins, and cotton balls, were, in their way, just as sophisticated as the equivalent Spanish presents of hats, balls, and glass beads. These indigenous people of the Bahamas were later destroyed by contact with the Spaniards. They were closely related to the Tainos, whom Columbus would soon meet in the Caribbean.[31] What immediately seemed significant to him was that they wore no clothes.

Columbus took possession of San Salvador in the name of the King and Queen of Spain.[32] He also raised the flag of those monarchs: a green cross with an F and a Y (for Ysabel) crowned on a white background. He did not seem to think that these might be acts of war against the Ming Emperor of China, the shogun Hosokawa of Japan, or the Mogul Emperor. Presumably he supposed that the island was one of the many that Marco Polo had reported lay off the coast of Asia, without benefit of protection by a superior power.

The natives were amazed at the beards of the Europeans, especially the white one of the Admiral. They themselves seemed to be of the same color as the Guanches, the natives of Tenerife, had long hair, and were good-looking. Some had painted themselves black or white (sometimes their whole bodies, sometimes just their faces). All seemed to be under thirty and carried wooden spears. Some of these had a fish tooth as a blade. One or two of these "Indians" had obviously been wounded in battles, perhaps with neighbors who had tried to capture them. Columbus immediately thought, most surprisingly, that they would make good Christians.[33] They had long canoes made from "marvelously carved" tree trunks.

A few of the people of San Salvador had gold hanging from holes pierced in their noses. Columbus was told by sign language that to the south there was a king who had much more of that metal, even ships made of it. The Admiral tried unsuccessfully to persuade the people of San Salvador to lead him there. After all, he had not sailed three thousand miles in difficult circumstances merely to discover an island of gesticulating savages. The reaction of these natives was intelligent, however: to suggest that there was gold some way to the south was the best way of freeing themselves from the strangers—a trick used by many other peoples in the next few generations.

On October 14, Columbus coasted along *la isleta,* saw other villages, and met other "Indians" whom "we understood to be asking if we came from the sky." Of these, Columbus seized seven, whom he proposed to take home to Castile to be taught Spanish, so that later they could become interpreters. Two of them managed to escape the next day. But several other indigenous people were seized in the course of the next weeks. One of them, who was given the name "Diego Columbus," remained an interpreter with Columbus for two years.[34]

The Admiral thought that he might send the whole population to Castile—as slaves presumably—because he considered that with fifty armed men he would be able to subjugate them all.[35] He reported that they "were very timid" and "artless in respect of weapons." That would surely make them "good subjects."[36]

Columbus, now for a time in unquestioned command of his three ships, stopped at several more islands in what is now the Bahaman archipelago. The first of these he called Santa María de la Concepción, two others Fernandina and Isabela. It is unclear which islands these were: Rum Kay?

Crooked Island? Long Island? All were flat and offered little temptation for colonization or agriculture. He did not take possession of all these places formally because he seems to have assumed that if he had annexed one, he had annexed all.[37] But he gave them all names, though they had indigenous designations already. He received presents of cotton and, in return, gave his usual glass beads and trinkets, which were well received. He wrote enthusiastically in his log of the trees, the scents of the flowers that blew offshore, as in Corsica, and of the clean houses, the "hammocks" (a local word henceforward used in Spanish), the small dogs, as well as the short cotton skirts worn by the women over their private parts. He asked constantly for gold, which he optimistically assumed would be found on the next island, and he only decided to leave the Bahamas when he realized that "there is no goldfield here." Columbus regretted that he could not identify all the herbs that he came across, though he thought he did find aloes. He made constant comparisons to Andalusia in April. The singing of birds on Long Island was "so sweet that no one could want to leave the place."[38]

On October 24, Columbus left for what he thought would turn out to be Cipangu, or part of it: "another very large island . . . they call it Colba. . . . But I am still determined to proceed to the mainland and to the city of Quinsay [Hangchow] to present the letters of your highnesses to the Great Khan." "Colba" turned out to be Cuba. The natives of Guanahaní said that one could not sail around it in twenty days, a comment that suggested they could circumnavigate it in a few more—a lesson Columbus did not learn. The Admiral spoke of that new island as being "larger than England and Scotland together," though in truth it is smaller than England alone.[39] But he did think of it at first as an island.

When he reached Cuba on October 28, Columbus decided that it must be part of the Asiatic mainland.[40] He called it "Juana" all the same. He sailed up what he took to be a beautiful river that would seem to have been the Bay of Bariay, not far from what he called the Rio de Mares: "Never have I seen such a beautiful thing." The land, he thought, resembled Sicily. There were magnificent palm trees of a kind different from those of Spain and of Guinea. He found more dogs, which did not bark, and fishing tackle.[41] In another town, he found good houses with palm roofs and little female clay figurines, and interesting reed ornaments; the river was as placid as that of Seville and full of frogs. He also observed silver ornaments hanging from the noses of the indigenous people.

Did this coast have the coconut palms, the sea plums, the seaside lavender, the beach morning glory, the bay cedar, and the *Strumpfia maritima* that we admire as we arrive in eastern Cuba in our day? Surely the answer was yes. The mangrove and the mahoe were also seen for the first time by Europeans.

At the beginning of November, Columbus sent inland Rodrigo de Xerez of Ayamonte and Luis de Torre of Murcia with two Indians, one from San Salvador and the other a local one. Luis de Torre "had lived with the *adelantado* of Murcia [Fajardo] and had been a Jew—presumably he was one no longer—and knew both Hebrew and Chaldean as well as a little Arabic." From his name, the odds must be that Xerez was also a *converso*.[42] They returned after four days, having found a large village of fifty big wooden huts, thatched with palms, shaped like tents, in which many people lived as in a dormitory.[43] This was the first serious town encountered by the Spaniards in the New World. The people were Tainos.

The principal came out to greet these Spaniards and sat them down on *duhos* (chairs of wood, in animal shapes), and the people kissed the hands and feet of the newcomers, "believing that they came from Heaven." Torre and Xerez encountered tobacco ("certain herbs the smoke of which they inhale"), a crop whose role in future history was to be so important. They found cotton, which was gathered from ceiba trees. The Admiral thought that Spanish merchants might make much of that commodity.

This was, of course, a voyage of discovery, and Columbus was anxious to see more. On November 12, he set sail for what turned out to be Inagua Grande, where, on a hill, he saw crosses that were used to warn of an approaching hurricane but which gave the Europeans a curious sense that they must be near a Christian society. Then they sailed west to a point near Puente Malagueta before returning to Cuba, where they spent another two weeks, kidnapping a few more Indians to take back to Spain. They found wax, which Las Casas later believed must have come originally from Yucatan, suggesting that there was contact with the mainland.[44] Columbus sent down divers for pearls but found that though there were oysters, of pearls there were none.

By this time the Admiral had experienced another, and serious, rebellion: the ambitious Martín Alonso Pinzón had sailed off on November 21 on the *Pinta,* without leave. He had gone to look for gold on his own. His action, the culmination of a growing sense of frustration at having to follow Columbus's orders, was a blatant act of indiscipline. Columbus prudently kept quiet about the matter, biding his time, and seems to have maintained the loyalty of Pinzón's brother Vicente.[45]

Left with only two ships, the *Santa María* and the *Niña,* the Admiral found himself at the eastern end of Cuba, at Baracoa, which he named

Puerto Santo and which he described with special exultation. He left there on December 5, finding a wind to carry him to "Haiti," as the indigenous people called it, or Little Spain, "La Española," the name Columbus immediately gave to the island because of the vegetation. Even the fish were much the same as those he knew in Spain.[46] La Española seemed to Columbus "the best land in the world." He believed it to be Cipangu (Japan), and it appeared to produce some gold, to be found in river sands or rocks. That alone surely made his journey worthwhile. The place also seemed to boast a cultivated society—more so than that in Cuba. There were several principalities, all of which produced stonework, woodwork, ball courts, stone collars, and pendants. Columbus thought that "all the islands are so utterly at your Highnesses' command that it only remains to establish a Spanish presence and order them to perform your will. . . . I could traverse all these islands without meeting opposition . . . they are yours to command, and make them work, sow seeds, and do whatever else is necessary to build towns. They could wear clothes and adopt our customs."[47] Columbus talked continuously of seeing the Great Khan's ships and other signs of Chinese civilization; but he still never seems to have considered how he could with impunity seize that powerful sovereign's people and land.[48]

Had no gold at all been produced, or had no ornaments been made from it, the Spanish interest in the Indies would have evaporated. As it was, a preoccupation was aroused that would never go away.[49]

But alongside these amiable people, the Tainos, there turned out to be also in the Caribbean many warlike eaters of human flesh. On December 26, 1492, the word *caribe,* or "cannibal" (the two words were looked upon for a long time as synonymous), first appears in Columbus's log: he and his captains were dining with a local prince, a so-called *cacique* (also a local word, and like *hamaca,* it passed into Spanish).

> After they finished eating, the prince took the Admiral to the beach and the Admiral sent for a bow and arrows, and he made one of his company shoot the arrows; and the prince, who did not know of such a thing, thought this wonderful, and then he said that he wanted to talk of the Caniba, whom they were wont to call Caribs. The Admiral indicated by signs that the monarchs of Castile would seek to destroy the Caribs . . . and then the Admiral had a lombard and an arquebus also fired.[50]

The lombard both fascinated and terrified the Indians. The prince was much comforted when the Admiral indicated that he would use the weapons in his defense. He gave Columbus some masks with golden eyes

and large ears of gold.[51] Columbus thought these natives were "such an affectionate and generous people and so tractable [*convenible*] that I assure
your Highnesses there are no better people or land in all the world. . . .
[True] they go about naked . . . but . . . they have very good customs and the
prince keeps so wonderful a state and displays such dignity that it is a pleasure to observe him."[52] Columbus also thought the peppers that he found on
the island superior to those brought by him from Guinea and Alexandria.[53]

On Christmas Eve 1492, the largest of Columbus's ships, the *Santa
María,* on which he himself had crossed the Atlantic, was wrecked on a coral
reef off the northern shore of La Española, near what is now Cap Haitien in
Haiti. Columbus was asleep at the time and reported that the mishap was
the fault of a boy left in charge. Then he blamed the duplicity of the "men of
Palos" who had, he thought, given him a bad ship. (But the *Santa María* had
been built in Galicia.) Columbus's lieutenant, his Córdoban mistress's
cousin, Diego de Araña, arranged with the *cacique,* Guacanagari, with whom
they had dined, to send men to help the Spaniards disembark the goods that
were on board before the ship sank. That was done, but the shipwreck left
the Admiral with only one ship.

Columbus now made a fateful decision. He had had no expectation
when he set off from Palos that he would occupy territory. But faced with
the impossibility of carrying all his men back to Spain in one small boat, he
did so. He founded a "city," which he named "La Navidad" because it was
Christmas Day, for thirty-nine men who, he thought, would remain collecting gold samples and await the next Spanish expedition. Columbus represented the site of Navidad as the product of a revelation, not because the
Santa María had gone aground there: "God plainly wanted a garrison there,"
he remarked, and with the planks from the wrecked ship he built a wooden
tower and a moat.

On January 4, 1493, Columbus left this first European town of the Americas in the hands of Diego de Araña, along with the thirty-nine inhabitants.[54]
A doctor, "Maestre Juan," was also abandoned. Among the others was Luis
de Torre, the interpreter *converso,* who had been one of the first two men to
see tobacco smoked. Columbus left other things, too: to a *cacique* whom he
encountered offshore, he bequeathed a coverlet that he had used on his own
bed, "some very good amber beads," some red shoes, "a flask of orange
flower water," and a bead on which he had had carved the heads of the King
and Queen taken from a coin, the *excelente,* then current in Castile.[55]

7

"Tears in the royal eyes"

> There were tears in the royal eyes. . . .
>
> *Bartolomé de las Casas's comment on what*
> *occurred when the King and Queen received*
> *Columbus in Barcelona in 1493*

Columbus now planned to return to Spain, a brave, even reckless act considering the bad weather in spring in those parts. Sailing east along the north coast of La Española, Columbus on the *Niña* with fifteen men encountered the errant Alonso Pinzón and the *Pinta* near what is now the town of Montecristi just inside the Dominican Republic. Pinzón, with his twenty-six followers, rejoined the expedition, bringing 900 pesos' worth of gold that he said he had gained through trade. He gave various unconvincing excuses for having deserted, and Columbus pretended to believe him.

In an inquiry of 1513, a number of witnesses said that Pinzón had reached Maguana[1] and visited the houses of several princes, one named Behechio, and another, Caonabó, "where they found great stores of gold."[2] He was also said to have found chili, cinnamon, pearls, pineapple, and tobacco. Canoes and hammocks abounded. Columbus took home with him on the *Niña* ten Indians, according to Peter Martyr, of whom one died at sea.[3] He confided to his log on January 1 that he had definitely found what he had been looking for.[4]

The return journey to Spain was not without incident. On January 13, when the now reunited expedition of the *Pinta* and the *Niña* reached a peninsula off La Española named Samaná, the Spaniards had their first armed clash with indigenous people in the New World. Perhaps the Europeans, in search of slaves, attacked, and the Indians defended themselves. At all events, heavily painted Tainos used long and straight yew bows and arrows of cane, with arrowheads of sharpened wood sometimes finished with a fishbone, and sometimes coated with poison. The resistance convinced the

Admiral that these were some of "those carib[e]s who eat men."[5] His indigenous friends had, after all, told him that

> cannibals, also called Caraibes, were accustomed to land amongst them
> and pursue them through the forests, like hunters chasing wild beasts.
> The cannibals capture children whom they castrate, just as we neuter
> chickens and pigs which we wish to fatten for the table; and, when they
> are grown up, they eat them. Older persons who fall into their power are
> killed and cut into pieces for food; they also eat the intestines and the ex-
> tremities, which they salt. They do not eat women. . . . If they capture
> any women, they keep them and care for them, in order that they may
> produce children, just as we do with hens, sheep, mares, and other ani-
> mals. Older women when captured are made into slaves. . . . The island
> inhabited by these monsters [the peninsula, actually] lies toward the
> south and halfway toward the other islands. . . .[6]

Thus another myth was born. For the next generation, any native who resisted the Spaniards would be considered a cannibal, fit to be enslaved.
Columbus named the bay and the cape "de las Flechas"—of the arrows.

To begin with, Columbus had difficulty finding a way through the winds
bearing on him from the east. Then he sailed northeast through the Sargasso
Sea, finding the seaweed so thick that some of his men thought they might
be held fast. He nevertheless sailed east to the Azores. On the way, they met
a storm, and once again the two ships "of glory" were separated. This was by
far the worst weather they had encountered since they had left Palos the previous year. On February 14, Columbus wrote two letters: one to Luis de Santangel,[7] the treasurer and his chief backer, another to the Aragonese treasurer
Gabriel Sánchez. The letter to Santangel described how, in thirty-three days,
he had reached the Indies, how he had found many well-populated islands,
giving them the names of San Salvador, Santa María de la Concepción, Fernandina, Isabela, Juana (Cuba), and La Española. Returning, he had found
six other islands but not the mainland. Columbus put this letter to Sánchez
in a barrel, with a note saying that anyone who found it should deliver it to
King Fernando and Queen Isabel.

The purpose of these actions was to ensure that "if his ship were lost in
the storm, the monarchs would still hear of his achievement. . . ."[8] The pre-
caution turned out to be unnecessary, for on February 17, 1493, the *Niña*
reached the harbor of Santa María in the Azores. But the *Pinta*, with Martín
Pinzón, had once again disappeared.

Ten of Columbus's men went ashore in the Azores on Ash Wednesday to give thanks to Our Lady. They were promptly arrested by Juan de Castañeda, the Portuguese captain of the island. The Admiral had difficulty in securing their release, for the relations between Spain and Portugal were then poor. But in the end he was successful. He showed to the Portuguese authorities, "at a distance," his "letter of privileges" of April 30, 1492.[9] He left the Azores on February 20 and then reached Lisbon, the nearest European port, on March 4.[10] That day, Columbus added a postscript to his letter to Santangel, saying that he was stopping in Portugal because of bad weather.[11] He repeated that he had reached the Indies "in thirty-three days and explained that he had returned in twenty-eight."[12]

He also wrote a letter to the King and Queen announcing the discovery. It was much the same as that to Santangel. In it he made the interesting request that the King should demand, for Columbus's son Diego (still a page of the Infante), a cardinalship from the Pope when (as Columbus expected that he would) Fernando wrote to Innocent VIII about the discoveries, "just as the young Giovanni de' Medici, son of Lorenzo, obtained one in 1489 when only fourteen. . . ."[13] He did not send this letter till he reached Spain. Columbus wrote several other letters recounting his achievements: one to his friend of 1490, the Duke of Medinaceli, another to Juanotto Berardi, the Florentine merchant of Seville.

Before returning to Spain, on March 6, the Admiral called on King João of Portugal in the convent of Santa María das Virtudes in the Valle del Paraíso, about thirty miles from Lisbon. The King had gone there because of an outbreak of plague in the capital. Later Columbus naturally came under suspicion in Castile because of the visit. For he was, indeed, greeted enthusiastically by João, who predictably argued that Columbus's new lands must belong to Portugal, not Spain, by the terms of the treaties between the two countries.[14] Columbus also called on the Portuguese Queen Isabel, who was Spanish in origin, being the eldest child of Fernando and Isabel, in the convent of San Antonio at Vila Franca de Xira.[15] King João offered horses to the Admiral to take him to Castile if he wanted to return by land, but Columbus preferred to travel by sea.

After he had left for Spain, on March 13, King João interrogated extensively the two Portuguese who had been with Columbus and who had remained in their native land. He decided immediately to send a fleet under Francisco de Almeida to search for the lands found by Columbus.[16] One Portuguese chronicler, Rui de Piña, says that some courtiers of João suggested that Columbus should be murdered on his way to Spain so that they could take advantage of the success of the expedition.[17]

The news of Columbus's return reached the King, Queen, and court of

Spain by March 9. A Milanese businessman, Anibal Zennaro (Ianuarius), also in Barcelona, wrote about the expedition to his brother, who was ambassador in Milan. He reported that Columbus had come back, had disembarked in Lisbon, and had written to the King, who had summoned him to Barcelona.[18]

The text is interesting:

Last August, these monarchs, as a result of the requests of a certain Columbus [Colón], agreed that he should arrange for four [sic] caravels to sail in the great ocean and travel in the westward direction . . . until he arrived in the East, because, the world being round, he was bound eventually to reach the East.[19] And so he did . . . and, in thirty-three days, he arrived at a great island where there were inhabitants whose skin was the color of olives, going about naked, with no disposition to fight.[20]

By late March the news was everywhere. The Florentine Tribaldo de Rossi announced the discovery of the Indies in his *Libro de Conti,* a kind of primitive news sheet, presumably deriving the information from one of his many compatriots who lived in Seville.[21]

The monarchs had left Granada and Santa Fe at the end of May 1492, during Columbus's ten-month absence from the court. They had gone first to Córdoba and then traveled north, stopping occasionally until they reached Barcelona on October 18, where they remained till the end of January 1493, largely to supervise the diplomatic negotiations for the recovery of Roussillon and Cerdagne that Fernando's father, Juan II, had mortgaged to King Louis XI of France in the 1460s.[22] The Queen, meantime, was preparing her reform of the monasteries, which went far toward making a Reformation and dissolution of monasteries unnecessary in Spain. Had Isabel read the best seller of the year, Diego de San Pedro's *Carcel de Amor* (*The Prison of Love*)? It would not be surprising, since it had been dedicated to one of her dearest friends, the commander of the royal pages (*alcaide de los donceles*), Diego Fernández de Córdoba.

In December 1492, Fernando had been attacked by a man with a knife in the Plaza del Rey in the Catalan capital. Fortunately, the King wore a heavy gold chain that turned away the weapon and he survived the attack. The deranged attacker, Juan de Cañamares, confessed that the devil had told him to kill the King because the kingdom was rightfully his. The Queen "flew in search of her husband," but not before she had commanded war galleys to be rowed to the embankment in order to protect the Infante. An "entire battalion of doctors and surgeons has been summoned," Martyr wrote, "we swing between fear and hope."[23] After some days of fever, Fernando recovered. The would-be assassin died a dreadful death, the details of which were concealed from Isabel until it had happened.[24] Isabel wrote to her onetime confessor Talavera: "Thus we see that kings too may die."[25]

On January 19, 1493, the two monarchs signed a treaty with France by which the latter returned to Aragon the contested provinces of Roussillon and Cerdagne. In return, Spain agreed to allow King Charles VIII to cross into Italy to challenge Fernando's nephew, Ferrante, King of Naples, in a trial by combat. Fernando and Isabel went to Perpignan to be present at an act celebrating the restitution of the provinces, though Isabel wrote a long letter complaining of the tedium of dining so often with French ambassadors.

During all these months, the monarchs had remained apparently as uninterested in the possible achievements of Columbus as they were impervious to such news as was brought to them of the tragedies suffered by their late subjects, the unbending Jews. Many of these were seized by corsairs and sold as slaves in the very port whence they had set out, while others found themselves in the slave markets of Fez or Tangier. A few returned and then willingly converted on their arrival.[26]

The monarchs did, of course, take into account that, following the death of Pope Innocent VIII at the end of July 1492 and his swift interment in a tomb designed by Pollaiuolo, the conclave in Rome had voted for Cardinal Borgia, of the same Valencian family as Calixtus III (his uncle), who thereupon assumed the papacy as Alexander VI at the age of sixty-one. "A victory obtained," said Guicciardini, "because he openly bought many votes, partly with promises of benefices and offices."[27]

Everyone knew that Borgia was not going to be the "angel Pope" whom a few dreamers had optimistically predicted would appear in 1493—a man who could be expected to seek no temporal power but be concerned only with the good of souls. Profligate simonist and hedonist though Alexander might be, worldly and charming as he certainly was, unapologetically sensual and a lover of women as he had always been, great promoter of his family, including his murderous son Caesar, as he would show himself, he had the advantage, as far as Fernando and Isabel were concerned, of being half Spanish. Peter Martyr commented ribaldly that if Borgia had made his eldest son Duke of Gandia when he was a mere cardinal, now surely he would make him a king.[28] He feared that even though Alexander was Spanish, the monarchs hated the thought of his "wickedness, lewdness, and ambition for his children."[29]

Yet there were definite advantages for the monarchs of Spain in having Alexander as pope: the language preferred in Rome was now Valencian, and

that lasted throughout his reign.[30] Fernando, who liked him, was not the
man to have objections to anyone on moral grounds. As vice-chancellor to
Pope Sixtus IV, Borgia had influenced Rome's policy to support Fernando
and Isabel ever since his visit to Spain as papal legate in 1472, hoping to secure active Spanish support against the Turks. It was Borgia who had persuaded the young Cardinal Mendoza to side with Fernando and Isabel in
1472 and to desert King Enrique. He had brought the bull enabling these second cousins to marry, and he had approved of Fernando seizing for himself
the Mastership of the Order of Santiago in 1476 after the death of Rodrigo
Manrique. Further, so the Florentine historian Francesco Guicciardini
thought, Alexander possessed "singular cunning and sagacity, excellent
judgment, a marvelous efficacy in persuasion, and an incredible dexterity
and attentiveness in dealing with weighty matters." Guicciardini considered,
nevertheless, that these things were outweighed by his "obscene behavior, in-
sincerity, shamelessness, lying faithlessness, impiety, insatiable and immod-
erate ambition, a cruelty more than barbaric, and a most ardent cupidity to
exalt his numerous children."[31] The historian Infessura commented that immediately after he became pope, Alexander gave away all his goods to the
poor—that is, to the cardinals who had voted for him, of whom Ascanio
Sforza was the leader.[32]

The monarchs sent a generous letter of congratulation to Columbus on his
way to Barcelona. They were pleased that "God has given you such a good
end as you began, whereof He will be greatly served, and ourselves as well,
and our realms will receive so much benefit."[33] They requested that Columbus make haste to Barcelona and referred to him by all the grand titles that
he had obtained from them: Admiral of the Ocean Sea, Viceroy and Governor of the Indies.

Columbus went first, though, to Palos and then to Seville, where he was
cheered in the street by, among others, the young Bartolomé de las Casas,
the future historian, agitator, and apostle of the Indies. He then made for
Barcelona, going triumphantly via Córdoba, Murcia, Valencia, and Tarragona. He had seven of his Indians still alive to exhibit in Barcelona.[34]

Martín Alonso Pinzón had also arrived in Spain with the *Pinta*, at
Baiona, in Galicia, near Vigo, a few days before Columbus reached Seville.
He was ready to cause difficulty by disputing Columbus's story and would
indeed have been able to claim he was the first to return from the New World
to Europe. He wrote to the monarchs that he had discovered what he knew
to be the mainland (China?) as well as islands, whereas Columbus consid-

ered that he had only found islands. But Pinzón died as soon as he reached Seville, perhaps from syphilis; and, at any event, the monarchs wanted to welcome their Admiral. Still, in other circumstances America might perhaps have been called Pinzonia.

Columbus was in Barcelona probably on April 21. Las Casas said that the streets were full and that the monarchs received Columbus as a hero, allowing him to ride with them in processions. He added that in appearance the Admiral resembled a senator of the old Roman Empire.[35] Peter Martyr, who was present, wrote that "Columbus was honorably received by the King and the Queen who caused him to sit in their presence, a token of great love and honor among the Spaniards." He added that he was like "one of those whom the ancients made gods."[36] The cartographer Jaume Ferrer, who was also there, thought that the Admiral was like an apostle doing for the West what St. Thomas had done in India.[37] There was a Te Deum in the monarchs' chapel, and Las Casas reported that there were "tears in the royal eyes" as the two rulers knelt in emotion.[38] Isabel received from Columbus presents of hutias (the ratlike wild animals of the Caribbean), chili peppers, sweet potatoes, monkeys, parrots, some gold, and six (no longer seven) men wearing gold earrings and nostril rings, men not white but "the color of quince jelly."[39] These Tainos were baptized, the royal family acting as godparents, one of them, "Juan de Castilla," becoming a page, though, alas, "God soon called him to Himself."

These events occurred in the Salon del Tinell, the throne room, in the royal palace in what is now known as the Plaza del Rey, where indeed the attempt to murder Fernando had happened such a short time before. The hall had been designed by Guillén Carbonell in the mid-fourteenth century and has remained unaltered. The discoverer of America would doubtless have seen the curious Gothic murals on the walls of this vaulted place. When the monarchs were absent, the palace was used by the Inquisition.[40]

A copy of the letter of Columbus to Gabriel Sánchez was published by Pedro Posse in Barcelona a few days later. A Latin edition translated by Leandro del Cosco soon appeared in Rome, and it was printed no less than eight times in 1493 (three times in Barcelona, three times in Paris, once in Antwerp, and once in Basle).[41] Such a wide distribution of the letter could not have occurred, of course, had it not been for the new invention of printing, which over the next generation everywhere stimulated excitement at geographical discovery.

In this and in all his letters of that time, Columbus spoke of God's gift to Castile. How convenient to have such a present so close to the Canaries! How ideal the Indians were to receive the Christian faith![42] Columbus wrote that he had heard the nightingale everywhere in Cuba. He said that in La Española the people had no religion, yet believed that power and goodness dwelt in the sky.[43] He had found no monsters and had seen that the people were well made and that all spoke the same language, a fact that would be useful when it came to converting them to Christianity. He reported that he had left behind a strong fortress, Navidad, and taken possession of a large town where he had established good relations with the local king.[44] What that town was is rather obscure. He spoke also of the Caribs, who, he said, traveled around in canoes doing damage as well as pleasuring the women of "Matinino" (presumably Martinique, which he had neither seen nor visited) once a year.

Columbus concluded that as a result of his discoveries, he would be able to give their Highnesses all the gold they needed "if they will render me some very slight service." Also:

> I will give them all the spices and cotton which they want, and I will bring back as large a cargo of mastic [like that of Chios] as their Highnesses desire. I will also bring back as many aloes as they ask for and as many slaves, who will be taken from among the idolators. I believe also I have found rhubarb and cinnamon. Thus the eternal God, Our Lord, grants to those who walk in his way a victory over apparent impossibilities. . . . So all Christendom will be delighted that our Redeemer has given triumph to our most illustrious king and queen and their renowned kingdoms in this great matter. They should hold celebrations and render solemn thanks to the Holy Trinity, with many solemn prayers for the great feat which they will have by the conversion of so many peoples to our faith and for the temporal benefits which will follow, for not only Spain but all Christendom will receive encouragement and profit.[45]

Columbus, of course, considered that he had been to Asia. But most astute Italian commentators immediately assumed that his discoveries were antipodean: he had taken the name of Christ to the Antipodes, which "we did not even previously think existed." Someone in Florence spoke of the discovery as "the other world opposite our own."[46] That was because the idea fitted in with the general stream of ideas among Italian humanists of the 1490s. The fifth-century ecclesiastical writer Macrobius had written commentaries on Cicero that suggested that an "Antipodean landmass might exist in the northern as well as the southern hemisphere"—and Macrobius had recently been published; while a fifth-century encyclopedist from North Africa, Marciano Capella, had suggested the same in his curious allegorical novel *De Nuptis Mercurii et Philologia,* also now available (the cosmographer Pierre d'Ailly had thought that the Antipodes might be a landmass continuous with the known continents). Peter Martyr in Spain also wrote that Columbus had been to "the Antipodes": "There has returned from the western Antipodes a certain Columbus, of Liguria, who barely obtained from my sovereigns three ships for the voyage, for they regarded the things which he said as chimerical." (Since "Antipodes" implies something directly opposite, it would have been difficult to find the western Antipodes!)

Martyr also said that Columbus had been to "places unknown," which presumably meant that he at least considered that they were not Asiatic.[47] Columbus wrote in September to his onetime benefactor, the Count of Tendilla, and to Archbishop Talavera, without whose advice (he flatteringly, though inaccurately, added) he would not have done what he had done: "Raise your spirits, wise men, and hear about the new discovery! Remember, because you should, that Columbus, he of Liguria, has been traveling along a new hemisphere in the western antipodes."[48] A month later he wrote, even more appropriately, to the Archbishop of Braga in Portugal that, as to his finding the Indies, "I do not deny it entirely, though the magnitude of the globe seems to indicate something else."[49] In a letter to Cardinal Ascanio Sforza, of November 1, 1493,[50] Martyr was using the accurate expression "new world"—*novi orbis*—about the places where Columbus had been.

The Admiral himself in his letter to Luis de Santangel spoke of how "in thirty-three days I reached *the Indies.*" In the same letter, he wrote that he had "passed over to the Indies [*sic*] with the fleet which the most illustrious King and Queen our Lords gave me."[51] Why not India? Because, presumably, Columbus wanted "to use the vaguest, most inclusive term he could find to suggest the East, without doing violence to the public imagination at home";[52] and Fernando Colón, the clever son of the Admiral, thought that he used the phrase "the Indies" "because they constituted the eastern part of India, beyond the Ganges, to which no geographer had set bounds on the east. . . ."[53]

Columbus continued to think in terms of the Indies, and no one challenged him. But, of course, he had discovered something different. Fernando and Isabel as well as the court knew what had happened. They soon began to act as Peter Martyr would have desired.

8

"They love their neighbors as themselves"

The Tainos were "affectionate and without covetousness. . . .
They love their neighbors as themselves."

*Columbus's comment on the indigenous
inhabitants of La Española, 1492*

The two continents now known as "America" and the many islands off them "discovered" by Columbus were first settled by certain Asiatic peoples who, before 15000 B.C., reached what is today Alaska, over a tongue of ice that then linked it with Siberia.[1] The sea did not flow through what we now think of as the Bering Strait until after the Ice Age, about 8000 B.C.

Those Asiatics seem to have traveled in packs of about fifty or so, in a manner characteristic of men in the long age of hunting. Perhaps they went east first in pursuit of animals, such as mammoths, just as Columbus went west in search of gold and spices.

In physical appearance, these people probably resembled Mongols or Tartars. Perhaps some looked like the Ainus of Japan. A woman whose skeleton was found near the city of Mexico in A.D. 2002 seemed, however, to have a long head, more European than Asiatic. Archeologists will devote much time thinking of the significance of this. At all events, many people of Asiatic origin slowly journeyed down the Americas, living as nomads.

New men and women kept on coming from Asia until the opening of the Bering Strait made the journey more difficult. But that did not stop some continued migration; for example, the Eskimos did not reach their present habitat until about A.D. 100. Some of these wanderers may have reached Mexico about 10000 B.C.

Several sedentary centers of culture were eventually established: in the valley of Mexico, in Yucatan, and in Peru. All these were made possible by the discovery of agriculture. That itself seems either to have followed or been necessitated by the extinction of the large mammals, the pursuit of which may have led to man's coming to America in the first place.

In Mexico, the age of agriculture began about 5000 B.C., no doubt when some family discovered that the planting of seeds could assure a regular production of crops. This first crop was certainly maize, which is indigenous to Mexico and has been the North American continent's most important contribution to the world's prosperity. Even in A.D. 2000 it was still providing over half of Mexico's food. Maize soon began to be grown on terraces. Other plants of old Mexico were avocados, beans, and chili peppers, though wild fruit, fish, and game also played an important part in the diet. Pottery began to be made not long after 5000 B.C., and cotton was being used for cloth by about 3000 B.C.

These events occurred much later than they did in the Old World (planting seeds for an anticipated harvest began in the Near East by about 10000 B.C. or earlier). Nor was this agricultural revolution in the Americas accompanied by the domestication of animals, as it was in Asia. The primitive American dog remained an object of game. Horses were indigenous to the Americas, but they no longer existed by 8000 B.C. There were in the Americas no beasts of burden except, to some limited extent, the llama in Peru, until the Europeans brought them.

As in Asia, the coming of agriculture in the Americas led all the same to the intense concentration of human beings in towns. There emerged organized religions, complex political systems, and, at least in what is now called Mesoamerica (Central America and Mexico), commerce. Among the first objects of trade in what is now Mexico, obsidian, a fine, hard, black stone, was preeminent, which last played an exactly similar part in ancient Mesopotamia.

When Columbus and his Spanish friends reached the Caribbean in September 1492, they found people called the Tainos in the Bahamas (known then as the Lucays); on the island that he called La Española, anglicized as Hispaniola, but which the indigenous people called Haiti or Quisiquey (which signified "than which nothing is larger"); in Cuba, which has retained its indigenous name; in Puerto Rico, which was then known as Boriquen; in Jamaica (a word signifying "land of wood and water"); and in the northern islands of the Lesser Antilles.

These Tainos have been called the Arawaks, but that is an incorrect usage; people of that name did exist, but they lived in the Guianas and the island of Trinidad. The word "Taino" meant "good" in the language of the people concerned: several Tainos used it to Columbus to insist that they

were not "bad" Caribs.[2] But no one in the sixteenth century took much notice of these niceties.

In the Lesser Antilles, to the south of Guadeloupe, the Spaniards, as we
have seen, would encounter other, less sophisticated but fiercer people, the
Caribs.

All the peoples of the Caribbean came originally by canoe from the continent of South America along the chain of islands known as the Antilles, or
the West Indies, via Trinidad and Tobago. The winds in the region favored
travel from south to north and from east to west. The strong currents of the
River Orinoco may have swept these people into the West Indies to begin
with. Trade winds from the northeast also blow in that region most of the
year. Taino myths, however, insisted that the inhabitants were spawned from
certain magic caves on La Española.

In the far west of Cuba, beyond Pinar del Río, the Spaniards would find
a few people of another race, the Guanahatebeyes, sometimes called Ciboneys, of whom little is known except that they remained nomadic. They
were savages who lived in caves, without settled villages or politics, and ate
turtles, fish, and birds.[3] They were probably early inhabitants pushed to the
west by the Tainos when they came up from the Lesser Antilles, but they
seem to have vanished early in the Spanish occupation. Now the Tainos have
followed the Guanahatebeyes into the shades, though the blood of some of
them (perhaps of both peoples) flows among both the immigrant black and
white inhabitants of all the Caribbean islands, especially in certain Cuban
pueblos near Bayamo and among certain aristocratic Cuban families (such
as the Recios); and there are Caribs in reservations on what is now the island
of Dominica. A few Taino words also linger on in Spanish and even in English (hammock, canoe, hurricane, savannah, cannibal, barbecue, and, of
course, cacique).

There was little contact between these Tainos and the civilizations on
the mainland. The strait between Cuba and Yucatan is little more than 120
miles wide, but the currents there prevented regular communication, even
though the Mayas in the latter territory had strong vessels capable of crossing seas. On the other hand, the islands of Tobago and Grenada are about
sixty miles from the mainland to the south, and that journey is easily made
in a canoe, while even the one hundred miles from St. Vincent to Guadeloupe presents no difficulty.

The people of Mesoamerica were far more sophisticated than the
Tainos, but in their legends and writings (as collected by the Spaniards after
their conquest), there is almost nothing about traveling east, save that the

ancient Mexica believed that one of their gods, Quetzalcoatl, vanished into the Mexican Gulf on a raft of serpents.

The intercourse between Mesoamerica and the Caribbean islands was modest, but it did exist. On the Mexican island of Cozumel, Cortés's Spaniards found a woman from Jamaica who had been shipwrecked there.[4] The horizontal drum of the Mexica, the *teponaztli*, was known in Cuba when Columbus reached that island in 1492. Columbus himself claimed to have found in Cuba a nose ring of worked silver; if so, the ring must have originated in Michoacan, the only nearby center of silver, in what is now Mexico.[5] Then the first Spanish governor of Cuba, Diego Velázquez de Cuéllar, wrote to the King of Spain in 1514 that he had been told by people on his island that Indians had come over the sea to the northwest of Cuba from land five or six days' canoe journey distant.[6] The people concerned could have come from Yucatan or the territory of the Mexica.[7] In a few centuries, the Tainos, if left to themselves (a big assumption), might have mastered this strait and begun to trade with Yucatan. But then they might have been conquered by the Mexica as easily as they were by the Spaniards.

Scholarship veers wildly about numbers of these first Americans, between thinking that there were in the islands "at contact" with Europeans either 8 million Tainos[8] or only 200,000.[9] The historian, agitator, saint, and preacher Bartolomé de las Casas extravagantly guessed that 3 million Indians died in La Española between 1494 and 1508; and in 1519 the Dominicans stated that Bartolomeo Columbus, the Admiral's brother, estimated that there had been 1,100,000 Indians in La Española in 1494.[10] The lower figures are definitely more likely. There is much documentation about the early days in Santo Domingo, but no anxiety was expressed about the decline of the population until 1511. Most people agree that by the year 1510 there were about 35,000 people on the island.[11] The Spaniards were unsentimental, but they were not so insensitive that they would not have noticed a 99 percent decline between 1493, when the new settlers arrived, and that year. In 1499, Columbus was still thinking it possible to export 4,000 slaves a year from the island. So let us guess that there were between 40,000 and 100,000 in La Española and another 100,000 in Puerto Rico, Jamaica, Cuba, and elsewhere in the Caribbean islands.[12]

These people usually lived in large villages of between one thousand and two thousand people. Columbus told the King and Queen of Spain that the Tainos were less civilized than the Japanese and Chinese. That was true, though the Admiral's knowledge of the Orient was minimal. Each village in the Taino world was governed by a chief, or a *cacique*, to use their word.

Their houses, always large enough for several families, were made of wood and thatch, with mud or earth floors, similar to the *bohíos* that survive in Cuba today, though now they are smaller. The houses were usually ranged irregularly around a central plaza. The chief's house was larger than that of the others. The chiefs concerned themselves with storing surplus food in a special warehouse. These leaders, incidentally, might have been either male or female, a complete deviation from the usual among primitive peoples. Ancestors were always traced matrilineally, though there was polygamy.[13] Thus the role of women in the ancient Caribbean was stronger than in most countries, sophisticated or the reverse.

Inside these houses there were hammocks for sleeping made from cotton. The word *hamaca* for these things was to be general in South America (cotton was one of the plants to be found on both sides of the Atlantic before the voyages of Columbus). Baskets hung on the walls. *Caciques* would receive visitors seated on a well-carved wooden stool (*duho*), as they had received the *conversos*, Luis de la Torre and Rodríguez de Xerez, on the voyage of Columbus in 1492. Tainos were good woodworkers (and, indeed, workers in other materials, too—carved skulls were sometimes worn as pendants). A queen in La Española would send fourteen of these stools to the brother of Columbus in 1494, and he himself sent some ebony ones to Spain, to be admired by Peter Martyr. Chiefs would be carried in hammocks if they went anywhere by land. The villages were grouped into districts, and the districts into regions, over which an over*cacique* would "reign." But he did not have the power of life and death over the people, which the village chief did—an engaging example of the principle of subsidiarity in reverse from which perhaps we have much to learn.

The names of several regional monarchs in La Española have come down to us through Spanish chronicles. There was Caonabó, who reigned in the hilly country in the center of the island known as La Maguana to the Spaniards and Cibao to the Indians, the site of the supposed gold mines that Columbus sought indefatigably. That *cacique* was married to Anacoana, sister of Behechio, who ruled the west. Then there was Cayaca, an old queen who dominated the east. The last important monarch was Guarionex, in the large and fertile plain in the north of the island. Subsidiary to each of these were another seventy or eighty *caciques,* of whom Guacanagarí, who remained friendly with the Christians, was lord of the territory on which Navidad had been founded by Columbus and who, according to his own account, had tried to protect the settlers there. In consequence he was hated by the others, especially by Behechio and Caonabó, who had each stolen one of his wives. All these monarchs or leaders accepted the principle of heredity as if they had been Europeans.

One of Columbus's companions, a Jeronymite hermit, Father Ramón Pané, who accompanied him to La Española in 1493, wrote an account of the religion of these people. There were two supreme gods, or *zemis:* Yúcahu, god of salt water and of cassava; and Atabey, his mother, goddess of fresh water and fertility. There were other gods of lesser importance. All were often depicted by little statuettes of bone, wood, and pottery, and chiefs kept copies of these in special houses, which served as primitive temples, guarded by priests who, however, did not constitute a special class. Shamans or medicine men, whose task was to cure the sick, used the *zemis* in their ceremonies.

Annual celebrations were held to honor the *caciques,* at which there would be dancing and drumming, and a procession through the town. Music and dancing always went together. Both male and female Tainos also played ball games (separately), using rubber balls, enacted in special courts with different regions or villages contesting together. Perhaps this was another mark of contact with the mainland, for in Mesoamerica, too, ball games were played in splendid walled courts.

Taino society was divided into two classes, the lower one consisting of workers who seem to have had no rights. There were, however, no slaves—almost a unique qualification. Las Casas, though, who knew Cuba, would say that the Ciboneys were "a simple and gentle class of people who were held *as if* they were slaves."[14]

The Tainos had some knowledge of metallurgy, for they found gold in rivers and beat it into plates. They could not smelt metals, but they traded with peoples on the northern shore of South America, where that craft was known, in order to obtain a cheaper gold made with a copper alloy (*guanin*), which was worn as ornaments by chiefs. These Tainos made fire by using a wooden drill; they knew how to make pottery and could weave cotton into cloth.

In general, the men went naked but sometimes wore cotton loincloths, while the women wore cotton skirts and, if unmarried, bands over their hair. Chiefs liked feather headdresses, sometimes elaborate, as was the case in other parts of the Americas before Columbus arrived.

The Tainos had devised a successful form of agriculture, whose main characteristic was a mound of earth (*conuco*) three feet high and about nine feet round, on which they grew root crops. Their only tools were digging sticks. The main crop was cassava or yucca (*casabe manioc*), followed by the sweet potato (*batata*). From the former, a flour was made that was turned into an unleavened flat bread that could last a long time. Columbus described yucca as "their life."[15] He was right. The sweet potato was also eaten as a vegetable. Maize was grown, too, on a small scale, but the bread made from it did not last long.

Other products included pineapples, peanuts, squashes, peppers, and beans, as well as tobacco. The latter was smoked, in the form of cigars, for pleasure, a habit swiftly picked up by the Spaniards. The Tainos had, however, no alcohol. They went fishing with nets. They ate iguana, parrots, and the now extinct rabbitlike rodent, the hutia, one of which, it will be recalled, was presented to Queen Isabel by Columbus. Turtles were held, especially in south Cuba, in shallow corrals. These would be described by Michele Cuneo, one of Columbus's most observant Genoese companions in 1493, as "infinitely large, enormous."[16] There were no domestic animals, but small dogs that did not bark but were kept as pets and eaten. The Tainos used canoes and, for the purpose of trade, took to the sea much more than the modern inhabitants of the Caribbean. These canoes were hollowed out of ceiba trees with stone tools and were often well carved and ornamented. The Tainos had paddles but no sails. Some of these canoes could carry 150 people, Columbus thought.[17] There seem to have been many variants of the Taino language. Thus those who lived in the northern part of La Española spoke a different language from those in the south.

These Indians were not warlike. Columbus described them as "affectionate and without covetousness." "They love their neighbors as themselves," he remarked; "they have the sweetest speech in the world." But even had it not been for the Spaniards, the Tainos were probably nearing the end of their time as an independent people, for they were constantly faced by Carib raiders from the east, who were busy stealing girls for brides. To fend off such attacks, the Tainos, having painted themselves red, placed effigies of their gods on their heads. They fought with sticks, bows and arrows, and spears propelled by throwing sticks. But though they were mild people, they suffered from endemic syphilis; ancient Taino stories include the tale of a legendary oarsman setting off for South Africa in search of a cure for it.[18]

The main islands of the Tainos' enemies, the Caribs, were Guadeloupe and Martinique. These people, of whom little is known, have given their name to the sea and the region unjustly. The Carib men and women apparently lived in segregated houses, as in an old-fashioned boarding school. They had the same crops as the Tainos, and they made a kind of wine from pineapples.[19] They also bred ducks, which the Tainos did not. They raided all other islands to obtain wives, but like the Tainos, they principally traded with the north coast of South America. Their main weapon was the bow and arrow. They ate parts of the warriors whom they captured—not for pleasure but to acquire their valor. Their language was Arawak, that is, a South American tongue distinct from Taino. The Spaniards tended to call anyone who fought them, and did not accept Christianity, Caribs, but they thereby confused the issue, for the Caribs raided other islands but were not found settled north of Guadeloupe.

For all sorts of reasons, which will be considered later, these indigenous people of the Caribbean, like those of the Canary Islands, have disappeared. It is therefore impossible for us to know exactly what they were like. They live only in history, and it is only just that history has treated them well. Yet they were not saints. Had it not been for the Spanish invasions, it is likely that the Caribs would have destroyed the Tainos as the Tainos had destroyed the Ciboneys. Some have written of the ancient Caribbean as if it had been Elysium. But it was an Elysium with savagery in the wings.

9

"We concede the islands
and lands discovered by you"

> So we concede to you and your heirs and successors the islands and
> lands discovered by you . . . with the same rights, privileges, faculties,
> and immunities.
>
> *Pope Alexander VI to the Catholic Kings, 1493*

João, King of Portugal, was not slow to awaken to what he had lost by having been so discouraging in his discussions with Columbus in 1485 and 1488.
Allegretto Allegretti, a Sienese senator and historian, did not comfort him
when he wrote to the King that America was just another Canary Island.[1] On
April 5, 1493, even before Columbus had reached Barcelona, João dispatched
to Spain Rui de Sande, chief magistrate of Torres Vedras, the little wine-
growing town where the Portuguese court had spent Easter. He was to tell
Queen Isabel and King Fernando that, having talked to Columbus in Lisbon,
King João considered the lands that the Admiral had discovered to be Portuguese. All the relevant treaties confirmed his impression. As we have seen,
he had secretly sent a boat west as soon as he heard of Columbus's feat, and
according to some imaginative scholars, this vessel brought back news of the
existence of Brazil.[2]

Fernando and Isabel for their part sent an emissary to Lisbon. This was
Lope de Herrera, who was to say, first, that the Spanish monarchs thought
they ought to meet to discuss with the Portuguese any difficulties that might
arise between the two countries because of Columbus's achievements. He
was to add that the Crown of Spain would threaten with reprisals anyone
who set off for the Indies without their permission, in just the same way as,
since the Treaty of Alcáçovas, the Spaniards had respected the Portuguese
monopoly of the route to El Mina, on the Gold Coast, and elsewhere in
Africa.[3] Lope de Herrera was to inform or instruct Lisbon that no Portuguese should do anything in these new Spanish Indies that had been discovered by Columbus.[4]

The request was sensible, for, at the end of April, the new Duke of Medina Sidonia, Juan de Guzmán (Duke Enrique, who had been reluctant to help Columbus, had died in the summer of 1492), would inform the monarchs that he had heard King João wanted to send another expedition under Francisco de Almeida with ships to investigate Columbus's discoveries.[5] In reply, on May 2, the monarchs asked the Duke to organize his caravels in southern Spain to prevent Portugal from so acting.[6] A royal armada from Biscay (six ships, served by nearly nine hundred men), under a Basque, Íñigo de Artieta, was also ordered to the coast of Cadiz.[7] (Another of its missions would be to escort poor King Boabdil to Africa.)[8] All these moves were soon known in Lisbon because of an efficient Portuguese network of spies in Seville.[9]

The astute Spanish monarchs were also in touch with the papacy. The Spanish agent in Rome, Bernardino de Carvajal, was a nephew of that Cardinal Juan Carvajal who had been one of the Church of Rome's hardest-working legates, especially in central Europe: *Animo Pectore Caesar erat* had been inscribed on his tomb. Bernardino, a lesser man, had greater opportunities. The Carvajals came from Plasencia, in Extremadura, and were connected with the great families of that region, such as the Bejaranos, the Orellanas, and the Monroys. Bernardino Carvajal was asked to tell the Pope that if the new islands discovered by Columbus turned out to be on the same latitude as the Canaries, they would be naturally Spanish. But what if they turned out to be the mysterious "Antilla" or "Atlantis," of which so many old sailors had talked? Legend at least gave those "islands" to Portugal. Where, seriously, could one draw a line between Portuguese and Spanish interests? Columbus himself proposed a line a hundred leagues west of the Azores where he thought that he had noticed a change of climate; beyond that line, Carvajal was to argue, Spanish influence would begin.[10]

Carvajal and Diego López de Haro, the ambassador of Fernando and Isabel in Rome, were with the Pope in the Vatican. López de Haro, a minor poet from a great family, had privately criticized the Pope for promoting war in Italy, for condoning corruption in the Curia, for harboring *conversos* who were really Jews,[11] and for simony. Carvajal was now to insist that, by the will of God, the Canaries had been subjugated by Spain, as had "many other [islands] toward India, until now unknown . . . and it is expected that they will be converted to Christianity in a short time by persons whom the monarchs are sending there. The latter, therefore, request bulls from the Pope that would confirm the Indies to them. They ask, too, for papal permission to devote the proceeds of the bulls of indulgence that had been intended to finance the war against Granada to the conversion of newly found peoples."[12]

Pope Alexander, world-weary though he was, had been excited by the news of the expedition of Columbus, "seeing that such ample gates onto the Ocean had been opened up, and seeing that the world which had been hidden was shown to be overflowing with an infinite number of nations, for so many centuries concealed in such a way that one would hope that the empire of Christ would now be augmented and increased."[13] On May 3, 1493, he issued "a brief" on the subject of the new islands, changed the next day into the bull *Inter Caetera Divinae*. By this he allocated everything discovered by Columbus to the Crown of Castile, on the condition that the monarchs set about propagating the Christian faith there, and provided the lands concerned were not already occupied by another Christian power—that is, Portugal. Spain thus received the same rights as had been bestowed on her neighbor for her exploitation of Africa. Possibly the speed with which this statement was made was assisted by the present of a little Spanish gold, some of which had been brought back by Columbus and given to the monarchs in Barcelona. Certainly the story has been that the first gold brought to Rome from the Americas was used for the decoration of the panels in Santa María Maggiore, these being the most charming Roman works of their kind.[14]

Secondly, Pope Alexander described the rights of Spain in detail and dwelt on how these "newly found barbarous nations" might be introduced to the Christian faith. He spoke enthusiastically of Fernando and Isabel's victory over the Moors (*los saracenos*) and talked of the need to propagate Christendom (*el imperio Cristiano*). He mentioned, too, how

our dear son Columbus, not without great labor, danger, and expense, ensured that, with ships and men suitable for the task, he was able to find remote and unknown lands across seas where no one previously had sailed.

In consequence of which, having considered everything and, above all, thought of the exaltation and propagation of the Catholic faith as is natural for Catholic kings and princes, you [that is, Fernando and Isabel] have decided, according to the customs of your progenitors, kings of illustrious memory, to submit to us the said lands and the islands and their inhabitants and those who dwell there and to convert them with the help of divine charity to the Catholic faith. . . . [So] just as some kings of Portugal discovered, and acquired, the regions of Africa, Guinea, El Mina on the Gold Coast, and other islands . . . so we concede to you and your heirs and successors the islands and lands discovered by you . . . with the same rights, privileges, liberties, faculties, and immunities. . . .[15]

It was notable that this grant was made exclusively to the realm of Castile. Aragon was given no part. The exclusion did not seem to trouble King Fernando, who presumably expected to rule Castile for his lifetime.

Perhaps because some of these statements seemed vague, and possibly on the suggestion of Carvajal, the Pope added on May 4 another statement that omitted all mention of Portugal and included further compliments to Columbus. Alexander also declared that "we give, concede, and assign all the lands and islands discovered, and to be discovered, and to be found toward the west and the south, making and constructing a line from the arctic Pole which is in the north, to the Antarctic pole which is in the south, the line lying at a distance from what we vulgarly call the Azores and Cape Verde, one hundred leagues away."[16]

These declarations conferred on Fernando and Isabel priority in regard to the territories discovered by their Admiral. "As nowadays, patents are given for inventions, and copyrights for literary production," wrote a historian of Rome, so "a papal bull, enforced by the censures of the Church, protected the laborious discoverer from having the hard-won fruits of his own toil wrested from him by a stronger hand."[17]

This decision, as a Castilian judge, Alonso de Zuazo, would put it a generation later, "cut the world in two, as if it were an orange, between the king of Portugal and the monarchs of Spain." Had the Pope not been of Spanish blood, had Portugal had a stronger negotiator in Rome, the decision could have been different.

But what precisely did the Pope mean by his donation? Did he anticipate a missionary task or that Fernando and Isabel should have "full, free, ample, and absolute authority and jurisdiction"? Further, one could easily argue, as Magellan later did, that this arbitrary division of the world covered not only the Western Hemisphere but could be interpreted also as dividing the Eastern Hemisphere between Spain and Portugal. Thus the Spice Islands, the Moluccas, in what became the East Indian archipelago, the supreme goal of the era of discovery, would also lie in that section of the globe belonging to the Spaniards.[18]

King João of Portugal pretended not to know of these concessions by the Pope and tried to negotiate directly with Isabel and Fernando. These matters, however, were left on one side while the Crown of Castile encouraged Columbus to plan a second voyage to the new Indies.

After showing off his treasures and his captives, and explaining how he had left behind Spanish colonists at his "fortress" of La Isabela, the Admiral returned from Barcelona to Seville, taking with him a "letter patent" of May

23, which decreed that no one should go to the New World or take any goods to it without permission of the King and Queen, or of himself or of Archdeacon Juan Rodríguez de Fonseca.[19]

This last had just been ordained a priest and was of a good family, descended from the royal house of Hungary, so the genealogists said. A royal marriage in Spain in the eleventh century? Everything seemed to have happened to the Fonsecas. Our Fonseca was a cousin of a notorious if generous absentee Archbishop of Santiago. An aunt of his had married a Castilla, a royal bastard, and so he was a cousin of the late Queen Juana's lover. His father, Fernando, had died at the Battle of Toro, fighting for Castile, while an uncle, Alonso, had been a powerful archbishop of Seville in the 1470s. The vast brick family castle of Coca, near Medina del Campo, repays a visit even now.

A pupil of the great grammarian Nebrija at Salamanca as well as a protégé of the royal confessor Talavera, Juan Rodríguez de Fonseca had in 1492 crossed France in disguise to organize the marriage of the Infante Juan to the Habsburg princess Margaret, as well as the wedding of the Infanta Juana with the Habsburg prince Philip. Talavera took Fonseca as vicar-general to Granada also in 1492 when he became archbishop there, and he sought to train him so that, it was said, "in his service, he could learn to be a saint." But Fonseca learned managerial skills, not saintliness.

The Archdeacon was thus already a tried diplomat. He was ordained in March 1493, though he had been born in 1451, the same year as both Columbus and the Queen. The Queen allocated great responsibilities to him, and as a result of hard work and dedication, he dominated the history of Spain's relations with the Indies for a generation.[20] He has been called a "minister of the Indies" without the title, but essentially he was a civil servant rather than a politician. His brother Antonio also played an important role in Castile, receiving lands after the conquest of Ronda, in which he participated, and becoming, among other things, chief accountant (*contador mayor*) of Castile.

By the new arrangements, the position of Columbus seemed at one level enhanced. For instance, he was granted a new coat of arms, which would have above it "a castle and a lion whose colors and standing were to be carefully and grandly described. . . ."[21] He would be paid 10,000 maravedís a year for life for having been the first to see and discover the new lands.[22] His titles, rights, and powers as proclaimed in the *"capitulaciones"* and the "privilege" of April 17 and 30, 1492, were confirmed, and he was specifically compared to "the viceroys and governors which have existed and exist in our said kingdoms of Castile."[23] The Admiral was also confirmed as "Don" Cristóbal. His rule (*dominio*), it was said, would begin at a line drawn from the Azores and the Cape Verde Islands to both the North and South Poles, which was a more generous version of what had just been proposed by the Spanish diplomats at Lisbon.[24] Another letter spoke of Columbus as a "captain-general."[25]

The monarchs also addressed Columbus by his grand new titles and accepted as their own "the islands that he has discovered in the Indies." It was essential, they thought, to find more *tierra firme,* some part of this "new Asian mainland." All the same, in document after document, decree after decree, as a modern historian points out, the monarchs were now beginning to establish the bases for a new colonial government, naming public officials, recruiting peasants and laborers for specific works, and setting up their own monopoly in the Indies.[26] Whether they realized that Columbus had discovered a new world, not the far eastern end of the old one, is still not quite clear. But it is obvious that their civil servants and secretaries (among whom Fonseca was preeminent) were being practical.

Fernando and Isabel issued several other instructions on May 23, 1493. Thus Columbus was required with the help of Fonseca to prepare a new fleet, and they were to collaborate with Juan de Soria, who had been appointed the accountant of the expedition. Soria had once been an efficient secretary to the Infante Juan and also a magistrate charged to investigate how the Jews of León and Zamora had fled to Portugal, taking with them all their possessions, which had been against the law.[27]

Hernando de Zafra, a senior royal secretary who had been responsible for carrying through the terms of the surrender of Granada, was also ordered to choose, from among the members of the new Hermandad of that city, "twenty reliable knights, five of them with spare horses (mares)," to go with Columbus to the New World. They were to be paid the same as the treasurers of the Hermandad paid their colleagues—though this was a new departure for them.[28] These were modern knights, a light cavalry, it might be said, their armor reduced to a cuirass and steel helmet, much as the Granada cavalry's had been, to give them increased mobility. This instruction astonished Columbus, who began to sense his independent command crumbling beneath him.

That same May 23 the King and Queen ordered Columbus's fellow Genoese, the banker Francesco Piñelo, to act as paymaster for the expedition.[29] He also agreed to pay a salary of 200,000 maravedís every year to Archdeacon Fonseca.[30] The royal attitude toward that Genoese banker was, in fact, almost humble; for example, on August 4, 1493, they wrote to him thanking him for his services.[31] These were, indeed, considerable.

Similarly, the monarchs ordered Fernando de Villareal and Alonso

Gutiérrez de Madrid, the new treasurers of the Santa Hermandad, both young bankers, both probably *conversos,* to give the 15,000 gold ducats that they had collected for the Hermandad to Francesco Piñelo for the costs of the new armada.[32] Gutiérrez, whose wife was the niece of two Grand Masters of the Order of Calatrava, would have a long career in relation to Atlantic commerce. The monarchs also decided to use a confiscated sum of 1.545 million maravedís, which two other Genoese bankers, Octavio Calvo and Bernardo Piñelo (a kinsman of Francisco), had wished to send (in the name of a Toledo merchant, Alonso de Castro) to an expelled Jew, Iya Beneniste, already in Portugal, to help the expedition instead.[33] Finally, the Florentine friend of Columbus, Juanotto Berardi, the Seville agent of Bartolomeo Marchionni, was asked to buy a caravel of between one hundred and two hundred tons and make it ready for the Admiral.[34]

On May 29, Columbus received his formal instructions for the new expedition. This document discussed the fleet to be prepared and also the organization of the colony to be founded in La Española. The Admiral was to control all ships and crews, and could send them where he wanted, both to trade and to discover territory. He was to appoint magistrates (*alcaldes*) and constables (*alguaciles*).[35] Essentially, the colonists would be mostly workers, paid by the Crown and overseen by Columbus. There would be a few officials but no women: Isabel feared that any such would become prostitutes. The unplanned consequence would be, of course, to cause the Spaniards to seek Indian girls—hence the beginning of a mestizo population throughout the New World.[36]

The monarchs expected to be thought of, on the voyage and in the colony, as "sovereign emperors [*emperadores soberanos*] over all the kings and princes and kingdoms of all the Indies, islands, and *tierra firme,* discovered and to be discovered."[37] The phraseology was new but it passed unnoticed. The conversion of the new countries to Christianity was put forward as the consideration closest to the monarchs' hearts.[38] The instructions show that the Crown expected Columbus and his lieutenants to treat the Indians *"muy bien e amorosamente"* (the repetition of a word used in the surrender of Granada), without causing them any kind of "annoyance." Anyone who treated the Indians badly was to be severely punished.

The essence of these instructions was, after a section devoted to the needs of evangelization, the disciplined organization of the future colony, with provisions to ensure an economic monopoly for the Crown, and loyalty and obedience to it. The word *rescate* (ransom) summed up the economic life. No one was to carry off goods *"de rescate,"* neither of gold nor of anything else. That could only be done by the Admiral himself or the royal treasurer, in the presence of a royal accountant. There would be a customs house in La Española that would store all the goods the government would send from Castile, while another would be set up in Cadiz to hold everything sent from the Indies. The prime purpose of the expedition was agriculture and commerce, even though gold was, of course, not forgotten. All expeditionaries would be paid. Presumably the able Fonseca was the real author of these words. Here we find the beginning of the Spanish commercial system as it evolved in the next hundred years.[39]

There followed a firm instruction on June 7 to Bernal Díaz de Pisa, who was to be deputy to the royal accountant in the Indies, and to Juan de Soria.[40] The former's orders were elaborate: he had to list everything sent in the ships; he had to note, too, the people who were to travel; he had to record everything loaded en route, and also to enumerate what was sent home and when. It was he who was to establish the customs house in the Indies.

On June 12, the monarchs wrote to Columbus assuring him of the good intentions of the King of Portugal.[41] But in a sermon in Rome on June 19, the diplomatic Bernardino Carvajal all the same declared: "It pleased our Lord Jesus Christ to subject to the empire [*imperium*] of the kings of Spain the Fortunate [Canary] Islands whose admirable fertility is so noticeable. And now the Lord has given many other islands lying in the direction of India, previously unknown, but it appears that there are in the whole world none more precious or more rich."[42] He talked of the prophecy in the book of Isaiah that the lion would lie down with the ox, recalling that the latter was the emblem of the Borgia. This sermon was widely distributed.

Soon after this, Carvajal's brother, García López Carvajal, who had not previously played any part in diplomacy, and the protonotary Pedro de Ayala presented themselves before João II in Lisbon with a Castilian counteroffer to the scheme that Rui de Sande had taken to Barcelona. This derived from an idea of Columbus's but was somewhat altered: a latitudinal division in the ocean would run west from the Canaries. To the north would be the possessions of the Crown of Spain, to the south those of Portugal, with the exception of lands previously granted. Had this plan been adopted, only North America would have been Spanish.

Pedro de Ayala was furious at the proposal that he was charged to offer, since it would have given such a large slice of the New World to Portugal, whose possessions, he and others had hoped, would be confined to Africa. On the other hand, King João II was irritated by the obstinacy of the Spaniards and said: "This delegation has neither hands nor feet." He thought Carvajal a fool and complained that Ayala was lame. All the same, the negotiators were successful, since they could point out that Columbus would not be returning through Portuguese waters. The consequence was that a committee was named in Portugal to consider the rights of the two countries.

Fonseca, the bureaucrat-archdeacon, had already left for Seville to "help Columbus prepare for the new voyage."[43] Probably he owed this mission to the support of Talavera, the Archbishop and confessor for whom he had worked previously. These preparations were marked by arguments, and not only the Archdeacon but also Juan de Soria was every day more irritated with the Admiral, so much so that the monarchs had to write and tell them both to treat Columbus with all respect, because it was he who would, after all, captain the fleet.[44]

The King and Queen had their representatives on this second expedition of Columbus's in the form of priests and monks. They were to be given all the powers that they needed.[45] The monarchs were fortunate to obtain the attention of His Holiness to such concerns in those days, for he was busy with the wedding in the Vatican of his daughter, the beautiful Lucrezia, to Giovanni Sforza.[46] Still, there was time for the drafting of the bull, named *Pius Fidelium*, of July 25, 1493, the basis for the recruitment of missionaries. It authorized a prominent churchman, Fray Boil, to go on Columbus's expedition and removed any prohibition on founding monasteries without license from the Holy See.[47]

The same day, Fernando and Isabel wrote to Fonseca urging speed in arranging the departure of Columbus.[48] Pero Dias and Rui de Piña, ambassadors from Portugal, were now proposing to the monarchs in Barcelona a new line (*raya*) dividing the Portuguese from the Spanish possessions. They said that unless the Admiral suspended this second voyage of his, the King of Portugal really would send ships west—the threat being that some Portuguese captain would go to Cuba, say, and assert his control. But the Spanish armada of Vizcaya seems to have prevented the latter threat from being tried.[49]

For this reason, on August 18, 1493, Isabel wrote to Columbus himself, asking him to set off as soon as possible because a delay of one day now was like twenty a little time ago, and because "winter approaches. . . ." There was real anxiety about Portugal. Columbus heard that King João was sending a caravel from Madeira toward Spain. The monarchs thought it wise for Columbus to be prepared for this with some of his own ships, but he was to take care not to touch Guinea—an instruction that suggested a very inadequate grasp of the geographical implications of the first journey of Columbus.[50]

On September 5, 1493, Isabel wrote again to the Admiral mentioning her concern about Portugal and asking him, in a friendly style, always to let her know what he was doing.[51] The same day both monarchs urged Fonseca to insist on an early departure.[52] Yet another letter from them both to Columbus implored him to leave without further delay. They told Columbus about the state of negotiations in Lisbon over the line dividing the zones of influence, and talked of recent Portuguese discoveries. For that reason alone, they said, in yet another letter of the same date, they needed to know the degrees within which "fall the islands and land which you discover and the degrees of the path which you traveled."[53] Not all these letters arrived, or, at least, not in time. For on September 25, Columbus had left on his second voyage, with seventeen ships.

IO

"As if in their own country"

Lured by the ease of taking possessions of those islands and by the richness of the booty . . . many of the Spaniards began to live there as if in their own country.

Guicciardini, HISTORY OF ITALY

Queen Isabel and King Fernando spent most of the autumn of 1493 in Barcelona, with the exception of a journey in September to Gerona, Figueras, and Perpignan. As usual, they were accompanied by dukes, counts, secretaries, confessors, bishops, soldiers, archives, chests, and tapestries.

Columbus, triumphant, was on a different expedition. His ships included the *Niña,* the *San Juan,* and the *Cordero,* under his own direct captaincy. The latter were carefully chosen by the Admiral for their lightness: he did not want another clumsy large vessel, such as the *Santa María.* But in the end he had five big ships along with twelve small ones. It was a diverse fleet: fifteen of his vessels had square sails, while two had triangular lateens.

Probably between 1,200 and 1,500 men and a few women sailed on these caravels. A complete roll has never been made,[1] but the crews were recruited much as those of 1492 had been and, as before, paid 1,000 maravedís a month if they were experienced, 600 if not. The majority of crews were again from Niebla or Palos; but there were a few more Basques than in 1492. Some of those who sailed were Genoese, including Columbus's brother Diego (Giacomo), always dressed as if he were a priest; a childhood friend, Michele Cuneo, who would write an account of the voyage;[2] and another "Ligurian," Tenerin, who became *contramaestre* (boatswain) of the *Cardena.* Several other old friends of Columbus were officials of one sort or another. About twenty-two of his new companions had been with him on the first voyage.[3]

The accountant, Bernál Díaz de Pisa, a childhood companion of the Infante Juan, who was very much a royal appointment, also sailed, as did Sebastián de Olano, who later succeeded him. Thus the finances of the expedition depended on the Crown, whatever authority the Admiral might suppose that he had. Other friends of the monarchs included Antonio de Torres, brother of the Infante Juan's nurse, Juana Velázquez de la Torre, and a veteran member of the Infante's circle if, too, a mature courtier. Columbus intended him to command the fortress at La Isabela, but he had instructions from the monarchs to return to Spain with some of the ships as quickly as possible.[4] His mission was to see La Española for himself as if with the eyes of the monarchs. But Columbus's son Fernando thought highly of Torres and called him "a man of great prudence and nobility."[5]

The chief inspector was Diego Marquéz, a hidalgo from Seville who had once been a page to Archdeacon Fonseca—another appointment to make the Admiral wary.

There were also about two hundred unpaid volunteers, probably among them footloose aristocrats such as Diego de Alvarado, son of a *comendador* of Hornachos, in Extremadura, and the uncle of the Alvarado brothers later so important in the history of Mexico; Diego Velázquez de Cuéllar, the future governor of Cuba; Juan de Rojas, future founder of Havana, like Velázquez from Cuéllar, in Castile; as well as Jaime Cañizares, a young lawyer, who years later would be chamberlain of the Emperor Charles V. Another aristocrat with Columbus, who had been sent to Rome as ambassador, was Melchor Maldonado, of Seville. There were also from that city Pedro de las Casas and his brothers Gabriel and Diego de Peñalosa, both notaries, as well as their fourth brother, Francisco de Peñalosa.[6] These were respectively the father and the uncles of the historian Bartolomé de las Casas, and all were *conversos*. Another knight was Juan Ponce de León, a cousin of Rodrigo, Count of Arcos, and future conqueror of Puerto Rico; and Sebastián Ocampo from Galicia, later the first circumnavigator of Cuba. These men were to be among those who in the next generation laid the foundations of a vast empire.

Another courtier who captained a ship was Pedro Margarit, who came from a noble Catalan family, with a property at Montgri, a mountain castle that can be seen from miles away in the Ampurdán. He was the great-nephew of a famous bishop of Gerona, Cardinal Joan Margarit, who had worked for many years in the Roman Curia on behalf of both Kings Alfonso V and Juan II of Aragon, had protected Queen Juana Enríquez and her son Fernando in 1461, and had once remarked that the administration of a monarchy requires prudence, not morality. The Bishop had been an eloquent humanist, interested in the idea of Hispanic unity.[7] A cousin succeeded him as bishop of Gerona. Another cousin, Luis Margarit, was in the 1480s the King's councillor for Catalonia. Pedro Margarit was among the oldest as well as the best connected of the expeditionaries. As early as 1477, he himself had been in Saragossa as a magistrate, and in 1478, he had fought in a famous tournament in Seville, in honor of the monarchs during their stay there. He had also performed some services for the Crown in the war against Granada, for which the King gave him the right of receiving the tolls for cattle (*montazgo*) in the city of Daroca, in Aragon.[8]

A more ambiguous character among the captains of this second voyage of Columbus was Alonso de Hojeda, a man of about twenty-five from Cuenca, in Castile, whom the Admiral had first met in the house of the Duke of Medinaceli in the Puerto de Santa María in 1490. He was a clever, good-looking man, small in build, with large eyes, always the first to draw blood in any fight and, according to Las Casas, "uniting in his person all the bodily perfections that man could have, despite his small size."[9] Columbus admired him but would have much trouble from him in the future, partly because he transferred his loyalty from Medinaceli to Fonseca. The Queen also admired him; in her presence, he had walked out along a beam of the scaffolding encasing the Giralda, the 250-foot-high Muslim tower, during the building of the cathedral in Seville, without any sign of vertigo.

Most of these men were more experienced in the ways of the court in Spain than was Columbus, and were by instinct certain to be loyal to the Crown rather than to the Genoese who was in command.

Then there were twenty knights, five of them, with two horses each, from Granada. They had been members of the Hermandad of that city and had, as we have seen, been specifically named by the royal secretary, Hernando de Zafra. All seem to have been connected with later individuals whose names would figure in the history of the early Spanish Empire: Coronado, Cano, Arévalo, Osorio, Leyva, Sepúlveda, and Olmedo.[10] The presence of these men-at-arms, not sought by Columbus, as well as the two hundred knightly volunteers, troubled the Admiral: they were of a different class from men to whom he was used.

Two doctors traveled with him: first, Diego Álvarez Chanca, from Seville, who had once been a medical adviser to the King and Queen and who underestimated the likely discomforts of the voyage. The monarchs seem to have paid him a salary. He had been a member of the household of the successful knight Rodrigo Ponce de León, and would later write an important letter about what he saw. The second doctor was Guillermo Coma, from Barcelona, who would also write of his experiences.[11]

The majority of these men were people whom Columbus had never met before and who surely found their Genoese Admiral a curious leader: a wonderful sailor, no doubt, but with many odd fancies that he would express in his strange Portuguese Spanish. In general, "So many offered themselves that it was necessary to restrict the number . . . ," wrote Columbus's son Fernando.[12]

As we have seen, Columbus also had with him several priests and monks, and some of them seemed to be royal agents. Their leader, Fray Juan Boil (Buil), an Aragonese who had begun life as a Benedictine, had been a childhood friend and secretary to King Fernando and ambassador to France and Rome; he then joined the "Minims," the hermits of St. Francisco, a society that had grown up in the mid-fifteenth century around Francisco de Paula, a holy man from Cosenza. Boil had negotiated with France on behalf of Fernando and Isabel the future of Cerdagne and Roussillon in 1490, a most delicate task. He was therefore a man of weight and reputation. Boil became the self-styled "Apostolic Vicar for the Indies." His mission is not quite clear; perhaps the monarchs wanted a continuous supervision of their protégé, the Admiral. Fernando and Isabel had written to Columbus: "We send our devoted father Boil, together with other religious persons, so that . . . the Indians may be well informed about our faith and understand our language."[13] How the good father was going to communicate was uncertain; and perhaps his long experience of life on the fringes of power made him more a political commissar of the expedition than a priest.[14] Further, he neither liked nor admired Columbus, and conditions at sea (as later on land) were intolerable for him, austere hermit though he proclaimed himself.[15] At all events, the combination of Margarit and Boil meant that King Fernando had agents in the most important positions on Columbus's second voyage.

Other religious men included Fray Pedro de Arenas, who would celebrate the first Mass in the Indies;[16] Fray Jorge, commander of the Knights of Santiago;[17] and a Jeronymite anchorite, Fray Ramón Pané, a Catalan whose Spanish was imperfect: "a simple-minded man," Las Casas wrote of him, "so that what he said was sometimes confused and of little importance."[18] All the same, he would write the first account of the deities of La Española.[19] There were also on the expedition Father Juan de la Deule and Father Juan de Tisin, both Belgian, Franciscan lay brothers of the Picardy connection, as well as Juan de Borgoña, another Franciscan, from Dijon.[20] Thus the expedition had a broad, almost cosmopolitan foundation.

A few women sailed in 1493; we hear of them in the Admiral's diary: "And I ordered him to give a native boy discovered in one of the Lesser Antilles to a woman whom I had brought from Spain."[21] Who these women were is obscure: servants, nurses, or mistresses, anything is possible.

Columbus also took back with him three Indians whom he had captured in 1492 and of whom Peter Martyr wrote: "All this was recounted through the native interpreters who had been taken back to Spain on the first voyage. . . ."[22] He had originally kidnapped more Indians to train as interpreters, but by now the others had died. There may also have been some African slaves, berbers, mulattoes, or negroes from West Africa.[23] Las Casas certainly thought that there were black slaves on board. According to the historian Bernáldez, Columbus carried twenty-four horses together with ten mares and three mules, but presumably these included the mounts of the knights.[24] There were other animals: some pigs, goats, and sheep.

The majority of the expedition were laborers whose plan was to till the soil of La Española or to find, and mine, gold there. They were going in order to make money, to become someone, if not a hidalgo. The royal secretary, Hernando de Zafra, had been asked to seek in Granada "twenty country laborers and one other who knows how to make irrigation ditches. And he was not to be a Moor."[25] These men were also to bring horses, mares, mules, and other beasts, as well as wheat and barley seeds, and all kinds of "little trees and fruit bushes."[26] Las Casas later wrote, "If these men had known what the work would be, I do not believe that any one of them would have gone!"[27] But Columbus planned a trading colony in the Genoese tradition (such as he had seen in Chios and in Guinea), able to send home mastic (a gum that he thought he had seen on his first voyage), cotton, and gold, as well as enslaved cannibals.

Perhaps we see here already a divergence between the Crown's and Columbus's expectations. The Crown hoped for political control of territory. Columbus wanted with him family men who would give stability to the colony, and also craftsmen and industrious prospectors. "Even the Nereids and the Sirens were stupefied when the fleet set off," wrote Dr. Guillermo Coma.[28] In these respects, as in many others, the Crown was copying in the Indies what had been done with success in the Canary Islands.[29]

On October 2, Columbus's fleet reached Gran Canaria, where they repaired a leaking ship.[30] They also stopped at the island of La Gomera, where Columbus bought eight pigs at 70 maravedís each, three mules, and some chickens—birds and beasts that, after a few years' breeding, would transform the new Caribbean in a way that astonished all the Europeans. There was a celebration in honor of the acting governor, Beatriz Bobadilla.[31] The one thing that Fonseca had underestimated, the need for a year's supply of food for two thousand people, was partially, though not completely, made up for.

On October 13, 1493, the expedition sailed from the Canaries. Columbus had decided this time to approach the Caribbean from the southeast, not the northeast. He does not seem to have discussed this plan with the monarchs or with Fonseca, or indeed with anyone in authority. His star at that time was standing so high that his will was automatically accepted; and that was to try and visit some of the other islands of which he had heard talk, much of it wild talk, of Amazons and giants—neither of whom the other Spaniards particularly wanted to meet.

After only twenty days' sail, the expedition encountered several islands that the Admiral took to be those of the Caribs. The first was one that he named La Deseada, for the innocent reason that he and his crew desired so much to see land again; the second, the mountainous Dominica, because it was a Sunday, Domingo, when they saw it; and the third, María-Galante (named after the flagship), where they soon found a suitable anchorage: "The Admiral and many people with him, and with the royal standard in their hands, took possession of the place."[32] Here the inspector, Diego Márquez, went inland with eleven men and was lost for several days, but Columbus dispatched Alonso de Hojeda and forty men to find him. They had seized twelve fat but beautiful indigenous girls and two slave boys who, they said, had been castrated by cannibals. All these "Indians" were eventually sent to Spain.[33]

These wonderfully green islands were about halfway up the Lesser Antilles, and so Columbus on this journey missed visiting Martinique. According to what Antonio de Torres told Peter Martyr, Columbus was (again) assured that there were Amazons in that latter island, being visited by men at regular times of the year. If attacked, the women repaired to secret caves where they defended themselves with bows and arrows. That was not good news: the Amazons were thought to constitute the most potent of dangers to the Europeans.[34] Amazons had been known (if that is a permissible way of putting it) in Greek mythology, a people always on the edge of the civilized world. Alexander was said to have met the Amazon Queen beyond the River Jaxartes, which flows into the Sea of Aral. Columbus was thus in good company.

The fleet then sailed on to Guadeloupe (which was now named after the Jeronymite monastery in Extremadura) and anchored in a bay that is today known as La Grande Anse (the Great Bay). They found a fine waterfall and also houses with straw roofs in which were parrots and human bones: the first sign of anthropophagy. The idea of the Carib as a man-eating savage was strengthened. Some natives were captured, including a boy, with twenty female Tainos who had been seized in "Boriquen," or Puerto Rico. The

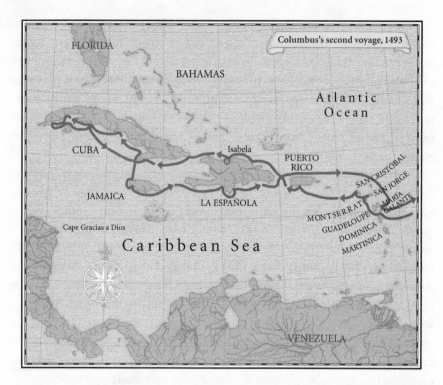

Castilians also came upon calabash, geese, and parrots, as well as stores of provisions and well-woven cotton cloth. There were canoes, but the Spaniards found that ten of them had been taken to raid other islands, for in the words of Dr. Álvarez Chanca,

> the people are all friendly to one another as in one large family. They do not harm each other but make war on the neighboring islands. They then carry off all the women they can. In fifty houses, we found no males again except for two castrated youths. More than twenty of the captives were girls. These said that they had been treated with a cruelty that seems incredible.

The Caribs were reported by Álvarez Chanca to think that

> human flesh is so good that there is nothing like it in the world; and this must be true, because the human bones which we found in their houses were so gnawed that no flesh was left on them except what was too tough to be eaten. In one house, a neck of a man was found still cooking. They castrate the boys whom they capture and use them as servants till they

are men. Then, when they want . . . a feast, they kill and eat them. They say that the flesh of boys and of women is not good to eat.[35]

Antonio de Torres, the *alcaide*-designate of the fortress of La Isabela, later related much the same: "In their pots [were] geese mixed with human flesh, while other parts of human bodies were fixed on spits, ready for roasting. . . . [In] another house, the Spaniards found bones that the cannibals carefully preserve for points of their arrows; for they have no iron. . . . The Spaniards discovered the recently decapitated head of a young man still wet with blood."[36]

On this island, Miguel Cuneo was given a beautiful girl by his fellow Genoese, Columbus. He wrote that he had had to beat her to accept his advances, but in the end, "we came to an agreement" and "she appeared to have learned her arts in a school of whores."[37] This was the first account of lovemaking in the New World.

These encounters gave rise to foreboding. Perhaps conquests would not be so easy after all. Yet the evidence that these bones and this flesh were of humans is weak. Could sailors from Seville have told the difference between the flesh of men and that of monkeys?

After six days in Guadeloupe (November 4–10, 1493) Columbus sailed on to Santa María de Montserrat, so named because its central mountain seemed to resemble that on which there stands the famous monastery in Cataluña and whence captives said that the Caribs had removed the whole population. Nearby, at Santa María la Redonda, which gained its name from its rounded hills, they dropped anchor but, again, they did not land. They continued to Santa María de Antigua, so called by Columbus after the famous Virgin in the cathedral of Seville. Finally, they landed at what the Admiral designated San Martín, which seemed well populated. A canoe remained motionless "two lombard shots" away, her crew of seven stupefied at the sight of the Castilians. The Spaniards captured these men with ease, though not quite without a battle. Two of Columbus's men were wounded and one, probably a Gallego, killed—the first casualty of the voyage. They then proceeded on November 14 to Santa Cruz (now Saint Croix): "Very high and mostly barren: it seemed to be the sort of place where there might be metal, but we did not go ashore." It appeared uninhabited.[38] Nor did they go ashore on any of the pretty islands that Columbus named "the Virgin Islands" after St. Ursula, martyred in Cologne with, allegedly, "eleven thousand" virgins in the third century (the figure derived from a medieval misprint for eleven).[39]

The next day they reached Boriquen, a word that means "crab" in Taino and that Columbus now called San Juan Bautista. It became Puerto Rico within a generation or so, and San Juan remains its capital. Álvarez Chanca thought it

> most beautiful and appears very fertile. The Caribs come here in raids and take off the people. The natives have no canoes [that was not the case] and no knowledge of navigation, but according to Caribs whom we captured, they use bows very like their own, and if they manage to capture any of the raiders, they eat them in the same way as do the Caribs themselves. We stayed in a harbor on this island for two days, and many of our people landed. But we were never able to have speech with the people, for they were terrified of the Caribs and all fled. . . .[40]

This place was probably Aguadilla, on the western coast facing what later became the island of Mona and the perilous straits there. Columbus himself simply said that the inhabitants ate human flesh, for which accusation there seems no other evidence.[41]

Columbus also christened in these days a number of other islands: Nuestra Señora de los Nieves, later Nevis; Santa Anastasia (now Saint Eustatius); and San Cristóbal (now Saba).

At last, the expedition reached La Española. With it were now about thirty Indian prisoners from the lesser islands that Columbus had just visited. The possibility of a serious trade in slaves captured in these islands was every week becoming more appealing in the mind of the Admiral.[42]

The fleet went first to Samaná Bay or Cabo Engaño, on November 22,[43] then to Monte Cristi from November 25 to November 27, and finally on the twenty-eighth reached the colony founded on the previous journey, Navidad, to which such expectant thoughts had been directed. It had been destroyed.[44] The expedition "found all Navidad reduced to ashes, while a profound silence reigned over the place. The Admiral and his companions were deeply moved . . . thinking, and hoping, that some of the settlers might be still alive and, wandering inland, he ordered guns to be fired, so that the noise of these formidable detonations might serve as a signal of his arrival. . . . It was in vain; for all were dead."[45] In a village of seven or eight houses on the coast, Columbus's men found many possessions that had once belonged to their compatriots; among them were a Moorish cloak that had not been unfolded since it had been bought in Spain, some stockings, and some cloth, as well as the anchor of the shipwrecked *Santa María*.

The first battle in the New World between Europeans and indigenous people was thus won by the latter. The truth of what had happened never became known, but a brother of Guacanagri, the local *cacique,* later said that the Spaniards under Araña had gone on a campaign of stealing women as well as of hunting for gold. Many men were killed, and Guacanagri had himself been wounded. The battle had been less than two months before, judging from the state of the bodies that were found. But Columbus thought that Caribs from another island might have been responsible. Some of his party, including the austere Minim Fray Bernardo Boil, wanted to avenge the dead by seizing Guacananagri, but Columbus merely visited him and obtained some gold by barter.[46]

In early December,[47] probably either the seventh or the eighth, the Admiral "decided that we should turn back up the coast by which we had come from Castile because the news of gold was from that direction . . . [but] with the bad weather, many weeks passed before we landed."[48] Las Casas says that the "people arrived at another place of disembarkation very tired and the horses exhausted."[49] Probably some of the horses never recovered.[50]

After this difficult voyage, the Admiral and his ships at last arrived in early January in Monte Cristi. Columbus went ashore some forty miles to the east, where he disembarked nearly everyone on the expedition, twenty-four horses, ten mares, and three mules—very few men had as yet been lost.[51]

The Spanish expeditionaries were soon restored by eating yams and some local fish. The place where they had landed was well populated by Tainos, whom Álvarez Chanca found so well disposed "that they could be easily converted if we only had an interpreter, for they imitate everything that we do. They bend their knees at the altars at the Ave María and cross themselves. They all say that they wish to be Christians. Yet there are idols of all kinds in their houses which they say belong to the sky."[52]

Columbus set about founding a settlement, which he christened Isabela, after the Queen. He chose the site because it was close to the inland valley of Cibao, where he understood, from the encouraging report of Martín Alonso on the previous voyage, that there were gold mines.[53] About two hundred cabins or huts were shortly built on a rectangular plan that would have pleased or amused Vitruvius. The water was good, though Columbus exaggerated, as he so often did, when he said that it came from "a powerful river with water better than the Guadalquivir from which, by a ditch, one can carry it into the central square of the town, making use of a large vale to the southeast of that place. There is here wonderful land incomparably superior to anything in Castile, and it has tall grass. . . . Two leagues from the town, there is a marvelous beach and the best port in the world. . . ."[54] In fact, Isabela had a bad harbor, and the site had been chosen foolishly. The river was unsuitable for building water mills.

Columbus showed himself incompetent as governor, and he was unable to control the rapacity of his followers. He had no experience of civil administration and had developed none of the arts of the politician. The Spaniards with him had been chosen at random or had chosen themselves. Most of them had no idea what to do, and they expected to be paid, but that did not prove to be immediately possible. Columbus's aim had at first been to exploit La Española for its gold, making the local chiefs responsible for its collection as a form of tribute. The plan assumed that there was much gold (there was not) and that the Indians were weak (they were not, only good-mannered). Some of the settlers wanted to go home. Others were brutal to the Tainos while a few (including enemies of Columbus such as Fray Boil and Pedro Margarit) were critical of any ill-treatment of them. When hostilities with the local Indians began, as a result of generally worsening relations in which the kidnapping of Taino women played a part, some slaves were taken. The mood was one of confusion. The idea of substituting a slave trade for the pursuit of gold became appealing. The same idea had occurred to the Portuguese when their captains in Africa found that people ready to be enslaved, or indeed already slaves, were more available than precious metals.

Within a week of landing at Isabela, in the "middle of January," the Admiral sent Alonso de Hojeda, the good-looking captain from Cuenca, with Ginés de Corvalán as his second in command, into the interior with fifteen men to seek gold. This immediately brought the Admiral into difficulties with "the *jinetes*" (knights) provided by the Hermandad of Granada. Columbus wanted their horses for Hojeda, but they refused to surrender them. Even those who were ill after the voyage were adamant that they were going to keep control of their mounts. This insubordination, for such it was, caused Columbus, in a fit of pique, to cut off the supply of fodder for the horses. With such petty preoccupations did the conquest of the world begin.[55]

Hojeda set off on foot with his fifteen men, and walked sixty miles toward what is now the town of San José de las Matas. He and his companions were lucky: when they returned, they reported overoptimistically, "Wherever you look in this province, you will find gold." Hojeda talked of "much gold in three or four places." Álvarez Chanca became carried away and wrote home that "our sovereigns can certainly consider themselves henceforth the richest and most prosperous rulers on earth, for nothing comparable has ever been seen or read of till now in the whole world. On the next voyage which the ships make they will be able to carry away such quantities of gold that those who hear of it will be amazed."[56] At last the explorers seemed to have discovered what they most needed: the physical attraction of gold exercised men's minds in those days in a way impossible now to recapture.

Michele Cuneo commented that "the pursuit of gold was what had really inspired the journey that Columbus had embarked upon."[57] He recalled that the Admiral now told the monarchs he could find as much gold in La Española as there was iron in the Basque country. Cuneo also said that though conditions were bad on Columbus's first journey inland in 1494, "the desire for gold caused us to maintain ourselves strong and magnanimous."[58] The historian Fernández de Oviedo, at that time a mere page at the court of the Infante Juan, would later say of the majority of the *conquistadores* whom he came to know: "They are the sort of men who have no intention of converting the Indians or of settling and remaining in this land. They come only to get some gold or wealth in whatever form they can obtain it. They subordinate honor, morality, and honesty to this end and apply themselves to any fraud or homicide and commit innumerable crimes. . . ."[59]

The conquistadors' thirst for gold was less commercial than it was comparable to the Moorish and Christian warriors' hunger for loot in the Middle Ages. The desire was not for credit or for wealth in the abstract, but for the actual golden metal. Yet a modern historian qualified these matters: "The incentive provided by the gold of the Indies was doubtless a great attraction; but the dream of great personal achievement . . . was a stimulus more in the foreground. . . ."[60]

On February 2, 1494, Antonio de Torres, the monarchs' man in La Española and whom Columbus had intended to command the fortress of Isabela, sailed home to Spain with twelve of the expedition's ships (leaving Columbus with five), taking back a formal "memorial," or letter, from the Admiral, a letter from Álvarez Chanca, and indeed Álvarez Chanca himself, as well as gold worth 30,000 ducats, some cinnamon, some peppers, some wood, a few Indians who had been enslaved, and sixty parrots. Torres also took back several hundred of those who had set out in 1493 and had expressed their disillusion. This was, as will be seen, the voyage that carried syphilis to the Old World—the first negative contribution of the New World to the Old.[61]

This "memorial" of Columbus to the monarchs was a rambling document which insisted that Hojeda and Ginés de Corvalán (who were among those returning to Spain) had found "rivers of gold." He explained that the homesickness, which Torres would report, was caused by a change of air inevitable on arriving in new territory. Columbus also explained that he was sending back cannibal slaves so that their Highnesses could place them in the hands of those who would teach them Spanish. Columbus was equivocal about cannibals, for he also said, in relation to the settlement of bills for cattle and other supplies that he hoped would thenceforth be brought every year from Castile, that they might be paid for in slaves, who seemed wild but were well proportioned (a "people . . . suitable for the purpose"). He was sure that if they could only rid themselves of their "savagery," they would prove to be the best slaves of all. By this time he was talking of "Indians" without any embarrassment.[62]

This letter included admissions that some of his expectations—about gold, climate, and the Indians—had been excessive. But even now Columbus predicted that, in the future, the island could be planted with wheat, sugar-cane, and vines and that Castilian livestock would prosper there. He urged the dispatch of laborers who had worked in the mercury mines of Almadén. He made some complaints about the knights' insubordinate refusal to contribute their horses to the expedition's general purposes, saying, too, that the accountant, Juan de Soria, had at the last minute slipped in on the boats some bad horses that Columbus had not been able to inspect. Columbus was in two minds over what to say about the knights: on the one hand, he needed them to defend the camp at Isabela, but, on the other, he did not want them to consider themselves beyond his authority.

We henceforth see the poor Admiral trying vainly to cope with the problems of administration on land for which he had no gift, and no doubt longing to return to the sea, which he saw as his own.

II

"Mainland, no island"

I held this land to be mainland, no island.

Columbus sailing along the coast of Cuba, 1494[1]

On March 12, 1494, Columbus set off with five hundred men to explore what he thought of as "the gold country" of La Española,[2] traveling to the Puerto de Cibao (near San José de las Matas) and Santo Tomás, on the River Jámico. All the able-bodied men not needed to guard the ships that remained of the fleet rode or walked with Columbus. Conditions were hard, but "the desire for gold kept them strong and vigorous."[3] The Indians acted as beasts of burden, helping to carry baggage and arms, and assisting those who could not swim across two rivers.

The royal controller, Bernal Díaz de Pisa, had by now quarreled with Columbus, apparently not realizing that "gold may never be had without the sacrifice of time, toil, and privations."[4] Seizing two ships, he tried to return to Spain as soon as Columbus had left for the interior, on March 12. But he never left port and was imprisoned by Columbus's brother Diego, with a few "accomplices," as a traitor.[5]

On his inland journey, Columbus took with him not only his team of foot soldiers but also what he called "the necessary horsemen," which may have meant that he agreed to take some of the knights: and henceforth he grudgingly allowed their horses the fodder that they needed.[6]

Columbus reached what he hoped would turn out to be the magically golden Cibao after four days, on March 16; he found it stony and unwelcoming, though bathed by streams. Having discovered some signs of gold, he decided to establish a fort there at a place that he named San Tomás.[7] Pedro de Margarit, the Catalan, and Fray Boil, representatives of both Crown and Church, were left behind as the local commanders, for once in agreement. Cuneo reported that on this journey some traitors made themselves known; but they betrayed one another and the Admiral had no difficulty in coping with them, whipping some, cutting off the ears of a few and the noses of others, so that, Cuneo wrote, "one felt very sorry for them."[8] Columbus had one Aragonese, Gaspar Ferriz, hanged. Presumably Ferriz and his friends had sought to overthrow Columbus by force.

The Admiral then returned to Isabela, arriving there on March 29. Two days later, on April 1, a messenger reached him from Margarit saying that "the Indians of the neighborhood had fled" and that King Caonabó seemed to be preparing to attack the fortress. So, the following day, Columbus sent back to San Tomás seventy men with ammunition.[9] He seems to have used this occasion as an excuse to rid himself of more of those knights who were ready to challenge him. He also ordered Margarit to capture the *cacique* Caonabó, whom he now supposed to have been the author of the death of the Spaniards at Navidad. The seizure was to be effected by arranging that one of Margarit's men, Contreras, should treat him well until he could be captured. Margarit refused to be a party to this plan, not on moral grounds, it seems, but because he thought that it would damage the overall Spanish standing with the Indians. So, after another week, Columbus sent, on April 9, further reinforcement to San Tomás, consisting of all the healthy Castilians who remained, except for officials and artisans. These totaled about 360 men and the remaining 14 knights. The commander would be the handsome Alonso de Hojeda, with Luis de Arriaga as his deputy.

This was a demotion for Margarit, who, however, was asked to lead an expedition around the island. That made him the man responsible for supplying food for about five hundred men, causing him to seem, as a modern historian put the matter, "the captain of hunger."[10] Margarit was to "reconnoiter the provinces and people." He was "to take good care of the Indians and ensure that no evil or hurt was done them, nor should they be captured against their will. But, rather, they should be honored and kept in safety so that they do not rebel." But if they stole anything, they should have their ears and noses cut off "because they are parts whose loss one could not disguise."[11] Margarit was told by Columbus to ensure that "Spanish justice was much feared."[12] If the Spaniards could not buy food, it should be seized "as honestly as possible."

Alonso de Hojeda, meanwhile, had few doubts about moral issues, and when he reached the neighborhood of San Tomás, he tricked Caonabó and two or three of his relations into capture. He sent them back, bound, to Columbus at Isabela.[13] One of these princes was tied up in the square of the new town, in front of everyone, and had his ears cut off. The Admiral was determined to send Caonabó back to Spain as a trophy, but the ship on which he was stowed sank offshore while embarking slaves. Caonabó, the prize, was drowned.[14] By this time the Admiral felt certain that the shipment of Indians to Spain was necessary as a means of providing some kind of wealth for the Crown, even though they constituted the very labor force on which he had proposed to rely. The right of the Christians to behave in this way derived from Columbus's belief, shared by the priests, that, not having received baptism, all Indians were in a state of sin.[15]

The consequences were predictable. The natives ceased to collaborate with the Europeans. They stopped supplying fish, just when the flour that had been brought from Spain came to an end, as had other supplies. There were no good new European crops ripening as yet—even though the Admiral's son Fernando would report that chickpeas, wheat, sugarcane, melons, cucumbers, and grapes were all beginning to be grown near Isabela. In the short term, rationing had to be introduced. The climate seemed far from perfect for European crops, and sickness was frequent. Gold was not being found at all regularly.

Columbus refused to confront the crisis. Thinking of himself first and foremost as "Admiral of the Ocean Sea" and a sailor-explorer, he decided to leave to others his role as "governor" and "viceroy"; and on April 24 he set out on a journey of discovery west to the lands, such as Cuba, on which he had touched so briefly on his first voyage.

The Admiral left his new colony in the hands of his brother Diego and Father Boil, who would preside over a council on which would also serve Pedro Fernández Coronel, the *alguacil mayor;* Alonso Sánchez Carvajal, Columbus's friend from Baeza; and a onetime member of the royal household, Juan de Luján.[16] Columbus explained, before leaving, that food would soon be coming from Spain, but he did not wait to see if that prediction had validity. This seemed an act of desertion to those he left behind. After all, he only allowed them two ships, for the remainder of the fleet had returned with Antonio de Torres or had sunk with Caonabó. Columbus's authority never recovered.

Before setting off, the Admiral wrote to the King and Queen in Spain. This letter was full of interesting exaggerations: the River Yaquí was described as being more broad than the Ebro, the province of Cibao was said to be larger than Andalusia, and in this Cibao there was more gold than anywhere else in the world. Once again he said that nothing was preventing him from converting the Indians to Christianity save that he did not know how to preach in their language. (Actually, "Diego Colón," an Indian whom he had captured on the first voyage, by now knew the elements of Castilian, so at least the Admiral had an interpreter into Taino.)

This letter of Columbus could not be immediately sent back to Spain. No ship was ready to sail. So for the moment the "memorial" of Columbus to the monarchs taken back by Torres was the basis for the latest that the court had about the new Indies.

Torres with his twelve ships had taken thirty-five days to reach Cadiz, arriving on March 7, 1494.[17] Some of those who returned with him brought bad news: so many of Columbus's claims were laughably exaggerated, there was a shortage of food at Isabela, Columbus had unjustly jailed the controller Bernal Díaz de Pisa, and the system of tribute imposed on the Indians was not working. There was little gold and no mines.

The monarchs and the court were at this time at Medina del Campo, staying in the brick castle of La Mota, built some sixty years before, the courtiers being billeted in the grand houses of the town whose owners had been made wealthy by the wool trade to Flanders. One belonged to the family of the novelist Garcí Rodríguez de Montalvo, author (or renewer) of *Amadís de Gaula,* whom we must presume to have been even then at work on that astonishing masterpiece, and another to the family of the future chronicler of the conquest of Mexico, Díaz del Castillo. The Queen had always liked Medina del Campo; it was no distance from her birthplace, Madrigal de las Altas Torres, and was close to Arévalo, where she had been brought up.[18]

The two rulers of Spain had many preoccupations at that time apart from any concern that they might have had about the Indies. They were being urged by the Inquisitor-General, the Dominican Fray Tomás de Torquemada, to make over the site of the old Jewish cemetery in Ávila for a new convent, to be named for San Tomás.[19] Several *autos-de-fe* were held and other strange punishments given to those who confessed their theological guilt.[20] From a judgment made that month, the Pope confirmed that his view of the Inquisition was disagreeably close to that of the Queen.[21]

Torres, clever though he was, brought only a little more than 11 million maravedís' worth of gold from Columbus, as well as some inferior spices and urgent requests for supplies.[22] Fernando was disappointed, for he needed money in Europe and he had been dreaming of using Indian gold for Italian purposes. When, in April, Torres arrived at court, Peter Martyr and a courtier from Seville, Melchor Maldonado, talked with him. There also came Peralonso Niño, the pilot, and Ginés de Corvalán, who had been with Hojeda on his expedition into the interior of La Española in search of gold. All rather surprisingly spoke positively about the Admiral, for Martyr, impressed, wrote to an Italian friend, Pomponio Leto, about the quantity of gold to be found: "a great abundance."[23] The Crown also welcomed the second son of the Admiral, Fernando, as a page to the Infante Juan as well as his elder brother Diego.[24]

Ten days later, on April 13, the monarchs wrote to Columbus encouragingly and ordered the Admiral's brother Bartolomeo Colón to prepare to go to the Indies with three caravels of provisions. Bartolomeo was at last back from his frustrating journeys to France and England, and was anxious to join his elder brother. Columbus's Florentine friend Berardi advanced Bartolomeo what he needed for his voyage.[25]

Bartolomeo set off, loaded on board a hundred head of sheep in Gomera, and was on his way across the Atlantic by May.[26] In the meantime, one of the royal secretaries, Fernando Álvarez, on behalf of the Crown, replied to every chapter of the "memorial" sent by Columbus through Torres. In doing so, he passed on one or two rather demanding requests to Fonseca, who was still the royal official in charge of the Indies—for example, that "in respect of the meat to be sent to the Admiral, please make sure that it is of good quality."[27]

A more pressing consideration for the monarchs in the early summer of 1494, however, was their negotiation with Portugal about their joint rights in the New World. Several Portuguese courtiers reached Medina del Campo in April. One of them was Ruy de Sousa of Sagres, a confidant of King João and an experienced sailor and diplomat, who had not only been ambassador to England but had commanded a fleet that had sailed to the Congo. It had been he who in 1475 had taken to Queen Isabel the declaration of war in the name of King Afonso V. With him went also his son Pedro, chief constable of Portugal; and Aires de Almeida, also an ex-ambassador to England. These three men were all members of the Portuguese royal council.

Four "experts" accompanied them: Duarte Pacheco, a famous sailor and cartographer, who had been to Guinea and would, in his book *Esmeraldo de Situ Orbis* (to appear ten years later), make a major contribution to the geography of Africa; Rui de Leme, who had been brought up in Madeira and whose father, Antonio de Leme, had been one of those said to have discussed the Atlantic with Columbus in the 1470s; João Soares de Siqueira; and Estaváo Vaz, a secretary to João II who had endeared himself to the Spanish monarchs by taking a cargo of gunpowder to assist them in the siege of Malaga. Later he had been in Castile as an ambassador charged to tidy up the affairs of the Duke of Braganza after the latter's execution in Lisbon as a traitor. All knew the eastern Atlantic well.

Castile, on the other hand, was represented by grandees whose knowledge of the Atlantic was sparse. There was thus Enrique Enríquez, *mayor domo* of the court, uncle of the King, and, despite his title of Admiral of Castile, an aristocrat without knowledge of any sea. His presence is only explicable because he was the father of María, the bride of one of the Pope's sons, and a correspondent of his co–father-in-law, Alexander Borgia.[28] There was Gutierre de Cárdenas, the chief accountant, the long-standing courtier who had introduced Fernando to Isabel in 1474 and had made money, especially in the Canaries, from the import of the lichen orchil, but whose knowledge of marine matters probably did not even stretch to the journey from Cádiz to Gran Canaria. There was also Rodrigo Maldonado de Talavera, a lawyer of the Council of the Realm, and three geographical experts: *comendadores* Pedro de León, Fernando de Torres, and Fernando Gamarro. Perhaps Jaume Ferrer, the Catalan cartographer, was present some of the time, as suggested by Cardinal Mendoza. But man for man, the Portuguese representatives were superior in quality to the Spanish ones, and the history of the world ever since that time would reflect that.

The negotiations took place at the convent of Santa Clara in Tordesillas. On May 8, 1494, Queen Isabel, King Fernando, and the court reached it from Medina del Campo. The distance was a mere morning's ride of fifteen miles. The court would remain there till June 9. The monarchs formally met the chapters of the Orders of Santiago and Calatrava, and then discussions began.[29] There is a picture of the meeting, or at least of the conclusion reached, in the Museo de la Marinha, Lisbon, depicting a group of wise men presiding over a confusion of maps, under the coat of arms of the two kingdoms. The "Treaty Houses," Casas del Tratado, the buildings where the discussions occurred, can still be seen.

After a month's talk, on June 7, agreement was reached between Castile and Portugal, first, about the rights of the two Crowns to the navigation, commerce and fishing, and establishments in the Canaries and on the coast of Africa. This was no more than a confirmation of the treaty of 1479 at Alcáçovas.[30] But the same day another treaty was concluded for the "division of the ocean" (*partición del mar*). The Portuguese had obtained a substantial change, in their favor, in respect of the arrangements agreed with the Pope a year before. A new line would be imagined: "a partition or a line drawn from the North to the South Pole, not 100 leagues, but 370 leagues, to the west of the Cape Verde Islands."[31] To the west of the line all would be Spanish; but to the east, with the exception of the Canary Islands and the African territory opposite, all would be Portuguese. "To cut the air with a saber or cut the sea with a knife": that was one definition of the Treaty of Tordesillas. With this, Portugal was given a substantial segment of what would eventually become Brazil. A mixed commission, as the modern world would express it, of one or two caravels from each side was to establish the line in "the ocean," but alas that body never took shape.

How did this Portuguese victory come about? The rulers of Spain, after

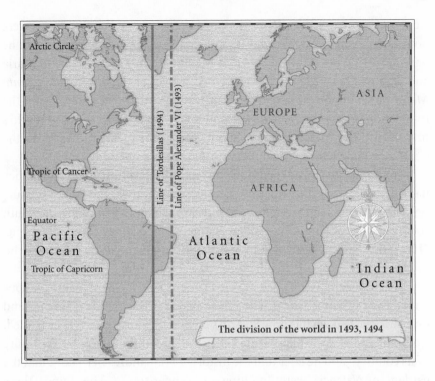

The division of the world in 1493, 1494

all, were used to getting their way internationally. Spain's first defeat at Tordesillas was to accept that there was need for a new agreement. The Spanish monarchs, or at least their advisers, also seem to have been unduly worried about the possibility of a Portuguese fleet leaving for the Indies. But Columbus had not been consulted, nor indeed had Antonio de Torres, who might have been supposed an ideal adviser and who was then in Castile. Could Portugal's insistence have been because Brazil had already been secretly discovered?[32] That would seem fanciful. The Portuguese were preoccupied by the African route. They wanted to guarantee their way to the lucrative Spice Islands, as charted by Bartolomeu Díaz. The allocation to them of 370 leagues westward—270 more than in 1493—meant that their ships could sail south in a broad arc and so avoid the winds and tides off the African coast. It is not clear how the distance of 270 leagues was reached, but such matters constitute the essence of diplomatic compromises. One historian thinks that probably each side thought that the other had been deceived.[33]

While these important decisions were being made, Columbus, who, of course, was the man who created the need for the negotiations, was off the coast of Cuba with his three caravels, one (the San Juan) of seventy tons, the other two much smaller. With him were one or two friends, such as Miguel

Cuneo of Genoa; Fernán Pérez de Luna and Diego de Peñalosa, who were both notaries from Seville; and Juan de la Cosa, the Cantabrian whom he had met in the house of the Duke of Medinaceli in Puerto de Santa María and who had been the master, indeed co-owner, of the doom-laden *Santa María* on Columbus's first voyage but was now a simple sailor, laying the foundations of his fame as a cartographer.[34] There was also the New World's first tourist, the "rich and pious abbot" of Lucerne, who had come to the Caribbean "solely for his own pleasure and to see something new."[35]

Columbus and his expedition first found a beautiful island that they named Tortuga, for the rather obvious reason that there they saw a big turtle. They then sailed through the Windward Channel and along the south coast of Cuba for a thousand miles. No mere island surely could be so long: "I held this land to be mainland, no island," commented the Admiral, who found the footprints of what he believed to be a griffin.[36]

The Admiral's fleet passed the now famous Bay of Guantánamo and observed five big canoes there. Then they made for the island of Jamaica and on May 5 reached what is now St. Ann's Bay, on the north coast. They landed. Columbus named the place Santa Gloria on "account of the extreme beauty of its country," and he later told the historian Fray Andrés Bernáldez that the gardens of Valencia were "nothing in comparison."[37] The Tainos there seemed benign, for they had no experience of war; the Caribs had as yet never reached there. After spending a night offshore, they sailed west to "Discovery Bay" where he was faced in fact with a hostile group of Tainos. Columbus set a dog on them. He also used crossbows, and formally took possession of the island, which he called Santiago. The Tainos then came forward and gave the Spaniards a feast. On May 9, the Admiral sailed west to reach El Golfo de Bueno Tiempo (Montego Bay), then sailed away, arriving back in Cuba at Cabo Cruz (which Columbus so named) on the eighteenth. Passing through Los Jardines de la Reina (as he called the islands) he reached San Juan Evangelista (the modern Isle of Pines) about June 13.[38] There the Spaniards spent ten days, and for the first time came upon the iguana.

Just before this, while at the mouth of the River Sabaló,[39] Columbus secured a statement, drawn up by Fernán Pérez de Luna, the notary of the flotilla, and signed by his sailors and passengers (including Juan de la Cosa) that they had seen the mainland, *la tierra firme,* at the beginning of the Indies, probably the province of Mangi (China) or just possibly the Golden Chersonese (Malaya). (The island would still be called Terra de Cuba Asiae Patris as late as 1516.)[40] They formally swore, too, that if they had gone farther, they would have seen the mainland of China; and they promised to maintain their opinion, on pain of a fine of 10,000 maravedís and the cutting off of their tongues.[41] Nearly everyone signed. Miguel de Cuneo was allowed not to take the oath as a Genoese (though that information did not appear in his own account), and the "rich and pious abbot" of Lucerne refused on the ground that he did not know where he was. Columbus, for his part, was determined to be able to say that he had discovered the Asian mainland even though he had been told by the Tainos of the north of the country, on his first voyage, that Cuba was an island. In insisting thus, he was probably seeking to please the Catholic Kings, for they always thought that "the mainland must contain greater benefits, riches, and secrets than the islands."[42]

At the end of June or the beginning of July 1494, Columbus was back on the east coast of Cuba, regaining Cabo Cruz on July 16. He then again cruised around Jamaica, which he found "extremely fertile and populous . . . the natives," he thought, rather oddly, "have a keener intelligence and are cleverer in the mechanical arts as well as more warlike [than the people of La Española]. . . ."[43] On August 20 he sighted the west end of La Española, which he named Cabo San Miguel after his companion Cuneo (it is now Cabo Tiburón). He sailed along the south of the island and made for "Saona" (named after the Ligurian city of Savona, which he had known in his childhood). He was back at Isabela on September 29, where he remained ill for five months—perhaps it was gout, perhaps dysentery, perhaps both.[44] Columbus found the island, says his son Fernando, in a "pitiable state": his fellow Christians had committed outrages for which they were now hated by the Indians, who refused to obey them.[45]

While he was away, there had indeed been trouble in the colony. The supplies that the Admiral had promised never arrived. Isabela was short of food, Cibao even more so. The harvest of the new crops originally brought from Spain was discouraging. Many Spaniards, perhaps half of Margarit's men, had died of syphilis, caught from Indian girls.[46] Diego Colón was unpopular; he could scarcely speak Spanish. To the tales of his incompetence were added stories of ghostly, well-dressed men taking their heads off with their hats and saluting the hungry survivors.[47] The Indians were suffering, too, from having to put up with Spaniards drifting about the countryside, stealing women and food—though there were some fine moments, as when an Indian offered two turtles to Margarit, who gave him "various glass beads" as a result. (Margarit subsequently released the turtles because there were not enough for all, and he did not want to eat alone.)[48] Shortly afterwards, he decided to withdraw from Cibao and make for Vega Real, only thirty miles from Isabela, intending either to subvert or insist on joining the council that Columbus had set up to manage the settlement. Margarit had,

improbably, become the leader of those enlightened Spaniards who wished
to insist that the Indians should be treated as human beings with souls.[49]

All the same, there was an Indian rebellion: a fort under construction at
a crossing of the Yaque River between Cibao and Isabela was attacked, and
twelve Spaniards were killed. This was the first serious battle in Columbus's
La Española. A punitive expedition was sent out from Isabela, of course, and
several hundred Indians were captured for the benefit of the home market in
slaves.

The only positive thing to which Diego Colón could point in his time as
acting ruler of the colony was the building at Isabela of a water mill, which
did begin to grind wheat sown the previous year though the stream that
powered it was sluggish.

At last, on June 24, Bartolomeo Colón sailed in from Spain with three
caravels. With him came food and other supplies, and also an Aragonese nobleman, Miguel Díaz de Aux, and perhaps Juan Ponce de Léon, who probably had first gone to the Indies on Columbus's second voyage, had gone back
to Spain with Torres, and now returned. Díaz de Aux, who had been born in
Barbastro, was probably the first Aragonese to reach the Indies. He came
from a family well known for its public service in that realm. He was also related by marriage to Juan de Coloma, the influential secretary of the monarchs who had drawn up the *Capitulaciones* for Columbus in 1492.[50] He
would play a substantial part in the next few years' history of La Española.

Bartolomeo immediately took over command of the colony from his
younger brother Diego. While they were not surprised, many Spaniards
began to feel resentful of this Genoese invasion. Yet Bartolomeo was a more
competent administrator than Christopher, his elder brother, and nearly as
good a sailor. He was also an excellent cartographer. The hostility toward
him had little to do with his qualities. It was a consequence of his critics' national pride.[51]

The arrival of Bartolomeo Colón coincided with the return of Margarit
to Isabela with his men, including the rebellious knights. That meant an immediate challenge between two groups of hungry men, of whom some
under Margarit had been reduced to eating the wild dogs that they had
found on the island. Bartolomeo tried to persuade the knights to help finish
his brother's water mill—a task they thought was beneath them. They also
thought that their much-prized horses should not be asked to work a mill.
Was this a typical clash between Italians interested in technological development and Spaniards interested in honor? Worse, Margarit, though still in
charge of the army of Cibao, was in the end not invited to join Columbus's
council.

So it was not surprising that, a few weeks later, with Columbus still ill and with Bartolomeo Colón still in control, in the middle of September 1494, Margarit, accompanied by the difficult and resentful Father Boil, finally "deserted." Seizing the three ships in which Bartolomeo Colón had arrived, they sailed home to Castile. In part they blamed the Admiral's cruelty (for example, his hanging earlier in the year of the Aragonese Gaspar Ferriz for treason)[52] and in part the problem of food supply. "All the main troubles derived from hunger," wrote Las Casas.[53] This was when, also according to Las Casas, people in Isabela began saying, "Please God, take me to Castile!"[54] They took with them some of the monks who had come to the colony in 1493 and also some of the knights (of whom three had died), leaving no priests in the colony and only one monk, the poor Catalan anchorite Fray Ramón Pané.

Those Spaniards whom Margarit left behind at San Tomé or Cibao seem to have scattered into various Indian communities; as a result, wrote Fernando Colón, "each one went where he willed among the Indians, stealing their property and wives, and inflicting so many injuries upon them that the Indians resolved to avenge themselves on any Spaniards that they found alive or in small groups. Thus the *cacique* of the Magdalena, Guatiganá, killed ten Christians and secretly ordered fire to be set to a hut that housed forty sick men. . . ."[55]

The only bright sign was that Fray Ramón Pané did carry out a successful proselytizing mission. He went first to the fortress in the interior that Columbus had named Magdalena (then captained by a Castilian named Arteaga), where there were converts to Christianity, the servants of the *cacique* Cuanóbocon, who had been martyred.[56] Pané became the godfather of one *cacique*, Guaicavanú, who was baptized Juan. He then went on to La Concepción, where the Spanish captain was Juan de Ayala and where he instructed the *cacique* Guarionex in Christianity. Guarionex was at first a good pupil but then drew away, and Pané moved on to try to convert a *cacique* named Maviatué, all of whose household said that they would like to become Christians. But Guarionex obstructed this evolution.[57] The expedition showed, at least, that conversion to Christianity was possible as an alternative to conquest. Pané's report was not only the first study of Taino religion but the first work of literature written in the Americas.[58]

Since Columbus continued to be ill, Bartolomeo Colón remained in control. The Admiral named him "*adelantado*"—an office used in Castile for a general with administrative powers in a province that had been occupied, and that was within Columbus's rights to grant.

The most encouraging development of these months in La Española

was the return from Spain of Antonio de Torres with four new ships carrying supplies, in October 1494. He brought with him the monarchs' letters to
Columbus of August 16 and 17, both written in Segovia and both drafted by
Fernando Álvarez de Toledo, the clever *converso* secretary who now spent
most of his time dealing with international matters.[59] In the first, the monarchs told Columbus what had been agreed with Portugal.[60] They also wrote
to say, rather surprisingly, that "one of the principal things which gives us so
much pleasure is that . . . it seems that everything which from the first you
said could be done has been achieved and that all has turned out for the
most part to be true, as if you had seen it before you spoke of it."[61] The
Queen added that she was thinking of sending a monthly ship to the Indies.
Fernando, meanwhile, demonstrated that he was at last showing some interest in the New World when he asked if Columbus would send him as many
falcons as he could.[62]

The monarchs in Spain seemed from these letters to be in other ways
satisfied with their new dominions. Thus on October 22 they contracted
with Andrés Quemada and Juan de Cartaya, both of Jerez de la Frontera, to
go to La Española to inspect the soil, to find out the best place for agriculture, and then to plant as seemed appropriate.[63]

That autumn the monarchs were mostly in Madrid, with brief visits to
Guadalajara (in late September), partly to visit Cardinal Mendoza, now on
his deathbed—an anticipation of what would turn out in the end to be the
best place for a Spanish capital.[64]

All the same, the King and Queen were not deceived by Columbus's reports. That was made evident from a letter of theirs in early December 1494
that they wrote to Fonseca, saying what a pleasure it was for them to hear of
the arrival from the Indies of Margarit and Boil. No reproach was addressed
to either of them for irregularly seizing the ships in La Española and returning without permission from Columbus. They asked Boil to present himself
at court.[65] Las Casas says that when he did so, the monarchs were informed
more graphically than before of what had been told them by Antonio de
Torres: that all the stories of the riches of the Indies were "a mere tease"
(*burla*); that there was not much gold; and that their Highnesses' costs were
unrecoverable.[66]

The King and Queen of Aragon and Castile were concerned with, to
them, a far more pressing problem. Fernando's cousin Ferrante, King of
Naples, died in January 1494. He was succeeded by his son, Alfonso, who had
married a daughter of Ludovico el Moro, Duke of Milan. It was the signal for
King Charles of France to revive his ancient if complicated claim to that
throne; and on September 3, 1494, as he had promised, Charles crossed the

frontier between France and Savoy with over thirty thousand foot and another ten thousand or so on ships.[67] This well-armed force amazed his contemporaries. A considerable amount of artillery was also carried. The invasion was a threat to the Spanish possession of Sicily and, of course, to Fernando's kinsman, King Alfonso.[68]

It was for centuries said that this was when modern history began. The historian Guicciardini describes alarming auguries in Italy: in Puglia one night three suns appeared in the sky, with awful thunder and lightning; in Arezzo an infinite number of men on enormous horses were seen in the heavens, with a terrible clamor of trumpets and drums; many sacred statues sweated; monstrous men and other animals were sighted; and people became terrified of French power.[69] Fernando, however, had partly benefited from the rumors of these events. As earlier explained, he had recovered Roussillon and Cerdagne for Aragon. But he had not expected King Charles to reach Naples in triumph. Yet that monarch entered the cathedral there, carrying the imperial orb (the Empire of the East) in his left hand and the sceptre (of Naples) in his right, even if a few days later, with half his army, he began his retreat, the rest of his troops remaining under his cousin, the Duke of Montpensier.

What was most shocking about this new stage in European history was Charles VIII's method of war: at Monte Giovanni, the French committed massacres. Guicciardini reported that "after having given vent to every other kind of savage barbarism, they resorted to the ultimate cruelty of setting buildings on fire." That way of making war had not been used in Italy in the Middle Ages, and it filled all the kingdom with "the greatest terror. . . ."[70] The Battle of Taro in 1495 was a good example of the change: the French lost two hundred, the Italians several thousand; it was the first time for generations that such battles had happened in Italy.

Fernando saw that war had to replace diplomacy, and he dispatched in September a fleet of more than forty caravels under Garcerán de Requesens. With him was the hero of the last stages of the war against Granada, Gonzalo Hernández de Córdoba, "El Gran Capitán," who soon set out for Calabria where he began a long career of legend. The fleet of Requesens had, unsurprisingly, been well organized by the ubiquitous Fonseca.[71]

Something else occurred, too, in Italy, which was related to the achievements of Columbus. To quote again from the admirable Guicciardini:

This was the same time when there first appeared that malady which the French called "the Neapolitan disease" and the Italians commonly called either "boils" or "the French disease." The reason was that it manifested itself first among the French when they were in Naples and then, as they marched back to France, they spread it over Italy. This ailment showed itself either in the form of the most ugly boils that often turned into incurable ulcers or in very intense pains all over the body. And since the physicians were not experienced in dealing with such a disease, they applied remedies that were not appropriate, indeed often were actually harmful, frequently inflaming the infection. Thus this disease killed many men and women of all ages, and many became terribly deformed and were rendered useless, suffering from almost continual torments.

This malady was syphilis, from which Columbus's men had already suffered in the New World, which Antonio de Torres had brought back to Spain and which would now begin a long life in European culture.[72] The word was coined by Girolamo Fracastoro when he published his poem "Syphilis Morbus Gallicus" in 1530. By that time the malady was well known, and the crippling sores so caused soon darkened the lives of emperors and clowns, Frenchmen and Turks, bishops and businessmen, as well as soldiers and missionaries. The disease was more prevalent among the upper classes than the lower: a punishment, as it seemed, to greater sinners.

12

"Whether we can sell those slaves or not"

We want to inform ourselves from . . . theologians and canon lawyers whether we can sell those [slaves] or not.

Fernando and Isabel to Juan Rodríguez de Fonseca,
April 16, 1495

By 1495 the King and Queen in Spain were coming to realize that the discoveries of Columbus would impose new responsibilities, as well as new opportunities, on themselves. So they began to fumble toward an imperial policy. A decisive influence in this, as in most other matters, was that of Jiménez de Cisneros, the Queen's new confessor, and, after January 1495, Cardinal Mendoza's successor as primate and archbishop of Toledo.[1] As archbishop, this able, austere, and effective churchman still lived as if he were a hermit. He walked barefoot; and he continued to devote his attention to his reforms of the Franciscan Order, which caused an upheaval—especially when he insisted that friars lead an ascetic life. Some of them are said to have gone to North Africa in order to convert to Islam rather than abandon their mistresses.[2]

The executive official, however, who ensured that decisions about the Indies taken by the wandering court were put into effect in Seville or Cadiz, was another prelate, Juan Rodríguez de Fonseca, the onetime archdeacon of the former city who in these years became a "minister for the Indies" without the name. In 1494, he had been named Bishop of Badajoz, though he never went to live in that city of Extremadura since his work for the Crown kept him in Seville. He was paid an annual salary of 200,000 maravedís for this. He also became a member of the Council of Castile, which brought him another 100,000 maravedís. He was competent and resourceful, but his effectiveness was vitiated by his dislike of Columbus, whose genius he never saw and of whom he could only observe the foibles.

This was something that everyone noted at the time. Las Casas wrote of

Fonseca: "He was much more successful in planning fleets than presiding at masses"[3] and added, "I always heard and believed and, indeed, saw something of the fact that he had always been contrary to the activities of the Admiral. I do not know with what spirit and with what cause. . . . I must say that, justly or unjustly, the Admiral was against him, and that I don't have any doubts about. Yet the Bishop was a man of good stock and of a generous spirit, and very close to the monarchs."[4]

Fernando Colón was stronger in his criticism. He reported that Fonseca had always hated his father and his enterprises, and he was "always the leader of those who spoke badly of him at court."[5] He felt at ease only with people of good family, so adventurers, even if clever, suffered, and aristocrats, even if foolish, prospered in consequence of his appointments. Antonio de Guevara, a Franciscan who in 1495 was a page to the Infante Juan, but was later a senior preacher and historian to the court (as well as the secret author of *The Golden Book of Marcus Aurelius,* one of the most successful books of the sixteenth century), would write candidly to Fonseca:

> You ask me, *señor,* what they are saying about you here, and all say at court that you may be a very solid Christian but that you are a very peevish (*desabrido*) bishop. Also, they say that you are fat, prolix, careless, and indecisive in the contracts which you have in your hands, as with the petitioners who appear before you and, what is worse, many of them return home exhausted and unconsidered. They also say that you are a bully, as well as proud, impatient, and high-spirited. . . . Others admit that you are a man who deals in truth, that you tell the truth and are, indeed, the friend of truth, while a liar never has you as a friend. They admit that you are direct in what you do, just in how your decisions are executed, and that, to be honest, you have no prejudice in favoring, and no affection for, anyone. They also comment that you are compassionate, pious, and charitable. Don't marvel at what I say, since I am shocked by what you do. There is no virtue more necessary in a man who runs a republic than patience. Whether you are a prelate or a president, you have to live modestly and be long-suffering.[6]

That said, Fonseca, like others of his illustrious family, was an enthusiast for the arts, especially Flemish painting, as can be seen from the depiction of himself in the cathedrals of Badajoz and of Palencia, especially the latter, where the Fleming Juan Joest de Calcar painted him on the reredos.[7]

The need for a clear policy toward the empire was forced on the Spanish Crown by Columbus's policies in La Española, especially in respect of the enslavement of Indians. For by 1495, Columbus, despairing of finding gold in any quantity, was seriously trying to compensate by securing slaves to send home. He himself, his brother Bartolomeo, and the handsome Alonso de Hojeda carried out cruel armed drives to almost every part of La Española in order to kidnap Indians. But the indigenous people were not prepared to accept such seizures meekly. Nor did the Spaniards distinguish between peace-loving Indians, who might have a future as Christians, and Caribs, who were presumed godless, cannibalistic, and brutal.

The campaign of Columbus to obtain Indian slaves gave rise to one of the most soul-searing of paragraphs in the works of Las Casas, who added that in this way was destroyed two-thirds of the population. That was a typical exaggeration of that author, though his enemy, the historian Oviedo, also spoke of innumerable victims.[8] This led to a spontaneous decision by many Indians in La Española to flee to the mountains. This "rebellion," as it was misleadingly called, led Columbus to seize about 1,660 "souls both men and women," as Miguel Cuneo put it, and to send 550 of them home to Castile in the second home-going fleet of Antonio de Torres, which left Isabela on February 24, 1495. The Atlantic slave trade thus began in an east-west direction, not from Africa but from the Caribbean to Europe.

On this second return voyage, Torres was accompanied by Columbus's younger brother, Diego Colón, and his childhood friend Miguel Cuneo. It was a far from triumphal journey. But it was swift: Cuneo reported that the journey from Puerto Rico (Boriquen) to Madeira took only twenty-three days. Yet about two hundred of the Indians who accompanied Torres died from the cold when they entered Spanish waters.[9] The rest landed at Cadiz, though another half of them were ill. Cuneo reported: "They are not accustomed to hard work, they suffer from cold, and they do not have a long life."[10]

Nine prize Indians were given to the Florentine Juanotto Berardi, whose instruction was to hand them over to someone appropriate so that they might be able one day to act as interpreters. The remaining prisoners were left to be sold in Seville, even if a number seem to have escaped. But even before they arrived, the Catalans Margarit and Fray Boil, who had abandoned Columbus without leave, had been developing a theory that the Indians were potentially Christian subjects of their Highnesses and, therefore, should not be enslaved.[11] This arose from their observation that Taino religious manifestations, from the offering of food to the gods, their adornment, the processions, the dancing, the singing, and the distribution of bread to heads of families, had something in common with Christian practices.[12]

Bernal Díaz de Pisa, the accountant whom Columbus had imprisoned, was summoned to court to contribute to the collective knowledge of what was going on in La Española. Several knights who had returned complained, too, that the brothers of the Admiral had seized their horses.[13] Others said that Columbus had told some of the gentlemen volunteers that those who did not work could not eat—a statement that no Spanish gentleman could receive tranquilly, especially not from a Genoese of unknown birth.[14]

Columbus knew nothing of such intrigues at court, though having spent so much time there, he could have imagined them. By the time of Torres's arrival in Spain, he was already back in La Española, his plan being now to occupy the whole island in the name of the Spanish Crown. His original idea that there would simply be trading posts for the delivery of merchandise, precious metals, and slaves, in the style of Portuguese expansion in Africa, had been pushed aside in favor of a more Castilian interpretation of the desirability of expansion: to occupy land and to seize populations.[15] One has the strong sense that both the Admiral and his royal masters were being forced to reconsider their assumptions in consequence of the actuality of settlement and its difficulties.

Columbus left Isabela on March 25 with two hundred men, twenty horses, and a number of dogs to "occupy" the center of La Española—not trade with it. He was accompanied by his brother Bartolomeo and by his indigenous ally, the *cacique* Guacanagarí, and some of his Indians. He divided his forces in two and attacked a large Indian army. They defeated them easily; Fernando Colón wrote that these were dispersed "as if they had been birds."

Columbus then set about founding fortresses at four places: Concepción de la Vega (Santo Cerro), Esperanza, Santiago, and Santa Catalina. These were built of wood, of course, owing more to the art of carpenters than of masons. All the same, Concepción became a center of pilgrimage—and of miracles. In his will, Columbus remembered it and hoped that Masses would be said there in a chapel every day. By the time he died, however, it had reverted to jungle.[16] Much of the remaining small Spanish population of Isabela moved inland to garrison those fortresses. Excellent fish were easy to catch, as has always been the case in the Caribbean. Cotton, linen, and various other domestic products began to do well under Spanish direction, and a few Castilian transplants were also successful: wheat, vegetables, some cereals, vines, and even sugarcane had all been planted; some survived. Pigs and chickens were also flourishing.

In the course of that spring and in the summer, Columbus arranged with friendly *caciques* that all adult Indians between the ages of fourteen and seventy would undertake to provide regular tribute to the Spanish Crown in the form of the appropriate produce of their locality. Thus the Indians of Cibao and Vega Real agreed to give Columbus over 60,000 pesos of gold in three separate payments. Those who lived in cotton-growing regions would each contribute a bale. All tributaries would wear a disk when they had paid their due. In return, Columbus undertook to restrain his followers from roaming fecklessly.[17] In the meantime, some of his followers had begun to settle down inland with Indian women.

The *caciques* gave what they could but then begged for mercy if they did not produce what they were asked for. Guarionex offered to plant a huge agricultural plot (*conuco*) all the way from the north to the south of the island if his people were released from the tribute of gold. Columbus considered the matter. Of course, he preferred gold.

Whether Columbus would have survived in the long run as the commander in chief, governor, or viceroy of this little world is something that cannot be known, for by the end of the year 1495, he learned that the Crown's policy toward him was changing. As early as April of that year, the monarchs were beginning to look on La Española and other islands in the Caribbean as if they were extensions of Andalusia.[18]

This was in part the consequence of the dispatch to Spain of the Indians— slaves, as Columbus believed that they should be considered. It should have been an easy task to have arranged for their sale in Spain.[19] Andalusia was accustomed, after all, to the auctioning and purchase of slaves of many origins. Valencian merchants, such as Juan Abelló and Antonio Viana, could have dealt easily with these cargoes, as could those in Genoa—for example, Domenico de Castellón and Francisco Gato.

The Crown did not seem hostile in principle; thus the monarchs wrote to Fonseca in Seville on April 12 that "in respect of what you write to us about the Indians who came in the caravels, it appears to us that you can sell these better in Andalusia than anywhere else and you ought to sell them as best you can."[20] But the Crown went back on that decision. Probably that was because of the influence of Boil and Margarit. The Queen's confessor, Cisneros, may have played a part. His attitude toward the Indians, whom he did not know, was always more humane than it was toward Jews and Muslims, with whom he had associated. At all events, just four days later, on April 16, 1495, the monarchs sent another letter to Fonseca delaying the sales:

> We want to inform ourselves from *letrados*, theologians, and canon lawyers if, with good conscience, we can sell those [slaves] or not, and we cannot do this until we have seen the letters that the Admiral has written

to us . . . and those letters are in the hands of Torres but as yet he has not sent them to us; therefore, the sales of those Indians should be suspended for a brief spell.[21]

It was, however, a long time before that learned opinion was forthcoming. Nor is it clear how, of whom exactly, and even whether the opinion was formally sought. What does seem to have happened is that fifty Indian slaves were quickly made available to Admiral Juan Lezcano Arriarán for use in the royal galleys, and a few more were allowed by Fonseca to be sold by Berardi, while the rest died in Seville while waiting for a decision about their future.[22] The monarchs, for their part, continued to think that a distinction could be drawn between good and bad Indians. Cuneo, in a letter written to a friend in Seville in the autumn of 1495, mentions this distinction, speaking of cannibals being found as soon as he arrived at Santa María Galante on the second journey of Columbus.[23]

This was the beginning of a debate about the identity of Caribs and the possibility of enslaving them. But what is remarkable about these royal doubts is that both monarchs knew that they, too, were governed by law and that they could not invent it. Autocrats they might be, but they were law-abiding.

It was becoming increasingly clear to both of them, too, that they would have to reduce Columbus's franchise. Fernando and Isabel had not presided over the unification of the peninsula in order to allow a Genoese adventurer to establish a private suzerainty under their authority. All the same, on April 10, 1495, the monarchs issued a decree in Madrid that authorized anyone— any Castilian, that is—to equip expeditions to discover islands, even continents, in the Indies or the Ocean Sea. The rules for those who wanted to go to the Indies were these:

> Since we hear that various persons, our subjects, want to go to discover other islands and parts of the mainland other than those which, by our mandate, have already been discovered in the said part of the Ocean Sea, and to barter gold and other metals and other merchandise; and inasmuch as others would like to go to settle in La Española, which has already been discovered . . . and recalling that no one is to go to the Indies without our license . . . we establish, first, that every ship which sets off for the Indies must leave from Cádiz and not from anywhere else, and that those who set out must register themselves there with the appropriate officials; second, that anyone who wants to go and live in the Indies without a salary can do so freely and can receive maintenance for a year,

keeping for himself a third of the gold that he discovers, the other two parts being for us, while of all other merchandise they must give us a tenth; third, that anyone who wants can go and discover new islands or *tierra firme* other than La Española, but they must register at, and leave from, Cádiz;[24] and fourth, that anyone can take whatever they like in the way of supplies to La Española, but on all ships a tenth part of the burden must be of our goods, etc.

Columbus would always be able to carry an eighth part on all ships. But this was a document of capital importance. It broke Columbus's monopoly.[25] The beneficiary was, however, first, his Florentine friend Berardi, who by another decree was enabled to hire twelve ships to carry nine hundred tons of goods to sell at a cost of 2,000 maravedís per ton. He would have the decisive advantage of dedicating half his fleet to the person dreaming of finding unknown places, with a previous benefit assured. This was the only way of working out an efficient method for costing the attempts at discovery, the return journey, and so on.[26] Naturally Columbus complained of this decree when he heard of it. But he only heard late, and his complaint was ineffective. The decree ensured six years of liberty for traders and emigrants, a liberty that, in fact, would not be seen again for 250 years.[27]

These decisions followed much royal correspondence about the Indies earlier in the year. Thus, in February, the monarchs had ordered Fonseca to send four ships to the Indies full of supplies.[28] On February 14, Sebastián Olano, a courtier who had sailed with Columbus in 1493, wrote to the monarchs saying that, far from the Admiral having prohibited the distribution of goods in the absence of the accountants, as Columbus had apparently alleged, he had ordered the contrary.[29] In March, a flotilla of three ships for Santo Domingo had been planned by Juan Aguado, a chamberlain of the court, who had also been with Columbus in 1493 and had returned with Torres. Columbus had looked on him as a friend, but he seems to have been firmly on the side of Fonseca in all doubtful questions. Pedro de Mata, constable of the Inquisition in Seville, gave to Juan Lucero of Moguer 40,000 maravedís from the Inquisition's funds to finance this caravel to the Indies.[30] Then in April, the Crown charged Juanotto Berardi to resupply the colony in La Española, and a contract was exchanged by which the Florentine agreed to send twelve ships with merchandise in three journeys. But they were delayed. The Crown still at this time thought they could seek to maintain commerce with the New World as a monopoly between Columbus and themselves.[31]

Berardi wrote to the Crown saying the problem of the colony was that all or nearly all the expeditionaries of La Española wished to come home, while their debts amounted to 10 or 12 million maravedís. He proposed an arbitrary settlement to deal with both problems. By amortizing 2 of the 12 million, the Crown could buy about ten or twelve caravels so that the colonists of La Española could discover and even settle in other islands. With another five caravels the Crown could buy all the food needed. With the remaining 5 million maravedís, the monarchs could invest in merchandise to be sold to the residents of La Española. Everyone on that island could be provided for adequately for two years, although those who found precious metals or pearls would pay their fifth (*quinto*) to the Crown. On every ship henceforth there ought to be a notary. All ships of exploration would return to La Española and all, as the monarchs would prefer, would be built in Spain, not in the Indies. The plan would go ahead slowly; the first four caravels would be sent with food and merchandise, and afterwards they would go two by two. At the end of six months, the products of the *quintos* would pay for everything.[32]

We see in these proposed rules the beginning of the bureaucratization of the discoveries that would subsequently dominate the Indies.

Soon after this, the monarchs sent their first serious admonition to Columbus: on June 1, 1495, they wrote to him from Arévalo, "We have learned that, in recent days, especially when you were away from La Española, the available supplies were not shared out to the settlers. So we order you to divide these up as agreed, and please do not change this rule except where a grave crime has been committed by someone, such as would be worthy of a death penalty and which would be equivalent to an abbreviation of such supplies."[33] It turned out that those responsible for the past "abbreviation" were not Columbus and his brother but his deputies in control of supplies, Alonso Sánchez de Carvajal and his successor, Juan de Oñate, a Sevillano. All the same, this letter was the first indication the Admiral had that the Crown had its own ideas about the government of his Indies.[34]

The remainder of 1495 passed in Spain with the monarchs seeking to devise a policy toward Naples as well as the New World. They did issue a series of decrees affecting the latter, which did not suggest consistency except that overall responsibility was vested in the Crown. Columbus would be seen henceforth as just one more public servant and a difficult one at that. We also find the Inquisition giving Fonseca substantial sums that were seized from departing or condemned Jews for the benefit of the exploitation of new discoveries.[35] Other regulations followed. Anyone who wanted to go to the New World was now supposed to subordinate himself to an authorized commander, who would obtain a license to "conquer and settle" some island or coast. That individual would have to raise money to finance everything. Royal officials, however, would be attached to him. Often, though, he would have his title (say, "governor") for his own life and perhaps that of his son. He was expected to provide missionaries and priests, and, of course, he had to obey royal decrees. He also had to explore as well as develop his proposed colony, to establish towns, to discover gold mines, and to turn the natives into good Christians. The Crown, which could offer no protection, would still expect a fifth of the gross value of all products, with no expenses taken into account. If the booty derived from a tomb, the royal share would be one-half. Really, anyone who obtained one of these licenses had to be a gambler or a visionary, one who might pawn everything to set off at the head of a gang of interested men, some of them being ruffians. Most of his followers would receive no income and have no specific loyalties.

On August 5, 1495, Juan de Aguado, the butler royal, left Seville for La Española with four ships, with supplies but also with the explicit task of carrying out a *residencia* (an inquiry into the mandate) against Columbus.[36] That was normal Castilian practice, used often in relation to *corregidores;* but the proposal was a striking change of royal policy toward Columbus, and the end of his dream of a private empire.[37]

Aguado carried with him a document listing exemptions and rights. From this Columbus would know that his monopoly was henceforth limited to La Española and that the rest of the Indies, including places he had already discovered, would be governed by a different system. Even in La Española, the Crown had restrictions to impose; for example, it seemed to the court that the number of persons who were receiving a salary was excessive. Would it not be desirable to establish a maximum of five hundred such settlers?

Aguado's sailors and the captains of his four vessels were instructed to return after only a month in the Indies. But their ships were all wrecked at Isabela soon after they arrived, in a hurricane in the autumn of 1495. The reports of this functionary were lost then too, but hearing of them, the Admiral began to think that he could deal with his enemies only by returning to Spain.[38] On October 15, he wrote to Fernando and Isabel from Vega de la Maguana. It was a letter mostly about the *cacique* Caonabó and his crimes, and about how Aguado's ships had been lost. But he did suggest that the monarchs should send out to the Indies "some devout friars who were above greed for the things of the world"—presumably a reproach to Fray Boil, whom he now saw as the chief of his enemies.[39] It is true that there was much sardonic comment at court about the Admiral's claim to have found "the Indies." On August 9, 1495, Peter Martyr in Tortosa was wondering, in a letter to Bernardino de Carvajal, whether La Española was, after all, the Ophir of Solomon.[40]

The achievements of Columbus were all the same beginning to catch the imagination of many thinking people in Castile. Thus Juan del Encina of Salamanca (where his father had been a shoemaker), who had joined the household of the Duke of Alba as actor and courtier as well as poet, wrote an introduction to his book of ballads (his *Cancionero*) called *The Art of Castilian Poetry,* which was dedicated to the Infante Juan. This included the splendid words: "Since, as the most learned maestro Antonio de Nebrija says (he, that is, who flung out . . . the barbarisms that had grown in our Latin language), one of the reasons which moved him [Encina, that is] to devote himself to romance was that our language up to now is more exalted and polished than it has ever been, so much so that one might fear that the descent might be as fast as the rise. . . ."[41] Language of empire, indeed!

Columbus decided finally to go back to Castile. On March 10, 1496, he left Isabela with 30 Indian slaves and 225 disillusioned Spaniards, including most of those who had gone out with Aguado and who had not been able to return before. This return journey was made in two ships that had been built in the Indies—the first such, it seems.[42]

Just before he left, Columbus found a new goldfield south of Vega, to which he gave the name San Cristóbal. He again left his brother Bartolomeo as governor. Diego Colón would be the second in command.

In a letter to Fernando and Isabel two years later, in 1498, the Admiral explained that at this time "evil words arose in Spain with a belittlement of the enterprise which had been begun, because I had not at once dispatched home ships laden with gold, not allowing for the brevity of the time that had elapsed or everything else I had said of the many problems . . . for my sins or for my salvation, I was placed in abhorrence, and obstacles were erected against whatever I said or asked. I decided, therefore, to come before your Highnesses and to show my incredulity at this and also to show that I was right in everything." He also recalled how Solomon had sent ships to the Orient to look for Ophir; how Alexander had sent others to seek the government of "Tapóbrana"; and how Nero sent others still to find the sources of the Nile, and even the kings of Portugal caravels to discover Guinea.[43] Columbus considered himself in excellent company.

"Malevolent jokes of the goddess Fortune"

These shouts of laughter and malevolent jokes of the goddess
Fortune . . .

Peter Martyr[1]

Columbus sailed home through the Lesser Antilles, stopping on April 10 at
Guadeloupe, where he seized some Caribs to be slaves, and leaving on April 20.
He visited no islands that he did not know and reached Cadiz on June 11.

The Admiral then made his way, dressed, surprisingly, as a Franciscan
monk in gray, toward Seville. He had always seemed something of a friar and
had had excellent relations with the order ever since his sojourn at La
Rábida. He stayed for a time in the house of Andrés Bernáldez, the priest of
Los Palacios, later the author of *The History of the Reign of the Catholic Kings*,
whose chapter about the discovery of the Indies and the second voyage was
much influenced by what the Admiral now told him. Bernáldez's parish was
fifteen miles south of Seville, but he was all the same a chaplain to, and protégé of, Fray Diego de Deza, Columbus's friend at the court of the Infante
Juan. He was anti-Jewish, and his laughter at the sufferings of the Jews who
in 1492 left Spain for Morocco makes sad reading.[2]

When he arrived in Seville, Columbus would have observed his old comrade of the first voyage, Peralonso Niño, making ready to leave for the Indies
(he did so on June 16). It was Fonseca's new fleet, consisting of two caravels
and a Breton vessel, as well as a brigantine bought in Cadiz, with fourteen
oars. Like other such flotillas, they were to buy a hundred sheep and some
goats in La Gomera.[3] They were to sail out to La Española and sail back; nothing was mentioned about further expeditions. Here was a voyage that had not
been authorized by the Admiral-Viceroy, and he was ignorant of it before it
sailed. Columbus would have learned, too, that Alonso Fernández de Lugo
had completed his conquest of Tenerife at last in 1496; and how in June he
had paraded his Guanche captives before the monarchs at Almazán, the town

on the River Duero and on the border of Castile and Aragon that would become the seat of the short-lived court of the Infante Juan.[4] He would have
found that, however important his own enterprise had seemed in 1492, four
years later it was just one more activity of the monarchs, perhaps as interesting as the Canary Islands but nothing like as tempting as Italy.

Columbus found, however, that on the surface there was no real weak-
ening of the support that the King and Queen were giving him. They wrote
a friendly letter from Almazán.[5] Columbus, still in his Franciscan robe, traveled to meet them in Burgos at the beginning of October. They saw him in
the Casa del Cordón, a splendid palace begun by the late Constable of
Castile, Pedro Fernández de Velasco, and completed by his widow, Mencía.
The Admiral gave them a "good sample of gold . . . and many masks, with
eyes and ears of gold, and many parrots."[6] He also presented to the monarchs "Diego," the brother of the dead *cacique* Caonabo, wearing a gold collar that weighed six hundred *castellanos*.[7] This hint that more gold might be
forthcoming was most encouraging to them. Legend also insists that some
of the gold brought back in 1496 was given to Diego de la Cruz to gild the
retablo in the chapel of the Carthusian monastery of Miraflores, outside
Burgos, where the mad, sad mother of Queen Isabel, who at last died in 1496,
would shortly be interred.

The Admiral wanted to return to the Indies immediately, and the King
and Queen thought that he should indeed go, with eight ships, to discover
more of the mainland—that is, presumably, Cuba and South America.
Columbus must have rehearsed his achievements as an explorer eloquently,
for despite the criticisms of Margarit and Boil that the monarchs had previously heard, his "Privileges" of 1492 were again confirmed. Peter Martyr was
as usual at court and wrote to Bernardino de Carvajal in Rome enthusiastically of Columbus.[8] The latter's brother, the unpopular Bartolomeo, was
confirmed by the Crown as *adelantado*, the grand office that had been given
him by the Admiral.

There were delays, however, before Columbus returned to his new lands.
Fonseca was reluctant to authorize any further voyage by Columbus, and he
made excuses in order to obstruct him. Completely unsentimental, he knew
that discovery was one thing, administration another. He thought that for
the moment Columbus was best occupied in Castile; and, sitting about in
the court and following the monarchs through Burgos, Valladolid, Tordesillas, and Medina del Campo, the Admiral had time on his hands, and he
seems to have spent it with books (much of his serious reading probably
dates from these years). It was in 1496 that he obtained from England his
copy of the *The Travels of Marco Polo* (which he probably now read for the

first time) and that he bought Albertus Magnus's *Philosophia Naturalis,* as well as Abraham Zacuto's *Almanach Perpetuum.*[9] These purchases are a happy reminder that now for the first time the ordinary man could buy real, printed books. Next year Columbus would send for the latest information about the Venetian John Cabot's recent crossing of the North Atlantic to Newfoundland from Bristol (a journey probably only made because of the news of Columbus's success).[10]

Columbus now made new summaries of the size of the world and compared its shape to a walnut, with the sea the shell. He talked, of course, and he may even have listened; presumably he took in that, in December 1496, Pope Alexander had granted Fernando and Isabel the joint title of "the Catholic Kings," *Los Reyes Católicos,* an action that infuriated King Charles of France, who was already known as "the most Christian King." The gesture was the consequence not only of the war in Granada, but also of the commitment of the two to send an army to Naples and to assist the papacy against France (so Alexander VI interpreted the landing of the Gran Capitán and his men in May 1495).[11] They received no such formal designation for their patronage of Columbus in the New World.

Columbus probably participated, in early 1497, in the celebrations that attended the arrival in Spain of "the so much desired archduchess Margaret" (Martyr's words), the seventeen-year-old daughter of the Emperor Maximilian, in order to marry the Infante—the culmination of the monarchs' dynastic policy, complemented by the long-awaited marriage of their daughter Juana to Margaret's brother Philip. "The white throats of the Queen and her ladies were heavy with jewels," Peter Martyr wrote in the same exaggerated style as Columbus was wont to write of the Caribbean landscape.[12]

Columbus would also have witnessed the court's sadness after the death of the Infante Juan in October of the same year in Salamanca, in his father's arms, bringing to an end not only that remarkable little court of Almazán organized so imaginatively by Fray Diego de Deza, but also the old royal family of Spain.[13] There was no legitimate male heir to the house of Trastámara, and it seemed certain that the throne would pass to the Habsburg descendants of the Infanta Juana. We observe now the exquisite tomb of the "hope of all Spain" in the Dominican *convento* of St. Thomas at Ávila, designed by the Florentine Fancelli—it was his first major commission—and can still imagine the consternation that marked his death.

Neither Fernando nor Isabel recovered from this tragedy, which was soon to be compounded by the death the next year, in 1498, of their eldest daughter, Isabel, the Queen of Portugal, and then (in 1500) of her infant son, Miguel.

After the Infante's death, the monarchs went to stay with Cardinal Jiménez de Cisneros at the episcopal palace at Guadalajara, where they remained in virtual seclusion for six months, till April 1498. This was the time when Cisneros, even though busy with his plans for the new university of Alcalá (the Complutense University),[14] confirmed his position as the de facto chief minister for the Crown. One must assume that he comforted the monarchs with prayers. Or were they more cheered by being reminded of verses written by Jorge Manrique to recall his own dead father:

> Popes, emperors
> And Princes of the church
> Are treated by Death
> As if they are poor
> Cattleherds.

Or:

> Our lives are rivers
> Which run into the sea
> Of Death.
> There, too, go their Lordships.[15]

The Habsburg family would always assert that the prince died because he had made love too assiduously to Margaret. A more convincing explanation is that he ate a bad salad at the fair in Salamanca.[16]

The members of the court of the Infante, of course, sought other places of employment. Columbus's friend Dr. Deza became bishop of Salamanca and then archbishop of Seville, with other honors later falling to him. The young Columbus brothers, Diego and Fernando, sons of the Admiral who had been attached to the Infante as pages, moved to the household of the Queen. Most other members of the household had successful careers, some in the Indies, often dining out on their experiences with the Infante for the rest of their days, like Cristóbal de Cuéllar, the Infante's treasurer. He would frequently be heard saying in Cuba, as in Castile, that the wild happenings at Almazán "would have earned him one or two tumbles in Hell."[17]

The same autumn, Peralonso Niño returned to Spain from La Española. Rumor had it that he was carrying much gold, but in the event, his main cargo was only more slaves, sent by Bartolomeo Colón, as well as a little brazilwood. He handed over about three hundred of the former to Nicolás Cabrero, a merchant of Seville.[18] Peralonso Niño brought little in the way of news from La Española except that Bartolomeo Colón had put to death some of the *cacique* Guarionex's men because they had buried some Christian images.[19]

Columbus was still trying to organize his new, third, voyage. He was given financial backing of 6 million maravedís by the Crown, but that seemed to him inadequate. Had not the monarchs spent that sum merely defending Perpignan against the French? Columbus was also now finding it difficult to enlist volunteers to accompany him. Too many bleak stories had been told of the rough life in the Indies. Those who had been in La Española made bad propaganda for the cause; they were, said the historian Oviedo, "of the color of gold, but they did not have its shine."[20] At this time the "Catholic Kings"—they fully embodied that title now—asked Antonio de Torres to take over from Fonseca as chief organizer of the expeditions to the Indies. That marked a triumph for Columbus, since Torres at least knew the Indies, which could not have been said of Fonseca. The King and Queen also wrote saying that Columbus was to be allowed to buy what he wanted.[21]

But whether Fonseca or Torres constituted their executive arm, the monarchs were determined to impose their own conditions on Columbus. The colony had to be constructed as a collaboration between soldiers and workers, and the Crown wanted to be able to say who these should be and how many there should be. As for policy toward the indigenous people, that was to be characterized by conversion: natives were to be made to serve the Crown peacefully "in benign subjection . . . so that they could be converted to our Holy Catholic faith."[22] A few monks and priests, "good people," would administer the sacrament to those who were there, as well as convert the Indians to Christianity, and would take with them what was needed for the administration of the religion.[23] By a special decree, many criminals could take part in the new colonial experience. But murderers, counterfeiters, arsonists, "sodomists" (any kind of homosexual), traitors, heretics, and anyone who had illegally exported money from Castile were excluded from such possibilities.

Other decrees followed throughout the summer of 1497, sometimes emanating from the castle at Medina del Campo, sometimes from the monastery of La Mejorada, sometimes directed at Columbus, sometimes at Torres. Reading the texts, we get a sense of the outlines of an imperial policy being painfully worked out by monarchs feeling their way in quite new circumstances. Of course, the reconquest of Spain from Islam and the conquest of the Canary Islands were precedents of a sort, but not entirely so. Soon, Fonseca would return to direct the affairs of the Indies, for Torres imposed so many conditions for his collaboration that the monarchs became annoyed.[24] But that did not stanch the flow of decrees.

In one of these, the Crown went back on its general permission to Castilians to equip expeditions for the New World and once again accepted Columbus's monopoly. But Columbus himself had also changed his mind on this score: "It seems to me," he wrote, "that permission ought to be given to all who want to go." Perhaps this opinion derived from his realization that he was losing money from his insistence on monopoly, recalling that he could have an eighth share of every cargo shipped on vessels not his own to the New World.[25] The consequence seems to have been that, in the next few years, many captains received permissions, some perhaps finding new territories without leaving a record.[26]

More significant perhaps, on July 22, 1497, Columbus was given the authority to distribute land in La Española, provided that the new proprietors committed themselves to four years' work on the property concerned, growing wheat, cotton, or flax, or building sugar or other mills. All metal-producing estates and those that could produce brazilwood would be reserved to the Crown, and everywhere else, if not fenced, would be looked on as common land.[27] That in theory meant that Columbus would be able to create something like a landed oligarchy.[28] Columbus was also asked to found a new town in La Española near the gold mines.[29]

The Admiral's third journey continued to be delayed. He spent much of the summer of 1497 at La Mejorada, the Catholic Kings' favorite Jeronymite monastery, near Medina del Campo. Fernando and Isabel were also there for a spell in July.[30] We may imagine that they sometimes met in the vast courtyard or the cloisters. Columbus wrote a brief to support his masters in a protest that they were planning against any breach of the Treaty of Tordesillas. The document talks of how he "had gone to the said islands and mainland of India,"[31] and how he had had to put into Lisbon at the end of his (first) voyage. Then without success King João of Portugal, having been informed of the journey, sent his own fleet to those same lands with the help of Portuguese sailors who had been with the Admiral.[32] But it did not seem to have reached the Caribbean.

The Admiral also wrote an interesting summary of the events leading up to Tordesillas. It pointed out that since the world was round, there was still a doubt about what would happen in the East. Where in the Far East (it was not so called at that time) was the dividing line between the Portuguese and Spanish zones?[33] Surely that matter was one that should be resolved as soon as possible.

That summer, incidentally, the dominions of Spain were expanded in a new way—not in the "Indies" but in Africa, for this was the year when Pedro de Estopiñan, a captain in the household of the Duke of Medina Sidonia, besieged and occupied the Moroccan port of Melilla, which was near Tafilat, a hub of the gold exchange between the coast and the Sahara.[34] The monarchs were also busy with the creation of a new currency and the coordination of the monetary situation in Castile, which had been untidy since the reign of Enrique IV.[35]

Columbus was at Seville in the winter of 1497–98, obviously supposing that he would soon be off to his Indies. His son Fernando later wrote that the delays were the clear responsibility of Fonseca, who hoped to prevent the proud, unpredictable Admiral from ever returning to La Española.[36] The ships earmarked for him had even been used by Pedro de Estopiñán. Later, the Admiral would say that he undertook his third voyage in order to provide some alleviation to the Queen for her sorrow at the death of the Infante, a claim more loyal than exact.[37]

That winter Columbus seems to have written down his ideas about the size of the earth for the first time; he thought that the circumference was 4,000 miles, "as confirmed" by José Viziñho, the Portuguese cosmographer. (It is 25,000 miles at the Equator.)[38] Columbus was still determined to prove that he had reached Asia, recalling again and again Pierre d'Ailly's statement in *Ymago Mundi* (which he attributed to Aristotle) that "the sea is small between the western part of Spain and the eastern part of India and is navigable in very few days."[39] That must have proved his point.

But Columbus's protractions continued: in January 1498, his friend Pedro Fernández Coronel, who had been constable (*alguacil mayor*) on the second voyage, set off for La Española with two supply ships. They included the *Vaquina,* of which "half belonged to your Highnesses and the other half to a widow in Palos."[40] It was understood that this flotilla was an advance guard for Columbus himself. But still the Admiral tarried, not yet having found the backing that he required and having had personal matters to attend to. Thus, in February he drew up an entail (*mayorazgo*) for his estate, presumably a sign of continuing royal favor.[41] His titles were to go first to his son Diego, and if Diego had no heirs, to his son Fernando. His brothers Bartolomeo and Diego would be the residual beneficiaries.

In this document, Columbus spoke warmly of Genoa as "a noble and powerful city on the sea."[42] He also compared himself to the Admiral of Castile.[43] He "recalled" that it was the Holy Trinity "which put into my mind the thought, which later became perfect knowledge, that I could sail from Spain to the Indies by crossing the Ocean sea to the west." He insisted that he had been granted 25 percent of the yield of the New World (the Crown never had conceded more than a tenth of their royal fifth). Columbus also spoke of his share of the Indies as beginning a hundred leagues to the west of the

Cape Verde Islands. He wrote as if he had never heard of the treaty of Tordesillas.[44]

On April 29, 1498, Columbus was finally able to write to his son Diego,
saying goodbye, ending: "Your father loves you as much as he does himself."[45] On May 12, having slipped down the River Guadalquivir with five
ships, and being already at Sanlúcar de Barrameda, he wrote to his new confidant, Fray Gaspar Gorricio, to say that he had loaded his cargo but so many
people wanted to travel with him that he needed another vessel; hence his
further delay.[46] (Fray Gaspar was a Carthusian from Novara, near Milan, and
was then at the monastery of Las Cuevas, just outside Seville.) On May 28
the Admiral wrote again to Gorricio saying that he had bought an extra ship
in Palos but he still could not leave, since the French were known to be raiding on the high seas and had even seized a Spanish ship full of wheat destined for the Indies.[47]

Finally, he left Sanlúcar de Barrameda, sailing, he said, in the name of
the Holy Trinity, on May 30, 1498, with five caravels—the *Castilla,* the
Rábida, the *Gorda,* the *Garza,* and the *Santa María de Guía,* all of which had
been built in Palos.[48] These ships carried over two hundred men, including
eight men-at-arms, forty-seven crossbowmen, and sixty sailors. There were
also twenty civil servants, ten gardeners, thirty gold-panners, and, in the
end, about twenty women (at least two of whom were Gypsies). Another
fifty agricultural laborers, a few priests, and some other specialists made up
the numbers. Columbus had had all his old rights confirmed. He would be
allowed to divide the land among his followers. Native rights were this time
not mentioned.

This "third voyage" was financed largely by the Genoese bankers the
Centurione, Columbus's old employers in the 1470s and a family ever more
important in Seville. Another Genoese associate, Bernardo Grimaldi,
helped. Columbus's voyages would never have occurred had it not been for
the backing of these imaginative and independent-minded Genoese, who
have never received the credit they deserve.[49]

Columbus and the Crown still had divergent views of the purpose of
colonization in the Caribbean. To Columbus's mind, the ideal was still that
La Española would become a trading colony in which, though there would
eventually be Castilian crops to feed the colonists, the main task would be
the procurement of primary goods such as gold, cotton, dyestuffs, spices,
and slaves. But the monarchs, commending this new voyage to, for example,
the cities of Spain, spoke of colonizing the island of La Española and the
other islands "which are in the said Indies, because thereby Our Lord God is

King Fernando and Queen Isabel pray, attended by the royal children,
Juan and Juana. St. Thomas Aquinas and St. Dominic hover in the wings.

Fernando the Catholic, King of Aragon.
Macchiavelli considered him the cleverest
monarch of the age.

Isabel the Catholic, Queen of Castile.
"Her will was of iron."

Fernando preferred Italy
to the New World after 1492.

An older Queen Isabel. Public triumphs
were spoiled by private tragedies.

The second wife: After Queen Isabel's death, King
Fernando married again. Germaine de Foix, thirty
years his junior, failed to give him an heir.

The Infante Juan, "the prince
who died of love."

Philip the Fair. The infidelities of this heir of the Habsburgs were as extensive as his realms.

Juana "la loca" (the mad), who was unhappy as a princess, queen, and prisoner; but her son founded a dynasty.

Above Margaret, the talented archduchess. Married when young to the King of France, then to the heir of Spain, then to the Duke of Savoy, she became governess-general of the Netherlands and brought up her nephew, Charles V.

Top left The banker Jacob Fugger, the richest man of the century, financed the election of Charles to become Holy Roman Emperor, and never allowed that to be forgotten.

Left The new king, crowned Charles I of Spain in 1516, when aged seventeen, became Holy Roman Emperor Charles V at nineteen.

King Fernando met his son-in-law Philip the Fair in 1506 at Remesal, a tiny place in northwest Castile.

A bullfight at Benavente offered in honor of Philip the Fair.

Cardinal Cisneros led Spanish troops to capture Oran in 1509.

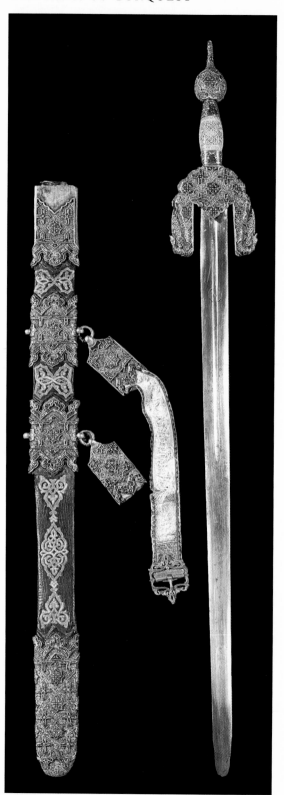

The Spaniards took over their enemies' weapons: This is a sword for horsemen, perhaps Muslim in origin.

A crossbow, as effective in the sixteenth century as it had been in the Middle Ages.

The pike was still in use during the Renaissance.

Right Victors: Cardinal Mendoza, Queen Isabel, and King Fernando enter Granada.

Bottom left Fadrique, Duke of Alba, King Fernando's most reliable friend.

Bottom right Íñigo López de Mendoza, poet, statesman, and grandfather of the Castilian aristocracy.

Our Lady protects Granada, about 1498. The city would soon be changed
by the appearance of new churches.

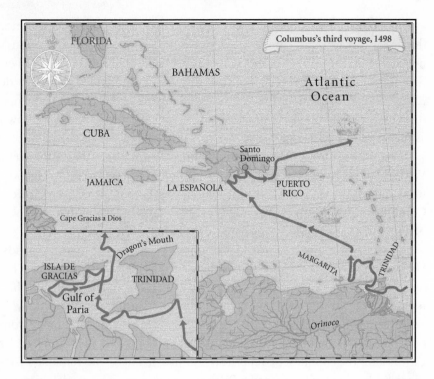

served, His Holy Faith extended, and our own realms increased."[50] They still wanted Columbus to share out La Española among the settlers, much as the Canaries had been distributed. They also seem to have wanted in the Indies a new agriculture in the style of the Canaries (with sugarcane), and they wanted to obtain the precious metals and the brazilwood (for dyes).

As for the Indians, Columbus was told to

> try, with all diligence, to inspire and draw the Indians into the paths of peace and tranquillity, and impress on them that they have to serve and live beneath our lordship in benign subjection and, above all, that they may be converted to our Holy Faith and that to them and to those who go and live in the Indies be administered the holy sacraments by the clerks and friars who are or shall be there.[51]

There was nothing in these instructions that talked of discovery of other lands, though it soon became obvious that that was what Columbus himself now had in mind.

The Admiral divided his men into two flotillas of three ships each. One would be led by his friend Alonso Sánchez de Carvajal, who had once been a *regidor* (council member) of Baeza and who had already done many minor things for the Admiral. One of his ships would be captained by Columbus's nephew Juan Antonio Colombo, who was probably an illegitimate son of either Bartolomeo or Diego.[52] Another ship was commanded by Pedro de Araña, a cousin of Beatriz, the Admiral's old mistress in Córdoba. These first three ships would go direct to La Española via what would soon be known as the Dominican Passage.

The other ships, under Columbus himself, would go first to the Cape Verde Islands and from there across the Atlantic to approach La Española from the south. He had with him his old companion Alonso de Hojeda. Columbus's aim was to explore the veracity of tales in Lisbon that there was between the Indies and Europe a new continent "in the south."[53]

On the way to the New World, Columbus visited all the Atlantic islands. He was in the Azores on June 7. Then he visited Madeira, where his wife, Felipa, had long ago died giving birth to his youngest son, Diego. He also had memories of working there selling sugar for the same Centuriones who were now financing him. Next he sailed to the Canaries, also known to him from other journeys. By that time the entire archipelago had been annexed by Castile after the conquest of Tenerife by Alonso de Lugo, who remained governor both of Tenerife and of La Palma. Lugo was not an especial friend of Columbus, even if he was already being accused of favoring the Genoese and Portuguese instead of his fellow Castilians. The fact is that those Genoese had the capital that the Canaries needed. Portuguese laborers and farmers were also made welcome, especially if they had experience of sugar manufacture in Madeira. But the Genoese were as ever prominent as entrepreneurs.[54] The local people, the Guanches, soon vanish from history, but slaves from there must have had descendants in Spain.

Finally, Columbus made for the Cape Verde Islands, where he arrived at Fogo on July 1. There were there about fifty settlers, mostly criminals. The Portuguese Governor, Álvaro da Caminha, was busy buying and selling slaves from nearby Africa, copper objects, and sugar. He also had with him at that time two thousand Jewish boys and girls who had been separated from their parents in Lisbon after King Manuel had introduced laws expelling the Jews the previous year, at the time of his wedding to the princess Isabel of Spain. The parents of these children had not had enough money to pay the fine necessary to ensure their continued residence in Portugal. The scene in Fogo must have been colorful: impoverished lepers seeking turtles' blood, mingling with optimistic gatherers of orchil for dyes. On the island of Boa Vista there were wild goats. The Admiral had been there in the 1480s but this time thought that these islands were "so dry that I saw nothing green."

But he was impressed that the worst African slave could be sold for 8,000 maravedís.[55] That perhaps influenced him to buy some slaves himself.

On July 5, 1498, Columbus set off westward. The ships hit the doldrums, met terrible heat in a calm that rotted some of the supplies, and then, on July 31, reached an uncharted island that the Admiral named Trinidad (he saw three hills there and, anyway, he had dedicated this journey to the Trinity). Columbus first anchored off the east end of the island (Punta Galeta) and took on water. A canoe with twenty-four men on board appeared, "armed with bows and arrows and wooden shields, the people being fairer than other natives that I had seen," the Admiral commented with his usual enthusiasm. They wore what seemed to be Moorish headdresses. Columbus tried to attract them by shining swords or even saucepans at them, but they were even less attracted by Juan de Guadalajara, who played a tambourine and whose charming music (to which some of the Spaniards danced) led them to begin shooting arrows. Columbus ordered crossbows to be fired. The natives rowed away.[56]

The Admiral next sailed south to a cape that he named the Puente de Arenal, which must have been close to the present-day Punta Araguapiche. There he saw the colossal outflow of the Orinoco, by far the largest river the Europeans had yet seen in the New World. This suggested that they must be off some kind of mainland, a judgment confirmed by the sight of a volcanic wave that the Admiral feared might sink his ship.

In 1513, in the here often-cited inquiry in Seville into Columbus's activities, witnesses were asked whether they thought that when the Admiral said he had discovered Paria on the hinge of Venezuela, he had only touched the island of Trinidad. Alonso de Hojeda said that the Admiral had sailed to the south, expecting to find islands about which he had been told by Indians, and that he had passed between Trinidad and the mainland through a strait that was soon named "the Dragon's Mouth," at the end of the Gulf of Paria. Then Pedro de Ledesma, a pilot in 1498, testified (in 1513) that Columbus did not discover any land that could be called Asia but instead saw (and did not land on) the island of Margarita before turning north for La Española.

In fact, the fleet anchored off what was undoubtedly South America, and Pedro Romero de Torreros took possession of the territory in the name of the Catholic Kings.[57] Hernando Pacheco, a Sevillano, who was fifteen at the time, had been among those who had leapt onto the land and helped to raise a cross, at which the natives marveled: "The Admiral asked the pilots where they thought they were, and some said that they thought that they were in the sea of Spain, others in the sea of Scotland." But the sailors added that "it must have been the devil who had persuaded them to sail with the

Admiral."[58] Hojeda said that "he saw cats in Paria and footprints as big as those of a mare and also goats and pigs."[59] Some of the Spaniards found the trees were "as lovely as the orchards of Venice in April."

The people whom Columbus met were friendly, wearing "pearls around their arms and gold around their necks. We went to see them in a very large house with a double-pitched roof. We drank some of their intoxicating beer." Some of it had obviously been made from maize, of which crop Columbus had already brought some back from the Caribbean, so that there was now "much in Castile."

This discovery of alcohol—of which there was none in La Española or Cuba—was almost as interesting as that of the gold.[60]

The Spaniards were given two dinners on shore, one by a father, one by his son. They were told that both gold and pearls came from islands farther to the west. But they were advised not to go there, since the people were cannibals. This was when the Admiral decided that the earth was not round "but shaped like a pear which is round everywhere except at the stalk, where it juts out a long way; and that, though it is generally round, there is a part of it on which there was something like a nipple." That protuberance, he thought, lay below the Equator and in the Atlantic Ocean, "at the farthest point to the east." (It may be recalled that the sphericity of the earth was first conceived of by Anaximander in the sixth century B.C.)

The Admiral and his companions considered that the mouths of the River Orinoco were, like those of Paradise, four in number. It had been assumed during the Middle Ages that East Asia did harbor the Garden of Eden. Columbus was sure that the Orinoco was one of these four rivers and that he had found the original site of the terrestrial Elysium, "which none can enter, save with God's leave. . . . It lies at the summit of what I have described as the stalk of a pear, and . . . by gradually approaching it, one begins . . . to climb. . . . I do not believe that anyone can ascend to the top. . . . If this river does not flow out of the earthly paradise, the marvel is still greater, for I do not believe that there is so great and deep a river anywhere."[61]

All the people whom Columbus met at this time, both in Trinidad and on the mainland, were part of what is now known to anthropologists as "the Caribbean family of tribes." They were sophisticated, for they depended on an advanced type of horticulture. Bitter manioc was the staple product, and the coca tree was the most prized of those cultivated, being grown for its leaves. Another tree was produced for resin. Maize, sweet manioc, sweet potatoes, calabashes, chili peppers, pineapples, and guava were also grown extensively. These people had a regular system of canals and ditches, even though their fields were customarily abandoned after being used for two years. Many wild fruits were also gathered. Deer, porcupines, rabbits, squirrels, tapirs, rats, and tortoises were killed for food, as were many birds (quail, doves, ducks, partridges), the main weapon being a longbow with arrows tempered by cane. Hunters used both nets and fire. There seem to have been turkeys. A kind of palm wine was made, as well as maize beer. It is hard to believe that reckoned by diet their standard of living was below that of Europe.

As a rule, villages consisted of about two hundred large round houses shaped like tents and with roofs of bark, palm leaves, reeds, or straw. They were usually arranged around a central square. *Caciques* might control a large collection of buildings, including room to accommodate a substantial harem, as was the case of the *cacique* Guaramental on the River Urare. Inside the houses in this territory, hammocks would be found for sleeping, and sometimes at night fires were lit underneath them to keep off mosquitoes. Many houses boasted carved ebony stools.

Men wore decorative cottons around their private parts, sometimes a cotton loincloth that stretched to their knees, sometimes aprons, and women wore the latter also. Often women tied tight plates around their breasts. Both sexes might wear strings of teeth or claws of animals that they had killed or other necklaces, anklets, bracelets, earrings, pearls, coral beads, and flowers. Both men and women painted their bodies and sometimes covered themselves with resin, to which they attached feathers.

Like the Tainos, all the peoples of the northern shores of South America used canoes, which they paddled dexterously.

The customs of these Indians were unexpected. Homosexuality was accepted, widows were inherited by the dead man's brother, and women harvested, spun, and made pottery. But they also went to war and apparently managed bows and arrows expertly. Old men were respected. *Caciques* were sometimes hereditary, sometimes elected. Justice was usually placed in the hands of the injured person. Unlike what obtained in the Caribbean, slavery was usual, while war was ceremonially announced. Drunkenness was permitted in wild bouts, tobacco was smoked, drums as well as flutes and rattles were used at dances, while the year was divided into lunar months.[62]

Columbus sailed along the territories where these peoples lived as far as the island to which he gave the name of Margarita, for there he found pearls. A little later he wrote that this was "another world" (*otro mundo*). So it was, but he never realized or could accept that it was a new continent, something utterly new to his experience.[63]

This discovery of pearls was the most important consequence of this third voyage of Columbus. It changed the judgment of people at home in respect to the financial promise of the New World and led to great interest in it in the next few years, something that Columbus could not control.[64] Columbus's landfall of August 1, 1498, on the south of the peninsula of Paria, marked the discovery of South America, however much others have sought to disprove both the landing and its significance, which (it is true) Columbus did not himself appreciate. He wrote on August 13, 1498: "I believe that this land is a large mainland [*tierra firme, grandísima*] which, up till now, no one knew existed."[65] Yet the Admiral still thought that he was in the East.

A few days later he turned north to La Española, since his eyes were suffering from a disease that he had apparently caught in Cuba some years before and that had revived. This voyage alone was a remarkable feat of seamanship, for no European had ever before sailed north across the Caribbean.

Arriving in Santo Domingo on August 31, 1498, Columbus found that, while the ships that he had sent with Hernández Coronel in January had reached the colony, and while the criminals on the first of these were already at work in the gold mines at the center of the island, the other ships, those of Sánchez de Carvajal, had only attained Jaragua, to the west of the island, and with their cargoes ruined. There they had become engaged in an intractable quarrel that had arisen in relation to Bartolomeo Colón, in his brother's absence.

The high point of Bartolomeo's stewardship of La Española had been in 1497, when he agreed to give freeholds (and the services of Indians in the places concerned) by a division of land to the conquistadors. In order to exploit the new goldfields on the island, Bartolomeo established a new town, Bonao, a hispanization of an indigenous word. With royal permission (and Columbus's backing, by letter)[66] he then began to build the city of Santo Domingo on fertile land on the southern shore of La Española as an alternative capital and center of administration in place of La Isabela.[67] Most of the Spaniards who had remained in Isabela moved south to this new city, which began to be constructed in the traditional shape of a gridiron. There was to be a church, a town hall, the Governor's Palace, and a prison, all facing a central square. The men charged to direct this new attempt at "populating" a territory were a Basque, Francisco de Garay, who had been a notary, and Miguel Díaz de Aux, the Aragonese who had come out with Bartolomeo.

But this change provoked a rebellion headed by the chief magistrate of Isabela's, Francisco Roldán, an Andalusian from Jaén (Torre de Donjimeno) who, apparently angry that his own new city would lose importance, denounced Bartolomeo as "a hard, sharp man, as cruel as he was greedy."[68]

The real cause of this rebellion remains mysterious. Roldán had been a favorite of the Admiral's, but overnight he became for him, as well as for his brother, an ingrate.[69] What was the source of Roldán's resentment? Had Bartolomeo perhaps gone too far in reproving Roldán for seducing the wife of the *cacique* Guarionex? Or had he otherwise stood in the way of an *affaire de coeur*?[70] Roldán later said that Bartolomeo had governed with "such rigor" that "he put the people in such fear as caused him to forfeit all their love." It seems probable that he was simply hostile to the superior power that Bartolomeo did not hesitate to use over him.

At all events, this protest occurred when Bartolomeo was in the west of the island, near Jaragua, having left Roldán as his lieutenant, under the authority of his brother Diego. Roldán decided that he wanted to send a ship back to Spain for reinforcements. Diego refused the idea, citing the lack of equipment. Roldán accused Diego and Bartolomeo of limiting his freedom to act and of employing Indians as they wished. Then, when Bartolomeo returned, he imprisoned Barahona, a friend of Roldán's, for no good reason.

Seventy or a hundred joined the rebellion.[71] Roldán disputed with the Columbus brothers the best use of land and the exploitation of the inhabitants. He seems also to have opposed the idea of exacting tribute from the Indians. Instead of building fortresses, Roldán appears to have thought that it was desirable to seek to work with the natives. Perhaps left to himself he could have become a benign influence.

Diego Colón sent Roldán with forty men to pacify the Indians near Concepción. Roldán thought that he could make that phantom town his own headquarters and take over the island. But the commander of the fort there, a venerable Catalan, Miguel Ballester, from Tarragona, remained loyal to the Columbuses and told Bartolomeo what was afoot. Bartolomeo went to Concepción, where Roldán confronted him and demanded that he allow the caravel to return home. Bartolomeo said that Roldán knew nothing of ships, nor did his men. Roldán refused to settle their differences and refused, too, to resign as chief magistrate.[72]

He then went to Isabela where, finding that indeed he could not launch the ship, he plundered the arsenal and storehouse, and then set off for Jaragua, in the west, which he knew was in the "pleasantest and most fertile part of the island and with the most civilized natives, as well as the best-looking and best-natured women."[73] As he journeyed, he released Indians whom he met from the tributes that they had assumed in their relation with Bartolomeo.

Eventually, Bartolomeo allowed these Spanish rebels—with their Indian servants and mistresses—to live virtually independently at Jaragua. Roldán secured that "his" Indians paid no tribute to Bartolomeo. Here we see the beginning of a tragedy, for the abolition of these tributes in food combined with the disruption of traditional supplies soon led to famine in the colony.

Roldán, in his part of the island, also took an important step in establishing a division of land, giving both Indians and property to his followers. But the decision to do this was taken without viceregal, much less royal, consent. Roldán as chief magistrate acted as the controller of his own territory, while he allowed it to be understood that the holdings he allocated would be hereditary.[74]

Freed of these difficult colleagues, Bartolomeo busied himself with completing a line of seven forts between the north and the south coast of the island, and he then moved west, looking for brazilwood. He was well received by the *cacique* Behechio, with Anacoana, the widow of the unfortunate Caonabó. Behechio offered the Spaniards cotton and cassava bread. But some other Indian leaders (such as Guarionex and Mayobenix) were seized, and the former was held as a slave until he could be shipped to Spain. That was a mistake, since the amount of tribute naturally fell even more sharply once there were no *caciques* to deliver it.

Bartolomeo succeeded in establishing Santo Domingo, on the south coast, as an administrative capital, beginning what would become an efficient shipyard, and also a store of food. His chain of fortresses, each manned by about ten Spaniards with a specially appointed commander (*alcaide*) and under the overall control of the *adelantado* himself, was intended as the guarantee for the tribute.[75]

On his return to La Española for the third time, Columbus assumed that power had reverted to him, and he proceeded to try to deal with Roldán. He compromised. He and his brothers had too few trustworthy followers to do anything else. He issued a decree on September 12 promising food and free passage home to all who desired it.[76] Then Miguel Ballester reported from Concepción that Roldán and two rebel leaders (Pedro de Riquelme and Adrián de Mújica) were in the neighborhood. Columbus tried to persuade them to make their peace with him, offering them free travel home if they so wished. He also sought to capture Roldán. But his plan did not work. Roldán had most of the arms in the colony, and his strength had been reinforced by recent arrivals. He said that he would only negotiate with Hernández de Carvajal, whom he knew. That approach merely caused the Columbuses to suspect Carvajal, who, like Ballester, now saw no way out other than to treat with the rebels.

Two months after Columbus's return, a new flotilla of five caravels went home to Castile from Santo Domingo. To the Admiral's surprise, three hundred Spaniards took advantage of his offer to go home. Columbus permitted each of them to take back one Indian slave, and some other slaves were also sent. The Queen was not pleased when she heard of this concession: "What power of mine does the Admiral hold to give my vassals to anyone?" she demanded, asking that all the Indian slaves be freed.[77] For the issue of the legality of enslavement had still not been decided. The learned men allegedly asked to pronounce on the matter had not reported.

The returning colonists also took with them letters from Columbus to the monarchs in Spain in which he suggested that 20 million maravedís a year could be obtained in La Española merely by cutting brazilwood. A large-scale trade in Indian slaves should also be profitable. All Europe, he pointed out, was longing for slaves of one sort or another, and though many West Indian slaves had died in Spain, a similar mortality had been noticed, to begin with, in respect of Berbers and blacks from Africa and Canary Islanders. Four thousand slaves could probably be sent home a year.[78] They could be sold at 1,500 maravedís each. Columbus boasted that in his colony "there is no lack of anything except for wine and settlers."[79]

The Admiral added that

> our people here are such that there is neither a good man nor a bad one who has not two or three Indians to serve him, and dogs to hunt for him and, though it were perhaps better not to mention it, women so pretty that one must wonder at it. With the last of these matters . . . I am extremely discontented, but I can do nothing about it, nor the habit of eating meat on Saturday [*sic;* presumably Friday] and other wicked practices that are not good for Christians.[80]

Columbus suggested to the Crown the dispatch of friars to "reform the faith in us Christians" and afterwards to convert the Indians. He wanted fifty good men in every new fleet; he would send back in exchange fifty idle and insubordinate ones.[81] As a "poor foreigner," he also suggested that a *letrado* should be sent, "a person experienced in matters of law" (*persona experimentada para la justicia*), though whether he thought that this person would assist or replace him was unclear.[82]

In the meantime, Hernández de Carvajal was negotiating successfully with Roldán. He had at one point almost persuaded that adventurer to meet with the Columbus brothers. But Roldán's friends prevented that, and the war of words between them continued. In his new improbable role as the champion of the Indians, Roldán said that Columbus had to release all the Indians whom he had captured. He also wrote to Archbishop Cisneros on

October 10, 1498, to accuse the Admiral of wanting to hand over La Española to the Genoese.[83] A week later he and his friends sent Columbus a letter blaming Bartolomeo for their actions and asking to be allowed to establish an independent principality.[84] Columbus wrote back avoiding the last idea but representing himself as tolerance personified, saying that "anyone can come to me and say exactly what they like."[85]

Eventually, Roldán did meet Columbus after he had secured a safe conduct and, a few weeks later, sent a list of articles of agreement between them. Columbus published an amnesty on the doors of the church at Concepción and gave a safe conduct to all who wanted to go back to Castile. In return for Roldán's renewed, if purely formal, allegiance to Columbus as the Crown's representative, it was agreed that he and his friends, the ex-rebels, should be able to settle virtually where they wished. Most of them established themselves in the center of the island, though Roldán himself, named chief magistrate of the whole colony, remained in the west, at Jaragua.

Almost without being noticed, a new form of land grant was agreed in the wake of Roldán's rebellion: a given *cacique* and his people would be asked to serve a specific conquistador. The grant of men would be called an *encomienda*, as had existed in a different form in old Spain during the reconquest of the land from the Moors. (The difference was that, in medieval Spain, local people were not given away; nor was there any obligation in old Spain for the landowner to provide for the conquered people's religious instruction.)[86] Most of the surviving Indians in the conquered areas would be included in the system. Roldán, it might be said, thus submitted to Columbus on the understanding that he and his friends would receive not only land but also the services of the Indians working on it.[87]

But Columbus did not have much time to enjoy the relative peace that he and his friend Sánchez de Carvajal had with such difficulty achieved. New rebellions against him by Spanish settlers broke out. Then, on March 21, 1499, Francisco de Bobadilla, member of the Order of Calatrava, chamberlain of the Catholic Kings, brother of the Queen's best friend Beatriz, and for a time *mayor* of the new city of Santa Fe, was named to discover who had risen against the Crown in La Española and to proceed against that individual and others responsible. Columbus himself had, after all, asked for someone knowledgeable of the law, a *letrado*, to be sent to the Indies. Francisco de Bobadilla was that man.[88]

Book Three

❧❧❧

BOBADILLA AND OVANDO

Philip the Fair greets his bride,
Princess Juana, upon her arrival in Flanders in 1498.

14

"To course o'er better waters . . ."

To course o'er better waters now hoists sail the little bark of my wit, leaving behind a sea so cruel.

Dante, PURGATORIO, I, *recalled by Vespucci, 1499, when off Guiana*

Francisco de Bobadilla was an experienced public servant. His connections were excellent. He had been an effective leader in the war against Granada and then mayor of Santa Fe at the moment of the surrender of the Moorish city. His father and grandfather had both served kings of Castile.[1] He himself had held numerous public appointments. His nomination to the Indies, therefore, seemed appropriate. To the court it was an indication that the new conquests were to be seen like the old ones. To the friends of Columbus the nomination must have appeared to be a confirmation of the importance of the Admiral's achievements.[2]

The terms of Bobadilla's appointment did not suggest anything untoward. The royal text read:

Know that Don Cristóbal Colón, our Admiral of the Ocean Sea, has sent us a report that, while he was absent from the said islands in our court, a number of people who were there, among them a magistrate [Roldán], rose in the said islands against the said Admiral and against the justices who, in our name, have appointments in them, and notwithstanding that they were asked to desist, they did not do so, but rather did they continue the said rebellion and go about the island robbing and doing other damage and carrying out crimes to the disservice of God Our Lord, giving a bad example and being worthy of blame and punishment. . . . In consequence, we command you to go to the said islands and the said mainland of the Indies [*sic*], and you will find out who the people were who rose against the Admiral and our magistrates, and you should seize them and confiscate their goods, and when they have been made prisoners, you should proceed against them.[3]

That should have seemed clear enough. Columbus, it is true, was not referred to as Viceroy or as Governor, just as Admiral; but the decree accepted
that what he had discovered was the "Indies," and the term continued to be
used both officially and unofficially. Nor did there seem any doubt in the
mind of the Crown that the criminals were Roldán and his friends, not Bartolomeo Colón and his.

But later documents altered Bobadilla's orders. For example, on May 21,
1499, a new instruction was issued that did not mention Columbus but
merely stated that Bobadilla would henceforth direct the government of the
New World. All fortresses, arms, horses, ships, and even houses were to be
made over to the new Governor.[4] A letter of May 26, 1499, from the Catholic
Kings told Columbus that Bobadilla had instructions from them to which
they asked him to listen.[5]

Thus the age of Columbus in La Española was over. Martyr thought that
the monarchs, wearied by so many complaints and because so little gold had
hitherto been found, had decided to name someone new as governor to establish order.[6] Perhaps the fact that Columbus continued to send back slaves
against the Queen's wishes was a reason for his replacement;[7] five ships
bringing another installment of six hundred slaves reached Seville that same
May.[8] Part of the explanation may be that a wave of xenophobia was sweeping through the court, and most evils were blamed on foreigners.[9] This
mood had a special effect in the Canaries, where it was laid down that no
foreigner should be able to own property worth more than 500,000 maravedís.[10] (The Genoese negotiated a compromise excluding them from this
rule, but they continued to feel threatened.) Father Bernáldez reported rumors (in Seville) that Columbus was keeping for himself all the gold that he
found, and repeated the story that he was thinking of giving away the island
of La Española to his fellow Genoese.[11]

There was, however, an interminable delay between the issue of instructions to Bobadilla and his departure from Spain. In part, that was because
the ever more powerful Archbishop of Toledo, Jiménez de Cisneros, still the
Queen's confessor, wanted to ensure the evangelical role of Spain in the Indies. With that in mind, he sought friars who would accompany Bobadilla
and, in the end, arranged the passage of one Benedictine (Fray Alonso de
Viso) and five Franciscans.[12] The mission of these men would be to convert
the infidels and to build churches, but they were also to work as officials for
Bobadilla. The most interesting of this group was "El Abulense," Fray Francisco Ruiz, future bishop of Ávila, then aged about twenty-three; he was the
son of a seller of olive oil in Toledo and had first been a chorister in that city,
then Cisneros's secretary, and a professor at the Franciscan convent at Al-

calá. On Cisneros's recommendation he was asked by Queen Isabel to find out what was really happening in the New World under Columbus.[13]

Another reason for the delay of Bobadilla in Seville was that the King was busy in the mountains south of Granada, the Alpujarras, directing operations against Moorish rebels—Muslims who were refusing to accept the choice offered to them either to convert to Christianity or to leave the country. Neither Jiménez de Cisneros, who claimed to have converted no less than four thousand Moors in Granada in 1499, nor the King could have had much time to deal with Indian matters.

Cisneros was now the most influential man in the country. Martyr again commented: "This man [that is, Cisneros] is he who through his advice makes everything happen in Spain. Through his dynamism and his talent, through his gravity and his wisdom, through outdoing in holiness all the cenobites, hermits, and anchorites, he has much more prestige with the monarchs than anyone has had before. They judge it a sin to contradict his counsel, for they do not believe what he says comes from the mouth of a mere man. . . ."[14]

In addition, he seemed "to the Queen to be so wonderfully decisive in everything he did, moments of self-doubt never held him up, and he impressed all by seeming to be able easily to combine meditative spirituality with efficient modern administration, a combination of qualities that had so impressed Cardinal Mendoza when he was young." The Queen continued to rely on Cisneros for everything. His influence was to be seen in all her actions. The sixteenth-century historian Jerónimo Zurita said of him that not unnaturally he was unpopular at court—outside the circle of the monarchs—because he had a mind "that soared with great thoughts more usual for a king than for a mere friar."[15] His mass conversions were a foretaste of other such actions later carried out with equal fervor, partly in his shadow, by other Franciscans in the New World. They were certainly a contrast with medieval Castilian practice in which the three "peoples of the book" had often lived side by side in separate but neighboring districts.

Francisco de Bobadilla was still in Seville in the summer of 1500. Just before he left for Santo Domingo, the monarchs, on June 20, decided to free some of the slaves sent home by Columbus who remained alive in Spain. Bobadilla was asked to take these back to La Española.[16] A courtier, Pedro de Torres, was made responsible for delivering as many of them as he could find to the *corregidor* of El Puerto de Santa María, Gómez de Cervantes, who was organizing Bobadilla's flotilla. Torres managed to find twenty-one Indians for a return voyage. Of these, one was declared too ill to travel. Another, a girl, insisted not only that she wished to continue her education in the house of Diego de Escobar, a Sevillano who had been on Columbus's second voyage, but that when her education was finished, she wanted to remain in Spain. Perhaps she dreaded another voyage. The remaining nineteen Indians, of whom three were females, were handed over for safekeeping and safe travel to Fray Francisco Ruiz.

These twenty-one were, however, only a minority of the surviving Caribbean slaves in Spain.[17] Those left behind after the departure of Bobadilla must have numbered at least five hundred. Presumably the Queen, Cisneros, and Fonseca would have seen them as having been fairly enslaved since they were said to be (or to have been) cannibals, or at least cannibalistic, or had been captured in some good cause. There seem to have been Taino as well as Carib slaves available in Granada in 1501, put up for sale by Genoese merchants. Nor were all the Taino slaves brought back by other adventurers in the Caribbean ordered to be freed.[18]

While Bobadilla delayed, new expeditions began to set out for the New World. This was a sensational development for which the Admiral was unprepared, though he knew most of those involved. The first of these was one led by Peralonso Niño of Moguer, which left Palos for the "Pearl Coast," the north coast of South America, at the beginning of May 1499. The second was that which left Cadiz later that month, directed by Alonso de Hojeda, in the company of the Cantabrian Juan de la Cosa and a Florentine who had been living in Seville, Amerigo Vespucci. The third was that of Vicente Yáñez de Pinzón and Juan Díaz de Solís, which left Palos in November. A fourth was that of Diego de Lepe, which left Seville the following month. Then Rodrigo de Bastidas, a young *converso* merchant of Triana, having been on one of the expeditions of 1499, probably that of Hojeda, received permission to sail to the north coast of South America. Finally, in July 1500, Alonso Vélez de Mendoza was authorized to set off for what was Brazil in the Portuguese zone of the Americas. But all the commanders on these journeys had orders both to avoid territory that had already been discovered by Columbus and to take into account the Treaty of Tordesillas; so Mendoza had to return with no claims on what he had seen.

We should no doubt mention a seventh journey, a magnificent Portuguese one that left Belem, outside Lisbon, in March 1500 and, directed by Pedro Alvares Cabral, set out for the true India and, making a big curve to the west, inaugurated the Portuguese penetration of Brazil.

There does not seem to have been any difficulty in finding sailors to embark on these journeys. Men who in the past would have spent their lives waiting for some opportunity in the Canaries or in the war against the Moors were now catapulted by Columbus's deeds in the 1490s into performing acts of world significance. Thus Peralonso Niño of Moguer, who had accompanied the Admiral on his first voyage as captain of the *Santa María*, had been on the second voyage as a sailor, and had seen on the third voyage the promise of the pearls in the region of the island of Margarita. When he returned to Spain, Niño sought permission for a personal journey there, finding financial help from a financier of Triana, Luís Guerra. He set off from Palos, in one ship only, with about thirty men, in the company of Luís Guerra's younger brother Cristóbal and of Juan de Veragua, a confidant of the latter.[19]

Later, as already intimated, there was debate as to where Columbus had earlier been in this territory and whether Peralonso Niño and his comrades had a prior claim to have discovered the South American mainland. They went to many of the places where Columbus had been in 1498, but reached several hundred miles farther west. From Cubagua or Curiana on the Paraguaná peninsula, in what is now Venezuela, south of the island of Aruba, they obtained a substantial quantity of pearls. They visited a number of markets on the north coast of South America, and they also discovered that gold, from what is now Colombia, was freely traded: Peter Martyr said that Peralonso Niño later recalled that "in making their offers and their bargaining and disputing, the natives conducted their commercial affairs in just about the same way as our women when they are arguing with peddlers."[20]

Peralonso returned, accurately thinking that "this land is a continent."[21] He also came back "loaded with pearls, as other people come loaded with straw." The Spaniards traded hawks' bells, glass beads, and scarlet cloth in return for all kinds of fruit, cassava, maize, and a little gold. It was a most profitable journey. Peralonso seems to have tried to avoid paying the Crown its royal fifth by returning to Castile via Baiona, at the mouth of the Miño, in Galicia, as Martín Pinzón had done in 1493. He was accordingly arrested there by Hernando de Vega, the Viceroy, a relation by marriage of the King, who had assumed many administrative tasks in that province after the royal visit of the 1480s. Guerra, who treacherously informed the Crown officials of Peralonso Niño's hopes, brought back and sold in several cities of Andalusia a number of Indian slaves, which action the Catholic Kings as usual criticized since "they were our subjects." Once again the monarchs tried to ensure that these slaves were handed over to the next expedition that returned to La Española to be freed.[22] Meanwhile, nothing was proved in the end against Peralonso Niño, who was duly released.

· · ·

The second of these independent journeys, that of Hojeda, la Cosa, and Vespucci, was the most interesting, though it is obscure in detail. Hojeda, whom we have of course often met before, was then the best-known captain of New World voyages after Columbus himself, and though impetuous and negligent of human life, was by now experienced in dealing with the Indians of the Caribbean.[23] Juan de la Cosa, of Santoña, was also a veteran of the first and second of Columbus's voyages. On the second he had been asked by Columbus to make maps. Vespucci, on the other hand, had not been to the Indies before (though there were stories for many years—several hundred years—that he had sailed there in 1497, even that he had discovered Mexico).[24]

This Florentine was then about forty-five and had lived in Seville since 1494.[25] He and Hojeda, with Juan de la Cosa, set off in four caravels from Cadiz on May 18, 1499, and crossed the Atlantic as usual, via the Canaries.[26] It does not seem that Vespucci was a captain of any of the boats to begin with. The leaders of this expedition went to find pearls at Margarita, but they also sailed even farther west than Peralonso Niño and touched at islands that were by then called "the Frailes" and "the Gigantes," stopping at Coquibacoa (now the peninsula of Guajiro). They were thus approaching the boundary of modern Colombia and Venezuela. Hojeda later claimed that he discovered Maracaibo, the so-called gulf of Venezuela. They found gold as well as pearls.

Vespucci sent a report to his employer in Florence, Lorenzo di Pierfrancesco de' Medici, about this voyage. He seems to have become separated, however, or perhaps he broke away for a time from the main expedition, with two ships and sailed not west but south from near the island of Trinidad to the Demerara, Berbice, and other rivers of Guiana.[27] Here he found wonderfully aromatic trees and forests, as well as a freshwater lake.[28] He also saw marvelous birds and splendid trees. Just as Columbus had, he thought that he was in an earthly paradise.[29] He sailed up one of the rivers where, in comparison, "the current at Gibraltar or at Messina was a mere fish bowl." Perhaps this was the Courantyne or the Marouini. Watching the stars and trying to interpret their changed aspect, Vespucci remembered with affection the first verse of Dante's *Purgatorio*, which figures as the title of this chapter.[30]

Turning back eventually to the north, the Florentine came to Trinidad, where he found naked and beardless natives: they were cannibals. They did not eat one another, however, but went on long journeys to find appropriate victims.

> They do not eat women except for female slaves. They have bows and arrows, and are excellent archers. They took us to a town where they gave us food, more through fear than by good will, and after spending a day with them, we left. We went on and saw the Gulf of Paria and the Orinoco, where we saw what we thought was a great town and where we were received with love. There we drank a wine made from fruit, and very good it was. They gave us a few small pearls and eleven big ones.

Vespucci, like Columbus, still thought that South America must be "on the extremity of Asia" (*los confines de Asia*).[31] He wrote most enthusiastically of the women whom he encountered, a fact that helped make his letter, when published in Florence in 1502, very successful.

> Having traveled 400 leagues [he continued] we began to meet people who did not want our friendship. Indeed, they awaited us with weapons, trying to prevent us from landing, so that we had to fight them. Often it happened that sixteen of us had to fight two thousand of them. Once a Portuguese [sailor] aged fifty-five rallied us while we were running away, saying: My boys [*hijos*], show your face to our enemies so that God will give us victory.[32]

This simple reflection turned the tide, and "soon it was they who fled, and we killed 150 of them and burned 180 houses."

Shortly after this, Vespucci seems to have rejoined Hojeda and Juan de la Cosa. They sailed westward and brought back several of the emeralds for which Colombia remains famous. They landed, too, on the islands of Curaçao (where they found some exceptionally tall people) and Aruba, where there were numerous natives living in houses standing in the sea "like Venice." Hence they spoke of the mainland there as "little Venice," Venezuela. The name has survived. Only Vespucci of the captains could have been to Venice, and even that is uncertain. But Hojeda received credit for the designation.

Then they started for home, since the crews of the ships were tired of "tempting sea and fortune."[33] They returned via La Española, even though they had been told to avoid it because it was under Columbus's control. In September 1499, Hojeda landed at Yaquimo, near Jaragua, and immediately gave out that he was Fonseca's man in the Indies. On Columbus's orders,

Roldán marched against him. Yet, after some arguments, Hojeda talked that individual out of taking any action; they were, after all, old friends. But de la Cosa and Vespucci, who had seized 232 natives as slaves in various places to be sold at Cadiz, returned home via the Azores. Vespucci wrote to his Medici chief that he took thirteen months for the return journey, an estimate understandably challenged by some who insist that he was back by the end of November or early December,[34] and others who say that it must have been June.[35] The uncertainty added to the mystery of Vespucci's career, which will be discussed later. Whenever he returned, the pearls that he carried he gave to the Queen.[36] He had lost only two men (killed by the Indians) on his entire voyage.

Vespucci concluded his account to Lorenzo di Pierfrancesco de' Medici of what he had seen by saying that he hoped he would soon be able to start on another such voyage and perhaps find the island of Ceylon (Taprabana).[37] He added that he was sending a map and a globe to Tuscany with a Florentine, Francesco Lotti, who was with him in Seville. He also wrote to Lorenzo di Pierfrancesco about the recent voyage of Vasco da Gama to India, and explained that he had heard, when in the Cape Verde Islands, of that of Cabral.[38] When disembarking in Lisbon, Vespucci wrote again to Lorenzo, saying: "We arrived at a new land which, for many reasons enumerated in what follows, we observed to be a continent." The fact that he described what he had seen as a new land, not just an eastern extension of Asia, enables Vespucci to be looked upon as an innovator. Juan de la Cosa made a chart on his return that was much valued thereafter.[39]

The third voyage at this time was that of Juan Díaz de Solís, with Vicente Yáñez Pinzón and with the latter's nephew Arias. The first-named apparently came from an old but impoverished family in Asturias. He was born in Lebrija, near Sanlúcar de Barrameda, and had been in the Portuguese service. He was said to have left Lisbon to escape being charged for the murder of his wife, but that is the kind of story frequently bandied about in ports.

Yáñez Pinzón had, of course, been on Columbus's first two voyages and came from the premier maritime family of Palos.

The two captains built four caravels in the latter town and set off from there on November 18, 1499, with Pedro de Ledesma as chief pilot.[40] They sailed to the Canaries, then to the Cape Verde Islands, and finally, after being blown fast by a gale in the wrong direction, found themselves at the end of January 1500 in Brazil. They had reached the estuary of the Amazon (Cabo

San Agustín) at the extreme east of the South American continent, which they baptized Santa María de la Consolación.

There Pinzón and Solís took possession of the territory in the name of the Catholic Kings, though they must have known that it was in the Portuguese zone of influence. The natives killed eight of their number, including a pilot, and the Spaniards saw what they claimed were footsteps "twice as large as those of a medium-sized man." They believed themselves to be "at the other side of Cathay, on the coast of India, not far from the river Ganges." They found much brazilwood and cinnamon bark trees ("as efficacious for driving off fevers as the cinnamon that the apothecaries sell . . .") and trees so big that sixteen men holding hands could not encompass their trunks.[41] They named a great river the Marañón, presumably for some private reason long forgotten.[42] Surviving terrible storms, they turned north to La Española, which they eventually reached on June 23, 1500.[43] Returning to Spain three months later, they reached Palos with a cargo of twenty slaves and some logwood. The journey was important, since the collaboration between two such skillful captains was successful and would be repeated in other voyages. But they had lost many men.

The fourth journey, undertaken by Diego de Lepe, who seems to have been related to the Pinzons and to have been born in Palos, appears at first sight of less importance than those of his predecessors. Lepe left in December 1499 with two ships, went down to the Cape Verde Islands, and then sailed about 1,500 miles to the southwest, until he reached a bay in Brazil to which he gave the name of San Julián. There Lepe found no one with whom to treat or even talk. He sailed a hundred miles up an astounding river, the Amazon, the Santa María de la Mar Dulce, as he curiously named it—an achievement that should have made him famous forever. Returning to the coast, he sailed north to the River Marañón and thereafter went farther north still to Paria, where he seized some Indians whom he took home as a present for Bishop Fonseca.[44]

Rodrigo de Bastidas of Triana was twenty-five when, in 1500, he set off for South America with two ships, the caravels *Santa María de Gracía* and *San Antón*.[45] Half of his sailors were Sevillanos, half Basques. There were nineteen backers of the expedition, all Sevillanos except a certain Alfonso de Villafranca from Valladolid.[46] With him was Juan de la Cosa, who had been much the same way with Alonso de Hojeda, and an adventurer, Vasco Núñez de Balboa, who would play a great part in the future of the Spanish Empire. It is unclear where exactly they made landfall; they perhaps sailed to the island of Margarita and then the Río de la Hacha, the lovely bay that is now known as that of "Cartagena de Indias," and the Gulf of Urabá, which turned out to be a center of Indian trade. Probably Bastidas or Juan de la Cosa was responsible for the christening of Cartagena.[47] They established themselves there for a few weeks and found gold and some emeralds. They may have reached Nombre de Dios, on the isthmus of Panama, where Núñez de Balboa would later make himself the "first caudillo of the Americas."

Then, making for La Española since their ships had been damaged by termites, they were wrecked off Jaragua. Bastidas and his companions walked two hundred miles across La Española to Santo Domingo, presumably with Indian bearers carrying what treasure they had. He (and de la Cosa) returned to Spain in 1501 on the vessel *Aguja,* which survived the hurricane of 1502.[48] Though he had lost money, Bastidas dutifully gave a fifth of what he had (including emeralds, pearls, and gold) to the monarchs at Alcalá. This booty excited much attention. At last the Indies seemed to be productive. The discoveries seemed less remarkable. But Bastidas had sailed along the north coast of South America and probably discovered the isthmus of Central America. At any other time in history his account of this journey would have seemed epoch-making.[49]

The last of this series of early independent voyages was that of *comendador* Alonso Vélez de Mendoza, a hidalgo of Moguer, who left Spain on July 20, 1500. He had with him two ships, one owned by another citizen of Triana, Luis Rodríguez de la Mezquita, the other by the Ramírez family. Mendoza had to add the cost of the salary of the inspectors insisted upon by the monarchs to that of the armament of his journey. His instructions were similar to those given to Bastidas except that the lands that were forbidden to him were not only those discovered by Columbus, the King of Portugal, and Cristóbal Guerra but also those by Hojeda. The monarchs again would get a fifth part of all profits.[50] Luis Guerra accompanied Mendoza. In the event, he much extended the knowledge in Europe of the coastline of Brazil, where he made landfall near Cabo Santo Agostinho, and then perhaps reached as far south as what is now São Francisco by Christmas.[51]

The Portuguese fleet of Pedro Alvares Cabral, which sailed from Belem on March 9, 1500, had nothing directly to do with the Spanish Empire. Yet it affected it immensely. This expedition was large: thirteen vessels—the biggest

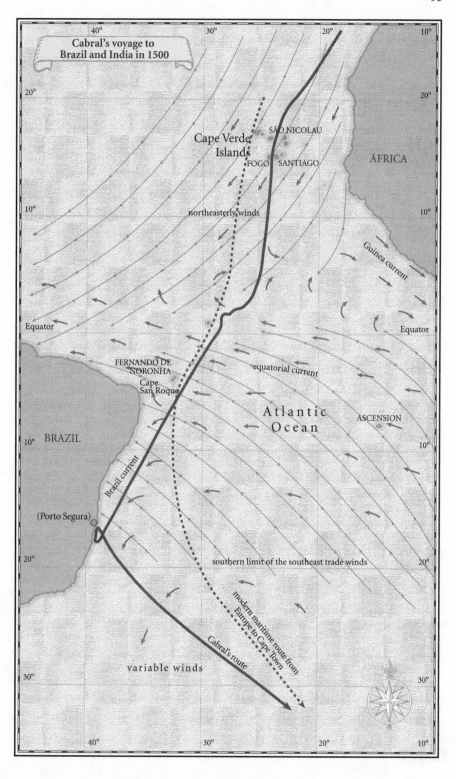

Cabral's voyage to
Brazil and India in 1500

40°   30°   20°   10°

20°   20°

Cape Verde   SÃO NICOLAU
Islands   ÁFRICA
            •FOGO   •SANTIAGO

10°   10°

            northeasterly winds   Guinea current

Equator   Equator

      FERNANDO DE
      NORONHA   equatorial current
      Cape
      San Roque
                                                    A t l a n t i c
                                                    O c e a n   •ASCENSION
10°   10°
BRAZIL

      Brazil current

(Porto Segura)

20°   southern limit of the southeast trade winds   20°

                              modern maritime route from
                              Europe to Cape Town
                    Cabral's route

      variable winds

30°   30°

40°   30°   20°   10°

that Portugal had mounted in the Atlantic. It was intended for India, following the successful journey there, two years before, of Vasco da Gama. On board these ships were 1,500 men, including Frei Henrique Suárez de Coimbra, once bishop of Ceuta, nine priests, and eight Franciscans.[52] They sailed first to the Canary Islands (on March 14)—without landing, because the Canaries were Spanish—and then to the Cape Verde Islands, which they left on March 22. They then made for India on May 2 in a broad arc, but sailing rather to the southwest instead of the southeast. On April 22 they found themselves in Brazil. Nicolás de Coelho, who had sailed with da Gama in 1498, had landed in front of a steep mountain, which they named Monte Pascual. Cabral took possession of this territory on behalf of the King of Portugal; he named it Terra Sanctae Crucis, stayed ten days, and sent a ship back to Portugal to announce the discovery. (This was the *Anunciada*, which belonged to the Florentine merchant Bartolomeo Marchionni. We note that without surprise, for at that time he had his hand in every undertaking.)[53]

In comparison with these voyages, that of Bobadilla to take over the reins of government in the only place as yet settled by Europeans in the New World, La Española, seemed a sedate operation. Yet to seize control from Columbus was something sensational. Bobadilla set off from Seville in July 1500 with four ships. On board were his priests and his freed Indian slaves. He reached Santo Domingo after about a month, on August 25, 1500, to find Diego Colón in control of the new city. The body of Adrián de Mújica hung in the breeze from a gallows on the right of the River Ozama and that of another, unnamed Spaniard hung on the left. Altogether seven Spaniards of Roldán's party had been hanged the previous week, and two more, Pedro Riquelme and Hernando de Guevara, were in the castle of Santo Domingo awaiting death. Columbus himself and his brother Bartolomeo were in the interior of the island hunting other rebels, the Admiral being in the neighborhood of Concepción, the *adelantado* in the west near Jaragua.

During the last year or so, since Columbus's return to La Española and the relative peace he had established with Roldán, he and his family had managed the colony with constant criticisms ringing in their ears when there were not actual rebellions. The difficulties with Roldán were never properly overcome. Many letters had passed between the two men, in the course of which Columbus not only accepted that fifteen of the ex-rebel's friends should be permitted to return to Castile by the next ship but also that Roldán, far from being punished, should be named magistrate of Jaragua for life. Roldán seems to have had by then the backing of about a hundred settlers, and they covered the richer, that is the western, part of the island (present-day Haiti). Columbus also agreed to Roldán's idea that the land in La Española and elsewhere should be divided among the settlers. A settler would be responsible for organizing the Indians' security and protection against Caribs, as well as for educating them in the Christian religion; in return, the *caciques* would work for him, ensuring both service and a form of tribute. The word used for these divisions of land, *repartimiento,* was well known in Old Castile. For example, the conquest of Andalusia had been characterized by that name.[54] Conversion seems to have taken second place to contumely. It is true that the Belgian Franciscan father Juan de Deule, who had sailed with Columbus in 1493, claimed that by 1500, two thousand Indians had been baptized in La Española. But that still constituted a tiny minority of the Tainos available.[55]

The Admiral had recently sent home several ships (one captained by Miguel Ballester), taking letters, slaves, and a few other products. He still hoped to develop the slave trade. He also thought in terms of making money by granting monopolies; for example, he gave permission to a Sevillano, Pedro de Salcedo, to sell soap in the island.[56]

Columbus would later insist that these years, 1498–1500, had been decisive for the development of the colony. He had completed the line of forts, begun by his brother Bartolomeo, across the island of La Española, from Isabela, in the north, to Santo Domingo, in the south. In the center of this line, at Cibao, which had been christened La Vega Real, gold was regularly obtained. Columbus had established a stud for breeding horses, cattle, and pigs; and had agreed with Roldán that two heifers and two mares, as well as twenty pigs, would be permanently retained for that purpose. Surely, he argued, these were considerable achievements? In a letter of May 1499, Columbus told the King that the failure of the colony to produce more gold had been the fault of the greed of those who had come to the Indies to try to make a quick fortune: they thought that gold and spices could be gathered by the shovelful, and they did not reflect that, though there certainly was gold, it was buried in mines.

Columbus believed that his system of government would have functioned had he not remained so long in Spain. Casting about for a scapegoat, he blamed *conversos* for subverting his authority, though nothing suggests that Roldán, Margarit, and Boil were such. Some of the royal secretaries certainly were. But they had not initiated policies against him. Columbus added that he did not have to worry too much since no one who had shown malice toward him had been left unpunished by God.[57] Then, in February 1500, the Admiral wrote to the monarchs another, more bitter letter: "It appears that my communications," he said, "do not reach your Highnesses." He talked wildly of the desirability of restoring the Temple of Jerusalem with gold from Ophir. He recalled the efforts of his backer, Fray Juan Pérez of La Rábida, by then dead, to assist the Catholic Kings not only in respect of the New World but in the conquest of Granada and the expulsion of the Jews.[58]

Any apparent neglect by the monarchs of the affairs of Columbus at this time was, in fact, natural: not only were they planning war with France in Naples, but they were still dealing with the Muslims of the old city there. There was a rebellion of Muslims not only in the Albaicín, in Granada, and in the Alpujarras (October 1500) but also in Ronda (January 1501). All were inspired by hostility to compulsory conversion. The King was busy conducting a war, which ended in 1502 with a decree by which all Muslims living in Castile were given two months to convert to Christianity, and those who refused would be sent to Africa with their goods. The Queen, on the other hand, was in Seville, but even her mind was on the Muslim rebels, not on the affairs of the Admiral in La Española.[59]

After Bobadilla landed in Santo Domingo, he and his train went directly to the house where Diego Colón was staying and presented him with his royal letter of appointment. Columbus's secretary, Diego de Alvarado, seems to have been ready alongside the commander of the fortress, Rodrigo Pérez, to fight the newcomers, but both were restrained.[60] Diego Colón abandoned the place and sent messengers for his brothers. In a ceremony on September 15, Bobadilla again presented his letters of credentials, this time to the Admiral. Numerous settlers were present. Columbus said that he had a royal letter stating the contrary to what Bobadilla's letter specified. Perhaps he thought that there would be, as so often had happened, a long debate at the end of which he would emerge victorious. But he also seems to have told Bobadilla that he considered him just one more Andalusian traveler. Whatever he said, Bobadilla immediately put him and his brothers into an improvised dungeon and had them chained. With the Columbus brothers was Miguel Díaz de Aux, the Aragonese who had become commander of the fortress of Santo Domingo.

Bobadilla then carried out an investigation of the actions of Columbus and his brothers and heard innumerable complaints.[61] Their chief offense was that they had executed Spaniards without the authority of the Council of Castile. Perhaps some of those so killed had been friends of Bobadilla. Had it not been for the loyalty to Columbus of a cook (his name was Espiñosa), life would have been hard for him. As it was, the indignity seemed outrageous, for within a few weeks, Bobadilla sent these illustrious prisoners home on the boat on which he himself had traveled to the Indies. He asked its captain, Andrés Martínez de la Gorda, to deliver the Columbus brothers still "in chains" to Bishop Fonseca.[62] They set off for Spain in October.

Bobadilla then made some more radical decisions in his colony. First, he revived the gold mining in the center of the island by permitting anyone to go there, with only a modest limitation—to pay an eleventh of what they found to the Crown. The mines of San Cristóbal were expanded, and nearly three hundred kilos of gold were found in 1501 alone.[63] Then the Governor issued a decree that stated that the Indians of La Española were free vassals of the Queen. That meant, in practice, that any conquistador could make use of any Tainos, provided that he could persuade them to work for him. The rebels who had been condemned to death by Columbus were reprieved. Roldán was dealt with harshly but with respect.

By these and other measures, the confidence of the island, which had much declined during the near–civil war between Roldán and the Columbus brothers, revived. Bobadilla was effective even if he was ruthless. The colony, for such it now clearly was, was run much better by him than it had been by the Columbuses, whose qualities were different. The drain of settlers back to Spain stopped. Kidnappings of Indians for slaves ended, though the Indians were worked hard in the mines and gained little from it. Judging discretion to be the better part of valor, Bobadilla did not interfere with Roldán's *repartimientos* in Jaragua. Indeed, he encouraged each settler to find a different *cacique* for his own use, basing his power first on the act of conquest and threat of punishment; but he also took account of how many Spaniards had settled down with the daughters of the native leaders.

Las Casas wrote that "the three hundred Spaniards who were here [in 1502] . . . used seduction or force to take the head women of the villages or their daughters as paramours, or servants, as they called them, and live with them in sin. Their relatives or vassals believed they had been taken as legitimate wives and, in that belief, they were given to the Spaniards, who became objects of universal adoration."[64] Thus began the tradition of interbreeding that thereafter characterized the Spanish Empire, in contrast with what happened later in the Anglo-Saxon world. It was encouraged by the obvious attraction of the Spaniards to the Indian women.

Columbus, meanwhile, reached Spain. He and his brothers had remained in chains throughout the crossing. They were accompanied by Father Franciso Ruiz, Cisneros's clever secretary, who had not been able to tolerate the Caribbean climate. Landing in Cadiz on November 20, 1500, the Admiral wrote to the monarchs, in a not unnaturally plaintive note, saying that he had arrived home. He explained: "Bobadilla sent me here in chains. I swear that I do not know, nor can I think why, save what God, our Lord, wants me to do for your Highnesses. . . . I did only what Abraham did for Isaac, and Moses for the people of Israel in Egypt."[65]

The monarchs in Granada were apparently dismayed that Bobadilla had gone so far. Despite their preoccupation with the problem of the Moors, they wrote back on December 17, asking for the Admiral to be released from chains immediately, and instructed him to come to Granada. Columbus sulkily kept on his impediments until he shuffled, wearing them, into the presence of the monarchs in the Alhambra. The Catholic Kings insisted that it had not been their wish that Columbus be so treated and imprisoned.[66]

Columbus wrote, too, to Juana de la Torre, the onetime governess of the Infante Juan and sister of Antonio de Torres. "If my complaint against the world is new, its practice of ill treatment is old,"[67] he began. Then he described how everyone he had met had been incredulous: "But the Lord gave to the Queen the spirit of understanding. . . . Seven years passed talking and then came nine when I was engaged in the enterprise itself. . . . Then I arrived back, and there was no one so vile but wanted to denounce me." He said that he had often "begged their Highnesses to send someone out at my expense to take over the administration of justice; and when I found the chief magistrate [Roldán] in revolt, I begged them once more for some men or at least for a servant bearing their letters."[68]

The monarchs had remained in Granada most of 1500 and much of 1501. Their preoccupations were still with the Muslim population. The old administration in the city of Granada was abolished in 1501, and a single city government formed with few concessions to the Muslim population. The Supreme Court that had been established in Ciudad Real was soon also moved to Granada. Most Muslims submitted to baptism as Christians, though some went to the mountains or fled the country altogether, convinced that the monarchs had broken the terms of the peace of ten years before. A low-level guerrilla war continued in the sierra to the south, with some support for the Muslims from across the Mediterranean. Christians and converted Muslims (*Moriscos*) alike suffered, and the Granada silk industry fell into decline. The Inquisition of Córdoba began its activities in Granada, causing much resentment and inspiring the hostility of the city's benign governor, the Count of Tendilla. The Muslims of Spain in general ceased to be the self-confident people they had been until recently.

It was against this background that the Catholic Kings turned their attention again to the Indies. Columbus had been treated harshly, and Bobadilla had shown himself intemperate. It is true that the arrival of new imports of gold suggested that "the enterprise of the Indies" was at last beginning to be worth the effort of managing it. The monarchs, after all, needed money, not least for their confrontation with the Turks in the Mediterranean. The threat to Christianity from the Ottoman Empire had not vanished with the fall of Granada. So a fleet was needed, and a fleet needed money. The Indies could produce some of it, if not as much as the Admiral had once promised. The Mediterranean as well as the Balkans remained a theater of war. Those considerations were on everyone's mind in the European courts, including the papal one.

In the circumstances, the monarchs decided that it was essential to appoint a serious, new, loyal, and effective proconsul who could mend the divisions in La Española, which seemed to have been pushed farther apart by Bobadilla. Perhaps they found it easier to come to a decision on this at a time when, in the summer of 1501, their most experienced adviser on Indian affairs, Bishop Fonseca, who had been responsible for nominating Bobadilla, had gone to Flanders to assist Prince Philip, the husband of the Infanta Juana. It must have been a difficult assignment for Fonseca, who was used to the sobriety of Spain. Now he found himself in a court where love and marriage were not always partners, and where mistresses played important parts in the lives of noblemen as well as of the royal family. In Fonseca's stead in Spain for a time, there was the less ambitious Diego Gómez de Cervantes, the *corregidor* of Cadiz, with whom Columbus had good relations through Alonso de Vallejo, who had accompanied him from Santo Domingo.[69] In addition, Peter Martyr, the Italian courtier who had always taken such an interest in the affairs of the Indies, had gone to Egypt as Spanish ambassador.

So Fernando and Isabel went ahead with a nominee of their own to take over Santo Domingo: this was Fray Nicolás de Ovando, commander of Lares in the Order of Alcántara. Though Bobadilla thought that he was doing well and was making money for the Crown, he would be relieved of his authority. Probably the then president of the Council of the Realm, Álvaro de Portugal, played a part in the new nomination, as did Cisneros. This announcement was followed by the proclamation of a bull by the Pope in November, at the royal request, that the Crown would receive all ecclesiastical tithes in the New World on condition that the governors carried out the instruction and conversion of Indians as well as the maintenance of churches.[70]

One or two further journeys to the Indies were approved before Bobadilla knew of his dismissal. Thus in February 1501, two supply ships were sent quietly to Santo Domingo by Francesco Riberol of Genoa[71] and Juan Sánchez de Tesorería, a well-connected Aragonese merchant of *converso* origin: his uncles included Gabriel Sánchez, treasurer of Aragon after 1479, and Alonso Sánchez, treasurer of Valencia.[72] There also shared in this voyage Francesco de' Bardi of Florence (he had married Briolanja, the sister of Columbus's long-dead wife, Felipa) and three other businessmen. This was the first purely commercial expedition to the Indies, and its profits were said to have been between 300 and 400 percent.[73] The cargo was mostly clothes, but it included horses, sheep, and cattle.

There were also journeys to the New World from Lisbon. The most interesting was that of Gaspar Corte-Real with his brother, Miguel, and was composed of two vessels that set sail in the summer of 1500. Gaspar Corte-Real had sailed in search of new islands, even a new continent, before 1500. He was the son of Joam Vaz Corte-Real, captain-general of southern Terceira, in the Azores, by a girl from Galicia whom his father had kidnapped. Joam was also said to have been "a great land stealer."[74] His son seems to have reached Labrador, then Newfoundland, very "close to England," reflected Las Casas rather curiously.[75] He went on another expedition in 1501 with three ships, apparently discovered Greenland, returned to Labrador, and then probably died in Hudson's Strait. His brother, Miguel, went to look for him but also died in an arctic part of Canada.[76] The interest of these journeys is that they show Portuguese captains were determined to discover new lands but at the same time were reluctant to break into territory accepted as Spanish. There was no suggestion by Corte-Real, any more than there had been with Cabot, that the travelers thought they were off Asia. Other journeys undertaken, or at least financed, by members of the family of Corte-Real continued, indeed, throughout the century.

It seems certain that in these years there were further journeys to the New World unauthorized by any government, some of them leaving Spanish ports, some Portuguese, and some even setting off from England or France. In an affidavit of June 19, 1505, for example, signed at Rouen by a certain Binot Paulmier de Gonneville, we hear of "mariners from Dieppe and St. Malo as well as other Normans and Bretons who, for years past, have gone to the West Indies in search of dyewood, cotton, monkeys, parrots, and other articles."[77] He was not the first French pirate to dispute the terms of the Treaty of Tordesillas. To the modern world it must seem curious that no captain bound for the Americas could by law raise anchor in any European port without seeking official permission. But so it was, since all governments wished to tax ships on their way out as on their way in. The consequence was inevitable: illegal journeys.

15

"The greatest good
that we can wish for"

We wish that the Indians be converted to our holy Catholic faith,
and that their souls be saved, for that is the greatest good that we can
wish for.

Instructions to Nicolás de Ovando,
governor of the Indies, 1501

Fray Nicolás de Ovando was fifty-two when he was selected by the Catholic
Kings to succeed Bobadilla as commander in chief of Spain in the Indies.
The Order of Alcántara, to which he belonged, like that of Santiago and Calatrava, had been in the vanguard of the Castilian armies in the Reconquista
and was now, for obvious reasons, losing its importance. But all the orders
still had prestige and their lands brought profit. It was symbolic that the new
Governor of the Indies should be an official of an order founded to garrison
newly conquered Christian outposts in Old Spain.

Ovando was known as honest and straightforward in his person, as in
his acts, and "an enemy of greed and avarice."[1] His place in the Order of Alcántara gave him standing in the court. But he was wellborn, too. Through
his ancestors, the Blázquezes, he descended from a bastard of King Alfonso
IX. A Blázquez (originally of León) had been given the city of Cáceres when
it was liberated from the Moors. Nicolás's father, Diego de Cáceres Ovando,
"El Capitán," had also received many concessions when Queen Isabel visited
Extremadura in 1477 during the war against La Beltraneja and the Portuguese.

Ovando's mother had been Isabel de Flores Gutiérrez, a lady of the bedchamber of Queen Isabel the Catholic's mother, the Portuguese Isabel. She
came from Brozas, a town in the northwest of Extremadura, near Alcántara,
where Ovando was brought up and where he had his house.

Fray Nicolás had been a companion of the household of the Infante
Juan. He had been among the ten knights always with him. He was also the

first of many Extremeños to play a decisive part in the history of Spain in America.[2]

Ovando was named governor on September 3, 1501, when the court was still in Granada. The order appointing him repays examination.[3] He was given the government and magistracy of the new Spanish islands as well as the right to appoint lesser magistrates, mayors, and constables.[4] But he would not be asked to govern that part of the mainland of South America where Alonso de Hojeda and Vicente Yañez Pinzón had been and where their responsibility had now to be considered.

Ovando was charged to see if there were foreigners in his new fief and, if so, to send them back to Spain: the New World was not to be exploited by an international brigade but by Castile alone. If, though, some foreigners had reached the Indies in the service of the Admiral, their status would be considered, and, anyway, Ovando was allowed to take five Portuguese with him.[5] He was specifically prohibited from carrying to the Indies "Moors, Heretics, and any Jews who had been punished for trying to pretend that they were not so [reconciliados] and conversos." But he could take "black and other slaves who had been born in the power of our Christian subjects."[6] Though one or two black African slaves may have slipped into the New World before,[7] and as we have seen, Columbus may have carried some on his third voyage, this was the first reference to them in an official document.

Some other relevant decrees were issued on the same September 3, including one that prohibited journeys to the New World without royal permission. Anyone who carried out such a voyage would be punished. Licenses would henceforth always be required.[8] This was not only because the Crown wanted port taxes but also to control the size of the population of the new empire. It was a reversal of the liberal policy that had been introduced in 1495. No doubt, as in respect of so many laws, there continued to be many breaches of it. Perhaps that was one of the reasons for it. But this rule was one that would last.[9]

Ovando's instructions were refined when another royal document was issued on September 16, 1500, signed by Gaspar de Gricio, the royal secretary for imperial matters, who had succeeded Fernándo Álvarez de Toledo in that position.[10] This gave Ovando certain absolute powers: no one was to establish or even seek gold mines without his permission; and of the product, half (later reduced to a third and later still to a fifth) would go to the Crown. All the same, production was to be stimulated. Miners would go about the settlement in teams of ten under a reliable leader. All grants made by Bobadilla would at the same time be revoked.[11]

Another order for Ovando included the statement:

We wish that the Indians be converted to our holy Catholic faith and their souls be saved, for that is the greatest good that we can hope for and, because of this, they must be informed of the details of our faith. You are to take great care in ensuring that the clergy so inform them and admonish them, with much love and without using force, so that they may be converted as rapidly as possible.

Ovando was to assure the surviving *caciques* of the protection of the Crown, and they were to pay tribute in the same way as the rest of the Crown's subjects. That tribute was to be agreed with the *caciques* so they would know they were not going to be treated unjustly.[12]

Ovando was naturally to carry out an official inquiry (*residencia*) into the rule of Bobadilla and his officials and then send them back to Spain in the same fleet in which he himself had come.[13] The new Governor was to be paid twice what his predecessor received (360,000 maravedís a year instead of 180,000), and a hundred new officials would be selected by Ovando.

The instructions were signed not only by the King, Queen, and Gricio, but also by the Archbishop of Granada, the Queen's sometime confessor, Talavera, and by Licenciado Luis Zapata. Zapata was an important intriguer, a Madrileño *converso*, of small build, soon to be spoken of, because of his importance, as "El Rey Chiquito" (as Boabdil had been), known to be both corrupt and miserly, if mellifluous in speech. He was an official who protected in Spain all the "Aragonese clique" that would soon succeed in establishing itself in La Española.[14]

None of these arrangements was kept secret. They were indeed proclaimed in Seville on October 2, 1501, by the town crier, Francisco de Mesa, on the steps of the cathedral (the famous *gradas*), in the presence of various notaries of the city. The same was done in Gran Canaria.[15]

The expedition of Ovando was organized by Diego Gómez de Cervantes, the *corregidor* of Cadiz, one of those essential officials in the royal reforms increasing the Crown's authority in municipal councils. Jimeno de Briviesca, a *converso* who had assisted Juan Rodríguez de Fonseca in the overall administration of the Indies, was to be in command of expenditure in Seville.

Several other voyages were approved at this time. Thus Luis de Arriaga, a hidalgo of Berlanga, in Castile, who had been on Columbus's expedition in 1493, and had served for a time as deputy to Margarit and then commander of La Magdalena (where he had resisted some serious Indian attacks headed by a *cacique* whom the Spaniards called Juatinango), was ordered to try to colonize La Española with sound Spanish families.[16] There would be four towns with fifty settlers in each, two hundred people in all.[17] They were not to have any income. But they would be given free passage and, after five years, would receive as their own the property that they had been allocated. The cost of seeds, cattle, and so on would be theirs to bear. They would be permitted to explore further coasts.[18] This expedition left Seville in February 1502, at much the same time as that of Ovando.

The persistent adventurer Alonso de Hojeda also again left Cadiz early in 1502, with four ships. Two of his vessels were wrecked either in Bahía Honda or Santa Cruz Bay in Cuba at the beginning of May. On a third, Juan de Vergara sailed off in insubordinate rebellion, bound for Jamaica. Hojeda went in pursuit, as the responsible captain, on the caravel *La Magdalena*, but he was captured by his enemies, who carried him, bound, to Ovando, by then in Santo Domingo.[19] The Caribbean was beginning to seem like Extremadura before the coming of the Catholic Kings.

Columbus, meanwhile, was in Spain arguing for a new approach to the recapture of Jerusalem, which he thought, optimistically, would constitute the court of "the last world emperor."[20] After all, the world would soon end, as St. Augustine had predicted. Columbus had an elaborate correspondence on the matter with his Carthusian friend Fray Gaspar de Gorricio. He also wore down the monarchs with his continual demands and letters: "I would rather be to your Highnesses a source of pleasure and delight," he wrote, "than of annoyance and surfeit." This touching letter was full of dubious scientific reflections about the consequence of the world being a sphere.[21]

Then the Admiral received from the monarchs permission, in January 1502, for "another voyage in the name of the Holy Trinity," as he put it to both the Pope and the Bank of Genoa. For on March 14 the monarchs wrote him a most friendly letter from Valencia de la Torre: "Your imprisonment was very displeasing to us, as we made clear to you and to all others, for as soon as we learned of it, we set you free. You know the favor with which we have always treated you, and now we are even more resolved to honor and to treat you very well. All that we have granted you shall be preserved intact . . . and you and your heirs shall enjoy them, as is just. . . . Pray do not delay your departure."[22] The King and Queen obviously realized that Columbus excelled at discovery as he was incompetent at administration.

In these months, Columbus's correspondent Pope Alexander confirmed his interest in what his compatriots the Spaniards were doing. Thus, on December 16, 1501, the bull *Sinceritas Eximie Devotionis* repeated the "Privi-

leges" granted in 1493. The Pope also guaranteed the grant of tithes in the Indies to the Catholic Kings, not the Church.[23] Columbus himself wrote again
to Alexander in February 1502 that he had wanted to come and "talk personally to His Holiness about his discoveries." But he had been prevented from
doing so by the difficulties between the monarchs of Spain and the King of
Portugal. Still, he wanted the Pope to know that he had discovered 1,400 islands and had found that there were no fewer than 333 languages on the
tierra firme of Asia, where there were also all kinds of metals, including, of
course, gold and copper. As for La Española, it should be thought of as a
combination of "Tharsis, Cethia, Ophir, Ophis, and Cipanga." He recalled
that he had also been to some land to the south of these territories and seen
"the earthly Paradise" where there was, appropriately, a large oysterage, with
pearls. But Satan had disturbed the proper management of these things,
Columbus added: "The government that had been allocated to me forever
has with fury been seized from me."[24]

Ovando, for his part, sedately left Sanlúcar de Barrameda on the *Santa
María de la Antigua* on February 13, 1502, with twenty-seven ships. It was far
the largest fleet that had yet set out for the New World—bigger even than
that of Cabral. It carried 2,500 would-be settlers, including many women,
priests, Franciscans, and artisans. It shipped enough mulberry shoots to permit the foundation of a silk industry, and much sugarcane.[25] Arriaga followed with another three ships, taking with him seventy-three of his
planned two hundred families. Fonseca gave him the right to collect tithes in
La Española. On the fifteenth, Alonso Vélez de Mendoza, the hidalgo from
Moguer, who, as we have seen, had been down the coast of Brazil into what
was plainly Portuguese territory in 1500, set out on another expedition that
was intended to be a copy of Arriaga's.[26]

Twelve hundred of Ovando's "settlers" seem to have come from Extremadura, including several from his own town of Brozas. Some were hidalgos, such as his secretary, Francisco de Lizaur,[27] and Sebastián de
Ocampo, from Noyia, Galicia, who may also have been on Columbus's second voyage.[28] Many were poor men driven to consider emigration as an alternative to an uncertain economic future at home, a consequence of poor
harvests or perhaps the royal favoring of the Mesta, the famous wool monopoly. Ovando had, as his second in command, Antonio de Torres, that
well-connected and experienced captain who had been back and forth so
often across the Atlantic. (He had been governor of Gran Canaria for a year
before this new mission.)

The accountant of the expedition was Cristóbal de Cuéllar, a Castilian
whom Ovando had known in the household of the Infante Juan at Almazán,

with his six servants. The supervisor was Diego Márquez of Seville, a onetime page of Fonseca who had had the same role on the second expedition
of Columbus. The *fundidor* who was responsible for melting down gold was
Rodrigo del Alcázar, a member of a rich *converso* family of Seville, who took
with him nine servants.[29] A kinsman of Ovando, Francisco de Monroy, of
that talented but undisciplined Extremeño family, traveled as factor, with six
servants.[30] Rodrigo de Villacorta, from the Castilian pueblo of Olmedo, famous in the civil wars of the previous century, was treasurer. He had been
with Columbus in the same capacity on his second voyage. The Admiral regarded him as "a hardworking person and very loyal to the service of the
Crown."[31] Alonso Maldonado of Salamanca went with Ovando as chief
magistrate. He turned out to be the best of the early judges of the New
World, according to both of the historians Oviedo and Las Casas, for once
united in their judgment.[32] He took two servants.

The commander in overall charge of the ships was Andrés Velázquez,
who had two servants. He was presumably from the large Velázquez family
that played such a key part in the early history of Spanish America. Alfonso
Sánchez de Carvajal, the factor of the Admiral, returned to La Española with
Ovando to take charge of the Columbus family's possessions. On board, too,
were Cristóbal de Tapia, a protégé of Bishop Fonseca from Seville, and Rodrigo de Alburquerque from Salamanca, men who, with Francisco de Puér-
tola, were to command the three new fortresses that they were instructed to
build along the line from Isabela to Santo Domingo.[33] Others included the
comendador Gabriel de Varela, Cristóbal de Santa Clara, a *converso* merchant, and a Sevillano *converso* named Pedro de las Casas and his son Bartolomé, the future apostle of the Indies. The twenty-year-old Hernán
Cortés, another remote relation of Ovando's from Extremadura, planned to
travel with him, but at the last minute he hurt his leg jumping out of the
window of a lady in Seville whom he had been trying to seduce, and could
not leave.[34]

There were also on these ships seventeen Franciscans[35] and four priests.[36]
The former were to found the first house attached to their order in the New
World. While important, certainly, as the beginning of Atlantic commerce,
this was also going to be a serious journey in search of souls. Nearly sixty
horses sailed, too.[37] The monarchs optimistically forbade any who traveled
with Ovando to resell the slaves that he was taking home. This was the first
occasion that Indian slaves already in Spain were returned to the New World.

Ovando sailed away attended by celebrations and music, as was normal
when major expeditions left Spain. The port that he left, Sanlúcar de Barrameda, was now established as the daughter city of Seville in respect of its

trade with the Indies, for most of the cargoes were loaded there, and many passengers preferred to ride there or travel there by a separate boat rather than board the fleet at Seville. The benefit for Juan de Guzmán, the Duke of Medina Sidonia, who had his palace on the hill behind the town, was considerable, since many profits of the commerce with the Indies flowed into his hands. It is easy even now, as one stands on the shore at Sanlúcar looking at the little group of houses at Las Paletas, at the mouth of the River Guadalajara, to imagine the fleet of Ovando disappearing into the sunset over the sea.[38]

The music died down and for a few days all was both calm and happy, but then, eight days out, halfway to the Canary Islands, on February 21, Ovando's fleet encountered a terrible storm. One ship, *La Rábida,* was lost with 120 passengers, while the crews of many of the others felt constrained to throw their merchandise overboard. All the vessels were dispersed. Many chests were washed up on the coast of Andalusia. The news reached the court that the entire fleet had to be supposed lost.

Fernando and Isabel, fearing the worst, did not talk to anyone for eight days.[39] Their lives, so triumphant in politics, had been so sad in private that this new tragedy seemed to imply a new curse on their endeavors.[40] But shortly they learned that only one ship had actually sunk. The vessels that were scattered might be recovered. The King and Queen resumed their usual arduous journeys. They soon left Seville, and Andalusia, too, for the north, passing through the Sierra Morena to Toledo, where they spent the summer of 1502. The royal mood warmed a little as their daughter and heir, Juana, reached Spain with her husband, Philip von Habsburg. This royal pair reached Fuentearrabia after having left Flanders in July 1501. They took the land route, which meant endless acts of obeisance to the King of France, including the gift of coins in token of vassalage.[41] They were, of course, now the heirs to the kingdom. They were greeted by Fernando, and Isabel met them at Toledo. There followed a state banquet, tourneys, and, on May 22, the Cortes and other leaders took an oath to Philip and Juana as "Princes of Asturias."[42] Some complained that Philip did not speak Spanish. But with the realization that through him the monarchs now at last had grandchildren, including male descendants (Charles, Juana's eldest son, had been born in 1500), such qualms were forgotten. More troubling was the inability of Prince Philip to ignore any pretty girl on whom his blue eye happened to alight, as well as the inability of the Infanta to rise above such flexibility on her husband's part.[43]

Ovando, meanwhile, regrouped most of his ships in Gran Canaria. He found much evidence of enterprise then at work on the island. Batista de

Riberol had been building an important sugar mill, and his fellow Genoese Mateo Viña was doing the same at Garachio in Tenerife.[44] Many Portuguese farmers and laborers had been welcomed as colonists—several of them after a stay in Madeira. Using the services of the island to help him repair his fleet, Ovando again set off. He reached Santo Domingo with half his ships on April 15, 1502. The remainder of his expedition, with the sad exception of those lost on *La Rábida,* followed two weeks later, led by the veteran Antonio de Torres.

Ovando found that the Spanish population of La Española amounted to only about three hundred on his arrival. A few were established at Concepción de la Vega, Santiago, and Bonao, and some, like Roldán, in the far west of the island, but most were established at Santo Domingo. Many of these colonists, as we have seen, had settled down with native mistresses, and had mestizo children. There were rudimentary churches with thatched roofs in both Isabela and Santo Domingo. (The priests there, however, were not entitled to carry out confirmations.) Power among the Indians theoretically remained with *caciques,* but by then Guacanagarí and Guarionex had been subdued, and Caonabó was dead. In Higuey, in the eastern part of the island, Cotubano was delivering tribute in kind—of a varied sort—to the Spaniards, as in Jaragua, while in the west, in what is now Haiti, the king named Behechio was doing the same.

Gold was still being produced from the valley of San Cristóbal. The other products of value were cotton and brazilwood.

Two of Columbus's friends, Francisco de Garay, a Basque, and Miguel Díaz de Aux, a hardworking Aragonese, had made themselves rich in consequence of the gold.[45] The Admiral had sent these entrepreneurs down the woody slopes of Bonao, and there, on the banks of the River Hayna, a woman resting near a stream had found a lump of gold weighing thirty-five pounds, a famous *pepita* (nugget) of gold that helped give these two northern Spaniards a fortune. They were reputedly the richest men in the colony. Garay had begun to build the first private house of stone in the city of Santo Domingo.

As soon as he arrived, Ovando carried out the required inquiry (*residencia*) into the actions of Bobadilla. The Cortes of 1480 in Toledo had ruled that, after the dismissal or resignation of a magistrate, especially a senior one, he would remain in his "residence" for a month ("thirty days and no more") while anyone who chose could complain about or praise his actions during his time of office. Sometimes these inquiries were drawn out, some ended quickly. Occasionally, if the subject of the inquiry proved to have behaved badly, a criminal charge might be preferred.[46] The practice was a direct transfer of Castilian practice to the New World.

The *residencia* of Bobadilla was finished in the regulation period of thirty days. No doubt Ovando wanted to send his predecessor home as quickly as he could. Bartolomé de las Casas, in La Española for the first time, marveled at how people competed to attack Bobadilla. Yet the outgoing Governor did not seem to have enriched himself personally. By the end of June, the ships under Antonio de Torres were ready for the return journey; with the papers relating to the *residencia* safely packed on board, Bobadilla and his staff were preparing to embark for home. There were others who wanted to return. Then the disquieting news came that Columbus, the hated "pharaoh," was offshore with a small flotilla of four ships.

Columbus, it will be recalled, had been encouraged by the monarchs to set off on a new, fourth journey—one of exploration only. He was not to think of administering what he had discovered. But he was to explore further the territory of South America. It was to be hoped that he would find a strait that would lead to Asia. He himself expected to reach the Spice Islands. On March 21, the Admiral wrote to Niccoló Oderigo, the ambassador of Genoa in Spain, telling him that he had left a copy of his recently confirmed "Privileges" with Francesco de Riberol, another copy with his Carthusian friend Fray Gaspar de Gorricio, and another in his own house in Santo Domingo. He sent a fourth to Oderigo himself. The list of recipients shows how his friendships then stood. Riberol, for example, was one of the richest of Genoese merchants, with his wide interests in sailcloth, soap, sugar plantations, and wheat. He farmed the monopoly of Canarian dyestuffs, such as orchil, for Gutierre de Cárdenas, the great courtier, and he had by now an interest, too, in the oldest sugar mill in the Canaries, El Agaete.[47]

On April 2, Columbus wrote to the Bank of San Jorge in Genoa: he assured them that, though his body might travel to many places, his heart was always with them. God had granted him the best gifts that He had given anyone since the age of King David, and now he was going to return to the Indies in the name of the Trinity.[48] He wrote also to his son Diego, saying that he hoped Diego would use everything that belonged to him in Santo Domingo, and would look after Beatriz Enríquez, Columbus's mistress in Córdoba, paying her 10,000 maravedís a year or half what would be earned by each of the three commanders of the new fortresses in La Española who were accompanying Ovando. Another 10,000 maravedís was to be paid to his sister-in-law, Briolanja Muñiz.

He told Diego, too, about four friends from Genoa: Riberol; Francesco Doria, who sold more wheat in Seville and bought more olives than anyone else; Francesco Cataño (Cattaneo), concerned in exporting sugar to Milan, and whose brother Rafael had done the accounts for his third voyage;[49] and finally, Gaspar d'Espinola, whose interest had hitherto been dried fruit from Granada. These friends provided Columbus with the goods that he was now taking to the Indies.[50]

Columbus set off with four caravels and with not only his two brothers, Bartolomeo and Diego, but also Fernando, his clever, illegitimate, still very young son by Beatriz Enríquez. His first mission was to "reconnoiter the land of Paria." He had told the monarchs that he might very well meet Vasco da Gama, the Portuguese captain who had sailed east. They had written back: "We have written appropriately to the King of Portugal [Manuel I], our son-in-law, and send you herewith the letter addressed to his captain as requested by you, wherein we notify him of your departure toward the west and say we have learned of his [da Gama's] departure eastward and that if you meet, you are to treat each other as friends. . . ."[51] The prospect was appealing, the possibility imaginative.

Columbus's fleet of four ships was led by the *Santo* (or *Santa María*), the flagship, whose captain, Diego Tristán, had been on the journey of 1493 and who came from a family of leather merchants in Seville. The master was Ambrosio Sánchez, a sea captain now embarking on a career of many years of crossing the Atlantic.[52] There was also the *Santiago de Palos*,[53] on which Francisco de Porrás was captain, while his brother, Diego de Porrás, was the notary. They had been on the expedition to Paria of Cristóbal Guerra and Peralonso Niño in 1499, and had been placed on this fourth voyage of Columbus at the request of the treasurer of Castile, Alonso de Morales, who, it is said, was in love with their aunt—though whether that insistence was because he wished them out of the way or desired to offer them a chance of glory is not evident. They were of a *converso* family—a fact that did not endear them to Columbus.[54] The third ship was the *Gallega*, captained by Pedro de Terreros, who, like the master, Juan Quintero, had been on all Columbus's previous three voyages. Quintero, who came from a well-known seafaring family in Palos, was the brother of Cristóbal Quintero, who had been the owner of the *Pinta* on the voyage of 1492.

Finally, the *Vizcaína* had as her captain Bartolomeo Fieschi, from a famous Genoese family. Fieschi was the only Genoese to serve as a captain under Columbus at sea. The pilot was Pedro de Ledesma, also a veteran of the Admiral's third voyage. The crews totaled 140 on the four ships.[55]

The pilots included men who would be found navigating the Caribbean one way or another for the next generation. One such was Antonio de Alaminos, later the pioneer of the use of the Gulf Stream, who now began his maritime life with Columbus as a cabin boy;[56] and Juan Bono de Quejo, a Basque, from San Sebastian.[57] The chief clerk of the fleet was Diego Méndez, an old ally of Columbus, a Sevillano of Portuguese origin who, having fought on the losing side in the civil war of La Beltraneja, had accompanied Lope de Alburquerque, Count of Peñaflor, in a long exile in France, Flanders, and even England.[58] There was at least one black slave, a certain Diego, who sailed with his master, Diego Tristán.[59]

Columbus had been instructed not to go to Santo Domingo, though he was to be allowed a short stop there "on the way back, if you think it necessary." He had intended sailing due west along the north coast of South America from Paria, but on June 15, at Martinique, he turned north because he wanted to exchange one slow, heavy ship, the *Santiago de Palos,* for a better, lighter one, at Santo Domingo. (This was quite contrary to his instructions and it is not surprising that it brought him difficulties.) The Admiral sailed to the island of San Juan (Puerto Rico) on June 24, reaching Santo Domingo on the twenty-ninth, where he sent ashore Pedro de Terreros, the captain of the *Gallega,* to tell Ovando about his needs. He also thought that he should advise Ovando not to let the homeward-bound fleet under Torres set off because a storm was in the offing.

Ovando read out Columbus's letter to him in a mocking voice before a group of colonists, refused the Admiral's request, and did not delay the sailing of Torres's large fleet of nearly thirty ships. His attitude was determined by the resentment still entertained toward the Columbus family by the majority of the settlers in Santo Domingo. Antonio de Torres, the *cacique* Guarionex, the ex-governor Bobadilla, with the papers relating to Bobadilla's *residencia,* the famous *pepita de oro* found by Garay and Díaz de Aux, and the rebel Francesco Roldán, with many of his followers, then set off gaily on June 30 for Spain. At the last minute, the young *converso* merchant from Triana, Rodrigo de Bastidas, who had walked two hundred and more miles to reach Santo Domingo when his own ship had been wrecked off Jaragua, also joined the homebound armada, in a small vessel, the *Aguja,* along with Columbus's agent, Sánchez de Carvajal, who had come out with Ovando.[60]

Columbus, furious at being denied entry into what he regarded as his own island, took refuge along the coast in what would become the Bay of Azúa de Compostela: "Was there a man born who would not die of despair—excepting Job himself—at being denied refuge at the hazard of his life and soul . . . in the very land which, by God's will, and sweating blood, I won for Spain. . . ."[61] Columbus sailed close to the shore. He was at Azúa when the hurricane came.[62]

This storm was destructive. The town of Santo Domingo, built by Bartolomeo Colón on the east side of the River Ozama, was practically razed.[63] Columbus wrote that "the storm was terrible and, that night, my ships practically fell apart. Each ship pulled at its anchor without hope, except for death. Everyone thought that the other ships were bound to have been lost."[64] But thanks to the skilled seamanship of both Columbus and his brother Bartolomeo, their four vessels survived, after a fashion.

The fleet of Antonio de Torres was less fortunate. Having already reached the deep and dangerous Mona Straits between Santo Domingo and Puerto Rico, twenty-three or twenty-four ships, including those carrying Antonio de Torres himself, Bobadilla, Roldán, and many of his friends, and even the *cacique* Guarionex, were lost,[65] together with 200,000 pesos of gold; so were the *pepita de oro* and all the documents about the outgoing governor. Three ships warily returned to the ruined harbor of Santo Domingo. Only one vessel of the fleet, and that one of the smallest, the *Aguja,* with Bastidas and Sánchez de Carvajal on board, eventually reached Spain, with 4,000 pesos of the Admiral's gold. Bastidas's treasure made an impression, as we have seen.[66] But it did not compensate for the losses.

Despite this bad beginning, Ovando's government in La Española soon took shape. He sent criminals back to Spain. The disappearance of Roldán and many of his followers made everything much easier. Ovando immediately began the rebuilding of Santo Domingo on the west bank, not the east, of the Rio Ozama, where the city has stood ever since and where a fine statue commemorates him. He laid out a plan (*la traza*) of the new capital, embarked on a fortress there, and arranged for the building of twelve houses of stone. He imposed a new tax, in addition to that paid since 1498, of one ounce on each three ounces of gold mined, a proportion especially unpopular with colonists dedicated exclusively to mining. This coincided with an increase in the price of both food and tools caused by the sudden failure of communication with Castile. Ovando also made an enemy of a protégé of Fonseca's, Cristóbal de Tapia, who, before the building of the new city, had bought land where most of the new Santo Domingo was to be built. But he was not compensated for it.[67]

Most of Ovando's new men made quickly for the goldfields in the center of the island, in the region of Cibao, by now treated as a Spanish province. But these new settlers, as full of enthusiasm as they were covetous, died nearly as fast as the Indians whom they secured to work for them—as a result of dysentery caused by the new diets more than anything else. The gold-seekers would return to Santo Domingo crowing over a tiny speck of gold that they believed they had found. It was hard for them to realize that "gold was not to be found like fruit on trees, to be picked as soon as they arrived."[68] It was harder still to find that when the Indians fled, which they often did, "they had themselves to work on their knees, loading carts with potentially interesting rocks, even carrying burdens on their own shoulders."[69] The euphoria of the new arrivals, therefore, lasted only a short time: heat, fatigue, even hunger took their toll. Then an epidemic of syphilis, or a variation of it, broke out in Cibao. So by the end of 1502, a thousand of the newcomers had died, another five hundred were ill, and Ovando's colonists had been reduced to little more than a thousand.[70] Most of these soon abandoned the gold mines both for want of indigenous labor and because their lack of technical knowledge prevented them from enjoying any success in directing the works themselves.[71]

The consequence was that the three hundred veterans, men like Diego de Alvarado and Diego Velázquez de Cuéllar, who had reached the island on the second or third voyage of Columbus, were the masters of the situation, for they not only had experience and access to food but also the service of Indians whom they needed.

The search for, discovery, and washing of gold soon became a systematic undertaking. Official places for the melting of gold every year were designated, two in the new gold zone of Buenaventura, near Santo Domingo, where each marco was worth between 50 and 60 million maravedís; and two in the first gold territory, at La Vega or Concepción, where rather more than that was usually measured.

After the initial setbacks, Ovando's policy began to be successful. After the unhappy reign of the "pharaoh" Columbus and his brothers, followed by the harsh days of Bobadilla, it seemed as if this conversion of the Caribbean into an outpost of Extremadura by Frey Nicolás de Ovando was at last creating a treasure house comparable to what Columbus had predicted. In 1504, 1506, and 1507, respectively, only 15.3 million, 17.5 million, and 16.8 million maravedís' worth of gold were sent home.[72] All the same, the colony seemed in these years to be organized (as a modern historian has pointed out) like a "large mining farm in which the entire active population was imprisoned."[73] Actually, agriculture did well, too: cassava, garlic, and pigs were now the main concerns.

Castile still dominated no more than the center of the island of La Española. The Spaniards did occupy, however, a broad sweep of land running from the old capital of Isabela, every day in greater decay, to Santo Domingo. Both to the west and to the east, indigenous principalities survived in a lesser or greater degree of independence. Ovando put an end to this cohabitation with indigenous rulers. Bartolomé de las Casas, who, as has been seen, came out with Ovando, wrote that his commander was "prudent, slow, modest, and equable," but his acts seem to challenge that judgment for, from the beginning, Ovando had bad relations with the Indians, whom he could not begin to understand.

In late 1502, the new governor decided to investigate the territory to the east of Vega Real, the goldfield in the northern center of the island, where there had been little fighting in Columbus's day and where Ovando thought that he could persuade the indigenous population to work for the Spaniards. He also began to build a new port on the north of the island, at Puerto Plata, a place that still bears that name. It lies in a bay that offers the best harbor in northern La Española and was superior for maritime purposes to Isabela. It gained its name because Columbus, sailing past on his first voyage, imagined that the mountains there resembled silver.

Then, after a preliminary investigation by a voyage of eight men, the Governor sent an expedition around the eastern end of the island. It stopped at the island of Saona, where Columbus had been in 1493, in order to buy cassava. One of the Spaniards' dogs, perhaps a mastiff, possibly a lurcher, even though called a *lebrel* (greyhound), killed a local *cacique*. Not surprisingly, a "rebellion" of Indians followed and eight Spaniards were killed. Ovando sent a party of four hundred men under Juan de Esquivel, a Sevillano with a cold heart, to pacify this territory.[74]

Esquivel, like so many of the first generation of settlers, came from a *converso* family, being the son of Pedro de Esquivel and Constanza Fernández de Arauz, herself the daughter of Gabriel Sánchez, a *converso* who had been the controller of customs in Seville. Pedro de Esquivel had been captured by the Moors in the mountains of Ajarquía, north of Malaga, when the Order of Santiago had met such a bad defeat in 1483 and, having escaped, for that reason benefited from royal favor. But the Esquivels never quite escaped the stigma of being *conversos*.[75]

Juan de Esquivel's instructions were to impose peace with the Indians. But King Cotubanamá, the *cacique* of the east of La Española, with his headquarters more or less at the site of the present city of Higuey, was not disposed to consider any terms. His people, including his women, prepared for war. But their armaments were inadequate, they were defeated, and Saona was depopulated. Many were made slaves, "legally" because they had been captured in "a just war."[76] Esquivel and Cotubanamá eventually agreed that the port near Higuey would now supply such Spaniards as stopped there on the sea with the cassava they needed. Cotubanamá accepted a position as a tributary.

In the west of the island, in the autumn of 1503, Ovando embarked on an even more ferocious pacification. Some unattached Spaniards left behind by Roldán still had their illegal *encomiendas,* and they were reluctant to accept control from Santo Domingo. There were also misunderstandings with the Indians. The indigenous leader there was now Queen Anacoana, sister of Behechio and widow of Caonabó. She did what she could to charm the Spaniards, but she was unable to discipline her own people, who often skirmished with the settlers and interfered with their optimistic attempts to create a new agriculture reminiscent of that of Castile.

Ovando resolved to put an end to what he judged to be a double-headed disorder and set off for Jaragua with seventy horsemen and three hundred foot soldiers. Ovando seems to have decided to conquer the whole island and reduce all the Indians to subjection. He believed that they would live better under Spanish direction than under their own *caciques,* whom he regarded as cruel and incompetent wastrels. Las Casas wrote kindly of him that he was indeed "worthy of governing many people but not Indians."[77] He was determined to introduce a system of subservience deriving from the practice of the military orders with which he was familiar in Spain.[78] This implied the enlightened management of land by a disinterested upper class—a form of nationalization, it might be said. Ovando thus made his decision to bring to an end the old polity, apparently without any consultation with his monarchs and without any discussion even in Santo Domingo. As governor, his word was law, though perhaps he had discussed the future of Spanish rule in La Española privately with Fernando and Isabel before leaving Spain.

Oblivious of impending doom, Anacoana gave a fiesta in honor of Ovando. She summoned a substantial number of her noblemen (perhaps a hundred) and many other of her subjects, and received the Governor. There were entertainments, prolonged dances, and an elaborate game with sticks (*juego de cañas*). The music of the Spanish guitars and the parading of the horses mingled with the native dances and the games. There seemed a mood of real friendship. This lasted for three days.

But then there were rumors that the Indians were mounting a conspiracy. Such reports would play a major part in the history of the Spanish conquests in the Americas.[79] (They were not all delusions: the Spaniards in 1503, as often in the future, were heavily outnumbered.) Ovando's men came to suspect that they would be attacked at night, and slaughtered to a

man. The Governor promised a display of arms. The Indians were delighted at the idea. Then Ovando's men opened fire when their commander placed his hand on the gold cross of the Order of Alcántara, which he
wore around his neck. Horsemen surrounded the large house in which the
caciques had gathered, and the foot soldiers prevented anyone from escaping. Then the house was set on fire. Anacoana was captured and later
hanged in the Plaza de Santo Domingo for "rebellion." The resistance of
the surviving Indians in Jaragua was bitter but ineffective; forty Spaniards
were killed, but the conquest was complete.[80] Castile was now in full control of the west of the island.[81]

Ovando appointed as his deputy for that territory Diego Velázquez de
Cuéllar, a conquistador who had sailed to the Indies first with Columbus in
1493. He had been present at the massacre, but the responsibility lay with
Ovando. All the same, Velázquez had participated in what had happened,
and it was never suggested that he had been unwilling to participate in the
brutalities.

Ovando, the Governor, was now the unquestioned ruler of a large island
that had been discovered only eleven years before. All the native rulers encountered by Columbus in his first years were dead. Ovando was building a
house for himself, now the Hostal Nicolás de Ovando. The church in the
center of Santo Domingo still had a thatched roof, but there were plans for
a serious cathedral—though it was not embarked upon for another twenty
years. The Capilla de los Remedios preceded it. The *convento* of San Francisco was soon under way, too.[82]

Other buildings in what is now the center of Santo Domingo were
begun by Ovando, including the so-called Governor's Palace, now the
Museo de las Casas Reales. Ovando founded the Hospital de San Nicolás de
Bari, for many years a popular asylum though until 1508 it seemed just one
more large, thatched-roofed *bohío*.[83] Another big house was that of the Genoese merchant Jerónimo Grimaldi, who established himself with his uncle
Bernardo as the most powerful entrepreneur in the Indies. (Bernardo had
helped finance Columbus's third voyage.) The Grimaldis had originally
been shippers of wool. Now their interests were multiform. Ovando also
began the building of a large, open, triple-towered fortress (the Fortaleza de
Santo Domingo) on a bluff overlooking the point where the Ozama flows
into the Caribbean.

These buildings, of which some survive, were the first examples of Spanish architecture in the New World. Columbus had left nothing behind.
Ovando's work marks the beginning of a great tradition. Sweeping changes
have come to the peoples, the landscapes, and the economic circumstances

of the vast territory soon claimed, and then ruled, by Castile. New countries have come into being. Eccentric, revolutionary, intransigent, military, brutal, and sometimes liberal governments have had their day. But buildings such as those ordered by Ovando still cast their magisterial shadows over the centers of decaying capitals, the bolts on their doors still call up long memories, and the very stones suggest legends of endurance.

"Teach them and indoctrinate them with good customs"

Our main aim was to arrange the introduction there of our holy
Catholic faith and to ensure that the people there accepted it, and
also to send prelates, monks, and priests and other learned people
who fear God to instruct the people in the faith and to teach and
indoctrinate them with good customs.

Codicil to the will of Queen Isabel, 1504

Among those who observed the massacre in Jaragua was Diego Méndez,
who had been with Columbus on his fourth voyage to La Española as chief
clerk, and who had now returned to Santo Domingo by canoe from Jamaica
after some extraordinary adventures. He was able to tell Ovando that the
Admiral was then not far away, in Jamaica. Ovando was unimpressed. Like
most Spanish hidalgos, he thought of "the pharaoh" neither with respect nor
with enthusiasm. He did nothing to help him; but help at that time was what
Columbus needed.

From his refuge in the storm of 1502 in the bay of Azúa, fifty miles west
along the coast from Santo Domingo, to which his four ships had been refused entry,[1] Columbus not only saw and weathered the hurricane that destroyed the city and homegoing fleet, but while in the bay of Santo
Domingo, he also saw the recent charts of Bastidas, then returning home.
Las Casas says that he witnessed the encounter.[2] Then Columbus set off on
July 14, first to Yaquimo, in the west of La Española, a place known for its
brazilwood, and then farther west still. His aim had been, apparently, to go
first to Jamaica and then to strike land in Central America at a point close to
where Bastidas had been. In the event, he and his vessels were carried by the
storm through the islands that he had himself named the Jardines de la
Reina, off Cuba, and then past Cayo Largo and the Isle of Pines to other islands of Central America, now known as the Bay Islands, off Honduras.

The journey across the Caribbean was appalling. The Admiral himself recalled:

Rain, thunder, and lightning were so continuous that it seemed the end of the world. . . . During eighty-eight days, this intolerable storm continued in such a way that we saw neither the sun nor the stars as a guide. [It could have been nothing like that length of time.] The ships were lying open to the skies, the sails broken, the anchors and shrouds lost, as were the cables . . . and many supplies went overboard; the crews were all sick and all were repenting their sins and turning to God. Everyone made vows and promised to make pilgrimages if they were saved from death, and, very often, men went so far as to confess to each other. We had experienced other storms but none had been so terrifying. Many who we had thought were brave men were reduced to terror on more than one occasion.

The distress of my son [Fernando] who was with me racked my soul, for he was only thirteen years old, and he was not only exhausted but remained so for a very long time. But the Lord gave him such courage that he cheered the others, and he worked as hard in the ship as if he had been a sailor for eighty years. He comforted me, for I, too, had fallen ill and was many times at the point of death. I directed our course from a little shelter that I built on the deck. My brother [Bartolomeo] was in the worst and most dangerous ship, and my grief was even greater because I had taken him with me against his wish.[3]

Eventually, after this dark journey, Columbus and his friends reached the north coast of what is now Honduras, Central America, probably the island known as Guanaja, forty miles offshore. There, he mended the boats and gathered supplies, while the local people told him, by signs, of gold mines to the south, just as the natives of San Salvador had done in 1492. Columbus assumed that he was in a land that Marco Polo had called Cochinchina. He heard of a province of great wealth, which would appear to have been Yucatan.[4] But he also believed that he was only ten days' sail away from the River Ganges.[5] By this time most people in Spain and Italy, and no doubt elsewhere in Europe, realized that Columbus had discovered something new. But the poor Admiral still lived in his world of Oriental dreams.

These "local people" who talked of gold were either Paya or Jicaque Indians, probably the former. They had a "slash-and-burn" method of agriculture, and planting was done by women with digging sticks. Pineapples and sweet and bitter manioc were their main products. The latter was ground into flour, then made into dough and baked. Men used four-foot-long bows and obsidian-tipped arrows for hunting, and both men and women used bone hooks for fishing. Fish were sometimes shot by arrows, and large specimens were caught with harpoons. Honey and liana sap were used as the basis for a light alcohol. Live turtles, as in Cuba, were kept in corrals behind stockades in shallow water. The villages of the Paya Indians usually had about one hundred to five hundred inhabitants, who lived in elliptically shaped communal houses that appear to have contained beds placed on platforms.

Clothing customarily consisted of only a loincloth and a poncho. Women usually wore a knee-length bark-cloth skirt, wrapped around the body. Paya Indians wore their hair short. Men painted themselves black and women red, both as decoration but also to protect themselves against insects. These people made baskets of wickerwork, pottery of clay polished by pebbles, wooden spoons, wooden stools, and blowguns. They were highly inventive.

It seems that political leaders were elected by village elders. As in most places in the Indian world, dancing and music went together, almost never one without the other. The Paya and Jicaque believed in two benevolent deities and in a female god of evil. After death, the Paya imagined a journey by the soul to a lower world of plenty. All believed that the natural world was full of spirits.[6] All in all, these Indians lived a peaceful life in which wars only rarely figured.

The meeting between the Indian and the Spanish worlds occurred thus. One of the Admiral's sailors, Ramiro Ramírez, recalled that "the Indians left two girls on the beach, and the Admiral ordered them to be captured and put in one of his boats and he made them dress and put shoes on, and then he left them where he had found them . . . and the Indians returned for them and took their clothes off. . . ."[7]

But by far the most interesting event in this part of Columbus's journey was his encounter, while still in the Bay Islands, with "a canoe as long as a galley and eight feet wide, made of a single tree trunk . . . freighted with merchandise from the western regions around New Spain. . . . It had a palm leaf awning like that which the Venetian gondolas carry; this gave complete protection against the rain and waves."[8] On this canoe the Spaniards encountered twenty-five traders from what has usually been identified as the Mayan territory of Yucatan. They were carrying embroidered shirts of dyed cotton, cotton cloaks, loincloths, long swords of wood with a groove on each side into which

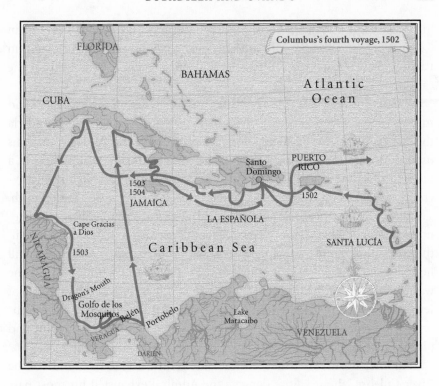

flints had been set, good copper hatchets, what seemed to be hawks' bells of copper, and "a certain wine made of maize, like the beer of England."[9] This was, as we now know, pulque. Women and children traveled under the awning, surrounded by tools of onyx and some of the cocoa beans that were used in the land of the Maya as a form of coinage. The Indians displayed "admirable modesty" because, "if one had his loincloth taken from him, he would immediately cover his genitals with his hands ... while the women covered their faces, as if they had been Moorish women in Granada."[10]

This meeting made a considerable impression on the Spaniards, especially, one must assume, on one of the cabin boys, Antonio de Alaminos, who would spend most of the rest of his life as a pilot pioneering expeditions in this region. The sophistication of these people was much greater than that of the Tainos or the Caribs; and what a relief to the Spaniards to find alcohol among indigenous people. "Columbus took one old man, a certain Yumbe, from among them as a translator and detained him until the ships reached the Costa de las Orejas, beyond which his language was not spoken, and then he sent him home."[11]

At this point, Columbus made a decision for which he was later reproached. He sailed along Central America not north and west, toward the higher civilization of the Maya, but east and then south. This route took him past Cape Gracias a Dios, Nicaragua; Caray (now Puerto Limón in Costa Rica); and the Bay of Chiriguí, to the bay he named Portobelo, in Panama, which Bastidas and Hojeda had once reached, coming from the east.

Columbus took this route because the natives whom the Spaniards had met at Guanaja had talked of a strait that Columbus thought must lead via the "Chersonese" (Malaya) to India.[12] He recorded this journey with his usual superlatives. He heard Mass on the coast in northern Honduras at a place to which he gave the name of Costa de las Orejas, and then he discovered Caray, "the best country and people that we had yet seen." To the south, "Veragua" (a territory probably so called after an ill-remembered indigenous name), in what is now western Panama, seemed to have gold. From it, the Columbus family eventually took a title that their descendants still hold.[13] Columbus wrote from there to the Catholic Kings optimistically; he was convinced that his masters were "just as much lords of this land as of Jerez and Toledo."[14] He had found a building of stone and lime, and he observed the extensive planting of maize. Lower down the coast, palm and pineapple wine flowed.

Another storm drove the Admiral and his little fleet to the mouth of the River Culebra, about whose dangers the Admiral exhausted his most passionate adjectives. They entered the Bay of Portobelo, which over the next few centuries was to be the scene of so much commerce and so many naval encounters. They continued to another bay, which they named Nombre de Dios, and then returned to Portobelo and Veragua, where they were in time to celebrate the Epiphany in 1503 in a valley that Columbus christened Belén. There they attempted to trade with the Indians. An expedition under Bartolomeo Colón found some signs of gold up the river, but waterfalls made it impossible for the boats to reach it. The Admiral thought of leaving Bartolomeo near Portobelo and returning again to La Española, against instructions, in order to mount a proper gold expedition, but the mood of the local Indians was turning sour, so he thought better of it.[15] To make matters worse, he observed that his ships had been damaged by termites.[16]

In desperation, Columbus went up to the crow's nest of his ship, where he communed with God at some length and also, it would seem, effectively.[17] In a short time, he managed to set sail for Santo Domingo. They reached the Jardines de la Reina at the beginning of May 1503, touched at Macaca, Cuba, near what is now known as Cabo Cruz, and finally arrived in Jamaica at the end of June, with crippled boats that could be sailed no farther. They anchored off Puerto Bueno, first, and then Santa Gloria (St. Ann's Bay), where Columbus had been in 1494.

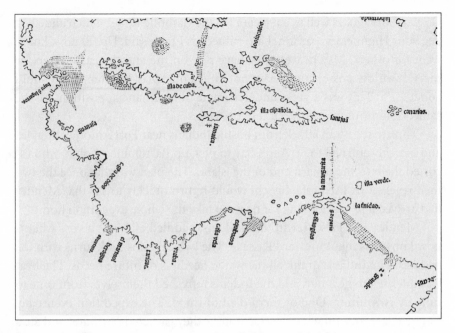

What was known and unknown in 1511: the official map of the time.

The Admiral had no choice but to build shelters from the timbers of the wrecked ships and fit them with straw roofs. When the expedition had divided the last rations of wine and biscuits, Diego Méndez, Columbus's great friend, set off into the interior and procured food (cassava bread and fish) from the natives. Indeed, he made arrangements for food to be brought every day. But how could the expedition return to Castile? By canoe to Santo Domingo across 120 miles of sea? No one volunteered save for Méndez, who at first had said that the journey was impossible. Then he told Columbus:

> "My lord, one life have I and no more. I am willing to risk it in your lordship's service and for the welfare of those present, because I have hope that our Lord God, seeing the good intention with which I shall do it, will deliver me, as He has done many times before." When the Admiral heard my decision, he arose and embraced me and kissed me on the cheek, saying, "I well knew that there was none who would dare to undertake this enterprise but you."[18]

In July 1503, Méndez left in a canoe with six Indians, accompanied by Bartolomeo Fieschi, the Genoese captain of one of Columbus's four caravels.[19] He took with him letters, including one from the Admiral to Fray

Gaspar Gorricio, as well as a *relación* for the Catholic Kings, which ended: "I beg your Highnesses' pardon. I am ruined, as I have said. Up till now, I have wept for others. May heaven now have pity on me and the earth weep for me. Of worldly possessions I have not even a maravedí to offer for my soul's good. . . ."[20] This was a gross underestimate of his financial position. All the same, Columbus evidently felt it to be true.

Threatened by an attack from hostile Indians near Port Antonio, Méndez and Fieschi returned to St. Ann's Bay to pick up Bartolomeo Colón, who escorted them to the eastern end of the island. The plan was that once the two men reached La Española, Fieschi would return quickly to say that Méndez had arrived and was looking for boats to take the whole expedition home.

Méndez and Fieschi, with the Indians, paddled all night across what is now known as the Windward Passage. The two captains took turns with the paddles. The Indians drank all the water, heedless of future needs. The heat was intense the next day, and the Indians refreshed themselves from time to time by swimming. One of them died of thirst. The expedition eventually found a bare rock on which, miraculously, they gathered rainwater and ate a few mollusks. They arrived exhausted at Cape San Miguel, at the western end of La Española, four days after their departure.

Fieschi, heroically, wanted to return there and then to Jamaica to tell Columbus of his and Méndez's success, but the Indians refused to go with him: they never wanted to paddle again. So both Méndez and Fieschi set off for Santo Domingo on foot, just as Bastidas had done a year before. They had reached Azúa, on the south coast of La Española, the bay where Columbus had sheltered from the storm the previous June, when they learned that Ovando was in Jaragua, 150 miles to the west.[21] Leaving Fieschi to go on alone to Santo Domingo, Méndez walked back to Jaragua, and found the Governor, who "kept me with him several months."[22] Ovando promised nothing. He was in no hurry to do anything to assist Columbus. So Méndez walked back the 200 miles to Santo Domingo. There he waited until some ships came from Spain. There was a long delay before three at last arrived. One of these was bought by Méndez in order to send it to Jamaica with supplies. But that was not till May 1504.

Back in Jamaica, there were many grumbles and denunciations. Food was a constant preoccupation. The Admiral and his companions ate rabbits, rats, and cassava bread. Finally, a rebellion broke out, led by Francisco de Porrás (once the captain of the *Santiago de Palos*) and his brother, Diego (the notary).

The Porrás brothers had been unwelcome to the Admiral from the beginning. They had been imposed on him by Morales, the royal treasurer, as will be recalled. One day at St. Ann's, Francisco de Porrás went to see Columbus and said, "*Señor,* what do you mean by making no effort to return to Castile? Do you wish us to stay here and perish?" The Admiral realized that this was a challenge, but merely replied that he knew no way of going home till a ship was sent. If Porrás had a good idea, he should submit it to the next council of captains. Porrás said that there was no time to talk; the Admiral should decide either to embark or to stay. Then he turned and shouted, "I'm for Castile. Who's with me?" All the men outside said, "We're with you," and running about in great disorder, these rebels soon occupied the castles and roundtops of the mainmasts of the wrecked ships, some wildly crying out, "To Castile, to Castile!" or "Death to them!" or "*Señor* captain, what now?"

The poor Admiral was at that time so crippled with gout that he could scarcely stand. But even so he hobbled forward with his sword drawn. His servants, however, dissuaded him from fighting and even prevailed on his more bellicose brother Bartolomeo to drop his lance. Porrás and his friends thereupon seized the canoes that Colón had procured, first to use themselves, and second to prevent their being seized by the Indians. They set out for Santo Domingo as gaily as if they had been sailing in a regatta. Many desperate men who had not been mutineers piled into these boats. Later, they picked up a few Indians and ordered them to paddle. The few loyal men and the sick remained behind, aghast.

The Porráses' expedition had to turn back less than twelve miles out from the east of Jamaica. The boats were overloaded and the winds variable; the mutineers became frightened and decided to lighten the boats. The obvious thing was to kill the Indians and throw them overboard. This they did; eighteen were so disposed of. They then landed at an Indian village in eastern Jamaica, near what is now Port Antonio, and made two further efforts to cross to La Española. They failed again because of contrary winds. So they made their way back sixty miles on foot to Columbus, robbing Indians as they went.[23] Then, as Columbus wrote with justifiable complacency, they were all "delivered into our hands. . . ."

While the Porrás brothers and their friends were absent, Columbus broke up a protest by local Indians who wanted to stop supplying him with food. He did this by predicting successfully, after consulting his books, an eclipse of the moon.[24] The Tainos were impressed, and for a time the Admiral could do no wrong. Finally, in May 1504, Diego de Escobar, a Sevillano, arrived from La Española on behalf of Ovando to verify Columbus's plight. He had been a gentleman volunteer on the Admiral's second voyage and afterwards a rebel with Roldán against Bartolomeo Colón. He brought a bar-

rel of wine and a haunch of salt pork, a modest contribution, it might be
thought, to the marooned expedition, as well as a friendly letter from
Ovando. He sailed off again almost immediately, taking with him a reply in
which the Admiral stated his "hope . . . that you will not spare yourself to
save me."[25] Columbus later explained that he had encouraged Escobar to sail
home quickly because his ship had been too small to take everyone off. The
Porrás brothers continued to plot, living separately, even coming to think
that the caravel of Escobar had been a myth. Surely a real caravel would not
have left so soon. Bartolomeo went to negotiate with them, but they attacked
him. But instead of the swift victory that they had expected, several mutineers were killed by Bartolomeo and his friends, including the chief pilot,
Juan Sánchez de Cádiz. Francisco Porrás was captured. On May 20, 1504, he
and his companions sued for peace.

At last, in June, two ships did arrive from La Española, thanks to Diego
Méndez, though Méndez himself had judged it better to return to Spain to
tell the monarchs what had happened. All the Spaniards left Jamaica on June
28. They had a difficult journey across the Windward Passage but arrived in
Santo Domingo on August 13. Ovando decided at last to appear generous
and lodged Columbus and his brothers for a day or two in his own house.
But, Fernando wrote, that was a "scorpion's kiss" since Porrás was released
by Ovando, and he vowed to punish those responsible for his previous imprisonment.

On September 12, Columbus, with his brother Bartolomeo and his son
Fernando, left for Spain. When at sea, the mainmast of the first ship of the
flotilla split. Another mast also broke in a storm. Yet the skill of the Columbus brothers was such that they arrived safely in Sanlúcar, where they
learned that the Queen, Columbus's benefactor in so many ways, was on her
deathbed in her favorite city, Medina del Campo.

During the years that Columbus was away, the monarchs had shown as
usual only a sporadic curiosity about the new empire in the Indies. No one
even called it an empire yet, and the maintenance of Spanish interests in
Naples (to which cause King Fernando gave increasing attention) seemed
more imperial as well as more important. But the Crown now plainly conceived of the New World as theirs, not Columbus's, and certainly not as belonging to its indigenous monarchs. That world was still thought of as "the
Indies." Whether it was still believed that these Indies were close to the real
India is curiously difficult to ascertain. As early as 1494, Francisco de Cisneros, a clerk of Seville, had declared that "these new islands . . . are not in

India but are in the Ethiopian ocean sea, and are [should be] called the Hesperides. . . ."[26] Peter Martyr always thought much the same. But Columbus continued to insist that he had been to India, Malaya, and China, as well as Japan, and he still enjoyed the fame of being the great explorer, however bad he had shown himself to be as an administrator. A bull of 1504 in Rome mentioned the conquests by Spain as having occurred "in parts of Asia," and even named three new episcopal sees there.[27]

Spain's links with La Española were by then continuous. Despite the delay in 1504 that had so distressed Diego Méndez, twenty or thirty ships a year seem usually to have plied between Seville, or Sanlúcar, and Santo Domingo or Puerto Plata.[28] Sometimes Ovando would send back *caciques* to Spain to learn Spanish; they would be received by a friend of his, Juan Vázquez, and would stay for two years. Some of them later returned with Juan Bermúdez, who had been captain of the *Santa Cruz* on Columbus's third voyage to the Indies and would soon give his name to the lonely island due east of what became Georgia.

Commerce was growing every year. Thus, on September 12, 1502, we find a license granted to Juan Sánchez de la Tesorería, a prominent Aragonese merchant (a *converso*) and dealer in olives in Spain, and Alonso García Bravo, described as a messenger of the Queen, to take five caravels to La Española with a varied cargo of goods. The two merchants had to give the royal secretary Jimeno de Briviesca proof of the value of their goods so that, once these were sold, the Crown would receive a quarter of the profit.[29] Columbus, or his representatives in Spain, would still be able to contribute an eighth of the goods carried, and Governor Ovando would also be able to carry seventy tons free of tax. One ship on this voyage carried a rood screen on which were depicted scenes of Spain and Flanders, done by two painters of Seville, Diego de Castro and Francisco de Villegas. But the most important items taken to the Indies were clothes, many made in northern Europe, sometimes in London; and there was Dutch linen, and velvet from Flanders. These ships indeed took the most complete range of goods that "one could imagine."[30]

The monarchs were at Toledo in early 1502, and Fernando spent part of the summer in Aragon, where he persuaded the Cortes in Saragossa to accept his daughter Juana as his heir if, as now seemed inevitable, he had no son. Both monarchs then went to the Alcázar at Madrid, where they remained most of the rest of the year. News was brought to them sporadically of the Indies, but their minds were more concerned with things nearer at hand, such as a famine caused by harvest failures. They must have heard that in Aznalcóllar, twenty-five miles northeast of Seville, the populace went to the mayor to demand the wheat that they knew to be in a warehouse; "if they were not given the wheat, they said, they would break in and take it in order to avoid seeing their children die."[31] The monarchs also approved an innocuous-sounding decree that provided that authors had to obtain a license and pay a fee to magistrates before printing books. The import of books from abroad would also thenceforth require a license from the Council of Castile.[32] The shadow of censorship began to lie across the life of Spain. But it was still faint in a world where books themselves were such novelties.

The problems of Jewry and *conversos* also affected the Queen: she had to face the fearful rumor that Archbishop Talavera, her longtime friend, adviser, and onetime confessor, as well as the bishops of Jaén and Almería, the chief ecclesiastical judge, Juan Álvarez Zapata, and royal secretary, Juan de Zafra, not to speak of the treasurer Ruy López, were all "crypto-Jews," plotting, according to their accusers, to send preachers of the Mosaic law to the court to announce that not only Elijah but the Messiah himself had come.[33] (There is nothing that recalls Isabel's reaction to these alarming accusations.)

Presumably, too, in these months the Queen learned of various punishments inspired by the Holy Office; how in July 1502, in Tablada, just outside Seville to the southwest, five people were burned at the stake. Three of them were women punished for heresy, "one of those being the mother of Diego de la Muela, one of the royal accountants. . . . *Deo gracias.* . . ."[34] But there was no chance that the Queen would intervene in such matters, and, anyway, in the summer of 1502, she had begun to suffer from a severe illness that was probably a form of cancer. All the same, she was still active for many months. For example, in October 1502, she ordered the *corregidor* of Toledo and the treasurer of Madrid, Alonso Gutiérrez, to begin an inquiry into the way that so much gold was leaving her kingdom because of the activities of bankers.

Gutiérrez was one more important person close to the court who was a *converso* in origin. He was a councillor (*veinticuatro*) of Seville, where he lived after 1510, and was also treasurer of the mint and then of the Santa Hermandad, in which capacity he had swiftly resolved the question of the payment to the knights whose horses were taken by Columbus to La Española in 1493. He and a colleague, Fernando de Villareal, had also been asked to pay 15,000 ducats, which would otherwise have gone to the treasury of the Hermandad, toward the costs of Ovando's armada to the Indies.[35] In the next twenty years, Gutiérrez would accumulate a fortune and become a controversial individual of considerable influence.[36]

This investigation into the loss of Spain's gold began in the early months of 1503. Special attention was paid to Francisco Palmaro and Pedro Sánchez of the Bank of Valencia, which, with its easy access to Italy and other Mediterranean markets, seemed responsible. After the inquiry, the papers were passed to the Council of the Realm to initiate a trial. Bail of 10 million maravedís each was given for Palmaro and Sánchez.[37] In fact, at that time the Queen personally owed them 12 million maravedís. The prosecutor of the Council presented a criminal accusation against the two men, stating that they had taken 150 million maravedís in gold out of Spain in the last four years, and asked for a death sentence. As so often happened, the sentence was approved but never carried out. The simple reason for the flight of the gold was that Italians, especially the Genoese, sold more products in Spain than they exported.[38]

Fernando spent most of 1503 in Aragon trying to shore up his position in southern Italy, which had been diminished by an arrangement concluded by his unpredictable son-in-law Philip. This arrangement had stipulated that Naples would pass to Philip's son, the baby Charles (the future Charles V), and the French princess Claudia, the daughter of the heir to the French throne, Louis, Duke of Orléans, whom Charles was expected to marry. In the meantime (which might be a long time), Naples would be ruled jointly by the Flemings and the French. Fernando was not prepared to accept that arrangement and was soon sending more troops to his general in Italy, the brilliant Gran Capitán. This dispute between father-in-law and son-in-law augured badly for their future collaboration in Spain.

In 1502, meanwhile, the Indies forced themselves upon the monarchs' attention when one of Columbus's friends in Seville, Francisco Piñelo, whose multitudinous commercial activities have been amply noted, wrote a paper entitled "What Seems Necessary to Regulate Business and Contracting in the Indies."[39] This sketched out a plan for what would become the Casa de Contratación de Indias (the House of Trade in the Indies). That would be to some degree a copy of the Casa da Guiné, a body in Lisbon that organized the African trade of Portugal (Lisbon had since 1498 also had a Casa de India). It would owe something, too, to the Consulado of Burgos, established in 1494, and there were similar organizations in Valencia, Palma de Mallorca, and Barcelona. (Burgos was then the major wool city of Castile. Though one hundred miles from the sea, it organized shipments of wool from Basque and Cantabrian ports such as San Sebastián and Laredo.)

To direct this proposed new institution Piñelo proposed that there would be an agent, or factor, a treasurer, and two accountants, who would be able, with specialist's eyes, to inspect ships to ensure that they were not overloaded and, where necessary, advise the captains bound for the Indies as to the best route to take.

As a consequence of Piñelo's memorandum, the Catholic Kings, on January 20, 1503, ordered this "Casa de Contratación" to be established in Seville.[40] The institution followed closely the proposals of the previous year, though there would be only one accountant. Francisco Piñelo himself would be the first factor, and a Sevillano canon, Sancho de Matienzo, from Villasana de Mena, in the foothills of the Cantabrian mountains, where he had founded a monastery, would be the first treasurer. No doubt his Burgos antecedents commended him. Jimeno de Briviesca (Fonseca's *converso* assistant) would be the first notary. The Casa would initially be set up in part of the Alcázar of Seville known as the Atarazanas, but it was soon moved to another part of that palace, facing the river. The square in front of the Casa would soon be known as the Plaza de Contratación, as it is today. By March 1503, Piñelo and Matienzo were both installed, and Briviesca was about to arrive. Matienzo was a competent civil servant; one who has studied the accounts of the Casa said that "his work surpassed that of any treasurer or comptroller who followed him."[41]

If partly inspired by Burgos, the connection with Aragonese precedents made the Casa more of a Spanish national institution than at first appeared. Its responsibilities were extended to include trade with the Canary Islands and the Barbary coast, while the mint in Seville was charged in July 1502 with coining the gold that the Casa should give it, though only a third of the gold of the Casa was to be treated in Seville, the rest being dealt with in Granada or Toledo.[42]

The Casa began to function on February 25, 1503. Despite the advocacy of Piñelo, the motor behind this scheme was undoubtedly Fonseca, whose capacity for hard work and administration were shown to advantage.[43] The establishment of the Casa in Seville also confirmed that city as the de facto capital of the Indies. A decree of January 20 had confined the government's dealings with the New World to this new Casa, which was to be at once a market, a magistracy, a registry of ships, a center of information, and a registry of captains.[44] A postal service was organized from it to ensure that the court, wherever it might be, would be informed of events affecting it within forty-eight hours. All trade with the New World was required to pass through the Casa. At the beginning, ships were allowed to receive their cargoes elsewhere and then go to Seville to register them, but after a while that was found impossible. All ships thereafter had to begin their journeys at Seville.

Within a year or two an official map of the New World, the so-called Padrón Real, was being drawn and regularly revised by the cosmographer at the Casa for sale to the public.

The Casa de Contratación's powers were defined in a declaration from the Queen in July 1503.[45] The Casa could from then on impose fines, send malefactors to prison, demand bail, and deviate from the city of Seville's requirements. A decree of January 1504 allowed the officials of the Casa to issue licenses on whatever conditions they thought fit. Power was in their hands.[46] But the words of the first declaration were as vague as they were far-reaching. Legal disputes between the Casa and Seville followed, and not until 1508 was it agreed that the judicial authorities in the latter should not intervene in the affairs of the Casa. In 1503, the disputes were continuous, as was to be expected with a new institution whose officials were feeling their way.

Cadiz, with its deep bay, had, to be honest, a better, more accessible harbor than Seville. Ships leaving Seville had to pass Sanlúcar de Barrameda, where the bar was dangerous, while the journey from there up the River Guadalquivir to Seville was difficult. But Seville had many advocates. It was easier to defend against piratical attacks than was Cadiz, on its peninsula, and it was closer to internal Castilian commerce. The goods that the settlers in the Caribbean wanted—wine, flour, olive oil—were more easily obtained in Seville than in Cadiz, which had no hinterland. The ports of the Río Tinto, such as Palos and Moguer, were too small and too close to the frontier with Portugal to be serious alternatives, for hard-won gold might have been easily smuggled thence to Lisbon if the Casa had been founded there. So, for two hundred years and more, the Casa de Contratación remained at Seville; and for two hundred years cannon would fire a signal indicating that within six hours heavily laden caravels bound for the Indies would cast off their moorings and begin to drop down the river to Sanlúcar and the sea.[47]

The first dispatch of a ship for the Indies under the control of the Casa was in November 1503, when Pedro de Llanos, an old friend of Columbus's, went out as factor to Santo Domingo to succeed Francisco de Monroy, who had died. Thereafter, as a matter of course, all emigrants to the New World registered first at the Casa.

In March 1503, meanwhile, another decree provided that no more slaves—Berbers or black slaves from Africa—should be sent to La Española from Spain. The reason was that some of those who had been sent had rebelled and helped similar risings by Indians.[48] The question of slavery in the Americas was left for a later decree. How many black slaves had already gone to La Española is obscure; such papers as refer to the matter are inconclusive. If the number exceeded fifty, it would be surprising.

At the end of that same month, the monarchs dictated a detailed rule for the education of Indians into a civilized Christian life. The decree was entitled "Of Innocence and Confusion."[49] It seems to have been a reply to a report of Ovando's, now lost. Cisneros must have collaborated in the drafting. The Indians of the islands in the New World were not to be allowed to disperse; on the contrary, they should be brought together to live in families in towns, so that they could be more easily instructed in Christianity. Each Indian family was to have a house. There would, as a rule, be a church, a chaplain, and a hospital in every settlement, all under a Spanish protector, the *encomendero,* to avoid the injustice of the *caciques.* The Indians would be taught by the chaplain to respect the property of others, and the *encomendero* would protect his charges against exploitation. Indian children would be educated in the faith and instructed how to read and write. The Crown also supported mixed marriages between Spaniards and Indians.

All Indians would be encouraged to dress decently, and there would be no blasphemy (an injunction, of course, as necessary to insist upon in respect of Spaniards as of Indians). All would pay tithes and taxes. All fiestas would be Christian festivals, and there would be no naked bathing. All would be baptized and informed how best to renounce pagan customs. To protect the Indians, they were not to be able to sell property to settlers.[50]

Another decree of late March 1503 embroidered these rules. It provided that "in each of the said towns, and next to the said churches, there should always be provided a house where the children in those towns should go twice a day and where a chaplain would be able not only to teach them to read and write, but also to make the sign of the cross, and learn the Lord's Prayer, the *Ave María,* the Apostles' Creed, and the *Salve Regina.*"[51] This instruction explains why 138 short primers (*cartillas*) were sent to the Indies in 1505, probably written by Hernando de Talavera, still the Archbishop of Granada—the addressees being Indians, not Spaniards.

The regulations for Indians working in mines, however, contradicted these utopian visions. Another instruction to Ovando, for example, urged that Indian towns should be established close to mines.[52] It would seem obvious that neither for the first nor for the last time in imperial history the government was speaking with two voices: two different people were advising the monarchs.

The royal adviser concerned with economic matters was Fonseca. But the one who was preoccupied with ensuring the peace of the souls of the indigenous people was Cisneros. In relation to Muslims, the Cardinal had been inflexible. But his record in respect of the New World was benign. In the same way, the Dominicans would show themselves harsh to Jews at home, benevolent to Indians abroad.[53]

Another important declaration concerning the relations of the Spaniards with the Indians in the New World, of October 30, was addressed by the Queen at Segovia to the future monarchs, Philip and Juana, her daughter and son-in-law.[54] It was supposed to ensure that

> the King, my lord, and I, with the aim of ensuring that everyone who lives in the islands and mainland of the ocean sea [a somewhat strange way, it may seem, of expressing the matter] become Christians and be converted to our Catholic faith, have sent a letter stating that nobody of our administration should dare to take prisoner anyone, or any people, of the Indian inhabitants of those territories, to carry them to these my realms or anywhere else.
>
> And in order to convince those who are Christians to live as reasonable men, we have ordered some of our captains to go to the said regions and to take with them some monks in order to indoctrinate and preach our holy Catholic faith . . . to those places where there are a people who are known as cannibals,[55] and who never wanted to hear them or welcome them, defending themselves with arms, and in that resistance have killed one or two Christians and afterwards, in their brutality and pertinacity, have made war on the Indians who are in my service, taking them to eat them[56] . . . and . . . it must be right for the cannibals to be punished for the crimes that they have committed against my subjects.[57]

Isabel added that she had asked her "council to look into the matter and discuss it," and the council had thought that, because of the cannibals' "many crimes" and their reluctance even to hear the propagation of the Christian doctrine, "they could be captured and taken to the other islands" so as thereafter to be converted to Christianity effectively.[58]

That was a double-edged statement. Indigenous people would be well treated, provided they were submissive and accepted Christianity as well as Spanish rule; but if they resisted and fought, they would be called cannibals and denounced for eating their captives, and so enslaved. There was, however, no racial distinction between the two: a rebellious Taino, such as the Spaniards would encounter in Puerto Rico, might be described as a cannibal; and a docile Carib, if one were to be found, might be a good Indian. Before the contradictions behind this declaration were resolved, the Indians of the Caribbean were, for other reasons, which will be explored later, close to extinction.

Following these decrees, there was some discussion in the court while it was at Medina del Campo at the end of 1503 as to the basis of Spanish rule in the Americas. Members of the Council of the Realm and other lawyers and theologians took part. Fray Diego de Deza (now Inquisitor-General of Castile as well as Bishop of Salamanca) was present. They made little progress. It is true they decided that Indians "running away from the Christians, and from work, would be treated as vagabonds." They carefully considered the statements of Pope Alexander VI and seem to have agreed, in the presence of the Archbishop of Seville, that it was in accord with divine as well as human law that Indians should serve Spaniards.[59] But all present seem to have realized that the issue was far from settled.

Another decree, issued at Medina del Campo by the Queen on December 20, 1503, regularized the idea of the division, *repartimiento*, of Tainos among the Spaniards, making the surviving *caciques* responsible for the recruitment of the workers.[60] Those who worked in mines were to be there not more than six to eight months and were then, by a rule known as "the delay," to be sent back to their villages, where they could busy themselves again in vegetable-producing allotments. A visitor would be named for each town to ensure that the work was fairly carried out. Perhaps Ovando had been influenced to achieve these so-called *encomiendas* on the basis of what he knew of them from being a *comendador* of the distinguished Order of Alcántara.

This was a refinement on the earlier arrangements of Columbus and Roldán. For the plan now was that each native would be given over for exploitation to an individual Spaniard, unless he was assigned to the Crown for work in the mines or in agriculture. In theory, the Tainos as subjects of the Crown would only work for wages. They were to be known not as slaves but as *naborías*, a word that derived from the Taino language.[61] In practice, they were treated much as if they had been slaves, or even worse since their masters had no incentive to treat them well.[62] It has been suggested that the status conferred on the Indian was one of "pupil" of the Crown, with rights and duties. The state would undertake, through the settler, to protect, feed, and "civilize" the Indian, looking after his physical well-being as well as his everlasting soul. But the settler had the right to the work of the "pupil" in return.

Encomiendas in Spain in the Middle Ages had implied a grant of jurisdiction as well as of manorial rights, and *encomenderos* had received rights to services from the people concerned. In La Española and later elsewhere in the Indies, an *encomienda* now included an obligation to instruct Indians who worked on land on which landlords were beginning to produce cattle, pigs, cassava, yams, and sugar.

The Indians must have looked on the matter differently, for in practice they were worked beyond their strength. If they ran away, they were treated much the same as fugitive slaves. People soon began to notice a demographic decline, though when that was first remarked upon is surprisingly obscure.

These were also difficult years in Spain. The monarchs were still much more worried about the country's economy, bad harvests, hunger, and the high mortality in the peninsula than about what was happening to a few thousand emigrants to the New World. The harvest in Castile of 1504 was so bad that the price of wheat went up to 600 maravedís per *fanega*.[63] Galicia, Asturias, and Vizcaya had never been able to feed themselves, but now even Castile was becoming reliant on foreign grain. Partly, this was a consequence of laws such as that of 1501 by which all land on which migrant sheep had pastured was reserved forever for the sheep cooperative, the Mesta. Vast swathes of Extremadura and Andalusia were therefore kept from agriculture. Royal encouragement of wool meant the ruin of arable farming. Ironically, 1504 was the year when there appeared the successful pastoral poem *Arcadia* by Sannazaro, about the charms of country life.[64]

But not all the news was bad.[65] The monarchs could rejoice in the remarkable series of successes in Italy achieved by the Gran Capitán; thus, in May 1503, he entered Naples in triumph after defeating the French at Cerignola. On December 28, 1503, he gained another victory over the French at Garigliano. On January 1, 1504, Gaeta capitulated. The French recognized that they had lost Naples forever. Southern Italy was confirmed as the eastern bastion of Spain's possessions. Naples and Sicily were henceforth part of the Spanish Empire.[66] Like the Caribbean, they remained so for generations.

These victories were the consequence of the Gran Capitán's transformation of his troops into a powerful infantry—itself the result of good protective armor, such as cuirasses and light helmets. A skillful reconstruction of the army was achieved on the basis of colonelcies of four companies supported by cavalry and artillery. New weapons such as lombards and arquebuses had also been added to the swords, spears, and javelins of the past. Henceforth, Naples (like Sicily and Sardinia) was run by viceroys appointed by the Aragonese Crown.

These victories went some way toward compensating Spain for the loss of a friend at the Vatican: Alexander VI (Rodrigo Borgia) died, and following the brief papacy of Pope Pius III, who died only ten days after his coronation, Cardinal Juliano della Rovere, the French nominee, a magisterial Genoese who was a nephew of Pope Sixtus IV, succeeded as Julius II—a prince of the Church determined, as the Venetian ambassador Domenico Treviano would put it, to play "the world's game"—and play it he did.[67]

The Queen finally took to her bed at Medina del Campo in May 1504. She seemed to suffer considerably. Thus Peter Martyr wrote in October that "the doctors have lost all hope for her health. The illness spread throughout her veins and slowly the dropsy [hidropesia] became obvious. A fever never abandoned her, penetrating her to the core. Day and night she had an insatiable thirst, while the sight of food gave her nausea. The mortal tumor grew fast between skin and flesh."[68] She ceased to see ordinary documents and now only signed important ones.

The Queen signed nothing at all after September 14 except her will. That document of October 4 began by begging her daughter and her husband—in that order—to dedicate themselves without rest to the conquest of Africa and the crusade against Islam. After all, one could argue that the Visigothic kingdom of Spain had included Morocco. She wanted to be buried in a habit of St. Francis in the Franciscan monastery of St. Isabel. Her heirs were never to alienate the marquisate of de Villena, which Isabel had won for the Crown, or indeed Gibraltar. Her oldest daughter, Juana, would be her heir: "Conforming with what I ought to do and am obliged to do by law, I order and establish for her, my universal heir . . . to be received as the true Queen and natural proprietress." She expressed gratitude for what King Fernando had done in Castile and reaffirmed his rights to all his Castilian undertakings.[69] Fernando was also to have half the income that Isabel had received from the Indies.

A codicil to the Queen's will, dated November 23, 1504, added an allusion to the New World: "At the time when we were conceded by the holy apostolic see the islands and mainland of the Ocean Sea . . . our main aim was to arrange the introduction there of our holy Catholic faith and to ensure that the people there accepted it, and also to send prelates, monks, priests, and other learned people who fear God to instruct the people in the faith and to teach and indoctrinate them with good customs."[70] This codicil suggests that she considered her title to the Indies secure.[71] Later, the Dominicans used these paragraphs to confirm that the Crown had accepted the mission to convert the Indians as the chief aim of Spanish rule in the New World.

Isabel's last actions in relation to the Indies were to approve a new expedition to the north coast of South America directed by Juan de la Cosa and Pedro de Ledesma[72] and to appoint, on September 30, 1504, the ambitious son of Cuenca, Alonso de Hojeda, as governor of the Colombian bay of

Urabá and its surroundings, on what is now the border of Colombia and Panama. It was one of the most desperate assignments ever granted by any Crown. Urabá then, as now, was unfit for human life. The heat and humidity were intolerable. Yet it was to be the first colony on the mainland. Tribute to the monarch would be paid on the sixth part of everything sold. Hojeda's backers were a curious combination: the *converso* merchant Juan Sánchez de la Tesorería; Lorenzo de Ahumado, a lawyer who may also have been Jewish in origin—a Catalina Sánchez de Ahumado had been *"reconciliada"* in 1494; the heirs of Juan de Vergara, who had sailed with Hojeda in 1499 and whose mother had been condemned to perpetual imprisonment in 1494 as a false Christian; and García de Ocampo, an Extremeño who alone of these men seems to have been an old Christian. But this improbable undertaking had made no headway before Isabel's death.

According to Columbus, just returned to Spain after his terrible fourth voyage, the "nobles of the realm now sharpened their teeth as if they had been wild boar, in the expectation of a great mutation in the state." In a letter to his son Diego, Columbus mentioned again how "Satan" had upset his own destiny; and he insisted that he had served their Highnesses with such diligence and love as to deserve to live in Paradise.[73]

Columbus never saw the Queen again, for on November 26 she entered "Pluto's tenebrous kingdom," as the author of *Tirant lo Blanc* would have put it. She received extreme unction from the Prior of La Mejorada. Fernando was present. She gave freedom to all her personal slaves—no doubt they included blacks from Africa, Berbers as well as Negroes, not to speak of Canary Islanders and men and women captured at Malaga and in Granada.[74] Her body was taken to Granada and was interred there in the royal chapel of the new cathedral on December 18, her ex-confessor, the Archbishop Talavera, presiding. Subsequently, the Florentine Domenico Fancelli sculpted her likeness for a magnificent tomb.

Isabel had been a great queen. With the help of her husband, Fernando, she had established peace at home. She had tamed the nobility. Her ecclesiastical reforms alone should cause her to be remembered for her intelligence. She chose her advisers intelligently. Castile in 1504 was unrecognizable to anyone who remembered the bellicose disorder of 1474. Her reputation assisted the unity of the kingdom. Her support for Columbus had been essential to secure the "enterprise" of the Indies. With the assistance of her husband, she established institutions that lasted. For Isabel, Christianity represented truth itself. Peter Martyr wrote of her as "the mirror of virtues, refuge of good things, scourge of evil," adding that "under the body of a woman she had always a manly spirit."[75]

But great queens, like great men, make great mistakes. Her reliance in her last years—from 1492 to 1504—on Cisneros made for intolerance as well as virtue. She therefore not only sponsored the Inquisition, but also the expulsion of both Jews and Muslims. Her tomb in Granada shows her in tranquillity. It was something she never obtained in life. The death of her only son, one of her daughters, and a grandson, and the unpredictable quality of Juana la Loca cast heavy shadows over her. She suffered as well as celebrated.

"Children must constantly obey their parents"

King Fernando said, "You, my dear daughter, as sovereign of the realms, must choose the place where you would like to live." In reply, Juana ventured, "Children must constantly obey their parents."

Peter Martyr, 1507[1]

The death of Queen Isabel in November 1504 threw her kingdoms into confusion. For a time, indeed for nearly two years, it seemed that the old bad days previous to her reign might be returning. Fernando of Aragon had been King of Castile while his wife lived. Afterwards he had no claim. That throne was now in the hands of Philip and Juana.

Part of the difficulty, however, was caused by Isabel herself, for, most surprisingly, her will was confused. In respect of the regency in Castile after her death, the Queen in her codicil even contradicted the will itself. Should Fernando, Philip of Flanders, or Cardinal Cisneros act for Juana, who was now presumed incapable?[2] Fernando might now be merely ex–King Consort and King of Aragon. Yet he had banners raised for Juana as "*la Reina propri-etaria*" as she was proclaimed, and he had himself proclaimed both governor and administrator. He returned to his favorite monastery of La Mejorada, near Medina del Campo, at the end of November 1504, went to Medina del Campo itself on December 10, and then repaired to Toro, where he remained until the end of April 1505, in order to meet the Cortes of Castile. Philip and Juana, meanwhile, remained in Flanders, the Habsburgs' rich and creative principality, which the Emperor Maximilian, Philip's father, had inherited from his late wife, Mary of Burgundy.

In the confusion in Castile, caused by the infirmity of poor Juana, crowds rioted in cities; noblemen seized towns to which they had no right; city councils, split into factions, were paralyzed; people sought ways to influence Juana and Philip; and even men of integrity found it difficult to know how to act.[3]

On January 11, 1505, Isabel's will was read to the Cortes assembled at Toro, which declared it law, took an oath to Fernando as "*administrador e gobernador*," and agreed that were Juana to be declared ill, Fernando should be permanent Regent, Philip being informed of the decision. Fernando had Castilian coins stamped "Fernando and Juana, King and Queen of Castile, León, and Aragón."[4] But all the same, many grandees, seeing the way that the wind seemed to be blowing, went to Flanders or sent messages there, to curry favor with Philip and Juana, who were both displeased at Fernando's self-assertions. A few months before, the country had seemed full of strong men. It suddenly appeared to be peopled by vacillating dwarfs. The movement of so many aristocrats toward Philip's side can only be explained by their longstanding suspicion of Fernando, who was, with Cisneros, the only man of quality left.

At the end of April 1505, that monarch set off, via Arévalo, for Segovia, where he remained nearly all the summer—until, indeed, mid-October. Again the harvest was disastrous; wheat in Castile was selling at 375 maravedís the *fanega*, while in Extremadura it was again up to 600.[5] Then, because he was still desirous of having a son, Fernando contracted to remarry, to most people's amazement and shock—to King Louis of France's niece, Germaine de Foix. Their wedding was celebrated in Valladolid on March 22 of the next year.[6]

This marriage marked a reversal of Fernando's usual policy of alliances against France. Germaine was then a pretty girl of eighteen, Fernando fifty-four. Heirs seemed likely. Further, Germaine was a Navarrese, a fact that would assist Fernando in policies toward Navarre, which he coveted. The marriage had been agreed by Fernando in return for Louis's abandonment of any claim to Naples. Naples was, however, Germaine's dowry. If she died childless, the damaging French claim could be revived. That said, the marriage risked the unity of the realms of Aragon and Castile that had been so carefully put together by the Catholic Kings. But a male heir would guarantee that Aragon at least would remain in the hands of a Spanish prince, not in those of a Habsburg. For Fernando, appearing as a patriot, the stakes seemed high.

It also seemed likely, meanwhile, that there might be a major quarrel between King Fernando and his son-in-law Philip over details of policy. The issue of Naples already divided them; and in September 1505, Philip, still in Flanders and desirous of breaking with the past, suspended the Inquisition in Castile. Fernando complained to the Pope.[7]

But then he was able to reach an agreement, the so-called Concordia de Salamanca, with the Fleming de Veyre and Andrea del Burgo, two representatives of Philip. A combined government for Castile would be formed of the three monarchs, Juana, Fernando, and Philip. The Cortes now swore allegiance at Toro to Juana and Philip as *"reyes proprietarias"* in their absence and to Fernando as *"gobernador perpetuo."*[8] On January 7, 1506, Philip and Juana embarked at Flushing, on their way to Spain. Considering that the Low Countries were Castile's best customer for wool, and Castile was one of the Netherlands' best export markets, there was a certain logic to the new arrangement.

As for the Inquisition, the new Inquisitor-General (Cisneros had given up), Archbishop Deza, Columbus's old friend, wrote the following year to Philip and to Juana that he was delaying all "the suits that were pending in that year in both Seville and in other cities until their Highnesses had properly considered what they wanted to do in relation to the Holy Inquisition"—which, "pleasing God, one might hope would be soon."[9] In June 1506, Deza, in Astorga, explained that the suspension only affected criminal charges, and minor cases would continue.[10]

Philip and Juana were shipwrecked off England and only arrived in Corunna, in Galicia, on April 26, 1506. They stayed in the city, recovering from the journey, for a month, till May 28. Probably they went to Galicia to avoid Fernando's coming to meet them at Laredo, or elsewhere on the northern Castilian coast. Corunna was already a major port, with a fine harbor. With his usual agreeable habit of exaggeration, Peter Martyr would say of it that "it has no equal. It has capacity for all the ships that plow the seas."[11] Many nobles went to greet these monarchs, if that is what they were, including the Duke of Infantado; the Admiral, Fadrique Enríquez; and even the Constable, Velasco, who had previously hesitated as to whom to support. Many bishops, including Cisneros, also gave their loyalty to Philip. Columbus wrote sycophantically to explain why he had not gone to meet them.[12] Fernando's position as ruler of Castile seemed to be crumbling.

Philip was, as Peter Martyr wrote, "harder than a diamond."[13] But that, he thought, was no bad thing in a king. He also thought that there was no one on earth more agreeable than Philip, none more brave among the princes of the time, nobody more handsome. His bearing was wonderful, his verbal subtlety impressive.[14] Furthermore, any king in Spain could expect loyalty from his nobles. Yet Philip had long ago claimed, to Juana's constant distress, the usual princely freedom from his wife.[15] He was also dreaming of bringing Portugal under Spanish control, an ambition that might have occurred to any hot-blooded Fleming who had no knowledge of the real differences that existed between those countries.

King Fernando then made a curious journey. Determined to confront his son-in-law and daughter, he left Valladolid on April 28 for Dueñas, Torquemada, Palencia, Carrión de los Condes, Sahagún, and then León. At León, he sent emissaries to Philip and Juana. Among them was Peter Martyr, who, according to his own account, sought to persuade Philip not to quarrel with his father-in-law.[16] A complicated dance followed, with Fernando visiting many places that no monarch had previously visited or, indeed, would ever visit again.[17] Finally, in the far west of Castile, on June 20, in a farmhouse at Remesal, in the valley of Sanabria, near the Portuguese border, he met Philip, who had come equally slowly, but more directly, from Corunna, through Galicia, passing splendid Betanzos, superb Santiago, curious Ribadavia, with its deserted *judería* (Jewish quarter), delectable Orense, with its sacred hot waters, on the River Miño, with its exquisite wines, and finally Sanabria.[18]

Philip arrived at the remote rendezvous at Remesal with an army, Fernando with patience. Perhaps Juana, who spoke perfect French due to her ten years in Brussels, acted as an interpreter, as she had done in 1502 during her and Philip's first journey to Spain.[19] Fernando agreed with Philip that, contrary to what the will of Isabel had stipulated, it would be unwise to expect Juana to rule. He accepted thereafter that in Castile his son-in-law Philip should have exclusive power. Afterwards, Fernando left for Villafáfila, a tiny town in León, where, on June 27, he agreed to abandon his regency of Castile in favor of his "most beloved children" Philip and Juana. His withdrawal was an act of realism and was not what he had desired. Even the Count of Tendilla in Granada began in self-interest to turn toward Philip. Fernando went to Tudela del Duero and Renedo, where, on July 5, he again met Philip and Juana (they had come via Benavente and Mucientes). He now agreed to retire to Aragon, where he immediately, if secretly, renounced the agreement of Villafáfila.[20] He was protected on this journey by the lancers of the Duke of Alba, a service that he never forgot: Alba could always count on the King afterwards for what he wanted.

Philip took over authority as King Philip I of Castile. He made his way to Valladolid, effectively the capital, and was confirmed by a Cortes there on July 12. The parliamentarians (*procuradores*) swore allegiance to Juana as Queen Regnant ("*reina titular*"), to Philip as her husband, and to their six-year-old son, Charles, far away in Flanders, as their heir. The courtier Juan Manuel, who had cultivated Philip so extensively in Flanders and was a master of intrigue, would be their chief minister. "As astute as he was energetic" was the verdict on him by a historian of the papacy.[21] Fonseca, who had up till now never left the side of King Fernando, abandoned his charge of the

Indies and withdrew to his bishopric of Burgos, while his assistant, Lope Conchillos, of whom Martyr speaks as being "good-natured and clever, of proven loyalty to the royal family," was imprisoned and tortured in the castle of Vilvorde.[22] With Fonseca he had plotted to try to keep Philip from power.

Philip and Juana remained in Valladolid until July 31, when they went to Cogeces de Iscar, a little town between Valladolid and Segovia. Juana feared that if she stayed in the castle there she would be locked up in it, and refused to remain, a curious but successful measure of self-preservation. On August 8 they moved to Tudela de Duero, where, remarkably, they spent three weeks. It had had a pretty Jewish quarter, now empty. Philip sent Archbishop Deza back to Seville and told him to delegate his powers as inquisitor-general to the Bishop of Catania, Diego Ramírez de Guzmán.[23] The young joint monarchs, husband and wife, then went to Burgos. By that time, Fernando had reached Barcelona.

After spending a month there, Fernando set off on September 4 for Italy, to which he had never been though he had devoted such extraordinary care to it. He was interested in the reorganization of the political structure of Naples and anxious to replace the Gran Capitán, of whom Fernando was said to have become jealous because of his marvelous achievements, with another commander. He also had Aragonese officials in Naples whom he wished to substitute—hence the Collateral Council of Naples, at first constituted by just two lawyers, the "regents," both imported from Aragon.[24]

Of Philip and Juana's short life back at Burgos, there is little to record. King Philip played pelota at the Carthusian monastery of Miraflores. He exerted himself too much. On September 25, he played again, drank iced water afterwards, and within hours suffered a shivering fit, which grew worse. He was dead before dusk. As a biographer of Juana expressed it, the conquistador was himself conquered.[25] His funeral was held the next day in that same Miraflores, an austere place for a dandy to die in. Poison was naturally alleged as the cause of death, the assassin being said to have been Luis Ferrer, a gentleman of the bedchamber, acting on behalf of Fernando. It is inconceivable. Much has been said against Fernando, but despite his enthusiasm for his Italian possessions, he has never been supposed capable of murder.

The news of the young King's death inspired fresh riots and many difficulties, for his widow, Juana, then twenty-seven years old, was demented with grief, whatever her previous state; and her father, King Fernando, was beyond reach on the sea, having stopped at Palamos, Port Vendres, and Collioure, in Catalonia, and then at Toulon. When Philip died, Fernando was at Savona, near Genoa, the port where Columbus's father, Domenico, was once supposed to have had an inn.

Juana came from a family that had experienced its full share of depression, and the memory of her grandmother Isabel of Portugal, who had lived demented for so long in Arévalo, alone must often have occurred to her and her family. She had what Peter Martyr calls "mental turbulence" and had certainly several times behaved uncontrollably, as when she insisted on remaining outside castles for fear of being imprisoned inside them. She had the fair hair cut off a pretty Fleming whom she suspected, probably rightly, of having an affair with her husband.[26] She had failed to respond to recent offers of help from her sister Catalina (Catherine of Aragon) when in England. Still, she had often shown herself to be determined during her years in the Low Countries. She was cultivated, having been taught by the humanist Geraldini, who had been appointed to be her tutor by Queen Isabel. She had acted as a good nurse to Philip. She also had had six children by him, all of whom lived into adulthood—though perhaps that was less of a consolation to her than her youngest son, Fernando, thought it should have been.[27]

But after Philip died, Juana retreated into apathy, indecision, silence, and neglect of her person, passing days without eating. No one could make sense of a conversation with her. Perhaps she was not mad in the modern sense of the word—if indeed there is such a sense. But in 1506 she seemed incapable of governing, and after her opening of the tomb of her husband in the Carthusian monastery of Miraflores, Burgos, and her escort of the body toward Granada in the winter, her retreat to a monastery seems appropriate even though the treatment meted out to her by, for example, the "odious" Aragonese guardian Luis Ferrer (the man suspected of Philip's murder) and even the Marquis of Denia, Fernando's cousin, seems to have been inhuman.[28] The story of Juana la Loca is one of the most tragic in history. Here was a pretty and educated princess, daughter and eventual heir of the greatest of queens, once married to the heir of an empire, who seems deliberately to have chosen solitude, silence, and alienation.

The Council of the Realm in Castile faced the crisis caused by the death of Philip and the incapacity of Juana with unexpected self-confidence. A regency took shape under the chairmanship of Cardinal Cisneros, supported by the Constable, Velasco; by the Duke of Alba, Fernando's closest friend; and by the Duke of Infantado. They sought to insist that administration remained in their hands. The "Flamencos," on the other hand, the old supporters of Philip—the Duke of Nájera, the Marquis of Villena, and Juan

Manuel—called on the Holy Roman Emperor, Maximilian, Philip's father, to assume the regency in the name of Charles of Ghent, eldest son of Philip and Juana, the boy heir to the throne of Castile and, in the long run, of Aragon unless Queen Germaine had an heir. These plotters tried to procure the abduction of Philip's and Juana's second son, the Infante Fernando, from his lodging in the castle of Simancas. They were unsuccessful.

Everywhere, though, the royal law seemed for a time to falter. The now elderly Marquesa of Moya, Beatriz de Bobadilla, seized the Alcázar de Segovia, while the old rebel of the 1480s in Galicia, the Count of Lemos, besieged Ponferrada. Cardinal Cisneros had to place a hundred cavalry in Burgos to guard Juana in the castle; in the circumstances, she was less a queen than a prisoner, and so she remained. The Duke of Medina Sidonia laid siege to Gibraltar, of which he had been dispossessed by the Crown in 1502 and which was guarded by the commander Garcilaso de la Vega, who, in turn, asked for help from nearby noblemen. From Granada, the Count of Tendilla organized an expedition to relieve the place, but the Marquis of Priego refused to help him until Juana herself gave the order. Such an instruction was difficult to obtain, but Tendilla did attain his goal.

Medina Sidonia then formed an alliance with the Archbishop of Seville (Deza), Priego, and the counts of Ureña and Cabra, who declared that they intended to free Juana from the control of Cisneros. Archbishop Deza resumed his generalship of the Inquisition. (He even defended the cruel inquisitor Lucero, against whom there had been a riot in Córdoba.) But then Juana, in a lucid moment and advised by the Cardinal, annulled all her husband's decrees on the Inquisition.

The year 1506 was yet another terrible one for the supply of food in Spain, with wheat selling at nearly 250 maravedís per *fanega* in comparison with under 100 maravedís in 1501.[29] It would seem that in October alone, eighty ships arrived with grain from Flanders, Brittany, Barbary, Sicily, and Italy.[30] Then Basque shippers brought wheat from Flanders, and others followed, including Genoese merchants such as Bernardo Grimaldi, Giuliano Lomellini, Francesco Doria, Gaspare Spinola, and Cosmo Ripparolo (Riberol)—all the great names of Genoese commerce, many of whom were already associated with the Indies and others would soon be.[31] (Bernardo Grimaldi, an old supporter of Columbus, gave the King 30,000 ducats in January 1507 for the right to be considered Castilian and to trade freely in America. He was the only foreigner with such rights, though they turned out to mean little.)[32]

This widespread confusion played into the hands of King Fernando. He calmly sailed on from Savona to Genoa and then to Portofino, in whose charming bay he received an urgent message from the regency in Spain asking him to return immediately to act as governor of the realm. But with the serenity that was one of his attributes, he continued to Naples, promising to incorporate himself in future in the government of Castile if he was needed, and endorsing such actions as the regency might take. He wrote to the Council of the Realm accepting that Cisneros should remain in charge until he returned. He also appointed the Count of Tendilla as viceroy in Andalusia and the Duke of Alba as his lieutenant in Castile. Those two, along with Infantado and Velasco, now committed themselves fully to Fernando. Juana remained in Burgos till the end of the year. It was Cisneros, however, who had saved the day. The great Cardinal showed himself at his best: he never shied from decisions, he reveled in both crises and the exercise of power, he was at ease with every kind of demand.

Fernando reached Naples on October 27, making a solemn entry on November 1, with his new queen, Germaine, receiving the homage of the Gran Capitán, Fernández de Córdoba, whom he would shortly dismiss.[33] The King remained in Naples till the summer of 1507. There is no way of knowing whether he observed that all the beautiful things said about this city were true. But he was plainly pleased to be in command there.

Back in Castile, the Duke of Alba and Constable Velasco reduced the confusion. Once again the former's lancers acted decisively for Fernando; and in the winter of 1506–07, the Duke of Infantado established peace among the factions in Toledo. Tendilla did the same in Andalusia, ultimately securing the main ports of Malaga, Gibraltar, and Cadiz for Fernando. The nominal Queen, Juana, even began to travel in her supposed dominions, if to little effect.

Fernando waited in Italy till his allies had restored his position in Spain. Then he left Naples on June 5, stopping at Gaeta, Portovenere, Genoa and Savona (where he met King Louis XII of France), Villafranca, Cadaqués, Tarragona, Salou, and, finally, El Grao de Valencia, which he reached on July 20. He was accompanied by the Gran Capitán. Fernando had embraced him "as if he were another monarch."[34] But the flattery was ephemeral. Fernández de Córdoba never had another appointment under the Crown. Fernando did not stop at Ostia to meet Pope Julius, though the latter had gone there specifically to see him.[35] But he did make a solemn entry, with Queen Germaine, into Valencia on July 25.[36] There Pedro de Fajardo, the *adelantado* of Murcia, the most splendid nobleman of the region, greeted him with five hundred horsemen.

Then Fernando reentered Castile, at Monteagudo, where on August 21 he resumed the government in the name of Juana. He was generally accepted as Regent in place of Cisneros and his colleagues, and made his way slowly to Burgos, stopping briefly at such places as Aranda de Duero, Tortolés (where he met Juana on August 29), Santa María del Campo (where he stayed from September 4 until October 10), and Arcos (where Fernando saw Juana again and introduced her to his new wife). He reached Burgos on October 11, where he remained till early February 1508. The only serious exchange between father and daughter was when Fernando said, "You, my dear daughter, as sovereign of the realms, must choose the place where you would like to live." In reply, Juana ventured: "Children must constantly obey their parents."[37]

All in Spain now agreed that Juana would never be able to govern and that Fernando should therefore act as Regent for his eight-year-old grandson, Charles of Ghent. Secretaries still spoke of "la Reyna Doña Juana," but her letters were written on Fernando's orders, and Juana herself remained behind closed doors in Tordesillas. The nobles had thus to choose between returning to support Fernando or seeking, like Juan Manuel, to ingratiate themselves with the Flemings, who seemed likely in the future to play a part in the politics of Spain; the heir of both Juana and Fernando, Charles, was then being educated by Fernando's clever and interesting ex-daughter-in-law Margaret, the sister of the late Philip and widow of the Infante Juan.[38]

Fernando now revived his old group of advisers on matters relating to the Indies. He decreed that all dispatches about these dominions should again go first to Bishop Fonseca, who had maintained his distance effectively during the reign of King Philip, or to Lope Conchillos, who was now out of prison where he had suffered so much. Fonseca was a member of the Council of the Realm, which had a collegiate character, but he acted in respect of the Indies in a high-handed and quite independent manner.

Can one say that Fonseca and Conchillos constituted already a fledgling Council of the Indies? Not really, for the other members of the Council of the Realm—García de Mújica; Francisco de Sosa (Bishop of Almería); Fernando Tello, a Sevillano; and the lawyer, Juan López de Palacios Rubios—were responsible for all judicial matters, whether related to Castile or to the Indies. Yet Fonseca and Conchillos were considered essential as far as the administration of the new lands was concerned, and while King Fernando lived, they had their way. Though they themselves benefited financially from the arrangements (as the list of *encomiendas* in La Española in 1514 would show), they were efficient. For example, they arranged a new postal service, modeled on the innovation made in respect of the Casa de Contratación, by horseback between Seville and the court, wherever it might be; this took only four days, inspiring an arrangement whereby every city had to have a boat always ready to cross rivers "at whatever hour the postboy arrived without any delay."[39] The King trusted them, and he had the gift of being able to delegate effectively.

Thus stability in Castile was restored by the beginning of 1508. But the interval since Isabel had died had been long, and more than one change had occurred. First and foremost, in respect of the history of the Indies, there had been the death of Columbus.

It will be remembered that he arrived back in Seville after his fourth voyage only a few weeks before the death of the Queen. He had planned to go to the court, which he supposed would be at Valladolid. To take him to that city, he gained approval for his use of the same stretcher that had brought the dead body of Cardinal Hurtado de Mendoza down to the cathedral at Seville to be interred: "If I travel on a stretcher, I think it will be by the silver road [la plata, that is, the road north from Seville]," Columbus wrote to his son Diego, telling him a few weeks later that he had not been paid anything for his last voyage, and in consequence he was so poor that he "lived on loans." (As usual, this was a gross misrepresentation of his true wealth.) He hoped that Diego at court would inform Archbishop Deza of any difficulties.

Columbus as usual delayed before traveling. It was not until May 1505, six months after the death of Isabel, that he set out for the court, accompanied by his brother Bartolomeo and by much luggage. But King and court were on the move, so it was hard to catch up. Columbus did not abandon his aims. He wrote to the King in June 1505 that "the government and the possession that I had was the height of my honor; I was unjustly expelled from there; very humbly I beg[40] your Highness that you give orders to put my son in possession of the government which I once had."[41] The King received Columbus courteously in August but, according to Fernando Colón, treacherously, for he was determined now to establish his own control over the Indies. He proposed a new contract with Columbus, but for a time the idea was dropped because of his need to face the arrival of his son-in-law Philip.[42] Columbus, meanwhile, wrote to Philip and Juana asking to be looked on as their royal vassal and servant.[43]

On May 20, 1506, Columbus died in his bed in Valladolid. Of old age? He was only fifty-seven. No disease was obvious. His will, which spoke chiefly of

Genoese friends, had been dated the previous day. In a codicil, he still wrote of his own share of the Indies as beginning "a hundred leagues" (three hundred miles) west of the Azores and the Cape Verde Islands.

Columbus's body was first interred in Valladolid. In 1509, it was taken to the Carthusian monastery of Las Cuevas, Seville, and thence it traveled first to Santo Domingo; then in the nineteenth century to Havana; then, after 1898, back to Seville, where it probably remains in its splendid tomb in the cathedral.[44]

Columbus's achievements had been "marvelous," to use his own favorite word. He had persuaded the Spanish Crown to support an expedition that he had himself conceived and that led to the conquest and settlement of half the Americas by Spain. He died still thinking that the large continent south of the Caribbean that Vespucci had called a New World was part of Asia; he had no idea that the continent of North America existed. He was, though, in addition to being a wonderful sailor, a man of vision and determination who prevailed upon the monarchs of Castile to do something for which they had no inclination. It is easy to say that if it had not been for Columbus, someone else would have discovered the New World, since it was so obvious a thing to sail westward once it was known that the world was round. But the obvious is not always done.

For much of the last part of his life, Columbus was preoccupied by what he thought would occur in respect of the expected coming of the Antichrist and the last judgment of mankind. In 1498, when drawing up plans for an entailed grant (*mayorazgo*) for his son, he talked of his hopes for the recapture of Jerusalem. That had earlier appeared as an injunction at the beginning of one of his favorite books, Mandeville's *Travels*. In his *Book of Prophecies*, a collection of fancies written in 1501, Columbus wrote to the Catholic Kings that Jerusalem and Mount Zion would soon be rebuilt by Christian hands and, as the Calabrian abbot Joachim of Fiore had prophesied, those would be Spanish ones.[45] Columbus was a dreamer. Had he lived longer, he would have concentrated, probably, on Jerusalem more than on plans for the Indies. But his magnetic personality had attracted the Catholic Kings precisely because he was partly a seer. In his time, much favor was shown to Sor María de Santo Domingo, the "Beata de Piedrahita," a laywoman of the Dominican Third Order. She became, thanks to Cisneros, the reforming visitor of the Dominican monasteries in Castile. Columbus must sometimes have seemed to the monarchs a comparable person.

King Fernando wrote to Ovando seeking to ensure that the gold and other income that were the due of Diego Colón the younger should be made over to him. He would inherit the title of Admiral, after all, and he had been at court most of his life.[46] Columbus had not died poor, however much he complained. His property in La Española was considerable, and he had enjoyed a substantial subsidiary income from many concessions. On November 26 of the same year, 1506, Fernando wrote to young Diego repeating his assurance of friendship.[47] That was shortly to be confirmed in a striking way.

"You ought to send one hundred black slaves"

The Governor wrote to me that you had sent him seventeen black slaves and that you ought to send more. It seems to me that you ought to send one hundred black slaves and a person in your confidence ought also to go with them.

King Fernando, 1507

The political confusion in Castile, meanwhile, gave Ovando a free hand in La Española. During the brief reign of King Philip, there had been no guide on the subject of the Indies. Fonseca's letters were few and far between. The Governor found a friend in Cristóbal de Santa Clara, whom he appointed chief accountant of the colony after the death of Pedro de Villacorta. Santa Clara was a new *converso*, since his father, David Vitales, had been a well-known Jewish merchant of Saragossa and the bones of his mother, Clara, had been buried as having been those of a heretic in 1495.[1] But that dubious origin did not prevent him and his brothers Bernardo and Pedro from having long, prosperous careers in the Indies. Cristóbal was known for extravagance: once he served a dinner in Santo Domingo where the saltcellars were filled with gold dust.

Ovando's successful but brutal rule had seen the increase of the Spanish population of La Española from three hundred to several thousand. That was partly because the Crown had made evident in a decree of February 2, 1504, that "our will was, and is, to populate and ennoble those islands with Christians." That in turn permitted all future residents to import to the island, free of taxes, all kinds of clothing, cattle, mares, seeds, food, and drink needed for their maintenance and the development of their land. Only slaves, horses, arms, gold, and silver objects were excluded from the concession.[2] Andalusia naturally was the chief beneficiary of this emigration. Soon, Ovando would ask that no one else for the moment be sent to the island because there was no more work there. Two *procuradores*, Diego de Nicuesa

and Antón Serrano, returned to Castile in 1507 to discourage further settlement. (A *procurador,* in the past in the New World as well as now in Castile,
was supposed to represent the ordinary citizens with the Council of the
Realm and to ensure that what was discussed there was for "the common
good.") Nicuesa and Serrano had, too, the mission to secure permission
from the King to import slaves from neighboring islands, such as, for example, the Bahamas, then known as the Lucays, or "the useless islands."[3] They
were "useless" only because they had no gold. But the people who lived there
were of the same race as the Tainos of La Española.

Ovando had already begun to organize the island of which he had made
himself the supreme authority, as if it were one large estate. Cattle increased
fast on the pastures, which the decline of the Indian population made possible. So did horses and hogs. Yucca provided all the cassava bread that was
needed. Ovando obtained oxen to help the natives carry goods from the
mines to the boats, and he also concerned himself with roads.[4] He sent back
to Spain a substance that appears to have been rubber, as well as roots that
may have yielded the dye madder. The Crown, in return, sent seeds, hoping
that silk would eventually come from the mulberry trees that were being
planted.[5] Ovando also thought that he had found copper near Puerto Real.
He had "a hardworking foreigner" (probably an Italian) soon busy at work
on the matter.[6]

Tainos captured in the wars in Higuey or Jaragua had been defined as
slaves and were the property of those who had captured them. Ovando had
secured royal approval of this interpretation.[7] He also persuaded the Crown
that they would obtain more wealth in the long run if they accepted only a
fifth of profits of harvests and mines in the colony. This *quinto* became a
permanent feature of colonial rule in 1508.[8]

The conquests of Jaragua, in the west, had been followed by a new war
in the east, near Higuey, the consequence of a fire in a wooden fortress and
the death of eight Spaniards out of the nine who were there. Ovando sent a
new punitive expedition. It was again led by the Sevillano Juan de Esquivel.
His two subordinates were, first, Diego de Escobar (Columbus's reluctant
savior), who came in from Concepción; and, second, Juan Ponce de León, a
bastard member of the great family of Seville of that name, being a cousin of
the redheaded Rodrigo, who had been such a hero in the war against
Granada.[9] The forces led by these men came together at Yacyagua, near
Higuey. They totaled four hundred, supported by Indians working as
porters or servants. The battles with the untamed Indians were as usual unequal because of the superiority of Spanish weapons, especially their swords.
The Christians sought to corral the Indians as if they had been bulls and

then kill them. But there were some single combats. The Indians sometimes threw themselves into ravines in order to tempt the Spaniards into similar leaps, and some Indian women killed themselves. Cotubanamá was seized—the last of the indigenous *caciques*. He was hanged in Santo Domingo. Most of those captured were made into slaves, as the conquistadors thought fit; and a fifth of them were sent home as slaves of the Crown.[10]

With Higuey and the east of the island of La Española crushed and as subservient to Castile as the west, Ovando busied himself with founding towns. As mentioned earlier, the royal plan was that "the Christians living on the said island should not live isolated." Ovando agreed with this; he knew that dispersal under Columbus had wrecked all hope of the Crown's policies being put into practice.

These new Spanish communities were mostly built near old Taino ones and were known as *villas,* in contrast with the Indian towns, which were known as *pueblos.* The new places (founded or confirmed) were Bonao, Concepción de la Vega, and Buenaventura, all service stations for the pursuit of gold; Puerto de la Plata (subsequently Puerto Plata), the new port on the north coast; Salvaleón de Higuey and Santa Cruz de la Haniguayana, the headquarters in the east of Ponce de León and Esquivel, respectively; Puerto Real, near Columbus's Navidad; Lares de Guahaba, also in the northwest; and San Juan de la Maguana, near the old capital of the *cacique* Caonabó. There were, too, Santa María de la Vera Paz and Villanueva de Yaquimao, both close to Jaragua; and, finally, in the west, Salvatierra de la Sabana, the headquarters of Ovando's deputy, Diego Velázquez de Cuéllar.

All these places were given councillors, justices, notaries, and coats of arms, as if they had been cities in Old Spain. Two of the towns concerned, Concepción de la Vega and Buenaventura, had two foundries each. Ovando was as ever seeking a revised version of a peninsular tradition. The main element in the recovery of land from the Muslims in Spain had been the creation of cities, usually Christian establishments on Moorish foundations. Ovando and other conquistadors would also found Castilian towns on, or near, indigenous sites, give them some legal being, and place their friends in the municipal offices. As in Castile, the towns would be laid out in the style of a gridiron, except in the center, where the main square would have upon it a mayor's house, a town hall, a church, and probably a prison. The town would dominate the neighboring countryside. The grandees of the place might farm or use (but not own) sections of the country, but they would still probably live with their families in houses near the main square.[11] Towns based on these principles would soon be seen everywhere in Spanish America. Ovando had also been granted the right to name all the officials in his cities. This in effect negated an agreement made, for example, with Alonso Vélez de Mendoza, according to which all the residents should elect their own *alcaldes* and other officials.[12] But Ovando was the proconsul of the moment, and his decisions were as important as they were long lasting.

Santo Domingo, meanwhile, was beginning to look more like a capital. The building of the new city, on the west bank of the Ozama, was nearly complete. By 1507, a stone fortress, the Torre del Homenaje, was in position. It had been designed by an Italian architect, Juan Rabé. When, in August 1508, another hurricane hit the port of Santo Domingo and destroyed half of the transatlantic fleet and damaged the city, the Governor decided to substitute stone houses for wooden houses roofed with straw: "It is a noble thing for the city to have houses of stone," wrote Juan Mosquera, a notary who was one of the councillors. The architect of the victories in the east of the island, Juan Esquivel, said the same: "It's a matter of honor for the place."[13] Thus by 1509 there were in Santo Domingo at least four private mansions of stone: those belonging to the Basque Francisco de Garay; to Fray Alonso del Viso, of the Order of Calatrava; to a well-known pilot, Bartolomé Roldán; and to a *converso* merchant from Seville, Juan Fernández de las Varas.[14]

The Spaniards in the new towns needed entertainment. To serve them, books, those new jewels, began to be imported. Thus we hear how, in January 1505, there left from Sanlúcar the caravel *Santa María la Antigua,* belonging to Alonso Núñez and Juan Bermúdez, the discoverer of Bermuda, with "138 sheets of paper for reading; fifty Books of Hours, thirty-four romances, all bound, and sixteen works in Latín."[15] These romances would probably have included the most famous of them all, *Amadís de Gaula.*

This romantic work of chivalry was the supreme literary success of the early sixteenth century, being soon published in all the main European languages, including French, German, Italian, English, Dutch, and Portuguese, as well as Hebrew. Originally composed probably at the end of the thirteenth century, *Amadís* had been rewritten at the end of the fifteenth by Garcí Rodríguez de Montalvo, a town councillor of Medina del Campo, the famous mercantile city in Castile. It was probably first published in the mid-1490s, though the first surviving edition is that of the printer Coci of Saragossa, of 1508.[16] But there were earlier editions, and we can assume that any shipment of novels to Santo Domingo in 1505 would have included copies of it.

The book would have introduced its readers on the cramped boats and in the makeshift lodgings in the New World itself to a heroic knight, Amadís, a love child of the King of Gaul, who has fallen in love with Oriana, daughter of Lisuarte, King of Great Britain. He is not only the epitome of the seven virtues but also very successful as a warrior. He kills everyone who challenges him, both as a knight errant and as the commander of an army. He is faithful to his delightful lady Oriana, with whom eventually he goes to bed and to whom he soon gives a son, Esplandián. Since Amadís's birth is unacknowledged, he has to prove himself and travel the world—Europe, that is—engaging in duels, carrying out rescues, killing both monsters and evil knights, and capturing enchanted islands.

There are some charmingly amatory scenes in *Amadís*, even if they do not dwell on the details of seduction. The leading characters are nevertheless allowed nights of love with their beloveds in a way that, because of the influence of the Reformation and Counter-Reformation, would be surprising to meet in Spanish literature again till the nineteenth century. These moments take second place, however, to the tremendous combats.

Amadís remains a wonderful story, compulsive in its appeal. No doubt some Spanish adventurers who traveled with a copy of *Amadís* in their traveling chests allowed it to influence them. Some perhaps thought that if Amadís could kill one hundred thousand men with no difficulty, so could they—hence possibly the wild exaggerations (of numbers) in Bernal Díaz's famous book about the conquest of Mexico. Some were probably as besotted by it as Cervantes represents Don Quixote to have been—and, indeed, that great novel was in its way a tribute to *Amadís* (Cervantes gives his book, as epigraphs, some poems purportedly by characters in *Amadís*).

One of the cities of the New World founded by the Portuguese in Brazil, Olinda, is named after a princess in *Amadís*. The magic word "California," the realm of Queen Califia, derives from episodes relating to Amazons in a sequel to *Amadís, Las Sergas de Esplandián,* published first in 1510. The word "Patagonia," the southernmost of the Spanish dominions in the Americas, comes from another novel, while the great River Amazon takes its name from the fact that the intrepid Extremeño Orellana identified the river with a place where Amazons lived.[17]

The success of *Amadís* led many people to copy it, and would-be sequels as well as parallel series soon began to appear, such as that featuring Palmerín de Oliva, whose first publication was in 1511. The author was probably a certain Francisco Vázquez.

The reading public of the sixteenth century was entranced by these chivalrous stories. Those readers constituted, we should never forget, the first generation of men and women able to read books as a source of entertainment. The brilliant Spanish commander in Italy of the next generation, Fernando de Avalos, read *Amadís* as a boy and himself said that in consequence he was inspired to deeds of glory.[18] Other Spanish soldiers in Italy read *Amadís* with profit.[19] Garcilaso de la Vega, who wrote the first true American history, *The Royal Commentaries of the Indies,* also loved these novels as a youth.[20] Nor was it just adventurers with time on their hands on long voyages across the Atlantic who became so preoccupied. For example, St. Teresa of Ávila wrote that as a child she, too, "began to fall into the habit of reading them [the romances of chivalry] . . . and it seemed to me that it was not wrong to spend many hours of the day and night in such vain exercise, though I concealed it from my father. I became so absorbed that if I did not have a new such book to read, I did not feel that I could be happy."[21] St. Ignatius had a similar experience: when wounded at the siege of Pamplona in 1521, he asked to be given a copy of *Amadís,* and perhaps it influenced his life as the founder of the Jesuit order. Certainly the coming together of himself and his first followers in the crypt of Sainte-Marie in Montmartre had much in common with the establishment of a band of knightly brothers.

Other entertainment in the New World was provided by drink; and we find the veteran of the expedition of 1501, Rodrigo de Bastidas, from Triana, now more of a merchant than an explorer, not only selling wine—perhaps the popular fortified wine of Calzada de la Sierra—to Santo Domingo but obtaining a 300 percent profit.[22] In 1508, Alcalde de Espera would tell a royal pilot (*comitre*), Diego Rodríguez, that the goods that he had given him to sell, worth 600 ducats, had raised 2,000 ducats—a profit, that is, of over 200 percent.[23]

Ovando by now thought his achievements were such that he ought to be able to retire: on May 20, 1505, he wrote to his brother Diego in Castile: "May God be praised that this island is now so pacific and with such desire to serve His Highness . . . I really believe that this will give me a license [to return home]. . . ."[24] But he did not receive that for many months.

On September 18, 1505, Fernando, having heard good reports about the possibility of finding copper in La Española, dispatched three caravels from Seville[25] with all the equipment needed for such an enterprise. He sent not only equipment, but a hundred African slaves.[26]

Ovando had been hostile at first to the idea of black labor because he had found that Africans created trouble among the Indians. But he had come to realize that African slaves could contribute substantially to all these undertakings. Everyone in La Española noticed how the few black Africans there worked harder than the indigenous Indians, who were developing many clever ways of avoiding the excessive work that the Spaniards wanted of them. Two days before, King Fernando himself had told the officials of the Casa de Contratación that "the Governor wrote to me that you had sent him seventeen black slaves and that you ought to send more. It seems to me that you ought to send one hundred black slaves and a person of your confidence ought to go with them."²⁷

As we have seen, a few black slaves had been sent to the New World in the first years of the sixteenth century. But previously they had gone in twos and threes, never as many as a hundred. So 1507 marked a new phase in the history of the Indies, of Africa, of Europe, and of human population.²⁸

The island of La Española had by now been divided among the conquerors. It was well organized in respect of the discovery of gold, its first preoccupation. The benefits gained by those who produced this were considerable: the *quinto* of the Crown alone in 1505 had been over 22 million maravedís. The total must therefore have been about 110 million.²⁹ The years 1503 to 1510 would produce in total nearly 5 million grams of gold, which was something that impressed the King.³⁰ Those were the years when Ovando was also bringing in cattle to the colony, at his own cost, ensuring that they were kept for breeding.³¹ By 1507, he could even write to the King saying that it was not necessary to send any more mares: there were already enough horses to enable the conquest of nearby islands.³² Ovando had also commissioned the experienced pilot Andrés de Morales to draw a map of the coasts of the Antilles. His maps were soon thought to be the best and most accurate available. Morales, who was probably from Seville and in 1508 would have been just over thirty, was also the first man to describe methodically the ocean currents in the West Indies.

Ovando began to be criticized, however. For example, he mishandled the case of Cristóbal Rodríguez, a conquistador who had learned the Taino language, having spent several years without talking to any Spaniards. He had gone to treat with Roldán, at the request of Columbus, and he had been the first to go down to the port in Santo Domingo on the Admiral's behalf to see who Bobadilla's fleet was bringing in. He had interpreted at a wedding in 1505 between a Spaniard, Juan Garcés, and an Indian, at Concepción. For acting thus without permission, he was fined 100,000 maravedís by Ovando and sent back to Spain. But the King saw him and warmed to him, and decided that Rodríguez would be of value to the colony. To Ovando's displeasure, he was sent back to La Española, with a horse and even a mare, and with instructions to try to work out a constitutional arrangement for the Indians. Rodríguez then challenged Ovando on the benefits of his recent allocation of Indians.³³

More serious was Ovando's quarrel with the Tapia brothers of Seville. Cristóbal de Tapia, backed by Bishop Fonseca (of whom he was a distant relation), reported from Santo Domingo to the King that Ovando "did not fulfill the instructions in the letters that their Highnesses sent him asking him to allocate Indians to various specified persons." Yet at the same time the Governor was treating his own Extremeño friends very well, among whom even "the assistants to the assistants of the cooks have Indians in large numbers."[34] Ovando had made his cousin, Diego de Cáceres, the commander of the fortress in Santo Domingo in place of Cristóbal de Tapia, who had lost his land on the west bank of the Ozama. The truth was that Ovando preferred Extremeños, especially men from his own towns of Brozas and Garrobillas, to Sevillanos. He even named an unknown young notary from Medellín, Hernán Cortés, his own distant cousin, to be notary of the new town of Azúa soon after he reached La Española in October 1506.[35]

The Tapias were supported in their accusations by Miguel Pasamonte, an Aragonese *converso* from Judes, near Ariza, who arrived as royal treasurer in 1508 and was henceforth to represent Fonseca's interests in the Indies.[36] He acquired power in La Española and was responsible for many grants of Indians and franchises from which money could be made.

A sign of the King's growing interest in the Indies was his determination to assure himself of control of the appointments of bishops in the New World. It was an important change, for he had more authority over these prelates than any monarch had ever had anywhere. Yet it was three more years before any such were named. By that time, there were three projected monasteries, one of which, the Franciscan, was already nearly finished in Santo Domingo. There were no churches of stone as yet, but hospitals of that material had been constructed at Buenaventura and Concepción and a provisional one, of St. Nicolas, in Santo Domingo itself. The authority of religion was something that the monarchs could increasingly count on in their plans to control both Indians and settlers.

By the summer of 1508, Cristóbal de Tapia considered that he had enough material to use against Ovando to return to Spain and present Fonseca with the case for that Governor's dismissal. Fonseca proposed that Francisco de Tapia, brother of Cristóbal, should take over as commander. Cristóbal, delighted, returned to Santo Domingo to collect more material against the Governor. The rumor even spread that he was planning a rebellion of settlers. Ovando held up a letter he had intercepted on its way home to the King that purported to prove this. He sent Tapia to jail, and confiscated his Indians. Fonseca ordered Ovando to free Tapia. Conchillos came to hear of the censored letter and inspired the King to state liberally: "All who want to write to us should be free to do so, and any information received we will inquire about and make our decisions on the basis of the whole truth; and the truth once known, we shall decide on the issue."[37] This seemed a blast in favor of liberty of expression on the part of the Crown. But it was not to dictate a rule.

The King, who went in state to Seville in 1508 with his new wife, Germaine, decided to replace Ovando. In Arévalo, Castile, where the young St. Ignatius was at that time learning the arts of life and chivalry as a member of the household of Juan Velázquez de Cuéllar, the King explained on August 9, 1508, that he had asked Diego Colón, the new Admiral in succession to his father, to go and live in and govern the Indies.[38] Diego's formal nomination (in Seville) was on October 29, 1508. The letter instructed all the officials of the New World to make the oath necessary to the said Diego and receive him as "my magistrate and governor of these isles and mainland."[39] Diego was thus confirmed in his hereditary title of admiral, but nothing was said about his being viceroy. He was called Admiral of the Indies, but not of the Ocean Sea. Were these mistakes?[40] Surely not. Fonseca and Conchillas did not make mistakes of that kind. Diego Colón's powers were being deliberately limited.

The explanation for this appointment was no doubt that the King, sensitive to opinion at court, perceived, thanks to the complaints that he had received, that Ovando's time was up. He had, after all, been governor for seven years, since 1501. As to the appointment of Diego Colón, Fernando felt warmly toward him, having seen him often at court, first as a companion of the dead Infante, and afterwards as a member of the household of Queen Isabel. Fonseca, too, must have been in favor of the nomination.[41] But more important, Diego Colón had recently married María de Toledo, the niece of the Duke of Alba (she was a daughter of Fernando de Toledo, *comendador* of León). What Alba requested in these days was usually immediately granted by a King always grateful to him for his support in times of danger—a support that, indeed, it might be necessary to call upon again.

Fernando gave his instructions to Diego Colón on May 3, 1509, and the same day he gave permission to Ovando to return to Spain, something for which that proconsul had often asked but that seems, as often happens in such cases, to have surprised him.

Ovando left the island of La Española Spanish but cowed. All authority was in the hands of the governor. No alternative source of power survived. But partly as a result of that eclipse of indigenous governments and the consequent communal melancholy, the native population had begun to decline. No one had thought much about this while Ovando was in office, even if it would soon become the main preoccupation of the settlers.

"And they leapt onto the land"

They all went very happily and contentedly and they leapt onto the
land. They went to the *caciques* of the Indians and were there talking
with them till the sun went down.

Francisco Rodríguez, in evidence for Juan González
Ponce de León, 1532

On April 24, 1505, while at Toro, some months after the death of Isabel, King
Fernando agreed to name the old companion of Columbus's, Vicente Yáñez
Pinzón, of Palos, to be *corregidor* and captain of the Isle of San Juan. Puerto
Rico, as it soon became known, Boriquen, as the Indians called it, was the island next door to La Española; before 1492, Tainos in the west of La Española
had made daily visits to Boriquen across the deep and narrow sea.[1] San Juan,
it was thought, could become a new colony if enough Castilians declared an
interest in going there. It was about 150 miles long and 75 wide. Much as had
happened in La Española, the land would be divided among the new settlers,
who would have to undertake to stay at least five years. Yáñez was to build a
fortress of which he would be governor.[2]

Vicente Yáñez visited the island, landing probably on the south coast,
built a stockade, and took livestock there. But he did nothing more permanent. He could not even have seen the central mountain range that forms
such an interesting variation to other Caribbean landscapes. For the moment, no one declared an interest in settling there. La Española, small
though it is, seemed large enough. Also, like Columbus, Yáñez was a great
sailor, not a colonial administrator, though he, again like Columbus, was
tempted by land grants: to an adventurer, land is always an attraction. Yet
one important point had been made: La Española would not be simply a
colony on its own, it would be a center for expansion.

Nothing happened in Boriquen until August 12, 1508, when Juan Ponce
de León, having sailed out from Higuey, in eastern La Española, which he
had helped conquer and where he had been living, disembarked in the

pretty bay of Guánica, on the southwest shore of Puerto Rico, with forty-two potential settlers and eight sailors.[3]

Ponce de León, as has been explained before, was a cousin of Rodrigo Ponce de León, Count of Arcos, and he was indeed a Ponce de León on both sides.[4] He had fought against the Moors in Granada and had been a page at court. Apparently a volunteer with Bartolomeo Colón in 1494, he was also probably among those so optimistic emigrants on Columbus's second voyage in 1493.[5] He was a friend of Bishop Fonseca. He helped his fellow Sevillano Esquivel in his campaign to conquer Higuey. Settled there, he obtained an *encomienda* and for a time made money selling cassava bread to passing Spanish ships, perhaps operating this business from a house that still stands and is recalled as his.[6] Ponce de León himself owned (with Alfonso Sarmiento) at least one ship: the *Santa María de Regla*.[7] He persuaded Ovando to give him authority to conquer Puerto Rico.

Ponce's personality escapes us. Las Casas allows himself to say no more than that he was "very clever and served in many wars."[8] Oviedo was more expansive, saying that he was "spirited, sagacious, and diligent in all warlike matters" and "a hidalgo and a man of elegant and high thoughts."[9] The naval historian Samuel Eliot Morison, the pride of Harvard, said that he was a typical Andalusian, but gave no reference for that innocent reflection.[10] Judging by his actions he was obviously resilient, strong, and brave, but he was probably unimaginative.

The conquistadors who accompanied him included his own son, Juan González Ponce de León (who had apparently learned the language of the Tainos), who sailed as interpreter, and some other captains, such as Miguel de Toro, who had also been in La Española with Columbus, and Martín de Ysasaga, a Basque. There also traveled several Sevillano servants of the Ponce de León family. One adventurer who accompanied Ponce de León was an interesting free black of Portuguese origin, Juan Garrido.[11] The King designated Ponce as interim governor of the island. He was given the old title of *adelantado,* a designation that had been given by Columbus to his brother Bartolomeo and that meant the holder had political as well as military duties. The long list of other responsibilities and powers that went with the title had in this instance no significance.[12]

There seems to have been no justification for the invasion other than conquest. Perhaps, though, Ovando perceived a need to avoid having the island next to La Española as a potential base for Caribs. Of course, he hoped to convert the Indians. But the ambition of Juan Ponce de León to possess a colony of his own probably played a part. Possibly, Ovando desired to see that adventurer established in another island. The terms of the agreements concluded with Ponce de León seem to have imagined the indefinite survival of indigenous principalities.

The best description of the conquest of Puerto Rico derives from a declaration by the son of Ponce de León, Juan González.[13] The account makes obvious that the expedition of his father was intended from the beginning "for the conquest and settlement" of the island. After landing at Guánica, the party reembarked and made for Aguadilla, at the extreme west of the island, near a river known to the indigenous people as the Guarabo—where Columbus had anchored on his second voyage in 1493, perhaps indeed accompanied by Ponce de León. There Juan González talked to some Indians armed with bows and arrows, apparently successfully, and took two back to the fleet to meet his father, who gave them combs, shirts, beads, and mirrors. (Andrés López, a servant in the Ponce de León household, later said that these presents included diamonds, but that would seem improbable; probably he did not know a diamond when he saw one.) The next day, Juan González returned to Aguadilla, and his father and most of his followers accompanied him. A witness, Francisco Rodríguez, recalls that they all went "very happily and contentedly and leapt onto the land," Juan González with them. "They went to the *caciques* of the Indians and were there talking with them till the sun went down when they set about embarking. Many Indians accompanied him as far as the boat. Juan González told his father how he had talked to many *caciques* and lords and how they were happy with our coming."

This was the territory of the *cacique* Agueybana, an Indian leader who at first impressed all the Spaniards who met him as "human and virtuous." He welcomed Ponce, offered to exchange names with him, and they reached various territorial understandings. He even explained where gold could be found.[14] Again according to Andrés López, this gold was used by the Indians "for earrings and nose rings."[15]

Juan González, the interpreter, and twenty Spaniards then sailed off to discover a better port, and they found it, a hundred miles to the east in what became the Bay of San Juan. There they transferred their equipment and baggage, the Indians helping. They found gold in several streams nearby. But then the Indians attacked.

The historian Oviedo has a story of how the indigenous people of the island supposed that white men could not die. A small group of Indians persuaded a certain Salcedo to go with them to a beautiful place on horseback and then seized him and pushed him underwater and held him there. They found that the Spaniard quickly died and, after three days, began to smell.

That persuaded the people that their previous information was wrong. They, therefore, prepared for war with the Spaniards.[16]

Juan González Ponce de León disguised himself successfully as a native, painting his skin and dyeing his hair, and, according to his own account, eavesdropped on the plans that the Indians were making. He also canoed out farther toward the east, passing Culebra and Vieques, into the pretty archipelago of the Virgin Islands (as Columbus had named them) and seized some Caribs, whom he later took back as slaves to Santo Domingo. He reported that he had heard Indians say they intended to kill all the Spaniards.[17]

The Indians soon destroyed the little Spanish settlement at Aguadilla, where they killed most of the colonists. Juan González escaped with thirty-six arrow wounds. This marked the parting of the ways, for the Spaniards never forgave such a violent reaction. It was the beginning of a brutal war.

There seems to have been about a year of skirmishing and traveling, during the course of which, again according to his own account, the skillful Juan González was always in and out of the enemy quarters in one disguise or another. A new settlement was established at San Germán, in the southwest, named after Fernando's new queen, Germaine de Foix. Juan González also ensured the capture of some seventeen *caciques* who were sent to Santo Domingo by his father. This seems to have marked the end of the resistance. Ponce de León established himself near what is now San Juan, at Caparra, which still bears that name and where tiles from Triana, the port opposite Seville on the River Guadalquivir, which were introduced in these early days of empire, can still be identified.

Further proclamations confirmed Ponce de León's position on the island, though he was specifically forbidden by the Crown to use Indians in any mines. He established himself in a hacienda at Toa, near San Juan, where he undertook numerous plantings.[18]

The arrival of Diego Colón in Santo Domingo altered matters in San Juan. The new Governor of La Española had apparently not known of the King's designation of Ponce de León as governor of Puerto Rico (or pretended not to have) and wanted his own man there. So the new Admiral named a comrade, Julio Cerón, to that post, with an old friend of his father's, Miguel Díaz de Aux, one of the few Aragonese to interest themselves in the Indies, as chief magistrate.

Cerón expelled Ponce de León from Puerto Rico, even from Toa, his new property. But Ponce had his grant of office sent to the island, and in the subsequent confusion, he seized both Cerón and Díaz de Aux and, accusing them of "excesses," sent them home to Spain as prisoners in a boat belonging to Juan Bono de Quejo, a Basque captain who was a friend of his. In a politically astute move, Ponce de León also named one of Diego Colón's friends, Cristóbal de Sotomayor, as his own chief magistrate. An aristocrat of Portuguese origin (he was a brother of the Count of Caminha and a kinsman of the first governor of the Portuguese colony of São Tomé, Álvaro de Caminha), Sotomayor had been a secretary to the late King Philip and became an effective second in command. He had come out to the Indies in a flotilla of his own in May 1509.

Ponce de León did his best to have his authority in the new colony confirmed. For example, he gave a gold entrepreneur, Gerónimo de Bruselas—presumably a Fleming, and a protégé of Conchillos—permission to bring in Indians from outside the island. A similar license was given to Sotomayor.[19] But a bigger provider of Indians to the colony was the Triana *converso* who had initiated the pearl trade, Rodrigo de Bastidas, now established in Santo Domingo, who was laying the foundations of what would become a great fortune.[20] Ponce de León then did all he could to ensure the final conquest of the island.[21]

The Spanish upheavals and uncertainties, however, had provoked the indigenous Indians of Puerto Rico to protest, and at the beginning of 1511 the *cacique*, Agueybana, previously looked upon as amiable, convertible, and friendly, organized a rebellion of what were said to be about three thousand men, apparently including some Caribs from Santa Cruz, probably brought to Puerto Rico by Sotomayor after a murderous trawl through the Lesser Antilles. They burned the hacienda of Sotomayor and killed both him and his nephew Diego, an event that led to a cruel "pacification" carried out by Captain Juan Gil of Corunna on behalf of Ponce.

The Spaniards had been drawn into war with the natives and the Caribs largely because of the settlers' desire for slaves from the Lesser Antilles, and Puerto Rico, therefore, was very exposed.[22]

The Council of the Realm in Castile, meanwhile, decided in favor of Cerón as governor and Díaz de Aux as chief magistrate, and Ponce de León was pushed to one side. He was substituted for as lieutenant-governor by Rodrigo de Moscoso, and then by Cristóbal de Mendoza, another aristocrat of whom Oviedo thought highly: "a man of good birth and a virtuous one, suitable for the job, and even for something much more important."[23] Yet Mendoza soon gave up and was succeeded by Pedro Moreno, from Seville, who imposed an effective calm on the island, the Indians being cowed and their leaders either dead or enslaved. A judge of *residencia* and member of the large Velázquez family, Sancho Velázquez, arrived as supreme magistrate in 1512.

Two years later, Ponce de León, back from other adventures, principally in Florida, was again formally named deputy governor—but in effect governor—of Puerto Rico.[24] An ambitious intriguer, Francisco Lizaur, Ovando's ex-protégé, was named chief accountant in San Juan.

At the end of 1515, the only two surviving *caciques* of San Juan, Humaco and Daguao, again rose against the Spaniards, the cause being an attempt by Íñigo de Zúñiga to conscript ten Indians to help him against the Caribs. These fights against the Caribs were the most serious of the battles to date with the Indians in the Caribbean, in which the Governor's large red dog, Becerrillo, played a famous part. He received a salary of the rank of a crossbowman. By late 1516 the lovely island of Puerto Rico (once Borinquen) was finally in Spanish hands.[25]

Columbus had discovered and almost circumnavigated Jamaica in May 1494. He had spent a most uncomfortable time there in 1503–04 at what is now St. Ann's Bay. That made it even more irritating to his son Diego Colón that, in 1508, the King should have granted the use of it as a base to Alonso de Hojeda and Diego de Nicuesa, two adventurers with whom he was not on good terms. What his father had discovered, he thought, belonged to him. Had not the Admiral spoken of Jamaica as "the most beautiful of the many islands which I have seen in the Indies"?[26] (He had, of course, said much the same about Cuba.) This memory led to Diego Colón's determining to have Jamaica conquered under his own auspices. He put this in the capable hands of Juan de Esquivel.[27]

Esquivel is even more anonymous in history than Ponce de León. We have no likeness of him, and little is known of his life. As has been noted, he was a *converso* of Seville, of a family converted in the late fourteenth century. He probably came to the New World on Columbus's second voyage. He had been responsible for the subjugation of the east of La Española, with Ponce de León as his deputy.

Pánfilo de Narváez, Esquivel's second in command in Jamaica, was, on the other hand, a figure larger than life. He came from Old Castile, being born in the village of Navalmanzano, between Cuéllar and Segovia. He seems to have come out to the New World with one of the minor expeditions of 1498, perhaps with Peralonso Niño. Bernal Diaz wrote of him as a man with a natural authority, tall, with fair hair and a beard tending to red, honorable, sometimes wise but more often imprudent, a good conversationalist with a deep voice, and a good if often careless fighter. He was, as an incident in the later conquest of Cuba made clear, alarmingly capable of serenity when in difficulty.[28]

At the request of Diego Colón, and again without any apparent royal instruction, Esquivel and Narváez established the settlement of Sevilla la Nueva, in the north of Jamaica, near the Bay of Glory (La Bahía de Santa Gloria), close to where Columbus had been wrecked in 1503.

There is a distinction to be made between two accounts of the subjugation of this island. Las Casas wrote that as usual the conquerors treated the Indians with brutality based on trumped-up accusations, and immediately assigned them to properties in order to produce cassava, maize, and cotton for the other islands.[29] Oviedo, however, thought that Esquivel carried through his mission as "a good knight," placing the island under the Spanish flag through the use of force, of course, but also by persuasion, without shedding blood unnecessarily.[30]

In 1510, King Fernando was informed of the inadvisability of letting Indians be captured in Jamaica by Spaniards from other islands, because, unlike the Bahamas (Lucays), it was not a "useless island"; it was relatively large and therefore agriculturally promising.[31]

Esquivel remained on the island for about three years after its conquest, until he fell from favor both with the Crown and with Diego Colón. He was succeeded in quick order by two hidalgos who were friends of Diego Colón, a certain Captain Perea and then a Burgalés, Captain Camargo. But they lasted only a short time, since the rich chief constable of Santo Domingo, Francisco de Garay, had other ideas. Ambitious and competent, he had married an aunt of Diego Colón, Ana Muñiz de Perestrelo, sister of Columbus's Portuguese wife, Felipa. He, like Esquivel, had probably come to the New World in 1493 on Columbus's second voyage. He had found gold and was famous for building one of the first private houses of stone in Santo Domingo. He now returned to Spain and persuaded the King to name him governor of Jamaica. Garay, who had earlier tried and failed to establish a settlement in Guadeloupe, was a Basque. He founded two more settlements in Jamaica that he named Melilla and Oristán; afterwards, he brought cattle, pigs, and horses, many of which ran wild over the island. Peter Martyr, who would soon receive an improbable nomination as abbot of "New Seville," near St. Ann's Bay, described the island, from hearsay, as a garden of Eden.[32]

Juan Ponce de León, meanwhile, traveling back again from the Old World, made an effort to seize Guadeloupe. This was the largest of the Lesser Antilles and had received its name from Columbus in 1493. But he received a severe check. Peter Martyr left an account:

> When the [Caribs] beheld the Spanish ships, they concealed themselves in a place from which they could spy on all the movements of the people who might land. Ponce sent some women ashore to wash shirts and linen, and also some foot soldiers to obtain fresh water, for he had not seen land since he had left Hierro in the Canaries. . . . The cannibals [sic] suddenly attacked and captured the women, dispersing the men, a small number of whom managed to escape. Ponce did not venture to attack the Caribs, fearing the poisoned arrows that these barbarous man-eaters use with fatal effect. The excellent Ponce, who had boasted that he would exterminate the Caribs as long as he was in a place of safety, was constrained to leave behind his washerwomen and retreat before the islanders. . . .[33]

Among the conquistadors here was the veteran Portuguese black Juan Garrido, who had already been with Ponce de León in Puerto Rico and Florida, and had also been in Cuba.[34] The lost women were most probably Canary Islanders.

But it was not only the West Indies that received the attention of the new generation of conquistadors-cum-explorers. There was *tierra firme,* that mysterious mainland that people were coming to realize, *pace* Columbus, was nothing like India or Asia. Thus Juan de la Cosa, with Pedro de Ledesma as constable, set off in 1505 with four caravels for the north coast of South America, which he had visited before, in 1499, with Hojeda and Vespucci. It was la Cosa's fourth journey across the Atlantic, for even before 1499, he had been on two voyages with Columbus.[35] Ledesma and Martín de los Reyes, of Seville, were the financiers.

As had become de rigueur, the expedition stopped in the Canaries, went toward Guadeloupe, and made landfall in the pearl island, La Margarita. There they offered the usual presents of beads and mirrors to a diversity of Indian *caciques* and received in exchange parrots, cochineal, pearls, and a great new luxury, potatoes, whose potential was not immediately appreciated. They sailed on to the nearby island of Cubagua and, in the Gulf of Cumaná, found few pearls but much brazilwood. They seized some Indians as slaves and continued on to what later became Cartagena de las Indias, in whose ample bay they met, to their surprise, a flotilla of four ships, led by Luis Guerra of Triana. His elder brother, the merchant Cristóbal, had just been killed by the Indians, and Luis longed to go home. Their expedition had sailed the year before to the Pearl Coast. La Cosa gave him two-thirds of his supply of brazilwood to take back to Spain, as well as half the slaves he had seized.[36]

La Cosa and Ledesma sailed on until they reached the unhealthy Bay of Urabá, on what is now the hinge between Colombia and Panama. An Indian anxious to please showed them a town recently abandoned by a local *cacique,* who had left behind in a basket some kettledrums of pure gold and six gold masks.

Returning to Cartagena, they discovered that one of Luis Guerra's ships, captained by a certain Monroy—who came, no doubt, from a bastard branch of the wild family of that name in Extremadura—had been wrecked. Luis Guerra had long ago left for Spain. La Cosa and his friends went to help Monroy, but they, too, soon met trouble, and la Cosa's own ships ran aground. The commander gave orders that everything savable should be taken ashore, where a settlement of perhaps two hundred Castilians was temporarily established. They sought to arrange a means of sustenance, but even in those conditions, did not forget the search for gold; as Oviedo put it, "One cannot eat it, but it gives pleasure and the hope of eventual rest."[37]

But, all the same, these early involuntary Spanish settlers of what became in the end Colombia suffered from terrible shortages of food, and month after month went by without relief. In the end, Juan de la Cosa and Juan de Ledesma set off eastward in two brigantines with the entire colony, and some small boats in which the ill and suffering traveled, under the direction of Martín de los Reyes. Before leaving Urabá, the Spaniards buried their heavy equipment, such as anchors, lances, a few lombards, and crossbows. They assumed that they or other Spaniards would return.

The winds were hostile, progress was slow, morale low, food still short, the death rate high. Oviedo tells us that three Spaniards caught and killed an Indian and ate him, receiving a reprimand from la Cosa but no punishment.[38] A fresh wind divided the little fleet. One small boat was swept to Cuba, while the brigantines found themselves on the shores of Jamaica, presumably on the south coast near what is now Kingston. La Cosa went on one of his vessels with the sick to Santo Domingo, under a captain, Juan de Quecedo, and a pilot, Andrés de Morales, while twenty-five more or less healthy Spaniards remained in Jamaica to be rescued later, though not without further mishaps. For example, in order to frighten the Indians who were pressing them, la Cosa agreed to burn a house in an indigenous town, but the fire spread, fanned by wind, and the settlement went up in flames.

"Call this other place Amerige"

Since Europe and Asia have received the names of women, I see no
reason why we should not call this other place Amerige or America,
after the wise man who discovered it.

The cartographer Martin Waldseemüller, 1508

To discuss how to take best advantage of these lands, which suddenly began
to seem without limit, a meeting was held in 1508 at Burgos, in the Bishop's
Palace. Present were the King, Bishop Fonseca, and several important
mariner-explorers, including the experienced Juan de la Cosa, Juan Díaz de
Solís of Lepe (who, it turned out, had once sailed in the East in the service of
Portugal), Vicente Yáñez de Pinzón of Palos, the great survivor of Columbus's expeditions, and the Florentine Sevillano Amerigo Vespucci.

Vespucci had been on a long journey since he had last been seen at the
Spanish court in 1501. For he had gone in 1502 to Brazil in the service of King
Manuel of Portugal. It would seem right to dwell for a moment on his life,
since his Christian name at least has become so well known.

The Vespuccis were among the most successful of Florentine families,
with a fine property outside the city at Peretola, a village now ruined by the
establishment there of an international airport. They had made money in
the silk trade. The Vespuccis had a palace in Florence, conveniently sited to
the northwest, near the Porta del Prato (then known as the Porto della Cana)
in the district of Santa Lucia di Ognissanti. Members of the family had held
important offices in Florence over several generations; for example, another
Amerigo, in the mid-fifteenth century, had been chancellor of the Signoria,
and his son Nastagio (Anastasio) held the same office.

In 1472, Nastagio commissioned the youthful Domenico Ghirlandaio to
paint a picture dedicated to St. Elizabeth of Portugal (the art historian Vasari
recounts it was his first commission). In the center is the Madonna of Mercy,
Misericordia, and around her are portraits of the donors, members of the
family. The picture was intended for the Vespucci Chapel, which later be-

came the church of San Salvadore d'Ognissanti. Here we can see Nastagio's brother, the priest Giorgio, a "mirror of Florentine piety and probity," a collector of books, a scholar, and a humanist; and Nastagio's sons, including Antonio, who followed his ancestors by becoming an official in the Signoria; a notary, Girolamo; a future wool merchant, Bernardo; and looking directly forward, as if he were a painter in a self-portrait, the eighteen-year-old Amerigo Vespucci, named after his grandfather. This Amerigo studied under the direction of his uncle Giorgio, who in turn talked to him of Ptolemy and Aristotle, and he probably met Toscanelli, the Florentine geographer and merchant whose correspondents had included both the King of Portugal and Columbus.

Some of the Vespuccis had already taken to the sea (one cousin, Bernardo, had been captain of a Florentine galley; another, Piero, had been commander of a Florentine fleet that fought against the corsairs of North Africa); and another cousin, Marco, was married to the beautiful Simonetta, the beloved of Giuliano de' Medici and probably Botticelli's model for the *Birth of Venus* and the *Primavera*.

The young Amerigo started his career first in Paris as private secretary to yet another cousin, Guidantonio Vespucci, the Florentine ambassador there, and later he went to Rome and Milan in the same capacity. Then Guidantonio became the chief magistrate, or *gonfaloniere,* of Florence. But Amerigo began to work for the younger branch of the Medici family, at that time headed by the youthful Lorenzo di Pierfrancesco de' Medici and his brother Giovanni. He traveled on business to different parts of Italy and made several visits to Spain before settling in Seville in the autumn of 1492, while Columbus was away on his first voyage.[1]

In the following years, Amerigo collaborated with Juanotto Berardi, his "special friend," and an associate of the Medici since 1489. According to one of Amerigo's biographers, his ambition "had been fired by what Columbus had attempted"—and failed, as he believed—to do: to find a western passage to India. Hence his participation (already noted) in the expedition of Alonso de Hojeda in 1499 to 1500; and hence his acceptance of a commission to follow the coast of the South American continent, on the orders of the King of Portugal, between May 1501 and the summer of 1502. He then sailed down the Brazilian coast from what he named Cape San Rocco (where he was on August 16) past Bahia and Rio de Janeiro, to Cananor (which he reached in January 1502). That, he decided, was the farthest point west to which, by the Treaty of Tordesillas with Spain, the Portuguese could aspire. He then sailed on south toward the River Plate, in the Spanish zone of influence.

When Vespucci returned from Brazil, he declared that the land along which he had sailed extended much too far south for it to be India. He wrote to Pierfrancesco from Lisbon: "We arrived at a new land which, for many reasons that are enumerated in what follows, we observed to be a continent." He was sure that he had found a quite new land, not just an eastern extension of Asia.[2] He could henceforward have argued that what Columbus had found was in truth a new hemisphere that blocked the way to Asia by the west, unless a passage could be found through it. This astonishing new development was first realized in Lisbon, and there the court, the cartographers, and the merchants soon took this into consideration. Thus the excellent Portolano Map of 1502 shows the new continent in two unconnected sections. Asia ended with another ocean that would lie between it and "the New World." It also showed that Cuba, island or no, was definitely not a part of Asia.

Vespucci returned to Seville. A Florentine merchant friend, Piero Rondinelli, wrote that he had "endured labor enough and has had little profit."

It was later said that Vespucci wrote two more letters: one, *Mundus Novus,* was allegedly to his friend Lorenzo di Pierfrancesco. This was published in 1504 and purported to be an account of his activities in the New World. It was a mixture of inaccurate and false statements, with a few scientifically peculiar observations. It also contains some vulgarisms untypical of Vespucci's style. That it was addressed to someone whom Amerigo Vespucci knew to have been dead at the time of writing should have put people on their guard. By that time, after all, Vespucci was famous. The Signoria of Florence had ordered that the house in which he had been born should be lit up for three nights, while the Vespucci family were to be allowed to attach a beacon to their residences. A letter purporting to be by him would surely sell well. Indeed, *Mundus Novus* did so.

Another letter was published a month later, in September 1504. This took the form of a missive to Piero Soderini, a new *gonfaloniere* in Florence, and was dated September 4, 1504. Soderini was a new man, "feeble and timorous, unequal to the moment," and jealous of the Medici, with whom Vespucci had been associated.[3]

In his previous letters to Lorenzo, Amerigo had spoken of having made two voyages to the New World. To Soderini he is said to have spoken of four. The new letter was soon published as *Quattuor Americi Vesputi navigationes* (*Four Voyages of Amerigo Vespucci*)—that is, in 1497–98, 1499, 1501, and 1503—of which the first and last journeys were myths. The letter of September 1504 was full of inaccuracies, illogicalities, grammatical errors, and a few words that read like Italian hispanicisms. There were also some stories about defecation more suited to a popular English newspaper of the twenty-first century than to the Renaissance. The author was probably the Florentine hack journalist Giovanni Gicondoco. No one at the time realized that the letters were forgeries and that Vespucci had nothing to do with them.

The second of the forgeries had an extraordinary history. It was sent early in 1505 to, among others, René II, Duke of Lorraine, a Maecenas interested in geography. That Duke René was the nephew of the more famous "Bon Roi René," a titular king of Sicily who had lived in France, at Angers and Chanzé. He, like his nephew, had been interested in geography, and, indeed, he had had maps of the world painted on the walls of his chateau. He was especially proud of his Latin translation of the book of the geographer Strabo recently completed by Guarino of Verona.[4]

Duke René in turn gave his copy of "Vespucci's" last letter to a group of clever men known as the Gymnase Vosgien, in Saint-Dié, a small town in the Vosges in Alsace.[5] They were a circle of intellectuals who met regularly in what the Spaniards would have called a *peña*. One of these men, Gauthier (Walter) Lud, acted as secretary to the Duke. He owned a printing press. Another member of the group, Martin Waldseemüller, had already decided to publish a new edition of Ptolemy's *Cosmographia* (with a third friend, Mattheus Ringman, a professor of Latin). Waldseemüller, who had been working on these ideas for many years, wrote an introduction, *Cosmographia Introductio*, into which he inserted these *Navigationes*, having had them translated from Italian into Latin by a canon of Saint-Dié. In this he wrote:

> Today these parts of the earth, Europe, Asia, and Africa, have been completely explored, and a fourth part has been discovered by Amerigo Vespucci, as may be seen in the attached charts. And since Europe and Asia have received the names of women, I see no reason why we should not call this other place Amerige, that is the land of Amerigo, or America, after the wise man who discovered it.

Whether Asia and Europe are called after women is doubtful. "Asia" has been said to stand for the land of the "rising sun" or "land of light," but it more likely derives from "Assiuva," the Hittite word for northwest Asia Minor; while "Europa" indicates not only the beautiful daughter of Agenor, King of Tyre, with whom Zeus fell in love, but also, in the Greek mind, central Greece, then the Greek mainland, and, finally, the landmass behind it. "Africa," on the other hand, was apparently a derivation of a Phoenician or Carthaginian place-name, and the Roman province had that name.

But Waldseemüller did consider that all these continents derived from the names of women and that was what caused him to choose a man's name for the New World. His new *Cosmographia* was accompanied by a planisphere made by himself, alongside which there was an engraving of Ptolemy facing east and of Vespucci facing west: "We have proposed in this little book to write a kind of introduction . . . which we have depicted both on a globe and on a chart, very succinctly, of course, on the globe, where space was wanting, but more fully in the map of the world." On this map (reproduced on pages xvi–xvii of this history), the new hemisphere across the Ocean Sea was named "America" for the first time.

This new edition of Ptolemy's geography was published by Gauthier Lud on April 25, 1507. The woodcuts for the map were made fifty miles away at Strasbourg and printed in Saint-Dié.[6] These later much influenced other mapmakers, including Mercator in the 1540s.[7]

Waldseemüller had no intention of diminishing the achievement of Columbus. He said as much in his foreword to Ptolemy. On his large map, indeed, he wrote in the Caribbean section: "These islands were discovered by Columbus, an admiral of Genoa, at the command of the King of Spain." On the section dealing with South America, he wrote: "Here is a land discovered by Columbus, a captain of the King of Castile, and by Americus Vespucius, both men of great ability, which, though a great part of it lies beneath the path of the year and of the sun and the tropics, nevertheless extends about nineteen degrees beyond the Tropic of Capricorn toward the Antarctic pole."

There were some astonishing elements in the map: an inset presented much of the northern part of what we now know as the Americas as well as the south. South America is well drawn. The two, North and South America, are connected, though on the larger map, not the inset, where they are separated by a hypothetical strait roughly where the Panama Canal now lies. Even more interesting, both the inset and the map present a large ocean between Asia and the New World—one even bigger than the Atlantic. It was an outstanding achievement to guess thus in 1507 when the Pacific had not even been seen by any European, much less crossed.[8]

Peter Martyr would soon write of South America that "this continent extends into the sea exactly like Italy, but it is dissimilar, in that it is not the shape of a human leg. Moreover, why should we compare a pigmy with a giant? That part of the continent beginning at this eastern point lying toward Atlas that the Spaniards have explored is at least eight times larger than Italy; and its western coast has not yet been discovered."[9]

Frederick Pohl, the best biographer of Vespucci, points out that the

word "America" is so euphonious and so happily parallel with the words
"Asia" and "Africa" that the idea of using the word became immediately appealing.[10] In 1509, it appeared on a globe, and others such followed, also carrying the magic name.

What an irony it is that the letter *The Four Voyages*, of which Duke René
was so proud and which so influenced the sages of Saint-Dié, should have
been a forgery! Vespucci's first alleged voyage in 1497 never occurred, and
Columbus did discover the continent of South America on his third voyage
in 1498. Waldseemüller seems to have realized the truth, and another edition
of Ptolemy, edited by him in 1513, gave more credit to Columbus. All the
same, the cartographer Mercator, in his first world map, the heart-shaped
Orbis Imago of 1538, applied the Christian name of Amerigo to the northern
continent, North America, as well.[11]

That *The Four Voyages* was fraudulent was not hinted at until 1879, and
it was not till 1926 that Professor Alberto Magnaghi of Milan, in a study of
Vespucci, showed that both it and the *Mundus Novus* were forgeries.[12]

Vespucci deserved his legacy, "America." In September 1503, after he had
returned from his journey down the coast of Brazil in the King of Portugal's
service, he declared that he had been to a new world[13]—which he would
christen *Novus Orbis*, "as the ancients had no knowledge of it."[14] He added
that he wanted one day to go back to that world, in order to reach the East
through the south by using the austral winds.[15] But he never did so.

The board of royal advisers—Vespucci, Juan de la Cosa, Vicente Yáñez de
Pinzón, and Juan Díaz de Solís—that met in Burgos in 1505 decided, first, to
create in the Casa de Contratación a position of chief pilot (*piloto mayor*), a
supreme geographer and cartographer who would chart the expeditions to
the New World.

That appointment would, in the first instance, be held by Vespucci, who
would be paid 75,000 maravedís a year, not a bad sum at that time though
Governor Ovando was receiving 360,000 (Ovando had far more responsibilities, of course). The King hoped that Vespucci would train and impart his
remarkable knowledge to all Spanish pilots and try to convince them to use
his astronomical methods of establishing longitude at sea rather than rely-
ing on their old custom of dead reckoning.[16] All masters of ships, before obtaining advances of money for voyages to the Indies, were to present
themselves to Vespucci at the Casa de Contratación with details about the
capacity of their vessels so that officials could determine their value and the
amount that could be safely secured on them.[17]

On August 8, the King issued a patent that defined Vespucci's duties and gave him the power to compel all pilots to submit to him. The words were strong:

No one shall presume to pilot [our] ships or receive pay as a pilot, nor may any master receive them on board, until they have first been examined by you, Amerigo Vespucci, our chief pilot, and have been given a certificate of examination and approval by you. We order that those who obtain the said certificates shall be accepted and received as skilled pilots by whomsoever is shown them, for it is our pleasure that you shall be the examiner of all pilots. In order that those who are ignorant may learn more easily, we order that you are to teach them, in your house in Seville, everything that they need to know, you receiving payment for your work. . . .

Furthermore, we have learned that there are many charts by various masters on which are delineated the lands and the islands in our Indies, by our command recently discovered, and because these charts may give rise to confusion since they are very different from each other, both in the sailing directions and in the contour of coastlines . . . [we] order that there shall be made a general chart (*padrón general*), and so that that may be more accurate, we order our officers of the Casa de Contratación at Seville to assemble all the best qualified pilots who may be found in Spain at that time, and that in your presence, Amerigo Vespucci, our chief pilot, there shall be made a chart of all the islands and lands of the Indies . . . and this shall be kept in the possession of our aforesaid officers and of you, our chief pilot, and that no pilot shall steer by any other chart. . . .

Furthermore, we order all pilots . . . who voyage hereafter to the said lands of our Indies discovered or to be discovered that when they find new lands, islands, bays, harbors, or anything else, they make a note of them for the said royal chart and that, upon arriving back in Castile, they shall give an account to you, the chief pilot, and to the officers of the Casa de Contratación, that all may be correctly delineated on the said royal chart. . . . None of our pilots shall henceforth be without his quadrant and astrolabe and the rules for working them under penalty of being named incompetent to exercise the said employment. . . .[18]

The *piloto mayor* was therefore to be a kind of teacher who would conduct a school for captains at his house in Seville. Vespucci had by then established the reputation in Seville of being not only a great traveler but also "very skilled" in the art of making maps.[19] He carried out his new functions from a house in the Plaza del Postigo del Carbón that he rented from Bishop Fonseca, and he does not seem to have moved again.[20] A nephew, Juan (Giovanni), lived with him and his Sevillana wife, María Cerezo. So did five slaves, including two blacks and a Canary Islander, Isabel, who may have given two illegitimate children to Vespucci.[21] Like Columbus and like Isabel the Catholic, when he died (in 1512) he was buried in the robe of a Franciscan.

Another decision of the Burgos conference in 1508 derived from a determination to seek a strait in the Americas to establish the real western route to the Spice Islands. Given that Vespucci had searched most of the coast of Brazil and that la Cosa had sailed along the coast of northern South America as far as Darien, while Columbus had been from Darien to the Bay Islands, there were only three possibilities: one in the far south; a second in the center, to the north of the Bay Islands; and a third to the far north, where Cabot had sought to establish an English interest. In the event, Pinzón and Solís set off uncertainly on June 29, 1508, with two ships, the *San Benito* and the *Magdalena,* to explore the central route, close to where Columbus had turned south in 1502 after meeting the Maya merchants. They had with them Pedro de Ledesma, a pilot who had been with Columbus on his terrible fourth voyage. On this journey they almost certainly touched at Yucatan and probably sailed some way up what is now the Mexican coast.[22] They reached Spain again at the end of August 1509. The journey had much more importance than it has ever been given credit for.

Now that the difficulties attending the deaths of Queen Isabel and King Philip were over, and Diego Colón restored, as it were, to La Española, it seemed entirely possible to confirm Alonso de Hojeda and Diego de Nicuesa as the first governors of new provinces on the mainland, "Urabá" and "Veragua." Jamaica would be their base. Diego Colón was still displeased, since he thought both the nominations and the use of Jamaica constituted a violation of his rights. But he was brushed aside. Urabá would include Cartagena de Indias, and Hojeda would build two fortresses there. Veragua would constitute the east of what is now Panama. Neither place could be defined very well in Valladolid, however. Still, Hojeda and Nicuesa were believed to have been friends at least since they had sailed with Columbus in 1493, and that seemed to augur well for the success of what was considered in Castile a joint exercise.

Hojeda, with his combination of energy, cruelty, and ambition, needs no further introduction. Nicuesa, it should be realized, was a gentleman from

Baeza. He had once been in the household of the King's uncle, Enrique Enríquez, Admiral of Castile, and had it not been for the discovery of the Americas, would have remained there all his life. He was a gifted and charming man, good with horses, skilled on the old guitar (*vihuela*), and both rich and well meaning. Alas, he coveted a colony of his own. That was his undoing. Returning to Spain as *procurador* of Santo Domingo, he asked the King to give him the nomination to "Veragua." Fernando agreed.[23]

Hojeda, meanwhile, had already set off for the north coast of South America on December 18, 1508, and with him went the veteran Juan de la Cosa and several young men, such as the resourceful brothers Pedro and Diego de Ordaz from Castroverde del Campo, near Benavente. They stopped in the Canaries and at La Española, where they picked up more men, including Francisco Pizarro, the illegitimate son of a hidalgo from Extremadura who was known for his achievements in the wars in Italy. This Pizarro had first set off for the Indies with Ovando.

The expedition dropped anchor at Turbaco, near Cartagena, where the local Indians had dark memories of the brutal visit there of Cristóbal Guerra. Hojeda thought of entering the nearby harbor of Calamar, in order to capture Indians as slaves and send them to La Española to settle various debts that he had there. Juan de la Cosa, as captain-general, remembered the poisoned darts that he had encountered in the past and advised against any such effort. But Hojeda insisted and made a surprise attack on the place, capturing sixty natives. Those who escaped fled to Turbaco.

The Castilians pursued them and reached the settlement, but Hojeda found himself isolated. His men were left behind in the mountains, and the Indians, regrouping, attacked in surprisingly well-directed waves. Hojeda fought bravely, but in the end, he committed himself to flight and ran to the safety of the nearby ships. But Juan de la Cosa, hero or villain of so many voyages to the New World, was surrounded in a hut, and on February 28, 1510, was killed by arrows, along with perhaps seventy others. He was then sixty years old.[24]

The men left behind on the boats eventually went in dinghies to look for the refugees. They found Hojeda fainting in a mangrove swamp. The brothers Diego de Ordaz and Pizarro also saved themselves. This Battle of Turbaco was the first serious defeat of the Spaniards since Navidad in 1493.

At this point, Diego de Nicuesa hove into sight with two *naos* and three brigantines, as well as several hundred fresh soldiers. Thus in a sense reinforced, Hojeda returned to the battle and even to Turbaco, which he destroyed. He burned the huts and cut the throats of those inhabitants whom he captured. He then set off for the Bay of Urabá, where he established a

rudimentary settlement, San Sebastián. He sent a ship back to Santo
Domingo with a cargo of captured Indians, some of them coming from the
island of Fuerte, just offshore.

Nicuesa, on the other hand, sailed on to what he presumably hoped
would turn out to be Veragua. His old friendship with Hojeda does not seem
to have survived this act of kindness on his part.

The conditions in San Sebastián de Urabá—the first attempt at the establishment of a colony on the mainland—were discouraging. Hojeda's supplies ran out, the local Indians pursued him and his men with more
poisoned arrows, and disease took its usual appalling toll. Fortunately for
the Spaniards, a ship of seventy refugees from justice in La Española, all
criminals, captained by Bernardino de Talavera, soon appeared. They had
stolen a ship from Genoese merchants at Punta del Tiburón. But they were
helpful to Hojeda.[25]

The colony soon used up the supplies brought by Talavera, and Hojeda
decided to return to Santo Domingo in the stolen ship with about half the
expedition. As for those left behind, if help had not arrived in fifty days, the
survivors, under the command of Francisco Pizarro, who had been a resourceful second in command to Hojeda since the death of la Cosa, should
do what they could to save themselves.

Hojeda with his new ally Talavera went first to Cuba. There, on a beach
known later as the Bay of Pigs, they were attacked by Tainos, whose *cacique,*
however, received them well. Pedro de Ordaz sailed from Cuba to Jamaica in
search of help, and from there the Governor, Juan de Esquivel, sent a well-
supplied caravel under his second in command, Pánfilo de Narváez, which
took Hojeda and his companions to Santo Domingo. But the latter never recovered his health, and he died impoverished in 1515, having in his last moments of life become a Franciscan.

Hojeda had crossed the Atlantic about seven times and had explored
most of the northern coast of South America. His casual cruelty blinds us to
his considerable achievements. Las Casas was harsh: "Had he not been born,
the world would have lost nothing."[26] He was irrepressible, however, and has
a good claim to be considered the first pure adventurer to sail to the New
World.

Diego de Nicuesa, meanwhile, had left for what Columbus had called
"Veragua" and its supposed gold; and, after various tribulations, his party established themselves about four miles to the west of the Bay of Urabá, at Las
Misas, so called because the first Mass on the mainland of the New World
was celebrated there. There Nicuesa divided his expedition into two, always

an unwise move. Nicuesa left the bulk of his men and most of the ships under the command of a cousin, Cueto, another hidalgo from Baeza. He himself, with a single caravel and brigantine captained by a Basque, Lope de Olano, who had been a rebel with Roldán against Columbus in the late 1490s, sailed north with ninety men in a further search for "Veragua." The journey proved unsuccessful even though Nicuesa had with him some of the pilots, such as Pedro de Umbría, who had been with Columbus on his fourth voyage in those same waters.

Two months passed during which Cueto and the people at Las Misas heard nothing of Nicuesa. They sent out a search and, after finding a message left in a tree by him saying that he was well, came upon Lope de Olano, who said that the commander had sailed off alone in a canoe after a bitter argument with one of the pilots as to the whereabouts of "Veragua." If he were not telling the truth, that pilot commented, he hoped that his head would be cut off.

Cueto and Olano then set off northward themselves in search not of "Veragua" but of Nicuesa, and founded, as they went, a settlement on a river that Columbus had named the Belem. Eventually news of Nicuesa came from a comrade, Diego Ribera, who had deserted him on an island some miles off the coast that he had named El Escudo. A brigantine brought him back, and though Olano now had visions of personal power and arrested Nicuesa when he arrived in rags, hungry and ill, Gonzalo de los Reyes, a benign captain, took him to recover on a hill overlooking the place that became known as Nombre de Dios. These journeys were, of course, all completely new experiences for Europeans.

It will be recalled that Alonso de Hojeda had allowed the remaining settlers in the colony of San Sebastián de Urabá to remain for fifty days after his own departure for La Española.[27] The commander left behind the rough Extremeño Francisco Pizarro, who lingered longer than his appointed time and then, in September 1510, set sail for Santo Domingo. But in the Bay of Calamar, near what became Cartagena de Indias, he met by chance a boat carrying the geographer Martín Fernández de Enciso. That explorer had been on Hojeda's original expedition. He and Pizarro returned together to the settlement of San Sebastián, but found it had been razed to the ground by the Indians. On the suggestion of Vasco Núñez de Balboa, a clever conquistador from Jerez de los Caballeros who had stowed away on Enciso's boat to escape creditors in Santo Domingo,[28] they sailed to Darien, which Balboa knew from having been there in 1501 with Rodrigo de Bastidas. Despite resistance from Sinú Indians, the three conquistadors Pizarro, Núñez de Balboa, and Fernández de Enciso founded the city of Nuestra Señora de la Antigua in the Gulf of Urabá, at the mouth of the River Atrato, just inside what is now Colombia.[29]

This new settlement was a mistake. Martyr, on the basis of later conversations with those who went there, commented:

> The site is badly chosen, unhealthy and more pestiferous than Sardinia. All the colonists look pale, as if they are men sick from jaundice. It is not exclusively the fault of the climate, for in many other places, situated at the same latitude, the climate is wholesome and agreeable; clear springs break from the earth, and swift rivers flow between banks that are not swampy. The natives, however, here make a point of living in the hills and not in the valleys. The colony founded on the shores of Darien is situated in a deep valley, completely surrounded by lofty hills, in such a way that the direct rays of the sun beat upon it at midday, and as the sun goes down, its rays are reflected from the mountains, in front, from behind, and all around, rendering the place insupportable. The rays of the sun are most fierce when they are reflected. . . . The unwholesomeness of the place is further increased by the malodorous marsh surrounding it. To tell the truth, the town is nothing but a swamp. When the slaves sprinkle the floors of the houses with water, toads spring into action. . . . There is not even the advantage of a good harbor . . . for the distance . . . to the entrance of the gulf is three leagues and the road leading there is difficult. . . .[30]

Still, here was a Spanish colony in a remote and unknown place. What courage, what determination were needed to establish such a settlement! Once it was properly set up, several of the expedition headed by Rodrigo Enríquez de Colmenares, and accompanied by Diego del Corral and Diego Albítez, went to look for Diego de Nicuesa at Nombre de Dios. They found him "the most wretched of men, by now reduced to a skeleton, covered with rags." They embraced and Nicuesa returned with them to Urabá. After arriving there, newly confident and encouraged by Colmenares and the others, Nicuesa showed himself intent on reasserting his authority. The new settlement, he argued, was in his zone of command. He wanted to confiscate the goods of Balboa and his friends. But Balboa conducted himself cleverly. He encouraged Nicuesa to sleep in his room, and after about three weeks, Nicuesa was placed on board one of his own brigantines and ordered to sail off again, back to Veragua. He left, furious, on March 2, 1511, sailing east, not north, and was never seen again, probably being killed by Indians at Cartagena, where he landed to look for fresh water. Two of his men—a lay brother, Jerónimo de Aguilar, from Écija, near Córdoba, and Juan Guerrero, from Lepe, near Huelva—continued on the brigantine only to be wrecked off the coast of Yucatan. Both survived to play a part in the expedition of Cortés to Mexico.[31]

Lope de Olano, who also challenged Balboa's authority, was punished in a different way. He was made to grind maize in the streets of Darien in the style of Indians. As for Fernández de Enciso, Balboa had him expelled. He had never been a friend since he had threatened to have Balboa placed on a desert island when he was discovered as a stowaway on his vessel from Santo Domingo. Balboa thereby acquired temporary peace of mind but made an enemy of a powerful individual with the capacity to injure him. All the same, he now assumed command of the colony. Francisco Pizarro was his deputy.[32]

Balboa sent two adherents, Valdivia and Martín de Zamudio, to explain his conduct to Diego Colón, and he was confirmed in his command on December 23, 1510, by the King himself. Zamudio went on to Spain, but Valdivia returned to Darien. His ship was wrecked, and he and some of his men were captured by the Maya Indians in Yucatan.[33]

Balboa was the first caudillo of the Americas, in the sense that he made himself leader through sheer determination and strength of character. He followed a policy of relative friendship with the indigenous people, which, in general, worked well (though there were some exceptions, such as when he had the *cacique* Pacra torn to pieces by dogs). The leaders of the Indians at Urabá were similar to those in La Española in that there were recognizable *caciques*. But in most other ways, with their palm and pineapple wines, their beer made from maize, and their glittering gold ornaments, they were more sophisticated. The houses of their chiefs were rectangular, often built elegantly in trees, and their gold objects (sometimes the accumulation of generations) were frequently elaborate. Like all sophisticated people, they had slaves. They did not possess the bitter yucca of the Caribbean and therefore had no cassava bread, but they did have the staple of Mexico, maize, sweet potatoes, and sweet yucca. They also bred turkeys and dogs to be eaten.

They provided Balboa and his three hundred men with both food and girls. He traveled extensively, usually accompanied by Colmenares, and found gold in the foothills of the Andes, the origins of the myth of Eldorado. Once, the *caciques* planned to murder the Spaniards, but a sister of one of them was Balboa's mistress, and she betrayed her relations.[34]

Balboa also clashed with the eldest son of a *cacique* named Comogre, who struck the scales in which the conquistadors were weighing the royal fifth of gold, and asked:

> What thing is this, Christians? How is it possible that you set such a high value on such a small quantity of gold? Yet you nevertheless destroy the artistic beauty of these necklaces, making them into ingots! If your thirst for gold is such that, in order to satisfy it, you destroy peaceful people and bring misfortune and calamity among them, if you exile yourselves from your own country in search of gold, I will show you a country where it abounds and where you can satisfy the thirst that torments you. But to undertake this expedition, you will need numerous forces, for you will have to conquer powerful rulers who will defend their country to the death. More than all the others, King Tumanamá will oppose your advance. . . .
>
> On the other side of those mountains there is another sea that has never been sailed by your little boats. The people there go naked and live as we do, but they use both sails and oars. . . . The whole southern slope of the mountains is very rich in gold mines.

King Tumanamá even had a golden kitchen, the young Indian said. Gold was considered there of no more value than iron was in Europe, he went on airily. Young Comogre offered to go as guide. He said: "Summon a thousand warriors, well armed for fighting, so that by their help and assisted by the warriors of my father . . . we may shatter the power of our (and your) enemies. . . . In this way, you will obtain the gold that you want." "The love of gain and the hope of gold fairly made our men's mouths water . . . ," commented a sailor who talked to Peter Martyr.[35] There were, of course, many parts of this story that owed much to the imagination.

An expedition to what is now Florida was mounted in 1513; the Spaniards called it Bimini. The indigenous people there were tougher than the Tainos in the Caribbean; their arrows were poisoned, unlike those of the Caribbean Indians and, indeed, those of Mexico. They were hunters, but nevertheless they grew maize and corn. They may have been similar to the mysterious Guanahatebeyes in Cuba, with whom they perhaps had some contact.[36]

Juan Ponce de León was commander of the Spanish expedition.[37] Presumably that was a compensation for having been dismissed as governor of Puerto Rico. He took three ships, first the *Santiago,* commanded by Diego

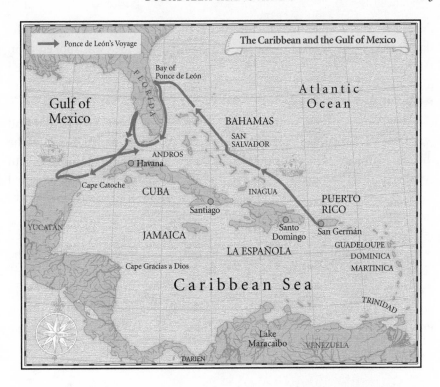

Bermúdez, a brother of the Juan Bermúdez who had discovered the island of Bermuda. Antonio Alaminos was the pilot—an outstanding sailor who had been with Columbus in 1502–04 and would later be the pilot of the conquest of Mexico.[38] The second ship was the *Santa María de Consolación,* whose captain was Juan Bono de Quejo, a Basque from San Sebastián who would also have a long history of marine activity in the Caribbean, ending with the conquest of Mexico, in the second phase of which he also participated. The third ship was a brigantine, the *San Cristóbal.*

Two women sailed on the *Santiago,* in what capacity is obscure. Among the others was Juan Garrido, the black Portuguese who had been with Ponce in Puerto Rico and Guadeloupe and had fought in Cuba. He would afterwards sail with Cortés and be the first European to plant wheat in the New World.[39] Ponce de León also took with him his son, Juan González Ponce de León, who had been the interpreter in his father's conquest of Puerto Rico.

Ponce de León's expedition set out in March 1513 and made landfall in Florida near what is now Palm Beach on Easter Sunday, March 27. He sailed south past the sites of famous modern resorts—Cape Canaveral, Daytona Beach, and Miami—and then turned north into the Gulf of Mexico. He was looking, Peter Martyr tells us, especially for "a fountain of youth"—a fountain with the miraculous power of restoring to old men their fading capacities.[40] This marvel had been mentioned in the work of Sir John Mandeville, the mythical traveler of the fourteenth century. The idea was spoken of in *Palmerín de Oliva*, a romance that had appeared in 1511, where it was alleged to have been found on the magic mountain of Artifaria, belonging to Palmerín, King of England.

But Ponce de León found neither fountain nor gold. What he did find was the Gulf Stream, as important a discovery as Florida itself, though he did not know it.[41] On his way back to Puerto Rico, he stopped in Yucatan (probably near Progreso, Mérida)[42] while the pilot Alaminos returned through the Bahamas (the Lucays). Ponce de León, however, seems not to have explored anywhere in Yucatan. He reached Puerto Rico on October 10, 1513, completing a journey that had been far more important than expected or than its commander, thwarted of his fountain, reported. He named the "island" that he had discovered to honor the day he first saw it: Easter Sunday, otherwise the day of the spring festival (La Pascual Florida). Then, in 1514, Ponce de León returned to Spain to receive a confirmation of his title to Puerto Rico.[43]

Book Four

DIEGO COLÓN

A captain says a prayer.

"A voice crying in the wilderness"

I . . . am a voice of Christ crying in the wilderness of this island . . . the freshest voice that ever you heard, the sharpest and hardest and most awful and dangerous that you ever expected to hear. . . .

Advent sermon of Fray Antonio de Montesinos
Santo Domingo, 1511

Diego Colón, the elder, legitimate son of the Admiral, arrived in Santo Domingo from Spain after a happy voyage on the *Que Dios Salve* with "a large household"[1] including María de Toledo, his fashionable wife, the Duke of Alba's niece, on July 9, 1509. María brought with her a number of well-born girls who would be maids of honor suitable for the wife of a viceroy.[2]

Diego was then aged thirty. Like all Spanish proconsuls, he came to his new mission with new friends in addition to his younger brother, Fernando, and his uncles, the once notorious Bartolomeo (who became chief constable) and Diego, not to speak of cousins, such as Juan Antonio and Andrea Colombo. It was a measure of the success of Ovando's administration that the return of these old members of the Columbus family did not inspire a revolution on the island. Diego had with him, too, an experienced magistrate, Marcos de Aguilar from Écija, whom he made chief justice. Important merchants of Castile sent goods with him, for example, Alonso de Nebreda, a successful trader of Burgos, connected by blood with all the important *converso* businessmen of that city. Among others who accompanied Diego Colón was García de Lerma, an entrepreneur of Burgos who has been described as a pioneer capitalist in the Caribbean.[3]

Diego was a courtier, not a sailor. He had spent his entire life either at the court of the Infante Juan or at that of the Queen, and subsequently at that of the King. His father had been fond of him, usually ending his letters with the phrase "Your father who loves you more than himself."

Columbus had had dreams for Diego. It may be remembered that in 1493 he asked for a cardinalate for him. Then he had hoped that Diego might marry Mencía, a daughter of the Duke of Medina Sidonia, who wielded such power near Gibraltar. But the King refused his permission. In the end, he made an even more advantageous match in 1508 with Maria de Toledo. Las Casas wrote of Diego Colón that he "was more the heir to the anguish, the labors, and the setbacks of his father than to the status, the honors, and the privileges that had been gained with such effort."[4] It was true. Diego was recognized as hereditary admiral, but nothing was said about his being viceroy. There were other privileges in relation to his father that had been included in the famous contract of Santa Fe in 1492 that were missing in Diego's designation in 1509. So he embarked on a lawsuit against the Crown that was a curious accompaniment to his departure on his new mission.

He took with him elaborate instructions.[5] First, he was told that it was desirable to rely on the treasurer, Miguel de Pasamonte, for everything to do with the Church. A second clause spoke well of Ovando—"I am informed that Fray Nicolás had a very good way of conducting himself." Diego Colón was asked to obtain from his predecessor, Ovando, a memorandum as to how he had conducted the government of the island.[6] Then the new Governor was enjoined to look after the hospitals that had been founded at Buenaventura and La Concepción.

The King added that his main desire for La Española was to convert the Indians and to keep them Christians, and to that end there had to be in every town a clerical person, not necessarily a priest, with a house near the church. The Governor was also to assure the Indian *caciques* that he wanted them to be "well treated, not robbed." They in turn had to look after their own Indians generously. The Indians were not to have fiestas except "in the style of the other people of our realms," that is, in Spanish style. Everyone, Spaniards and Indians alike, was to live in towns. Indians who inherited property were not to sell it below its value. No Spaniard was to sell or give arms to Indians.

The Governor and the treasurer, Pasamonte, were also to ensure that they obtained as much gold from the mines as possible. The gold was to be melted down by teams of about ten men, or whatever number was thought right, under the control of a trustworthy person. Fernando hoped that a third of the male Indians on the island of Española would be employed in the discovery of gold, to be found in the sandy beds of rivers or in rock. Diego Colón was to find out how many Indians there were on the island and carry out a census—unless, indeed, that had already been done by Gil González Davila, a courtier of the royal household who had been named accountant. The rise and fall of the population was to be noted. The Governor was to ensure that no one was idle, because "idleness was dangerous."

Diego Colón was further to ensure that no foreigners established themselves in the Indies. Neither Moors nor Jews nor heretics nor anyone who had been castigated by the Inquisition (*reconciliados*) nor people newly converted should go there; though, if they were black slaves or others born in Christianity, they could do so, provided a license had been obtained for them. Even descendants of those punished by the Inquisition were also prohibited from going. Two fortresses, approved in the days of Ovando but not carried through, were to be built, one at Concepción, the other at Santiago; and no one was to go about exploring the island without royal permission. The Governor was to find out and write at length and often about "everything that was going on."[7]

As was often the case, these instructions gave a better impression of what the Crown hoped would happen in La Española than what Diego Colón would achieve. But they did show that the Crown assumed that much of the real power would be exercised by the treasurer, Pasamonte, and that the Governor would be a figurehead.[8] Perhaps it was assumed in Spain that he would be happy to sit in the new stone house built for Ovando and read. For he and his friends had set out with many books. Even the new apothecary took five books of medicine; Cristóbal de Sotomayor, the future deputy governor in Puerto Rico, took nine books, of which eight were bound in gold, a map of the world, and a bundle of other unbound volumes. He later gave Fernando Colón two manuscripts, a sure sign of friendship. The lawyers also took their books: Álvaro de Sandoval had the *Siete Partidas,* the legal code of King Alfonso X, while Marcos de Aguilar had three boxes of unnamed books.[9] One or two copies of the novel *Amadís de Gaula,* in its edition of 1508, were perhaps among them.

In keeping with the tradition of disasters that most of the early governors of La Española encountered, nearly all the ships in which Diego Colón arrived were destroyed in a storm in the Bay of Santo Domingo soon after he arrived. As a result, the colony was unable to communicate with the mother country until October. Diego did not mind, since he was determined to control all the movements of his fellow countrymen in the Caribbean. No new expedition was to occur unless it and its leader had been approved by him, at least while he was himself in litigation over the fate of the whole New World, which he believed he had inherited.

Despite the overbearing presence of the treasurer, Pasamonte, Diego Colón set about preparing his own solutions to the problems of the island. He was advised by three Franciscans: Fray Alonso de Espinal, who had come to La Española with Ovando and had managed to arrange that his own order should be able to receive lands in the New World despite their vows of poverty; Fray Pedro de Melgarejo, a Sevillano, who would later take part in the second stage of Cortés's expedition in Mexico; and Fray Pedro Mejía, an Extremeño. With these men he set about inspiring a new general division of the land on the island. The idea was that the Governor would hand over one hundred Indians to officials and commanders of fortresses named by the Crown. Any *caballero* (knight) who brought his wife to the Indies would receive eighty Indians, while any foot soldier who brought his would receive sixty. Common laborers from Spain who similarly came with wives would receive thirty Indians. Diego was able to act without the fear that native rulers would interfere with his plans, for they no longer existed. But the decline of the native population carried its own anxieties.

The eighteenth-century historian Muñoz, who studied the archives on the matter, declared that this division concerned 33,528 Tainos. The details, however, seem to be lost. So there is no way of knowing how far that estimate of the Indian population was below the figure for 1492 and how many Indian slaves there also were. All calculations of population (suggesting a catastrophic decline) suffer from having been made by interested parties. It would seem certain that this number was below what was found at contact with the Europeans. But in 1509 there was little expression of anxiety about this, which makes it legitimate to think that it could not have been so very much below the previous figure. Had the decline been of the disastrous order suggested by Bartolomé de las Casas or, in the twentieth century, by the California school of historians (Lesley Byrd Simpson, Woodrow Wilson Borah, and Sherburne Friendly Cook), there would already have been alarm expressed, if not consternation.[10]

Instead, by a decree of 1510, the hundred Indians provided by the division for officials and commanders of fortresses was increased to two hundred.[11] Slaves, the King agreed, could be brought in from neighboring islands if they were necessary.

Slaves close to the European definition of the term were well known in the Americas before the Europeans arrived, though not in Taino societies. To the conquistadors, it was one of the many comforting similarities between the two worlds. The two main settled monarchies, the Mexica and the Inca (as yet undiscovered), both had substantial slave populations.[12] The Caribs, too, used Tainos and other captives as slaves.

So it was scarcely an innovation when a dozen colonists in La Española received permission in August 1509 to build caravels to seek slaves in neighboring islands.[13] That same month the Governor approved an offer by a consortium of merchants to procure Indians either from the Bahamas or the mainland. If the captives went willingly, they would be called *naborías* (indentured servants); if they resisted, they would be looked on as slaves.[14] But unlike the *naborías* in La Española, these Bahamians (Lucayos) did not have land of their own to cultivate. So the difference between them and slaves was slight in practice.

The leader of those interested in these adventures was the treasurer, Miguel de Pasamonte.[15] He was an official, but neither he nor any other contemporary civil servant supposed that public service should interfere with commercial dealing. In that view, he was supported by the accountant, Gil González Dávila. The fact was, as was said in a later court, in respect of Bishop Fonseca's protégé in Santo Domingo, Cristóbal de Tapia, "the properties of this land are nothing without Indians."[16]

The King was interested. Early in 1510 he wrote to Diego Colón: "I saw the letter that you sent home with your brother Fernando. . . . Now I reply to that section of it which concerns the mines. Since the Lord gives it [gold], and I need it for the war in Africa [against the Barbary pirates], one cannot discount what is produced. And because the Indians are feeble at breaking up rock, please put into the mines the [black] slaves, of whom I am sending you another fifty, through the officials of Seville."[17] On February 10, 1510, the King, by then in the pueblo of Guadarrama, gave permission for another two hundred African slaves to be sent to the New World.

Most of these had been brought back originally to Lisbon or Seville by the Portuguese from the Gulf of Guinea or the Cape Verde Islands. Some of them were Negroes, others were Berbers. A few of them, or even their fathers, had been in Europe a long time. Two hundred, however, was a substantial figure, and this decision of the King's, even more than the action in 1507 to which reference has been made earlier, was another important date in the history of the African slave trade to the Americas. At that stage no one worried about the condition of these Africans, who were admired as slaves wherever they went. As many as 150, bought in Portugal by the Genoese merchants of the Salvago family, Balian and Antonio, seem to have been sent in 1510, dispatched to La Española in boats belonging to the King.[18]

The King observed that every year the import of gold from La Española seemed to be increasing. Thus 445,000 pesos of gold had been imported in the three years 1503–05, of which 116,000 came from royal mines. Between 1506 and 1510 this figure grew to nearly a million, of which the contribution to the Crown was over 250,000 pesos.[19] This was a side of the Indies that interested Fernando; it was still hard to see what else did.

To take account of these opportunities, the *comendador* Ochoa de Isasaga, the new factor in the Casa de Contratación, who had succeeded the Genoese Francisco Piñelo (he had died in 1509), suggested some changes in the Sevillano institution's organization. Sitting in Monzón, where the court spent March, Isasaga proposed thirty-six new ordinances (approved on June 15, 1510, by the King, Fonseca, and Conchillos). They were important, but they did not mention the Indians. They insisted that all transactions had to be entered in a book. There would be records to account for all money, both incoming and outgoing, and another for the registration of all kinds of objects. Business would be conducted twice a day, from 10 to 11 A.M. and from 5 to 6 P.M. In the summer, the morning hours would be from 9 to 10 A.M.

The Casa had also to concern itself with the administration of the goods of those who had died in the Indies, which were to be kept in a chest with three locks, as was all the gold. Though still no one condemned for religious or other reasons would be allowed to go to the Indies, anyone else could go if they so desired, providing that they registered with the Casa de Contratación.[20] Every big vessel would henceforth have a notary on board. There was to be a clever manager in the Casa as well as a treasurer, an accountant, and, again, a notary. Anyone who wanted to set off for the Indies would have to have his vessel inspected first.[21] The benefits of these arrangements to the Crown included that those who went to the New World would be taxed.

Further refinements were added the next year, when the Casa de Contratación was given civil and criminal jurisdiction, and as much time as it needed to deal with all matters relating to the trade to the Caribbean. Prisoners of the Casa would, however, be held in the public prison of Seville.

Far more important in the long run than these bureaucratic arrangements was the dispatch of six Dominican friars to Santo Domingo in August 1510, as a result of a decree of King Fernando signed the previous November. These friars were all from the reformed section of the order, the "province of San Gabriel de Extremadura."[22] The idea of sending Dominicans to the Indies was that of Fray Domingo de Mendoza, a learned, pious preacher who knew how to put good ideas into practice.[23] At first, these Dominicans seemed a challenge to the Franciscans, who were by then well established in the island of La Española. But within a few months they would constitute as well a threat to the established order, for these friars were the great reformers of the early days of Spanish rule. Their magnificent monasteries, constructed over the next generation in the New World, were landmarks as important as cities.

The Dominicans did nothing immediately, and the years 1510 and 1511 passed uneventfully. Diego Colón's lawsuit over his inheritance was resolved by the Council of the Realm in Seville on May 5, 1511. The new Admiral's hereditary rights were recognized, not over all the territory west of the line of Tordesillas that he had claimed, but at least over the island of La Española and the other lands that had actually been discovered by his father—a not inconsiderable archipelago.[24]

This decision was not what Diego had hoped for; it merely meant that he was governor, with his rights as viceroy left unrestored;[25] but all the same it was enough for him to encourage explorations to begin again, and so Juan de Agramonte, a friend of his, was commissioned to set out for the northwest of the continent, toward and beyond Panama.[26]

The first *audiencia,* or supreme court, of the New World was also established in La Española in 1511. The siting of it in Santo Domingo allowed that city for several generations to remain effectively the capital of the Spanish Empire in the New World. The first judges named were Lucás Vázquez de Ayllón, who had had been in Santo Domingo as deputy to Judge Maldonado and had even been in business on the island; Juan Ortiz de Matienzo; and Marcelo de Villalobos. Of these, Vázquez de Ayllón was of a *converso* family from Toledo, where his father had been a councillor. Ortiz de Matienzo was a nephew of the treasurer of the Casa de Contratación, Sancho de Matienzo, to whom he owed his appointment, while Villalobos was a Sevillano and married to Isabel de Manrique, a kinswoman of the Duke of Nájera. All these judges believed their appointments enabled them to enter into business in the island, especially Vázquez de Ayllón. They also expected to have an important share in the administration of the colony. Spanish *audiencias* were more judicial. Diego Colón protested, though not about the commercial question. He did not think that there should be any appeal from him in his capacity as governor. If the judges had to stay, could they not serve as a gubernatorial council sitting under him?[27]

But before the judges arrived in La Española, several more Dominicans had reached the island.[28] There were now nearly twenty of these friars in the colony, more than there were Franciscans. Of these men, Fray Pedro de Córdoba, the leader, was a saintly individual, a man of prudence, well versed in theology. He came from Córdoba, of a good family, and he had a fine presence. He had studied in Salamanca and had been for a time at Torquemada's monastery of St. Thomas in Ávila. He was well received by the Governor.

For several weeks the Dominicans were the favorites of the settlers. Fray Pedro de Córdoba preached eloquently. Then, on the fourth Sunday in Advent, December 4, Fray Pedro inspired one of his colleagues, Fray Antonio de Montesinos, to preach in the large but still thatched wooden building that served as a church for the Dominican friars. He announced that the theme of his sermon would be St. Matthew, chapter 3, verse 3: "I am a voice crying in the wilderness" (*Ego vox clamantis in deserto*).

A Dominican preacher was still a novelty in Santo Domingo, so the church that day was full of settlers, including many old hands who had been on the island with Columbus and others who had come with Ovando as well as with Diego Colón. Dominicans had the reputation of being able to preach well. The sermon that day, however, posed an extraordinary challenge to all settlers. Fray Montesinos said:

> In order to make you aware of your sins against the Indians, I have come up to this pulpit, I . . . am a voice of Christ crying in the wilderness of this island . . . and, therefore, it behooves you to listen, not with careless neglect but with all your heart and senses; for this is going to be the most lively voice that ever you heard, the sharpest and hardest and most awful and dangerous that you ever expected to hear. . . .

Montesinos spoke so forcefully that some of those who heard him thought they were already listening to divine judgment. He went on:

> This voice says that you are in mortal sin, that you are living and may die in it, because of the cruelty and tyranny which you use in dealing with these innocent people. Tell me, by what right or by what interpretation of justice do you keep these Indians in such a cruel and horrible servitude? By what authority have you waged such detestable wars against people who were once living so quietly and peacefully in their own land? . . . Why do you keep those who survive so oppressed and weary, not giving them enough to eat, not caring for them in their illnesses? For, with the excessive work you demand of them, they fall ill and die or, rather, you kill them with your desire to extract and acquire more gold every day. And what care do you take that they be instructed in religion, that they know God, the creator, and that they are baptized and hear Mass, keeping Holy days and Sundays? . . . Are these not men? Have they not rational souls? Are you not bound to love them as you love yourselves? Do you not understand this? Do you not feel this? Why are you sleeping in such

a lethargic dream? Be certain that in a state such as yours, you can be no more saved than Moors and Turks. . . .[29]

Fray Montesinos then proudly left the church, his head high, leaving the colonists aghast.[30] They had never given much thought to their Indian charges, and they had never considered that they were doing wrong to them. Several prominent settlers (we may imagine among them Diego de Alvarado, Columbus's ex-secretary; Rodrigo de Moscoso; Juan Mosquera; Juan de Villoria; and Pedro de Atienza, to mention some of the other, richer landowners) went to call on the Governor in his palace, asking for the preacher to be punished as a scandal maker or as the sower of a new doctrine. Then they went to the Dominican monastery, where Fray Pedro de Córdoba assured them that Montesinos had spoken for all the Dominicans.

Diego Colón himself complained to Fray Pedro. Since he had spoken so harshly, the Dominicans themselves obviously ought not to own Indian slaves, the Governor commented. He asked the friar to tell Montesinos to withdraw his statements; otherwise he would receive an appropriate punishment. Fray Pedro replied by saying that Montesinos would preach again the following Sunday. Diego Colón assumed that he would retract his harsh words. But Fray Antonio's opening words were: "I will return to repeat what I preached last week," and he went on again to speak harshly, on a text from Job. He said that he and his fellow friars would henceforth no more hear the confessions of settlers and conquistadors than they would those of highway robbers. They might write home to whomever they thought right if they wanted to complain. The church was crowded with outraged settlers who, however, took no further action.[31] But the Spanish possessions overseas would never be the same again.

"Infidels may justly
defend themselves"

If an invitation to accept Christianity has not been made, the infidels
may justly defend themselves.

Matías de Paz, c. 1512

The sermons of the Dominicans in Santo Domingo had no immediate effect.
The island of Trinidad continued to be used as a source for slaves for La Española, on the understanding that the operations of slave merchants would
not affect the Pearl Islands. The natives of Trinidad were declared cannibals
on December 23, 1511, and their capture was therefore authorized.[1] The same
day, the King issued a decree in Burgos that stated that "one could fight and
take as slaves anyone who resisted, or did not wish to receive and welcome in
their lands, the captains and others who, by my mandate, go to those shores
to indoctrinate the people there in the holy Catholic faith."[2] This included the
Carib inhabitants of all the Antilles and the north coast of South America,
from Martinique as far as Cartagena.[3] The colonizers of Santo Domingo were
delighted. They knew very well (whatever people in Castile supposed) that
almost anyone could be designated a Carib and therefore was enslavable.[4]

The judges of the *audiencia* arrived in Santo Domingo. They did not
support the position of Montesinos and the Dominicans. The three—
Vázquez de Ayllón, Matienzo, and Villalobos—became indeed the most determined entrepreneurs in dealing in Indian slaves as well as in pearls,
setting a pattern for judicial involvement in commerce that affected Spanish
legal credibility thereafter. Two expeditions left Santo Domingo in search of
slaves in 1512, the first consisting of four caravels, two brigantines, and four
hundred men, organized by Diego Méndez, that valiant colonist who had
saved Columbus in 1502; and the second by Juan Fernández de las Varas, a
converso merchant of Seville connected with all the administrators. Two of
his ships were destined for the Virgin Islands and what later became Dominica, in the Windward Islands.[5]

King Fernando, having heard of Montesinos's sermon, told Diego Colón to reason with the preacher. If he and his fellow Dominicans continued in their error (which, said the King airily, had been denounced as such ten years before), the Governor would be ordered to send them all back to Spain.[6] A few days later, on March 23, Fray Alonso de Loaysa, the Dominican superior in Spain, wrote to reprove Fray Pedro de Córdoba and Montesinos, and called on the latter to stop preaching his scandalous doctrine. No more friars would be sent if such sermons continued.[7] It was scarcely a punishment, certainly not one that would have any effect.

There followed a prolonged discussion in Spain of the issues raised by these sermons. Both Dominicans and colonists sent emissaries to court, the Dominicans sending Montesinos himself, the colonists the Franciscan Alonso de Espinal.[8] Legal arguments about conquests were not unusual in Spain. After all, the conquest of the Canaries had been preceded by a justificatory legal declaration by Bishop Alonso de Cartagena saying that the islands had been part of the kingdom of the Visigoths.[9]

In August 1512, Fray Antón Montesinos, back in Spain, called in person on the Council of the Realm in Burgos. He said to the King, "Lord, may your Highness be good enough to give me an audience because I have to tell you things that are extremely important for your service." The King replied: "Say, Father, whatever you like."[10] Montesinos then gave a long list of Indian grievances. The King was impressed, even horrified, and summoned a group of theologians and officials to consider the matter. The establishment of a royal commission of this nature was, it will be recalled, what the Spanish Crown had decided on in relation to Columbus. The committee met more than twenty times in Burgos, probably in the house of the constable of Castile, the Casa del Cordón, a Moorish-style building with a rope carved above its portal. It was here that Fernando and Isabel had received Columbus in 1496, here that King Philip had died in 1506. The belt of St. Francis connected the coat of arms of the Velascos with the royal one. It seemed emblematically appropriate. The house had begun to be built in 1482.

Here some unusual things were said, and we should recognize that this debate was unique in the history of empires. Did Rome, Athens, or Macedon inspire such a debate in respect of their conquests? Would Britain mount a learned disputation in Oxford to speculate whether the wars against the Ashanti or the Afghans were legal? Or the French speculate similarly about their standing in Algeria? The idea is laughable.

These discussions had been preceded by a peculiar work entitled *The Commentaries on the Second Book of Sentences*, written in Paris by a Scottish philosopher, John Major, in 1510. This constituted the first extended theoretical treatment of the role of Spain in America. Major conceded temporal power to neither pope nor emperor, and declared that mere ignorance of the faith did not deprive men of their own autonomy, though armed opposition to the preaching of the faith did.[11]

The King's committee in Burgos was composed of Bishop Fonseca, Hernando de Vega, the eternal courtier and Viceroy of Galicia, Luis Zapata, the royal secretary Licenciado Santiago and Dr. Palacios Rubios (both learned men), Licenciado Mújica, Licenciado Sosa, two Dominican friars (Tomás de Durán and Pedro de Covarrubias), and a jurist of Salamanca, Matías de Paz: the great and the good of Castile.[12]

At this conference in Burgos, Fray Bernardo de Mesa, then the King's favorite preacher, of a noble Toledan family, presented a thesis in which he proved, to his own satisfaction at least, that the Indians of the New World were a free people. Yet they suffered from a disposition to idleness. It was the King's duty to help them overcome that. Absolute liberty was bad for them, so a form of servitude was desirable "to curb those vicious inclinations." Mesa justified the enslavement of the indigenous people with arguments deriving mostly from *The Rule for Princes* (*Regimiento de Príncipes*), a document usually then ascribed to St. Thomas of Aquinas but in fact written by one of his pupils, Ptolemy of Lucca.[13]

Then Fray Matías de Paz, a young Dominican professor of theology at Salamanca who afterwards taught in that university for many years, contended that the Indians could not be reduced to slavery, since they were not covered by the Aristotelian definition of natural law.[14] In fifteen days at Valladolid, Paz had written a major treatise on "the origins of the rule of the King of Spain over the Indies." This raised and answered three questions: first, could the King govern these Indians despotically or tyrannically? The answer was: "It is not just for Christian princes to make war on infidels simply because of a desire to dominate or to obtain their wealth. They can only do so in order to spread the faith. If the inhabitants of these lands (which have never before been Christian) wish to listen to and receive the faith, Christian princes may not invade their territory. . . ."

Second, can the King of Castile exercise political dominion? The answer was: "If an invitation to accept Christianity has not been made, the infidels may justly defend themselves, even though the King, moved by Christian zeal and supported by papal authority, is waging a just war. Such infidels may not be held as slaves unless they pertinaciously deny obedience to the prince or refuse to accept Christianity."

Third, could settlers who received substantial personal services from these Indians, treating them like slaves, be obliged to make restitution? The

An auto-de-fe. A tragedy of the age was the persecution of converted Jews who were accused of continuing their old practices.

Right Adrian of Utrecht was tutor to Charles, and later became Regent of Castile and pope. The Romans laughed at him because he liked beer.

Below Cardinal Cisneros, confessor to Queen Isabel, was hard, austere, honest, brave, and unyielding. He was twice Regent of Castile.

Middle right Guillaume de Croÿ, a Flemish aristocrat and chief adviser to Charles V, in whose bedroom he slept until the Emperor was twenty.

Below The Chancellor, Mercurino de Gattinara, inspired Charles to dream of world empire.

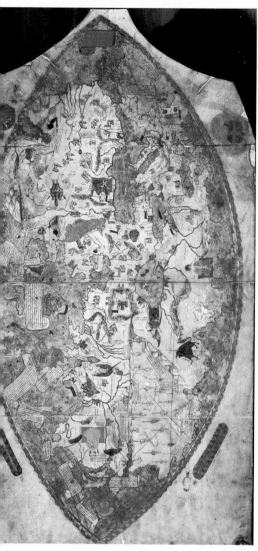

Toscanelli's map, which influenced Columbus.
Another Italian contribution to the discovery of
America.

In the cathedral of Seville, *Our Lady of La Antigua* was
an inspiration for explorers and colonizers, and gave
her name to boats, cities, and islands.

Christopher Columbus: His face is a mystery, his origins unclear, his deeds incomparable.

Bottom left Amerigo Vespucci, who gave his Christian name to "America."

Bottom right Bishop Fonseca, who, as de facto Minister for the Indies from 1493 to 1522, managed Spain's new empire.

Magellan, who in 1519 sought to be the first person to sail around the world, but was killed in the Philippines.

Left and below Hernán Cortés conquered Mexico and considered conquering China with Mexican troops. It was a mistake to refuse him a command in Europe.

PREPARATIONS FOR THE JOURNEY TO THE NEW WORLD

Careening the ship.

A captain awaits a favorable wind.

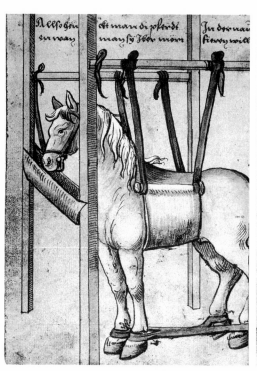

Horses are hoisted on board.

Strong wines from Jerez arrive at the quay.

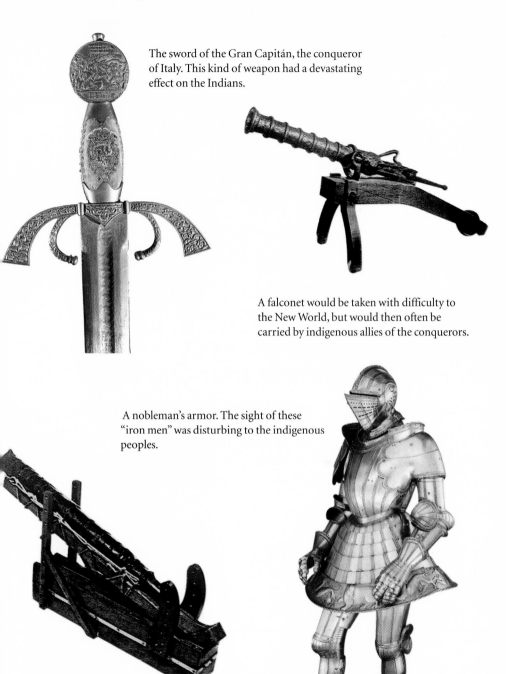

The sword of the Gran Capitán, the conqueror of Italy. This kind of weapon had a devastating effect on the Indians.

A falconet would be taken with difficulty to the New World, but would then often be carried by indigenous allies of the conquerors.

A nobleman's armor. The sight of these "iron men" was disturbing to the indigenous peoples.

The lombard, an inaccurate piece of artillery, made a noise that terrified the Indians.

The Wheel of Fortune is turned by a servant of the blind Goddess of Fortune. In the Renaissance she was believed in almost as widely as Our Lady.

Almost all the gold from New Spain was melted down. Here are some pieces that survived, found in Mexico in the 1930s.

reply was that only by the authority of the Pope would it be lawful for the King to govern these Indians and to attach them to the Crown. Therefore, Spanish settlers who oppressed Indians after they had been converted should definitely make restitution. Once the Indians were converted, however, it would be lawful, as was the case in all political circumstances, to require work from them. Even greater services, after all, were exacted from Christians in Spain, as long as they were reasonable—taxes, for example, to cover the costs of travel and other expenses connected with the maintenance of peace and the good administration of distant provinces.

Paz also cited, with approval, Henry of Susa, a bishop of Ostia ("Ostiensis") of the thirteenth century, who had argued that when heathens were brought to a knowledge of Christ, all their powers and rights passed to Christ, who became their Lord in the temporal as well as the spiritual sense. His rights subsequently passed to the pope. Paz added benignly: "I am told that there also exist in those [Indian] lands gentle people, not ambitious, avaricious, or malicious, but docile and potentially submissive to our faith, provided they are treated charitably. Some observe the natural law, and others pay tribute to the devil, with whom they maintain speech. Perhaps it was this that led God to inspire our King to send people to point out to these persons the way to salvation."[15] This liberal statement was not equaled, much less surpassed, for three centuries.

Next to intervene was Juan López de Palacios Rubios, a clever lawyer who had become a member of the Council of the Realm. He was by origin from Santander and had the calm efficiency of men from that region. He had been a professor of law at Valladolid. He had also been an unsuccessful ambassador of Spain to the Vatican, and he was president of the Council of the Mesta. No one was better connected, no one was better prepared for the discussion—save that he knew much more about Spanish sheep than he did about American Indians.[16]

Palacios Rubios thought it obvious that God had created all men equal and it was war that changes that situation. Those taken prisoner in a just war could always be looked upon as slaves. He had written an apologia for Fernando's recent claim for Navarre, in which he had argued that all goods acquired in that "very holy, very just war" against Navarre would become "the property of the conquerors"; though he had not suggested that captured men and women from Pamplona could be justly enslaved. In his "Of the Ocean Isles" of 1512, he would argue that the right of Spain to the Indies derived from Pope Alexander's gift of 1493. The Indians had to be required to come to the faith, but those who mistreated them had to make restitution. He spoke warmly of Indians and even argued that they had to be treated as if they were tender plants. He, too, accepted the idea that the pope had temporal as well as spiritual authority.[17]

Another professor of law, Licenciado Gregorio, was disdainful. He spoke of the Indians as "animals who talk." He quoted extensively from Aristotle, Aquinas, Duns Scotus, and Augustinus of Ancona to prove this point.[18] But Fray Antonio Montesinos did not gain many followers when he declared that he would preach from the text "Answer a fool according to his folly, lest he be wise in his own conceit." His eloquence was wasted. The Franciscan Fray Alonso de Espinal (with whom Montesinos quarreled in a street in Burgos) also spoke, as did Martín Fernández de Enciso, who had the advantage of having been to the Indies as second in command to Alonso de Hojeda.

In conclusion, this committee of Burgos decided that the Indians all had to be treated as free beings. All the same, they would be subject to coercion in order to be instructed in the Catholic faith. They would be obliged to work for their own benefit, their labor being paid for by the provision of clothes and houses. Grants of land to settlers were to be recognized "in view of apostolic Grace and donation and, therefore, in agreement with both divine and human law." But "no one may beat or whip an Indian nor call an Indian a dog, nor any other name—unless it is his real name."[19]

These debates led to the so-called Laws of Burgos, which were promulgated on December 27, 1512. The most important items were that all Indians were to be gathered in towns and villages, and in specially built new houses; their old homes were to be burned, "so that they might lose the longing to return to them although, in the removal, violence should not be used, rather, much kindness." (This echoed an ordinance in Ovando's time that had not been carried out.) Spanish landowners were to pay close attention to religious instruction, such as the teaching of the creed, the importance of prayer, and of confession. Churches were to be built and supplied with the right pictures and ornaments. When an Indian died, other members of his town were obliged to attend the funeral and to follow a cross. All Indian children should be baptized within eight days of their birth; and sons of caciques should be handed over to Franciscans for four years both to be taught to read and to learn about Christianity. In Santo Domingo, they would also be taught Latin by a certain Hernán Suárez.[20] A third of all the Indians were to work in gold mines, as the King desired, but care was be taken to ensure that they were neither ill-treated nor overworked. Pregnant women were not to be required to perform manual labor. All Indians were to be encouraged to marry.

Then came some prohibitions certain to be unpopular with Indians. They were not to be allowed to dance, since that might suggest a return to their old ceremonies and religions. Nor were they to be allowed to paint their bodies or to become drunk. In each new town, two inspectors would be appointed to ensure that the laws were complied with.[21]

Fray Pedro de Córdoba, the leader of the Dominicans in La Española and the inspiration for their brave challenge to the settlers, returned to Spain, studied these laws, and argued for amendments. Impressed, King Fernando agreed. A new committee was set up; the members were Fray Tomás de Matienzo and Fray Alonso de Bustillo.[22] (Matienzo had been to Brussels in 1498 to be the confessor of the Infanta Juana and give a report on her life there.)[23] Hence the so-called Clarification of the Laws of Burgos, promulgated on July 28, 1513.[24] This contained provisions for the further protection of Indian children and also insisted that Indians wear clothes. Children of Indians were to be allowed to learn trades if they wished. The latter were to be asked to give nine months' service a year to the Spanish landowners, "to prevent their living in idleness," but for the remaining three months they would be free to work on their own farms.

In order to tell the Indians in the new territories what was being offered them by the Spaniards, Palacios Rubios was now asked to write the famous "Requirement" (the *Requerimiento*), apparently influenced by the experiences of Alonso de Hojeda, who had felt the need for such a thing at Cartagena de Indias in 1509. The procedure had a firm peninsular basis: a town council in a dispute with a lord might read aloud a "Requirement" against a magnate in respect of a disputed boundary. A more aggressive "Requirement" had been used in the Canary Islands when the Governor had demanded that the indigenous inhabitants accept both Castilian sovereignty and Christianity. The final text of 1513 for use in the Indies derived from a discussion at the Dominican monastery of San Pablo, in Valladolid, an edifice of the previous generation, having been built by Juan and Simón de Colonia, two architects from Cologne, father and son, who had worked previously in Burgos. Palacios Rubios argued that the Spaniards had been allocated the Indies by God, just as Joshua had procured Canaan for the Jews. So "the King might very justly send men to 'require those idolatrous Indians' to hand over their land to him, for it had been given him by the Pope. If the Indians were reluctant to do so, then the King could justly wage war against them, and kill or enslave those captured in arms, as Joshua had treated the inhabitants of Canaan." But those Indians who gave up their lands should be allowed to live on peacefully as vassals.[25]

Present at these discussions were Conchillos and Matienzo, the King's confessor, as well as most of the Dominican monks of San Pablo.

By the "Requirement," the indigenous people would be asked to recognize the Church of Rome and the Pope as supreme rulers of the world and, in the Pope's name, the King and Queen Juana as "superiors" of these islands and the *tierra firme*. In addition, the Indians had to allow the faith to be preached to them. If that was not accepted, the Spaniards would calmly declare:

> We shall take you and your wives and children, and make slaves of them and, as such, sell and dispose of them as their Highnesses may command, and we shall take away your goods and do all the damage and harm that we can, as it is right to do to vassals who do not obey and who refuse to receive their lord, and resist and contradict him; and we emphasize that any deaths and losses which may result from this are your fault . . . and we request the notary present to give us his testimony in writing and we ask the rest of those present to be witnesses of this requirement.[26]

The document began with a brief history of the world until the gift of the Americas by Pope Alexander VI to the Catholic Kings.

The "Requirement" gave the Spaniards on sweltering riverbanks in the Indies, standing before arrays of ill-armed men and women, or before forests in which they suspected armed "cannibals" were hiding, the illusion that they had agreed with a higher authority on any action that they might want to take. It was intended as a justification for all Spanish actions in the New World: conquest, enslavement, conversion.

But what action might they take in the conquered territory of La Española, whose population now seemed to be declining? In 1514, Rodrigo de Alburquerque, a methodical lawyer from Salamanca, with the treasurer, Pasamonte, to help him, set about making another general division of the land and people on the island. Alburquerque, a relation of the royal secretary Zapata, who had probably arranged the new appointment for him, had gone to La Española with Ovando in 1502 and had been the first commander of the fortress at La Concepción. Now he had a quite new role.

This new division by Alburquerque reflected the balance of power in Spain. King Fernando, for example, was allocated 1,000 Indians, the Viceroy Diego Colón 300, his wife, María de Toledo, the same, the Columbus brothers, Diego and Bartolomeo, 200 to 300 each, the new judges and other officials, 200 each, while all magistrates, *procuradores*, councillors, and other officials would have fewer. And so it was, though the King received 1,503 Indians, not 1,000, and, in addition, the King's cousin, the courtier Hernando de Vega, Viceroy of Galicia and member of the Council of the Realm, received 300. Bishop Fonseca and Conchillos received 200 each. (They would obtain similar allocations in Cuba, Jamaica, and Puerto Rico.) No religious orders received Indians. Otherwise, the distribution in practice was as expected: there were altogether 738 properties, among which a little over 26,000 Indians were to be divided.[27] This did not embrace all the Indians, since slaves constituted personal property and so were not included in the division. A decree of 1514 shows that there was some anxiety about the Spanish population of the island: 250 Castilians were offered free passage to, and maintenance for a time in, Santo Domingo.[28]

The *Repartimiento* did not affect the already conquered Indians. Overwork and the collapse of traditional agriculture were all playing a part in the decline of the indigenous population. The birth rate had fallen, and suicide—rendered easy by the drinking of the poisonous juice of the bitter yucca—also played a part. The destruction of the old polities was not to be ignored. It is not obvious that disease was a factor before 1518 (when the first serious epidemic, of smallpox, occurred). But perhaps small bouts of typhoid and tuberculosis had an effect. Moving the Tainos from a familiar old village to an unfamiliar new one was, of course, another cause of their loss of faith in their future. As in other empires, the deliberate destruction of the memories of the past seemed necessary for the Spanish triumph; it was all too successful.

It is true that many Taino girls did settle down with Spanish conquistadors, partly because there were so few European women on the island. The division of 1514 suggested that half the Spaniards had indigenous wives. Many of these naturally had mestizo children.

Another destructive element was that the coming of cattle from Europe destroyed much native agriculture, for the newly imported animals were generally allowed to roam. It was with these considerations in mind, obviously, that Thomas More, in his *Utopia,* first published in 1516, wrote that "these placid creatures [sheep] that used to require so little food have now apparently developed a raging appetite and turned into man-eaters. Fields, houses, towns, everything goes down their throats." *Utopia* was in theory set near Brazil. But it could have been anywhere in the New World.

Here was a demographic catastrophe for which the Spaniards have naturally been blamed. They were also blamed at the time, and by Spaniards. Thus Pedro de Córdoba, provincial of the Dominicans in La Española, declared: "People so gentle, so obedient and good have been kept in excessive and unaccustomed labors. . . . Pharaoh and his Egyptians treated the children of Israel less badly."[29] For a time, it seemed possible to compensate for the shortage of labor by the seizure of slaves from elsewhere. On January 6, 1514, Diego Colón, with the judges of Santo Domingo and other officials, de-

cided to finance an expedition for slaves to the three islands of the Gigantes—that is, Curaçao, Aruba, and Bonaire, which on July 29, 1513, had
been declared, like the Bahamas, "useless isles." The voyage was organized by
Jerónimo Grimaldi, a Genoese Sevillano, helped by Diego Caballero, from
Sanlúcar de Barrameda and two other merchants, Juan de Ampiés and Lope
de Bardeci (who acted as notary as well as royal administrator), though one
judge, Marcelo de Villalobos, was also interested. Pedro de Salazar, experienced in slaving expeditions to the Bahamas, was named captain. The ships
were crewed by sailors from Santo Domingo who answered an appeal by the
town crier and were told to assemble at Salazar's house. The King approved
and even instructed his representatives to assist in the costs.[30]

The natives on the doomed islands at first received these expeditions in
peace, but when the designs of the captains became known, they fought.
This served them little, and most were captured. Two hundred were sent to
La Española in August 1514; Captain Salazar remained in Curaçao, and in the
following months, anywhere from five hundred to two thousand Indians
were sent to Santo Domingo from these islands. Two-thirds died either in
the crossing or on reaching their destination. Those who survived were
mostly held on a large property that Grimaldi had bought in Santo
Domingo, though a few were kept in the new building of the Casa de Contratación. They were sold by auction for up to 100 pesos a head. All were
branded with letters on their faces by their buyers. Judge Vázquez de Ayllón
was among those who bought them eagerly.[31]

Meanwhile, the opposition to the status quo in the New World had
gained a new leader.

Bartolomé de las Casas, one of the most interesting Spaniards in the first fifty
years after the discovery of the Americas, was a native of Seville. He was born
about 1484;[32] he was of *converso* extraction and was apparently a grandson of
a certain Diego Calderón, who had been burned as a Jew in Seville in 1491.[33]
He was the son of that Pedro de las Casas who had accompanied Columbus
on his second voyage of 1493. Pedro had received, in the division of Alburquerque, a grant of seven *naborías* and fifty-three Indians.[34] Bartolomé had
interesting uncles, for they included Juan de Peñalosa, the courtier who had
been asked, in 1492, to read out in Palos the decree enjoining the people there
to serve with Colón; Francisco de Peñalosa, also a courtier and favored by Isabel, who had been chief of the military contingent on the second voyage of
Columbus and was later killed in Africa; Diego de Peñalosa, a notary; and
Luís de Peñalosa, a canon of the cathedral in Seville.

Bartolomé de las Casas attended the school of San Miguel in the latter city. After that, he went to the classes of Nebrija in the cathedral school and became "a good Latinist."[35] He was in Seville to see Columbus in 1493, on his first return from the Indies with his Indian prizes, adorned with gold and pearls, with their green parrots.[36] He is also said to have enlisted in the militia charged to put down the Moorish rebellion in the Alpujarra Mountains.

Las Casas went to the New World in 1502 with Ovando, at the age of eighteen, accompanying his father (who was returning to a colony that he knew). It does not seem that he went in any way as a churchman. He may have been immediately concerned with mines, perhaps the mines nearest Santo Domingo, perhaps those richer ones in the province of Cibao.[37] When he arrived, he later wrote, the settlers of Santo Domingo told him that all was going well in the island and that a recent war had brought them plenty of slaves. The news caused much enthusiasm on his boat.[38]

Las Casas probably did not take part in the murderous expedition against Anacoana in Jaragua, though he did later write that he was united to Diego Velázquez "by the friendship that we had in the past in that island."[39] He participated, however, in the summer of 1504 with Juan de Esquivel in the subjugation of Higuey: "All these things and others far removed from human nature I saw with my own eyes."[40] He also seems to have been among the fifty men whom Esquivel took with him to Saona to destroy the native monarch, King Cotubanamá. After that, he was for a time in the business of furnishing supplies of food and clothing to the settlers.

He left La Española in 1506, intending to take orders, and he was in Rome, no less, in early January 1507. There he saw a fiesta of flutes, as always celebrated on the thirtieth day of that month, "with great licentiousness, attended by men dressed as women, masked and dancing. . . ."[41]

Las Casas returned to Santo Domingo in 1509, by then a priest, probably with Diego Colón, for he wrote that he observed the departure of Nicuesa for the mainland. Perhaps for a time he was again concerned with agriculture on his father's farm near the River Yasica. Later, possibly in 1510, he presided over a Mass at Concepción de la Vega: it was the first time in the Indies that a recently consecrated priest had celebrated his first Mass there, and for that reason, Diego Colón attended the occasion.[42] Las Casas was friendly with Don Diego ever afterwards. He also made friends with the Dominicans who arrived in September 1510, and probably met Fray Pedro de Córdoba in Concepción in November. He was with Pánfilo de Narváez in Cuba in 1511 (see chapter 23).

Las Casas went from Cuba to Santo Domingo between August and September 1515 and then sailed for home on the *Santa María de Socorro,* the royal pilot Diego Rodríguez Pepiño's vessel, in the company of Fray Gutierre de Ampudia, who had recently led a small mission of religious men to Cuba. He reached Seville on October 6 and, armed with a letter from Archbishop Deza, saw the King in Plasencia, which Fernando reached on November 28.[43] Las Casas told the Catholic King that the Indians of the New World would all die unless something was done to save them. The senior secretary Conchillos tried to divert attention from the issue, and Bishop Fonseca supported him. The King, however, promised to see Las Casas again in Seville. With that "the apostle of the Indies," as Las Casas soon became known, had to be satisfied.[44] To have seen the King was anyway a great step forward.

It is impossible to know how much of the controversy now beginning as to how to treat the Indians was followed by the King himself. He had been present for part of the discussions in Burgos, but he had then continued his usual travels around Spain, as he and his wife had always done. For example, in 1510 he spent some months in Córdoba, and then he moved to Écija, Carmona, La Rinconada, and Seville, where he remained from late October to early December. Always he would have with him his trusted staff of secretaries, above all now Pérez de Almazán and Conchillos, as well as the councillors Zapata and Galíndez de Carvajal, and a few other advisers, such as Fonseca and Hernando de Vega. In these years, substantial payments were made to courtiers and others for distinct services, including a million maravedís a year to the Duke of Alba.[45]

Thanks to his courtiers, Fernando's mind was kept principally on matters other than how to treat the Indians—his wars in Navarre or Italy, for instance.

Fernando's failure to have an heir by his second wife, Germaine, also caused him distress. In fact, Germaine gave birth to a son in 1509, but he lived only for a few hours. Neither Fernando nor anyone in Spain relished the idea of the throne of the united country, which he and Isabel had established and to which Granada had been added, passing to a foreign dynasty, the Habsburgs. Yet his only two male grandchildren, Charles and Fernando, the children of the incapable Juana, were of that imperial family.

Fernando had also to consider the war in Africa, where Cardinal Cisneros had mounted a major campaign to expand Spanish influence in the western Maghreb. That was a continuation of his desire to fulfill the terms of Queen Isabel's will, which called on Spain to establish her presence not in America but in Africa. In May 1509 at Ascension, the Cardinal, advised by a Genoese commander, Girolamo Viannello, entered Oran with an army, having found both the money and the men for the expedition in territory that belonged to his archbishopric. The chief captain was Pedro Navarro, previously known as the conqueror of Vélez de la Gomera, another strongpoint on the coast of North Africa. Entering Oran, the Cardinal joyfully recited Psalm 115: *"Non nobis, Domine, non nobis, sed nomini tuo da gloriam. . . ."*[46] There is a fine fresco depicting the scene by Juan de Borgoña in the Mozarabic chapel in the cathedral of Toledo. Afterwards, Diego Fernández de Córdoba, a kinsman of the Gran Capitán, took over as commander of the new possession.

Cisneros returned home with many Moorish slaves as well as a troop of camels laden with gold and silver, not to mention a collection of Arabic books, some dealing with astrology and medicine, as well as some baths, and also keys and candlesticks that had been used in the mosque. Some of these things can still be seen in the church of San Ildefonso in Alcalá.[47] But a defeat followed at Las Gerbes, where the son and heir of the Duke of Alba was killed. Fernando was tempted by the idea of going himself to Africa to avenge the setback. But he did not, being still far more concerned with Italy. He never devised a strategy for the colonization of North Africa and continually argued with Cisneros over the latter's plan to conquer the Maghreb up to the edge of the Sahara.

There had been difficulties with Pope Julius in respect to these as well as other matters. For example, in December 1510, bulls were presented to the Supreme Council of the Inquisition whereby Julius had allowed Pedro López de Águila of Seville to escape the restrictions imposed on *conversos,* even though he had been condemned by the Holy Office.[48]

Then the economy in his European dominions must have given the King many a headache. For example, between 1510 and 1515 there was a fall in prices, the only such case in the century, followed in 1515 by a sharp rise.

But Fernando, for his own narrow economic reasons, no doubt, seemed to have become more interested in the Indies than previously. Thus in December 1509, we find him ordering a report about the instructions, rules, and other commitments sent to the Casa de Contratación in order to make, where necessary, new dispositions. That order was repeated on January 22, 1510.[49]

On July 30, 1512, a royal order was issued to Diego Colón appointing Bartolomé Ortiz as "representative of the [Spanish] poor in the new world." His salary was the service of seventy Indians, a less than generous emolument in the circumstances.[50] On September 26, 1513, the King summed up the grants and other liberties that had hitherto been made available to settlers on La Española. In this, he commented that the island had been populated by old Christians, not new ones, and that no child or grandchild of a burned heretic or a son of a *reconciliado,* or even a son or grandson of a Jew or a Moor, could be given Indians on the said island.[51] Actually, in 1512 an arrangement had been made between the Crown and the *converso* communities in Córdoba, Jaén, and León: *conversos* could go to the New World if they paid the substantial sum of 55,000 ducats. Some did.[52]

But these orders were all drafted by Fonseca and Conchillos and put under the King's eyes purely for signature, we assume, even if, as seems likely, they coincided with Fernando's wishes. No doubt this was also the case when, in July 1513, the King asked his ambassador in Rome, Gerónimo de Vich, to establish a "universal patriarchate" in the Indies for Fonseca.[53] For Fernando the new possessions in the Indies certainly now constituted an obligation, but it is impossible to detect any sign of enthusiasm for them.

In May 1512, the King began to suffer from a grave illness that is impossible to identify but from which he never fully recovered.[54] He was fit enough, however, to send an army, under his friend the Duke of Alba, to occupy Navarre in July 1512. That was an act of realpolitik, which Fernando justified by claiming that a secret treaty between France and the family of Albret included a plan for an invasion of Castile. The removal of this French protectorate (as it seemed) south of the Pyrenees was a fulfillment of the strategically minded Fernando's long-term ambition. Pope Julius II obligingly blessed the invasion and the subsequent occupation, and also the transfer of sovereignty. (This only applied to southern, or Spanish, Navarre; French, or northern, Navarre remained an independent, if French, state under the Albrets.)[55]

Fernando remained in Valladolid nearly all of 1513, save for journeys to Tordesillas, Medina del Campo, and the monasteries of Abrojo and La Mejorada. He went hunting both there and later in León. But his infirmity was now his perpetual companion. He was henceforth too ill to perform his usual work, and this permitted his secretaries to increase their power further. Even old allies, such as the Count of Tendilla, lost their habit of direct correspondence with the King, since all his letters were drafted by secretaries. In these circumstances, Fernando tried to arrange that the Duke of Alba should be the Regent if he were to die—a violation of Isabel's will, which had stipulated that Cardinal Cisneros should so act if necessary. Tendilla supported Alba, but other powerful noblemen on whose approval so much hung, such as the Duke of Infantado and the Constable Velasco, backed Cisneros. The argument shows vividly the limitations imposed on even the most powerful of monarchs. Once again, meanwhile, Columbus's dominions in the Indies were allowed to develop on their own due to Spanish domestic preoccupations.

Fray Pedro de Córdoba, the Dominican leader in the New World, after being reprimanded by the provincial of his order, Alonso de Loaysa, finally won his argument with the Franciscan Alonso de Espinal. On June 10, 1513, he persuaded Fernando to allow him to lead fifteen missionaries to convert the Indians of the South American mainland between the Gulf of Paria and what was already known as "Venezuela *tierra firme.*" Córdoba would himself lead this mission. There was no specific grant of territory.[56] But in order to prevent clashes with Spanish slave-hunters, Córdoba convinced the King that no armada from Santo Domingo or Spain could, without his consent, sail to the mainland coast between Cariaco, just south of the island of Margarita, to what was then known as Coquibacoa, now the peninsula of Guajira. This was a stretch of about five hundred miles of coastline, covering most of what is now the western half of Venezuela. King Fernando was inspired to ask Diego Colón to give the friars everything they needed. That came to 400,000 maravedís' worth of goods, including many pictures of saints and the Holy Family, some by distinguished painters such as Alejo Fernández or sculpted by Jorge Fernández, both of Seville, as well as thirty copies of Nebrija's *Grammar.* (The pictures included depictions of Our Lady of Rosario, St. Dominic, and the thirteenth-century St. Peter Martyr.)[57]

Due to illness, Fray Pedro de Córdoba could not in the end lead the expedition on which he had set his heart. He asked the controversial preacher Montesinos to direct it instead. But though he accepted the daunting task, Montesinos, too, became ill in San Juan, and in the end, only one Dominican friar, Francisco de Córdoba, and a lay brother, Juan Garcés,[58] set off from Santo Domingo on the heroic mission. The two men disembarked at the seaward end of the valley of Chiribichi, in the east of their prescribed territory. There they were well received by the *cacique* "Alonso," who had been baptized by Alonso de Hojeda several years before.

Some months later, Gómez de Ribera, originally from Zafra, in Extremadura, sailed into Chiribichi with three ships. Ribera had been a notary in La Española, and in 1500, Francisco de Bobadilla had even asked him to carry out the *residencia* of the brothers Columbus. He had remained in Santo Domingo and, in the *division* of Alburquerque of 1514, he had seven *naborías* and twenty-five slaves. He was now looking both for pearls and for more slaves. There were several days of fiesta and for a time an amiable dis-

cussion between the newcomers and the Indians, at which the two missionaries were present. Then one of the members of Ribera's flotilla invited the
cacique and his wife to visit their flagship. "Alonso" accepted, with seventeen
Indians. They were immediately seized, and the ship raised her anchor and
set off for Santo Domingo.

The Indians on shore naturally arrested the two Dominicans, who explained that they would tell the captain of the next ship that passed to send
a message to Santo Domingo that their lives were at risk unless "Alonso" and
his companions were sent back. The message reached La Española, and a letter was taken to Fray Pedro de Córdoba. But by that time Alonso and his
friends had been sold and separated. Montesinos denounced these events,
and Gómez de Ribera fled to a convent of the Mercedarians in Santo
Domingo, where he was protected by a relation, Judge Vázquez de Ayllón. In
vain, Montesinos demanded the recovery of the Indians. As a result, after
only four months, in January 1515, the two missionaries, Fray Francisco de
Córdoba and Juan Garcés, were executed. A later inquiry, presided over by
Francisco de Vallejo, a conquistador who had first come out with Ovando,
ruled that the Dominicans had been killed by Caribs and, therefore, there
was no crime in continuing to enslave their leaders.[59] That dubious point established, the Dominican order was blamed for the deaths of their brothers,
for they had been warned not to go to Carib territory. But then it was said
that the Indians who had originally been kidnapped lived in the center of a
group of Caribs but were really a people called Guaitiaos. Some of those who
had been seized by Gómez de Ribera were then sent back to Chiribichi. This
unfortunate conclusion obscures the fact that the Dominican friar Francisco
de Córdoba and the obscure lay brother Juan Garcés were the first Spanish
settlers on the northern coast of South America, the forerunners of great
waves of emigration there and, in the end, of two large independent states.

23

"Without partiality, love, or hatred"

And if you know that the said *adelantado* Diego Velázquez, in respect of the Indians and their *encomiendas,* has maintained all fairness, giving them to those who merit them the most and without partiality, neither love nor any hatred . . . ?

Question 22 of the "residencia" taken of Diego Velázquez, 1525[1]

The large, long, beautiful island of Cuba, sometimes in those early days known as "Juana" and occasionally as "Fernanda," was circumnavigated in eight months in 1508 by Sebastián Ocampo, a caballero from Noia, Galicia, and a sometime member of the household of Queen Isabel.[2] Noia is near Padrón, where the body of St. James, in his stone coffin, was miraculously found in the ninth century. Hence the center of pilgrimage, Santiago de Compostela. Ocampo's achievement was one worthy of his origin. He had come to the Indies in 1493 on Columbus's second voyage.[3] Apart from a mysterious quarrel in Jerez in 1501, he seems to have remained in La Española thereafter.[4] In 1507, Governor Ovando wanted to know for sure whether Columbus had been right in insisting that Cuba was part of a continent, or whether Peter Martyr had been on the right track when he said in 1505 that "there are not lacking those who—Vicente Yáñez Pinzón, for example—declare that they have circumnavigated it."[5]

With two ships, Ocampo sailed around Cuba, entered Havana Bay, the admirable but to Spaniards as yet unknown port, passed the Punta de San Antón, visited a *corral* of mullet, and showed that Cuba was indeed an island—about as long as Britain. Cuba seemed to have copper, and Ocampo detected what he judged to be some signs of the presence of gold in the sierra in the east. He thought that the Bay of "Xagua," the modern Cienfuegos, could offer a safe harbor to one thousand caravels.[6] He also saw Baracoa and Manatí, the last point visited by Columbus on the island, where, on his first voyage, he careened his boats.

In fact, Cuba not only boasted a little gold but also nickel, cobalt, iron, manganese, and chromite. Nickel would one day seem particularly important. Las Casas, meanwhile, would say that Cuba was an island fresher and calmer than La Española.[7]

Early in 1511, the conquest of Cuba was carried through by Diego Velázquez de Cuéllar, a "corpulent and red-haired" hidalgo. Velázquez was, like Ovando, from a family of importance in medieval history. The cofounder of the military Order of Calatrava had been one Diego Velázquez, a monk who had offered to defend that city of La Mancha (Calatrava) against the Moors when the Templars had said they could not do so. A Ruy Velázquez had composed some of the best ballads in Spanish. Another Ruy Velázquez was the uncle in the story of the Infantes de Lara. Diego's own uncle had been a councillor to King Juan II of Castile, and a cousin, Cristóbal de Cuéllar, in Santo Domingo with Ovando as treasurer, had been cupbearer to the Infante Don Juan, the ill-fated heir of the Catholic Kings.[8] Another cousin, the Infante's chief accountant, commander of the castle at Arévalo, had been the preceptor of the young Basque Íñigo de Loyola, later the founder of the Society of Jesus. Sancho Velázquez de Cuéllar, a judge of the supreme court, was a member of the first national council of the Inquisition in 1484. Antonio de Torres, a captain in Columbus's second voyage and Ovando's second in command, the virtual founder of the regular sailings to and from the Indies (*la carrera de Indias*), had also been a close relation.[9]

Cuéllar, whence Diego Velázquez came, is an ancient, long-decayed Castilian city halfway between Segovia and Valladolid. It is too far from Madrid to provide a weekend life for that capital, and the countryside nearby, though there are pine woods, is too austere for the tourist. The ten thousand people who live there now work in the timber industry and in agriculture, especially with cattle. The nineteenth-century English traveler Richard Ford reported that Cuéllar's streets were steep and badly paved; and that judgment would apply today. But there are charming squares, churches and monasteries, some ruined, a colossal castle, and a few dilapidated mansions with crumbling but decipherable coats of arms over the doors.[10] One of these, in the Calle San Pedro, leading down sharply from the main square, was once that of the Velázquez family.

The castle at Cuéllar had been built by Beltrán de la Cueva, first Duke of Alburquerque, the favorite of King Enrique IV and the lover of his second wife, Queen Juana. Cuéllar had been a town whose taxes had gone to Queen Isabel when she was a girl. Though Cuéllar now seems remote, it was in the late fifteenth century a center for many complex plots. The contemporary decay is symbolized by the castle and the church of San Francisco, both in ruins. Even the fine tombs of the Alburquerques now rest in the museum of the Hispanic Society of America, in northern Manhattan.

Diego Velázquez was born about 1464, the year when the Crown ceded Cuéllar to the Duke of Alburquerque. Because of the civil wars that in those years divided the Castilian nobility, the conquistador's childhood must have been a turbulent one. There were also religious implications, for Cuéllar had a substantial Jewish district, one of whose rabbis was so eloquent as to draw old Christians to his synagogue to listen to his sermons, including, in the 1470s, the Governor of the city. We should assume, though, that Diego Velázquez's education would have included more stories of chivalry than of Jewry, and much reciting of ballads, many of them with classical themes, for that was the fashion.

Diego Velázquez figures in a list of those who fought in the last campaign against Granada. From that war, it is said, he emerged "ill and poor." But he seems to have recovered adequately to be one of the two hundred or so gentlemen colonists who accompanied Columbus on his second voyage to La Española, in 1493. He never returned to Europe, much less to Cuéllar.[11]

Don Diego became rich in Santo Domingo and was soon recognized as a leader of the new Spanish colony. He must have been physically strong, for most of his colleagues on the second expedition of Columbus died, and the majority of those who survived went home when they found that the gold available was modest. He became an especial friend of Columbus's brother, the austere Diego. He must also have been politically resilient, for few other leaders survived the disorganized days of the rule of the "pharoah" (as Columbus was known to the infuriated Spanish colonists), as well as the reforms of his successors.

Velázquez's role as deputy governor in charge of the west (that part of the island now known as Haiti) is a puzzle. Las Casas, a strict judge, talks of him as an easygoing, good-natured man and, if quick to anger, swift to forgive. Velázquez enjoyed Las Casas's sermons; Las Casas himself said so. Yet Velázquez must have been present at the brutal events that included the betrayal of Anacoana and her execution in 1503.

He was obviously an engaging man. Conversation with him when he was governor in Cuba was all banter, as often between undisciplined young men of good family who know one another well. Velázquez enjoyed banquets. He was also proud of his family, as his will made clear, and he passed that pride on to the many impoverished Castilian relations, most of them from Cuéllar or nearby, who accompanied him to the Indies.

After the pacification of Santo Domingo, there was discussion about the desirability of expanding Spanish rule to other neighboring places: Puerto

Rico, Jamaica, and to the west, of course, Cuba. Ponce de León went to Puerto Rico, Esquivel to Jamaica. Velázquez was keen to follow up his defeat of the Taino leaders of the west of La Española with an expedition to Cuba; one of those *caciques*, Hatuey, had fled to that island across the sixty or so miles of the Windward Passage. Velázquez's idea was backed by the all-important royal treasurer in Santo Domingo, Pasamonte. The King looked on Hatuey as a rebel, for there had been a time when it seemed that he was "in our service."[12]

Cuba is a big island. The idea of Castile absorbing such a large new territory should surely have been a matter for discussion in the Council of the Realm. It seems not to have been. The Spanish Empire expanded as if it had been a vast growth, locally driven, locally motivated. Diego Colón told the King his plans and received approval afterwards—the King objecting to Diego's first idea that his uncle Bartolomeo should lead the Cuban expedition.

In 1509, Diego Colón gave Velázquez authority to carry out the conquest of Cuba. The instructions do not survive. It would seem that, through Pasamonte, Velázquez maintained a direct connection with the Crown that circumvented formal dependence on Diego Colón: Fernando seems to have recognized Velázquez as an independent authority, and Velázquez wrote letters directly to the King, not to Diego Colón.[13]

Velázquez assembled a small fleet of ships and about three hundred Spaniards at Salvatierra de la Sabana, in what is now known as the Bay of Les Cayes in Haiti. He financed these himself. His secretary, the thirty-year-old Hernán Cortés, who must have played an important part in making the arrangements, had been a protégé of Ovando. Until then he had been a notary and planter at Azúa, one of the towns that Ovando had founded. Just as Ovando had accepted Velázquez, though he was a Castilian, so Velázquez used Cortés, though he was an Extremeño. The retirement of Ovando perhaps caused Cortés to suppose that he had no future in La Española and needed to look for future opportunities.

Bartolomé de Las Casas was also on the expedition. Though, as we have seen, he had been ordained a priest in 1508, he still seems to have been more interested in participating in conquest than in saving Indian souls. There were four Franciscans, too. The son of Ponce de León, Juan González, who had served his father as interpreter, also sailed with Velázquez.[14]

Velázquez established himself quickly on the far east of Cuba, near Baracoa, which, as "Asunción de Baracoa," became his first capital. The local Cubans resisted, but their bows and arrows made no headway against the

Spaniards. Velázquez soon seized Hatuey, the onetime *cacique* of La Española.

What happened next is part of Cuban myth. A captured enemy leader had to be executed. No one doubted that. One of the Franciscans offered Hatuey a Christian death and burial, provided he converted to Christianity. Hatuey listened to the arguments and is supposed to have said that if Christianity meant he had to spend eternity in the company of Spaniards, he would prefer not to be baptized. He was accordingly burned, as a pagan.[15]

The conquest of the island then began. It was not a difficult task, for though Cuba is much larger than La Española, the population was smaller. There were several political entities in Cuba, but they were not used to war except when it was necessary to mount a defense against raids by Caribs. Those were less frequent than in La Española. The Tainos had reached Cuba later than they had the latter island, and its soil was apparently well suited to being tilled by digging sticks. Thus the place had a sense of fertility.

As elsewhere in the Americas, bows and arrows and stones flung by slings were no match for Spanish weapons, including arquebuses, primitive artillery, horses, and even dogs, but above all those long steel swords that even now can cause a shiver of anxiety when we see them in military museums. How curious to imagine all these knights from Cuéllar, and other cities of Old Castile, riding across the beautiful tropical island. Unfortunately, the only real source for the feelings of the conquistadors is the history of Las Casas, who had his own priorities when he came to write his book.[16]

Velázquez was joined in Cuba by Pánfilo de Narváez, the fair-haired giant who had been second in command to Esquivel in Jamaica. Velázquez had probably known him since childhood because he came from Navalmanzano, a small town between Cuéllar and Segovia. Oviedo says of Narváez that he was a good man and good at war, but Las Casas was dismissive of most of his qualities.[17]

Narváez arrived in Cuba with a well-armed force of thirty archers. He landed on the south coast of the island and soon joined forces with Velázquez, who set out westward from Baracoa with a hundred infantry and about twenty horsemen. The two moved across what became Oriente Province toward Bayamo, where Narváez, in the vanguard, reported resistance. Velázquez sent him another fifty men, of whom ten were mounted. Narváez was to try to tell the natives that he had come only to see the country, inform them of the allegiance that they owed to Spain, and explain that the Christians' intentions were to convert, not injure.[18]

But Narváez could not keep to his instructions (so he said). On one occasion, he was ambushed and (so he reported) had to kill a hundred Tainos, thereby bringing Bayamo under Spanish rule. He followed the escaping natives toward Camagüey, killing a leader named Caguax on the way. The Indians of Camagüey were not unnaturally unenthusiastic about the newcomers. The people of Bayamo, on the other hand, quickly submitted to the Spaniards, offering them bone necklaces as presents.

Narváez returned to Bayamo to find that Velázquez had gone back to Baracoa leaving his young nephew, Juan de Grijalva, another citizen of Cuéllar, in charge, with Las Casas as chaplain. These conquistadors then pressed west again with several hundred men, supported by about a thousand fascinated and strangely willing natives, and they found signs of gold near Camagüey. While passing through a settlement named Cueiba, they had the encouraging experience of finding some natives worshipping an image of the Virgin that some shipwrecked Spaniards had apparently left there. They were reluctant to exchange her for a superior image offered them by Las Casas.

The Spanish strategy was to advance toward a native village, where Las Casas would try to persuade the natives to give up half the place to the Spaniards. They would also be asked to provide food in the shape of meat, fish, and bread. Las Casas would send an interpreter ahead to explain all this.

But at Caonao, near Camagüey, things went badly wrong. It was a large place, with what seemed to be two public squares. As a result of Las Casas's petition, cassava bread and much fish were prepared for the invaders. Two thousand people gathered and gazed, amazed at the—to them—extraordinary sight of the Spaniards and at their even more astonishing horses, while another five hundred observed from a large house on the square. Las Casas told the natives that the Spaniards wanted to enter that house, but they were offered more chickens to persuade them to remain outside. While the commanders were considering what to do, a certain Spaniard (Las Casas does not name him) ran amok and started killing. The mood was infectious. Narváez's captains (again we do not have their names) went to the large house and, breaking it open, started more slaughter there, until the street ran with blood. Las Casas saved forty Indians in the square, but his companions went away to join the fighting elsewhere. Narváez sat on his horse, "still as marble," while this was going on. When he saw Las Casas, he asked, "What do you think of our Spaniards, what they have done?" Las Casas replied: "I offer you and them to the devil." He bitterly recalled: "I do not remember with how much spilling of human blood that path was marked."[19]

After this massacre the Spaniards found no one in their way; the surviving natives of the town tried to escape to islands offshore, though they eventually came back. Las Casas said:

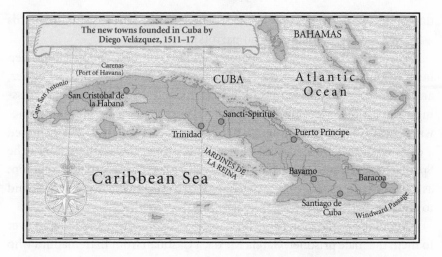

The new towns founded in Cuba by
Diego Velázquez, 1511–17

BAHAMAS

Carenas
(Port of Havana)

CUBA

Atlantic
Ocean

Cape San Antonio

San Cristóbal de
la Habana

Sancti-Spiritus

Trinidad

Puerto Príncipe

JARDINES DE LA REINA

Caribbean Sea

Bayamo

Baracoa

Santiago de
Cuba

Windward Passage

Men and women like sheep, each with his little bundle of poverty on his
back. . . . To see them return caused [me] joy for they were going back to
their own homes which was what they wanted, and it caused me pity and
great compassion, considering their meekness, humility, and poverty,
and what they had suffered, their banishment and their weariness,
brought upon them by no fault of their own, the murder of their fathers,
sons, brothers, and neighbors so cruelly accomplished—all, all being set
aside as done with and forgotten.[20]

This experience marked a turning point in Las Casas's attitude toward
the policies of his fellow Spaniards. All the same, he did establish a green-
turtle farm in a lagoon near Cienfuegos and seems to have remained there
during the year of 1512–13. But within a short time he was following the example of Fray Antonio Montesinos, the Dominican of Santo Domingo. This
may have been after the arrival in Cuba of three Dominicans from there:
Gutierre de Ampudia, Bernardo de Santo Domingo, and Pedro San Martín.
One of these is said to have refused Las Casas communion while he possessed slaves. On August 14, 1514, Las Casas denounced the conquest to the
settlers in Sancti-Spiritus: "I began to speak to them of their blindness, their
injustices, their tyrannies, and their cruelties."[21] Las Casas abandoned his
property to Velázquez and devoted the rest of his life to working for the good
treatment of Indians. So did his partner in the farm, Pedro de Rentería. The
fact that they had seen the savagery of the conquest of Cuba with their own
eyes determined their opinions.

Narváez established himself on the north coast of Cuba, where a little
more gold was forthcoming. This was probably near Santa Clara (a corrup-

tion of the words *casa harta,* "house replete," so called because the Spaniards were well fed there, apparently on parrots).

The natives there told of a Spaniard and two women who had long been held prisoner by some of their fellow Tainos. Narváez informed Velázquez, and the latter sent a brigantine along the north coast in search of the missing compatriots. Messengers held up white papers on high poles. Somewhere near Cojímar they found two naked Spanish women. These identified a chief who, they said, had treacherously drowned their companions. The Spaniards were about to burn him, but Las Casas protested, so they kept him as a prisoner in chains, and they went on to a stream whence gold was said to come.[22]

Another *cacique* soon came forward to welcome them and to hand over to them the male prisoner, García Mexía, a Castilian from Extremadura who had been lost for several years. He had almost forgotten Spanish, and gesticulated as the Tainos did. He and the two women were, it turned out, survivors from Alonso de Hojeda's expedition to Urabá in 1506, which had become separated on its way to Santo Domingo.

Narváez and his men went to meet Velázquez at Xagua, on the site of the modern Cienfuegos, on Christmas 1513. Then Velázquez sent Narváez back to Havana with sixty men and, thereafter, farther west still to what is now Pinar del Río. He returned along the south coast of Cuba, where, in January 1514, he founded Trinidad, of which a brother-in-law of his, Francisco Verdugo, from Cogeces de Iscar, about twelve miles west of Cuéllar, would become the first mayor. Then he sent a ship to Jamaica for cassava bread, and another to Santo Domingo for cattle, mares, and maize. The conquest, in the sense that Castilians could establish themselves wherever they wanted on the island, was complete.

Diego Velázquez continued as governor of Cuba for another eleven years, until 1524. During this time he, with his secretary Cortés at his side, founded the main cities of Cuba, settlements that have remained important to this day: San Salvador de Bayamo (founded in November 1513, though not on the exact present site of Bayamo), Trinidad (established in January 1514), Sancti-Spiritus and Puerto Príncipe (Camagüey), both also towns of 1514, as well as Asunción de Baracoa (1511), Havana, and Santiago. Havana was founded on the south coast of Cuba, near what is now the tiny town of Batabanó. It was later moved, together with its name, to its present site, previously known as Carenas, in order (probably) to meet the demands of shipping when returning home from New Spain via the Bahamas. The traveler to Batabanó will seek in vain for the remains of the first Havana. It is no longer even a legend. The date of the transfer is unclear but it seems to have been begun in 1519 and concluded in 1526.[23]

All these new cities, as in La Española, were built near to where Taino settlements had been. The paperwork to establish them (never to be neglected in Spanish matters) was probably performed by Hernán Cortés, a trained notary. These places were as usual planned with the same squares, churches, town halls, prisons, and governors' palaces that characterized the cities of La Española and whose outlines can often still be discerned.[24] It was, of course, Indians who actually erected the buildings. Velázquez told the King that those in Cuba were much "more inclined to the matters of our faith than those in La Española or Puerto Rico," and the King wrote back expressing pleasure.[25] Why Velázquez had this impression is obscure. But he always preferred to look on the bright side of things. He was much more tolerant after the early days in Cuba than had seemed at first likely.[26]

While busy with the foundation of this new colony, Velázquez was challenged by Francisco de Morales, a Sevillano protégé of Diego Colón's, to whom he had assigned the town of Manzanillo. He was an ardent supporter of the *encomienda*, as instituted in La Española and which Velázquez had not yet introduced in Cuba. Morales seems to have captured some Cubans in order to press for that conclusion. These natives rebelled, and some Christians were killed. Velázquez seized Morales and sent him as a prisoner to Santo Domingo.[27] Among those who appear to have supported Morales was the Governor's secretary, Hernán Cortés. Velázquez was at first tempted to hang him in consequence, but refrained, though he never worked as his secretary again.

Velázquez soon received permission from Castile to divide up the Indians of Cuba as they had been in La Española. Thus, Morales's policy was, in fact, pursued after his imprisonment. There were differences from the practice in La Española: to begin with, the Governor allocated Cubans to work for Castilians for a month only, at the end of which time they were sent home to their villages, with food for the journey. Velázquez also sent out expeditions of about twenty Castilians in different places with an interpreter to bring in the natives, who were to be held together in new towns dependent on Spanish landowners. He appointed inspectors whose task was to ensure that they were well treated. The King also sent instructions that the Cubans were to be treated less roughly than their companions had been in La Española and Puerto Rico, saying that he held them "in special esteem" and that he desired to convert them to the Christian faith. Fernando knew that if they were made into enemies, they would not produce much gold.

Velázquez, with his usual optimism, reported to the King that the Spaniards were in consequence "satisfied and had lost the ill will that they had incurred. . . ."[28]

Soon after, while Velázquez was again in Bayamo, he received a message from the King giving him permission to embark on a general division of Indians, being allowed to act without any consultation with Diego Colón, the formal Governor of all the Indies.

To begin with, Velázquez confined his divisions to Baracoa and Bayamo. Velázquez assigned to each Spaniard a specific *cacique* who was obliged with his men to serve him, in return for which he was fed, clothed, and instructed in Christianity. The maximum size of an *encomienda* would be three hundred Indians. That was for officials. Principal citizens would receive a hundred Indians; less important ones, sixty; and minor ones, forty. The royal secretary, Conchillos, and Diego Colón were among the absentees who received good allocations. Usually, though, the *encomenderos* were settlers, which meant that the Spaniards had the right to the land as well.[29] In addition to Indian tenant laborers there were, as usual, slaves: men and a few women taken in war.

In Cuba, as in La Española, the indigenous population soon began to decline. Some black African slaves had probably been brought in to replace Indians as laborers. But as in Santo Domingo, a Caribbean slave trade preceded the arrival of the Africans, many Indians being seized from those "useless" islands, the Bahamas, as well as from *tierra firme,* in this case from Darien/Panama or elsewhere in that doomed region.

Velázquez was in some ways original since, alone of early Spanish governors, he encouraged the growing of indigenous crops by the conquistadors. Proconsuls elsewhere had hesitated to do that, but the Governor of Cuba had no inhibitions about ordering the planting of cassava, maize, sweet potato, and malanga—a farinaceous root still much consumed in Cuba—as well as of rice. He also brought in sheep, pigs, and cattle. These animals multiplied fast. Velázquez boasted to the King that the small herd of a hundred long-legged swine that he had had to begin with had turned into thirty thousand in three years. Horses were also bred. To the conquistadors, the increase in the number of animals seemed to make up for the decline in the number of Indians.

Some gold was produced; Hernán Cortés and a friend of his, Francisco Dávila, for example, made fortunes near Baracoa in the first few years of Spanish occupation. Gold was also found near what is now Cienfuegos, in the valley of the Rio Arimao, a discovery that acted as a magnet for the emigration of many frustrated Spaniards in La Española.

Sometime before mid-April 1515, Velázquez moved his capital from Baracoa to the settlement that he and Cortés had already named "Santiago de Cuba," on the edge of a fine bay on the south coast. The Governor considered, but in the end rejected, the idea of establishing this headquarters halfway up the island, for example, at Trinidad, on the Bay of Xagua. Soon he would begin to build the house of stone in Santiago that is still associated with his name, but for the moment he improvised a wooden palace. The King declared that he wanted this settlement to be a permanent one, and other houses for long-term habitation began to be constructed. Married conquistadors sent for their wives from Spain. Velázquez established a warehouse to house the King's share of the proceeds—the royal fifth, the *quinto*—from the country. Velázquez thereafter presided over a little court in Santiago, mostly of adventurers who hailed originally from his own part of Castile—many of them relations, including at least three others who shared his surname.

A prominent member of Velázquez's court continued to be Cristóbal de Cuéllar, the treasurer. Since the Governor had married María de Cuéllar soon after he arrived in Cuba, Cuéllar had once been Velázquez's father-in-law. She in her turn had come to the Indies as one of the maids of honor of the wife of Diego Colón. Her wedding to Velázquez was the first Christian one on the island, but the bride died within a week.

The friends of Velázquez's who began to gather for nightly discussions at his home in Santiago de Cuba included Andrés de Duero, a tiny man from Tudela de Duero, secretary to the Governor in succession to Cortés; and also Amador de Lares, the Governor's accountant, who whenever asked (and often when not) would recall the days when he had been in the courtly household of the Gran Capitán, Fernández de Córdoba, in Italy. Occasionally, Velázquez himself would joke that when he returned to Spain, he would marry again, this time one of the two rich nieces of his patron, the Bishop of Burgos. No one seems to have had the heart to tell Don Diego that those nieces, by then middle-aged, had both long ago married. Sometimes the ex-secretary, Hernán Cortés, would be seen at these *tertulias*. Forgiven by Velázquez, he became a magistrate on the town council of Santiago. Courteous, even sycophantic, but obviously independent of spirit, "Cortesito," as his enemies in Cuba called him, was a prudent participant in these discussions.

Occasionally one or another of the Genoese merchants, a Riberol or a Centurione, who had by then developed interests in Cuba as they had in Santo Domingo and Puerto Rico, probably joined in these talks. Some of these merchants had obtained permission to live in the Indies, though others among them seem to have decided that it was not necessary to go through that formality. One or two *conversos,* such as Bernardino de Santa Clara, who may have come to the New World in the hope of escaping the attention of the Inquisition, might also have been present. (Santa Clara's brother had been that treasurer of Santo Domingo who had once filled the saltcellars at a banquet with gold dust instead of salt.) Velázquez, as befitted a tropical monarch, also had a buffoon, Francesillo, on hand to tell him disagreeable home truths in the form of jests.

These and other friends of Velázquez's would often smoke the new American herb tobacco, which they bought from the Indians, when they met to discuss the problems of the day. This plant would begin to be smoked at home in Spain also, and its famous names, "cigar" (*cigarro*) and "cigarette" (*cigarrillo*) would soon become attached to it because tobacco was smoked in *cigarrales* outside Toledo—little summerhouses so called because after dinner the call of the cicada (*cigarra*) was so insistent.

Velázquez had collateral descendants through his sister; and in the apartment of a modern Velázquez in Madrid there are the remains of a mahogany table that in the family is held to have been Diego's. It is improbable that Diego Velázquez was related to the seventeenth-century painter of the same name.[30]

Velázquez and his friends became accustomed to the tropics, whose foods (turtle, cassava bread, iguana, and cotora bird) began to please them in a way that never happened in Santo Domingo. The Governor seems to have neglected much of what was happening elsewhere on the island, though he had established ten or more haciendas of his own in several places, from Baracoa, in the east, to Havana, in the west, usually shared with others and managed by a majordomo who would receive a third, a fifth, or perhaps a seventh part of the profits. These farms were chiefly concerned with pigs, turtles, and different kinds of game.[31]

The decline of the Indian population was noticed, of course, as it had been in La Española, but no one—not even Las Casas, by now back in Spain—could think of a solution, except to bring in more black African slave labor. The problem was surely discussed at Governor Velázquez's evening *tertulias* in Santiago. The anxiety about the future of the labor force concentrated the minds of the settlers. Any Indian escaping into the forest would be followed by dogs in hot pursuit, for a slave was at least as important as a settler.

There was in Cuba an annual melting down of gold in the spring before the rain made all travel difficult. At that time, there would also meet in Santiago the representatives (*procuradores*) of the cities, and sometimes a *procu-*

rador general would be sent to Castile to report to the King what needed to be done. This was not exactly a democracy, but it was a liberal oligarchy as far as the Spaniards were concerned. Four Dominicans sent from Santo Domingo by Fray Pedro de Córdoba had little impact, even if they did preach against injustice to the indigenous people.[32]

One subject that must have come up for discussion at the *tertulias* in Santiago de Cuba was the question of what existed to the west and northwest of the island. Here there was a gap in knowledge. As we have seen, Ponce de León, the conqueror of Puerto Rico, had found a country that he christened the land of La Pascual Florida. To the west, he and, earlier, Pinzón and Díaz de Solís had stopped in a territory that sounded promising. That was surely Yucatan. Even Columbus, in 1504, had come upon sophisticated Maya merchants near the Central American mainland. But no one knew exactly whence they had come.

In 1514, Velázquez, in his first full report home after his conquest, wrote to the King that he had been told that on occasion certain Indians had come from the islands beyond Cuba "toward the north, navigating five or six days by canoe and gave news of other islands that lay beyond." This was a remarkable report to which little attention was paid. It suggests connections between the mainland of Central America and Cuba that archaeologists have not recognized.[33] Velázquez and his friends in their nightly talks did not know, of course, that these were marks of the civilization of Mesoamerica. But they suspected that profit might come from investigation. If nothing else, more slaves could be obtained who might help to make up for the shortage of labor. They had no inkling of the magnitude of the riches that awaited their compatriots in Mexico and Peru.

In Havana, in the Plaza de Armas, near the house of the Governor-General, there stands a small chapel that commemorates the foundation of the city in 1519, on the north shore of the island. Pictures by a nineteenth-century French painter suggest that Velázquez was present and that Bartolomé de las Casas celebrated the first Mass there. Little is true in this respect: Havana was probably not completely moved from the south to the north until after the days of Velázquez. Nor was Las Casas the first to celebrate Mass there. The confusion indicates the number of myths that attend the history of Cuba even at the beginning of its time as a colony. One thing, though, is sure: Columbus did not exaggerate much when, on his first voyage, he spoke of the island as a place of great beauty. But Spaniards in the sixteenth century wanted fortunes, not flowers, and rivers full of gold, not just streams carrying it.

Book Five

❦❦❦

BALBOA AND PEDRARIAS

How the Germans saw the New World. Woodcut, 1505.

24

"They took possession
of all that sea"

And in the presence of the natives they took possession of all that sea
and the countries bordering on it in the names of Fernando and
Juana.

Peter Martyr on Balboa's vision of the Pacific, 1513

Vasco Núñez de Balboa was the acting governor in the first permanent
mainland colony, of Darien. He unwisely sent home a report about his discoveries. It took the form of a most enthusiastic letter to the King, talking of
rivers of gold three days' march away in which there were also large pearls.[1]
At the same time, he sent Juan de Quevedo and Rodrigo de Colmenares as
representatives to La Española to beg for reinforcements and also for a
judge. Martyr says that these two *procuradores* were elected, but it is more
likely that Balboa chose them himself.[2] (He would apparently have liked to
go, but his followers refused him their votes—perhaps because they thought
he might not come back, perhaps because they needed his leadership.) Their
journey was difficult, for they were wrecked off Cuba and there encountered
the remains of Valdivia's expedition. On January 20, 1513, Balboa wrote again
to the King. It was a letter that would lead to his ruin. It owed a lot to his
imagination, for he said:

> In this province of Darien we have discovered many and very rich mines.
> There is gold in great quantity. We have discovered twenty rivers, and
> there are altogether thirty which have gold that stream out of a sierra two
> leagues from this villa. . . . There are in these sierras certain chiefs who
> have . . . gold that grows like maize in their huts, and they have it in bas-
> kets. They say that all the rivers in these sierras have gold and there are
> big nuggets on a large scale.[3]

These were the lands of the *gran cacique* Dabeiba. Balboa asked for the thousand men that the son of Comogre had suggested, "to conquer a large part of this world."[4] He also requested some ships.

This letter was taken home to King Fernando by Sebastián Ocampo, the circumnavigator of Cuba. But Ocampo delayed in Santo Domingo and died as soon as he reached Seville in June 1514, and though he transferred his powers to a cousin, Alonso de Noya (from his name, probably another Gallego), the two *procuradores* Juan Quevedo, ex-*veedor* of Nicuesa, and Rodrigo Enríquez de Colmenares arrived in Spain first, in May 1513. When they were presented to the King by Fonseca, Peter Martyr thought that "a mere look at these men is enough to demonstrate the insalubrious climate and temperature of Darien, for they are as yellow as if they had suffered from a liver complaint, and as puffy. They attribute their condition to what they have endured."[5]

Martyr reported, too, that among the things brought back there was a pineapple—the only one to last the journey. The King ate it. Martyr added,

> There are certain roots that the natives call *batatas* [sweet potatoes] that grow spontaneously. The first time I saw them I took them for Milanese turnips or huge mushrooms. No matter how they are cooked, roasted or boiled, they are equal to any delicacy and indeed to any other food. Their skins are tougher than mushrooms or turnips and are earth-colored, while the inside is quite white. When raw, they taste like green chestnuts, only sweeter.[6]

This was the first description of any form of potato, whose splendid history among Europeans now began.

Balboa also sent home yet another emissary, Martín de Zamudio, in order to expand on his merits to the King. But he arrived too late: the information of, first, Fernández de Enciso and then of the *procuradores* had been hostile to Balboa; and according to the historian Oviedo, Zamudio had to escape secretly from the court, the Council of the Realm even having given orders for him to be seized for apparently treacherous behavior.[7]

Before the *procuradores* from Balboa arrived, much was already known at the Spanish court about Darien. It was believed that the few surviving colonists "lived in anarchy, taking no heed to convert the simple tribes of that region to Christianity and giving no attention to gathering information. . . ." But now the story spread in Castile that "one could fish for gold in *tierra firme* with rods." The thought of "rivers of gold" was, of course, an intoxicating one, so innumerable men and some women set about trying to go

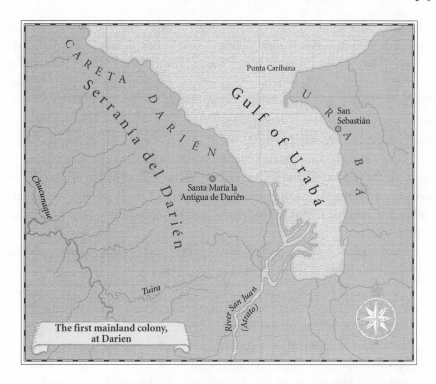

The first mainland colony, at Darien

"to fish" there.[8] Peter Martyr wrote a little later, ironically: "Spain need no longer plow up the ground to the depth of the infernal regions nor open great roads, nor pierce mountains at the cost of much labor and at the risk of a thousand dangers, in order to draw wealth from the earth. She will find riches on the surface, in shallow diggings. . . . Pearls [too] will be gathered with little effort."[9]

The creative enthusiasm of Balboa was his undoing. The King and Bishop Fonseca rechristened Darien as Castile the Golden, "Castilla del Oro." They immediately planned a new expedition to be headed by "an important person."

First, the King appointed Diego de Ávila, a *comendador* of Ávila, as leader but he decided not to go ahead. No one understood why. Then, thanks to the backing of Fonseca, the elderly soldier Pedro Arias Ávila (known at court as "Pedrarias"), was named governor of this new golden colony, his instructions making clear that a durable settlement was intended. There was no mention of any subservience to Diego Colón: Pedrarias would have a regime independent of the Admiral in Santo Domingo.

On August 2, 1513, instructions were prepared for Pedrarias as captain-general and governor "for the sea as for the land, to go to the mainland as we used to call it and as it must now be called golden Castile."[10] The instructions were that "the ships should not be overcrowded, that you go via the Canaries, that on the way you should touch on the cannibal islands [the Lesser Antilles], that a fifth [of all loot and harvests] should be paid to the Crown, that all new cities should be given names in conjunction with Bishop Quevedo, and that native women should not be seized, while cards and other games would be prohibited. . . ."[11] Bishop Quevedo was the churchman selected to accompany the expedition and found a see in the new land.

This was only the second expedition since 1492 that the Crown had financed (the first was Columbus's of 1493); all the others had been paid for by private enterprise. The arrangement enabled the Crown to begin a new era of Spanish conquest, and the rights of the Columbus family were further set on one side.

Efforts were made by both Balboa's critics and his friends to quash this nomination of Pedrarias. But Fonseca told the King:

> Pedro Arias, O most Catholic King, is a brave man who has often risked his life for Your Majesty and who we know from long experience is used to command troops. He signally distinguished himself in the wars against the Moors, where he comported himself as befits a valiant soldier and a prudent officer. In my opinion, it would be ungracious to withdraw his appointment in response to the representations of envious persons. Let this good man, therefore, depart under happy auspices; let this devoted pupil of Your Majesty, who has lived from his infancy in the palace, depart.[12]

But in the end Pedrarias did not leave Sanlúcar for "Castilla de Oro" until April 11, 1514. His expedition was delayed until a revision of the "Requirement" was complete, something that especially infuriated Fernández de Enciso, who planned to accompany Pedrarias in order to settle accounts with his enemy Balboa.

The preparation of this fleet of Pedrarias's was the responsibility of the Casa de Contratación. But, all the same, the Casa was only an executive body. Power to initiate policy remained with the advisers of the King, namely Fonseca and Conchillos. The King himself took an interest, and the concern in Seville all the summer of 1513 was great. A small group of soldiers had returned from Italy, and some of these, who had fought with El Gran Capitán, enlisted. On July 28, a curious decree was issued moderating any sign of luxury in the new expedition.[13]

Balboa, hearing of the proposed journey, determined himself to seek first the golden land spoken of by the son of Comogre. He set off by sea with a mere 190 men, landing in the territory of Careca, *cacique* of Coiba. He marched straight to the mountains through the territory of a *cacique* named Pomcha, who fled. Balboa sent messages and proposed an alliance that was eventually concluded. They exchanged presents. Balboa offered Pomcha hatchets of iron. "There is no such instrument that the natives appreciate as much, for they have none of them," wrote Martyr.[14] But they also liked glass beads made into necklaces, mirrors, and copper bells, and in return the Spaniards received 110 pesos of gold. King Pomcha offered guides to lead them through "inaccessible defiles inhabited by ferocious beasts."

The conquistadors scaled "rugged mountains and crossed several large rivers both by improvised bridges or by throwing beams from one bank to the other." They were challenged by Quareca, the lord of a territory of that name, who drew himself up in front of his naked horde and apparently said, "Let them retrace their steps if they do not wish to be killed to the last man." But he and his men were soon astounded by musket fire, which convinced them that the Spaniards commanded thunder and lightning, and "six hundred of them were slain like brute beasts." When Balboa discovered that Quareca's brother and some other courtiers were said to be transvestites, he had them torn to pieces by dogs; conquistadors were sometimes prudes.[15] (Since the Indians wore few clothes, transvestism implied imagination.)

Balboa embarked on the crossing of the peninsula, meeting on the way a beautiful Indian who served him as interpreter. Guided by her compatriots and after passing through dense jungles such as neither he nor any of his men had ever seen, in late September 1513 on a "bare hill" in what is now Panama, he first saw the long-desired "Southern Sea," the Pacific Ocean. Balboa was accompanied to the mountaintop by Fray Andrés de Vera, Licenciado Andrés Valderrabano, and the resilient Extremeño from Trujillo, Francisco Pizarro: a priest, a lawyer, and a great leader of the future.[16] Balboa "went to scale the peak, being the first to reach the top. . . . Kneeling upon the ground, he raised his hands to heaven and saluted the Southern Sea; . . . he gave thanks to God and to all the saints for having reserved this great opportunity to him, an ordinary man, devoid of experience and authority. Concluding his prayers in military fashion, he waved his hands to some of his compatriots and showed them the object of their desires. . . ." All his companions shouted for joy: "Prouder than Hannibal showing Italy and the Alps to his soldiers . . . he promised great riches to his men, saying, 'Behold the much desired ocean! Behold, all you men, who have shared such great efforts, behold the country of which the son of Comogre and other natives told us such wonders. . . .' "

As a sign of possession, Balboa had built a heap of stones in the form of an altar and "in order that posterity might not accuse them of falsehood, they inscribed the name of the King of Castile there and then on the tree trunks. . . ."[17] The lawyer Valderrabano drew up a statement of the discovery signed by all the Spaniards present, the priest Andrés de Vera signing first. A dog and a black slave are also believed to have been present.[18]

Intoxicated by this momentous experience, Balboa and his friends went on and defeated the *cacique* Chiapes, who had been determined to block their way. The Spaniards unleashed a pack of fighting dogs and discharged their guns. The sound of the latter reverberated among the mountains, and "the smoke from the powder seemed to dart forth flames; and when the Indians smelled the sulphur that the wind blew toward them, they fled in a panic, throwing themselves on the ground." The Spaniards approached in good order, killed some of the enemy and took more prisoners. They subsequently agreed to make peace with Chiapes, who gave Balboa 400 pesos of gold and received in return "articles of European manufacture. . . ." The Spaniards then went on to the shore of the much-longed-for ocean "and, in the presence of the natives, they took possession of all that sea and the countries bordering on it in the names of Fernando and Juana."[19] At first hearing of the formula, one laughs; at second, one stands amazed at the audacity of Balboa and his men.

Balboa left some of his men with Chiapes and set off with eighty men and some Indians in canoes built from tree trunks, up a river that led him to the land of the *cacique* Coquera. There he went through the usual procedure: the *cacique*'s attempt to fight was in vain; advised by a messenger from Chiapes, he gave in, and there was an exchange of presents. Balboa visited, and named, the Gulf of San Miguel, after the Archangel whom he supposed to be fighting for him. He then took to the open sea, where he and his men were nearly drowned. They took refuge on an island, and though they survived the night, the next morning they found their canoes damaged and full of sand. All the same they repaired them and crossed the land of a *cacique* named Tumaco, who presented them with four pounds of local pearls, which gave "the liveliest satisfaction." (A Basque, Arbolante, took these back to Spain and sought to persuade King Fernando to see that they proved the qualities of Balboa.[20] But it was then too late.)

Balboa found other beds of pearls for himself and extracted some beautiful smaller ones. He had further clashes with *caciques*, sometimes establishing good relations, sometimes killing them with dogs. These *caciques* almost always gave gold presents in return for beads or hatchets, which they continued to appreciate. As for the Spaniards, there was a price to pay for

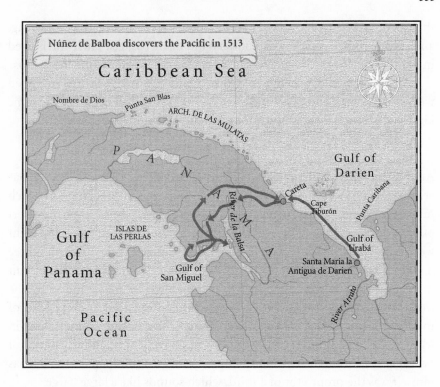

Núñez de Balboa discovers the Pacific in 1513

Caribbean Sea

Nombre de Dios

Punta San Blas

ARCH. DE LAS MULATAS

P   A   N   A   M   A

Gulf of
Darien

Careta

Cape
Tiburón

Punta Caribana

Gulf of
Urabá

ISLAS DE
LAS PERLAS

River de la Balsa

Gulf
of
Panama

Gulf of
San Miguel

Santa María la
Antigua de Darien

River Atrato

Pacific
Ocean

their acquisitiveness: "loaded with gold, as they were, but suffering intensely and so hungry they were scarcely able to travel. . . ."[21]

These were extraordinary journeys in utterly unknown territory, carried out with determination and imagination despite the hardships deriving from heat or attacks by insects and beasts of the jungle, as well as uncertainties about the route.

It is not easy to identify the tribes of this territory. But the region was inhabited by people speaking either Coiba or Cuera, or dialects of them. They cultivated many vegetables, with maize and manioc predominating. Meat was preserved by smoking—deer, iguana, turtles, and duck. Birds were caught in nets. Fish and shellfish were important in the diet. Chicha, beer from maize, was the customary drink.

These tribes lived in towns of often up to 1,500 people, usually fortified by log palisades and with houses of various sizes, those of the *caciques* sometimes being large. Inside there were, as usual among indigenous Americans, hammocks or benches, blankets, baskets, and aprons.

Most of these peoples painted themselves or were tattooed, and most leaders wore ornaments—helmets of gold, feather headdresses, nose plugs, labrets, necklaces, and so on. Metalworking was highly developed among these people, who had invented many methods of casting, plating, soldering, and cold-hammering. They had pottery and made baskets. Their chiefs lived in luxury; there were many slaves, unlike what prevailed among the Tainos.

All in this territory seem to have had standing armies of sorts, equipped with spears, darts, and bows and arrows. There were ball games of the same kind as those in the Taino territories, but the ceremonies were richer.[22]

After many delays and one or two false starts, Pedrarias left Sanlúcar de Barrameda on Holy Tuesday, April 11, 1514. He had twenty-three ships, of which nine were caravels (four Portuguese), two were old caravels for the transport of passengers or cargo, four were brigantines, similar to pinnaces, and eight were fishing boats. Fourteen of these vessels belonged to the King, and three had been privately hired (one jointly by Fernández de Enciso and a biscuit merchant, Juan López). One had been provided for merchandise by the Madrid banker Alonso Gutiérrez, who was then involved in every kind of maritime adventure. A *converso* from Burgos (and future conquistador in Mexico), Juan de Burgos, owned another ship, while the land distributor of La Española, Rodrigo de Alburquerque, possessed another, and Pedrarias himself was the proprietor of a third, which sounds like a large barge.

Another caravel, the *Santa María*, was added to the fleet in the Canaries. This carried a soldier, Juan de Zurita, and two other men whose mission was to train Canary Island soldiers who, it was thought, would play a helpful part in the conquest. This was the only ship in the fleet whose captain, Juan de Camargo, had permission to stop at Santo Domingo.

In the end, the fishing boats did not sail, nor did the brigantines, either because they were in a bad state or because they had been overloaded. Four other vessels were taken instead, under the command of a carpenter of Sanlúcar, Cristóbal Márquez.[23] All these were carefully stocked so as to avoid the overloading that was officially held accountable for the disaster that had occurred at the beginning of Ovando's journey in 1502.

The cost of the expedition was over 10 million maravedís, a figure that made it much the most expensive undertaking yet mounted by Castile in the New World.[24]

The commander, Pedrarias, was an unusual choice. Whatever justifiable complaints may be made about his cruelty, his arrogance, and his impetuosity, his audacity at leading a great expedition to the New World in his sixties cannot be gainsaid. He came from a very interesting and famous *converso* family of Segovia, though in behavior he was far from what is usually associated with Jewry, being turbulent, intemperate, unpredictable, and the reverse of an intellectual. He was the younger brother of the Count of Puñon-rostro, and had been variously known at court as "the Jouster," "the Gallant," and "the Great Courtier." His grandfather had been Diego de Arias, "Die-garias," treasurer of Castile under Enrique IV, while his father, the second Count of Puñonrostro, had also been known as Pedrarias "the Brave." An uncle, Juan de Arias, had been for years Bishop of Segovia and a pioneer of Spanish printing. Later, he became the effective leader of those in Segovia who protested against the high-handed behavior of the commander of the Alcázar, the favorite of Queen Isabel, the Marquis of Moya, Andrés de Ca-brera, by whom he was exiled. The Inquisition had preferred a charge of heresy against Bishop Arias in 1491, and the Crown supported the Holy Of-fice, winning a subsequent argument with the papacy. But Bishop Juan died before the matter could come to court.

Pedrarias the conquistador was tall, with a pale complexion, green eyes, and red hair. He had probably been born in 1450. Thus, in the words of Las Casas, he was "a man of a considerable age and was over sixty" when he went to the Indies.[25] He had been page to two kings of Castile, first Juan II and then Enrique IV. He married Isabel de Bobadilla, daughter of the Francisco de Bobadilla who had governed La Española between 1500 and 1502 and had been drowned after sending home the Columbuses in chains. She was there-fore also the niece of Beatriz de Bobadilla, the great friend of Queen Isabel, and had been a lady-in-waiting to Isabel's daughter, poor Juana, at her ill-fated wedding in Brussels.

Pedrarias had been one of the deputies to Pedro Navarro, the great spe-cialist in mines, in the African campaign of 1510. The grant of arms of 1512 mentions him as having been in "the Holy Conquest of Granada and Africa . . . in the capture of Oran where you stood out honorably and also in the capture of Bugía."[26] But there was more to report than just hard work by him in that war. Pedrarias having apparently been mortally wounded in Africa, his relations decided to bury him in the monastery of Our Lady of the Cross, on the outskirts of Torrejón, near Madrid, but when he was al-ready in his coffin, one of his servants, giving him a last embrace, found that he was alive. This incident decisively affected "the Gallant," and he obtained yet one more nickname, "the Revived One." Thereafter, every year he had a solemn requiem in a coffin to thank God for saving him at the last minute.

Pedrarias's salary in Castilla de Oro would be a little more than what had been paid to Ovando: 366,000 maravedís a year, with half advanced to him on his nomination.

His principal bankers and suppliers were Juan de Córdoba, the silver-smith of Seville who was a friend of the Columbus family, and the every-year-more-powerful Genoese bankers, the Centuriones and the Grimaldi.[27] Indeed from this time onward, Gaspare Centurione (Gaspar Centurión), whose money depended originally on the wheat trade to Seville, was to be found at the heart of every expedition to the New World. Other Genoese, Agustín Vivaldo and Nicolas Grimaldi, were expressly allowed to establish themselves and their agents in *tierra firme* and "conduct trade there as if they were Spaniards."[28] In addition, Pedro Báez, Pedrarias's majordomo, declared before leaving Castile that he had received 10,500 maravedís from another Grimaldi, Agustín, in the name of Bernardo, his brother, to buy supplies in Seville.[29] A conquistador named Hernando de Soto, from Villanueva de la Serena, in Extremadura, later famous in Florida, explained that he obtained a loan of 3,000 maravedís from Juan Francisco de Grimaldi, while Fernández de Enciso, Pedro Camacho, Juan Fernández de Enciso (perhaps a brother of the geographer), and the merchant Gonzalo de Sevilla undertook to return 225 ducats to Juan Grimaldi and Centurión, which they had been lent for the equipment of their ships.[30] Sancho Gómez de Córdoba, a courtier, gave authority to Juan Francisco de Grimaldi and Gaspar Centurión, as well as to Juan de Córdoba, so that they could take three black slaves with them. Thus this second great royal expedition to the New World had, even more than the first under Columbus, a distinctly Genoese flavor.

Despite this participation of the Genoese, the expeditionaries were of course mostly Spaniards. Peter Martyr even had difficulty in getting a passage for an Italian botanist, Francesco Coto; he finally did, thanks explicitly to the King.[31]

Pedrarias took with him about two thousand men, "all chosen from hidalgos and distinguished men,"[32] who included, according to Pascual de Andagoya, one of his captains, "the most lucid people from Spain that had ever left those shores."[33] Estimates for the number of participants also reach three thousand.[34] In fact, the original list had been fixed at eight hundred.[35]

The list of those who accompanied "the Gallant" included many of his special friends, among them Pascual de Andagoya himself, whose part in subsequent conquests in Peru would be important.[36] There were also Martín Fernández de Enciso, who was invited because "he had experience of the things of the mainland and also of the activities of the fleet."[37] Sebastián de Benalcázar, also later to become famous in Peru; Hernando de Luque, a lay brother who, too, would fight alongside Pizarro; Bernardino Vázquez de Tapia, who would fight at the side of Cortés in Mexico; Hernando de Soto, of fame in both Peru and Florida; Diego del Almagro, the ally and then the enemy of Pizarro; and Diego de Tovilla, a chronicler of Pedrarias's regime (in the book *La Barbárica*).[38]

There were, too, Alonso de la Puente, treasurer, once secretary to the Infante Fernando; Diego Márquez, accountant, general supervisor on Columbus's second voyage, who had been lost for six curious days on Guadeloupe in 1493; Juan de Tavira, supervisor and a protégé of the Queen of Portugal; and the future historian Gonzalo Fernandez de Oviedo, a protégé of Fonseca's who, though already thirty-six years old, had not yet found his métier. He was to concern himself with mines in Castilla de Oro and the melting down of gold.

Oviedo, whose family was from Asturias, seems to have derived from a long line of *converso* notaries. He had begun his career in 1485 as gentleman-in-waiting of the Duke of Villahermosa, bastard of King Juan II of Aragon and the first commander of the national Hermandades. He went in 1491 to the court of the Infante Juan and was then in Naples with Don Fadrique, Duke of Calabria. He married first Margarita de Vergara, said to have been the most beautiful woman in Toledo, whose fair hair was famous for reaching to the ground and who died in childbirth; and then Isabel de Aguilar, by whom he had two children. He had been notary of the Inquisition in 1507 and was then at the court of Naples. He would have liked to return to Italy but never did.[39]

As we have seen, a Bishop Quevedo also accompanied Pedrarias. That prelate had been designated bishop of "Betica Aurea" in Castilla de Oro, with his seat at Darien. He was supported by a dean, Juan Pérez de Zalduendo, the priest of Torrijos (who had already been to Santo Domingo) as well as an archdeacon, a precentor, various canons, three sacristans, and an archpriest, not to mention at least six Franciscans.[40] The Bishop was equipped with an episcopal ring, of course, a silver staff, and a pectoral cross, as well as chasubles, holy candles, carpets, missals, altars, incense burners, chalices, several silver crosses, and six religious pictures. No concession in these consignments was made to tropical living.[41] Pedrarias's passengers included many well-dressed Castilian gentlemen; some reached Darien in "silk tunics and many were in brocade."[42] Some of these gallants had been in the wars in Italy, where, as the King himself said, they had become "accustomed to very great vices."[43]

Travel was free for all passengers or emigrants, as were provisions for the first month after arrival. By then it was supposed that all would have found enough to live on. But in order to avoid shortages, food for another year and a half was also loaded, to be sold later at reasonable prices. For four years emigrants could take back to Spain, free of all taxes, salt, pearls, and precious stones—once the royal fifth had been paid, of course—and during the same period they could count on being free of all lawsuits![44]

Several native slaves originally from *tierra firme* (though not that part of it to which Pedrarias was going) accompanied this expedition, as well as fifty so-called Indians who had been shipped to Spain from La Española and who were supposed to know about gold mining.[45] Finally, the King, though ill and tired, invested 20.75 million maravedís in the journey and concerned himself in many details of the planning, more than in any other such endeavor since 1492. Like his subjects, he had been mesmerized by the letter of Núñez de Balboa that had told of the gold resources of the colony. He thought the enterprise "one of the most important in the world."[46] He believed that to delay departure even a single day would be a great loss to the expedition.

Money did not seem to be in short supply. Cristóbal de Morales, a painter from Seville who had decorated the audience room of the Casa de Contratación, designed for Pedrarias a splendid royal swallow-tailed pennon, with lions and eagles. There were, too, three silk flags painted by Pedro Ramírez, one of Our Lady of La Antigua, one of Santiago the Apostle, and another of the Cross of Jerusalem. Firearms were bought at the royal factory in Malaga, while most of the rest of the war matériel was obtained in Vizcaya. Diego Colón was asked to send interpreters to Pedrarias, though the order did not take into account how the languages of La Española differed from those of the Panamanian isthmus.

Pedrarias went out of his way to hire the best pilots: the pilot of his flagship, also appointed by the King, was Juan (Giovanni) Vespucci, a nephew of Amerigo, who, like his uncle, had been born a Florentine. Juan Serrano (afterwards with Magellan) became the chief pilot of the fleet. Vicente Yáñez de Pinzón was to have been pilot on the *Santo Espíritu* but had to withdraw for reasons of health, and was succeeded by Rodrigo Yáñez, probably his son.[47]

Most of these expeditionaries were attracted by the promise of land as well as of gold; after all, the King had said: "It is our wish that we will divide up houses, sites, lands, farms . . . making a distinction between infantry and foot soldiers, and those of a lesser grade and worth."[48]

The King recommended to the Casa de Contratación that neither the children of those "reconciled" with the Inquisition should be permitted to go to the Indies, nor the grandchildren of those who had been burned as heretics on the advice of the Holy Office. Several such persons in fact found their way on board, for example, Maestre Enrique, a Portuguese surgeon. The prohibition would have excluded Las Casas; perhaps that was one of the intentions. Lawyers were also forbidden, an unprecedented restriction.[49]

Numerous servants traveled with the expedition, some specially hired for a two-year period. There were also a number of black slaves, for example, twelve attached to Pedrarias himself, ten to Alonso de la Puente, and three to Sancho Gómez de Córdoba.

The military equipment is of much interest, since it was a mixture of the old and the new, for Pedrarias took with him forty arquebuses, two small falconets (light cannon), six *ribadoquines* (bronze cannon), nearly two hundred swords with decorated scabbards, five hundred pikes, fifty lances for use on horseback, eight hundred short lances, fifty iron maces, and two hundred daggers from Villareal, their sheaths sold to the expedition by a certain Bartolomé Muñoz of the Calle Sierpes in Seville.

There had been discussion as to what kind of armor would be best. Some thought that tortoiseshell was adequate; others favored a type of doublet padded with cotton or wool, known as an *escuapil.* The Indians, after all, never had more than this. In the end, that self-styled specialist in the Gulf of Urabá, Fernández de Enciso, had the last word: he recommended tin breastplates, with attached sidepieces, available at 500 maravedís each. Once arrived at Castilla de Oro, every man given this armor would be asked to pay 3 ducats for it, the equivalent of two months' salary. Pedrarias also took with him over seven hundred helmets with little wings. He bought one thousand wooden shields made from "dragon trees" from the Canary Islands.

Much of this equipment was supplied by Basque merchants, mainly from Azpeitia, Eibar, San Sebastián, and Durango.[50] Indeed, nearly 700,000 maravedís were spent in the Basque country, and with these purchases, families later so famous as the Aguirres, Motricos, Ibarras, and Arriolas enter into Spanish economic history. The guns themselves, however, came mostly from Malaga.

Pedrarias carried thirty-five pipes of wine and corn, two barrels of honey, sixty *arrobas* of vinegar, and sixty of oil. Licenciado Barreda and his chemist, Solórzano, stocked up with many medicaments for "the first pharmacy of the New World."[51] Carters were among those who profited—people who carried the goods from Sanlúcar el Mayor, Malaga, or the Basque country.

Pedrarias had planned to leave behind in Spain his wife, Isabel de Bobadilla. But she came of a tough, experienced family, and when he proposed this, she wrote:

> My dear husband, we have been united from our youth, as I think, for the purpose of living together and never being separated. Wherever destiny may lead you, be it on the tempestuous sea or be it among the hardships that await you on land, I should be your companion. There is nothing that I should more fear, nor any kind of death that might threaten me,

which would not be more supportable for me than to live without you and be separated by a great distance. I would rather die or be eaten by fish in the sea or devored on land by cannibals than to consume myself in perpetual mourning and unceasing sorrow awaiting not my husband but his letters. . . . The children whom God has given us [there were nine of them] will not stop me for a moment. We will leave them their heritage and their marriage portion, sufficient to enable them to live in conformity with their rank, and, besides, I have no other preoccupation.[52]

In the end, she took two of her children with her. Isabel was not the first governor's wife to accompany her husband to the New World. That honor had fallen to María de Toledo, the wife of Diego Colón. But Isabel went to a far more savage colony.

25

"A man very advanced
in excess"

He is very old for these parts and suffers very much from the great
illness that has never left him for a day since he arrived. He is a man
very advanced in excess.

Balboa on Pedrarias, 1515

Pedrarias's fleet set off, he himself on the caravel *Our Lady of the Conception*.
The most interesting ship's captain was Alonso Quintero of the *Santa
Catalina*. A native of Palos, he had been carrying passengers and merchandise from Seville to Santo Domingo for ten years and more. Among his
clients in 1506 had been Hernán Cortés, who by 1513 had of course moved
from Santo Domingo to Cuba.

Pedrarias sailed on a southerly route to the Caribbean and stopped at
the isle of Dominica on June 3, where, after christening a large inlet the Bay
of Fonseca, after the Bishop, he fought some Indians and, resisting the idea
of stopping at other places in the Lesser Antilles, made for what is now Santa
Marta, Colombia, which he reached on June 12.

There, on June 19, he caused the "Requirement" of the lawyer Palacios
Rubios to be read for the first time, by his notary Rodrigo de Colmenares.[1]
The Indians had been running backward and forward over the beach, armed
with poisoned arrows, waiting for the arrival of the Spaniards whose ships
they had observed at sea. They had painted their bodies and adorned their
heads with plumes. Some seventy Indians assembled, and both Pedrarias
and Rodrigo de Colmenares thought this an adequate audience for the new
legal declaration. The latter affected to know the language of the Indians but
all the same read his text with the help of an Indian girl who had been kidnapped on a previous expedition, perhaps by the Guerra brothers or by
Vespucci, and was now brought from Spain.

For the first time, Indians now heard the curious statements: how God,
our Lord one and eternal, had fashioned the heavens as well as the earth, and

how a certain Adam and Eve, from whom everyone, both emperor and clown, descends, had been created.[2] That had been five thousand and more years ago. God our Lord later gave the command of the world to one man, St. Peter. He had been called "Papa," and the present Pope was his successor.

One of the past popes had given these islands of the Caribbean and also *tierra firme* to the King and Queen of Castile. So, Colmenares went on,

> I ask and require you, who understand very well what I have been saying [!] . . . that you recognize the Church as the Lord and Superior of the universe and the King and the Queen, our lords, as superior to the lords and kings of these isles and mainland by virtue of the said donation. And if you accept this, I shall receive you with all love and charity, and will leave you and your wives, and children and farms, free without servitude. . . .[3]

The statement was naturally followed by silence. No one among the Indians had understood a word of it. Then a rain of arrows was dispatched over the Spaniards, who replied with gunshot. That effectively routed the Indians, who fled to the forested mountains.

Fernández de Oviedo said to Pedrarias: "My lord, it appears that these Indians will not listen to the theology of the 'Requirement' and that you have no one who can make them understand it; would your honor be pleased to retain it till we have one of these Indians in a cage, in order that he may learn it at leisure and my lord bishop may explain it to him?"[4] Then Oviedo handed the document to Pedrarias, who received it with much laughter, in which all who heard the speech joined; but all the same the "Requirement" continued to be read to trees and empty villages, sometimes to the beat of a drum; and sometimes from ships off an island.

Las Casas said that he did not know whether to laugh or to cry when he heard of this document.[5] Even its author, Palacios Rubios, would laugh when Oviedo told him of his own experiences.[6]

While he was making for the Bay of Cartagena, a storm diverted Pedrarias to Isla Fuerte, where he seized several Indians as slaves. On June 30, 1513, he reached his destination, Santa María la Antigua de Darien, on the west of the Bay of Urabá.

He found there a colony of a little more than 500 Spaniards with perhaps 1,500 Indians working for them as servants or laborers. The commander was, of course, Núñez de Balboa. The settlement seemed rich. Las Casas reported that the colonists had until 1512 made a profit of over 36 million maravedís, of which 7 million had gone to the King, while the voyage of

Núñez de Balboa to the South Sea had produced over 13 million maravedís. Oviedo thought that Balboa and his friends were living well and were on the way to enriching themselves. Balboa alone had made nearly 5 million maravedís.[7] He had also made the Indians reasonably content, if not entirely "as tame as sheep,"[8] as he later claimed.

Balboa, then three miles from the coast in Santa María, was informed by messenger of the new development: "Sir, Pedrarias has arrived in the port and has come to act as governor of this land."[9] Balboa said how pleased he was, and he organized a reception to greet the new Governor. Indeed, he and his colonists greeted Pedrarias with a *Te Deum Laudamus,*[10] the two leaders embraced, and then Pedrarias, his wife, and Bishop Quevedo made a solemn entry into the town, which must have seemed a most primitive place to those who had been born and bred in Segovia. The old inhabitants offered the newcomers rooms in their houses till the Indians could build them new ones. But that did not solve the problem of lodgings, for the building of the new houses took time.

Pedrarias went to the town hall, where he presented his credentials, and after dismissing all the old councillors who had been dependent on Balboa, nominated new ones. He had a long talk with Balboa in affable terms, asking for details of the land and passing on the gratitude of the King for all that he had done. Balboa replied on July 2 by giving Pedrarias a statement of the gold that he had found and the names of all the *caciques* whom he had reduced.

The *residencia* of Balboa then began, Licenciado Gaspar de Espinosa, who had accompanied Pedrarias, being the judge responsible. That provoked a long quarrel between the friends of Balboa and those of Fernández de Enciso, whom Balboa had expelled and who had now returned. But Espinosa refused to let Balboa's enemies determine everything that he himself did. Indeed, he soon saw that Balboa was a remarkable leader, as did Bishop Quevedo. Pedrarias, on the other hand, wanted to send Balboa home to Spain in irons because of his self-assertive spirit of insubordination. Quevedo managed to prevent this, with the result that he was accused of having private dealings with Balboa. Pedrarias was, meanwhile, incapacitated for a while by an infirmity, probably gout, which left him permanently an invalid.[11]

Martyr says that at Darien there seemed to be an atmosphere of prosperity. He wrote to the Pope:

> Everything that the Spaniards have planted or sowed in Urabá has grown
> marvelously well. Is this not worthy, Most Holy Father, of the highest ad-

miration? Every kind of seed, grafting, sugarcane, and slips of trees, and
plants, without speaking of the chickens and quadrupeds I have mentioned, were brought from Europe. O admirable fertility! The cucumbers
and other vegetables were ready for picking in less than twenty days!
Cabbages, beets, lettuces, salads, and other garden stuffs were ripe within
ten days; pumpkins and melons were picked twenty-eight days after the
seeds were sown. The slips and sprouts and such of our trees as we plant
in our nurseries or trenches, as well as the graftings of trees similar to
those in Spain, bore fruit as quickly as in La Española.[12]

But the geographical situation was less favorable: "The rustic township
of Antigua, made up of two hundred houses in indigenous style, and lived in
by the Spaniards of Balboa, could not easily include 1,500 new inhabitants.
Disease and hunger . . . finished off the lives of the population . . . ," wrote
Pascual Andagoya. He added: "The settlement had hitherto been small and
could support itself. But the new people could not be absorbed. . . . People
began to fall ill in such a way that they could not be cured and thus, in a single month, seven hundred men died either from hunger or from *modorra*."[13]
This was the first time that that terrible word was used in relation to a disease that so affected the early Spanish Empire. It was probably a form of
sleeping sickness, perhaps Chagas disease, a wasting infirmity transmitted
by insects.

There was also disquiet because the food that the officials in Seville had
specified should be sold was not regularly distributed.[14] This was because
much of the bacon and salt beef, even the biscuits and salted fish, that had
been carried had rotted on the journey. The supervisor Juan de Tavira gave
out what food there was in small rations, but some of those who received it
sold their share to richer emigrants. This period ended when the storehouse
burned down. The new colonists then began to ransack the houses of the Indians, sometimes offering a silk coat for a loaf of bread. Settlers from Seville
or from Burgos were said to have died shouting, "Give me bread." There was
an attack of locusts. The old colony regretted the new arrivals more with
every passing day, but the growing rivalry between Pedrarias and Balboa
prevented any rational approach to the potential catastrophe.

The "rivers of gold" in Balboa's letter still seemed far off. The new conquistadors, with their lack of experience, antagonized the Indians, and many
of these settlers left as soon as they could to return to Spain (the Franciscan
bishop Juan de Quevedo and the historian Oviedo were among them). Some,
though, went to Cuba and thence, like Francisco Montejo, Bernardino
Vázquez de Tapia, and Bernal Díaz del Castillo, to Mexico with Cortés.

The King, meanwhile, was pondering the kind of relationship that could be established between Balboa and Pedrarias. He asked the former to collaborate with the latter and to advise him of developments. Then he nominated Balboa *adelantado* of the Southern Sea and governor of Panama and Coiba. But even in these roles he would be subject to Pedrarias; the King specifically insisted that "in these parts there must be a single person and a single leader and no more."

Meanwhile, Pedrarias thought his only recourse was to send out his captains in all directions. These *entradas,* as they were called, were *razzias,* infernal manhunts in search of slaves, according to Oviedo, who added that he did not have time to explain all that the conquistadors did to trap the Indians. The *entradas* destroyed the reasonably good relations that Balboa had in general achieved with them. The "Requirement" was constantly used. It was read out in Spanish, usually at a distance. Once, when its meaning was explained to a *cacique* of the Sinú Indians by Fernández de Enciso, the *cacique* commented, "Oh, the Pope must have been drunk" to give away lands that were already in someone else's possession. Once Juan de Ayora, the most brutal of Pedrarias's commanders, had the declaration read when the Indians already had ropes around their necks.[15]

These long forgotten journeys by unremembered conquistadors into remote jungles constituted an extraordinary mixture of courage and cruelty. The names of both the Spaniards and their Central American discoveries— tribes, persons, places—defeat us. But that should not prevent us from recalling these astonishing and unprecedented events whose risks were great and whose losses vast.

The first important expedition into the interior was that of Luis Carrillo (a brother-in-law of the royal secretary Lope de Conchillos). Carrillo being inexperienced, Pedrarias gave him Francisco Pizarro, nothing if not knowledgeable, as his second in command. They set off with sixty men in a southerly direction, establishing a settlement on the River Anades, which they named Fonseca Dávila. But they did not find much of the gold of which Balboa had spoken: a mere 1,000 pesos, even if they captured many slaves. They returned to Darien, Pedrarias being angry at their inadequacy, but perhaps because of the relation between Carrillo and the royal secretary Conchillos, he did not punish them.[16]

The second important *entrada* to the west was that of Juan de Ayora, who took with him four hundred men. The aim was to further the work of Balboa, according to Oviedo, seeking the most narrow section of the isthmus and then building forts along it. Both the Governor and the Bishop gave express instructions that it was essential to be tolerant to the Indians.[17]

Ayora divided his army into three: one section, under Juan de Zorita, with 50 men, set off for Pocorisa, and another, led by Francisco de Ávila, 150 strong, made for the Pacific. The third group, under Ayora himself, went to investigate the Cueva Indians. Having been welcomed in Comagrem by the Indians there, and gaining their trust, Ayora and his men turned on their hosts, looking for gold and slaves, torturing and killing them with dogs. The chief of the Tubanama escaped and managed to attack the Spaniards in turn. In October, Ayora returned to Darien on the pretext that he was ill, leaving a lieutenant, Hernán Pérez de Meneses (who founded Los Anades, on the Gulf of San Blas), in control. This new town was soon destroyed, and many Spaniards were killed by furious Indians. María de Aguilar, a mistress of Ayora's who had gamely come out with her lover, was seized by a *cacique* who made her into his own mistress. She was soon killed by the *cacique's* other wives. Francisco de Ávila then founded a town at Tumaca, perhaps on the site of present-day Panama, but after falling ill, he abandoned the enterprise.

On these journeys Juan de Ayora treated the *caciques* whom he encountered so cruelly that they became implacable enemies. Driven to extremities, they killed the Spaniards sometimes openly, sometimes by setting traps for them. In places where commerce in the time of Balboa had been relatively normal and the *caciques* friendly, it became necessary to fight. Ayora, when he had thus amassed a quantity of gold by these means, decided to flee to Spain, Pedrarias apparently closing his eyes to this act of desertion.[18]

Two caravels then brought royal dispatches about Balboa's appointment as *adelantado*, as well as some new settlers. Pedrarias wanted to intercept these letters rather than deliver them to his rival. But both Quevedo and Balboa had heard about them, and Pedrarias had to convoke his local council. Bishop Quevedo criticized Pedrarias's disloyalty to the Crown, but Diego Márquez and Alonso de la Puente agreed that the letter should not be given to Balboa until the *residencia* on him had been completed. In the end, the letters were handed over on Bishop Quevedo's insistence. Thereafter, Balboa was indeed named *adelantado*, a title that made for the greatest difficulty: in an age where designations were all, Pedrarias felt indignant, since the nomination obviously threatened his position. Pedrarias wrote home complaining that Balboa had not explored the region of which he had been proclaimed the proconsul.

Meanwhile, the *residencia* against Balboa ended. Despite his growing admiration for Balboa, Espinosa found evidence of insubordination against the Crown and fined him 1,565,000 maravedís, which payment left him quite without funds. He began writing to the King. Of these letters, one remains, that of October 26, 1515, which took the form of a request for an investigation into what was happening in Darien—for, said Balboa, the *caciques* and Indians who had been like lambs "had turned into wild lions and God had been very badly served."[19] As for the Governor, he might be honorable, but he was very "old for these parts, and suffers very much from the great illness that has never left him for a day since he arrived." He was, thought Balboa, "a man very advanced in excess.[20] He never punished those who carried out damage in the various *entradas.*"

Balboa and Pedrarias also quarreled about a new decree that allowed for the sale of slaves captured on *tierra firme* in the islands. Balboa protested, but Pedrarias said that for the moment "it was better to accept it, since it gives the people something to do." Andagoya commented that in those days "no one was interested in making peace or in furthering the development of the settlement. All that people worried about was seeking gold and slaves."

Another *entrada* followed, that of Gaspar de Morales to the Pacific. He set off with Pizarro and captured the charming offshore isle of Terarequi, with its pearls. This was the occasion when Pizarro first heard of a rich territory to the south that turned out to be Peru. It was a beneficial expedition for the Spaniards. They found one extraordinary pearl: La Peregrina, or La Huerfana, which weighed thirty-one carats. Morales sold this to Pedro del Puerto, a merchant who, soon afraid of owning it, in turn sold it to Isabel de Bobadilla, from whom it passed later to Charles V's queen, the Empress Isabel, for 900,000 maravedís.[21]

Morales cut his way through the territory of new peoples such as the Tutibra, Chichama, Garchina, and Birú. His men showed great cruelty, capturing many slaves. Their fellow Indians tried to rescue them, and there was a fierce battle, in the course of which Morales killed all his "slaves" on purpose. He then returned to Darien and gratefully received permission to go home to Spain.

Balboa also went on a new expedition to the magic realm of Dabeiba, in the foothills of the Andes, which he had represented as being full of gold and of palaces. He set off with Luis de Carrillo and about two hundred men. The expedition was a failure. Balboa was nearly killed by an arrow in his head, while Carrillo died of wounds.

Next, Gonzalo de Badajoz set off in March 1515, with forty soldiers, toward the northwest, where he eventually reached Columbus's Cape Gracias a Dios and where he failed either to bribe or to persuade the *cacique* into helping him. He was then joined by Luis de Mercado with fifteen men. They decided to cross the mountains and take possession again of the Southern Sea. On the way they went to Javana, whence the *cacique* had fled, taking what riches he had with him. The Spaniards did capture some curiously branded slaves, however. They found, too, a good deal of gold and visited the *caciques* Totongo and Taracuru, and the latter's brother Pananome, as well as others named Anata, Scoria, and Pariza.[22] Badajoz then returned to Darien.

All these expeditions were badly planned attempts at enrichment. They were not much concerned with discovery, their attention to the souls of the indigenous people was not marked, and they brought their commanders little in the way of glory.

Finally, Pedrarias embarked on his own journey. After being inactive since his arrival, due to his continuous ill health, he set off with 250 men and twelve caravels on November 28, 1515. The party headed west, in the direction of the Gulf of Urabá, to look for a "conquistador," Gabriel Becerra, who had died there eight months before. The purpose was also punitive, for the whole region had risen against the Spaniards. Pedrarias and his men landed at Aguada and made their way inland to Aguila and then to Acla, known as "Huesos Humanos" (Human Bones) because it had been the scene of a battle in the past between the *cacique* Cartea and his brother Chima. There Pedrarias gave a banquet and wine flowed, and he founded a port that he thought was protected against shipworm. From there, he argued, one could go easily on foot to the Pacific. It must have been close to the modern city of Colón.

But Pedrarias became ill again, this time from what seems to have been hepatitis, and had to return to Antigua. There he arrived on January 26, 1517, leaving behind the experienced Lope de Olano with orders to complete the building of a port, and naming Espinosa to command the rest of the expedition. His *entrada* had been, as he thought, a success: there was booty of 45 million maravedís, and two thousand slaves were obtained for sale to La Española. Lope de Olano and his few men soon died or were killed, however, and the territory returned to Indian control.

Balboa secretly sent a friend, Andrés de Garabito, to Cuba to find more men in order to form another expedition to the Southern Sea. He had abandoned hope of finding volunteers among the expeditionaries of Pedrarias who would respect his leadership, *adelantado* though he formally might be. Garabito found sixty willing men in Cuba and Santo Domingo. They arrived silently, by night, but Pedrarias came upon them. Furious, he had Balboa arrested and placed in a wooden cage in his house. Bishop Quevedo again intervened in his favor. Quevedo suggested that peace in the colony was the only way ahead, and proposed that Balboa should marry one of Pedrarias's daughters. Pedrarias's wife, Isabel de Bobadilla, agreed, and in April 1516,

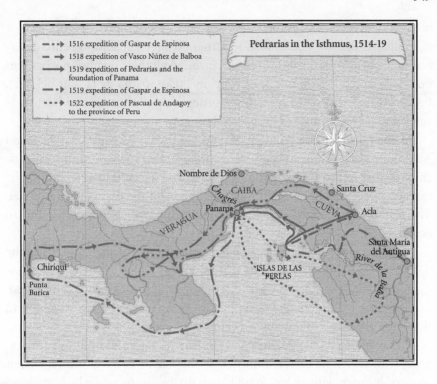

Pedrarias in the Isthmus, 1514-19

- - -▶ 1516 expedition of Gaspar de Espinosa
- - ▶ 1518 expedition of Vasco Núñez de Balboa
─────▶ 1519 expedition of Pedrarías and the
         foundation of Panama
- - ▷ 1519 expedition of Gaspar de Espinosa
· · ·▷ 1522 expedition of Pascual de Andagoy
         to the province of Peru

Balboa married María de Peñalosa by proxy. His bride was in a convent in Spain at the time, from which she did not emerge. In a few months, Balboa, freed from his cage, set off with his men to reestablish the settlement of Acla before moving on to the Southern Sea.

Espinosa remained in command of Pedrarias's expedition, killing and enslaving as he went. He still had with him two hundred foot soldiers and ten horsemen. He crossed the Sierra de Careta, reaching the upper canyon of the Bayano, where he killed many in revenge for their earlier murder of Spaniards at Santa Cruz and at Los Anades. Then he went on to the River Nata, where he and his followers remained for four months, living off the Indians' maize. He moved into Pariza country, where he had a series of skirmishes in which the sight of his horses so alarmed the Indians that they were decisively defeated. He returned along the peninsula of Azurero and in April 1517 went to Acla, then loosely but effectively governed by Balboa. Espinosa's men found Acla "in good shape and that they could eat there well, as if they had been in Seville."[23] There were many houses of wood, and the small Spanish population was well established on the basis of Indian servants and laborers.

In August 1517, Balboa made for the Southern Sea again with two hundred Spaniards, a hundred black slaves who had come with Pedrarias, and many Indians. Among his men were Andagoya, Hernando de Soto, Diego de la Tobilla, Andrés de Valderrábano, Hernando de Argüello, and Pedro de Arbolancha, of whom the last three had invested all their savings in what Balboa had named "the South Sea Company" (Compañía de la Mar del Sur). Pedrarias had wished to lead this journey himself, but he had been persuaded to desist because of his age and his gout.

Balboa ordered the building of a flotilla for this expedition. The wood was cut on the Caribbean coast. He had the timbers as well as the sails, anchors, tarpaulin, and rigging transported across the isthmus. He did this, he explained, because he thought that the timber on the east coast was better. The feat was herculean. Las Casas thought that over five hundred Indian bearers died; others put the figure at several times that number.

At all events, Acla now became the headquarters of Balboa. Thence the Spaniards and Indians set off to march seventy miles to Río de las Balsas (Sabanas) where, on a vast tract of level ground, a dockyard was prepared. But when the precious wood from the Caribbean reached there, it was found that, after all, much of it had been eaten by worms.

In October 1518, Balboa reached the Pacific coast and built two brigantines, with which he directed himself to the Isle of Pearls offshore. He left some of his men with orders to build two further ships, while he himself set out for the Gulf of San Miguel with a hundred men. They approached the Puerto de Piñas, but a school of whales prevented their landing. Balboa was plainly hoping to found his own independent colony on the Pacific, in a place that would have been more suitable than what was soon established at Panama, and where he would be able to leave Pedrarias behind.

Back at Darien, however, changes were afoot. As we have seen, Quevedo and Oviedo had returned to Spain. Both described how cruelly Pedrarias was permitting his followers to behave. Their stories convinced King Fernando that a new governor had to be found. Even Bishop Fonseca agreed: "I have already said that we must get that man out of there."[24] The royal choice for a substitute fell on a respectable official, Lope de Sosa, then the Governor of Gran Canaria.

Rumors that a change was planned soon reached Darien. For that reason, Balboa delayed on the Pacific, awaiting the arrival of the new incumbent. He sent an expedition of his friends (Garabito, Valderrábano, Luis Botello, Hernán Muñoz) to bring back more boatbuilding material from Acla, and also to discover whether the new Governor had come. Pedrarias feared that Balboa was planning a rising, and he sent a force to capture these men. He was half taken in by their innocent account. But then he convinced himself otherwise and, furious at failing to persuade Balboa to return, he sent his old subordinate, the ruthless Extremeño Francisco Pizarro, to arrest him. The surprise was complete: "But you are Pizarro," exclaimed the astonished Balboa. "You used not to come out and greet me in this way."[25] Knowing, however, where authority now lay in the last resort, Pizarro took Balboa to Acla as a prisoner, while Bartolomé Hurtado was sent to take over command of the *adelantado*'s troops still on the coast.

Judge Espinosa then embarked on a trial of Balboa, who with Luis Botello, Valderrábano, Muñoz, Argüello, Garabito, and Father Rodrigo Pérez was accused of treason. Garabito changed sides, perhaps because of his and Balboa's competing affection for the Indian princess Anayansi; he treacherously wrote to Pedrarias alleging that Balboa had planned a rebellion against the King as well as against Pedrarias. Balboa was also accused of engineering the death of Diego de Nicuesa in 1509 and of the illegal seizure of the powers of Fernández de Enciso in 1510. It was swiftly decided that he should be decapitated with his friends in the plaza of Acla. Garabito was forgiven, as was Rodrigo Pérez, because he was a priest.

Pedrarias visited Balboa in the makeshift jail and denounced him: "I treated you as if you were a son, because I believed in your fidelity to me and to the King. But then I found that you had decided to rebel against the Crown. Thus I can no longer treat you as a son but as an enemy, and so today you cannot expect of me more than . . . what I tell you."

Balboa replied: "Everything which has been said is a falsehood, because no thought of rebellion ever occurred to me. If such a thing had indeed happened, I had no need to answer your call to come back, for at my disposal I had three hundred men and four ships, with which, without seeing or hearing you, we could have gone on to the sea, for there is no shortage of land, both poor and rich. . . ."

It was a dialogue of deaf men. On January 1, 1519, Balboa and his four close friends (Luis Botello, Valderrábano, Muñoz, and Argüello) were taken to the improvised square at Acla. At the signal of a roll of drums, the first three and Balboa were executed. Argüello was pardoned at the last minute. Pedrarias watched. Balboa's head was left in the square for several days.[26]

Balboa had been a thorn in the side of Pedrarias since 1514, and given the unbending personalities of the two, some such denouement was probably inevitable. Balboa might have killed Pedrarias, but though fearless and imaginative, he was less ruthless.

This action left Pedrarias free to embark on his own adventures on the coast of the Southern Sea, a place that he realized, as Balboa had, was more promising as a settlement than Darien. Appointing Espinosa as his second in command, he traveled down the River Balsas as far as the gulf, reached the

Pearl archipelago, and took possession of the Isla de las Flores. Espinosa independently reached a point that he thought was "the narrowest stretch of land between one sea and the other." He sought to persuade Pedrarias to found a settlement there. So they jointly founded Panama on August 15, 1519, in a traditional ceremony, with a notary, Antón Cuadrado, taking notes as Pedrarias took possession in the name of Queen Juana and the new young King Charles. Pedrarias apportioned the blocks of the town to the four hundred Spaniards present, as specified in his instructions of 1513, and began to establish landowners through *encomiendas*, on November 5, 1519.

There were plenty of fish, including numerous sardines and mollusks, and abundant vegetation. The sea was a benign presence. The site, though, was probably less hospitable than where Balboa had been, and it is not clear why the new place was chosen. Perhaps chance played a part.

Innumerable Indians were unconquered in war, but no one knew quite how many were available. Still, Pedrarias found 25 political entities (*cacicazgos*), whose Indians could perhaps be divided through their leaders. Just over 100 Spaniards participated in this division of land, most of whom had to be content with less than 60 Indians each. Those who received more—between 150 and 300—were the Governor's friends.[27]

Pedrarias sent Espinosa northward with the pilot Juan de Castañeda, and they discovered the Gulf of Nocoya. They found, too, rich villages, a large population, and many deer, as well as many peacocks and geese in cages. Here they established yet another settlement, to which they gave the name of Santiago. Pedrarias also sent another expedition under Diego de Albítez to refound Nicuesa's Nombre de Dios, at the Caribbean end of what would soon become the main road between that sea and the Pacific, the so-called Camino Real.

Then the Governor returned to Darien, intending to dismantle it completely. He now knew that there were many more opportunities on the Pacific than on the Caribbean. But he found the inhabitants of Santa María de Darien quite opposed to another change.

The fleet of the new Governor, Lope de Sosa, at this point reached the port. What the existing Governor expected would happen is unclear. It made no difference. For no sooner had the ships come into the harbor than Sosa, who had been ill for most of the crossing, died, at midnight on May 7, 1520, presumably because of illness contracted on the journey. There was a grand funeral, at which officials and Franciscans were present, in the new but far from complete church of Darien. Pedrarias lavished many attentions on the son of the new Governor, who had accompanied his father, and his nephew of the same name who had been intended as his lieutenant, and also on the proposed chief magistrate, Juan Rodríguez de Alcarconcillo, who had been expected to carry out his own *residencia*. In the circumstances, it was natural that accusations should be made that Lope de Sosa had been murdered, perhaps poisoned by Pedrarias. But there is no evidence of it. Pedrarias was capable of crime, including murder, but on this occasion it was unnecessary.

A few months later, on July 20, 1520, the historian Gonzalo Fernández de Oviedo, who had been in Spain, reached Darien again. He returned thinking that Lope de Sosa would have assumed his post as governor and that he could again live peacefully in Darien. He had planned to travel from Spain with Sosa but came a month later, first going to Santo Domingo, where he heard of the new Governor's death. He continued with his wife and children to Darien, where Pedrarias received him amicably, though he must have known that Oviedo had done what he could to ruin his name in Spain.

In fact, Oviedo soon, improbably, became the leader of the opposition to any change of the Spanish capital from Darien and, in a spirit of defiance, built himself a luxurious house costing about 7 million maravedís. Pedrarias maintained his policy, though, moving the seat of government to the Pacific, as well as the seat of the bishop. Oviedo survived an attempt at assassination, which he thought must have been the work of Pedrarias because he had read the documents of the trial of Balboa that had afterwards disappeared. He eventually decided to return to Spain where, in 1522, he secured a royal order prohibiting the change of capital. But it was too late; by then Pedrarias had transported the remaining citizenry of Darien to the Pacific by force, except for a few old people who could not move. Soon afterwards, those last were killed by Indians who set the place on fire, leaving nothing save a few lemon and orange trees as evidence of this first European settlement on the American mainland.

Pedrarias—"Furor Domini," as he was known to his subordinates—wanted to remain governor. His equally determined wife, Isabel de Bobadilla, in no way dismayed by climate, diet, disease, and discomfort, went back to Spain to intercede, to this end, on behalf of her husband. She traveled with her eldest son, Diego, taking with her a chest carrying pearls and gold. When she arrived, the new King Charles had gone to Germany— the civil war of the rebel councillors (*comuneros*) was raging (see chapter 32)—and in September 1520, she quite easily secured a confirmation of Pedrarias as governor. No doubt the judicious use of the jewels in her chest played their part.[28]

One cannot applaud the conduct of Pedrarias, but his resilience and willpower were admirable.

Book Six

CISNEROS

The pride of Cardinal Cisneros: the polyglot Bible that
he commissioned showed the text in seven languages.

"King Fernando! He is dead!"

"¡El rey don Fernando!" "He is dead!" Three times this happened.
Then the thirteen Spanish knights in the cathedral threw their ban-
ners to the ground and shouted, "Long live the Catholic Kings,
Queen Juana and King Charles."

Cries at Sainte-Gudule cathedral,
Brussels, 1516

King Fernando spent the early part of January 1516 as usual, on his travels.
What roads he had followed since he had married Isabel in 1469, what
strange parts of their joint kingdoms he had visited! Everywhere in Spain except for Asturias! He had just been at Plasencia for the wedding of a bastard
granddaughter and was on his way to Seville. We find him at Trujillo, the city
of the Pizarros, on January 2, and on January 11 and 20 at La Abertura and
Madrigalejo, small towns scarcely marked on any map, old or new. La Abertura, on a hilltop, had a number of lovely streams nearby. Of Madrigalejo,
nothing so positive could be said. It is small today, as it was in Don Fernando's day. The house where the King lodged remains, a single-story building unchanged and unimproved by time. In the distance, the King could
have seen the high-towered Moorish castle of Montsánchez. Close by flowed
the River Pizarrosa. It was not a strong current. Charles, Fernando's grandson and heir, would say of his grandparents' lead-covered coffins, below the
royal chapel of Granada, that they seemed to fill a "small space for so great a
glory." He would have said much the same had he ever seen the little house
in Madrigalejo.

These towns were in Extremadura, the land of the conquistadors, of
men such as Núñez de Balboa and Hernán Cortés and Francisco Pizarro,
Castilian captains already established in Cuba and Darien, respectively,
though the great monarchies, Mexico and Peru, that the two would win for
Castile had not yet even been heard of.

In Madrigalejo, Death laid its icy hand on this most successful king. It was, because of the Extremeño connection, an appropriate place to end his life, but he would not have thought so, even though he did not complain. Fernando was the last person to be sentimental, though he might have remembered how his wife Queen Isabel had besieged the place in 1478, in the civil war against La Beltraneja, using lombards and siege engines, and how she had subsequently given orders to destroy the castle.[1]

More important to Fernando would have been the fact that between Madrigalejo and Seville there lay the valley known as the Serena, whence came most of the fine wool, from merino sheep, that was used in Seville's textile industry. The flocks of the Mesta spent the winter there, and the wool would be delivered in April and May. Lora del Río, to the far south, was an important market for connections between the Serena and Seville, and no doubt Don Fernando had intended to approach the latter city by way of it. The principal buyers of wool in 1516 would be Genoese, as had been the case for many years past: all the famous names of rich families from Columbus's city appeared in the list of wool merchants.[2]

Fernando had united Castile, of which he was still Regent, and Aragon, of which he was King, in a way that has endured, with some hiccups of separatism, ever since. He had also conquered all Navarre south of the Pyrenees, and that, too, would remain part of Spain. Naples, thanks to the Gran Capitán, Fernández de Córdoba, was also a Spanish viceroyalty. These territories were managed by councils, all depending on either the Council of the Realm or that of Aragon, which were now dominated by university-educated civil servants—to the irritation of loyal old noblemen.

Some of these "new" men were with Fernando at Madrigalejo: for example, Lorenzo Galíndez de Carvajal, the "chronicler" and lawyer from Extremadura who seemed to be "the most correct and wise politician of his time," with "possibly the best legal mind in Castile, being honorable and a little cynical"[3]; the important Licenciado Luis Zapata, "El Rey Chiquito," venal but mellifluous in speech; and Francisco de Vargas, the treasurer of Castile, a gray personage, typical of civil servants in modern states, who was one of the reliable pillars on which the regime had been built.

Some have sought to emphasize that Fernando's solution of the problems that he inherited in Catalonia—tensions between the classes, in particular—was based on the reinvigoration of traditional customs. He had certainly made no attempt to blend the institutions of the two realms of Aragon and Castile. Spending only four years in the former during his thirty-seven-year reign, he relied on deputies, viceroys, in those dominions. He had done his utmost to show himself a king of all Spain.

Fernando, of course, also had responsibility in his last years for the New

World, where the new Spanish Empire, without as yet that name, was being founded. There was no Council of the Indies, no formal committee to govern these territories, and Fernando continued to leave most decisions on the subject to Fonseca, now Bishop of Burgos, and his embittered assistant, the *converso* from Aragon, Lope de Conchillos. Already there was to be seen among the group of secretaries who concerned themselves with the Indies the astute Francisco de los Cobos, a poor hidalgo from Úbeda, who was signing royal documents on the matter by 1515. Fernando himself still seems to have had little idea of what the Indies meant and saw them as interesting primarily for the possible financial contribution that they might offer to his enterprises in the Mediterranean.

The neglect of the Indies was Fernando's only serious mistake. But he was not the last Spanish king to prefer the Mediterranean to the Caribbean. A greater mistake was to trust so implicitly Bishop Fonseca, who chose people according to whether they came from a good family in Spain; a Bobadilla, an Ovando, a Ponce de León, an Arias, or a Velázquez seemed superior to someone who had come from nowhere: a Columbus, a Balboa, or a Cortés.

The four largest islands of the Caribbean—La Española, Cuba, Jamaica, and Puerto Rico—were, nevertheless, Spanish governorships, the last three being formally subordinate to the governor of the first, though the long absence in Spain of Diego Colón, the second Admiral of the Ocean Sea, had left an interregnum in the first of these islands. The Castilian Diego Velázquez, the Basque Francisco Garay (in succession to Juan Esquivel), and the Sevillano Juan Ponce de León now controlled the other three. An inquiry, or *residencia,* into the "columbine officials," excluding Diego Colón himself, had been embarked upon. Then, on the mainland, Pedrarias, the Castilian with *converso* blood, "the Gallant," still reigned in 1516 in uneasy tandem with Núñez de Balboa in Darien and Panama, while the Dominican prior Pedro de Córdoba, father of the Dominican mission in the New World, was planning a saintly colony near the Pearl Coast of Venezuela. All these colonies would soon have their spiritual leaders; in 1512, three bishops had been designated, for Santo Domingo, for Concepción de la Vega (also in La Española), and for Puerto Rico.

The decline of the indigenous population had at last begun to seem serious to settlers in this New World, less, it would appear, because of the tragedy that this spelled for the people concerned than because of the shortage of labor that it implied. Expeditions were frequent to the Bahamas (the Lucays), to Trinidad, and to both the Lesser Antilles and the mainland in search of slaves, usually financed by the leading men of La Española, including, as has been seen, the judges of the *audiencia*.[4] Still, the Dominican preacher Fray Antonio Montesinos and the priest Bartolomé de las Casas were in Spain to put the case for a new order in the treatment of the Indians. In these years, it would be fair to recognize that the gold produced in La Española had started to justify the great investment of effort that had begun there, and as yet no one suspected that the unsteady prices in Castile had anything to do with the import of precious metals from the Indies.[5]

The King was certainly dying. Was it because the medicine given him by Queen Germaine de Foix—said to have been based on the testicles of a bull—to stimulate his virility and enable her to give him a male heir to the throne had damaged his heart? That medicine, if it existed, failed—so much for the unity of the Crowns. But Fernando himself in these last years seems to have hoped for a Spain divided between a Habsburg in Castile and a Trastámara in Aragon rather than one country under a German.[6] Perhaps, though, after so many journeys, so many wars, such intrigues and brilliant arrangements, so many nights in so many uncomfortable beds in remote lodgings, Fernando was exhausted.

He was in his middle sixties, a fine age at which to die in the Renaissance. He had his last confession with that Friar Tomás de Matienzo who had been a member of his enlightened committee of Burgos on Indian problems. Then he summoned Galíndez de Carvajal, of the Council of the Realm, the secretary Zapata, and the treasurer Vargas. (Galíndez de Carvajal had just been appointed chief of the post office of the Casa de Contratación, a job that entailed supervision of all transatlantic mail for a time.)[7] Together they advised him to alter the will that he had made in favor of his second grandson, Fernando, whom he knew well since he had been brought up in Spain. The counselors suggested that unity between the advisers of the throne and the nobility would only be achieved if the will were changed to favor the elder Infante, Charles of Ghent, whom Fernando had never met.

Fernando the King accepted this advice without complaint.[8] The responsibility of these advisers for avoiding the "Fernandine succession" was considerable. They may have been mistaken. The Infante Fernando would have made a fine king who would have maintained himself in Spain and the New World and left the Low Countries and the Holy Roman Empire to his brother Charles.

After King Fernando's death, and until Charles arrived in Spain, the will specified that Cardinal Cisneros would once more be Regent in Castile; and Fernando's illegitimate son, Alonso de Aragón, Archbishop of Saragossa, would have that office in Aragon. Legally, Fernando had no right to make such dispositions in Castile, for he was himself a mere Regent, and his daughter, Juana, was already Queen regnant. But King Fernando had long realized that Juana was at least half demented and that, above all, authority of some kind was necessary.

The King, in that rural, "undecorated, and unfurnished"[9] house in a small town, Madrigalejo, in an impoverished part of Castile, wrote on January 22 to his heir, his grandson the Infante Carlos (it was thus that the Spaniards liked to think of him), an affectionate deathbed letter. He began by explaining "that it had pleased God our Lord to put us in such straits that we are more a dead man than a live one." Fernando regretted that he and Charles could not meet and that Charles could not come to Spain before his death. He also hoped that Charles would look after "our most dear and most loved wife"—Germaine.[10]

The King died soon after midnight on January 23, 1516.[11] A message was immediately sent to Charles in Flanders. But long before that reached him, Cardinal Cisneros, knowing of the King's instructions in respect of the Regency, left his palace in Alcalá de Henares and set off for the monastery of Guadelupe, which he reached on January 29. There a quickly assembled Council of the Realm confirmed his authority and regularized the legal position of his new government. His first act was to confine the Infante Fernando, still a potential rival to his brother Charles, to his lodging; and he also placed under restraint Gonzalo Núñez de Guzmán, the longtime preceptor of Fernando's.[12]

Cisneros, with the Infante Fernando, Queen Germaine, and some members of the Council of the Realm, such as Galíndez de Carvajal, thereupon left Guadelupe, via Puente del Arzobispo, Calera, and Talavera, for Madrid, where they lodged in the house of Pedro Saso de Castilla (in the still surviving Plazuela de San Andrés), the court being partly lodged in the Alcázar and partly in the ample cloisters of the Convent of San Jerónimo.

The news of King Fernando's death reached Malines, fifteen miles north of Brussels, where the Infante Charles was living with his intelligent aunt, the Archduchess Margaret, on February 10, 1516. His principal adviser, Guillermo de Chièvres, Seigneur de Croÿ, summoned all the Spanish officials in Flanders and promised not only to confirm them in their positions but to triple their salaries.[13]

These advisers and their friends revolved around three personalities: Charles himself, then aged sixteen; the Archduchess, his aunt, who once so many years ago had been married to the Infante Juan; and Chièvres. There was also a fourth influence, the austere and erudite Adrian of Utrecht.

The young heir Charles had been born on February 25, 1500, in Ghent, heart of the old Burgundian principality, and he was given the name of his great-grandfather, the impetuous last Duke of Burgundy.[14] Almost no one in Spain had been given the name of Charles until that time.[15] His namesake, the old Duke, exerted an influence: "No one was so consciously inspired by models of the past, or manifested such a desire to echo them, as Charles the Rash. In his youth, he made his attendants read out to him the exploits of Gawain and of Lancelot. . . ."[16] The young Charles of Ghent did the same.

Charles had been christened in the splendid church of Sainte-Gudule in Brussels on March 7, 1500. No representative of the court of Spain was present. The only Spaniard there was, indeed, Diego Ramírez Vilaescusa, then chaplain to Charles's mother, the Infanta Juana, and later bishop of Malaga. Margaret of Austria, recently back from Spain after the death of her husband, the Infante Juan, was a godmother. Given this background, it is scarcely surprising that Charles was a prince who, for the first fifteen years of his life, had no desire to be other than a Burgundian nobleman.

The court of Burgundy was known for elaborate and serious ritual, and its example gave Charles all his life noble principles, the necessity of a courtly bearing, the cult of the ambience of a great prince, the idea of knightly honor, and of fighting for the Christian faith, as embodied in the code of the Burgundian Order, the Golden Fleece. Burgundy also inculcated in Charles a sincere piety and an attachment both to the ideals of chivalry and to a rigorous court ceremonial. Was that the ideal of the passing age? Or was it that of a New World?[17] Charles seems to have always lived between two eras.

Charles was more drawn to bodily than intellectual exercise, a preference shared by all his pages,[18] and early in life he mastered the arts of hunting, jousting, and falconry. He could soon splinter an opponent's lance without losing his seat on his own horse.

Charles's childhood had been chiefly spent at Malines. It was an education marked at first by austerity bordering on indigence, being directed by the saintly scholar Adrian of Utrecht, from whom much of his own piety derived. But from 1509, the influence of the aristocratic Guillaume de Chièvres grew, and after 1515, the demands of Burgundian splendor grew dominant. Charles always showed a tendency toward being dressed "very richly and very gallantly."[19] His chivalrous grandfather, the Emperor Maximilian, was proud of him and said that he was glad that Charles was making such progress as a huntsman, for had it not been so, it might have been supposed that the boy was a bastard.[20]

Charles was richly endowed with good qualities, but from his earliest youth he was surrounded by rapacious courtiers. Vincenzo Querini, the Venetian representative in Brussels, said of Charles that he was "in all his actions cruel and willful [*voluntarioso*]; he also looked rather similar to Charles the Rash, in imitation of whom he well captured the strong chivalrous spirit." He added spitefully: "He has no value of any kind and is completely governed by others."[21]

This negative comment was unfair, but another Venetian, Lorenzo Pasqualigo, said of Charles: "He was of a mediocre stature and so thin that one cannot believe it, pale, melancholy, always with his mouth open."[22] Juan de Longhi thought that Charles was an unhealthy mixture of passivity and impatience. One ambassador said that he looked as if his eyes had been glued onto too long a face. But in England, where he had been in 1513 to present himself as a possible candidate for the hand of the Princess Mary, he had impressed everyone by his lanky dignity. The comments made about Charles in his early youth are a striking contrast to what would be said of him when he was more mature.

He had been proclaimed of age as duke of Burgundy on January 5, 1515, when he was fifteen and Maximilian thought that he would be ready to exercise authority. The Archduchess Margaret's Regency was over. The court changed. Charles then traveled in a leisurely fashion around the Low Countries and established himself in Brussels. Challenged to a ceremonial duel by Charles de Lannoy over the accusation that the music he loved was effeminate, he chose to fight with lances on large horses, and though he won in the end, his horse fell and for a long time the Prince bore signs of injuries.[23]

The influence of Charles's aunt had been decisive till 1515. Margaret of Austria, born on January 10, 1480, had been named after Margaret of York, her own godmother, the last wife of Charles the Rash. As a result of the Treaty of Arras, of December 1482, between France and the burghers of Ghent, she, "Madame Marguerite," became "Madame la Dauphine," the putative bride of the Dauphin Charles, the future King Charles VIII of France, nine years older than she. Her dowry had been substantial: Artois, the Franche-Comté, Mâcon, Auxerre, Bar-sur-Seine, and Noyon. She went to France at the age of three, being welcomed into French society at Hedins as "La Marguerite des Marguerites." She was duly betrothed to Charles and stayed in France, at Amboise, until 1491 as, first, dauphine and then, after Louis XI died, really as queen, being advised by the King's daughter,

Madame de Beaujeu ("Madame ma Bonne Tante"). In those happy days of royal childhood, Margaret had as her chief companion a green parrot. But in 1491, the young but already callous Charles insisted, for dynastic reasons, on marrying Anne of Brittany to bring that duchy to France. Margaret left Amboise, staying for a time at Melun in semicaptivity, but returning to Malines in June 1493.[24]

The next chapter in this princess's remarkable career occurred when two years later, on November 5, 1496, she married the beloved heir of King Fernando and Queen Isabel, the Infante Juan. After spending a few days with her brother Philip (not yet married to her future sister-in-law Juana), in the abbey of Middleburg, Margaret set off for Spain on January 22, 1497, stopping in England at Southampton to escape storms. She reached Santander and then met the Infante. They went together to Burgos, where the marriage was reenacted on April 3, 1497, in the Convent of the Holy Trinity. The honeymoon in the monastery took place before the wedding. Peter Martyr wrote: "If you saw her, you would think that you were contemplating Venus herself." Martyr also recalled "our prince, burning with love," who persuaded his parents "to suspend protocol in order to enable him to obtain the desired embraces" before the ceremony. But on June 13, Martyr thought the prince was bearing himself sadly. He died on October 4: "There was buried the hope of all Spain," Martyr added. Perhaps, as mentioned earlier, he died from eating a dirty salad at the *feria* in Salamanca. But the Habsburgs always said that he had made love too often with his wife.

Margaret was pregnant, but she had a premature birth of a daughter who soon died, and once again she returned to the Low Countries.

The young widow was affianced again in September 1501, to Duke Philibert of Savoy. She traveled again through France to Dôle, where a marriage by proxy was celebrated, the "Grand Bâtard," Philibert's overbearing brother, standing proxy for the Duke. Then she went south and, at a convent near Geneva, met Philibert. She soon outmaneuvered the rest of the family and essentially took over the government of the duchy, controlling the administration from a château at the Pont d'Ain.

But once again tragedy struck, for, alas, Philibert too soon died after a boar hunt in September 1504, much as Philip, the husband of Juana, would die, drinking too much water when he was hot from exercise. Margaret had her pearls ground down to make the best medicine—to no avail. She comforted herself by creating a lovely memorial at the church at Brou, thereby fulfilling a vow made by her long-dead mother-in-law, Marguerite de Bourbon. But she lost her task of governing Savoy.

Margaret's brother Philip next sought to make her queen of England,

The Europe of Archduchess Margaret

Stockholm
Edinburgh
Dublin
Copenhagen
London   Middleburg
Southampton   Utrecht
Antwerp
Brussels   Malines
Aix-la-Chapelle
Paris   Prague
Melun
Amboise
Dole   Munich   Vienna
Bourg Brou   Innsbruck Budapest
Santander   Lyon   Geneva
Turin   Venice
Burgos
Lisbon   Salamanca
Rome

Countries successively under
the authority of Margaret

Savoy	lands of the Habsburgs
Low Countries	—— Holy Roman Empire
Franche Comté	

and a contract of marriage with the future Henry VIII was even signed in March 1506. Margaret wisely refused the entanglement, even if it might have been good for England if she had accepted. Maximilian then named her Regent of the Netherlands. She left the Duchy of Savoy and on March 18, 1507, was formally established in the government of one of the richest territories. She took numerous Savoyards to assist her, such as the hardworking Italian Mercurino de Gattinara. She also became foster mother to the Infante Charles and established herself at Malines, in a palace where Margaret of York had been happy until her death in 1504. The Archduchess surrounded herself with poets, musicians, and painters. Her library became famous. She played chess with the Savoyards, and backgammon with Chièvres.

Margaret soon became engaged in high diplomacy, and a famous alliance, the League of Cambrai against Venice, was her triumph. Her inclination was anti-French, pro-English, and somewhat aggressive, unlike that of the prudent Chièvres, who would succeed her as the prime mover of policy making. She had to withdraw from power after her imprudent arrest in 1513 of Juan Manuel, the leader of the Spanish courtiers in Flanders, who was a Knight of the Golden Fleece, and she had to defend herself at a angry meeting of the council of that order. But the accession to the throne of François I of France changed matters back in Margaret's favor. Her motto was *"Fortune, infortune fort une"*: Misfortune as well as good fortune makes one strong.

The dominant influence, however, over Charles by 1516 was Chièvres, who was by then grand chancellor of Burgundy. He was a cultivated aristocrat who had been ambassador to France. He was governor of Flanders in 1505 in Philip's absence in Spain. From 1509 onward, he was grand chamberlain to the future Charles V: "The truth is that, as long as he lived, Monsieur de Chièvres governed me," Charles himself once commented. Chièvres slept in the same room as Charles and thus could have his eyes on him all night as well as all day. Later, Charles told the accomplished Venetian ambassador Gasparo Contarini, future cardinal and essayist, that he had early learned the value of Chièvres and for a long time subordinated his will to his. Chièvres's fine, intelligent, and observant eyes and good manners made him an effective counterweight to Margaret, though he always seemed "haughty, ambitious, and immoral."[25] When asked by the French ambassador Genlis in 1515 why he made the prince work so hard, he said: "Cousin, I am the keeper and guardian of his youth. When I die, I want him to be free to act, but also to understand his own affairs and to have been trained to know what work is."[26]

Chièvres was the head of the government in Flanders between 1515 and 1520. He was staunchly pro-French, where Margaret had been hostile; his moment of glory would be the Treaty of Noyon, of August 13, 1516, between Charles and François I. That treaty, which ended the era of enmity with France, was intended to create eternal friendship between the two kings, resolving the problems of both Naples and Navarre. Charles, aged sixteen, promised to marry Louise, daughter of François I (she was then a year old), who would bring with her as her dowry all the claims that France had on Naples. Charles also undertook to hear the complaints of the old royal family of Navarre, the Albrets.[27] (Maximilian adhered to this treaty by the Treaty of Brussels of December 3, 1516.)[28]

The fourth adviser to Charles, Adrian of Utrecht, was dean of St. Peter's, Louvain, and afterwards bishop of Utrecht. He had been born Florencio Adriano Boeyens in Utrecht in 1459, the son of a ship's carpenter. He was a member of the monastic order known as the Brothers of the Common Life. He went to Louvain University, where he became a doctor of theology in 1491 and its chancellor in 1497. Named by Maximilian to be preceptor of Charles in 1507, he was sent by the Archduchess Margaret to be the ambassador of Flanders in Spain, when in 1515 the King seemed to be toying with naming his other grandson, the Infante Fernando, Charles's brother, as his heir. Adrian had a tranquilizing effect on Fernando; "a prudent pilot of a great ship given to rolling on the ocean," Peter Martyr called him.[29] He was now associated, though, as "ambassador," by Cisneros with his government of Spain, a role that he (and Charles, after hearing the will of his grandfather) accepted, but he was a timid councillor, for he was as ignorant of Spain as he was of Spanish. He could communicate in Latin, however, with those clerics and learned men who knew that language, such as, for example, Bartolomé de las Casas, whose command of it was good.

Cisneros, who was now eighty years old, received a friendly letter from Charles at the end of February 1517 (the first since Fernando's death),[30] and on March 9, Cisneros sent his first decree to the Indies, in respect of taxes, signed by himself (F. Cardinalis) and by Bishop Adrian (Adrianus ambasciator), in the name of Juana, there being no mention of Charles. All seemed calm. Cisneros was taking over command effectively. On March 4, the Council of the Realm had written sensibly to Charles saying that "there is no necessity during the life of the Queen, our lady, your mother, to entitle yourself King, since to do that would be to diminish the honor and the reverence that is due by both divine and human law [to her] . . . and because, in consequence of the death of the Catholic King, your grandfather, you have not acquired any more rights than you had before, since this realm was not his."[31]

The Regent of Aragon, Archbishop Alonso, however, sent his half-nephew Charles a warmer message of support, repeating that he had often urged the late King to insist that he come to Spain; while on March 8, Alonso Manrique de Lara, Bishop of Badajoz and one of Charles's supporters in Flanders, sent a long letter to Cisneros about the mood in Brussels: "Charles has a good disposition but he knows scarcely anything of Spain and is quite ignorant of its language, being completely under the influence of Flemish counselors, especially of Chièvres." The Bishop emphasized to Cisneros the greed of the Flemings. He also said that there were some Spaniards in Brussels who spoke critically of the Inquisition, "in such a way that people are beginning to ask if they could arrange for the Inquisition to be brought to an end." He denounced the excessive respect for France, which was the policy of

Chièvres, who, he recalled, had arranged for Charles to sign his letters to François I as "your humble servant and vassal. . . ."[32] Finally, he thought that Charles would soon be proclaimed king. That would have been news to Cisneros, to whom Manrique had once been chaplain.

On the evening of March 13, 1516, while Manrique de Lara's letter was still on its way to Spain, a procession lit by torches set off from the palace in Brussels to the cathedral, Sainte-Gudule, to mark the funeral of King Fernando, with Bishop Manrique presiding. The prince, in a cowl of mourning, rode on a mule. There was a requiem Mass, and Bishop Manrique, who not for nothing was a cousin of the poet Jorge de Manrique, preached a sermon on the vanity of human wishes. Perhaps he privately recalled that his grandfather Rodrigo had had as his slogan: "Our family does not descend from kings, but kings descend from us." The walls of the church were hung with black brocade, and there were hundreds of tapers.

Next day a quite different procession went to Sainte-Gudule. Thirteen Spanish knights bore the banners of Fernando's kingdoms, and three other knights carried a shield, a helmet, and a sword, the symbols of knighthood. Charles entered the cathedral last and sat in the chancel. Again, the Mass was introduced and sung by Bishop Manrique. The herald of the Order of the Golden Fleece then turned to the congregation and from the altar steps called, *"El rey don Fernando!"* From the depths of the church the reply came: "He is dead." Three times this happened. Then the thirteen Spanish knights in the cathedral threw their banners to the ground and shouted, "Long live the Catholic Kings, Queen Juana and King Charles." The new King flung off his mourning cowl and received a sword from the hands of Bishop Manrique. He brandished it aloft, and the congregation shouted, *"¡Viva el rey!"*[33] In a sense, this was something of a coup d'état,[34] since, as the Council of the Realm in Castile had tried to insist, the will of Fernando had left Charles as "governor" of Spain, no more. The extraordinary act of assertion was partly because Charles's Flemish advisers thought that he would stand a better chance of succeeding his other grandfather, Maximilian, as emperor if he were a king and not just governor of a realm. But for Spain the ceremony marked a decisive step toward the establishment of Charles and the Habsburgs on the throne of the Catholic Kings.

The news of this proclamation reached Madrid a week later, on March 21, accompanied by orders from Charles to Cisneros that he, the Cardinal and Regent, the Council of the Realm, the great noblemen, and the cities should immediately proclaim him king. Charles added that it was his "determined will" that he should be proclaimed thus. The letter named Cisneros "prince," not a title previously used in Castile, and gave him authority as regent until Charles himself arrived.

This decision of Charles provoked altercation among many leading people in Castile, who thought that he seemed to want to steal from the Queen the title that only she possessed. There was high talk at a meeting attended by both noblemen and the prelates in Madrid, a discussion that was cut short by Cisneros who insisted that "he had never had any intention of doing anything other than accept Charles as king";[35] and he summoned old friends of King Fernando, such as the Duke of Alba, the Admiral of Castile (Fadrique Enríquez), and the cultivated Marquis of Villena, and announced to them that he proposed to proclaim Charles as king. He repeated this at a meeting of the Council of the Realm in the Plaza de la Paja, opening the windows onto the balcony to show the noblemen his artillery in the square below, thus giving rise to a famous myth that he ordered his men to open fire before them, saying to the Duke of Infantado and the Count of Benavente: "With these powers that the King gave me, I am governing and shall govern Spain until the prince our lord comes to govern us."[36] He arranged that Charles should be proclaimed king in Toledo, where Pedro López de Ayala, the Count of Fuensalida, raised banners for him.

On March 31, a meeting in Madrid of counselors, grandees, and courtiers recognized Charles as king, if jointly with Juana, who was named first in the order. A few days later a brother of the Count of Fuensalida, Canon Diego López de Ayala, left Madrid for Flanders as Cisneros's representative to explain to Bishop Manrique and Charles what had been done. Cisneros and Adrian (now a cardinal) wrote from Madrid to all sources of authority (*las autoridades*) in the country, not just the municipalities but also the noblemen and leading clergy, saying that Charles would reign as king in conjunction with his mother.[37] Soon after that, the Infante Fernando, who never demonstrated any sign of independent action (he was still only thirteen years old), was confined to his house. Cisneros's decisive actions saved Spain for Charles. Had he not so acted, anything could have happened. A little later Cisneros sent a friend of his, Rodrigo Sánchez de Mercado, Bishop of Majorca, to Tordesillas to change the way that Queen Juana was looked after. There had already been local protests against the iniquity of her guardian, Luis Ferrer, and the Bishop ensured that he left forever. He also arranged that Juana, with her daughter Catalina, should have better access to gardens.[38]

Naturally pleased, Charles in Brussels approved what Cisneros was doing. The courtiers all preferred the Cardinal to what they considered to be a Jewish clique—the *conversos*—in Flanders. They were pleased that Cis-

neros had established order in Spain, that Adrian had been associated with
him in the government, and that the proclamation of the Infante Fernando
had been avoided.

Charles spent much of the next six months sending recommendations
to Cisneros for promotions of people whom he liked or who had worked
with his father. But he made no move to go himself to Spain. A fleet was assembled, but on October 10, Charles permitted those ships to disperse. He
did seek to interfere, however, in Cisneros's government. For example, outraged by the casual acts of violence willfully carried out by noblemen up and
down Spain, Cisneros conceived an idea of asking "the Men of Order" (*gente
de ordenanza*) to provide a militia to which each city would make a contribution proportionate to its population: Ávila and Segovia would thus send
2,000 men, Toledo 3,500, and so on. By this method there would have been
established something like a national army or police force of about 30,000,
able to intervene when and where the Cardinal thought right. The idea was
inspired by the old Hermandad. It was perhaps appropriate that in Spain a
cardinal should be the man to plan the first regular army. But the noblemen
were against the scheme and ensured that Charles, in Brussels, vetoed it.[39]
This was partly because of the influence of the Burgos *converso,* Bishop Ruiz
de la Mota, "el maestre Mota," the almoner to Charles.

Then there came a bombshell as far as the Indies were concerned: on
April 24, Cisneros dismissed Bishop Fonseca. This was more because Cisneros believed him to be corrupt than because he was against his Indian
policies. But Las Casas saw this as a vindication of his own and Montesinos's
ideas. A few days before, Cisneros had ordered Canon Sancho de Matienzo
in person to bring him forthwith all the gold and jewelry deposited in the
Casa de Contratación. Next, a friend of Las Casas's, Bartolomeu Díaz, royal
pilot (*comitre del rey*) in Seville, sent a report to Cisneros on corrupt practices in that body.

Las Casas himself, meanwhile, thwarted by the death of the King and of
his royal audience, had arrived at Cisneros's court in Madrid. It had been
his intention to travel on to Flanders to lobby the courtiers of King Charles
about the sufferings of the Indians, but before he left Madrid, about March
15, he sent a letter to "Ambassador Adrian" in Latin in which he gave a dark
picture of conditions in Cuba: he talked of excessive work in the mines, of
badly fed servants who were made to sleep on the floor, of the forced abandonment of women and children, of the employment of Indians as beasts
of service, of the absence of Sunday rest days, of hard work building roads,
and of cruel punishments.[40] Adrian was horrified. He went to Cisneros to
expostulate.

Cisneros already knew something of the tragedy in the Indies and received from Las Casas a Spanish translation of what he had sent to Adrian. Las Casas also wrote to King Charles about "possible reforms."[41] His letter made twelve suggestions for improving the welfare of the indigenous population.

This was the first of many such programs suggested by Las Casas in the next few years—ideas for reforms carefully worked out, meticulously written, wonderfully optimistic, read by the greatest men, and indeed generally well received. He proposed, first, the abolition of all *encomiendas* and other types of forced work; second, he wanted the maintenance of existing laws only if they protected the Indians. Third, all existing governors and officials should be replaced by others. Fourth, the Indians were to be collected into communities, each one of which was to have a hospital, shaped in the form of a cross, with fifty beds in each section and, in the middle, an altar so that all might see the Mass from their beds. If the Indians needed animals, the Spaniards were to lend them half of what they had.[42] Fifth, though the Indians would be free, they would continue to work for the Spaniards. But they would have time to cultivate their own plots. There would also be an annual rotation of Indians to serve cities and *villas*. The Indians would have the best land, even if it was already in Spanish hands. Sixth, some Indians would, of course, work as servants. Seventh, Spaniards dispossessed of Indians would be indemnified by the purchase of their cattle and other agricultural products, paid for with the first or second melting down of gold. Finally, all settlers could have their own sugar mills and seek gold on their own account. The King would grant licenses to import both black and white slaves, and African or other slaves were to be placed in the mines instead of Indians.[43] The fact that idealistic priests wanted to compensate for the shortage of Indian labor by introducing black slaves from Africa shows that the Renaissance was preparing to adopt classic behavior in more ways than one.

Las Casas also recommended the creation of mixed Hispanic-Indian communities. The new cities of the Indies would be reinforced by forty workers coming from Spain with their families, to each one of which there would be allocated five Indians. Of the benefits subsequently obtained, one part would go to the King, and the rest would be shared between the farmer and his Indians. In time, Indians and Spaniards would intermarry and so would form a single "republic," which would become the most peaceful and Christian in the world, "for the sons of one race would marry the daughters of the other." This encouragement to *mestizaje* was remarkable, being, like so many other aspects of the program, utopian. Las Casas thought that there were many poor Spaniards who would be delighted to find a new life in the

Indies: "Thus the land will be made fruitful and its people multiply, because they will plant all manner of trees and vegetables. Your Majesty's revenues will be increased and the islands ennobled and become, therefore, the best and richest in the world. . . ."

Meanwhile, ships going to the Bahamas would be controlled by the King, and each one would have on board both a Dominican and a Franciscan friar, who would decide which island was or was not habitable on Castilian terms. If they turned out to be inhabitable, a *"casa del rey"* would be built in such islands as a center of evangelization.

An ecclesiastic on each island would be available to protect the Indians and punish settlers who mistreated them. Indians were not to be punished for wrongdoings in the same way as Spaniards. All priests would be properly educated in matters relating to the Indians. Indians were not to be moved from one island to another. The Inquisition would be established, "insomuch as two heretics have already been discovered and burned there." Then "the books on Indian matters by Dr. Palacios Rubios and Maestro Matías de Paz, formerly professor of Valladolid," would be printed and sent to the islands "so that the Spaniards there may realize that Indians are men, are free, and must be treated as such."

Finally, a supervisor would oversee everything. Priests would instruct the Indians in religion. Graduates would teach them Spanish. Physicians, surgeons, and chemists would be drafted to serve them, lawyers would come to represent them in legal matters. Indians would be taught to sit on benches and to eat from tables. They were not to sleep on the ground. They would carry their hammocks wherever they went. Two or three beasts of burden would "always be kept on hand to be ready to bring in sick Indians [to the hospitals] wherever necessary." The seventy-four officials to be appointed would meanwhile cost over 3 million maravedís every year, apart from the cost of their animals.[44]

This remarkable letter can be compared to Macaulay's famous "minute" on education in India. Macaulay wanted Indians made into upper-class Englishmen. Las Casas wanted his Indians made into respectable and socially responsible Castilian Catholics. His scheme was put to a committee of the usual advisers on affairs of the Indies: the cousin of the King, Hernando de Vega; the secretary Zapata; the able Galíndez de Carvajal; the Dominican provincial Pedro de Córdoba; the lawyer Palacios Rubios; and the Bishop of Ávila, Francisco Ruiz, "El Abulense," Cisneros's adviser on Indian matters (who, it will be remembered, had briefly been in La Española with Bobadilla). All sorts of views were further considered: from those of settlers who wished to treat the Indians purely as beasts of burden, with no qualifications, to the curious idea that Aristotle was right that there were laws that proclaimed that white people were superior to those who were black and brown. Finally, the radical humanist approach, reflected by Montesinos in 1511 and by Las Casas himself in 1516, was also discussed.

Among the matters studied at the end of May was a memorial by Gil González Dávila, accountant of La Española, who urged that two sugar mills and a sawmill be built, as well as plantations of cotton and sugar. The cultivation of wheat and vines would be carried out in order to avoid import bills. González Dávila also suggested the encouragement as colonists of good Andalusians who knew about farming, for whom the passage would be paid. They would be given land on which to produce wheat. He suggested that there should be a melting down every two months for two or three days, not just once a year. He thought, however, that the position of escaped slaves would be easier if the universal enslavement of the Indians were declared.[45]

His memorandum led to another by Las Casas.[46] That took as its point of departure the then forgotten item in the will of Isabel in favor of the Indians. It argued that King Fernando ("to whom it was to be hoped that God would grant a good paradise")[47] had wanted the Indians to be looked after by benign *encomenderos*. Las Casas also demanded that the Laws of Burgos be fulfilled, and argued the benefit of restoring the officials of Diego Colón in La Española, while denouncing the protégés of Fonseca. Montesinos and a Dominican friar, Domingo de Betanzos, from Galicia, wrote to the court on June 4, 1516, recommending that they pay attention to Las Casas, and attacking the suggestion that Indians were unsuitable for marriage or for the faith: "The only Christians who said that were settlers who wanted the Indians for digging gold."[48]

Cisneros asked "the Abulense," Francisco Ruiz, to report on whether Las Casas was right. Ruiz wrote a paper on the matter. In this, he argued that Indians should be taken away from people who were absentees. Like Las Casas and, indeed, like Dávila, he agreed that workers in Castile should be sent to the islands. Ruiz also thought that the recently founded Santa Marta, in what is now Colombia, should become the main port of the Indies.

But he added: "Indians are malicious people who are able to think up ways to harm Christians, but they are not capable of natural judgment or of receiving the faith, nor do they have other virtues required for conversion and salvation. . . . They need, just as a horse or beast does, to be directed and governed by Christ."[49]

This intolerant view was reinforced by the arrival in Castile of Pánfilo de Narváez and Antonio Velázquez, the representatives (*procuradores*) from Cuba. The first, as we have seen, had been Diego Velázquez's second in command in the conquest of that island and before that of Esquivel's in Jamaica; while the second was one of the Governor's many cousins. The two accused Las Casas of being "a man of no weight, of little authority, and less credit, who speaks of what he does not know nor has seen, for reasons which are themselves contradictory."[50] Cisneros immediately cut this short: Las Casas's reputation now stood high with him. They were a curious combination: the austere Cardinal and the ever ingenious agitator. Yet the two served the Crown well.

27

"Go back and see
what is happening"

Cisneros asked: "In whom can we confide? Go back there yourself and
see what is happening."

*Cisneros to Las Casas at the time of the
mission of the priors to La Española, 1517*

At the end of June 1516, Cardinal Cisneros, surrounded by such contrasting
advice about what to do in the Indies, made a remarkable decision. He had
sought without success to find among royal officials a man who would truly
pursue justice in the Indies. So he decided to request certain priors of monasteries of the Jeronymite order to perform that task. In a letter to Charles explaining this unprecedented decision, he condemned new sinecures in the
Indies (for example, those of the courtier Hernando de Vega). He pointed out
that the Indians who worked as servants were free, not slaves, and should be
treated as such. He thought that the Crown should possess neither Indians
nor farms. He denounced the old courtiers and servants of the Catholic
Kings, an obvious reference to Fonseca and to Conchillos, without mentioning their names, who, he said, had been corrupted by the concession of too
many private interests. He referred to the visit of Las Casas to the late King on
his deathbed, "but since he had died, there could be no further remedy."

This letter probably owed much to Las Casas, who, because of his energy, charm, and persistence, was becoming every day more influential. The
idea of asking Jeronymite priors to form the government in La Española
was, however, that of Cisneros himself. Las Casas had suggested that Fray
Reginaldo de Montesinos, a Dominican, too, and a brother of Father Antonio, might be nominated. But Cisneros decided against nominating either
Franciscans or Dominicans, in order "to avoid what they might do in favor
of one or the other."[1] The Jeronymites had several advantages: first, they had
a good reputation as administrators; second, their recent statute of purity of
blood meant that there were few *conversos* among them. That counted posi-

tively with the austere Cisneros. Finally, the difficulties between moderniz-
ers and reactionaries that affected both mendicant orders did not exist with
the Jeronymites. The order had no experience, it is true, in the New World.
But that seemed an advantage to Cisneros.

Cisneros sent an emissary, Dignidad de Tesorero, to talk with the General
of the Jeronymite order, Father Pedro de Mora, who was then at the monastery of San Bartolomé de Lupiana in Guadalajara. He told him that the
Cardinal thought that up till then no one sent to the Indies had been free of
the "greed" that was so notorious. Now was the possibility for a real change.

In late July, Cisneros, Cardinal Adrian (now Bishop of Tolosa and, quite
inappropriately, Inquisitor of Aragon), and Bishop Ruiz of Ávila talked with
Gonzalo de Frías, prior of Santa María de Armedilla, near Cuéllar; Santa
Cruz, prior of La Sisla, near Toledo; and the prior of San Leonardo, near
Alba de Tormes. Cisneros explained to the priors that the Indians seemed to
be rational persons but that their cultural backwardness obliged Spain to
convert and civilize them, submitting them not to slavery but to a moderate
level of service. Cisneros asked his friends for the names of two or three men
who could govern but at the same time convert the Indians. He asked the
prior of the Jeronymite monastery in Madrid to provide him with similar
names.[2]

The court met these priors in that same monastery of San Jerónimo,
Madrid. The court (including Fonseca!) sat in the lower choir near the sac-
risty, where the priors of Sisla, Armedilla, Madrid, San Leonardo, and others
were gathered. Several priors were enthusiastic about the suggestion of Cisneros, including Fray Cristóbal de Frías, then the leading theologian of the
order. Shortly, three priors were nominated for the reformation of the Indies: Luis de Figueroa of La Mejorada, Olmedo, the favorite priory of Fernando and Isabel, who was originally from Seville; the prior of San Jerónimo
de Buenaventura, outside Seville; and Bernardino de Manzanedo, prior of
Santa Marta, near Zamora, an ugly but virtuous monk, who was balanced,
young, and still robust.[3]

Here in the Jeronymite monastery in Madrid, Las Casas first launched
his famous propaganda cannonade of figures. He insisted that Bartolomeo
Colón had said that there had been 1.1 million Indians in La Española in
1492. But now there were only 12,000.[4] Almost all Las Casas's statistics were
exaggerated, these more than most.

Cisneros asked the lawyer Palacios Rubios to help him work out a plan
for the good government of the Indies, and he consulted Las Casas, who
drew up a scheme, in collaboration with Fray Reginaldo Montesinos. This

plan, which bore a close relation to what Las Casas had suggested earlier, was accepted, with minor changes.[5]

Early in August 1516 the prior-proconsuls received their instructions. First, they were "to think and observe what was best for the service of God and the instruction of the Indians in our faith, for their own good, as also for the settlers of those islands and, whatever you think should be provided, provide it."[6] The benefit to the Indians was to be placed ahead of that of the settlers. Then, in any charges against the Christians for ill-treating Indians, Indians could thereafter be called as witnesses. Dominicans and Franciscans already in La Española were to be interpreters. The settlers and a few *caciques* should be called together and told that Indian rights were to be maintained: for example, the rights to life, not to be ill-treated, to personal security, to dignity, to culture—but not, of course, to religion. Indians, too, were to have the right to hold meetings and to talk with others. There would be in effect a "republic of Indians," living in free communities, and there would be a "republic of Spaniards."[7] One could not in the circumstances of that era have expected a more humane plan.

On August 8, 1516, Cisneros wrote to Sancho de Matienzo at the Casa de Contratación in Seville, asking him for "a good and secure ship that might take some Jeronymites to La Española." There were protests at these strange appointments. Antonio Velázquez and Gil González Dávila waited for the friars outside Las Casas's lodging in Madrid and shouted that he was their "chief enemy . . . a perverse and evil man." The friars went to stay at the hospital of Santa Catalina de los Donados, where several men back from the Indies tried to convince them to take the settlers' view of the position in the Indies, not that of Las Casas.

The friars went home to bid goodbye to their monasteries, but the prior of San Jerónimo de Buenaventura decided not to persist with the plan. There volunteered in his stead Alonso de Santo Domingo, prior of San Juan de Ortega, near Burgos, who had been an energetic reformer of the monastery of Uclés in 1504. By 1516 he was, however, aged and inappropriate. There was also added the equally old Fray Juan de Salvatierra. Fray Luis de Figueroa, prior of La Mejorada, would be the superior of the mission. Palacios Rubios talked to these three priors and was shocked to find that Fray Luis seemed to have already been won over by the friends of the treasurer in Santo Domingo, Pasamonte, and appeared disposed to be hostile to the Indians. Palacios went to Cisneros to tell him that whatever the merits of nominating priors, the actual appointments were mistaken. But Cisneros was suffering from colitis, and even Palacios Rubios was weakened by gout. The tragedy is that even before they set out, these Jeronymite commissars had begun to turn against what Cisneros wanted. But, as is often the case in politics, the Cardinal knew that it was too late to go back on what he had decided: Las Casas went to see Cisneros and told him of his and Palacios Rubios's doubts. Cisneros said, shocked, "In whom can we confide? Go back there yourself and see what is happening."[8] Las Casas maintained his optimism and prepared to set out once more, with his own instructions.[9]

Cisneros also named Alonso de Zuazo, a disciple of Palacios Rubios, a clever lawyer from Segovia who had been at the college of the Cardinal in Valladolid, as the official to conduct the *residencia* of the old judges of the *audiencia* of La Española, as well as of other officials. He was to operate under the direction of "the pious fathers." The instructions for the priors were signed on September 18, by Cisneros and Adrian. They contained no explicit order to be kind to the Indians: "You should know that we have been informed of the many injuries and wrongs that the Indians of these islands have received and are still receiving from the Christians who . . . are there, and the clamors from the part of the said Indians to the effect that they are in many ways merely prisoners." Cisneros wanted the Indians "to be properly indoctrinated in our Christian religion and live as men of reason."[10] The priors were to have the power to suspend officials and also to fill such places temporarily. They were to be neither governors nor judges, but "high commissioners for the protection of Indians." They were to think of themselves as in control of Cuba, Jamaica, Puerto Rico, and *"tierra firme"*—Panama/Darien—as well as of La Española.[11] They had in theory more responsibility in the Indies, therefore, than Diego Colón had had, since his writ had never extended to Pedrarias's principality on the isthmus.

In October 1516 the designated Jeronymite priors reached Seville. They showed themselves happy with the civil servants of the Casa de Contratación, but suspicious of Las Casas. The latter explained that he wanted to travel to the Indies on the same boat as they in order to inform them in detail of what was going on. But the priors said that Las Casas's presence would destroy their peace of mind. Actually, they delayed for some time in Seville and, against the explicit ruling of the Cardinal, embarked on a ship that was carrying fourteen or fifteen black slaves entrusted to the captain by their masters.[12] This vessel was the *San Juan,* a ship partly owned by Diego Rodríguez Pepiño and partly by Luis Fernández de Alfaro. They also delayed for eleven days at Sanlúcar de Barrameda and finally departed on November 11, 1516, seen off by the shipowners and López de Recalde, the accountant of the Casa de Contratación. Las Casas sailed on another vessel, the *Trinidad,* accompanied by four servants and his library. That vessel planned to stop in

San Juan, Puerto Rico, in order to deposit cargo. Among the other passengers was Gonzalo de Sandoval, from Medellín, in Extremadura, a youth who would eventually play a great part in the conquest of Mexico.

The co-owner of the *San Juan,* Luis Fernández de Alfaro, had been a sea captain and then a merchant. His career illustrates well the rise of a Sevillano captain to a position of significance in this first generation of the settlement of the New World. First of all, he was a *converso.*[13] He appears in records as master of the *San Juan,* bound in 1504 for Santo Domingo, borrowing 32,000 maravedís from a well-known banker, also a *converso,* Pedro de Jerez.[14] On August 29, 1506, the youthful Hernán Cortés paid Alfaro 11 ducats (4,125 maravedís) to take him to the Indies; and Cortés evidently maintained an association with Alfaro, who later sold him armaments and other goods, in combination with the silversmith Juan de Córdoba.[15] The same year there is a reference to Francisco de Morales, who, like Cortés, would go to Cuba after 1511, paying 12,000 maravedís to Alfaro for carrying him, his wife, and his daughter, as well as a "box of merchandise," to Santo Domingo.[16] Still in 1506, a certain Constanza Fernández sold this merchant "one black slave born in Guinea" (*una esclava negra natural de Guinea*) for 8,500 maravedís—presumably she came via Lisbon.[17] In the next year or two, Alfaro is remembered as going to the New World as both owner and master of ships, sometimes carrying back gold for the King.[18]

By his next appearance in the records of Seville, the following year, Alfaro had converted himself into a merchant: Francisco de Lizaur, the secretary to Ovando, and Licenciado Alonso de Maldonado, the judge, both of Santo Domingo, obliged themselves to pay him, as a "merchant," 27,000 maravedís of gold, which Lizaur owed him for an unnamed public contract.[19] In 1507, a well-known captain, Ambrosio Sánchez, agreed with Alfaro to carry "all the merchandise that he wanted to sell in La Española."[20] In 1512, we hear of the establishment of "a mercantile company composed of him, Gaspar de Villadiego, and Fernando de Carrión," with a capital of 1.6 million maravedís. By 1513, Alfaro had also become a banker and money changer, and he supplied Pedrarias's fleet bound for Darien with a large quantity of linen, from which to make cushions, sheets, pillows, and sailcloth, as well as all the barrels necessary for the water of the fleet. The company was closed down in 1517, with Alfaro making a profit of over 600,000 maravedís.[21] By that time he was co-owner of the *San Juan.* We shall find him busy again in relation to Cortés and the conquest of Mexico, having become by then a partner of the silversmith Juan de Córdoba.

Soon after the departure of Las Casas and the priors, a letter arrived at court from Fray Pedro de Córdoba directed to the first-named, saying that he thought the Crown should hand over to the religious orders (Dominicans and Franciscans) 100 leagues of the South American coast near Cumaná. If 100 leagues could not be provided, Las Casas was to ask for 10 leagues, or at least an island. Córdoba added that if these requests were not agreed, he would recall all the Dominicans from the New World, for it seemed no use preaching "when those Indians see those who call themselves Christians acting in opposition to Christian ideals." What the Dominicans desired was administrative responsibility for a large stretch of territory, for Fray Pedro was in no way downcast by the deaths of his namesake and the lay brother Garcés. Their experience told him that the mistake was to have such a small representation on the South American coast.

But Fonseca, who read the letter in Las Casas's absence, said that one could not give 100 leagues of savage coast to monks without making adequate provision for their defense. He was quite against making any such grant, but in the end, Córdoba never withdrew the Dominicans.

In La Española the interregnum continued, with Diego Colón in Spain, but with his wife, María de Toledo, maintaining something like a tropical court in Santo Domingo. The treasurer, Pasamonte, and the judges were the effective governors, though, awaiting the arrival of the priors, whom they expected to be able to persuade to accept their own point of view—about the nature of Indian labor, slaves, and mines. Presumably they had received news from their friends in Spain about the likely attitudes of the superior, Fray Luis de Figueroa. Their slaving expeditions were of course continuing. In 1516, there were eight such to the north coast of South America from San Juan alone.

One of these, organized by Antón Cansino, one more sea captain from Palos, that home of sailors, was denounced by the Dominicans, recalling the prohibition on the seizure of slaves in the zone of the missions. The government ordered the newly appointed judge—and the Governor of San Juan, Sancho Velázquez de Cuéllar (another member of that family so ubiquitous in the upper reaches of Spanish administration)—to leave the slaves in jail until their case was solved. But Cansino gave Judge Vázquez de Ayllón a present of pearls worth 22,500 maravedís, and he allowed the slaves to be sold. That same autumn of 1516, a similar expedition led by two captains from San Juan, Puerto Rico, Juan Gil and Maese Antonio Catalán, carried out such barbarities against the Indians that even the hard-bitten *Audiencia* in Santo Domingo condemned them. Gil was imprisoned in the common prison, where he died.[22]

The coast of Pedrarias's territory, and the land a little to its north in Central America, had become the focus of raids for slaves from Cuba: in 1516, for example, an expedition of two ships went from Santiago de Cuba to Guahabo. One ship seized its cargo and returned home via Havana. On the bay island of Santa Catalina, in the Gulf of Honduras, some captured Indians rebelled and managed to kill the Spanish crew, except for two whom they forced to sail back to Guahabo. Diego Velázquez sent a punitive expedition. There ensued a fierce battle in which the Spaniards defeated the Indians and returned to Cuba with four hundred slaves.[23] The pursuit of slave labor from the mainland for the islands was in fact becoming the stimulus for expansion.

In the summer of 1516, the authorities in La Española thus permitted a flotilla to go to the large island off the north coast of South America known, since Columbus's visit in 1498, as Trinidad. The only purpose was to look for Caribs who could be brought back as slaves. It was, as usual in such Spanish expeditions, a mixed enterprise: royal officials (including judges) and independent entrepreneurs collaborated. Some of the latter (Becerra, Bardeci, Bastidas) had wanted to manage the expedition, offering to bring back the slaves cheaply, giving away the children and the old. The judges rejected the offer, for they themselves wanted to share in the profits.[24] The commander of the expedition was Juan Bono de Quejo, an old hand in the Caribbean, a Sevillano but one who had been born in San Sebastián. He had been on Columbus's fourth voyage, as on Ponce de León's to Florida, and he had powerful friends in Spain. One of the captains of his three ships was a nephew of Diego Velázquez, Juan Grijalva, also from Cuéllar, near Segovia.

On arriving in Trinidad, the Spaniards were well received by the Indians, but they kidnapped a hundred and sent them in one of the ships to La Española. Their arrival provoked an immediate protest, not only by the Dominicans but also by some shipbuilders who had been prevented from joining in. The former demanded the return of the Indians, but these were proclaimed Caribs (cannibals) and so their capture was deemed legitimate.

In December 1516, Bono returned with his remaining two vessels to San Juan, Puerto Rico, with another 180 slaves. He arrived just when the three Jeronymite priors had reached there after a calm voyage. The San Juan had been expected to go straight to Santo Domingo, but in the event, it stopped in Puerto Rico for repairs. Las Casas then joined them on the Trinidad. On the beach in San Juan he saw Bono's 180 Indians, manacled, of course, and many of them wounded. Bono welcomed Las Casas, whom he had known for years, and, after offering him dinner, went straight to the point: "By my faith, Father," he said to Las Casas, "because I know that you would hand me over to destruction if you could, it is good for you to know that if you cannot capture slaves peacefully, you have to do so by war"[25]—the reference to destruction being a pun on the "instruction" he had received not long ago from the judges, his partners. Las Casas was furious that the priors did not seem interested in the iniquities of Bono, whom he hated: "Juan Bono, *malo*" was his rather obvious comment.

The priors sailed on to Santo Domingo on December 20 and put up first in the new monastery of the Franciscans, then in a building belonging to the Casa de Contratación. They summoned the three judges (Vázquez de Ayllón, Villalobos, and Ortiz de Matienzo), the treasurer (Miguel de Pasamonte), the factor (Juan de Ampiés, an Aragonese friend of Lope de Conchillos), the magistrates (Columbus's onetime secretary Diego de Alvarado and the *converso* Cristóbal de Santa Clara), as well as two councillors (Francisco de Tapia and Antón Serrano).

The priors wanted, of course, to know the local problems. They found that by then not all Ovando's cities survived: Verapaz, Salvatierra, Villanueva, and Lares had vanished. The population of La Española in 1516 constituted about 4,000 Spaniards, perhaps 6,000 fewer than in the days of Ovando, for many settlers had gone to Cuba in search of better fortunes. Apart from Santo Domingo, the cities that did remain still seemed to be labor camps at the service of the mines.[26] But it was the decline in the Indian population that constituted the most obvious catastrophe. Las Casas had argued that the population of working age had been 60,000 in 1509, Diego Colón 40,000 in 1510, while Peter Martyr repeated what had been stated by Las Casas in Madrid, namely that Bartolomeo Colón had estimated there to have been 1.2 million Indians in La Española in 1496.[27]

These figures are all guesses, or even just inventions, especially the higher ones, but that there had been a decline since 1509 is certain. Gil González Dávila had been saying in Castile that this was due to the constant moving of Indians from one place to another. Others more recently have thought that "the excellent but delicate ecological balance had broken down." The indigenous people had continued to live on cassava bread, but their fishing and hunting had been suppressed.

To begin with, the priors did their best. Las Casas had been too pessimistic about the new rulers' prejudices. They sought to distance themselves from the settlers and from officials such as the egregious Pasamonte. They attempted to encourage immigration and sought ways to convince more Spaniards to come out to the Indies, with seeds and cattle. They tried to do away with abuses and, following Cisneros's lead, set at liberty Indians belonging to absentee owners, even those who were the property of such powerful men as Fonseca and Conchillos.

The priors also traveled to the gold mines in the center of the island. They tried to arrange for surviving Indians who had been moved from the mines to be resettled in towns of four to five hundred people with a church and a hospital, where there would be common lands and where they would pay a fixed tribute as a tax. The priors thought that the Indians should cease to be asked to look for gold but should grow agricultural products instead— Spanish crops, for few Castilian settlers, except those in Cuba, were interested in American products, not even maize. As yet, sugarcane had only been grown on a small scale. But the success of that crop in the Canary Islands suggested that it could be planted in the Indies, too. There were over thirty sugar mills in the Canaries by 1515. Soon they would be built in the Caribbean, with Genoese capital playing the same kind of role that it had in Tenerife and Gran Canaria. It was the beginning of the long sugar history of the Caribbean, which is even now not quite finished.

The priors immediately, however, came up against the reality of America: the shortage of labor, the reluctance of the Indians to assimilate, the shortages of Castilian food and wine, the sweaty heat, the sense of distance, the uncomprehending ignorance of the settlers, and the deceptive beauty of the landscape. The arrival of Bono's slaves from Trinidad was accompanied by requests from the older colonists, backed by Franciscans and even some Dominicans, for artillery and gunpowder for defense against the cannibals. The priors, on the other hand, believed that such things were incompatible with "peaceful evangelization" and published another condemnation of the slave raids.

On inquiry, most sailors and others who had been to the Pearl Coast testified that the Indians carried back from there had been Caribs and had been given to the Spaniards by local leaders. But the Jeronymites were unconvinced and sought to ban all dealings with the Pearl Coast. They were constrained to relax their stand, however, and even to name Juan de Ampiés as responsible for that coast—a curious decision since, though certainly knowledgeable, he had been much implicated in the business of trading Indians. Two vessels were permitted by the priors to sail there, one of them owned by Diego Caballero de la Rosa, a powerful merchant and accountant in Santo Domingo (son of a *converso,* Juan Caballero, who had been "reconciled" at an *auto-de-fe* in Seville in 1488). The captains, Juan Ruano and Juan Fernández, kidnapped between 150 and 200 Indians and on their return, as in the past, declared that they were Caribs, though the priors insisted that they had to be considered free laborers. The individuals concerned were handed over to Ampiés.

The priors now decided to arrange an inquiry into the working of the colony. In April 1517 seven questions were put to the twelve oldest inhabitants.[28] Question three asked if the witness believed "that these Indians . . . are of such capacity that they should be given liberty. Would they be able to live in the same social circumstances as the Spaniards?" Could they be expected one day to support themselves by their own efforts, by mining or tilling the soil or performing daily labor? Did they know or care what they might acquire by such work, spending money only on necessities, as if they were Castilian laborers? Could they in fact become good Spaniards?

Marcos de Aguilar, the chief magistrate, from Écija, in Andalusia, a survivor from the days of Diego Colón, thought that continuous contact with Christians might eventually teach the Indians enough to let them live alone; but Juan Mosquera, a landholder who had received 257 Indians in Alburquerque's division of 1513, thought that most Indians were so steeped in vice that they did not even want to see Spaniards and often fled when they saw them coming. Jerónimo de Agüero, a councillor who had always been a strong supporter of the Columbus family (had he not been tutor to both Diego and Fernando Colón in his and their youth?) and the master of about eighty Indians, said that the Indians he knew could only be induced to work by large rewards. They lacked any sense of value: why, an Indian would exchange his best shirt for a pair of scissors or a mirror! Antonio Serrano, who had recently been to Spain as a *procurador,* thought that the curious lack of acquisitiveness of the Indians meant that it was impossible for them to live in society unless supervised by Spaniards. Juan de Ampiés said that even if Indians were beaten or had their ears cut off, they would not be considered any the less by their Indian friends; but Pedro Romero, another councillor, who had lived with an Indian wife for fourteen years, thought that if Indians petitioned for liberty, they should be given it. The treasurer, Pasamonte, on the other hand, considered that Indians should never be given full liberty because of the dangerous friendships many had with black slaves.

Gonzalo de Ocampo, an Extremeño who had been befriended by Las Casas, observed that the Indians must have had some capacity for self-reliance because after all they had raised crops, built houses, and made clothes before the Spaniards came. Judge Vázquez de Ayllón thought that it was better for the Indians to be tied servants than wild beasts who were free. Diego de Alvarado, from Extremadura, a former secretary of Columbus's and uncle of the famous Alvarado brothers who would be so prominent in the conquest of Mexico, believed that, left to themselves, the Indians would do nothing except drink, dance, and plot. Another landowner told a sad story: Ovando, when governor, had set at liberty two Indian *caciques,* giving them the names of Alonso de Cáceres and Pedro Colón. These men soon learned how to read and write, for they had lived with Spaniards for years. Ovando favored them, but afterwards Mosquera said that during the six years from 1508 to 1514, while they had had their freedom, they neither tilled the land nor raised pigs, nor could they clothe and feed themselves. So Alburquerque's division in fact removed their liberties. That first experiment ended "in poverty and without honor."

In another inquiry, witnesses such as the merchants Jacome de Castellon, Juan Fernández de las Varas, Sancho de Villasante, and Gonzalo de Guzmán gave a good picture of life in La Española. Guzmán also described the great slave hunts of the coast of what is now Venezuela in which he had participated; and Francisco de Monroy, of the Extremeño family of that name, told how in 1516 a certain Pedro de Herrera had raised the dangerous cry *"Viva el ynfante don Fernando. . . ."*[29]

While these inquiries were ending, leaving the priors even more puzzled as to what actually to do, new men reached La Española. The first was Judge Alonso Zuazo, who in April 1517 arrived with fourteen servants, a mule, and some costly luggage. He immediately began his *residencia* of the judges of the *audiencia,* but they succeeded in escaping denunciation, thanks to their experienced defense counsel, Cristóbal Lebrón.

At much the same time, fourteen Franciscans of mixed origins from the reformed division of Picardy also arrived in Santo Domingo, headed by the venerable French brother Fray Remigio de Faulx, a welcome addition to the monasteries of Santo Domingo and Concepción de la Vega. Las Casas thought they all looked like Roman senators. They came from several Franciscan groups: one of them, Ricardo Gani de Manupresa, was English, Guillermo Herbert was a Norman, while the provincial Tomás Infante was reported to be an illegitimate brother of Marie de Lorraine, Queen of Scotland.[30]

The priors were coming to an interesting conclusion. They may have been influenced by Las Casas, but there is no direct evidence of it. They wrote to Cisneros that having been in La Española six months and having observed the shortage of labor and the problems that resulted when the Indians were asked to work harder, they had no doubt that black slaves from Africa were needed—*bozales,* that is, slaves who had been bought in Africa, rather than bred in Europe: "because by experience one can see the great benefit of them." They suggested that the Crown should concede a license recognizing that "from this island, it would be easy to go direct to the Cape

Verde Islands or the land of Guinea, and they could arrange with a third person to export the slaves from there."[31]

But this request contradicted the expectations of the Flemish courtiers of Charles V: they knew that the slave trade could be beneficial to middlemen. Furthermore, it ran against the understandings in several treaties that trade with Guinea was a monopoly of the Portuguese. All the same, the request is of great interest. Since King Fernando had given his permission to introduce two hundred slaves into the Americas in 1510, a few black slaves had been sent every year. They had taken part in numerous expeditions. Diego Velázquez had had some African slaves with him in his conquest of Cuba. As we have seen, Vasco Núñez de Balboa is alleged to have had a black slave (Nuño de Olano) when he first saw the Pacific, and African slaves working for him in 1517 were building boats on that ocean.[32] Pedrarias had African slaves with him when he discovered a group of their fellows who had escaped from a shipwreck nearby a few years earlier.[33]

So it was scarcely surprising that in Spain a license was given in May 1517 to Jorge de Portugal, son of Álvaro de Portugal, that exiled Portuguese prince who had been a member of the Council of the Realm in the days of the late Queen Isabel. The new license was to take four hundred black slaves, presumably bought in Lisbon or Seville, directly to the Indies. No taxes were to be paid.[34] The number was later reduced to two hundred.[35] But Jorge de Portugal did little about the matter. He does not seem to have sent more than a handful. He was commander of the Inquisition's castle of Triana in Seville and appears to have been submerged in local politics there.[36]

The priors were so slow in doing anything else practical that Las Casas began to complain again. His letters were intercepted, and, obsessed, he became convinced that the priors were looking for an excuse to imprison him. He told the priors that he was going home but took refuge in the Dominican monastery. Fray Luis de Figueroa responded, "Don't go, because you are a candle that will burn up everything we are trying to do." Judge Zuazo told Fray Luis that he had to let Las Casas go home if he wanted to. Las Casas himself airily said that he had to return home to carry out some undertakings of his own.[37] On June 3, 1517, he did set off again back to Spain. He had with him letters—not only a long one from Judge Zuazo, but two others, one of May 27 from Fray Alonso de Santo Domingo, written in Latin and signed by the reformed Dominicans in the colony, as well as by the new Franciscan monks, and one of May 28, written by Fray Pedro de Córdoba. This last talked of the way that the Indian population was in headlong decline because of the brutalities of the conquerors, and said that the only way to resolve the problem was to allow the people to live freely.

On June 15, 1517, Zuazo, in the documents attached to his *residencia* of the judges, revealed the details of the slave-raiding fleets and demonstrated the active participation of the judges, above all of Vázquez de Ayllón.[38] The priors were perplexed as to what to do. In the event, Fray Bernardino de Manzanedo went home with Las Casas to tell Cisneros that he and his colleagues felt incapable of carrying out their mandate. They were beginning to see themselves as too unworldly to govern tropical settlers. After seeing Cisneros and delivering his letter to Conchillos, Manzanedo retired with relief to his monastery of Santa Marta, near Zamora. His letter was pessimistic. He thought that the Indians did not have the capacity to conduct themselves as if they were Castilians, but that to let them live in their old way would soon cause them to revive their ancient religions and ceremonies. To keep them in *encomiendas*, however, would lead to their extinction. It might be possible to delay disaster by avoiding the constant moves from master to master. Those recent grants of land might with advantage be considered permanent arrangements rather than be confined to a single generation and, if so, they should not cover more than eighty Indians per person. The indigenous population of La Española would be extinguished, and that could only be compensated for by introducing black slaves from Africa.

Las Casas saw Cisneros in Aranda del Duero, in July 1517. It was obvious that the great Cardinal had lost heart. He was ill. Las Casas decided that to talk more to him would yield little benefit and prudently thought that he would wait until King Charles came to Spain. If Charles did not come, he determined to go himself to Flanders. Reginaldo de Montesinos, a brother of the eloquent Fray Antonio, offered to accompany him if he went.[39] (In fact, Charles was at last planning his first visit to Spain.)[40]

Cisneros had already been modifying his Indian policies. His new ideas were contained in a letter of July 28, 1517.[41] This included encouragement to the bishops of the Antilles to reside in their dioceses; the establishment of judges for *residencias* in Puerto Rico, Jamaica, and Cuba (the priors to be free to name whomsoever they wanted, without Zuazo having a veto) and of the offices of factor and treasurer in Cuba; the naming of government inspectors to travel on all pearl ships to prevent abuses; the authorization to merchants to buy slaves on the Pearl Coast and sell them in the islands (provided that the Indians so obtained were well treated); the dispatch of workers from Andalusia as a result of appeals by a town crier; the admission of the legality of the trade in slaves from the Bahamas; a rebuke to the Dominicans for their condemnation of the *encomiendas;* the dispatch to Castile of Las Casas and an acceptance that, for the moment, there was no need to send Inquisitors to the Indies to seek out heretics or *conversos*. This policy was probably dictated by "the Abulense," Fray Francisco Ruiz, on whom Cisneros relied for advice on the Indies in the absence of Las Casas. It marked a definite retreat from policies articulating the Cardinal's original hopes.

The import of black slaves, however, was another matter, and Cisneros wanted the priors to await the arrival of Charles in Spain. He would decide. Perhaps the wise Cardinal saw the likely consequences of a commitment to import black Africans.[42]

So Cisneros allowed his enlightened imperial policy, inspired by Las Casas, to lapse—for example, there was no more consideration as to how laborers sent from Castile to La Española would be paid; nor of the complaints about the *almojarifazgo,* a sales tax that had become one of the benefits in the hands of the Aragonese clique; nor even how the grant that King Charles had made to Jorge de Portugal to carry four hundred black slaves to the islands was to be put into practice.

Cisneros then left Madrid with his staff, accompanied by the Infante Fernando and Bishop Adrian. He was heading for the northern coast of Spain, where he expected to meet the new King. Cisneros and his party stopped at Torrelaguna and then, crossing the pass of Somosierra, went to Aranda de Duero, arriving on August 15. Before leaving Madrid, Cisneros was able to see the first copies of his seven-language Bible, which had been partly paid for by gold from the Indies. Conceived in the tradition of the multilingual edition of the Old Testament of the learned Origen of the third century, it was to be his lasting memorial. Its first four volumes contained the Old Testament in Greek, Latin, and Hebrew, as well as the five books of Moses in Chaldean. Volume 5 was the New Testament in Greek and Latin, while the final volume had dictionaries and a Hebrew grammar.[43]

Cisneros also changed the entourage of the Infante Fernando. This was on the orders of Charles, who, on September 7—the day of his embarkation for Spain—wrote sharply to his brother from Middleburg: "Very often and in many ways I have been told that some people of your household are doing things that are of disservice to the Catholic Queen, my mother, and also damage the harmony between myself and yourself." He explained that he had sent instruction that Fernando's three closest associates, the Comendador Mayor de Calatrava, the Marquis of Aguilar (Pedro Manrique), and the Bishop of Astorga, should leave the court. Instead, El Clavero (the archivist) of the Order of Calatrava, Diego de Guevara, and Charles Poupet de Laxao, one of Charles's own Flemish advisers, should attend him. In the meantime, Alonso Téllez Girón, a reliable Andalusian and a brother of the Marquis of Villena, should remain with him until those gentlemen reached Spain.[44]

Perhaps Cisneros's inactivity in respect of the Indies had been influenced by the letter that he received from Judge Zuazo: "It was a pity," he wrote from Santo Domingo, "to find that the entire island before these judges, such as Ayllón, had arrived had been well populated and full of people. But now one only sees shepherds' shanties." The biggest town outside Santo Domingo had about 30 or 40 people at most. Thus San Juan de la Maguana had about 25 inhabitants, Azúa 37, and Salvatierra de la Sabana only 15. Concepción de la Vega had 40 citizens. Lares de Guahaba had disappeared altogether.[45]

On September 7, Charles at last embarked for Spain and the next day sailed from Middleburg with forty ships, the sails showing the Cross emblazoned between the Pillars of Hercules and the device *Plus Oultre*.[46] Charles had insisted on taking with him his sister, the Infanta Elena, who he had discovered was in love with one of his favorite jousting companions, the Count Palatine Frederick. Among others who accompanied the King was Wolf Haller of Nuremberg, representing the famous banking family of Fugger of Augsburg—the Fuggers' first entry into Spanish affairs.[47] He would later play a part in ensuring Charles's election as Holy Roman Emperor. There also sailed Charles's majordomo, Laurent de Gorrevod, the cultivated Governor of Bresse, in Savoy, and, since 1504, head of the court of the Archduchess Margaret. This courtier, who was also Admiral of Flanders and Marshal of Burgundy, to name merely a few of his remarkable collection of titles, would similarly have a brief but important role in Spanish American affairs.

On September 18, 1517, after losing all his horses on one ship during a storm, King Charles and his court arrived off the coast of Asturias. A lookout said that he could see the mountains of Cantabria ahead, and they made for land. The next day they realized that they were nowhere near Cantabria. Should they turn back to Laredo or land in Asturias? Given the weather, they decided on the latter course. The royal barge was lowered into the sea, and at five in the evening, Charles and the lovelorn Infanta Elena, as well as secretaries such as the increasingly important Francisco de los Cobos, were rowed past Tazones and up the tidal river that led to the town of Villaviciosa. There they disembarked a mile from the town and walked the rest of the way. The

Flemings, including Charles himself, were astonished by the rude manners of the Asturians, who, for their part, at first thought that the incoming fleet must be Turkish or French.

The men of Villaviciosa who assembled were armed. "Moors on the coast" was already a frequently expressed fear on Spanish beaches. But when they saw the ladies of the court, and the courtiers scarcely armed, their fears vanished. The King and his train reached Villaviciosa in the dark. The Asturians presented what they could: skins of wine, baskets of bread, hams, sheep. The Infanta Elena is said to have made a jam omelette while most of the company had to be content with a bench or straw for a bed. The courtiers busied themselves, too, to find horses to replace those lost at sea. The Belgian Laurent Vital said that in return for their hospitality, the King made the Asturians henceforth free of all taxes "as if they had been gentlemen." But though they might have been thus raised socially, the Asturians were not rich. Few wore shoes.[48]

Charles spent four nights at Villaviciosa—one can still see the house where he lodged—and then proceeded ten rough miles to Colunga, a small town where he and his sister stayed in two houses opposite each other. The journey was undertaken partly on foot, partly in oxcarts. How curious Asturias must have seemed to the two hundred courtiers, many of them from Aragon, some of them *conversos*, many being Flemings! None of them could ever have been to that birthplace of the Castilian nation. The fleet, meanwhile, set off to meet the court at Santander. Vital reported that the countryside was "like a desert and quite uninhabitable, and both difficult and dangerous to traverse."[49] Then they reached a pleasing seaport, Ribadesella, where a parade of people played music on the flute and the German tambourine. There was an orange fight.

On September 26, the party came to the cheerful port of Llanes, in eastern Asturias, where the King was joyously received. He stayed two nights, during which time he attended Mass in the fine church of La Magdalena and saw bulls running. En route he wrote several agreeable letters to Cisneros, drafted in French by Chièvres but translated by Cobos (who only recently had accused Cisneros of illegally holding on to the royal rents for the benefit of his own interests). One letter requested the Cardinal to remain at Aranda, for the King had not yet decided his final route. He was on the way to Santander, where he imagined that he would rejoin the rest of his followers.

According to Alonso de Santa Cruz, the Flemings of lesser rank behaved in those days as if they were conquistadors, even killing people for fun in the streets.[50] To avoid Charles knowing of such things, Chièvres "persuaded the King to keep himself to himself, talking to nobody, so much so that the people in the towns through which he passed began to call him a German, untalkable to [*inconversable*], and even an enemy of the Spanish nation."[51] Spaniards also began to think of the Flemings as people interested in stealing the wealth of Spain. The difficulty was that the Flemings and the Spaniards could not see eye to eye in any way. In matters of humor, for example, the bawdy conduct of the Flemings clashed with the solemnities of the Spanish court.

Cisneros remained at the Franciscan monastery of La Aguilera, near Aranda, expecting to meet the King at Valladolid. He began to recover his health by mid-September, receiving further amiable letters from Charles; for example, that of September 27, which sympathized with his indisposition: Charles hoped that he would do nothing apart from regaining his strength.[52] Then the King became ill himself at the pretty port of San Vicente de la Barquera, and he lingered there several days, receiving Francisco de Vargas, the royal treasurer, who brought money, and Archbishop Antonio de Rojas, president of the Council of the Realm, who had defied Cisneros's order to remain at Aranda. The doctors curiously decided that it must be the proximity to the sea that was upsetting Charles's health. Chièvres sent a message to the fleet at Santander to send the royal baggage to San Vicente de la Barquera, and when it arrived, after further trouble at sea, they set off south, inland, for Valladolid.

The King remained ill, ate nothing, and the weather was bad. Then they reached Reinosa on the Santander-Valladolid road. There they were met by Jean Le Sauvage, a protégé of Chièvres's, Grand Chancellor of the Duchy of Burgundy, who had come overland from Brussels. They moved on to Aguilar de Campóo, where they were met by Bishop Fonseca, his brother Antonio, the military member of the family, Councillor Zapata, Dr. Galíndez de Carvajal, and Hernando de Vega. Since the court was now in his diocese, Fonseca could ostentatiously receive the King in his capacity as bishop of Burgos. Cisneros, had he known, would have smiled derisively at these moves by courtiers to ingratiate themselves with the new administration. Charles, now recovered, met the grandees on October 22. Some archers and a hundred German noblemen came down from Santander. The secretaries asked if Chièvres would confirm their old positions; he said that could not be done until the court reached Valladolid. But there was anxiety lest Charles might be rejected by that city. So, taking advantage of an alleged rumor of a plague at Burgos itself, instead of going to Valladolid or Segovia, Charles decided to visit his mother, Juana, at Tordesillas. The Queen had recently been put under the control of Gil de Varacaldo, the father of Cisneros's secretary, and of Hernán, Duke of Estrada.

Cisneros, meanwhile, was traveling slowly north from Aranda to Roa, on his way to Valladolid, where, now ill with piles as well as with colitis, he lodged in the palace of the Count of Siruela. Years before, he had been a pupil of a priest who had taught him Latin in the same town. But by this time, all the couriers from Seville were directing themselves to the new court, not to Cisneros. Adrian of Utrecht seems to have fallen under the influence of Bishop Fonseca, whose star was rising again. On All Saints' Day, at Becerril, Charles met the Constable of Castile, Íñigo Fernández de Velasco, accompanied by his kinsmen, arrayed in gold cloth. They reached Tordesillas on November 4, and there the King, with his sister Elena, saw his mother for the first time since she had left Flanders in 1505 when he was five. They saw not only Juana but the coffin of their father, as yet not buried, in the convent of Santa Clara, as well as their sister Catalina, who had lived all her life with her mother. Catalina, then eleven, was dressed as a peasant with a country skirt, a leather jacket, and a scarf on her head.

Chièvres had a long conversation with Juana and told her how fortunate she was that Charles was now fully grown and capable of relieving her of the burdens of office. He had not known exactly what to expect. Suppose Juana had seemed sane enough to assert herself? But Charles left with the knowledge that he had nothing to fear from Juana, who showed herself quite uninterested in matters of state. According to the Belgian courtier Vital, Juana, when she first saw Charles and his sister Elena, asked, "But are these my children? And in such a short time they have grown so tall!"[53] Sandoval, the Marquis of Denia, a cousin of Juana on King Fernando's side of the family, would henceforth control the Queen as governor of Tordesillas. Charles wrote a letter to Cisneros, countersigned by Cobos, thanking the Cardinal for all his past services and asking to meet him at the little town of Mojados, where they could talk of current problems, and then, perhaps, Cisneros could take a well-earned rest.

Almost certainly before he received that letter, certainly before he could heed its instructions, Cisneros died, on November 8, 1517. The rumor survives that he had received another dispatch from the King, which has been lost, and which contained something so discourteous that the noble Cardinal would have considered death a providential solution to the conflict that must have seemed to lie ahead. This, together with the ingratitude of the new monarch, the unrestrained avarice of the Flemings (who were increasingly seen as looking on Spain as a new Indies to be sacked), and the cowardly abandonment of the grandees who had promised the new King their friendship, had driven Cisneros to lose his appetite for life.[54] But there is no evidence for such a letter.

Cisneros had been a hard, austere man, a decisive influence on Queen Isabel, possessed of a shining honesty and a determination to reach the right decisions. His intolerance toward Jews and Muslims was balanced by a belief that benign policies had to be pursued toward Indians. He was one of the greatest Castilians of his age. Pious but administratively competent, hard-working, and tireless, he did not shrink from audacity or from action at the head of an army. Even those who at the time hated Cisneros also admired him, at least in retrospect.

Book Seven

CHARLES, KING AND EMPEROR

An early newsletter from Mexico (1520):
a view of Tenochtitlan, the lake capital.

28

"The best place in the world
for blacks"

A license should be given for the import of blacks, ideal people for
the work here in contrast to the natives, who are so feeble that they
are only suitable for light work. . . . [La Española] is the best place in
the world for blacks.

Judge Zuazo, 1518

The lordly Flemings around the young King Charles hoped that the death of
the old Cardinal would remove the principal obstacle to their own authority. In reality, it took away the keystone in the arch of power in Castile. Neither Charles nor the Flemings regretted the death of Cisneros; but his
regency of eighteen months had created the possibility of a peaceful transi-
tion to rule by the new, foreign, and youthful monarch. The coming of these
northern Europeans seemed to many in Spain a disastrous consequence of
the termination of the native royal family. Still, Charles and even his new advisers and the new friendships in Flanders and Burgundy helped bring Spain
further into the general sweep of the European civilization of the Renaissance. Many of the Flemings were corrupt and covetous. But others were
magnanimous, open-minded, big-hearted, and cultivated.

On November 12, 1517, four days after the Cardinal died, Charles and his
court left Juana, his mother, at Tordesillas to go to Mojados, a village eighteen miles south of Valladolid, where, incongruously, they met not Cisneros
but the Infante Fernando, "the eternal younger brother" who always conducted himself impeccably, even if Charles feared that the contrary might
be true. Chièvres met, too, the Council of the Realm for the first time—
Archbishop Rojas, the calm president; Bishop Fonseca, the "Minister for the
Indies"; the learned and responsible Extremeño Lorenzo Galíndez de Carvajal; "El Rey Chiquito," Luís Zapata; and the gray treasurer, Francisco Vargas.
Chièvres did what they wanted: he confirmed them in their posts. The interpreter from French to Spanish was probably Cobos. The need for the ap-

proval of Chièvres may have seemed curious to some of these Spanish officials. But their loyalty was to the institution of monarchy. They could not
envisage any other frame to an ordered life than a royal one. They must have
approved the new court's next move to the Jeronymite monastery of Abrojo,
just south of Valladolid, while that city prepared for the King's ceremonial
entry. After all, the Catholic Kings, who had devised the form of monarchy
that they admired, had liked being at El Abrojo nearly as much as they had
at La Mejorada.

Charles entered Valladolid, the informal capital of Castile, at the head of
a triumphant procession on November 18, 1517. He stayed in the palace of
Bernardino Pimentel, a cousin of the Count of Benavente, next to the
church of San Pablo de Corredera. Most of the remaining members of the
court stayed nearby in houses of the Count of Ribadavia, a nobleman of
Galicia. Later, there were tournaments, banquets, dances, a javelin show, and
a mock trial at the chancellery, where two teams of lawyers debated in front
of the King. Charles learned that law could be an entertainment in Castile,
not just a vocation. All was arranged as if it had been a theatrical ceremony.[1]

With less fanfare but with determination, Fray Bartolomé de las Casas
and the Dominican Fray Reginaldo de Montesinos also arrived at Valladolid.
Fray Reginaldo had been proposed by Las Casas as an alternative to the
Jeronymite priors for the governance of the empire. He and las Casas
immediately approached the court once more, acting with the assistance of
the secretary Zapata. The latter was one of the members of the Council of
the Realm who was convinced, without having ever seen an Indian, that
such people were incapable of receiving the faith. All the same, like so many,
he was mesmerized by Las Casas's eloquence and seemed to have forgiven
Fray Reginaldo for insisting that his, Zapata's, view of the Indians was technically a heresy.[2]

Both Fray Bartolomé and Fray Reginaldo were present on December 11
at a meeting with the members of the Council of the Realm who had concerned themselves with the Indies. Fonseca, Zapata, Conchillos, and Galíndez de Carvajal were all present. The two friends of the Indians presented a
memorandum whose main point was a repetition of the declaration that the
"Indians are free," as stated at Valladolid in 1513.[3] Their suggestion was that
La Española and other Spanish colonies should be reconstituted with Indian
villages of at least ten Christian (Spanish) families and sixty Indians. The
Spanish territory in the Indies would be divided into provinces, and two
"visitors" and a constable (alguacil) would visit each town once a year.
Slaves, whether Indian or black, would be treated well. They could marry if
the idea had the approval of their masters.

These proposals were the fruit of a collaboration between Fray Reginaldo de Montesinos and Las Casas, both perhaps being influenced by what they had heard of Thomas More, whose *Utopia*, published in Louvain the previous year, might have been known, in Latin, in the library of San Gregorio in Valladolid.[4] Or were they perhaps impressed by Plato, who had influenced More? At all events, we see here a "Utopian" scheme for the development of the Spanish New World put forward in heroic terms by eloquent clerics.[5]

These exchanges did not result in much, however. As Las Casas reported, "The King was so new and had committed the entire government of the two realms of Castile and Aragon to Flemings, who knew neither who was important in Spain nor who was unimportant, and confided in nobody for fear they might be deceived by false information; and so, many of the activities of the state were suspended, particularly those relating to the Indies, which were further away and less well known."[6]

By December 1517, the administration of the Indies had been taken by Chièvres from Fonseca and placed in the hands of the Chancellor of the Duchy of Burgundy, Jean Le Sauvage. Chièvres was a clever man. Some sixth sense seems to have told him that Fonseca's judgments were often narrow and self-interested.

Le Sauvage came from a family of the lesser nobility dependent on Chièvres. He was indeed the executor of the latter's pro-French policies.[7] He had limitations: the late Professor Giménez Fernández considered him "the archetype of the modern state functionary, the blind assistant of absolute state control who, with his formal personal probity, was much more dangerous to society than old-fashioned prevaricating individuals of lesser quality."[8] Las Casas, however, regarded him as "a most excellent man, very prudent, most capable in all negotiations and of great authority and personality, whom we could imagine a Roman senator"—that last comparison being the highest of all praise for Las Casas.[9] Las Casas and Fray Reginaldo certainly welcomed him and sent him many letters in Latin.

The first document the receptive Le Sauvage received about the Indies, after reading the memorandum of Montesinos and Las Casas at the end of December 1517, was an "opinion" of the settlers that was probably written by Gil González Dávila, the ex-treasurer of La Española, but signed by various "*indianos*"—the word would soon be in use for someone who made money in the Indies and returned home—who happened to be in Spain at the time.[10]

The theme of this document was that "Indians have no natural capacity to live on their own."[11] But the only people who mistreated Indians were common or rustic people (from Spain) who had no virtue. If the King wanted to change the way that the Indians were managed, the costs would outweigh the benefits.[12]

Four things, the *indianos* said, had caused the fall in the population of Indians in La Española: first, the constant changes of governors; second, the moving of Indians from one place to another; third, the lawsuits between settlers; and fourth, the rumor that there was more gold in the Indies than was really the case. That had had the consequence of attracting too many white Spaniards to La Española. One solution might be that "many blacks should come or be allowed to come from Castile."[13] It will be seen how this idea was being gradually insinuated into Castilian public policy.

This "opinion" also seems to refer to what would become New Spain, or "Mexico": "If your Highness permits the islands which today are settled to be depopulated, it would be a great loss because, as a result of new adventures, other islands and lands much richer and better than those that have already been found will be discovered."[14]

This was an allusion to the first expedition from Cuba to Yucatan, that of Francisco Hernández de Córdoba, who had returned via Florida to Cuba in the spring of 1517.[15] Hernández de Córdoba was mortally wounded in a skirmish with Maya Indians, but he had seen interesting things, including the most interesting of all: golden jewels.[16]

The next year, Juan de Grijalva, a nephew of the Governor, Diego Velázquez, who some months before had accompanied Juan Bono de Quejo to the island of Trinidad in pursuit of slaves, left Cuba on a second expedition of four ships.[17] Grijalva had two hundred men altogether. They were away for only a few months, until June, when one of the captains, the magnetic Pedro de Alvarado, sailed home to Cuba. In the end, Grijalva himself decided to return there.[18] This journey is described in chapter 34, but it is as well to appreciate that these expeditions were being undertaken in 1518, King Charles's first year in Spain.

In February 1518, when Grijalva was preparing his journey, Charles's majordomo, Laurent de Gorrevod, was encouraged by some Spaniards (such as Francisco de Lizaur, who had become an adviser on the Indies to another courtier, Charles de Laxao) to ask the King a favor. This was to grant him a monopoly of trade to the new land just discovered by Hernández de Córdoba, that is, Yucatan, which he wanted to colonize with Flemings.[19]

It was not to be. The King would probably have liked to have given Gorrevod this opportunity—he was a firm friend of Charles's family—but a concession of that kind of new land of unknown size and wealth was excessive. It was not the last time, however, that Gorrevod sought to enter the Spanish market. Those who see his family's fifteenth-century mansion at Bourg-en-Bresse must stand astonished at the range of his activities. Gorrevod had been a friend of the Archduchess Margaret since her happy time as wife of Duke Philibert of Savoy, for whom he had been chief steward. She had already inspired a Gothic church to be built in flamboyant style, comparable to many Flemish churches, with a Burgundian roof, at Brou, outside Bourg, in the Bresse, which had been part of her dowry. She administered the duchy from Malines to commemorate her happy marriage, and Gorrevod, as governor of the province, was helping her with money as well as with local support. Beautiful marble and alabaster tombs for herself, her husband, and her mother-in-law had been commissioned from the Fleming Jean Perréal and the German Konrad Meit, who had also recently sculpted a famous head of Charles himself. Next to the new church would stand an Augustinian monastery. Gorrevod's brother, Louis, had also been named by Margaret as first (and only) bishop of Bourg.[20] Gorrevod would have his own chapel and tomb in the church. A stained-glass window dedicated to St. Thomas—in which we can see the successful impresario on his knees—commemorates him and his two wives there, but his tomb was destroyed in the French Revolution by ignorant radicals who probably had no idea who Gorrevod was. In 1518 he wrote regularly to Margaret to tell her what he had seen and done. His description of the clothes worn by the noblemen at Charles's proclamation at Valladolid would have delighted any fashion writer.[21]

Others who engaged in intense discussion about the Indies, from about January 1518, included Zapata, Adrian, and Fonseca, all of whom, as well as Le Sauvage, signed an order to the officials of the Casa de Contratación not to allow anyone to go to the Indies until "I [that is, the King] write to tell you what you have to do." In consequence of the many conflicting opinions as to what indeed had to be done, Le Sauvage asked Juan de Samano, one of the secretaries who had worked with Conchillos (and who had naturally received some petty sinecures in Cuba) to summarize all the different points of view, which he did. For this purpose, Las Casas wrote another memorandum, saying: "Nothing is killing the Indians except melancholy, which derives from seeing themselves in such servitude and captivity, and the bad treatment that they suffer, including the seizing of their women and children, and their being made to overwork, with food not as plentiful as is necessary."[22] Las Casas said that every year seven or eight thousand Indians were kidnapped on the mainland or in the Bahamas and carried off to La Española. He was never accurate with figures, as we know, but he did add, "Their highnesses ought to give generous licenses to settlers to carry there as many black slaves as each settler wants."[23] That Las Casas's ideas were even considered by Le Sauvage infuriated the *indianos* in Valladolid. They wrote a joint "memorial" attacking Las Casas as an indiscreet person. But it will be noticed that even he was toying with the idea of African slavery.

Then there was an opinion from Bishop Fonseca.[24] He bluntly opposed the idea of liberty for Indians. Like López de Recalde in the Casa de Contratación, Fonseca thought that a single commissar should be appointed to rule the new Spanish possessions. He agreed that "the Indians belonging to the Crown, to Fonseca himself, to Diego Colón and the judges should be given up."[25] But those who had been allocated *encomiendas* should be allowed to keep them. The slave trade in Indians from other islands and the mainland, the Bishop thought, should be maintained and legalized.

The priors were in communication, too. On January 18, 1518, after they had been in Santo Domingo just over a year, they wrote that they were still trying to settle the Indians in towns between four and five hundred strong, with instructions that they should plant their own crops and manage their livestock (a new departure), with permission renewed for both hunting and fishing. The priors added that they had encouraged the building of three new sugar mills, and concluded with yet another request that the new King "send us a facility to go and seek black slaves direct from the Cape Verde Islands and the coast of Guinea."[26] Could not the boats that were then going to the Gulf of Paria for slaves go on to Guinea? The request does not suggest much maritime knowledge on the part of the priors, since that journey would have been against the wind. Yet it shows again how the idea of importing slaves from Africa was growing.

Not only the priors were writing from the Indies: the Segoviano judge of the *residencia,* Alonso Zuazo, told the King on January 22, 1518, that the condition of the natives when he had arrived a year before had resembled that of "a man on his deathbed who was abandoned by doctors, and a candle placed in his hand." Zuazo urged that married couples be asked to come from Spain so that they could develop a real love of the land: "At present, two out of three conquistadors are without their wives [if they had them], and so have no real home here." Farms should be founded to take the place of depopulated mining districts. Unlimited immigration should be allowed, with the proviso only that the people concerned should be Christians. Zuazo wanted the commerce of the Indies to be open to all who wanted to participate. His description of La Española gave the impression that the place was potentially a paradise, capable of producing sugar, cotton, cassia pods, Oriental peppers, and wild cinnamon. But a reliable labor force was obviously needed. All the troubles of La Española were, in Zuazo's view, due to the avarice of the colonists. He wanted the return of Diego Colón to the governorship and the dismissal of all the other officials who were there, especially Miguel de Pasamonte, whom he thought venal.

The soil in La Española, he added, was the best in the world; there was neither cold nor too much heat—nothing, indeed, to complain of. Everything was green, and everything grew.[27] "Christ, in the great Augustan peace," continued Zuazo, "came to redeem the old world." The judge continued a little unctuously that there was something similar in the coming of King Charles to redeem the New World.

Zuazo, like the priors and Las Casas, was also beginning to think that the solution to the shortage of labor in the Caribbean was the import of Africans. La Española, he insisted, was "the best place in the world for blacks: *"la mejor tierra que ay en el mundo para los negros."* His main recommendation was that a general license should be given for the "import of blacks, ideal people for the work here, in contrast to the natives who are so feeble that they are only suitable for light work, such as looking after plots of land or plantations."

It was foolish, Zuazo added, to suppose that if brought to the Caribbean, "these blacks would revolt; after all, there is a widow in the isles belonging to Portugal [Madeira or the Azores] who has eight hundred [African] slaves. Everything depends on how they are managed. I found on coming here that there were some robber blacks and that others had fled to the mountains. I whipped some, cut off the ears of others, and, in consequence, there are no more complaints." Zuazo added that already near Santo Domingo there were excellent plantations of sugarcane. Some grew cane as thick as the wrist of a man. How wonderful it would be if large factories for making sugar could be built![28]

He reported, too, that of the fifteen thousand Indians taken to La Española as slaves from the Bahamas over the years, thirteen thousand had died. One of the evils was that under the guise of making discoveries, expeditions were often armed to go to the mainland to capture slaves. Zuazo reported that he had called a meeting of the *procuradores* of the island so that all could discuss the problems. The so-called Cortes of La Española would continue until April.

Chièvres, weary of hearing all these conflicting views, sought out Las Casas in Valladolid and asked him to dine. The Flemings, it seems, liked doing business over meals.[29] Las Casas was received amiably. There were several other advisers present. Las Casas told Laurent de Gorrevod that to obtain the contract he wanted in Yucatan, it would be best to talk to Diego de Velázquez, the Governor of Cuba, who had his eye on the mainland. He spoke expansively of what seemed to have been recently discovered—by

Hernández de Córdoba and Grijalva—and Gorrevod declared himself well pleased; and, sure enough, within a few months there arrived at Sanlúcar de Barrameda, at the mouth of the Guadalquivir River, ships sent by Gorrevod, full of working men from Flanders ready to populate the "territory of Yucatan"[30]—an improbable assignment since Yucatan had not yet even been explored, much less conquered. Those who spoke of it thought it an island.

Diego Colón heard of the proposed grant of Yucatan to Gorrevod and said that no one could receive such a thing since he himself possessed, through his father, all the rights. Fearing prolonged litigation, the King suspended the idea of so helping his Savoyard friend and began to consider an alternative benefit for him.

Francisco de los Cobos had been appointed to succeed Conchillos as Secretary of the Indies. Conchillos himself seems to have approved: he wrote from Toledo on April 5, 1518, to the Council of the Realm resigning his post on the ground of "certain ailments" that have come upon him "in the service of the Crown." He suggested that his successor should be Cobos, who "knows better than any other secretary what is best for the Indies and the policy that should be followed. I humbly beg your Majesty that, in my place, you entrust this office to the aforesaid secretary. . . ."[31]

Cobos, then in his late thirties, came from Úbeda, a city that his own subsequent wealth later embellished. Francisco obtained his entrée into the court through his aunt Mayor's husband, Diego Vela Alide, an accountant of Queen Isabel. Hernando de Zafra gave him various appointments, such as that of royal notary at Perpignan. Then he succeeded Zafra as accountant at Granada in 1510, though that did not mean he left the court. On the contrary, it became his task to record all payments, grants, and rewards of the King. He began to sign the Crown's documents in 1515, and then worked for Conchillos, who used him as an intermediary in difficult negotiations. His income was already 65,000 maravedís a year. He was named notary of the bedchamber in 1515. In 1516, he made an excuse to go to Brussels and remained there throughout Cisneros's regency. It was a sagacious move. Ugo de Urríes, one of the secretaries of the Council of Aragon, introduced him to the all-important Chièvres, who immediately took to him and for whom he began to work—against Cisneros, although the Cardinal did not seem to realize that. Chièvres liked Cobos because he was good-looking and seemed easygoing and bonhomous, but was hardworking and meticulous. As important, he could never be a rival to Chièvres, for he was far from being an intellectual. He did not know Latin and never so much as mentions Erasmus in the many letters of his that survive. He was also among the few Spanish civil servants in Brussels who had no *converso* blood.

In early 1517, Chièvres made Cobos secretary to the King at an annual salary of 278,000 maravedís, considerably more than the other secretaries. Charles told Cisneros that he had appointed Cobos "to take and keep a record of our income and finances, and of what is paid out and consigned to our treasurers and other persons, so that all is done in conformity with the rules that you have yourself established and discussed."[32]

Las Casas described Cobos as "surpassing all the other secretaries because Monsieur de Chièvres became fonder of him than of the others, because in truth he was more gifted than they, and he was also very attractive in face and figure."[33] López de Gómara said of him that though he "was diligent and secretive . . . he was also very fond of playing *primera* [a perverse card game in which the cards had values that bore no relation to their own declared significance]."[34] He greatly liked talking to women and indeed everything to do with them, though the names of his loves do not seem to have come down to us. Everyone said that he was charming but prudent. He never gossiped. His control of the royal bureaucracy in respect of the Indies flourished for twenty-five years.

Early in February, Charles's first Cortes met at Valladolid. The King asked his chancellor, Jean Le Sauvage, to preside, supported by Bishop Ruiz de la Mota. Juan Zumel, the *procurador* of Burgos, protested. He denounced the presence of foreigners, especially Le Sauvage as president, and he became for a week or two a national hero—if a questionable one, since he was the creature of the Constable of Castile, Íñigo Fernández de Velasco, Duke of Frías, who dominated Burgos. After that, Le Sauvage did not appear and Ruiz de la Mota, who originated in the same city, presided, assisted by García de Padilla, a member of the Council of the Realm who had been a protégé of the late King Fernando and who, like so many others, had emigrated to Flanders after the death of that monarch, "in order to secure the permanence of his job."[35]

The main subject of all such meetings, as in England and elsewhere, was the need of the Crown for money. The Cortes decided on eighty-eight other matters, of which some merely repeated petitions of the past, but one included a polite request to the King that he do his subjects the honor of speaking to them in Spanish. (Despite the efforts of Spanish councillors, such as Luis de Vaca in Flanders, Charles's Castilian at this stage was modest.)[36] The Cortes also wanted Charles to marry as soon as possible in order to provide an heir; they hoped that he would choose Isabel, Princess of Portugal, and not wait for another favored candidate, Louise de France, to grow up. They begged Charles, too, to maintain his control of southern Navarre and never to think of giving it back to France.

The Cortes considered next a petition that the sixteen-year-old nephew of Chièvres, who had, remarkably (even for those times), been appointed to succeed Cisneros in the archbishopric of Toledo, should at least live in Spain, if not necessarily in his diocese. Chièvres had at the same time arranged his own nomination as chief accountant of Castile, though he sold the office soon to the rich Duke of Béjar for 110 million maravedís. Despite these extraordinary actions, he managed to deal cleverly with the *procuradores*, even the difficult ones. More important, by hard work and eloquence, he secured for the Crown from the Cortes a subsidy of 225 million maravedís a year for the next three years. The Cortes, all the same, ended their session not at all happy because of the continuing dominance of Chièvres and the Flemings in the country.[37] It was an anticipation of twentieth-century resentment at rule by "Brussels."

Charles was then proclaimed king in San Pablo, Valladolid, the church of the Dominican convent that had been restored by Cardinal Juan de Torquemada (the theologian who was the uncle of the first Grand Inquisitor), who had himself taken orders there. The leading Spanish noblemen accompanied the King on foot. The Infante Fernando, the Infanta Elena, the *procuradores,* the bishops, and the nobles all took the oath to Charles on February 7, 1518. Soon after, the first bullfight was arranged for the King: "a wonderful thing to see." A great deal of money was spent on silk and gold cloth, reputedly 150 million maravedís. The historian Santa Cruz wrote without apparent irony that "his Highness was beginning to show himself very generous."[38]

Even as Charles, his court, and Chièvres worked to establish their legitimacy in Spain, voices continued to remind them of their troubled possessions abroad. Fray Bernardino Manzanedo, writing from his monastery in Zamora, repeated his demand that a license should be given to the priors to import blacks to La Española, "because the Indians are insufficient to sustain them in the island." He urged that as many black women should be sent as men. All had to be *bozales*—that is, slaves straight from Africa, for slaves bred in Castile often turned out rebellious. They had to come from the best territories in Africa, too—that is, from south of the River Gambia—to avoid any Muslim taint.[39] The stability of La Española, he repeated, depended on a supply of labor, and labor was precisely what was not available.

More sensational, though perhaps less significant, was a sermon about this time in San Tomás, the Dominican college in Seville, by Fray Francisco de San Romá, against the tyranny of Pedrarias in Darien, Panama. The preacher said, with the exaggeration that characterizes fanatics through the ages, that he had himself seen forty thousand Indians put to the sword or the dogs.[40] Fray Reginaldo de Montesinos wrote an account of this homily to Las Casas, who in turn described it to Le Sauvage, who asked Las Casas to show it to Bishop Fonseca, which he did. On March 20, Le Sauvage, his calm shaken, told Las Casas: "The King our lord orders that you and I put the Indies in good order. So send me your recommendations."[41]

This conversation occurred as Las Casas was coming out of the royal quarters in the palace of Bernardino Pimentel, in Valladolid. The exchange gave Las Casas new hope for his struggle on behalf of the Indians, if not of African slaves. For the second time the fate of the Indians seemed in his hands. What a victory for his eloquence, his persistence, his hard work, and no doubt, his charm!

The King and the court left Valladolid for Aragon.[42] Their progress was slow, since there was an elaborate reception almost everywhere they passed, to mark the royal visit. The King again went first to Tordesillas, to greet his mother, Juana; to Aranda de Duero; to Almazán, once the seat of his dead uncle Juan's court; and to Calatayud, to bid farewell to his brother.[43] On April 20, that sad but loyal Infante Fernando set off from Santander for Flanders, where he became Archduke of Austria, leaving forever not only his beloved sister Elena but his chance of becoming king of Spain. The brothers embraced. Fernando always maintained his interest in Spain, where he had passed a happy childhood, and we owe to his subsequent instinct for collection many wonderful objects.[44] The letters of his agent in Spain, Martín de Salinas, constitute an admirable source of information on life at the Spanish court from 1522 onward.[45]

On May 9, 1518, the King and his court reached Saragossa. Here the Cortes of Aragon assembled. They discussed at length whether it was right to speak of Charles as "king" in the lifetime of his mother, Juana, and the subsidy that the Aragonese were being asked to pay to Charles, whether he was king or regent: 750 million maravedís. These issues kept the Cortes together until January 7, 1519; and the court remained in Saragossa also until then.[46]

Las Casas retired to a convent at Aranda de Duero. There he prepared yet another of his many memoranda, to meet the request of Le Sauvage.[47] In this, he spoke primarily of the mainland rather than of the islands, and put forward a plan to which, in one form or another, he remained attached for several years. It seems, however, to come from the pages of a chivalrous novel rather than the brain of a political reformer, for Las Casas suggested the establishment, along the Caribbean coast of what is now Spanish America, of a chain of fortresses and towns, a hundred leagues apart. One hundred Christian settlers would be established in each place, each under a captain. No *entradas* into the interior were to be made, under pain of severe penalties. The Indians would be guaranteed freedom, and all those who had been seized in the region in the past as slaves would be freed. There would be liberty of commerce, though the Indians would be told that the Spaniards wanted above all gold and pearls. Bishops would be named, friars from either the Dominican or Franciscan orders would go there, and those orders would control the evangelization. In La Española, Cuba, Jamaica, and Puerto Rico, all *encomiendas* would be abolished, and the Indians told that they were entirely free to live where they wanted. Every Spanish laborer who wanted to go to this part of the Indies could do so. Prizes would be given for the successful introduction of new crops such as silk, sugar, spices, vines, wheat, and cinnamon. Further, each Christian in the Indies "could have two black male slaves each and two females."[48] The ground was thus further prepared for a slave trade in Africans.

While Las Casas was dreaming of a utopian future, the reality of life in La Española was approaching what seemed at first the end of autocracy. The two remaining priors, Figueroa and Santa Cruz, rousing themselves positively to their responsibilities, were arranging that *procuradores* in La Española be directly elected by the settlers. Those representatives were to make such joint petitions as they thought right, and there do seem to have been elections of a limited kind, though the electors were never more than about twenty male settlers or so. These men—and, of course, they all were men—were partly followers of Pasamonte, and partly "of the Columbus family." They were not especially humane, but they were certainly representative of Spanish society in La Española. When they assembled in April 1518, in the monastery of San Francisco in Santo Domingo, they had, first, to name a *procurador-general* to go to Castile to represent their wishes. By seven votes to five, on May 18, the *"pasamontista"* judge, Vázquez de Ayllón, was elected over the *"colombista"* merchant, Lope de Bardeci. The judge of the *residencia*, Alonso Zuazo, argued that that idea was illegal, because, being a judge, Vázquez de Ayllón could not leave the island. Pasamonte, Judge Villalobos, the accountant Alonso Dávila, and Vázquez de Ayllón himself opposed that interpretation and accused Zuazo of being "the executor of the passions of Diego Colón" against the needs of good people.

The *procuradores* asked for many things in Santo Domingo; most important, they urged once again the introduction of black slaves directly from Africa. The Crown, they expected, would benefit from the organization of any such slave trade. The importation of Indians as slaves from the Bahamas, as from the mainland, should also be freely permitted, and settlers in coastal towns should be allowed to go and seek them without let or hindrance.[49] All *encomiendas* allocated to the Crown, to absentee landlords, such as Hernando de Vega and Bishop Fonseca, or to officials in Seville should be abolished, in the hope that this would make for better treatment of Indians. The obligation to send Indians to the mines should be ended, or if that was impossible, the time that they spent there should be reduced. At the same time as improving the conditions for Indians, the settlers wanted to insist on the perpetuity of the *encomiendas*, making them inheritable and increasing their number by reducing the allocation of Indians to eighty as a maximum. *Procuradores* should henceforth be freely elected by councils, and the concentration of authority in the city of Santo Domingo reduced, though the authorities there would continue to be responsible for building roads. Merchants there should be able to trade anywhere in the Indies. Vines and seeds of cereals should be loaded on every ship from Castile, and sugar factories should be encouraged by the Crown by tax-free loans.[50]

The detailed examination of these ideas was prevented, first, by Las Casas's bout of typhus, and then by the death of Le Sauvage from the same disease, on June 7, 1518.

Le Sauvage's death was not regretted in Spain. He was thought to have accumulated nearly 20 million maravedís during his stay in the country. But it marked a setback for Las Casas, since the eternal bishop, Fonseca, was returned to power after (so it was said) a payment by himself and his brother Antonio, the chief accountant of Castile, to Chièvres. The latter was the person to bribe; even Anne, his wife, received a present of 160 *marcos* of pearls from the Indies from *conversos* desirous of diminishing the power of the Inquisition.[51] She and a friend, the wife of Charles's equerry, Charles de Lannoy, also obtained passports to take out of Spain three hundred horses and eighty mules laden with jewelry, gold, and clothes.[52]

Fonseca acted fast. The very day that Le Sauvage died, he and his protégé Cobos prepared eighteen decrees, which purportedly were drawn up by Le Sauvage without his having had the time to sign them. In fact, they were the work of Cobos. Among other things, Judge Zuazo was suspended without a salary. He was also ordered (in June 1518) not to leave La Española until a *residencia* had been completed against him. Yet it will be remembered that he, Zuazo, had arrived in the Indies in order to carry out a *residencia* of the other judges! All power in the Indies seemed suddenly to rest again with Fonseca, who now acted with the connivance of Chièvres and the silent neglect of Jean Carondelet, the Flemish nobleman, who, in addition to being dean of the cathedral of Besançon and Archbishop-Elect of Palermo, was acting chancellor. Knowing that Mercurino Gattinara, a Savoyard protégé of the Archduchess Margaret, had been appointed the successor to Le Sauvage and was about to leave the Low Countries for Spain, Fonseca and Cobos realized that they had to do what they wanted while they could. In such circumstances, Las Casas could for a time no longer count on access to authority. In these weeks, indeed, the secretaries García de Padilla and Zapata did what they could to ruin the whole plan of Cisnerian reform.[53] The priors lost their judicial power, Conchillos had his income from the benefits of the melting down of gold in the Indies restored, and many new licenses for slaves were granted for the benefit of old bureaucrats.

But soon Las Casas began to be listened to again, first by Cardinal Adrian, still in Spain with a rather uncertain brief—he could not be "co-Regent" after the arrival of the King—and then by Charles de Laxao, the Flemish courtier who had been sent by Charles to be close to Cisneros but who had been suborned by old friends of King Fernando, such as the Duke of Alba and also even to some extent by Bishop Fonseca.[54]

It was to Cardinal Adrian that Las Casas spoke of a letter from Fray Pedro de Córdoba in Santo Domingo. This told how the survivors of a new massacre of Indians in Trinidad had been sold in Santo Domingo. Córdoba managed with difficulty to persuade the priors to withdraw these from the market and take them back to the lodgings of the dealers who, he believed, put them up for sale secretly. He suggested that all Indians henceforth should be encouraged to stay a hundred leagues away from Spanish settlements.[55]

On receiving this letter, Las Casas wept as he talked of its contents to Fonseca and the Council of the Realm, while Fonseca drily responded that the King would be mad to follow Fray Pedro's advice. How would Spaniards survive without Indians? He said to Las Casas, "You, too, were once involved in the same tyrannies and sins as those that you now denounce." Las Casas answered: "If it's true that I did once imitate or follow those unfortunate ways, do me the justice to accept that I did at least abandon them and the other robberies, murders, and cruelties which continue to this day."[56] Las Casas understandably never talked much about his own actions as a young man in the Indies, even if he never sought to escape blame for them.

By the summer of 1518 all responsible people in the Indies as in Spain had become convinced that the only viable solution to the problem of labor in the new empire was the provision of African slaves. These seemed stronger than Spaniards when faced with tropical diseases, and they were able to cope much better with work in the heat. How odd it should have been that no one seemed at this time to have any hesitation about using Old World slaves, including Africans, while many were skeptical about the morality of enslaving Indians of the New World! Yet Africans were far closer to Europeans in their knowledge of animals and agriculture than Indians were.

No one put the contrary view. On matters of the Indies, King Charles and his advisers found it natural to accept the recommendations of the purportedly humane Judge Zuazo, the benign Las Casas, and the wise priors. If they agreed in their recommendations, could they be gainsaid? The only question seemed to be, how many African slaves were needed?

Fonseca, Carondolet, and, no doubt, Cobos consulted the Casa de Contratación in Seville. That was, effectively, Juan López de Recalde, the accountant there, who sent back the suggestion that for the four main islands of the empire (La Española, Puerto Rico, Cuba, and Jamaica), four thousand Africans would be adequate to begin with. Las Casas agreed.[57]

The court was then still at Saragossa, where the King was trying to placate the Aragonese. Subsequently the most conscientious of monarchs, he was at that time only eighteen years old. He was only King Charles I of Spain, for his imperial grandfather, Maximilian, was still living. As far as policy in the Americas was concerned, he was in the hands of his advisers. On August 18, 1518, a decree signed by Fonseca and Cobos gave permission to none other than Gorrevod, the protégé of the Archduchess Margaret and the Governor of La Bresse, to import the four thousand black slaves. "The second most avaricious of the Flemings" (after Chièvres), as he was considered by the Spaniards, Gorrevod had wanted (as we have seen) to receive, as a commercial opportunity for himself, the market of Yucatan, which Hernández de Córdoba and Grijalva had visited.[58] But now, as a compensation for not receiving that benefit, he was to be allowed to carry these four thousand slaves, direct from Africa if need be, to the new territories of the Spanish Empire.[59] A subsequent document (signed by the King, Fonseca, Cobos, and García de Padilla) instructed the royal officials not to collect any taxes on these slaves.[60] This of course was a far higher number of slaves than had been sent altogether to the New World until that time.

The young King signed the document approving Gorrevod's *asiento* (contract), and if he thought twice about the matter, he probably considered that he was acting to save the lives of the American Indians by agreeing to the petitions of the priors and to the eloquence of Las Casas. All those people who knew anything of the Indies, and who were usually in disagreement, seemed to speak with one voice when they talked about the need for black slaves. Charles must have been pleased, too, at last to assist, as he must have thought it, one of his aunt Margaret's friends and supporters. Gorrevod did not mention the contract in his letters to Margaret. In July 1518, indeed, a month before the signature of his contract, he ended a letter by saying: "I know of nothing further worthy to tell you."[61]

Gorrevod seems only to have been interested in the money to be made from his license, not in the social consequences, good or evil, for he soon sold his great privilege to Juan López de Recalde of the Casa de Contratación in Seville; he was, indeed, the very man who had suggested that four thousand slaves was a reasonable figure to send. But that official himself then resold the contract in turn to others, using as negotiator the *converso* banker Alonso Gutiérrez of Madrid, who, as we have seen, had been concerned in commerce in the Indies from the beginning; he was the man who in 1506 had resolved the question of the final settlement to the knights who accompanied Columbus in 1492. He would have his difficulties in the end with the Holy Office, but for the moment his wealth, influence, and public standing prevented any such thing.[62]

Gorrevod, we can assume, placed the money that he made in his coffers in Bourg-en-Bresse. Some of it he would surely contribute to the Archduchess Margaret's favorite project, the building of the exquisite church and monastery at Brou on which she had set her heart.

The buyers of Gorrevod's advantageous contract from López de Recalde were two Genoese merchants and one Spaniard established in Seville. These were Domingo de Fornari, who bought the right to carry one thousand African slaves to the New World; and Agostín de Vivaldi and Fernando Vázquez, who together acquired the right to carry the other three thousand slaves.[63] These last two also sub-sold their rights, to Juan de la Torre, of Burgos; to Gaspar Centurión (an even more famous Genoese, though a Castilianized one); and to Juan Fernández de Castro, of Burgos, but then in Seville.[64] They bought the rights for a little over 9 million maravedís, that is, 2,250 maravedís a slave.[65]

The first of these men, Domingo de Fornari, belonged to a Genoese family long active in trading slaves of all kinds from Chios, and he was already also known in the Portuguese slave trade from Guinea as a provider for the tropical island of São Tomé, in the Gulf of Guinea.[66] He was, therefore, a past master in the matter of providing black slaves. Agostín de Vivaldi (Ribaldo, sometimes, in Spain) was a man of the same background as Fornes. Vázquez was a native of Toledo who had always had many commercial interests in Seville. Juan de la Torre had been well known in Seville for a generation, a partner of the adventurer Francisco Barrionuevo, who would soon become a military commander in La Española. Juan Fernández de Castro was a businessman connected with all the important commercial families of Burgos. Finally, Gaspar Centurión was, by 1518, the most important Genoese merchant in Seville, with long experience in Santo Domingo. Renting a palace (in what is today the Plaza de Doña Elvira) from Jorge de Portugal—that palace was, indeed, the modern square—he had come to Seville as a trader from Naples about 1507 and was now a banker, being concerned in innumerable bargains, such as wine from Guadalcanal, with Juan de Córdoba, and loans to the geographer Martín Fernández de Enciso and even to Hernando de Soto, another brilliant captain on Pedrarias's expedition.[67] He was also the banker of Bishop Fonseca. Centurión was often associated with his fellow Genoese Juan Francisco (Giovanni Francesco) de Grimaldi, and the two were always making money by advancing loans to captains or Indies-bound merchants. Even churchmen, even Juan de Santa María, archpriest of the church in Concepción de la Vega, in La Española, owed Centurión money.[68] So did Juan Ponce de León.

Las Casas complained about the contract with Gorrevod: he thought that the license should have been given to Spaniards, because his countrymen were poorer than both the Genoese and the Flemings.[69]

This first major consignment of African slaves for the Americas was thus, in every sense, a pan-European enterprise: the grant of the Flemish-born Emperor was to a Savoyard, who sold his rights through a Castilian to Genoese and Spaniards, who in turn would have to arrange for the Portuguese in Africa or Lisbon to deliver the slaves. It will be remembered that no Spanish ship could legally go to Guinea. The monarchs of the two countries were then allies, and, anyway, only the Portuguese could even think of supplying four thousand slaves at one time. Several of those concerned, such as Gutiérrez, probably Fernández de Castro, and possibly Juan de la Torres, were *conversos*.

This grant was not, in fact, a monopoly, for some minor licenses to import slaves were also soon given: for 10 slaves to Pedro de Velasco in 1520, for 50 each to the royal secretaries Cobos and Villegas the next year, as well as one for 200 to the same Álvaro de Castro who had received a license in 1510 and who would use another Genoese, Benito de Basiniana, as a supplier.[70] Álvaro Pérez Osorio, Marquis of Astorga, obtained a license in September 1518 to send 400 black slaves to the New World, which permission he, too, sold to Genoese bankers.[71] But Gorrevod's license was a turning point. No larger contract was signed for many years. The settlers in the Caribbean thought that their problems of labor had been resolved. So in a sense they had, for what Charles and Gorrevod, in their relative innocence, began, the Atlantic slave trade, leading to the sale of millions of Africans, continued for another three and a half centuries.

"It is clear as day . . ."

> It is clear as day that had it not been for me, you would not have been able to obtain the Roman Crown.
>
> *Jacob Fugger to Charles V, April 24, 1523*

The return of Bishop Fonseca to authority in Castile as a result of the death of the Fleming Le Sauvage did not prevent the interminable circulation of further proposals for the improvement of conditions in the Indies. Thus, on September 10, 1518, even the Bishop promulgated an order on the subject of the "Privileges and Liberties granted to laborers who go to the Indies." This would provide an opportunity for emigration to all who lived in poverty in Spain. There would be free passage to the New World for all men and women concerned, free medicine and land, animals, seeds, and everything needed to support them till their crops matured. Taxes need not be paid for twenty years (except for the tithe, for the Church), assistance would be given to Indians who built the settlers' homes, and prizes would be presented to farmers who produced the first twelve pounds of silk, cloves, ginger, cinnamon, or other spices.

King Charles approved this and instructed López de Recalde, in the Casa de Contratación in Seville, to allow these privileges to any farmers who appeared there for passage to the New World. López de Recalde would inspect the applicants, "incite laborers" to go to the New World, and explain the possibilities. It was he who would ensure that each farmer had what he needed.[1]

Then, not to be outdone, certainly not by Fonseca, Las Casas, recovering from typhus, secured a royal order authorizing the foundation of towns of free Indians to live in a "political way like Spaniards." They were to pay tribute, like other vassals, and not be in an *encomienda*. He also secured an order that would make known to officials, judges, gentlemen, "good men of every city and town" in Spain, the purpose of Fonseca's plan to send farmers to the

Indies. No impediments were to be placed in the way of anyone who wished to go.

Las Casas had yet another curious plan up his sleeve for the promised land between Darien and the Pearl Coast—essentially from the Gulf of Urabá to the island of Margarita, off Venezuela. This enormous stretch of territory, he believed, should be reserved for the mendicant orders. This was not the first time that this astonishing idea had been put forward. Fray Pedro de Córdoba had launched it and Las Casas had already talked of it. But now he insisted that this was the best land that Castile possessed in the Indies, and within it there were surely hidden riches beyond counting. He then repeated his remarkable suggestion of the previous April for a chain of fortresses to be manned by a hundred men each, to be provided with sufficient goods to allow them to exchange with the natives both gold and emeralds. The commanders of these fortresses would slowly extend their authority over the interior, to increase both the evangelical work and the dominions of Castile. *Entradas* of the traditional kind would be prohibited, and no Indians would be enslaved. The costs would be met by confiscating some of the gold and silver already taken by the Spaniards.[2]

Having delivered this plan to the Council of the Realm, Las Casas set about trying to recruit people for Fonseca's scheme of colonization. He and some friends, therefore, left Saragossa on mules in October 1518 and went to many towns in Castile, making declarations in the churches on the benefits of the idea. They announced from pulpits that the King aimed to settle these new lands in the Indies. They spoke of the fertility, the freedom from disease, and the riches of the lands in question, and of the grants that the King would make to those who went there. They spoke in such a way, Las Casas himself said, that "the hearts of all rose up."[3] After all, he knew those places in the New World and so could talk with real experience. He reached Rello, a poor town consisting of thirty houses near Almazán that belonged to the Count of Corunna, a grandson of the Marquis of Santillana. There he recruited twenty people, including two old brothers with seventeen children between them. He asked, "You, father, do you really want to go to the Indies, being so old and tired?" To which the reply came, "By my faith, sir, I am going there to die and to leave my children in a free land."[4] Such a radical statement must have been as unexpected for Las Casas as it was to the Count of Corunna.

Las Casas was accompanied by Luis de Berrio, from Jaén, once a soldier in Italy. He had been recommended to Las Casas by Bishop Ruiz de la Mota.[5] Berrio, with the approval of Fonseca, recruited in Andalusia two hundred people whom Las Casas considered "ruffians, vagabonds, and idle people, not at all working men." They were sent by the Casa de Contratación to Santo Domingo, where they encountered many difficulties because, alas, the officials there had not been told in advance about them. Some died while they waited for approval of their journey. Some became thieves, robbing Indians, and some became tavern keepers, as they had been before.

Las Casas continued with his mission in Castile for two months. It was December when he arrived in Berlanga, a pueblo between Burgo de Osma and Almazán belonging to the Constable of Castile, Íñigo Fernández de Velasco. It had a population of two hundred. Las Casas, nothing if not eloquent, recruited seventy of them. They too explained that they did not want to go to the Indies "for lack of anything here, because each of us has 100,000 maravedís or more; but we want to leave our children in a free land."[6] The repetition of what he had been told in Rello of course much impressed Las Casas. On hearing of this exchange, Fernández de Velasco sent an infantryman to order Las Casas to leave the town. He asked Las Casas also to remove all his assistants from other places. Las Casas returned to Saragossa to tell Bishop Fonseca that he had gathered three thousand workers, a figure that could have been ten thousand had he not wished to avoid offending the grandees. For the moment, he had two hundred volunteers ready. Fonseca asked: "Are you sure, are you sure?" "Yes, sir, certain, certain," was Las Casas's answer. "By God," said Fonseca, "that's a great achievement, that really is!"[7]

By that time, however, a new authority was beginning to make itself evident in the conduct of business in relation to the Indies. This was Mercurino Gattinara, who had been named chancellor and who arrived at court on October 8. On October 15 he knelt before the King to take up his office. Though the Indies were always for him of less importance than was Spain, and much less significant than either Italy or Germany, Gattinara's clear brain soon caused him to realize the need for coherent policies in the New World.

Gattinara had been born in Vercelli, Piedmont, in 1465, into a family of the lesser nobility. He rose to eminence as a lawyer working for the Duke of Savoy, in Turin. He became president of the parliament of the Duke, bought an estate at Chévigny, near Besançon, in Franche Comté, and became a Burgundian subject of the Archduchess Margaret; and Burgundian concepts of honor always played a decisive part in his reactions. Yet the Venetian ambassador to Spain, Contarini, thought him essentially Italian, and he retained property in northern Italy. He was trusted by both Margaret and her father, Maximilian, and the latter sent him in 1509 to Flanders as ambassador. He aroused suspicions there for trying to impose a rigorous, if classical, system of justice on the Flemish nobility, who obtained his removal.

At the time of his appointment as imperial chancellor by Charles, Gattinara was president of the Parlement of Dôle and had also been for some years head of Margaret's Privy Council. He had a humanist conception of the Holy Roman Empire, which he wanted Charles to embellish and to which he hoped to give a new, Renaissance meaning. Christopher Scheurl, of Nuremberg, remembered him as

> an accomplished orator, an erudite jurisconsult, a faithful counselor, hardworking, gentle, charming, jovial, kind, and well versed in matters of polite learning. A bachelor but never dining alone, he is always revived by the company of feasting guests. He makes merry, laughs, converses, mixes jokes with serious matters when eating; he is most pleasing in his manner and most accessible and obliging. He honors those who visit him and listens indulgently.[8]

From now on, Gattinara was the adviser who would influence not only Charles's policies but also his character. His advice marked a change from the Francophile direction of Chièvres and Le Sauvage. In addition, he was the spokesman for Charles's right to be the Holy Roman Emperor, which in its religious inspiration had a Dantesque exaltation all of its own. He pressed for Charles to be the emperor in order to be able to use the title *"iustisimus"* and to dominate the globe. A great writer of memoranda, which he would pen in his neat, clear, careful handwriting, he dreamed of a world monarchy under a single shepherd.[9] He was not as yet in any way informed about the Indies. But his warmth of personality and capacity for imagination as well as hard work soon converted him into the most enlightened influence on all American questions.

Before Gattinara became fully engaged with overseas problems, Bishop Fonseca made some important decisions. He knew that the regime of the priors in Santo Domingo had failed, so he persuaded the King to bring it formally to an end. He proposed that Rodrigo de Figueroa (no relation that we know of to Prior Luis de Figueroa, who was still in La Española), a forty-seven-year-old lawyer from Zamora who had once worked for the military orders and had been in Seville as judge of *almojarifazgo* (the duty on imports and exports), take over as governor. The King agreed and wrote to the priors, thanking them for their numerous letters, explaining that the troubled position of Spain had made it impossible to write before, and asking them to remain where they were till their successor arrived.

Las Casas was named as the chief assistant to the new Governor Figueroa. Fonseca evidently wished to remove that turbulent priest from Spain in as effective a way as possible. He was indeed so enthusiastic about the chance of saying goodbye to Las Casas forever that for a time he was almost kind to him. Figueroa's instructions—in forty paragraphs[10]—meanwhile were dominated by the usual moralistic statements. The instructions included a discussion of the work that would be done in the fields and in the mines by the Indians, of the need to ensure their good physical treatment, of the requirement for their education in Christian doctrine, of the need to ensure that Indians had only one wife, and of the obligation to protect women and children and to limit the numbers of Indians assigned to a single *encomendero* to 150 maximum, 40 minimum. Figueroa was also to send the King the opinions of all "disinterested persons" in the colony on how to define Indian liberty.[11] These paragraphs may have been due to the influence of Cardinal Adrian, the latest to become convinced of the wisdom of Las Casas's judgment.[12]

Figueroa also received orders about the flotillas that were still leaving Santo Domingo to look for slaves: first, the regions inhabited by cannibalistic Caribs should be carefully marked out; second, Indians from non-Carib tribes should not be captured against their will; third, Figueroa should find out what had really happened during Juan Bono's expedition to Trinidad; fourth, the people of the Bahamas, Barbados, and the Islas Gigantes, off Venezuela (as it is now), should be looked upon as free; and, fifth, the details as to how pearls were found on the Pearl Coast should be made evident.[13]

But while the new ruler prepared himself in Castile and listened to a hundred speeches of well-intentioned advice, the poor priors in Santo Domingo were facing a new disaster: a smallpox epidemic in the winter of 1518 swept through the islands, in particular the new towns that the priors had founded.[14] This was the first full epidemic in the New World, though influenza, typhus, and measles had done damage before. Perhaps the priors' well-meant creation of new towns had inadvertently assisted the spread of the infection. It anyway now seemed as if the indigenous population, far from merely suffering from being overworked or losing faith in the future, was in danger of extinction because of a European epidemic, one to which the tough Spaniards, newcomers and established settlers alike, seemed immune. Indians and Spaniards joined together in sponsoring religious processions in the city of Santo Domingo, begging for divine protection. But prayers and ceremony proved inadequate.

The immediate consequence of the epidemic was to increase the demand for Lucays (from the Bahamas) and slaves from the Pearl Coast. The

Genoese Sevillano Jacome de Castellón (Castiglione) continued to send armadas north to the Bahamas and south to the Pearl Coast, in which there was a curious mixture of evangelization and criminality. There was also some conventional trading: arms and wine, especially the latter, were found in the hands of the Chiribichi in South America by 1518.[15] This also led the priors to repeat their requests for more black slaves.[16]

The deliberations at Saragossa concerning the Indies were interrupted. First, on January 7, 1519, the Cortes of Aragon gave Charles its support and its money. Charles, much relieved, then went to Cataluña to meet its Cortes, in Barcelona. The court traveled without fanfare via Lérida. But while in that Catalan city, he received on January 24 news of an event that transformed the history of Spain and of all her possessions: the King's grandfather, the Emperor Maximilian, who had seemed immortal, had died at Wels, in upper Austria, on the twelfth. The last months of the Emperor had been rendered uncomfortable by syphilis. His pains were only mildly reduced by the application of "Indias" wood (*madera de Guayana*), which, like the disease it was intended to soothe, derived from America.[17]

The candidacy of King François I of France for the empire was immediately announced, with support from the Medicean Pope, Leo X. But Charles was the critical candidate. In these circumstances, for several months it was difficult for anyone in Spain to gain the King's attention on any local subject, much less the Indies. The Chancellor, Gattinara, was even more possessed by the imperial dream than was Charles. So, many things happened in the New World without even being noticed in the home country.

Thus, early in 1519, Alvarez de Piñeda began to explore the coast between present-day Florida and the Mississippi. This region he called Amichel. His first vision of the River Mississippi entitles him to first place among the explorers of his generation. Alas, he seems to have left no description of what he saw. Then Diego Velázquez, the Governor of Cuba, promoted another expedition to the west, to follow up what had been discovered by Fernández de Córdoba and Juan Grijalva. This was entrusted to an ex-secretary of his own, an experienced Extremeño, Hernán Cortés (see chapter 35). Few in Spain learned of the expedition, and when they did, none paid attention to it. Even Las Casas was as ignorant as he was uninterested.

Judge Zuazo, in Santo Domingo, meanwhile agreed that further Indian labor was needed in La Española and, in the spring, gave a license to Diego Caballero, the chief accountant of the colony, to travel with Antón Cansino to what were engagingly called "prohibited lands" to seek slaves, as his *residencia* put it. He gave the same approval for other undertakings to such well-known merchants as Bastidas and Fernández de las Varas.[18]

The priors, still waiting for the arrival of Figueroa to free them from their responsibility, accepted this, though refusing to give any formal approval without the King's agreement. Then a decree was signed (on January 24) by Fonseca that allowed two other Sevillano-Genovese, Adán de Vibaldo (Ribaldo) and Tomás de Fornari, a brother of Domingo, the right to name a factor in the Indies, with the sole power to sell the black slaves conceded to them because of the contract granted to Gorrevod.[19]

The King, for his part, went to the monastery of Valdoncella, near Barcelona, and prepared for his official entry to that city. The secretaries Cobos and Padilla went ahead to begin discussions with officials there. After returning to Molins del Rey, they went back to Barcelona, with Dr. Galíndez de Carvajal.[20] The following night Charles went in, disguised, to see the city for himself. Next day he entered Barcelona in style, but even then his mind was on potential German empire, and in the choir of the cathedral, he showed his priorities by holding a ceremony admitting ten Spanish noblemen into the Burgundian order of the Golden Fleece.[21]

All the same, Gattinara and Laxao continued their discussions with Las Casas, and, indeed, they seemed to love hearing him talk. The King himself had also begun to warm to his ideas. Charles himself suggested that to decide on what Las Casas had proposed for the north coast of South America, there ought to be a committee of advisers whom the priest himself could choose. Las Casas chose Juan Manuel, the experienced and subtle diplomat who had led the party of King Philip, and Alonso Téllez (the brother of the Marquis of Villena) and Luís Manrique, both *letrados* of whom Las Casas approved. To these were added Francisco de Vargas, the treasurer of Castile. The preparation of this committee gave Las Casas time to refine his scheme. He made it even more fanciful, for he now wanted to send out fifty settlers, to be known as Knights of the Golden Spur—even more redolent of a chivalrous romance than his first proposal. They would be accompanied by twelve Franciscan or Dominican missionaries and ten Indian interpreters, and were to look for pearls, giving the King a fifth of the produce if the fishery was previously known but only a twentieth if it was new. Several imaginative financial arrangements would give both Crown and the colonizers an additional interest. A license would allow every partner to have three African slaves at the beginning and another seven later on.[22]

Discussion in the Council of the Realm then began on the subject and was prolonged by a personal campaign sponsored by Fonseca and his friends against Las Casas.

But these seemed small matters at the time. The most important event in the Spanish Empire was being played out in the Church of St.

Bartholomew, Frankfurt, where King Charles I of Spain was, in his absence, elected emperor as Charles V. (At that time there were seven imperial electors—four secular, three archiepiscopal.)

The victory had not been inevitable. François I, King of France, had, as we have seen, aspired to the imperial crown, and with his recent military successes, he was a compelling candidate. King Henry of England, still apparently sane and happy with his wife, Catherine of Aragon, King Charles's aunt, could not be excluded. One or two of the electors themselves were possibilities—for example, Elector Frederick of Saxony or Elector Joachim of Brandenburg. Indeed, the Pope, seeing that the King of France might not win, had begun to back the first of these two as an alternative candidate. He did not favor Charles for the simple reason that he did not want an emperor who was already King of Naples.

The King of France had earlier sought to leave the impression, through his able ambassadors, that his resources were endless; and François's rich mother, Louise de Savoy, had, indeed, given him much money. His administration was far more centralized than that of Charles, so it was easier for him to lay his hands on it. But François could not raise money easily in Germany. Jacob Fugger, the most powerful banker of the century, refused to cash his notes; and money, in cash, was what was needed to secure the imperial election. Each elector had his price.

Charles first approached the Welsers of Augsburg, and then Filippo Gualterotti of Florence, for their support and obtained promises of 133,000 and 55,000 Rhine florins, respectively, the loans being secured through the Fornaris in Genoa and Filippo Grimaldi of the same city. The contracts declared that the payments would only be made if Charles was elected emperor. Letters of promise were deposited in February 1519 with Jacob Fugger. They totaled over 300,000 maravedís, but that was not nearly enough.[23] (The Fornaris were among those who had benefited eventually from Charles's license to sell African slaves in the Americas, but there is nothing to suggest that there was a financial connection in 1518 between them and the King.)

The Archduchess Margaret, Charles's clever aunt and onetime foster mother, then directly approached Jacob Fugger, the nerve of the German banking system. After prolonged discussion, he made an offer of half a million florins. Four years later, Fugger would write a letter to Charles: "It is publicly notorious and clear as day that had it not been for me, you would not have been able to obtain the Roman Crown."[24] The same could have been claimed by the persuasive Archduchess, whose most remarkable achievement this was.[25]

The details of how the money so obtained was spent are extraordinarily interesting. Of the electors, the Archbishop of Mainz, Albert of Brandenburg, received 113,200 florins of gold—100,000 for himself, the rest for his entourage. Perhaps this enabled him to pay Albrecht Dürer for the fine engraving he made of him that same year. The Archbishop of Cologne, Hermann von Wied, received 50,000, and 12,800 went to his entourage; and the Archbishop of Trèves, Richard, was given over 40,000 florins, of which nearly 20,000 went to his staff. The Elector Palatine of the Rhine, the old love of the Emperor's sister Elena, received 184,000 florins.[26]

The Elector Frederick of Saxony received 32,000 florins, he being the only elector who had refused to say for whom he was going to vote—but the Spanish ambassador increased that sum by another 80,000 for his entourage, as well as paying off half of a debt contracted with the House of Saxony by the late Emperor Maximilian some years before. He, too, was a client and subject of Dürer, who also made an engraving of him a few years later. The King of Bohemia received over 40,000 florins, his vote being exercised by his chancellor, Count Ladislas Sternberg, who received 15,000. The King himself received a little over 20,000 ducats, and 5,000 went to George Szathmary, Bishop of Fünfkirchen, an old friend of the Fuggers.

The Elector of Brandenburg, Joachim I, supported the King of France almost to the end in what he called "this hay market." François had said that if he won, he would make him regent when he was absent. In the final reckoning, he voted for Charles, though he swore that he only did so "out of great fear." His cousin, the Margrave Casimir of Brandenburg, who had been at Charles's court and worked for him, received 25,000 florins.[27]

The Elector Palatine then found his share increased by another 30,000 florins.

Thus the electors received nearly 500,000 florins in all.[28]

The news of his triumph in Germany reached Charles in Barcelona on July 6.[29] Gattinara was also a victor of the day. He had always expected that Charles would become emperor. He spoke of the dignity conferred on his master that he thought made him "the most important emperor and king who has existed since the division of the empire made by Charlemagne, your predecessor, and putting you well on the road to achieve universal monarchy, so as to reduce the world to the care of a single shepherd"—a favorite expression of his.[30] He went on, in a guide to the monarchy (*De Regime Principium*), to tell Charles of the importance of having good officials.[31]

The imperial ambassador, the Count Palatine, and the brother of the Duke of Bavaria soon arrived at Barcelona with the original document that named Charles emperor and required him to go to Germany to receive the crown.

But in Castile, comment was critical: how could their monarch take up a foreign throne without consulting the Castilians? Their doubts were justified. If Charles had not been elected emperor, he would have had more time for Spain. Yet his interests in Burgundy and Flanders were vast, and whatever had happened in Germany, he would have played the part of a statesman of Europe rather than just one of the Spanish peninsula. If Juana had intervened, the situation would have changed completely. She did not do so. If the Medinacelis or the Enríquezes had claimed the throne of Spain in 1516, as heads of important branches of the old Spanish royal family, it would also have been a different matter. But they were not interested in such a suggestion.

30

"I was moved to act by a
natural compassion"

I was moved to act not because I was a better Christian than others
but by a natural compassion.

Bartolomé de las Casas to the King, 1519

In 1519, Spain had a king who was pleased to be an emperor, but he considered Europe his domain. He and Spain were on the verge of possessing an
empire in the Indies but did not yet realize it. In September, however,
Charles would declare, "By the donation of the Holy Apostolic See and other
just and legitimate titles, we are lord [*señor*] of the West Indies, the islands
and mainlands of the Ocean Sea already discovered and to be discovered."[1]
Those words occur in a decree sent in reply to a request of the settlers and
conquerors of La Española that affirmed Charles's sovereignty over the new
territories.[2] This seems to have been the first time that the expression "the
West Indies" was used—in contrast to the real Indies.

The standing of these colonies had risen at court recently, for the import
of gold from there had much increased since 1510: the official figures suggested that just over 9 million grams of gold had come in, and we can assume that this was an underestimate of the true total. Whereas before 1515
most of this treasure derived from La Española, after 1515 both Puerto Rico
and Cuba made their contributions: output in Puerto Rico almost equaled
that of La Española in some years, and Cuban production was about half as
great.[3]

To those islands now went Rodrigo de Figueroa, the judge from Zamora
named to succeed the Jeronymite priors. He did not have with him Bartolomé de las Casas, since that great agitating priest still thought it possible
to encourage free peasants to go to the New World from Spain; and he had a
hundred other ideas that he was still trying to propagate at court. Yet on the
boat out to the Indies, Figueroa talked with many experienced passengers—
men such as Juan de Villoria, of whom he could ask the real nature of the re-

lations between Judge Zuazo and Diego Colón. Such *petites histoires* must have consumed many hours of gossip on those high seas.

After arriving in Santo Domingo, Figueroa found only about a thousand colonists on the island: many had gone to Cuba. The Indians were still melting away. He talked extensively with the priors. Not all their experiments had failed. For example, with the funds obtained from the sale of Indians who had previously belonged to absentee landowners, they had been able to lend money to entrepreneurs such as Hernando de Gorjón, who had left Spain with Ovando, made a fortune in commerce, and now sought to found a college that would eventually become the University of Santo Domingo. With the help of the priors, Gorjón had built a sugar mill on his *encomienda* at Azúa, the new town where Hernando Cortés had been notary in Ovando's day. Figueroa also helped by asking Alonso Fernández de Lugo, the Governor in Tenerife, to send sugar technicians, and he exempted machinery needed to build mills from all taxes.[4]

Figueroa found that the overwhelming opinion among Spaniards in his colony was against the idea of giving Indians liberty of any kind. He did free those Indians who had been working in mines, only to receive many complaints from settlers who said that that would cut the gold produced to one-third of the previous year's output.[5] They knew that argument would be successful at home.

Back in Spain, Las Casas, meanwhile, had won the day in the Council of the Realm in the late summer of 1519 with a new, revised version of his romantic idea of converting the Indians of the north coast of South America—"the best and richest territory in the Indies"—into tributaries for ten years, with the foundation of ten model cities. Under this plan, the Crown would subsidize these places by up to 9 million maravedís, pay the cost of the journey of citizens and their equipment to those places, agree that for the time being there would be no taxes there, make easy the import of African slaves, and proscribe *encomiendas*. Diego Colón would have overall authority over them. These ideas were presented to the court in Barcelona, where the King then was.

The scheme fascinated the chancellor, Gattinara. Diego Colón also gave it his patronage, partly since he thought that it would increase his own power. But Fonseca knew how to counterattack. He was now critical of anything proposed by Las Casas and made thirty charges against him, accusing him of being inexperienced in government, of having deceived his patron Cisneros, even of being a "frivolous priest"—an accusation that would have been hard to substantiate, whatever one might think of Las Casas's ideas. Fonseca even accused his critic of robbery in Cuba and, worse, of plotting with Venetians and Genoese against Spain. Antonio de Fonseca, the military brother of the Bishop, was also a critic of Las Casas. He said: "Father, you really cannot say that these gentlemen of the Council of the Indies have killed Indians, because you have already taken from them the Indians they personally used to have working for them."

Las Casas replied: "Sir, these properties and these grants have not killed the Indians, it is true, even though many have died, but Spaniards have killed many, and your lordships helped them." The Council looked on, astonished, and Fonseca seemed shocked. The Bishop said ironically: "How fortunate the council of the King is if, while being the council, they have to have a lawsuit against Las Casas!" Las Casas responded: "Better off by far is this Las Casas who has traveled two thousand leagues, with great risks and perils, in order to advise the King and his council that they should not enter the inferno which, through their tyranny and destruction of peoples and regimes, they have achieved in the Indies." Gattinara said nervously to Las Casas sotto voce: "The Bishop is obviously very angry; please God that this business ends well."[6]

By this time in Spain, a Council of the Indies (Consejo de las Indias)—an informal group of members of the Council of the Realm—had really taken shape. It consisted of Fonseca (presiding), Bishop Ruiz de la Mota, the two secretaries García de Padilla and Luis Zapata, as well as Gattinara coming and going as he liked, with Cobos as the secretary.[7] Quite soon the organization of the royal secretariat came to consist of three councils: those of the State, of the Indies, and of Flanders. Gattinara was responsible for these changes.

One night in late September 1519, still in Barcelona, Gattinara asked his Flemish colleague Poupet (Laxao) and Las Casas to dine. He showed Las Casas a document that lay on his table: it was an attack on him by Fonseca. "You must reply," said Gattinara, "to these slanders and other things that are being said about you." Las Casas said, "What, my lord, they have been working for three months on these attacks, and I have to reply now in a second? Give me five hours."[8] Las Casas was permitted to prepare his defense. He asked Gattinara to read aloud Fonseca's criticisms one by one, and he would reply to each. They had begun on this when a messenger came to tell Gattinara that the King wanted to see him. Las Casas left but returned later and the two, the chancellor and the priest, spent the next four nights talking, with Las Casas defending himself. He acquitted himself successfully, and the King, who moved first to Badalona and then back to Molins de Rey, because of plague in Barcelona, was informed.

Fonseca had already left Barcelona for Corunna to prepare the King's

This page and next Christoph Weiditz was the first European painter to depict the indigenous people of the New World. Here we see their possessions, clothes, and games.

Aſlo Mamergans Indraniſche
Werber ſind mer dan aine herr
aus kumen

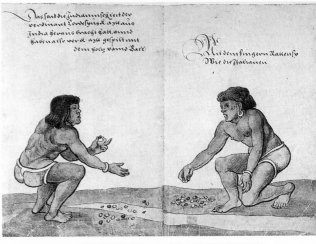

Das ſand die Indraner ſo gar der
verdinant Cortſchuſel d gthaus
India heraus bracht hat, und
haben alſo wer sk aʒt geſpilt mit
dem gotz und Ball

Wie
Wie den ſingern Ratten ſo
Wie die Italianen

Aſlo Wurfft er das holtz ober ſich mit
den fieſſen

Aſlo Empfaecht Er d Wider das
holtz auff die ves, ſo ers auff
geworffen gat.

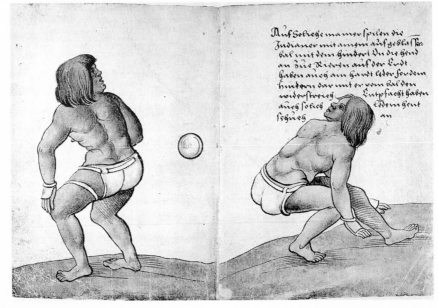

Auſ Solkche manier ſpilen die
Judianer mit ainem aus geblaſſen
bal mit den hindrei Dn die hend
an die Ritʒen auff der Erd
haben auch ain Hant leder ſo dem
hintern dar mit er vom bal den
widerſchweig Empfaecht haben
auch ſolich Elden heut an
ſchuch

Francisco de los Cobos, the charming supersecretary who ran the Spanish Empire between about 1517 and 1542.

Laurent de Gorrevod (kneeling), a protégé of the Archduchess Margaret, obtained the first major contract to transport slaves to the New World, in 1518.

Above "Civil servants decide": Dr. Sancho de Matienzo organized the commerce with the New World, 1503–1520.

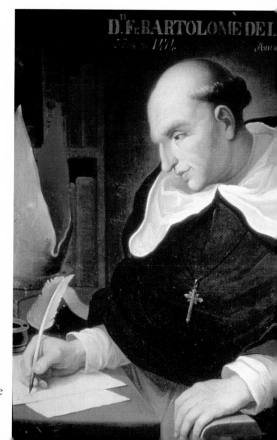

Right Bartolomé de las Casas devoted his life to the cause of the indigenous people of the Americas.

The wheel, here on a typical cart of Andalusia, was Spain's most obvious contribution to development in the Americas.

Right The Mediterranean plough was necessary for planting wheat, the main European cereal.

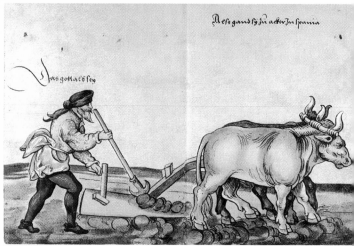

Bottom left A horse of the kind taken to the Americas, ridden by a typical knight.

Bottom right The knight's wife, whose clothes would have benefited from the dyes of the New World.

Above The guitar was the happiest European export of the sixteenth century.

Above Many Spanish conquistadors took their wives to the New World.

Right Wine was soon taken to the New World, where the indigenous peoples loved it.

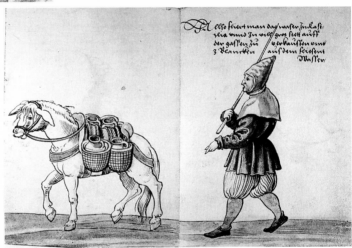

Black slaves were taken to the New World from about 1500.

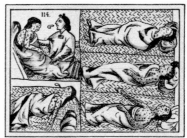

Scenes of war against the Mexica, from the Florentine Codex.

111. Burning of bodies of Mexicans slain in battle at Mt. Tonan (Chapter 27). 112, 113. Refurbishing of a temple in Tenochtitlan on the departure of the Spaniards (Chapter 28). 114. Smallpox plague (Chapter 29). 115-117. Return of the Spaniards to attack Tenochtitlan (Chapter 29). 118. Spanish brigantines (Chapter 30).

This page and next All conquistadors coveted gold. They found some, above all, in what is now Colombia and Central America.

A crocodile.

A man with a jaguar mask and crocodile motifs.

A man with a crododile costume.

A wizard with a drum
and snake.

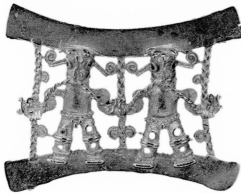

Double humans or twins.

A man with an
eagle costume.

fleet for Germany. Administration and preparation of fleets was, it will be recalled, his real specialty. In his fortunate absence, the King approved all the schemes that Las Casas had proposed. Las Casas, seeing that he ought to make some concession to avoid the persistent opposition of Fonseca and his friends, decided to exclude from his scheme the pursuit of pearls in Cubagua, in what is now Venezuela, so reducing the potential riches, though not much the size, of the territory that he sought. He spoke of hiring fifty associates "from the islands [Cuba, La Española, and Puerto Rico]" to carry through the plan. These would be for the most part "hidalgos or knights and persons of merit." How he would find these model gentlemen was not clear. The Franciscan and Dominican missions already in Cumaná would participate. In the territory under discussion, there was no gold that Las Casas knew of, except in the territory lived in by the Cenú, near Cartagena. Las Casas wanted to include that land in the west, with the River Essequibo (then known as the Río Dulce), in Guiana, as the eastern frontier. This was a colossal territory, including all present-day Venezuela and much of Colombia; it is not difficult to have some sympathy with Bishop Fonseca in his criticism. How could such a place be managed by an inexperienced priest and fifty friends, however worthy? More and more, Las Casas seemed to be demanding the conversion of the Indies into a romance.

There was no royal consultation on the matter with officials actually in the Indies. Yet Figueroa, in Santo Domingo, seemed for the moment reasonably public-spirited. He named a whole series of new officials; for example, his assistant, Antonio Flores (who had come with him), was to be chief magistrate of La Vega in order to investigate the illegal sales of "Lucays" in the north of La Española.[9] It transpired that there were many instances of slaves being sold instead of merely being exchanged. Another inquiry was into the nature of the Pearl Coast. Figueroa was determined to establish whence "the Caribs" came, since many slaves who had been carried to La Española under that designation were obviously not of that race. Were the people of Trinidad really "Caribs"? Many of the questions seemed, though, to be phrased to justify the seizure of slaves. For instance, one question ran: "Was it certain that Indians who have slaves sell them to the Caribs for eating or to be badly used by them?" Both cannibalism and sodomy continued too to be justifications for the kidnapping of any Indian by any Spaniard.[10]

The witnesses in this investigation included many experienced sailors, shipbuilders, and merchants, including Captain Francisco Dorta, of Moguer (who had by then been crisscrossing the Atlantic for more than ten years); Antón García (who as long ago as 1501 had accompanied Hojeda to Trinidad); the ineffable Juan Bono de Quejo, of Trinidad fame (who now insisted that all

Caribs were, conveniently, sodomites); and Francisco de Vallejo (the most experienced man on the Pearl Coast). Most were *encomenderos,* if on a small scale. The Dominicans Fray Pedro de Cordóba and Fray Pedro Mexía also testified. But the restless character of the indigenous peoples was causing both of these high-minded men to doubt the possibility of serious missionary work. The latter commented: "I see some merit in Fathers being there, but it is a very small merit." A modern historian thought grimly that "the friars already did not seem to be unconditional enemies of the seizure of indigenous people."[11]

The demographic diversity of northern South America was revealed in this inquiry for the first time: on the Venezuelan coast, for example, there turned out to be eight different major tribes, four definable as Arawak, four "Carib." The "Carib" territories were afterwards named as the four "provinces of the Gulf of Paria, and all the uncolonized islands of the Caribbean, except for the Lucays, the Barbados, the Gigantes, Trinidad, and Margarita." The capture of Caribs was to be allowed, but only if there was proper licensing.

The inquiry revealed, too, the precarious nature of the assignments on the Pearl Coast. The Franciscan mission there had closed, and a new Dominican one threatened to do the same when there came to be too few Spaniards to hear Mass. By October 1519, there was again only one Dominican on the coast along with a few lay brothers.

Figueroa also embarked on the *residencia* of Judge Zuazo, and in this connection, he examined numerous settlers, such as the ex-treasurer Cristóbal de Santa Clara. The chief accusation was that Zuazo had conceded licenses to capture slaves without telling the Jeronymites, and favoring friends.[12] He was also accused of having seduced an Indian girl, whom he had subsequently sold to Judge Cristóbal Lebrón, the judge of the *residencia* in respect of Marcos de Aguilar, the late chief magistrate. Zuazo replied with counteraccusations against the witnesses, for example that Cristóbal de Santa Clara had become a drunk who wanted to conceal the murder of Juan Pizarro (a brother of Francisco), whom Pasamonte had had killed; that the bachelor Juan Roldán was living with a witch; that Hernando Caballero was a *converso* and the son of a *reconciliado,* and so should not be in the Indies at all, while he accused Hernando de las Mallas of being a wizard. Zuazo insisted that all his licenses for slaves were for "Caribs," who could be legally enslaved.[13]

Figueroa's main anxiety was becoming much the same as that of the priors: if he treated the Indians well, the *encomiendas* would have to be abandoned. But if he abandoned them, most of the Castilians would leave for home. None of the four thousand African slaves planned under Gorrevod's famous grant seem yet to have materialized. As for the thirty Indian towns that the priors had planned, only four now existed.[14] Figueroa himself founded a few more places.[15] But he felt the shortage of labor was such that he would soon have to accept the arguments of the *encomenderos* and permit indiscriminate slaving in the Bahamas and on the Pearl Coast.

He soon had a report on the provenance of 108 Indians who had reached Santo Domingo in a boat belonging to Jacome de Castellón, one of the many hispanized Genoese who made such a major contribution to the first years of Spanish control of the Indies.[16] This showed that only twenty-eight were men, the rest women, some with babies still at their breasts. Their ages ranged from seven to thirty, though three women were over seventy. Two men were even older. Figueroa asked Bono de Quejo, Captain Dorta, and Antón García to examine these Indians. A *cacique* of Cumaná was the interpreter. Seventy-eight Indians were consulted. Those who could prove definitely that they were not Caribs were declared *naborías* and left as such with the factor Ampiés. Bono de Queijo announced that all were Caribs. The three examiners confirmed that estimate but, all the same, the Governor doubted it. He caused the magistrate Francisco de Vallejo and Antonio de Ojeda, who knew the areas concerned, to make a new inquiry. Spanish officials were thus becoming used to such investigations.

The conclusion of all these investigations was that the Crown allowed officials to participate in procuring slaves on condition that they did it alone, without business associations. The illegality of the sale of *naborías* was again proclaimed.[17]

But, benign though Figueroa might have been at heart, he himself sought to benefit from whatever commerce was available, to the exclusion of all the old shipbuilders. For example, he formed a society with Alonso Gutiérrez de Aguilón, of Azúa, an experienced planter, to build a new sugar mill, and sent his own nephew, Alonso de Aguilar, to do the same in the north of the island; and in 1519 and 1520, about thirty-four little fleets set off in the usual directions, north and south, in search of both pearls and slaves, bringing back about 1,500 of the latter. About twenty flotillas from San Juan to the Pearl Coast conveyed over five hundred *marcos* of pearls. Antonio Serrano, the *procurador,* returning from Spain, meanwhile busied himself with a scheme to make available slaves from the new Portuguese settlements in Brazil to La Española, to be carried in Castilian ships.[18] To a visitor from Mars, the search for Indian slaves on the mainland of South America might have seemed, in 1519, the prime concern of the new Spanish Empire.

Figueroa antagonized many of the older shipbuilders of Santo Domingo, who had powerful friends at home. Though lowly born, or perhaps because of it, he was haughty and declared, "There is no merchant here who has either a conscience or any sense of truthfulness,"[19] which, even if correct, was a remark scarcely calculated to please. The shipbuilders had the support of the three judges of the *audiencia*—Matienzo, Villalobos, and Vázquez de Ayllón—as well as friends at court. But then everyone had some friends at court; indeed, Las Casas, who was then dictating policy (if not activity) in the Indies, was permanently at court—wherever the court might be.

In October 1519, the court was still at Molins de Rey, outside Barcelona. Las Casas met Bishop Juan de Quevedo, the onetime peasant boy from the mountains of Santander who had gone out as bishop of Darien with Pedrarias, and who had been asked to dine by the royal almoner, Bishop Ruiz de la Mota. Juan de Samano, a notary and a protégé of Conchillos's who had survived the eclipse of his patron, and who would soon be named by Cobos as his deputy in respect to matters relating to the Indies, was also present. Las Casas went up to Quevedo and said, "Sir, because of my concern with the Indies, I am obliged to kiss your hands."[20] Quevedo asked Samano, who had some sinecures in Cuba, "Who is this priest?" "It's Señor de Las Casas." Quevedo asked: "Oh, Señor de Las Casas, and what sermon have you brought to preach to us?"[21] Las Casas said: "Certainly for days I have longed to preach to your lordship, but I assure you that I have a couple of sermons which, if you would only listen and consider them, would be more valuable than all the money that you bring back from the Indies."[22] Quevedo, furious, said: "You are lost, you are lost. . . ." Samano intervened to tell Quevedo that the Council of the Realm was pleased with Las Casas's ideas. Quevedo commented: "With good intentions, one can often do something dishonest and so commit a mortal sin."[23]

Las Casas was about to make an appropriate reply when Bishop Ruiz de la Mota came out of the royal bedchamber and carried off Quevedo to dine with him, and also Diego Colón and Juan de Zúñiga, a onetime courtier of the late King Philip and the future tutor of King Philip II.[24] After dinner, Las Casas approached Ruiz de la Mota, who was by then playing cards. They were all watching the game when someone who had been in La Española said that it was possible to grow wheat there. Quevedo denied it. Las Casas then took from his pocket some seeds that he said had come from an orange tree in an orchard in Santo Domingo. Quevedo asked him offensively: "What do you really know about anything? What is this business that you carry on? Do you know what you are talking about?"

Las Casas asked in reply, "Are my undertakings good or evil?" Quevedo demanded: "Are you so informed in arts and sciences that you dare to negotiate these undertakings?" Las Casas returned:

Do you know, my lord bishop, how little I know of the affairs that I am dealing with? That the learning which I think I have is less than you suppose? But I see my ideas as conclusions, and the first of them is that you have sinned a thousand times, actually a thousand times more than that, for not having put your soul at the disposal of your sheep, in order to free them from the hands of those tyrants who destroy them. And my second conclusion is that you eat the flesh and drink the blood of your own sheep. My third is that, unless you restore everything that you stole from the Indies, up to the last farthing, you cannot save anyone else except perhaps for Judas.

The Bishop saw that he could not make any headway with the intemperate Las Casas, so he began to laugh. Las Casas exclaimed: "You laugh, my lord bishop. Start to cry because of your unhappiness and that of your sheep. . . . Ah, if only I had tears in my pocket!"[25]

Bishop Ruiz de la Mota had continued playing his game while this unusual conversation was going on. Diego Colón and Zúñiga said something in favor of Las Casas, and Ruiz de la Mota then went to the King, whom he told of what had passed between Las Casas and Bishop Quevedo, suggesting that the King might like to listen himself to what "Micer Bartolomé" was saying about the Indies. The King agreed and suggested that the Bishop and Las Casas should both come to see him in three days' time.

The three days passed. The Bishop came upon Las Casas in the chamber that Charles used as a throne room and exclaimed: "Father, you here? Is it a good idea that friars wander fecklessly about the palace? Surely it is better for priests to be in their cells than in a palace?" Las Casas said: "In truth, it would be better if all of us who are friars were in our cells!" (Quevedo was a Franciscan while Las Casas for the moment was just a priest.) Bishop Quevedo suggested that Las Casas should leave so that the King should not find him there. Las Casas replied, "Silence, my lord bishop. Let the King come, and you will see what happens."[26]

The King soon entered and sat on his improvised throne, attended by Chièvres, Gattinara, Ruiz de la Mota, and three or four others, among them the historian Oviedo and Agustín Aguirre. The last-named was seeking land, and he would obtain it at Santa Marta, Colombia, but not the authorization to go there for one hundred members of the Order of Santiago that he had also requested. Las Casas had mocked that scheme, though he was scarcely in a position to do so, with his own suggestions for a specially instituted new order of knights. Oviedo had only just returned from the territory of Pedrarias, as the Bishop had done earlier, and he was, of course, experienced at court. Agustín Aguirre, Vice-Chancellor of Aragon (despite his Basque name), had been with King Charles since 1517. King Fernando had once imprisoned him, either because he had opposed the grant of a subsidy by the Cortes of Calatayud or, as some said, because he had been too friendly with the young Queen Germaine de Foix—who, aged twenty-nine in 1518, seems now to have enjoyed a brief love affair with the young King, who was still only eighteen and who, it may be remembered, had been charged to look after her by his grandfather, the late King Fernando.[27]

Gattinara said to the Bishop: "Reverend Bishop, His Majesty says that you are to speak now if you have anything to say about the Indies."[28] Thanks to Gattinara, the King was now addressed in Spain as "Majesty" rather than "Highness." Cobos had written to all Spanish noblemen and officials assuring them that that change did not mean the King intended to reduce the prestige of his Spanish realms. But letters to the monarch were no longer to be directed to the "very noble and powerful lord"; they were to be sent to "SCCR Majestad"—"sacra, cesaréa, católica, real Majestad." Gattinara had also wanted Charles to abandon the traditional Spanish royal signature "yo, el rey" for just "Carlos," but Charles, perhaps thinking of letters from King Fernando, refused.[29]

Quevedo then paid a compliment to the King in Latin, saying that his face, like that of Priam in the Iliad, alone made him worthy of an empire. Everyone present liked that, especially the King (they had forgotten what had happened to the King of Troy). Then Quevedo said that he had indeed many important things to say about the Indies, and asked that those who were not of the Council of the Realm be told to leave.

Gattinara spoke in the King's ear and afterwards repeated: "Reverend Bishop, His Majesty commands that you speak now if you have anything to say." The Bishop repeated that what he had to say was secret. Gattinara again consulted the King and then said, "Reverend Bishop, His Majesty commands that you speak now if you have anything to say."

Then, despite the, to him, offensive presence of Las Casas, the Bishop did speak. He spoke reverentially of the King's grandfather, the Catholic King, who of course had first sent a fleet to the New World. He said that he himself had lived in Darien for five years and that because the expedition had taken inadequate supplies, many of his friends had died of hunger. The first Governor of Darien, Núñez de Balboa, had, of course, been bad, but the second, Pedrarias, was worse—so "I determined to come home and give evidence to His Majesty about what I had seen." As for the Indians, "Those people are slaves by nature"—as the philosopher Aristotle had put it.

Then Las Casas was asked to speak. He said that he was one of the most senior of those who had gone to the Indies, having been there first in 1502, and he had "seen the greatest cruelty and inhumanity practiced on the gentle and peace-loving indigenous people, without any reason except for insatiable greed, thirst, and hunger for gold by the conquistadors—my father [Gabriel de Peñalosa] among them." These crimes, he said, had been committed in two ways: by unjust wars in which there had been no limit to the number of people, towns, and even nations that had been destroyed; and by subjecting Indians to unbelievably hard work to enable the extraction of gold. "I was moved to act not because I was a better Christian than others but by a natural compassion." He described how he had gone to tell King Fernando about these things and how he had approached Cisneros and, after him, Jean Le Sauvage. He repeated that "these Indians . . . are capable of Christian faith and, by nature, are free and have their kings and natural lords . . . and even if it were as the reverend Bishop says, we should recall that the Philosopher [whom he quoted, namely Aristotle] was a nonbeliever and is now, presumably, burning in Hell."[30] That remark had a considerable effect. No one talked critically, as a rule, of Aristotle. Las Casas added that the Christian religion concerned itself with equal treatment of all and that there were no people who are "slaves by nature." One should recall that Jesus Christ died also for those people.

This speech took three-quarters of an hour. Las Casas had a beguiling way of talking, and he completely held his distinguished audience. When he had finished, a Franciscan, Cristóbal del Río, who had just returned from Santo Domingo, was brought in to speak briefly, if with fervor, of the vexed subject of the decline of the Indian population. Diego Colón also was constrained to add some remarks about the damage that the Indians had suffered.

When the Admiral ceased, Bishop Quevedo rose and asked to reply. But Gattinara, again after consulting the King, said, "Reverend Bishop, if you have something more to say, you should write it down." The King then returned to his rooms and nothing more was said.

What an extraordinary conversation this was! We know of it only from Las Casas, and we should beware of trusting all that he says. Yet certainly the eloquence of Las Casas convinced not only the worldly Gattinara but also the inexperienced young King that a serious problem existed in the New World.

Quevedo did put his recommendations on paper. To everyone's amazement, they were quite close to the ideas of Las Casas's. First, he described the massacres that he had seen in Darien; and, second, he made suggestions for ending these evils. That was to bring an end to the *entradas* that had continued though they were formally prohibited.

Just before Christmas 1519, Gattinara summoned Las Casas, took him to his room, and, giving him one of the large candles that he had on a table, told him to read the memorandum of the Bishop. Afterwards, Las Casas said to Gattinara that he would like to sign the documents himself: "What greater cruelties have I described than these?"

In the event, then, Charles and Gattinara gave support to Las Casas's schemes. What a great opportunity now unfolded before the priest from Seville! The trouble was that although he had won the battle of ideas, his own schemes remained fanciful. He wrote in his *History:* "If it were not for the haste that the King, having been elected emperor, had to go to be crowned and confirmed as emperor, the future of the Indies would have been promising."[31] That was a self-deception. Las Casas was still, after all, pressing his scheme for the introduction of his Knights of the Golden Spur. These, he now thought, should number fifty. They were each to put up 75,000 maravedís, and with that money the colony would be founded. They would wear a robe of white on which would be a red cross, similar to that of the Order of Calatrava. They would control the one thousand leagues between Santa Marta and Paria.

The idea was opposed by Oviedo, who said that his own similar scheme could assure a more serious income. He had already come to dislike the fanaticism of Las Casas in a way that would eventually be reflected in his history of the Indies. But Diego Colón, like so many, had become fascinated by the priest, and wrote to Gattinara in favor of his ideas.

Another opponent wrote: "There is no assurance that the proposal of Las Casas will succeed, for it conflicts with the privileges of people now in La Española, and there are other weighty and secret reasons against Las Casas that cause me to recommend disapproval of this plan." But Gattinara was persuaded and advised the King to ignore both Oviedo and Fonseca. The situation was eased by the death of Quevedo on Christmas Eve 1519 from a fever probably contracted in the Indies. The outstanding questions raised by Las Casas—in particular, how exactly his plans would be put into effect— were left for a decision of the Council of the Realm, which, it was assumed, would soon be held at Burgos.[32]

"For empire comes from God alone"

At last, empire has been conferred on me by the single consent of Germany, with God, as I deem it, willing and commanding. For truly he errs who reckons that by men or riches, by unlawful canvassing or stratagems, the empire of the whole world can fall to anyone's lot. For empire comes from God alone.

The King-Emperor
Charles at Santiago de Compostela, 1520

While these learned discussions were under way at court, they began to be overshadowed by sensational international matters.

The question of what was going to happen in the German Empire was beginning to dominate the minds of Gattinara, Chièvres, and Charles. Ulrich von Hutten's dialogue *Vadiscus,* about the evils that the author thought had been caused to Germany by the Catholic Church, was a patriotic gauntlet flung down before Rome. It exalted the memory of ancient German liberty. On February 20, 1520, the electors of Mainz and Saxony wrote to Charles urging him to come quickly to help them. Unless he came soon, there would be a disaster such as had never been seen before,[1] and in March, von Hutten called on Charles V to lead the struggle against Roman oppression.

This was also the year when the Sultan Suleiman I came to the Ottoman throne and reversed the conciliatory policy of his father, Selim I, who had hitherto been desirous only of attacking Persia and Egypt, not the Christian Empire. Henceforth Charles was continuously at war with the Turks, who themselves were often in alliance with France, which seemed scandalous to the rest of Europe. At the same time, Barbarossa, a renegade Greek pirate, was also emerging as a formidable enemy in the western Mediterranean (he occupied Algiers in 1516).[2]

Gattinara was determined to ensure that Charles faced all these challenges and managed all his vast dominions efficiently. In early 1520, he penned another letter to the Emperor (as, of course, Charles now was), giving him further advice: "Each of the countries of which you are the ruler should be allowed to govern itself according to its ancient laws and customs. Each country, too, should try to arrange that its expenses do not exceed its income."[3] But Gattinara also thought that a controller-general should supervise all the royal finances.[4] The implications for the empire in the Indies were not mentioned.

On January 23, Charles and the Spanish court left for Burgos. On the way, at Calahorra, for years a Mendoza see, Secretary Cobos summoned a Castilian Cortes for Santiago de Compostela on March 20. The King as usual needed more money. Why Santiago? Primarily because the King wished to be near Corunna, which had been chosen as his port of embarkation. Perhaps, too, he wanted to be away from such a dangerously lively place as Burgos. Chièvres tried to persuade the municipal authority in Valladolid, independently of the Cortes, to make a direct grant immediately. But the city was in turmoil because the *procuradores* of Toledo had arrived and were trying to persuade those of their colleagues who cared to listen to oppose any new grant to the Crown until all their demands had been met.

Valladolid rang with rumors: was the King perhaps going to Corunna in order to abandon Spain forever? The bell of the church of San Miguel was sounded; crowds went into the streets in protest. The King received two *procuradores* from Toledo, Alonso Suárez and Pedro Laso, who asked him to hear their petitions. But Charles said he had to go immediately to Tordesillas in order to see his mother, Juana. He knew well that Valladolid was the most divided of Spanish cities. Chièvres, hearing the crowds in the streets, determined to leave there and then, in heavy rain. Some tried to prevent the royal escape by closing the gate. But the King's guard, small though it was, dispersed them, and Charles and Chièvres galloped the short distance of fifteen miles to Tordesillas, where they arrived at the end of the day. The court would eventually catch up to find a King shaken to the core, much as his great-great-grandson, Louis XIV, would be shocked by the Fronde, 130 years later.[5]

Charles, having seen his sad mother once again and consigned her to the far from considerate care of his cousin, the Marquis of Denia, left Tordesillas on March 9 and made for Galicia, stopping at Villalpando, once a Templar fortress, where he again found some of the difficult councillors from Toledo, now joined by the *procuradores* of Salamanca. They were received by Bishop Ruiz de la Mota and García de Padilla, the secretary to King Fernando, who had cleverly managed to intrigue his way back to influence with

Charles. (From 1518 he was to be found signing documents about the Indies and acted as temporary chairman of the little group of officials who dealt with imperial matters in the Council of Castile in place of Bishop Fonseca, who was in Corunna.) Ruiz de la Mota said that unless the Toledans explained exactly what their request was, they could not be received. They revealed something of what they wanted: they wished to be consulted—the demand of parliamentarians throughout the ages. So the Bishop told them to return at two o'clock in the afternoon. They did, and presented their petitions.

Ruiz de la Mota then told them that the King was leaving for Benavente. There they were received again, but by Antonio de Rojas, the Archbishop of Granada and president of the Council of the Realm, and Padilla, who told them peremptorily not to meddle in the King's affairs. They decided to continue to Santiago, where, indeed, the monarch and the court arrived on March 24, having spent nearly every night since leaving Tordesillas in a different place and having seen many of the wilder parts of Galicia. King, court, and *procuradores* were greeted by Bishop Fonseca's cousin Alonso, who, as his father and grandfather had been, was archbishop there. The Archbishop arranged fiestas with the fine fish, fruit, and other delicacies for which Galicia was always known.[6]

It seemed to most courtiers a mistake to hold the meeting in Santiago de Compostela, a remote place where only pilgrims ever went. Still, the assembly opened as planned on April 1 in a chapel of the cloister of the monastery of San Francisco, an institution said to have been founded by St. Francis in person.[7] The participants were eclectic, for the *procuradores* included many friends of the King: García Ruiz de la Mota, brother of the Bishop, and Juan Pérez de Cartagena, of the great *converso* family, attended from Burgos, and the royal secretary Cobos was one of the two representatives of Granada.[8] The ubiquitous courtier Hernando de Vega, for so many years viceroy in Galicia, was present, as were García de Padilla and Luis Zapata, the latter acting as secretary.

Here in the cloister Bishop Ruiz de la Mota made an astounding speech launching the imperial idea. It was apparently written by the royal doctor, the Milanese intellectual Ludovico Marliano, the best friend of Gattinara. Peter Martyr thought that he was "half Gattinara's soul." It was he who had devised for Charles the motto *Plus Ultra* and, as a reward (or so it was said), had been named to two Spanish bishoprics, that of Tuy and Ciudad Rodrigo. The first is one of the most beautiful of frontier cities. Charles, said Ruiz de la Mota, was more of a king than any other monarch had been, because he had more realms,[9] even if "Castile was the foundation, the protection, and the real engine of all the others." Looking back, he recalled that in the remote past Spain had sent emperors to Rome: for example, Trajan, Hadrian, and Theodosius. Now the empire had again come to seek in Spain its king of the Romans and its emperor.[10] Yet "the orchard of his pleasures, the fortress for his defense, the place to attack, his treasure and his sword, would remain his Spanish inheritance."[11] Ruiz de la Mota was one of those who had done his best to teach Charles Spanish—a good choice, since "nobody managed that language with more facility and elegance."[12]

Charles then spoke. His speech was probably written by Gattinara. He said:

> At last, empire has been conferred on me by the single consent of Germany, with God, as I deem it, willing and commanding. For truly he errs who reckons that by men or riches, by unlawful canvassing or stratagems, the empire of the whole world can fall to anyone's lot. For empire comes from God alone. Nor have I undertaken the charge of such great measures for my own sake, for I was well able to content myself with the Spanish *imperium,* with the Balearics and Sardinia, with the Sicilian kingdoms, with a great part of Italy, Germany, and France, and with another, as I might say, gold-bearing world [the Indies presumably; this was Charles's first public reference to the New World].
>
> But now a certain necessity compels me to set off on my travels. My decision is taken out of a proper respect for religion, whose enemies have grown so much that neither the repose of the commonweal nor the dignity of Spain nor the welfare of my kingdoms are able to tolerate such a threat. All these are hardly able to exist or be maintained unless I link Spain with Germany and add the name of *Caesar* to that of king of Spain.[13]

Charles then made two promises: first, though he had now to go to Germany, he would return to Spain within three years; second, he would appoint no more foreigners to Spanish offices. He added that he was in agreement with everything that Ruiz de la Mota had said.

The *procuradores* of Salamanca listened to these high-flown words with interest, but they had their own, more earthy demands. They did not want a foreigner such as Gattinara to preside in the Cortes at Santiago any more than they had wanted Le Sauvage to be at Valladolid. They refused to take the oath to the King unless their petitions were granted. They were then dismissed. Pedro Laso of Salamanca insisted that the King must heed the protests of the cities, while the nobles of Galicia were beginning to rouse themselves from their ancient lethargy to demand that their cities, too, should send *procuradores* to the Cortes of Castile. Why should that body be limited to the representatives of a few Castilian cities and exclude both Santiago and Corunna?

Chièvres sent Cobos and Juan Ramírez, the secretary of the Council of the Realm, to the lodgings of the men from Toledo to tell them that the King ordered them to leave Santiago. Led by Alonso Ortiz, those *procuradores* then saw Chièvres, who accepted a compromise: they would retire to El Padrón, twelve miles west of Santiago, the town where James's body in his stone coffin had been washed up in the River Ulla. But the King still refused to see them. He instead retired to the ancient Franciscan monastery of San Lorenzo for Holy Week. Ortiz continued to press Chièvres, Zapata, and Cobos. The debate went on. Cobos, in his improbable guise as member for Granada, proposed the grant of a generous subsidy to the Crown. Gattinara, in a later memoir, claimed that he had opposed Charles's request for a grant to pay for his journey to Germany, but the record shows that the Chancellor spoke several times in favor of it.[14] It does not suggest that this great Piedmontese felt the slightest timidity at speaking forcefully before a Spanish audience.

After Easter, the court left Santiago for Corunna. Charles ordered the Cortes, that is, the *procuradores,* to follow him the short distance to that port, which was already established on both sides of its elegant peninsula. The eastern side had a fine harbor, and the plan was that the King would sail from there to his northern empire with a brief, diplomatically useful stop in England on the way. In the interval between the meetings in the two cities of Galicia, Charles's courtiers cleverly persuaded most *procuradores* to support the subsidy.

The King himself spent much of his last days before going to northern Europe discussing the Indies. Thus on May 17, 1520, Charles reinstated Diego Colón as governor of the Indies without a clear definition of his power, for he would be governor and, at last, viceroy of the island of La Española, as of all the other islands that the Admiral—Columbus—had discovered in those seas. That seemed to imply that not only would Diego recover the islands in the Caribbean, Cuba, Jamaica, and Puerto Rico as well as La Española—but also the north coast of South America, from the Orinoco to present-day Honduras, which his father had visited in his third and fourth journeys, of 1498 and 1502.

This decree seemed to do away with the loose independence of Cuba, Jamaica, and Puerto Rico, based on the earlier nomination as "lieutenant governors" of Velázquez, Esquivel, and Ponce. But, in reality, nothing would change. The "lieutenant governors" would be the proconsuls on the spot, and Diego Colón would only constitute a distant court of appeal. One other concession was made to Diego: he would not be subject to a *residencia* when he abandoned his authority. But all the same, he was declared subject to investigation by *comisarios* who could institute what might seem to be a *residencia* without the name.[15]

The decree of May 17 relating to Diego Colón was detailed. It was signed by Gattinara, Cobos, Ruiz de la Mota, Luis Zapata, and a Dr. Joose, a new *letrado* from Catalonia. It included an Article 12 that declared, in words that read as if they had been written by Las Casas, that God had created the Indians as free men, subject to no one. Nor were they obliged to carry out any service to Spaniards.[16] Article 13 was equally positive, for by it the King and his council miraculously agreed that "the Indians were free men, ought to be treated as such and persuaded to accept Christianity by the methods that Christ had established."[17] Another article provided that Don Diego would receive a tenth of all the gold, pearls, silver, and other precious stones found in the Indies, as well as of all other products. The foundation of new cities and municipalities could not be made without Diego's approval. The empire might be built by and for free men, but their freedom of action was to be limited by Castilian rules.

Cardinal Adrian had been silent, even invisible, for many months but was now, improbably and unwisely, named as regent in Spain in the forthcoming absence of the monarch. Chièvres was responsible for that nomination. Adrian made a solemn and learned speech in Corunna in which he said that "by natural reasons, by the authority of divine law, and by the works of the Holy Fathers, as through human and ecclesiastical laws, the Indians were to be brought to a knowledge of God by peaceful means, not by Muslim methods"—presumably force.[18] Las Casas thought that this statement would enable him to go ahead with all his schemes of colonization. Diego Colón had by then made a de facto alliance with Las Casas and guaranteed himself to work for the evangelization of the Indians on the mainland.

The territory that Las Casas was now to think of as his own for special development was still that from Santa Marta to Paria, that is, most of the coast of what is now Columbia and all of Venezuela. He was not given the monopoly on pearls for which he had now decided to ask, and the recovery of those, as well as all violent actions against the Indians in South America, was prohibited. Once again, Las Casas pledged that Indians seized as slaves in the past from any part of this territory and now in La Española would be set free and taken home.

In return, Las Casas guaranteed to pacify and convert the Indians under his auspices and to organize them into towns so that within two years the King might have ten thousand or so new tax-paying vassals. Las Casas would pay the Crown a rent of a little more than 5.5 million maravedís after the third year, 11.25 million after the sixth, and 22.5 million after the tenth.

The fifty Knights of the Golden Spur, who were to articulate these splendid dreams and be the nerve of these operations, would be, in Las Casas's words, "modest persons, subject to reason, who would, by good will, concern themselves in such good work more for virtue and to serve God than by greed, though they could certainly seek to enrich themselves by legal means."[19] But such "modest" people in the sixteenth-century Indies were hard to come by.

The King also instructed the Governor of La Española, Figueroa, to give the appropriate Indians their freedom "with all reasonable speed." He was to begin with those who had been taken away from nonresident *encomenderos*. Indians left alone by the death of their *encomenderos* were also to be freed. Some "good Spaniards" were to be placed among these Indians to tell them how to live in the future. Free Indians would be provided with food and tools until they began themselves to produce crops. A priest and an administrator would be assigned to each place. Figueroa was to seek other Indians desirous and capable of living in those towns, even though their *encomenderos* might complain. These arrangements were to be repeated in Puerto Rico by Antonio de la Gama, a newly appointed judge from Seville.[20]

Another decision seemed less pressing at the time but in the long run was more significant than anything else agreed in Corunna in those May days of 1520. The previous autumn, two Spanish conquistadors, one from Salamanca, Francisco de Montejo, the other from Medellín, in Extremadura, Alonso Hernández Portocarrero, had arrived in Seville from the Indies. Montejo had first gone out there in 1514 with Pedrarias, and Hernández Portocarrero had gone to Cuba in 1516. In 1518, they had sailed with Hernán Cortés to the west. Then, on Cortés's orders, they had returned from Vera Cruz via Florida, guided by the famous pilot Alaminos, veteran of Ponce de León's expedition to Florida and of Columbus's fourth voyage.

To begin with, Montejo had seemed to be a friend of Diego Velázquez, but he had become an unquestioning supporter of Cortés and for the rest of his life his actions would be concentrated in what became New Spain. Hernández Portocarrero was a cousin of the Count of Medellín, in which city he was born. So he was probably an old friend of Cortés. His mother was a sister of Alonso de Céspedes, judge of Las Gradas, in Seville, a most useful connection, if a *converso* one.

These men, Alaminos included, came to Spain with some remarkable news and treasure, as well as some Indian slaves from the territory where, according to their reports, Cortés with about six hundred men seemed to be carving out a new colony. Cortés, it seemed, had been condemned for rebellion by Governor Velázquez, who had written of his outrage to Bishop Fonseca and to others in Spain; and Fonseca had wanted to arrest, perhaps execute, the two men who had come impertinently as Cortés's *procuradores*, technically representatives of a city that he had founded on the Caribbean coast and that he had named Vera Cruz.

Ruiz de la Mota and Cobos, both conventional but not always cautious, thought that the court should wait to see how matters were resolved between Cortés and Velázquez. They and their colleagues were much impressed by the treasure sent by Cortés, and as will be recalled, in his speech at Santiago a few weeks before, the King himself had referred to this territory as "a new land of gold." The so-called *procuradores* of Cortés had traveled with the court throughout the winter and the spring, and the treasure they had carried with them had been displayed not only in Seville but also in Tordesillas. The gold had been held in the Casa de Contratación. The pride of the exhibition was two large, elaborately worked "wheels" of wood covered with silver and gold. They were presents from the Mexican monarch Moctezuma to Cortés.

The Indians whom the conquistadors had brought back (they were Totonaca; see chapter 33) had been shown at court, too, and the King himself had been constrained to intervene to ensure that they were properly clothed against the Castilian winter. Montejo and Portocarrero were accompanied by Martín Cortés, Hernán's father, an ex-warrior in the war in Granada (and in the civil war between La Beltraneja and Isabel); while a cousin of his, Francisco Núñez, a lawyer of Salamanca, arranged a meeting between the emissaries of Cortés and that influential member of the Council of Castile, Lorenzo Galíndez de Carvajal, a distant cousin of Martín Cortés.[21] This meeting was second in importance in Carvajal's life to his talk with King Fernando the Catholic on his deathbed.

On April 30, the Council of the Realm discussed the requests of these emissaries. They merely asked that Cortés be allowed to continue his expedition free of obligations to Governor Velázquez. Present at the discussion seem to have been Cardinal Adrian; Gattinara; Hernando de Vega; Antonio de Rojas, Archbishop of Granada; Fonseca; and the Fleming Carondelet, along with such Castilian civil servants as Diego Beltrán, Zapata, Francisco de Aguirre, and García de Padilla. Galíndez de Carvajal was there, too, at least for part of the discussion. The council was now, if not well disposed to Cortés, at least not hostile, and though they did not rule on the main issue, they allowed Cortés's father and friends to receive from the Casa de Contratación in Seville 4.5 million maravedís for their expenses.[22] Cortés himself was not praised. But nor was he condemned; and so his friends felt that they had gained a famous victory.[23]

On May 19, 1520, the royal pilots in Corunna announced the wind right for England, and the King, Queen Germaine and her new husband (the Marquis of Brandenburg), Frederick Count Palatine, and the Duke of Alba set out for that northern country, being accompanied by such noblemen and courtiers as the Marquis of Aguilar, Diego de Guevara, Juan de Zúñiga, Galíndez de Carvajal, Bishop Ruiz de la Mota, García Padilla, Bishop Manrique, Cobos, and, of course, Gattinara and Chièvres. "With loud music from clarions and flutes, and with great demonstrations of joy [the court] weighed anchor and departed," in a hundred ships for England and Germany.

There remained behind, in a Spain "laden now with griefs and misfortunes," a new Council of the Realm, headed as before by Archbishop Rojas, of Granada, and including the eternal courtier Hernando de Vega, the Viceroy of Galicia, Bishop Fonseca, his brother the commander Antonio de Fonseca, and the treasurer Francisco de Vargas, while the Council of Aragon would be presided over by Juan, Archbishop of Saragossa (the illegitimate son and successor of the equally illegitimate Archbishop Don Alonso, now dead), and that of Valencia by Diego de Mendoza, Count of Melito, a legitimized bastard of Cardinal Mendoza.[24] Fonseca and Zapata would act as the officials for the Indies, together with Vargas, Pedro de los Cobos (cousin of Francisco), the notary Juan de Samano, and the Italian courtier Peter Martyr, who had talked so much with men who had been to the Indies, for the benefit of his brilliant letters to Rome. Fonseca now liked him: "The Bishop of Burgos in whom I have much confidence has been very amiable with me," Martyr wrote in September 1518.[25] These men were already acting as a subcommittee of the Council of the Realm. But they, like all other royal committees, would soon be challenged and nearly swept away by an unprecedented upheaval.

32

"The new golden land"

I have seen the things that they have brought the King from the new
golden land.

Albrecht Dürer, 1520

The King-Emperor Charles left Spain on May 20, 1520, stopping in England
as a guest of King Henry, his uncle by marriage—in Dover, Canterbury, and
Sandwich. Apparently he there showed off the treasures that he had received
from "the new golden land" of New Spain thanks to Cortés.[1] Alas, no record
seems to exist of what the English thought. Charles reached Flanders in June
and arranged to be crowned "King of the Romans" at Aix-la-Chapelle on
October 20.[2]

Charles was welcomed in Germany as if he were a new Messiah. Even
Martin Luther had high hopes of him. In August 1520, that reformer spoke
of Charles, in *An Address to the Nobility of the German Nation,* as the much
awaited "young and noble" chief. That was the year of Luther's two other
great works: *On the Babylonian Captivity of the Church of God* and *On the
Liberty of a Christian Man.* In the early autumn, the more radical Ulrich von
Hutten again made a direct appeal for support from Charles V, telling him
that the Church of Rome was the natural enemy of the German Emperor.
Charles did not react. Did he miss an opportunity? Perhaps. But he was too
good a Catholic to play with emotions.

While Charles was busy being crowned emperor at Aix-la-Chapelle, as
all his predecessors had been,[3] Cortés's Mexican treasures were displayed in
the town hall at Brussels. The Hungarian-German Albrecht Dürer, the favorite painter of the Archduchess Margaret, examined them with much
pleasure, writing of them fulsomely in his "Diary of His Journey to the
Netherlands." Dürer would have earlier almost certainly seen an account of
Cortés's conquests in a letter, *Ein Auszug Ettlicher Sendsbriefe,* published in
his own town of Nuremberg by a local printer, Friedrich Poel. So Dürer was
prepared. He now wrote: "I have seen the things that they have brought the

King from the new golden land."[4] Suddenly, the New World seemed, even to the hard-bitten courtiers around the new Emperor, to offer dazzling and exotic riches. Dürer met Erasmus, and that autumn the latter proposed a compromise in the Church whereby the Pope would suspend the bull (*Exsurge Domine*) that he had issued against Luther and submit the whole matter to a commission of wise men designated by the Emperor, his brother-in-law Louis, King of Hungary, and his uncle, the King of England. (The reputation of the future English rebel then stood high in Rome.) All would refrain from using any armed force while those wise men were sitting.[5]

For a time it seemed that this conciliatory policy might be successful. The world seemed, all the same, on the edge of profound transformations. The Emperor met Luther at the famous test of opinion known as the Diet of Worms. Charles appeared in person, as did Luther, who had a safe conduct, being protected by Elector Frederick of Saxony. Charles seems to have seen Luther as a heretic, but he implied that he did not oppose clerical reform outright. All eyes were on him and the papal conservatives, who were suspicious: the nuncio Gerolamo Aleandro even complained to the imperial court that Charles had agreed to listen to Luther at Worms. Chièvres replied: "Let the Pope fulfill his duty and let him not concern himself so much in our affairs and we will do what he wants."[6]

Luther appeared at Worms on April 16. He spoke badly. But then two days later he spoke well, representing himself as a man leading a revolution. He made a great impression. The Reformation had begun. But on Charles he had a wholly negative effect.

On April 19, Charles made a personal statement in French. He explained how he had inherited his loyalty to the Catholic Church from his ancestors and how he was determined to remain faithful to their memory. He had pledged his realms (including the empire), his possessions, his body, his blood, his friends, his life, and his soul to that cause. He thought that it would be a shame if any idea of heresy penetrated the hearts of his audience: "We have heard Luther speak, and I regret that I delayed in speaking against him. I shall never hear him again. Of course, he has a safe conduct, but from now on I shall regard him as a notorious heretic, and I hope that the rest of you will fulfill your role as good Christians. . . ."[7]

The great medieval scholar Menéndez Pidal thought that in this speech Charles was influenced by the memory of his devout grandmother, Isabel.[8] She certainly would never have stooped to an armistice with evil. At all events, any idea of compromise was at an end. Leo X's excommunication of Luther was thus seen as having been confirmed by Charles. On May 4, Luther was seized by soldiers of the Elector Frederick of Saxony and taken to the castle of Wartburg, in Saxony, where he was able to continue his writing in tranquillity.

Charles had other anxieties; for example, in April 1521, King François I declared war, and soon after, three Spanish transatlantic caravels heading for the New World were intercepted by the French. Defense of the new empire suddenly became a concern, especially when the next year French ships were observed for the first time off Santo Domingo. The age of diplomatic innocence in which Spain's only rival in the Indies was Portugal was coming to an end. Thanks to the diplomacy of the Spanish ambassador in Rome, the astute and courtly Juan Manuel, Charles organized a diplomatic reversal leading to an alliance with the Pope, Leo X, against France. An edict against Luther was also prepared. At the end of May, a different alignment was achieved by the marriage at Linz between Charles's brother, the Infante Fernando, now the Archduke Ferdinand, to Anne, sister of King Louis of Hungary, who himself at the same time married María, sister of Charles and Fernando.

Alas for the hope of friendship with France! Charles's master, Chièvres, who had slept in the royal bedroom for so long and who had always wanted peace with that country, which he respected as Burgundy's suzerain, died in May. He was replaced as grand chamberlain by Henry of Nassau, who never had much effect on policy. The Chancellor, Gattinara, was now in control, though, when in July 1521 he was away for some months at Calais to meet his fellow chancellors, the proud Cardinal Wolsey of England and Du Prat of France, Charles began to develop a taste for making his own decisions. He began to rely more and more on secretaries, such as the two experienced Aragonese Ugo de Urríes and Pedro García, as well as the charming Burgundian Jean Lalemand, Lord of Bouclans, once clerk of the Parlement at Dôle, of which Gattinara had been president. Lalemand would rise steadily under Gattinara's influence until, as often occurs in bureaucracies, he judged the time ripe to challenge his benefactor.[9] Cobos also from then on saw the Emperor regularly to discuss Spain and the Indies. When in late May the court left Worms for Brussels and stopped at Cologne, the Emperor gave Cobos a present: four of the heads of the eleven thousand virgins allegedly killed in that city during the first century A.D. Cobos took them as a treasured relic to his house at Úbeda. (As may be remembered, there had only been eight of them.)

While Charles appeared to be reaching for greatness in Germany, his first monarchy, Spain, seemed to be falling apart. On May 29, 1520, Whit Tuesday, nine days after the King had set sail from Corunna, a real rebellion of the *comuneros*, the councillors of the cities, began in Segovia.[10] Juan

Bravo, a determined man who had married a Mendoza, was the leader in that city. He raised a flag that appealed to many protesters: to those who wanted the King to remain always in Spain, to those who hated the Flemish and Burgundian advisers, to those who desired the preservation of the old Spain of greater urban independence, and to those who thought that the centralizing reforms of the Catholic Kings had gone too far. Like most movements of protest, that of the *comuneros* was Hydra-headed, and for that reason dangerous.

On June 6, Cardinal Adrian, the improbable Regent named by Charles, reached Valladolid with the Council of the Realm. Archbishop Antonio de Rojas, of Granada, the president, was already there with the Constable of Castile, Íñigo Fernández de Velasco. They discussed the problem created by the astonishing attitude of the *comuneros* in Segovia. All thought it essential to act decisively for fear that the unrest would spread.

But that was precisely what occurred: even remote Murcia peacefully proclaimed the *"comunidad"* (which implied increasingly the virtual independence of the city), while Juan Negrete "pronounced" in Madrid. Pedro de Coca, a carpenter, and Diego de Medina, a tiler, did the same in the Mendozas' capital of Guadalajara, while in Burgos the popular *corregidor* of Córdoba, Diego de Osorio, who had come home expecting only to meet his wife, Isabel de Rojas, also swept the city into rebellion. A mob demanded the burning of Bishop Ruiz de la Mota's house, because of what was seen as the destructive vote of that prelate in the Cortes of Corunna.

In the event, several palaces in Burgos were indeed sacked, including that of the commander of the Castle of Lara, Jofre de Cotanés (who, furious, said that he would rebuild his house with the heads of the *conversos* of Burgos, putting two heads for every stone destroyed; he fled but was captured by the rebels and hanged). Jews were not to blame: people of old Christian blood were the chief motors of turbulence. There were also successful risings in other cities of Castile and Extremadura. The representatives of Ávila demanded the dismissal of Chièvres, Ruiz de la Mota, Padilla, and Cobos because they were rumored to have carried off a fortune from the treasury. Adrian had already written to Charles saying that the *comuneros* were insisting that "money from Castile must be spent for the benefit of Castile and not of Germany, Aragon, Naples, and so on; and that his Majesty ought to govern each territory he controls with the money that comes from it."[11] Gattinara agreed.

In September, a junta of representatives of the rebel cities met at Tordesillas and set up a revolutionary government. Thirteen cities were represented: Toledo, Salamanca, Segovia, Toro, Burgos, Soria, Ávila, Valladolid,

León, Zamora, Cuenca, Guadalajara, and Madrid. The Council of the Realm was declared dissolved, and it was announced that Charles did not have the right to be named king during the lifetime of his mother. The new junta later began to issue decrees in the names of the *"comunidades"* and of Queen Juana, without mentioning the name of the King.

The old royal regime was thus experiencing its most severe crisis. What could the outcome be? Cardinal Adrian made intelligent concessions: the King would renounce the grants that had been voted in Corunna. No more foreigners would be appointed to any important posts, a concession that went a long way to satisfying the rebels. Then Gattinara, in Flanders, named two Castilians (the Constable, Fernández de Velasco, and the Admiral, Fadrique Enríquez) as co-regents with Adrian—a move that began to recover the great nobility for the King.

Before that order arrived in Spain, the *comuneros* had sent a detachment of soldiers to Valladolid with orders to arrest the old Council of the Realm. That they failed altogether to do, but they did catch two royal secretaries, Bartolomé Ruiz de Castañeda and Juan de Samano. The rest of the council—even the proud Bishop Fonseca—fled. The royalist forces, commanded by Bishop Fonseca's brother Antonio, who had a name for prudence gained in the war against Navarre, rallied to try to attack Segovia. They were defeated, and directed their efforts to finding artillery in the rich city of Medina del Campo. Fonseca failed yet again and was attacked by the townsmen. The city caught fire, and much of its famous market and royal quarter burned to the ground. The consequence was nearly fatal for the royalists, since the destruction of the market excited tempers in the hitherto quiescent cities of the south, for Medina del Campo had been the nerve center of the whole Spanish economy.

September 1520 saw an attempted coup in Seville, the de facto capital of the new empire in the Indies, by Juan de Figueroa, brother of the Duke of Arcos. The conflict of the *comunidades* there had the character of a new act in the ancient feud between the Ponce de León family and the Guzmáns, the former incensed by the alleged rapacity of the municipal treasurer Francisco de Alcázar and other *conversos* in power, who were assumed to be protégés of the Guzmáns. The Crown's representative, the *corregidor,* was afraid to return from Corunna, where he had voted for the King's subsidy, and such authority as there was lay in the hands of Andrés de Vergara, the chief magistrate, who established his headquarters at the palace of the dukes of Medina Sidonia. Other cities in Spain experienced similar eruptions: all might begin with new ideals, but old politics soon took over.[12]

In the Dominican convent of San Pablo in Seville on September 2, Juan de Figueroa and a group of disgruntled aristocrats, including the ruined treasurer Luis de Medina and Francisco Ponce de León, together with Pedro and Perafan de Villasis, proposed a massacre of *conversos*. Were there not many deserving citizens who had no income because the good posts had been seized by those most dubious Christians?[13] The first target was the Alcázar family, for the treasurer, Francisco de Alcázar, had recently raised local taxes.[14]

Figueroa led about four hundred followers to the cathedral along the Calle Sierpes. It is a route now familiar to those who attend Holy Week in Seville. But they found themselves barred by armed men near the convent of San Francisco. Though stopped, there were ominous cries for hangings, which created such a sense of panic that prominent *conversos,* such as Juan de Córdoba, the silversmith-banker, Juan Varela, the bookseller, and other worried businessmen of the Calle Génova prepared a letter of loyalty to the Crown, asking for the government's protection.[15] This would be later signed by many respected citizens, including the printers Tomas Ungut, Diego de Talavera, Gonzalo de Roelas, and Juan de Valladolid, several of whom were *conversos* and some even *reconciliados.*[16]

Figueroa was finally let into the Alcázar by its commander, Jorge de Portugal. But many of his followers deserted him and shortly he was surrounded, though offered a compromise by Archbishop Deza. He refused it, and the Alcázar was stormed by royal forces and captured, at the cost of five dead and Figueroa wounded. The latter became a prisoner of the Archbishop while two of his followers were hanged: a cheese merchant, Francisco López, on October 23, and a musician, Juan Velázquez, on November 6.

The extraordinary civil war in the rest of Spain was also far from over. Acuña, the Bishop of Zamora, with two thousand armed men, unleashed a powerful, popular, basically anti-aristocratic movement in the territory near his see. This bishop, appointed by Julius II, was the bastard of a late-fifteenth-century bishop of Burgos and had been an agent of the Catholic Kings in Rome.[17] In 1521, he set off for Toledo, which his men captured and whose townsmen were persuaded to name him archbishop. Also in February 1521, Juan de Padilla captured several key places. The rebels seemed increasingly successful, but their difficulty was that they did not quite know what to do with their sudden power. There was among them agreement that the old regime should be attacked, even destroyed, but no one knew what should succeed it. Extremists every day gained more authority, and a social revolution seemed certain. It would be a national social revolution, to be sure, one directed against Flemings and against Charles's imperial role. But many merchants, earlier sympathetic to the protests, now trembled at the thought.

The *comuneros* went to see Queen Juana in Tordesillas. They offered her everything that she wanted. Hesitant and confused, she expressed sympathy but nobly, regally, loyally, if (from her own personal point of view) foolishly, declined their offers. She thereby saved her son Charles but condemned herself to another thirty-five years of near-imprisonment in vile conditions.[18]

On April 23, the *comuneros,* who had now become an army as much as a political party, were forced to fight outside the little pueblo of Villalar, near Toro, by royal forces improvised by the new Regents, the Constable, and the Admiral of Castile. They were defeated. The three main *comunero* leaders, Juan de Padilla, Juan Bravo, and Francisco Maldonado, were captured and immediately executed. Within a few weeks most of the rebellious towns fell to royalists. Toledo held out the longest, under Padilla's widow, María Pacheco. But Bishop Acuña was captured and imprisoned in Simancas Castle.

A similar but in some ways more dangerous movement of protest was taking shape in Valencia, where a group of townspeople, principally artisans, formed a brotherhood, or "Germanía," that seized control of the city. Some, such as Juan Lorena, aspired to create there a "Venetian-style republic." Others, such as Vicent Peris, also wanted to destroy aristocratic power. Local nobles such as Pedro Fajardo, *adelantado* of Murcia and Marquis of Los Vélez, played with the idea of sympathy for the rebel cause, but soon abandoned it. In early 1522, the rebellion was defeated. Lorena had already died, but Peris was captured and executed.[19]

The upshot of the revolt of the *comuneros* was to reinforce an authoritarian element in the monarchy in Spain. Self-assertion by cities did not recur till the nineteenth century. Henceforward court and monarchy determined events. The Spanish Empire looked back across the Atlantic at institutions that never seemed to change. The monarchs did what they could to limit further the power of the Cortes. *Procuradores* continued to be elected, but they were impotent.

On May 20, 1520, the day that the King left Corunna, Las Casas went to see Cardinal Adrian. He met him as he came out from his lodgings, with the Bishop of Almería, Francisco de Sosa, who had once been a member of the Council of the Realm. Sosa had worked with Fonseca, and now he said to Las Casas: "Kiss the hands now of your most reverend lord [Adrián], because it is he alone who has given you the liberty of all the Indians." Las Casas laughed, replying in Latin, the language he had in common with Adrian.[20]

With the King on his travels, with Spain in flames, and with Adrian preoccupied by the rebellions, power in respect of the Indies remained with the eternal Fonseca, though he himself was out of touch with his responsibilities for weeks. All the same, when the court was eventually reestablished, Las Casas obtained concessions:

A special grant would be available for all who desired to participate in Las Casas's territorial adventure. He undertook to pacify ten thousand Indians in two years without having recourse to coercion; and he committed himself again to give the Crown a rising income every year. He agreed to build three settlements with fifty inhabitants each, "to report any discovery of gold," and to submit rigorously to the sovereignty of the Crown. An educated man (*letrado*) would be named for the administration, and both an accountant and a treasurer would also be chosen. A visitor could at any time be sent to supervise the work of Las Casas. In making these concessions Las Casas was showing that he retained some of the entrepreneurial qualities that he must have had in his early days as a settler in Cuba.

He himself was now ready to set off again for the New World, but the civil war prevented him from leaving even Valladolid. So while Spain boiled politically and while the friends of Fonseca were seeking refuge wherever they could, Las Casas took the opportunity to refine his plans, with the support of Cardinal Adrian.

Early in August 1520, the decree of May 17 restoring Diego Colón to the government of the New World reached Santo Domingo. The old judges resumed their places, and the old royal officials joyfully asked that Figueroa, whom they hated, be submitted to the usual *residencia*. Figueroa's lieutenant, Antonio Flores, was soon accused of innumerable wrongdoings in Cubagua, in what is now Venezuela, principally in relation to the pursuit of pearls—though Figueroa had reported that all was prospering on the Pearl Coast, thanks explicitly to himself! In truth, Flores had created a petty dictatorship on that coast, hanging the once helpful indigenous *cacique* Melchor and some others, acts that in themselves resulted in a revolt that killed two more missionaries and nine other Spaniards.

In the end, the judge of the *residencia*, Licenciado Lebrón, condemned Figueroa for his abuses. (Lebrón already had experience conducting an earlier *residencia* in La Española, against Judge Aguilar, and in the interim he had been a powerful lieutenant governor in Tenerife.)

Given the disturbances in Seville and a subsequent mood of distrust, more potential emigrants were interested in Las Casas's ideas than previously had been the case, especially since San Juan in Puerto Rico constituted the first stopping point of the voyage. If the idea of colonizing South America on Las Casas's lines proved unappealing, the settlers could return to

Puerto Rico. The Governor there now, comfortingly for Sevillanos, was Antonio de la Gama, a son of the lieutenant to the new *asistente,* the Crown's representative of Seville, Sancho Martínez de Leiva.[21]

Las Casas eventually left Seville for the Indies on December 14, 1520, accompanied by thirty-five companions.[22] Another twenty or so joined him at Sanlúcar, men who had "forgotten their spades and their cows and had already begun to fancy themselves gentlemen, especially on Sundays and holidays, together with their women and possessions . . . [including] many biscuits, much wine, and hams, as well as many gifts of one kind or another, all at the expense of His Majesty. . . ."[23]

On January 10, 1521, Las Casas once more reached San Juan, Puerto Rico. It had been a short voyage of only two and a half weeks. No one had crossed the Atlantic as often as he. Alas, the news of a "rebellion" of natives that had begun in September 1520 along the South American coast after the killing of the *cacique* Melchor, had spread to San Juan, following the murder of several friars at Chiribichi, on the Gulf of Santa Fe. Flores, still in Cubagua, had tried unsuccessfully to suffocate the rising. But in the process three captains and more than fifty Spaniards, including the experienced captain Francisco Dorta, had been killed by the Indians. Flores was preparing to leave Cubagua, and the settlers of that place were planning to abandon their houses.

There had also been a Carib attack on San Juan itself, probably by natives from the island of Santa Cruz. Thirteen Spaniards had been killed, and the Caribs seized fifty Tainos. A punitive expedition was prepared in Santo Domingo, to be led by the Extremeño Gonzalo de Ocampo, with San Juan as its first stop. Ocampo was an old friend of Las Casas's, and he arrived off San Juan on February 27, in time for the two to meet.

Ocampo was a citizen of Cáceres. Born in 1475, he was aged about forty-five in 1520 and was one of the many sons of a well-known landowner. He was also a brother-in-law of Francisco de Garay, the Governor of Jamaica. Las Casas said that he loved Ocampo and never had an exchange with him that was not one of happiness and laughter.[24] In 1502, Ocampo had gone to La Española with Ovando as Las Casas had done. That was when they had become friends. Ocampo was later concerned in trade with the Pearl Coast, and he collected slaves in the Bahamas, too. From 1504 to 1507, he was the representative of the Grimaldis, Genoese bankers, in Santo Domingo. He gave evidence to the priors' inquiry in 1517 as to whether Indians could be expected to benefit from liberty, even though he had an *encomienda* of thirty-three Indians in La Buenaventura, in La Española.[25]

Las Casas asked his old friend to desist from his enterprise of destroying the revolt on the mainland, because his instructions reserved the north of South America to himself. Ocampo said that though he would, of course, be generally influenced by the instructions of the King, as transmitted by Las Casas (whom he admired), he had to fulfill the orders that he had received in Santo Domingo; and so, on March 1, he went on his way. Ocampo's repression of the rebellion was rough, comprehensive, and effective. All the natives whom he captured were sent to Santo Domingo and sold as slaves.

Las Casas, meanwhile, having characteristically quarreled with La Gama, the Governor in San Juan, bought a caravel for 500 pesos and set off with his assistant Francisco de Soto for Santo Domingo, leaving behind in San Juan most of those whom he had brought from Spain. The grand schemes that had seemed so compelling to the Emperor and bishops in Spain now seemed to be unraveling. Could a great entrepreneur who expected to rule one thousand miles of seacoast be forced to buy his own ship? After he arrived in Santo Domingo, Las Casas found that his new friend, Diego Colón, had returned, but with the old treasurer, Pasamonte, as ever making imperious demands. Diego Colón was finding his old headquarters gloomy, even if a cathedral was being built nearby: the first stone of it had been laid. (Work had begun in 1512, the north door would be finished by 1527, and the building itself consecrated in 1541.)[26] To prevent Las Casas from returning to Castile to denounce everyone (which was always assumed might happen), the authorities in Santo Domingo arranged to deprive him of his ship. They even persuaded a Basque shipbuilder, Domingo de Guetaria, to ensure that it was not seaworthy.[27]

With the news of the royalists' victory over the *comuneros* at Villalar and the subsequent revival of the powers of Cardinal Adrian, the authorities realized that they would now have to make some token effort at least to assist Las Casas, who seemed to be a favorite of his. They fortunately did not at that stage know that the Crown had limited the impact of Las Casas's grant by giving licenses to seek pearls in part of his territory to two merchants who were protégés of Fonseca's (and Cobos's), Juan López de Idíaquez and Juan de Cárdenas, who was also the inspector of caravels in Seville. The Bishop no doubt hoped to profit from their dealings.

Las Casas was able to arrange an understanding of a sort with the powers that be. His friend Gonzalo de Ocampo would remain in charge of disciplining recalcitrant Indians, but Las Casas, as "administrator of the Indians on the Pearl Coast," would be the overall governor. His enterprise would be reconstituted as a trading company divided into twenty-four shares, six being held for the King by Ocampo, six going to Las Casas and his partners, three to Diego Colón, and one each to leading men of Santo Domingo, such as the judges Vázquez de Ayllón, Villalobos, and Ortiz de Matienzo. This list included most of Las Casas's old enemies as well as his friends.

Las Casas would decide where slaves and pearls could best be found. Two ships would be provided for him by his erstwhile enemy Domingo de Guetaria. One hundred and twenty men would be allocated to him as soldiers; the Spaniards would negotiate with the Indians and fight them only if Las Casas personally certified that they were cannibalistic or unwilling to accept the faith.

Actually, pearls were being brought back in a large quantity from Cubagua by Juan de la Barrera, a *converso* from the riverside port of Moguer, on the Río Tinto, who was becoming the most important entrepreneur at that time and who seems to have reached his own private (if separate) understanding with the authorities in Santo Domingo.

In July 1521, Las Casas at long last sailed for his designated Utopia accompanied by a small group only: the accountant Miguel de Castellanos; a priest, Hernández; his assistant, Francisco de Soto, from Olmedo, Valladolid; Juan de Zamora, a Castilian; and about six others. It was a sad decline in Las Casas's fortunes, which had seemed earlier to stand so high. It was as if his ideas themselves had been devoured by shipworms of the tropics.

The expedition stopped at the island of Mona and then at San Juan, where Las Casas did not find waiting for him the "modest and industrious farmers" whom he had brought from Spain to carry out his colonization. Some of these had died, others had vanished into the growing new society of Puerto Rico, and a few others had joined Juan Ponce de León in a new journey to Florida. But he and what remained of his old group of friends continued to Cumaná, on the north coast of South America, where they arrived on August 8. It was a very beautiful place, but savage.

There they found the wooden convent of the Franciscans where Fray Juan Garceto and his fellow fathers had been left largely unscathed by the indigenous "rebellion," and also a small town optimistically called Toledo, which had been founded by Ocampo. But the last-named place had been ruined, and the Indians there had fled.

Las Casas addressed the few Spaniards whom he found on the coast and told them of the changes upon which he was going to insist.[28] But not many of these wanted to stay in the Indies, much less do so in Las Casas's dreamland, and soon, despite repetitions of the eloquence that had so entranced everyone in Castile, from the Emperor downward, all left except the Franciscans, who in Cumaná received the "apostle of the Indies" with anthems and prayers. It was one thing to sound buoyant in Castile, another to remain so in the wilderness of South America. Las Casas built a house of straw and wood for himself, as well as an orchard with oranges, a vineyard, and a vegetable garden with fine melons. He then told the Indians what he was planning to do, speaking through "Doña María," wife of a *cacique* known as "Don Diego," who served as interpreter. To protect the water of the River Cumaná from use by other Spaniards who had established themselves on the island of Cubagua, Las Casas wanted to build a fortress, but he failed to achieve this, for those other Spaniards bribed the quarryman charged to carry out this task to be lethargic. Las Casas also failed to control those who secretly and illegally continued to trade slaves and pearls. The Spaniards in Cubagua had suborned the natives by the use of wine, "the most precious money which the Indians loved.[29] When they became drunk, they took up their bows and poisoned arrows, and became quite unpredictable."

Las Casas also had a conflict with Francisco de Vallejo, the previously named appointee of the priors in Santo Domingo, who, some miles away, claimed that he was the real lieutenant of Diego Colón on that coast. Further flotillas seeking slaves, belonging to such experienced merchants as Bastidas, Fernández de las Varas, and Jerónimo de Riberol, continued to sail in. Las Casas went to Cubagua and demanded unsuccessfully of Vallejo that he abandon his command and return to Santo Domingo. He refused. Las Casas complained by letter to the government in Santo Domingo, without making any impact, and he decided in the end to go there to protest in person.

He left in December 1521 on a ship of one of the slave seekers, Fernández de las Varas, leaving Francisco de Soto in command. In Las Casas's absence, and without his knowledge, Soto, with the two ships that he still had, began to look for gold and then for pearls and slaves. The prospect of establishing a chivalrous Utopia seemed daily more remote. Once Las Casas had gone, the Indians of Cumaná turned against the monks. The latter asked "Doña María" (the interpreter) to intervene. She told them that there was no danger to them, though signaling privately that there was. A boat looking for slaves appeared, and all the old followers of Las Casas sought sanctuary on it, but the Indians prevented the vessel in question even from anchoring. The Spaniards prepared artillery for their defense, but the powder was damp. The Indians eventually attacked, killed five of Las Casas's group as well as a Franciscan, and burned Las Casas's house, with the others inside. Soto was wounded, and he and the few remaining friars set off in a canoe, pursued by Indians. The Spaniards reached the open sea, took refuge on a beach protected by thistles, which the Indians would not cross, and were eventually saved by a passing Spanish slaving vessel. Soto died in the Caribbean on the way to La Española.[30]

Las Casas himself took two months to return to Santo Domingo, because as a result of a shipwreck he had to land at Yáquimo, in the west of La Española, and walk the rest of the way to the "capital." When he reached there, he wrote to the King, hoping that his problem had some solution. But the King was still in Germany. He received no response.

Rejected by all, his plans in tatters, Las Casas sought succor from the Dominicans, whose leader, or provincial, in Santo Domingo, an intelligent Gallego, Fray Domingo de Betanzos, told him tartly that he had worked enough for the souls of the Indians. Now was the time to worry about his own. Betanzos knew what he was talking about. After a wild youth, he had become a Dominican friar and had gone to La Española in 1514. Las Casas, who was then aged about thirty-eight, took sanctuary in the Dominican monastery at Santo Domingo and at the end of the year, without further comments or activity of any sort, decided to remain. His disillusion was complete, and he entered the Dominican order. For the next ten years he allowed himself to reflect on all these events.[31] The settlers, freed of the scourge of Father Bartolomé, as they saw it, thereafter carried on much as they wished despite the wonderful memoranda and the high-minded speeches far away in Castile.

Juan Ponce de León, meanwhile, made another journey in 1521. He had by then been outmaneuvered in Puerto Rico by Judge Sancho Velázquez, who was the de facto governor and was, as it were, again looking for new islands to conquer. (Ponce had the title in Puerto Rico of "captain-general," but that meant little.) He was now the only survivor from the early days of the settlements in the Caribbean, and he remained interested in Florida. He set out there once more in February 1521 from San Juan, with 250 men in four ships for which he himself paid. He carried some Franciscans with him, as well as a great deal of agricultural equipment, for he planned a colony. He wanted it to be established on Sanibel Island, at the mouth of the River Caloosahatchee, in west Florida (near present-day Fort Myers), but the Indians resisted the landing, and Ponce was wounded by a poisoned arrow. Carried back to Cuba, he died in pain near the present port of Havana in July, his remains eventually being transferred to Puerto Rico where they rest now in the Cathedral of San Juan.[32]

The expedition, and the plans for settlement, were abandoned.

At the end of May 1522, the King-Emperor Charles left Brussels and returned to Spain via England. This time he stayed in the latter country for several weeks, until July 6, when he embarked for Spain from Southampton, arriving at Santander ten days later. With him traveled four thousand German and Flemish soldiers. From there he went to Reinosa, then to Aguilar de Campoo and Palencia, which he reached on August 5 and where he held the first Council of the Realm after the rebellion of the *comuneros*. There was discussion about punishments after that conflict: Francisco de los Cobos and Bishop Ruiz de la Mota, like Bishop Fonseca and Hernando de Vega, took a hard line, while the men who had really saved the kingdom, Constable Velasco and Admiral Enriquéz, favored pardons.[33]

There followed a short period of repression during which occurred the execution of most of the leading *procuradores* and others who had led the *comuneros*: Alonso de Saravia, of Valladolid, for example, and Pedro de Sotomayor, of Madrid, as well as Juan de Solier, of Segovia. One of the last executions in the first list, on August 16, was that of Pedro Maldonado Pimentel, after an unsuccessful appeal for a pardon by his uncle, the Count of Benavente, supported by the Regents Velasco and Enríquez. Also executed were some of those who seemed to have inspired the risings. It may come as a surprise, though, to the modern reader, used in the twentieth century to long lists of dead men after civil wars in Spain as elsewhere in Europe, that those who died in 1522, either as a result of the executioner's axe or because of illness in prison, totaled about one hundred. There were few days in Spain in 1939 after the Civil War when that figure was not exceeded.[34]

In Seville, capital of the empire as it was about to become, the revival of traditional authority was warmly celebrated. The prostitutes of the Compás de Mancebía danced on the steps of the cathedral, bulls were run in the Plaza de San Francisco, and there was a regatta on the river.[35] It seemed as if the golden age was about to begin.

Book Eight

❧❀❧

NEW SPAIN

One weapon of the conquistadors in America was communication.
Here is Cortés talking to Moctezuma through his interpreter, Marina.

Book Eight

NEW SPAIN

"I am to pass away like a
faded flower"[1]

I am to pass away like a faded flower
My fame will be nothing
My fame on earth will vanish.

*A poem of ancient Mexico
as translated by Father Garibay*[2]

In the wings of Spain's imperial efforts in the Caribbean in the early sixteenth century were the two large and powerful societies of the mainland,
those of the Mexica (Aztecs) and the Incas. They were in some ways closer in
their wealth and sophistication to the civilizations of the eastern Mediterranean of antiquity than to the societies of the Caribbean. No one in Europe
knew anything of either of them before 1518.

About 1950, a fine German scholar, Richard Konetzke, invented a new
word for Mexico with Central America, in pre-Columbian days: Mesoamerica. It is a ponderous word that has not become part of the general vocabulary of well-educated people. It is useful, however, since it embraces the
many diverse peoples, speaking more than five hundred distinct languages,
who occupied these territories about 1500. There were probably 10 million
people living in 1519 in these lands.[3]

The history of old Mesoamerica can be divided into two eras: the time
that can be learned about only from archaeology or from other artifacts, including painted remains, such as can be seen in the sites of Bonampak or
Caxcala; and the era of the Mexica, whose regime survived into the sixteenth
century and of whom much can be learned by conventional historical
means, such as chronicles composed by persons with indigenous blood in
the sixteenth century.[4]

Many of the distinctive elements of ancient Mexico developed in the hot
territory near what we now call the Gulf of Mexico, the provinces of Tabasco
and Vera Cruz: for example, pyramids in ceremonial centers; human sacri-

fices on top of those pyramids; ball games; art based on clay figurines; hieroglyphs; arithmetic built around the number twenty; a solar calendar; a love of jade; and elaborate commerce, with markets. Later, societies developed in the higher, temperate lands, but those always seemed to need or to wish for tropical products: jaguar skins, say, feathers from fine birds, or cotton. But all these different peoples, in the coastal regions as in the temperate zone, participated in what can be represented as a single historical experience.[5]

Consider first the Olmecs, who flourished between about 1200 and 600 B.C. The immense stone heads to be seen in many of Mexico's museums, above all in the Garden Museum at Coatzacoalcos, much jade carving, and stone altars testify to these people's ingenuity. They obviously had knowledge of astronomy, they carved wood imaginatively, and they had highly decorated ceramics, colored by paints and dyes. By 650 B.C. they seem to have had primitive writing in the form of simple glyphs on a cylindrical seal.[6] They used drums, primitive flutes, and conch shells as musical instruments, and they had, too, awls, hooks, needles, and spatulas. The Olmecs lived in the coastal region, in what has been in the late twentieth century a zone for oil and known for its rubber; the word "Olmec" indeed signifies rubber in Nahuatl, the language used as a lingua franca in central Mexico in the early sixteenth century.[7] The Olmecs constitute a mystery, though, in many ways. We do not know, for instance, whether they had an empire or whether their physical type was close to the sculpted heads for which they are best known. Though they were in many ways at a high level of civilization, they lacked two essentials: domesticated animals and the wheel.

The reasons for this first "leap forward" of the Olmecs, comparable to what occurred in the Old World in Egypt or Babylon, are disputed. Probably the availability of water from rivers, lagoons, and rain was critical. The first constituted a channel of communication, the second were full of game and wildfowl. Also, malaria was unknown, as were yellow fever and the other tropical diseases brought by the Europeans and that afterwards flourished in these marshlands.

The second formidable society of old Mesoamerica was the Maya, whose golden age was between about A.D. 250 and 900. Much characteristic Maya work may have been done long before that, and, indeed, there are those who believe that they "could even have acted as an influence on the emergent Olmec society."[8] Whenever they first appeared on the large map of Mexican experience, the Maya seem to have been the most refined of the predecessors of the Europeans. The stucco bas-reliefs at Palenque, the paintings on the walls of Bonampak, and their painted vases almost recall the designs of ancient Greece. Maya achievements included palaces of limestone, with fine vaulted rooms based on a false arch,[9] as well as inscribed stelae that they placed in front of their buildings. The Maya were also mathematicians, able to make calculations as accurate as the Babylonians'. They had a solar calendar that began in the year 3133 B.C. that had an error of only 3/10,000ths of a day every year. Mayan scribes made beautiful painted books, of which five survive. They used turkey feathers to carry out this work, which they dipped into black or red paint.[10] They carved stone elegantly and built magnificent ceremonial cities, of which 230 have been identified. The largest of these, Tikal, in what is now Guatemala, with its three thousand buildings, was the home of anything between ten thousand and forty thousand citizens, on a site six square miles in size. Maya agriculture was primarily based on the so-called slash-and-burn method, but they probably relied on *chinampas,* an imaginative congeries of floating gardens—hence, perhaps, their use of the water lily as an emblem.

At the summit of their achievement, the Maya probably numbered about a million people. They worshipped 160 gods and enjoyed much trade. Their most splendid achievement is the Temple of the Sun at Palenque. The Temple of the Inscriptions in the same magical city boasted the only tomb in a pyramid in Mesoamerica—that of Prince Pacal, whose dead body was covered with the finest jade.

The end of the Maya civilization remains a mystery. But we do know that, in contrast with what was once supposed to be the case, these gifted people frequently fought among themselves. The paintings at Bonampak depict battles, and the annals of minor Maya tribes describe little else. But bellicosity was not the cause of catastrophe, any more than it would be in Europe. The Maya were probably conquered by a people from the north— from Teotihuacan. Toward the end of the seventh century A.D. there also appear to have been natural disasters—droughts, hurricanes—that led to social unrest. The ceremonial cities were abandoned. When the Spaniards began to arrive off the coast of Yucatan, the Maya constituted a collection of separate cities of a lower level of culture than their ancestors had reached five hundred years before. Just as modern scholars in Europe often cannot read Latin, it is not obvious that even their priests could read the inscriptions of their own golden age.

Before the fall of the Maya, and apparently unrelated to them, the vast city of Teotihuacan had been built in a fertile valley to the northeast of the present capital of Mexico. Founded about the time of Christ, Teotihuacan probably had a population of 200,000 people in A.D. 600, on a site covering two thousand acres. The place was a commercial center, with ball courts, palaces, several marketplaces, and good drainage. Skilled craftsmen worked feathers and obsidian there, and painted ceramics, while merchants organized trade over long distances in all directions. In Teotihuacan itself, the long Avenue of the Dead, with its pyramids dedicated to the Sun and the Moon (the one to the Sun was as large, though not as high, as the Great Pyramid in Egypt) was a nobler road than any in Europe at that time, while the regular pattern of the lesser streets would have delighted the Roman architect Vitruvius. Unlike the Maya, the people of Teotihuacan did not prize sculpture, but mural painters flourished. The city seems to have been a theocracy, with the plumed serpent, Quetzalcoatl, occupying a place of honor in a pantheon that included other gods who were still recognizable under different identities when the Spaniards came, such as Tlaloc, the god of rain. Teotihuacan was served by an agriculture that, like that of the Olmecs, relied on those wonderful floating gardens as well as terraces and irrigated fields.

As with the Olmecs, the politics of Teotihuacan constitutes a mystery since, despite its size and its high culture, no one knows who the people were who lived there or whether they had any connection with the Maya. As with the latter, no one knows if they had an empire. But all the same, the memory of this city dominated the imaginations of succeeding cultures much as that of Roma Antiqua influenced medieval and Renaissance Europe. Its influence stretched as far as present-day Honduras in the south and Colorado in the north, while the big pyramids of Cholula, to the east of the city of Mexico, and Tajín, on the coast, were probably built by colonists who came from Teotihuacan.

Another mystery comparable to the end of the Maya is what eventually happened to the city. One supposition is that the people lost faith when rain failed for several years. The divided city may then have fallen prey to barbarians from the north.

Teotihuacan became the archetype for subsequent societies in the country, even for modern Mexico. The city thus inspired Tollan, a military-minded state built on its ruins, and through Tollan it directly affected Mexico-Tenochtitlan.

The Toltecs, who lived in Tollan, were less creative than the people of Teotihuacan and the Maya. Until the 1940s, their capital was believed to have been Teotihuacan, but it now seems that modern Tula, a bleak, windy city to the west of Teotihuacan, is a more likely candidate. At all events, the Toltecs dominated the valley of Mexico during what in Europe would be called the high Middle Ages, say A.D. 1000 to 1200. Their significance is fourfold: First, their language, Nahuatl, became widely spoken in the region. Second, they were warlike, and some Toltecs captured much of Yucatan in the tenth century. There they established a new version of Mayan civilization responsible for such remarkable cities as Chichén Itzá. The expedition there is sometimes associated with the story of the flight of the god Quetzalcoatl, who was reputed to have fled Tollan, perhaps because he opposed human sacrifice. Third, the Toltecs passed knowledge of all the old cultures of Mesoamerica on to the Mexica. Fourth, they had a cult of death, with an increasing use of human sacrifice, and they began the curious custom of building ceremonial walls of skulls.

Probably there was a drought in Tollan in the twelfth century that led to political upheavals from which, once again, northern barbarians are said to have profited. The city is said to have fallen about A.D. 1175. Another Toltec city, Cualhuacan, also in the valley of Mexico, lingered longer.

By that time, a nomadic people of the north, who survived into historical times, had reached the great lake in the middle of the valley. They were at first considered barbarians by the other sedentary people around the lake. Legends at the time of the Spanish conquest in 1521 linked them with a legendary birthplace called Aztatlán, or "the place of cranes." (The Lake of Mexico was drained by the Europeans.)

These Mexica made their way south on the suggestion of the priests who accompanied them. They were apparently divided into clans (*calpulli*), and took about a hundred years to reach the valley of Mexico, which was by then studded with villages, and had been dependent on the Toltecs and, before that, on Teotihuacan. The prehistory of this people is unknown since it was reconstructed to serve contemporary politics in the fifteenth century. But it seems that when the Mexica arrived, the dominant people near the lake were the Tepaneca, who exerted their influence in the usual way, extorting tributes and threatening war. They had occupied all the best sites, so the newcomers found it hard to find a resting place. The Mexica first went, myths insist, to the hill of Chapultepec, "the hill of the locusts," now in the center of Mexico City, but then on the edge of what was the great lake. Expelled from there, they moved to a rocky island in the lake itself already known as Tenochtitlan. The priests told the Mexica that they were destined to settle there, since they had seen an eagle on it sitting on a cactus, eating a snake—a clear guide, as it seemed by the interpretation of legends, as to where to settle.

The Mexica remained the vassals of the Tepaneca for a hundred years. They absorbed from them much of what has subsequently been thought of as typically Aztec; for example, the cult of the god Quetzalcoatl and that of Tlaloc, god of rain, the use of the pyramids for sacrifices, the growth of a priestly class, commerce in obsidian and in feathers, craftsmanship in jade, and the use of calendars. The Mexica, as the Spaniards later found, were adept at copying other peoples' inventions. But they maintained some of their own traditions, such as the worship of their cruel god of war and of hunting, Huitzilopochtli, who became a co–supreme deity alongside Tlaloc—a most unusual cohabitation.[11]

Much as the Goths seized political control from their masters, the Romans, so did the Mexica from the Tepaneca. The decisive coup d'état occurred at the end of the 1420s. Itzcoatl, a Mexica leader apparently of Toltec blood, first killed his own appeasement-minded predecessor and then the last Tepanec monarch. He and his descendants—there were six emperors between him and Moctezuma II, who was reigning in 1519—established a bigger empire over central Mexico than any that had preceded them. It extended from the line of Guanajuato-Querétaro in the north to the Tehuantepec peninsula in the south. Within this territory about thirty identifiable peoples paid tribute to the Mexica in return for protection—protection from the Mexica themselves, if from no one else.

Like Rome, Tenochtitlan was a city-state writ large, and the center of power remained in the capital: an astonishing achievement of urban planning. Its central square was twice as large as that in Salamanca, or so said Cortés, while to the impressionable conquistadors the canals, markets, and palaces caused the place to resemble Venice.[12] But Mexico-Tenochtitlan was bigger than Venice was in 1519 and larger than any European city of that time, save perhaps Constantinople.

The Spaniards described the ruler of the Mexica as an "emperor." Despite some criticisms, the word has remained. The usage has its point, since the ruler of Mexico was the overlord of a number of other monarchs, who were usually referred to as "kings." So his standing seemed comparable to the relation of the Holy Roman Emperor and the subordinate electors and dukes in Germany. But the literal translation of the word that the ancient Mexicans used, *hueytlatoani,* is "high spokesman." The lesser states were ruled by *tlatoanis,* "spokesmen." The words remind us that the rulers of Mexico were expected, above all, to be able to talk eloquently. In the pioneering work of anthropology known as the Florentine Codex, compiled by the indefatigable Franciscan Bernardino de Sahagún in the middle of the sixteenth century, there are many examples of the kind of oration that the emperor or his colleagues at the court of the Mexica might have used.

Nahuatl, the language of the Mexica, was a rich one that, in its golden age, lent itself not only to sonorous sermons but to moving poetry that in translation resembles the French verse of the fifteenth century or its Spanish imitators, such as Jorge Manrique—being full of regrets that beauty dies, that youth passes, that warriors become weak. For example:

> I am to pass away like a faded flower,
> My fame will be nothing,
> My fame on earth will vanish.

Or:

> Ponder this, eagle and jaguar knights,
> Though you are carved in jade, you will break;
> Though you are made of gold, you will crack;
> Even though you are a quetzal feather, you will wither.
> We are not forever on this earth,
> Only for a time are we here.

Compare this to Jorge Manrique's:

> Gifts unmeasured, the royal buildings,
> Full of gold, dishes so burnished,
> The golden coins of the treasury,
> The caparisons of the horses and the finery:
>
> Where shall we find them now?
> What were they but the dew of the meadows?[13]

Such similarities have naturally suggested to some critics that those learned men who have tried to record the poetry of the Mexica must have been influenced by European examples. It may be so, but the Mexica plainly had sentiments comparable to those of their contemporaries on the other side of the Atlantic. Many of the political or economic arrangements of the Mexica seemed vaguely similar to practices that the conquistadors either knew of or could imagine. The Mexican Empire, for instance, had been maintained by armies whose predecessors had conquered the subject cities; and it was by the threat of force that those tributaries were persuaded to deliver biannual consignments of objects that their masters coveted. This was resented by those who paid (as the conquistadors would discover to their benefit). But, until the Spaniards came, the Mexica were regularly presented with an immense collection of goods. The best analysis of this system of tribute can be seen in the Codex Mendoza, completed about 1540 for the first Spanish viceroy of Mexico, Antonio de Mendoza, a son of that enlightened Count of Tendilla who was the first governor of Granada after its capture.

This "Codex" lists most things on which Mexico-Tenochtitlan came to rely: cloth, for dress and clothes generally, the fibers for which could not be grown in the valley of Mexico, though it was woven there (primarily by women) in a sophisticated way; feathers, for ceremonial decoration; tropical food; and, to a great extent, maize, the staple food that, though there were some fields of it near the capital, was not nearly abundant enough to meet the demand. Other Mexican goods dispatched to the capital included chocolate, soon to be a delightful revelation to the Europeans; cochineal (a red dye also extensively used in Europe); tomatoes, such a wonderful contribution to the diets of the Old World; and turkeys, so called by the English because the bird seemed exotic, even though it came from the West, not the East.[14] The Europeans were not used to this kind of tribute in the Middle Ages, but it was comparable to what was practiced in Oriental despotisms, such as those of the Mongols or the Tartars, and some conquistadors from Spain would have been familiar with it.

The emperors in Mexico were selected from a small group of noblemen, all of the same family. That was similar to the Scottish succession before Macbeth, the so-called law of tanistry. Some have creatively compared the way that one emperor succeeded another with the succession of modern presidents in Mexico within the "revolutionary family" of the Institutional Revolutionary Party. The emperor—like, indeed, the modern president of Mexico—though we should not dwell too long on such an agreeable anachronism—was a despot. He was limited, however, by an elaborate series of laws or rules that bound everyone else, and he was also the temporal expression of a civilization in which religion played the dominant part.

The Mexica had a social system that was easily recognizable by the conquistadors. There was a class of noblemen related to the Emperor, who seemed to have enjoyed, in the last few generations before 1500, lives of unexampled luxury—thanks to the system of tribute; a class of craftsmen, workers in stone or paint, apparently hereditary, as they had been in ancient Egypt; farmers, who were called on every year to an increasing extent to perform some kind of public service within the city, as well as producing maize on their plots; workers, who seem to have been the equivalent of serfs; and, finally, outright slaves, either captives in war or men or women who had been made slaves in consequence of some crime. Priests and generals were also a class apart. But the Mexica, who were neither slaves nor serfs, were obliged to fight in their country's wars when the emperor deemed it necessary.

The Mexica did not constitute the only authority in Mesoamerica. Close to them to the east lay the small, unconquered territory of Tlaxcala, which the Mexica had surrounded by the early sixteenth century but which remained independent. Its society was a modest version of what prevailed in its powerful neighbor, and its freedom to act was severely constrained by their close proximity. To the north there was the monarchy of the Tarascans, to give them the name used by the Spaniards, based on what is now Michoacan, before whose copper-tipped weapons the Mexica had fled in the 1470s. To the far southeast there were the Maya, that once superior society that, in the sixteenth century, was, as indicated earlier, a shadow of past glory. The Mexica traded with them and do not seem to have made any effort at conquest. It will be remembered that in his fourth voyage Columbus met some traders who seemed to be Maya, and he and his companions were impressed by them.[15]

Many things strike modern observers about ancient Mexico, but above all they are moved by the remarkable artistic achievement. In sculpture, for example, the Mexica prized and made relief and regular three-dimensional heads and ornaments, as well as monumental work. They designed delicate jewelry in gold, or gold combined with stones, of which there are still fine examples to be seen in Mexico (some of it found in the 1930s in the famous Tomb 7 in Oaxaca). There was remarkable featherwork, made by interweaving birds' feathers in mosaics, of which a few examples also survive (it is best represented in Vienna's museums).[16] A case can be made that this featherwork was, as poetry has been to England, the supreme achievement of the Mexica.

There were also mosaics made out of precious or semiprecious stones, of which turquoise was the most prized.[17] The Mexica were, too, skilled woodworkers, as one can see from their drums and spears. They used paint both to embellish stone sculpture and directly on stone, without sculptural additions. Ancient Mexico also used paint in its remarkable books, or codices, which, by means of glyphs and designs, not an alphabet, depicted genealogies and listed both conquests and quantities of tribute. The Mexica made music from instruments that the Spaniards would call flutes but that were more like recorders; from conch shells; and from at least two different kinds of drums. They danced often and extravagantly. Indeed, as elsewhere in the New World, there seems never to have been an occasion in Old Mexico where music and dancing did not accompany each other. The Mexica had games in which they used rubber balls that were much more elaborate than those used in the walled ball courts of the Caribbean islands.[18]

Ancient Mexico was a disciplined civilization: the streets were regularly cleaned and swept. That was a symbolic indication of a society that most remarkably—perhaps uniquely—provided some kind of education for all except slaves and serfs, and where everyone had a meticulously ordered place in society, much as they had had in ancient Egypt.

The complexity of Mexican religion does not lend itself to a swift summary.[19] As far as the common man was concerned, religion signified a large number of festivals: at least one a month in honor of a special deity, and marked by processions, dancing, and music. They were also attended by offerings and sacrifices, sometimes of birds such as quail and, increasingly, of slaves and other captives. As in earlier regimes, the human sacrifices were carried out on the summits of pyramids before shrines to the different deities. Priests, monarchs, and noblemen were called on to offer blood in other ways, from the ear, the wrist, or even the penis. Human sacrifice shocked the Spaniards, but it was an integral part of a series of ceremonies common to the region.

In addition to the worship of the regular gods, there were some, especially among the nobility of Texcoco, to the east across the lake, who seem to have been groping toward the idea of an impersonal deity whose goodness could not be expressed in pictures:[20]

> Everywhere is your house,
> Giver of Life.
> The carpet of flowers is woven with flowers by me.
> On it the princes worship you.

The life of the Mexica was obviously hard for the majority. But the upper class, as in most places, comforted themselves with alcohol such as pulque, a drink made from the sap of the maguey cactus; and there were hallucinogenitory mushrooms, flowers, and cactuses. These may have played a part in soothing victims before the sacrifice, and, like alcohol in Europe, they gave courage before battles.

The history of Mexico before the coming of the Spaniards prompts many interesting reflections—not least, on the similarities with the Old World. In Mexico as in the Old World, history told of the rise and fall of cities, of the preying by energetic nomads on sedentary states, of habits of adornment, and of festivals and ceremonies. But the differences were also great: the lack of domestic animals, either for war or for agriculture; the consequent employment of men and women as beasts of burden; the absence of wheels and of the use of metal except for decoration; and the pictographs that could begin to tell a story but were much less effective than the alphabets of Europe.

The relative similarity of the development of the Indians in Mexico (and also Peru) to what occurred in Asia has prompted many to argue that there must have been an earlier contact. The Chinese are said to have introduced

the art of weaving, the Japanese the art of pottery. Even the lost tribes of Israel are supposed to have given the Mexica a liking for law. St. Thomas is
thought to have brought the cross as a symbol in religion. All these ideas are
baseless. The Chinese, in the age of the Ch'in emperor, could have reached
the Americas in their big ships in the third century B.C., but they did not
choose to. Everything suggests that the American Indian peoples developed
their remarkable civilizations in isolation.

The Mexica believed, as their Emperor Moctezuma declared, that they
were the "masters of the world."[21] But they did not spend much time thinking of what lay beyond the wild tribes whom they called the Chichimeca in
the north, and the Maya in the south, although their merchants knew that
beyond the Chichimeca, turquoise could be obtained; south of the Maya
lived peoples who traded in jade and, farther on, in emeralds and gold,
which some of the Mexica's tributaries learned to work with incomparable
skill. From both the north and the south, slaves also were obtained by the
rulers of Tenochtitlan.

Nor did the Mexica have much interest in what happened beyond the
Eastern Sea—which we now think of as the Gulf of Mexico—though legend
insists that the intellectual and reforming god Quetzalcoatl had years before
disappeared there on a raft of serpents. The lack of curiosity was a mark of
Old Mexico distinguishing it from Europe.

But from about 1500, curious rumors began to reach Mexico from the
east. In 1502, some indigenous merchants, perhaps Jicaques or Payas, both of
them subdivisions of the Maya, as we have recalled, met Columbus, then on
his fourth voyage, off the Bay Islands in the Gulf of Honduras. Presumably
descriptions of well-dressed, bearded Europeans were carried back by the
Maya authorities to the Emperor of the Mexica in Tenochtitlan, just as
Columbus and his companions eventually carried back to Spain tales of the
merchants whom they had met off Honduras.[22]

Then, in 1508, as we have seen, two master sailors from Seville, Vicente
Yáñez Pinzón, who had been captain of the caravel *Pinta* on Columbus's
first voyage, and Juan Díaz de Solís, who would later discover the River Plate,
made landfall in Yucatan. They were looking for the strait that they believed
would lead them to the Pacific, hence to the Spice Islands and China. Perhaps they sailed along the Mexican coast as far as Vera Cruz or even
Tampico. Possibly their journey led to the depiction by a Mexican merchant
about that time of what looked like three temples floating in the sea on large
canoes. The sketch was sent up to Tenochtitlan, where Moctezuma consulted both advisers and priests about it.[23]

Then a canoe of Tainos, the indigenous people of Jamaica, was wrecked off the coast of Cozumel, itself off Yucatan, in about 1512. The survivors may have told, presumably by signs, something of what they had observed the Europeans to be already doing in the Caribbean.[24] A little later, a trunk washed up on the Gulf of Mexico somewhere close to Xicallanco, a Mexica trading outpost near what is now Campeche. Inside were several suits of European clothes, some jewels, and a sword. No one had ever seen such things before. What were they? Whose possessions were these? Moctezuma is said to have divided the trunk's contents with his cousins, the kings of Texcoco and Tacuba. But the mystery remained.

As we have seen, a Spanish settlement was established in 1510 at Darien, in Panama, directed to begin with by Vasco Núñez de Balboa, the first European to see the Pacific, afterwards by Pedrarias Dávila. The brutalities of the Spanish conquistadors under the leadership of the latter make it likely that some rumor of what was happening would have penetrated to the Mexica. Darien was eighteen hundred miles from Tenochtitlan as the crow flies, but merchants traveled far.

In 1511, Diego de Nicuesa, a merchant-explorer sailing from Darien to Santo Domingo, was wrecked off Yucatan. Several Spanish sailors survived, and two of these, Gonzalo Guerrero and Jerónimo de Aguilar, were for some years prisoners of the Maya, the former siding with his captors. So it was scarcely surprising that a magician in Tenochtitlan, later known to the Spaniards as Martín Ocelotl, predicted "men with beards coming to this land."[25]

Another Spanish landing seems to have occurred in 1513 in Yucatan when Juan Ponce de León stopped there on his return from his unsuccessful journey to Florida to find the Fountain of Eternal Youth. In 1515, there was yet another curious contact between Spain and the Mesoamerican world: a Spanish judge named Corrales in Darien reported that he had met a "refugee from the interior provinces of the West." This man had observed the judge reading a document and put the marvelous question, "You, too, have books? You also understand the signs by which you talk to the absent?"[26] Although Mexican painted books were inferior to their European counterparts, they had the same purpose.

The last years of old Mexico are full of legends of comets, predictions, and tales of strange visions. But more important were the signs of the Spanish presence growing ever closer.

In 1518, a laborer apparently came to the court of Moctezuma. He was said to have had no thumbs, no ears, and no toes: all had been cut off as punishment for some unrecorded crime.[27] He reported that he had seen a "range of mountains, or some big hills, floating in the sea." Moctezuma imprisoned the man presumably to stop him spreading such alarming tales but sent some trusted advisers to the coast to find out what was happening. They returned to tell their master:

> It is true that there have come to the shore I do not know what kind of people; there were mountains on the waves, and a number of men came in from them toward the coast. Some of them were fishing with rods, others with a net. They were fishing from a small boat. Then they got into a canoe and went back to the thing on the sea with its two towers and went into it. There must have been about fifteen of them. . . . Some had green handkerchiefs on their heads and others scarlet hats, some of which were very big and round, in the style of frying pans, against the sun. The skins of these people are very white, much more so than our skins are. All of them have long beards and hair down to their ears.[28]

These new people had come in 1518 from the Spanish island of Cuba, in a flotilla of four ships under the leadership of the Governor's nephew, Juan de Grijalva, a "charming young man, beautiful to look at and very well mannered," Las Casas thought, as well as being "a person inclined to virtue, obedience, and . . . very obedient to his superiors."[29]

An English poet once wrote some lines about these voyages of discovery and conquest that began:

> Doom-laden caravels slant to the shore
> And all her seamen land.

The most sensational event in the history of the Americas was about to begin.

34

"This land is
the richest in the world"

And we believe this land is the richest in the world, in stones of great
value, of which we carried back many pieces.

Father Juan Diaz in his account of the journey of
Grijalva to Mexico, 1519

The first Spanish expedition to the territory now known as Mexico was in
1517. It consisted of three ships (two caravels and a brigantine), and was led
by Francisco Hernández de Córdoba, who, with little more than a hundred
men, looked for Indians to kidnap and take back to Cuba as slaves. (This
voyage has been touched on earlier.) Hernández de Córdoba was a member
of an immense family from Córdoba from which derived the famous Gran
Capitán. He was "a close friend" of Las Casas and had arrived in Cuba with
Velázquez in 1511 from Santo Domingo.[1] Hernández de Córdoba, who may
have been forty-two in 1517,[2] persuaded two other captains to go with him
and help with his costs. These were Cristóbal de Morante, from Medina del
Campo, who had gone to Santo Domingo in 1514, and Lope Ochoa de
Caicedo, another Cordobés, who had left Spain in 1512. One who accompanied them (Ginés Martín) said that they had been setting out for the Bahamas but found the weather so bad that they went to Yucatan instead.[3] The
responsibility for this deviation may have been that of Antonio de Alaminos,
of Palos, Ponce de León's prize pilot, who had known the coast of Central
America since he was there with Columbus in 1502. According to Alaminos,
he was invited by Hernández de Córdoba and his friends "in order to seek
new lands."[4] So there were several motives behind this apparently simple
journey.

The expedition made for the Isla Mujeres, off what is now Cancún. Afterwards they sailed along the Mexican coast to the west, stopping at what
became known as Cape Catoche. Many friendly contacts occurred between
Spaniards and Indians, who told them that the name of the land where they

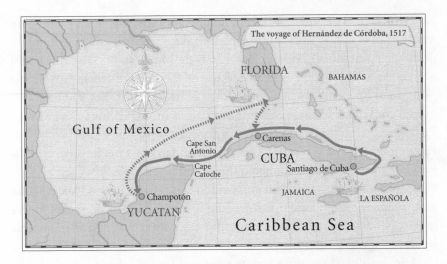

The voyage of Hernández de Córdoba, 1517

had arrived was Yucatan.[5] Hernández de Córdoba declared before a notary, Miguel de Morales, that he was taking possession of it in the name of Queen Juana and King Charles, her son.[6]

But he soon had to abandon his endeavors after a battle with the Maya near what is now Champotón. Twenty-five Spaniards were killed, a survivor, Pedro Prieto, later recalled. Hernández himself left for home mortally wounded, although his small force of arquebusiers made some impression on the indigenous enemies, who now smelled gunpowder for the first time. Hernández de Córdoba took back to Cuba some well-worked little gold objects, some small disks of silver, and some clay figurines. "Better lands have never been discovered," wrote a member of his expedition, Bernal Díaz del Castillo, a soldier who, like Cristóbal de Morante, came from Medina del Campo.[7] On reaching Cuba, Hernández de Córdoba said that he would like to return to Castile to tell the King and Queen what he had found, but he died before that could happen.[8]

In 1518, there was a second expedition to New Spain. This was led by Juan de Grijalva, a nephew of Governor Velázquez, who took a larger force with him than Hernández de Córdoba had, in four ships. He also took some artillery capable of firing twenty-pound cannonballs about four hundred yards.[9] With him too were arquebusiers, crossbowmen, and a few fighting dogs, probably mastiffs, but no horses. His instructions were apparently to sail along the coast of, and trade slaves in, Yucatan, rather than settle there. He did not have permission for any of those purposes from the Jeronymite priors of Santo Domingo, which probably he should have had.[10] But he did have with him the master pilot Antonio de Alaminos, who by now knew the waters of the Gulf of Mexico well. The four ships were captained by himself, Pedro de Alvarado of Badajoz, Francisco de Montejo, of Salamanca, and Alonso de Ávila, of Ciudad Real. Because of their roles later in Cortés's expedition to Mexico, they have gone down in history as if they had been immortal gods. Each of these captains invested in the expedition, as did Diego Velázquez.[11] Unlike Hernández de Córdoba, Grijalva had a priest with him, Father Juan Díaz of Seville, who wrote a brief diary of what he observed. Altogether, the expedition numbered three hundred people.[12]

Grijalva seems to have first gone out to Santo Domingo in 1508. He took part in the disgraceful quest for slaves in Trinidad of Juan Bono de Quejo's in 1516, but that apart, he had a reputation for honest dealing and honorable conduct.

His expedition set off in January 1518 and landed, as had Hernández de Córdoba's, at Cozumel, which they called Santa Cruz. There they found to their astonishment sumptuous houses, with stone doorposts (they reported them to be of marble), roofs of slate, tall temples, noble staircases, statues, and terra-cotta animals. A certain scent of incense hung over the island as if it had been Corsica in the old days. Then Grijalva, following in the wake of Hernández de Córdoba, turned north and west, and reached a spot near the present-day Campeche. There, a Mayan *cacique,* whom the Spaniards called "Lázaro," requested them to leave: "We don't want you as guests" was the comprehensible message. Perhaps he was the same *cacique* who had challenged Hernández de Córdoba. A skirmish followed, and the Indians fled at the sound of cannon. Grijalva, who lost two teeth in the fighting, did not pursue them. Instead, he continued to sail up the coast of what is now Mexico. Perhaps this was where Díaz de Solís and Pinzón were in 1508.

Grijalva was, however, soon sailing where no European had been before. He passed the port now known as El Deseado, and on the river that bears his name, he came upon a canoe from which the fishermen seemed to be using hooks of gold. The Spaniards captured a man, and the local chief offered him the weight of that man in gold; but Grijalva, "despite his companions," rejected the idea. A little later another *cacique* on the coast gave Grijalva a great number of ornaments, including golden shoes, gaiters and cuirasses of gold, and some golden armor.

The expedition then arrived at the Isle of Sacrifices, where Grijalva and his friends discovered what seemed to be signs of recent human sacrifices. They must have seen such things in Yucatan, too, but here the number of the victims was greater, and there were also decapitated heads and clear evidence of cannibalism. A local *cacique,* probably a Totnac, gave Grijalva a

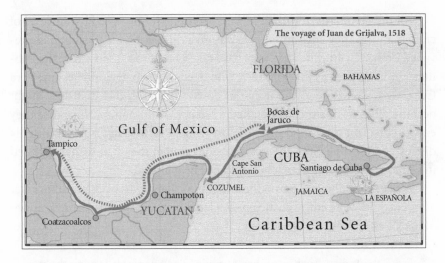

golden jar, some bracelets and golden balls, and other jewels. Yet another *cacique*, whom the Spaniards nicknamed "Ovando," gave them more beautiful objects of gold, such as a small statue of a man, a fan, and a mask, all carefully worked and with precious stones encrusted in the borders. They dined with the *cacique*, who also presented Grijalva with a beautiful, very well-dressed slave girl. Here they were close to the site of what would become Vera Cruz and eventually that of Tuxpan. Grijalva and his companions heard for the first time talk of a great empire, that of Moctezuma and the Mexica in the mountains.

Some members of the expedition, such as Martín Millán de Gamboa, wanted to remain where they were and establish a colony, but Grijalva quite correctly forbade it: his instructions from his uncle were different. Instead, he sent back Pedro de Alvarado to Cuba in his caravel to tell Velázquez what he had discovered. He took with him some of the gold that Grijalva had been given, including a breastplate and a mask. It was an astonishing story. The gold and the report of the empire of Moctezuma made a great impression on all who heard it in Cuba. This empire might not be that of China, but it did not sound so very different.

Grijalva sailed back down the coast as far as Cape Catoche, returning to Cuba on June 28. When he reached Santiago de Cuba, Velázquez criticized him on the ground that he should have stayed behind to settle the new territory that he had discovered, but Grijalva did not have the authority for such a thing, as Velázquez knew perfectly well.[13]

The noise of Grijalva's artillery had had a great effect on the Indians, and so did its effectiveness in destroying objects at a distance; its inaccuracy at close range seemed less important.

All the Spaniards, meanwhile, had been much impressed by the level of craftsmanship they encountered. It was on a different scale to what had prevailed in the Caribbean. They may have taken back, too, a sense that the tributary Indians, such as the Totonacs, who lived near what would become Vera Cruz, were so hostile to the imperial power of the Mexica that they might become allies of Spain. The detailed evidence of human sacrifice that they encountered on the island of Ulua, off what is now Vera Cruz, admittedly distressed everyone. Still, the positive side of what they had seen, expressed in so many interesting artifacts, could not be gainsaid.

Already by July 1518, only a month after Grijalva was back in Cuba, Peter Martyr could write enthusiastically in a letter to his ex-pupils, the Marquises of los Vélez and de Mondéjar:

> From the Indies much news has come in. The Spaniards leaving the island of Cuba—which is called by them "Fernandina"—toward the west but more toward noonday have encountered cities in which the subjects live according to law, there is commerce, and people go around dressed. They have books in whose pages they intersperse, between the lines of writing, figures of kings and idols, such as we see made by historians with prints or codices, with fabulous representations done in order to make them saleable. They have, too, streets as in any other city, houses built of stone and treated by lime, magnificent palaces and splendid temples where they offer sacrifices to their gods, similar to nocturnal phantasms. Annually they sacrifice an uncountable number of children, girls, and even slaves bought in the market.[14]

A real New World seemed thus to be opening before the Spaniards of the Caribbean: rich, because of the gold; savage, because of the human sacrifices; and cultivated, because of the illuminated books, the sculpture, and other works of art. The whole represented a temptation to all Spaniards in Cuba: the desire for glory, the desire for gold, and the desire to bring pagans to the true God.

35

"O our lord, thou has suffered"

O our lord, thou has suffered fatigue, thou has endured weariness,
thou hast come to arrive on earth.

Moctezuma to Cortés on the causeway
leading to Tenochtitlan, November 1518[1]

The third Spanish expedition to what is now Mexico was that of Hernán, or
Hernando, Cortés, to give him the name by which he was always known at
the time. Then in his late thirties, having been born about 1480, he came
from the town of Medellín, in Extremadura, and had first gone to the Indies
in 1506. He derived from an illegitimate and impoverished branch of the
wild Extremeño family of Monroy and was remotely connected by blood
with Ovando, the Governor of La Española. Another distant relation was the
councillor of the realm, Lorenzo Galíndez de Carvajal. Cortés had many
cousins but neither brothers nor sisters. Both his father and his maternal
grandfather were on the side of La Beltraneja in the civil war of the 1470s, his
grandfather Diego Alfon Altamirano having been a majordomo of one of
the leaders of the defeated party, the Countess of Medellín, a daughter of a
famous favorite of King Enrique IV, Juan Pacheco. The castle of Medellín
had been besieged by royal forces in 1476, and probably Cortés's grandfather
was in it at that time.[2] Thus the conqueror of Mexico emerged from a world
of rebellion, war, and conspiracy second to none.

Medellín, a town owned by the count of that name, is eight miles west of
Villanueva de la Serena, at the head of the lovely valley of the Serena, where
the archive of the Mesta was kept and where several hundred partners in that
sheep collective would meet once a year.[3] So Medellín was accustomed to
contact with the outside world. Cortés had been at the University of Salamanca and had mastered Latin there.[4] He may have been related to the dean
of the cathedral of Salamanca, Álvaro de Paz.[5] He then lived for a time in
Seville, acting as a notary. His life at Medellín had brought him into contact
with cultures other than Castilian, since in his childhood there were both

Jewish quarters and Muslim ones in the town. His grandfather's successor as majordomo in the castle had been Jewish, too, and had converted to Christianity in 1492 when Cortés was about twelve years old and when the Church of Santa Cecilia began to be built on the site of the synagogue.

As we have seen, Cortés had served his kinsman Ovando as notary in the new town of Azúa, on the southern coast of La Española, between his arrival there in the autumn of 1506 until 1510 or 1511. Then he had acted as secretary to Diego Velázquez de Cuéllar, who took him to Cuba and favored him. Cortés must have been present when Velázquez founded major cities in Cuba. Between 1516 and 1518 he had also been one of the magistrates of Santiago, by then the Spanish capital on the island; and he had made money from the pursuit of gold.[6]

Cortés was cautious and serene. He never troubled much about material comforts. He had a skillful way with his pen, as his artful letters to Charles V suggest: these are the only documents still worth reading of the large body of literature created by the conquests. At the same time, he was a voluptuary: the list of his women, many of them indigenous Mexicans, in the course of his war with the Mexica is long. The best portrait of him was a medallion by the Strasburger Christoph Weiditz.[7]

Cortés's expedition was a much more formidable undertaking than those of his two predecessors, for he took with him twenty ships and nearly six hundred men, including sailors. Like Hernández de Córdoba, he had arquebusiers. Like Grijalva, he had artillery. But unlike both of them, he also had horses. He had with him not just one priest, Father Juan Díaz, from Seville, who had also accompanied Grijalva, but also an agile Mercedarian friar, Bartolomé de Olmedo, from near Valladolid, in Castile, who must have helped him in gauging the reaction of the court in Castile to what he was doing. About twenty women also seem to have been with Cortés, as much fighters as nurses or mistresses (the role of "*conquistadora*" should be a subject for study). He had with him many young men fresh from Spain, such as Gonzalo de Sandoval and Antonio de Tapia, both from his own hometown of Medellín, as well as a free black warrior, Juan Garrido, who had been in many battles before in the Caribbean, in Puerto Rico, Guadeloupe, and Florida with Ponce de León, and in Cuba with Velázquez.

The majority of the expedition were men who had passed a few years in Cuba, but there were some who came especially from Santo Domingo, such as Juan de Cáceres, who became Cortés's majordomo. There also came some, like Ginés Martín Benito de Béjar (who played the tambourine so well) and Pedro Prieto, as well as the three chief lieutenants at the beginning (Alvarado, Ávila, and Montejo), who had been to Yucatan before, with either

Hernández de Córdoba or Grijalva, or indeed both. Some, such as Francisco de Montejo and Bernal Díaz del Castillo, had gone first to the Indies with Pedrarias but had made for Cuba when they found Darien an intolerable challenge to their health and patience.

Cortés was named to command this expedition as soon as Pedro de Alvarado returned from his journey with Grijalva. His instructions from Velázquez included the command to settle the lands discovered by Grijalva, to preach Christianity, to map the coastline from Yucatan to the north (and, by implication, to discover whether there was a strait there to the Pacific, then still known as the Southern Sea), and, wherever he landed, to take possession of territory in the name of the Spanish monarchs. There were also fantastic obligations: to find out about "the people with large, broad ears and others with faces like dogs and also where and in what direction are the Amazons who are nearby, according to the Indians whom you are taking with you."[8]

Cortés's men came from nearly every part of Castile, but the largest number came from Andalusia, say 36 percent, particularly from the city of Seville. Perhaps 16 percent came from Extremadura, and slightly fewer than that from Old Castile. The leaders, however, were mostly from the first of these last territories, including men whom Cortés had known all his life and who would back him unquestionably in moments of difficulty. Loyalty to the local leader was frequent among all the first generation of conquistadors. A few of Cortés's men came from Aragón and Cataluña, one or two from Valencia, almost none from Granada.[9] Cortés also brought with him a number of Cuban Indians as servants or slaves: Velázquez had given his approval.[10]

The leaders of his army, when it took shape as such, were Pedro de Alvarado, from Badajoz, nephew of that Diego de Alvarado who was one of the oldest Spanish inhabitants of La Española; Diego de Ordaz, from Castroverde del Campo, in Castile; Alonso de Ávila, from Ciudad Real; Andrés de Tapia, probably from a family of Medellín; and, later in the campaign, Gonzalo de Sandoval, who was also born in Medellín and who became in effect the second in command. None of these men had much previous experience of war, though some had participated in the fighting that had led to the Spanish control of Cuba. Diego de Ordaz had fought at the disastrous battle of Turbaco in 1509, in Hojeda's expedition, when Juan de la Cosa had been killed. Cortés himself had fought in Cuba and probably in La Española. Still, most of them came from families where the cult of arms dominated all conversations, and several, like Cortés himself, had fathers who had fought against Granada.

No doubt Alvarado had told Cortés of his impressions of this new world discovered by Hernández de Córdoba and Grijalva, and Cortés listened carefully.

Cortés and his expedition went first to Yucatan. There they recovered a lay brother from Écija, Jerónimo de Aguilar, who, wrecked in 1509 when on Nicuesa's expedition, had been for several years obliged to live with the Maya Indians.[11] One of Cortés's men, Angel Tintorero, described how on an island off Yucatan while looking for wild boar (so he recalled), he came across Aguilar in Indian clothes, clasping a worn Book of Hours.[12] Aguilar, who at first seemed so close to the Indians that no one recognized him as a Spaniard, spoke Maya. When Cortés was later presented with a Mexican slave, Mallinalli, or Marina, as the Spaniards named her, who spoke Maya as well as Nahuatl (the language of the Mexica), he was able to communicate with his supposed opponents through this double, clumsy, but effective system of interpretation.[13]

After several skirmishes in different places on the Mexican coast, Cortés set up a base near Vera Cruz, in defiance of the wishes of Diego Velázquez. There he fended off a rebellion mounted by some of the supporters of that Governor who were on the expedition and who seem to have wanted to go home. He established a good understanding with the people of the coast, the Totanacs, who had been tributaries of the Mexica. Already, he and his friends, like Grijalva before them, had seen signs of human sacrifice: "a sort of altar covered with clotted blood" was one of their disagreeable observations in Yucatan.

Cortés was approached by the Emperor of the Mexica, Moctezuma, who gave him presents but also tried to find out as much as he could of these surprising newcomers with long hair, sharp swords, and great physical strength. His magicians, who were, as we may suppose, his spies, reported that the leading Spaniards talked all night and at dawn were back on their horses. Now it was that Moctezuma presented Cortés with the two finely wrought, heavy gold and silver wheels almost certainly depicting the Mexican calendars (they were *repoussé* work). They had apparently been prepared for Grijalva, but he had sailed away before they were finished.[14] They seemed the great prizes of this stage of the conquest.

Cortés had the immense good fortune to land in the territory dominated by the Mexica in a year dedicated by the priests to the memory of the humane god Quetzalcoatl. He and his conquistadors came out of the same sea where legend had it that that deity had vanished long ago on a raft of serpents. Cortés played on these memories. There was a story, too, that Quetzalcoatl was always expected to return one day, though no evidence for the legend seems to exist that predates the conquest. The Mexica seem to have

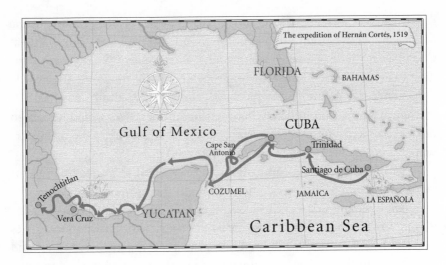

confused Cortés with the lost god. For that reason, Cortés was formally given clothing intended to resemble that of the god Quetzalcoatl.

Cortés now sent back two *procuradores,* Alonso Hernández de Portocarrero, from Medellín, and Francisco de Montejo, from Salamanca, to report his findings to the King. These men were only *procuradores* in the most simple definition of the word. They were certainly named by Cortés as his, not Vera Cruz's, representatives. No doubt they were selected since they would have been at home at court. Cortés avoided asking them to report to Diego Velázquez, but since Montejo had a property in Cuba, he stopped there for a day or two on his way to Spain. It was here that some of Cortés's treasure was observed by a friend who told the Cuban governor about it.

This mission was discussed earlier.[15] The treasure included the wheels presented by Moctezuma and a characteristic selection of Mexican works of art—wood carvings, turquoise, mosaics, feather mosaics, gold jewelry, and jade—except that there could not have been any of the large sculptures for which Mexico has been deservedly famous. The two also took back the news that Jerónimo de Aguilar, believed lost in Nicuesa's last expedition, was alive and well, and indeed serving the King as an interpreter.[16] (For their reception in Spain, see chapter 31.)

In August, Cortés left about a hundred of his men on the coast while, attended by many Totonacs as bearers, he led the rest over the tropical lowlands to the temperate zone of Mexico near Perote and across the mountains to the east of the city of Tenochtitlan, the Mexican capital.

Cortés and his army had some fierce battles on their way up to Tenochtitlan, on a scale much larger than Europeans had yet experienced in the New World. But they made friends with the people of Tlaxcala after fighting them. Tlaxcala was, as we have seen, a city-state that had often fought the Mexica, by whose empire they were surrounded. There was also a battle at Cholula, where the Spaniards assumed that the people of the city were planning to attack them. That seems improbable, but all the same, the heavily outnumbered expeditionaries may have genuinely feared such an attack: "If by chance we had not inflicted that punishment, our lives would have been in great danger," commented Bernal Díaz del Castillo, one of the many participants in this expedition who wrote about it.[17]

Then Cortés and his companions were received as guests by the Emperor Moctezuma. Their welcome was one of the most astonishing in history. The meeting occurred in November 1519 on the southern causeway, leading from the mainland across the lake of Mexico to Tenochtitlan. Cortés came with his four or five hundred Europeans, accompanied by bearers and servants from the indigenous, non-Aztec people who had flocked to serve him. Those people were happy to support a foreign military leader who might help them overthrow the Mexica.

The sight of Cortés and his fellow commanders, such as Pedro de Alvarado and Gonzalo de Sandoval, in their armor and on their fine Spanish horses made a great impression. Cortés had a few fighting dogs that were equally disturbing to the Mexica, and some cannon were probably carried up to Tenochtitlan on carts pulled by Totanacs, the usefulness of the wheel thereby entering the indigenous imagination for the first time in North America. In addition, there were arquebusiers, who could cause a violent detonation even when their fire was inaccurate.

Probably the Mexica would have heard of the long, strong, menacing swords of the Spaniards that had already been wielded to deadly effect on the journey up from the coast.

Cortés was received in person by Moctezuma, who was surrounded by many of the elaborately beplumed Mexican nobility. A man walked in front of the Emperor carrying a carved pole to indicate his authority. The Spaniards would have found that element in the ceremony familiar, and some might even have appreciated the admirable carving that probably adorned the pole. The Emperor may not have wanted to receive Cortés, but the local tradition of hospitality made it essential. The Mexica had impeccable manners: "as polite as a Mexican Indian" would be a typical phrase in the Spanish seventeenth century.

Moctezuma descended from his green litter, which according to the chroniclers was elaborately decorated with jewels, carving, featherwork, and other things for which his civilization is renowned. The Emperor probably wore an embroidered cloak, a green feathered headdress, perhaps comparable to the one that can be seen in the Museum of Mankind in Vienna, and on his feet gold-decorated sandals. He kissed his hand to Cortés after touching the earth.

Cortés apparently asked, "Art thou not he? Art thou not Moctezuma?" He then presented the Emperor with a necklace of pearls, probably made out of some gathered from the island of Margarita, off Venezuela, where Spanish pearl seekers had been so active.

Moctezuma gave Cortés in return a double necklace of red snails' shells from which hung eight shrimps made of gold. The color of this necklace may have confirmed that Moctezuma believed Cortés might have been a reincarnation of the lost god Quetzalcoatl, since red was one of that deity's favorite colors.

The Emperor then addressed Cortés. According to Fray Bernardino de Sahagún, a Franciscan who, after reaching Mexico in 1526, devoted his life to uncovering the nature of the civilization of the Mexica, it must have been the most remarkable greeting in history. Moctezuma is supposed to have said:

> O our lord, thou has suffered fatigue, thou has endured weariness, thou hast come to arrive on earth. Thou hast come to govern thy city of Mexico, thou hast come to descend upon thy mat, upon thy seat which for a time I have guarded for thee. . . . I by no means merely dream, I do not see in my sleep. I do not merely dream that I see thee, that I look into thy face. . . . The rulers departed maintained that thou wouldst come to visit thy city, that thou wouldst descend upon thy mat, upon thy seat.[18]

This translation from Mexican (Nahuatl) of the sixteenth century by Sahagún has invited many skeptical comments, but, all the same, some such elaborate words of welcome were surely made. "This is your house" is still a Spanish way of welcoming even a stranger on the peninsula.

Cortés and his men were allocated rooms in a palace facing that of Moctezuma, across the sacred precinct, on the site of what is now the state pawnshop. After a few days, fearing to be cut off and then murdered at the Mexicans' leisure, Cortés seized Moctezuma and held him captive in these lodgings. For an extraordinary time, between November 1519 and April 1520, the Emperor continued to govern Mexico, while Cortés ruled Moctezuma. Cortés taught the Emperor to use an arquebus, and they had numerous curious conversations recorded in subsequent accounts.

Relations between Cortés and Moctezuma became quite close, and on one occasion, Cortés remarked that with his weapons and generalship and with Mexican manpower, surely they could conquer the world together—or, at least, China.[19] All the same, there were tensions between the conquistadors and the Mexica, as when Cortés, Andrés de Tapia, and some others displayed images of the Virgin and St. Martin on the main temple on top of the pyramid, and broke some of the effigies of the Mexican gods, the remains of which were thrown down the steps of the ceremonial building.[20]

During this time, in January 1520, Moctezuma made a formal acceptance of his vassalage to the King of Spain, Charles V. The act, like many others in Cortés's time in the Mexican capital, has been questioned, and it has been plausibly suggested that the definition of being a vassal was quite different in Mexico to what it was in Spain. Yet the Mexica were, before the fifteenth century, the vassals of the Tepaneca, in the same way that Cortés now thought that they had become those of Castile. Several people testified to having witnessed the scene, and something like a concession of superior authority was probably given.[21] Moctezuma may even have agreed to become a Christian.[22] It has also been suggested that the aim of Cortés had always been to persuade Moctezuma to acknowledge himself a vassal of Charles V.[23]

This improbable cohabitation came to an end in April 1520 when about a thousand Spaniards, led by the veteran conquistador Pánfilo de Narváez—victor in Jamaica and deputy commander in Cuba—landed at Vera Cruz determined to capture or kill Cortés and establish the authority of the Governor of Cuba. Narváez had with him many experienced, swashbuckling adventurers, some known in battles in La Española as well as in Cuba. Once again, numerous Cuban Indians accompanied Narváez, either as slaves or servants.[24] Cortés told Moctezuma that these newcomers were principally Basques.[25] That was not so, even if there were a few Basques among them, such as Juan Bono de Quejo, one of Ponce de León's captains in Florida and leader of the infamous slaving exhibition to Trinidad in 1515.

Cortés left his deputy, Pedro de Alvarado, in Tenochtitlan and set off for the coast, where, at Cempoallan, near Vera Cruz, he surprised Narváez's Spaniards by a night attack. It was the first pitched battle between Spaniards in the Americas. About a dozen of Narváez's men were killed. Narváez himself was wounded, captured, and held as a prisoner at Vera Cruz for many months.

Then Cortés returned to Tenochtitlan, his forces swollen by most of the newcomers, who had seen no alternative to changing their allegiance to him. He also now had many more horses. In the meantime, though, Alvarado, in Tenochtitlan, fearing an attack, much as in Cholula the previous autumn, had massacred, in what modern strategists would term a preemptive strike, much of the Mexican nobility at a fiesta and was afterwards himself surrounded. Cortés entered Tenochtitlan and sought to raise that siege, but could not do so. The mood of the Mexica was quite different from what it had been the previous winter. Moctezuma died on a roof while trying to reason with his erstwhile subjects. That he was killed by a stone thrown from the ranks of the Mexica seems reasonable after reading the account of Fray Francisco Aguilar.[26] Cortés decided, after consultation with Alvarado, to leave the city surreptitiously at night.

A woman collecting water raised the alarm. In a fierce battle on the causeway leading from Tacuba into Tenochtitlan on the night of June 30, 1520, the so-called *noche triste,* many Spaniards were killed. Some seem to have been seized asleep in their lodgings, to be later sacrificed on the summit of the main pyramid.

The Spaniards were able to regroup, however, in the town of Tacuba, where the Church of Los Remedios now stands. Marching around the head of the lake of Mexico, they defeated the Mexica in an open battle near the town of Otumba. They were then able to recover fully on the other side of the mountains, in Tlaxcala. There, the indigenous enemies of the Mexica (the Spaniards' allies in this new territory) welcomed and succored them in return for a treaty that ceded Tlaxcala new authority in the valley of Mexico.[27]

Tlaxcala was the leading city-state that had successfully resisted incorporation into the Mexican Empire. Other peoples had been conquered and forced into a submission that they usually resented. Some of these seem to have seen the Spaniards' arrival as a heaven-sent opportunity to recover their old independence. Many Tlaxcalteca also saw the Spaniards as mercenaries from whose help they would benefit, and made what they thought was a hard bargain in return for their help.[28]

Cortés recovered from his wounds, as did his fellow commanders. He then devoted several months to the conquest of minor cities of the Mexican Empire, such as Tepeaca, to the east of the capital. He deliberately used terror as a deterrent against later resistance. Finally, his army, enhanced both by the help of indigenous allies and by new Spanish volunteers coming from Santo Domingo, in the spring of 1521 set about besieging Tenochtitlan.[29] One of the expeditions from Spain via the Canary Islands was sent at this time by two old *converso* associates of Cortés's, Juan de Córdoba, the well-known silversmith of Seville, and Luis Fernández de Alfaro, the merchant and one-time sea captain who had carried Cortés to the Indies in 1506 and whose life was discussed earlier.[30] Rodrigo de Bastidas also sent a large expedition from Santo Domingo.

Cortés could attack Tenochtitlan from the lake by commissioning a Sevillano, Martín López, to construct twelve brigantines. These were built at

Tlaxcala and were then carried over the hills in pieces to be assembled in a small estuary next to the lake of Mexico—an astonishing feat, a feat similar to that of Balboa in the isthmus of Panama.

The siege, a long battle, included many setbacks for the Spaniards. The fighting, often described, was on a scale unknown in the New World and ranks alongside some of the most bloody European battles; it was certainly one of the decisive battles of the world. The Spaniards captured control of the lake early on, through their use of the brigantines, and thereafter cut off the defenders from sources of food and other supplies. The battles led to the destruction of the city and the death from starvation, as well as in battle, of many Mexica. The latter almost certainly drugged themselves to fight with bravery, probably making use of sacred mushrooms and the peyote cactus.[31] But Moctezuma's cousin and successor, the youthful Emperor Cuauhtémoc, surrendered the city to Cortés on August 13, 1521. Many thousands of Mexica had been killed, and the people never recovered, though some survivors took part in subsequent wars of conquest, on the Spanish side. The Spanish losses since 1518 were probably about five hundred.[32]

Cortés's victory over the far more numerous Mexica has several explanations. The better-disciplined Spaniards were organized in companies and divisions, for which there was no Mexican equivalent. Cortés showed himself to be an excellent commander: always calm, particularly at difficult moments; always at the forefront of the battle; and always able to improvise imaginatively when things went wrong. He was as good a leader in a retreat as in an advance, and he could speak to and rally his men in a measured and inspiring tone. He could also explain in "a very excellent way . . . things about our holy faith" to the Indians.[33]

Communication of other sorts also counted. Bernal Díaz recounts how, during the siege of Tenochtitlan, Cortés was able effectively to correspond with Alvarado: "He was always writing to us to tell us what we were to do and how we were to fight."[34] The role of writing in all these conquests of the sixteenth century has been called "the literal advantage," or "perhaps . . . the most important" difference between the Spaniards and the indigenous people.[35] The part of Cortés's interpreter and subsequent mistress, Marína, was also critical.

Both sides were convinced of their own superiority. The Spanish conviction that they knew a unique religious truth that had to be imposed on those who sacrificed others counted for much. Even at the end Cortés had only three or four churchmen with him (the priest Juan Díaz, the lay brother Jerónimo de Aguilar, the Mercedarian Fray Bartolomé de Olmedo, and the Franciscan Fray Pedro de Melgarejo), but all his men were possessed by religion. That religiosity grew stronger as the conquest continued and as the extent of human sacrifice practiced by the indigenous people became known.

The Spaniards also had a capacity to improvise and think of new solutions that seemed nothing less than extraordinary to the Mexica. For example, after the conquest there was a severe shortage of gunpowder. Cortés's solution to this problem was to order two of his most reliable followers, Francisco de Montaño and Diego de Peñalosa, to lower a third, Francisco de Mesa, into the boiling volcano of Popocatepetl and obtain pitch in a bucket.[36]

Weapons and animals, however, constituted the determining factor. In order to prevent the Mexica from hiding on the rooftops of their capital and dropping stones into the streets, artillery fire by lombards or culverins, however inaccurate, came into its own. Horses were not effective in hand-to-hand fighting in the city, but they were decisive in combat in open country at, for example, the Battle of Otumba; and, to begin with, they seemed a terrifying innovation to the Mexica. Handguns, such as arquebuses, and older weapons, such as crossbows, did not make much difference to the course of battles, but the long, sharp Castilian sword was, as elsewhere in the New World, a vital element in the Spanish success. In comparison, the Mexica's swords of sharp stones slotted into wooden shafts were intended primarily to wound, not to kill, for their bearers hoped for wounded captives, not corpses, for sacrifice at festivals.

Artillery needs to be transported. Here the Spaniards were able to count on the help of their Indian allies. At the beginning, Cuban Indians probably helped. It is unlikely that Cortés could ever have left Vera Cruz for Tenochtitlan if he had not had such a supply of "sepoys." Even foot soldiers had servants and they, too, like their commanders, often had Indian girls with whom to sleep. The effect of these affairs, which founded the mestizo race in Mexico, was obviously beneficial for the morale of the Spaniards.

A further element in the Spanish success was contributed by the outbreak of a smallpox epidemic in Old Mexico in the autumn of 1520, which weakened indigenous resistance and killed several prominent leaders; in addition, the Spaniards seemed grandly immune. That may have had a serious psychological effect as well as reducing the superiority of manpower that the Mexica always had. The epidemic had been noticed in Spain in 1518, was destructive the following year in Santo Domingo, as we have seen, and was carried to New Spain/Mexico by a slave of Narváez's.

Moctezuma's ambiguous attitude toward his Spanish captors must also have had a negative effect on many of his fellow countrymen.

· · ·

After the conquest, Cortés set about reconstructing Tenochtitlan. He employed the surviving Mexica and several of his allies, such as the people of Chalco, who were known as competent builders from the days when they had previously worked on the Mexica's capital in the fifteenth century. The work was one of the great triumphs of Renaissance urban planning: in 1518, before its destruction, as has been pointed out, Tenochtitlan probably had been bigger than any western European city, and it was rebuilt within three years on a similar scale, on a plan devised by one of Cortés's friends from Badajoz, Alonso García Bravo.[37] The Indians worked, so the Franciscan monk Motolinía recalls, with enthusiasm and a will barely believable, no doubt because they were reviving what once had been their pride.

The indigenous people were particularly impressed by two Western devices introduced by the Spaniards: the wheeled cart and the pulley. Carts had been used by the Spaniards to transport guns during the war. Although the Mexica had the potter's wheel, they had not thought to use the wheel for the purposes of transport. Nor indeed did they have appropriate domesticated animals. Both the cart and the pulley, which transformed work on the building site of Tenochtitlan (it soon turned into just "Mexico"), were revelations. They helped the process of conversion to Christianity. If the foreigners had such technology, their gods (the Virgin, St. Martin, St. Christopher, as well as the Trinity) might be true, too.

The spiritual conquest of Mexico was the next stage after the material conquest. It was a triumph of proselytism. Many Mexica thought that the victory of Cortés meant a triumph for the God and the saints of Christianity. In most ways, they were right.

Cortés soon began also to allocate *encomiendas* to his followers. In a letter to King Charles, he explained that he would much rather not have done so, but the shortage of treasure with which to reward his followers was the explanation.[38] Among the first *encomenderos* were, of course, the heroes of the conquest, Andrés de Tapia, Pedro de Alvarado, and Juan Jaramillo.

In the spring of 1521, a detailed account of Tenochtitlan ("Venice the rich," Peter Martyr said the conquistadors had called it) reached Spain. Martyr wrote of it in a letter to his favorite correspondents, the Marquises de Mondéjar and de los Vélez.[39] In the autumn, two new emissaries of Cortés's arrived in Seville: Alonso de Mendoza and Diego de Ordaz. The first was a native of Medellín, an old friend of Cortés's, but no relation, or so it seems, of the dominant aristocratic family of that name. The second, Diego de Ordaz, born in Old Castile, had been a magistrate in Santiago de Cuba in

1518, at the same time as Cortés, and was one of his first commanders. These two told of the astonishing city that they were then besieging and of the empire of the Mexica, in what Cortés had already christened New Spain. They described how their commander was determined to seize it for King Charles and his mother, Juana. Castile was still considering this news when, six months later, on March 1, 1522, the message came that Cortés had indeed captured the Mexican capital. News of that event was described and published by the German printer of Seville Jacob Cromberger in a postscript to the second of Cortés's reports, or *Cartas de Relación,* to the King, which he must have had ready for printing.

A third letter, written by Cortés in New Spain in May 1522, gave a report of what had happened in the siege and the conquest of Tenochtitlan. It reached Seville in November 1522 and was published in March 1523. It had been countersigned as giving an honest account by a solid scion of an old family of Tordesillas, Julián de Alderete, the royal treasurer in Tenochtitlan, and two other conquistadors of repute, Alonso de Grado and Bernardino Vázquez de Tapia. It was a story that made even such novels as *Tirant lo Blanc* and *Amadís de Gaula* seem limited in their scope, though the latter was a book that Cromberger had also published. The attitude of Old Spain toward the Indies was transformed, and forever.

It has long been recognized that the study of the history of the conquest of Mexico is greatly facilitated by the large amount of original writing by the combatants. These included Cortés himself, Bernal Díaz del Castillo, Andrés de Tapia, Father Aguilar, Bernardo Vázquez de Tapía, and Father Juan Díaz (though he wrote only of the expedition of Grijalva). Fray Bartolomé de las Casas and Oviedo also wrote from personal experience of some of the people concerned in the conquest. But these names are merely the tip of an iceberg. Either as witnesses to the *residencia* of Cortés or as witnesses in their own right in inquiries into their actions during the forty years after the conquest, or acting as witnesses in others' inquiries, another 350 or so conquistadors left some kind of personal memory of what they had undergone or seen during the years 1519 and 1520. All the leading captains recorded something, so this is one of the best-documented conflicts in history. How often did it occur in some investigation twenty or more years afterwards that a judge would ask a middle-aged conquistador, "But how do you know of this?" and received the answer, "I was there. I saw it with my own eyes."[40]

Book Nine
❦

MAGELLAN AND ELCANO

Utopia by Thomas More was first published in 1516.
Here is an illustration from an edition of 1518,
probably designed by Hans Holbein.

36

"Go with good fortune"

You are to go with good fortune to discover that part of the ocean within our limits and demarcation . . . and, for the first ten following years, we shall not give leave to any [other] person to . . . discover by the same road and course by which you shall go.

Instructions to Magellan, 1520

Bartolomé de las Casas was in the rooms of the chancellor, Jean Le Sauvage, in Valladolid in March 1518 when a Portuguese captain, Hernando (Fernão) de Magalhaes (Magallanes in Spanish, Magellan in English), came in with a friend, Ruy Faleiro, who proclaimed himself an astrologer. They had arranged the audience with Le Sauvage thanks to the help of a corrupt but benign merchant from Burgos, the *converso* Juan de Aranda.[1] Magellan had with him a painted globe on which he had marked a westward voyage that he wanted to make. He seemed certain that he would thereby find a strait that would take him to the far south of what Waldseemüller had called America and, thence, to the Moluccas, "whence the spices come." He and Faleiro had worked out, to their own satisfaction, at least, that the line dividing the world between the Portuguese and the Spaniards would, if logically continued around the planet, give those Spice Islands to Spain.

Las Casas asked: "And if you don't find a strait, how are you going to pass through to the Southern Sea?"[2] Magellan said in that case he would take the old Portuguese route via South Africa, which he already knew from personal experience. Antonio Pigafetta, a citizen of Vicenza in the republic of Venice, who accompanied Magellan, later reported that that captain was convinced he would find a strait since he had seen a map drawn by Martín de Behaim in the library of the King of Portugal that showed it.[3] The famous globe, however, made by Behaim in Nuremberg shows no strait, nor does it show America. Waldseemüller's map showed the Pacific but no strait. Magellan must have seen something else.[4] More important, perhaps, in that commander's mind was the advice of a cousin of his, Francisco Serrano, a commander in the Moluccas who had convinced himself when he was in the East that there was a route to those islands via the West Indies.

Expeditions of discovery had been taken in this direction before. For example, Juan Díaz de Solís, the experienced sailor who succeeded the Florentine Vespucci as chief pilot, had also set out to look for a strait from the Atlantic into the Southern Sea.[5] Early in 1516, Díaz de Solís discovered the estuary of the River Plate, which he called El Mar Dulce. His was a great achievement, but the Plate was not "the strait." Nor was the river all sweet for, alas, resting triumphantly on the shore, Solís, together with eight others, were captured and subsequently eaten by Guaraní Indians: a tragic end for a great sailor.[6] Other members of the expedition were imprisoned, to be kept for later consumption, on the island of Santa Catalina, but some escaped. One of these was Alejo García, probably Portuguese, an astounding individual so characteristic of Europeans in this first generation in the years after Columbus. With four compatriots he reached the South American continent in an improvised canoe. They set off in search of "the White Man," a mythical figure of the interior whom they had been assured by local Indians possessed immense wealth. The author of *Amadís de Gaula* could not have done better. Followed for many miles by a large horde of Indians, whom he not only placated but fascinated, García reached the Peruvian Andes and made contact with the Incas—the first European to do so. Thence he returned and went somewhere near what is now Asunción, where he, like Díaz de Solís, was murdered by Guaranís about 1525.[7]

As for Magellan's plans for these waters, an arrangement (*capitulación*) was reached between him and King Charles (the document was also signed by the "Indian" specialists in Charles's court, Cobos, Gattinara, Fonseca, Ruiz de la Mota, and García de Padilla). Magellan saw not only Le Sauvage, but Fonseca and then Chièvres. The contract of April 19, 1519, stated that Magellan had wanted to offer to the Crown a great service within the limits of the agreed Spanish area of control. It continued:

> You are to go with good fortune to discover that part of the ocean within our limits and demarcation . . . and, for the first ten following years, we shall not give leave to any [other] person to . . . discover by the same road and course by which you shall go. . . . Also, you may discover in those parts what has not yet been discovered, but you may not discover or do anything in the demarcation and limits of the most serene King of Portugal, my very dear and well-beloved uncle and brother. . . .[8]

Magellan was to hand over to the King one-twentieth of all goods found and exchanged. The merchant Juan de Aranda would receive an eighth of the profits of the journey. Such were the benefits of important introductions. Magellan was granted the right to dispense summary justice in the event of disputes that might arise on land or sea. Before they left, both Magellan and Faleiro received nominations as Knights of Santiago.[9]

Magellan had been born in Villa de Sabroza, in the district of Villa Real, Trás-os-Montes, in northern Portugal, not far from Porto. He came from a family of minor nobility, his father, Ruy Rodrigo Magalhaes, having been for a time chief magistrate of Aveiro, while his grandfather Pedro Afonso also played a part in the administration of the province. Magellan was early attached to the service of the Portuguese queen Elena, who was a daughter of the Catholic Kings, and in 1505, he joined the expedition to India of Francisco de Almeida, who had fought for Castile against Granada. He took part in the conquest of Malacca and then sailed for the Moluccas. He was in India with the astonishing Admiral Afonso de Albuquerque and then in Azamour, in Morocco. As well as being a navigator of experience, he was also a military man. Yet he offended King Manuel, partly because he fell out with Albuquerque, and partly because of a trivial failure to hand over cattle captured from the Arabs in Morocco. For that reason he was not listened to when he approached the King of Portugal about his scheme for sailing to the Moluccas by a western route.

Thwarted in Lisbon, Magellan went to Seville accompanied by Ruy Faleiro, who was always full of interesting ideas. In Seville he was welcomed by a Portuguese merchant, Diego Barbosa, who was deputy commander of the Alcázar under Jorge de Portugal. He introduced Magellan to the Casa de Contratación and, indeed, to the society of Seville; and Magellan married his daughter, Beatriz.

King Manuel of Portugal continued to do what he could to create obstacles for Magellan. One of King Manuel's advisers, Bishop Vasconcellos, was even said to have suggested that Magellan might be killed. The King of Portugal's factor in Seville, Sebastián Álvarez, called on Magellan at his lodgings and, finding him arranging baskets and boxes of victuals for his journey, told him that he had embarked on a course in which there were as many dangers as spokes in the wheel of St. Catherine. He ought to return home. Magellan said that "for honor's sake, he could now do nothing else except what he had agreed upon." Álvarez said that a disservice to his own king could not be a matter of honor. But Magellan demurred and said that it was indeed unfortunate that he had been refused in Lisbon, but that it was now too late to do anything other than work for the King of Castile. Another agent of King Manuel wrote that he had told King Charles personally "how ill-seeming and unusual it was for one King to receive the vassals of another one, his friend, against his will—which was a thing that was not usual even among knights. . . ."[10]

On September 20, 1519, Magellan left Sanlúcar de Barrameda with five ships and about 250 men. They headed first, following the route of all explorers, for the Canary Islands. Then, two weeks later, they left Tenerife with another 26 men so that the total of the crews amounted to 276. About a third of his crew was not Spanish, and many bore the names of their birthplaces as their surnames: Jácome de Messina, Simón de la Rochola, and so on. About fifteen were Portuguese. There were among the voyagers some who knew the coast of Brazil; for example, an Italian named Juan Caravaggio. Rodríguez Serrano had also been to Brazil in 1500 with Vélez de Mendoza.[11] It seems that one of Magellan's men, "Master Andrés," a "constable," was an Englishman from Bristol. There were no women on board. Pigafetta, a citizen of Vincenza, said that Magellan "did not entirely declare the voyage which he was going to make to avoid his men, from amazement or fear, being unwilling to accompany him on so long a journey."[12]

Magellan's ships, which should live in legend as long as Columbus's, were, first, the caravel Trinidad (110 tons), of which the captain was Magellan himself. Pigafetta sailed as a passenger, as did Álvaro de la Mezquita, a cousin of Magellan's. Magellan arranged for a torch of burning wood to be placed on the poop of his boat so that the others should not lose sight of him. On his ship, Magellan carried good iron guns. Second, there was the San Antonio (120 tons), the captain being the inspector of the armada, Juan Pérez de Cartagena, who was said to have been a nephew of Bishop Fonseca.[13] Third, there was the Concepción (90 tons), whose captain was Gaspar Quesada, once an employee of Fonseca's.[14] The master was a resourceful Basque sailor, Juan Sebastián de Elcano, whose place in history is secure.[15] Fourth, there was the Victoria (85 tons), whose captain was Luis de Mendoza, a protégé of Archbishop Deza's. Fifth, there was the Santiago (75 tons), whose captain was Juan Rodríguez Serrano.

Magellan took with him a good supply of artillery: 62 culverins and 10 falconets, and he had some 50 arquebuses. He also carried 1,000 lances, 220 shields, 60 crossbows, 50 light guns (escopetas), and 50 quintales of gunpowder in barrels: this expedition was going to be able to defend itself. In addition, he had over 10,000 fishhooks, more than 400 barrels of wine or water, over 20 parchment maps, 6 compasses, about 20 quadrants, 7 astrolabes, 18 hourglasses, and numerous objects for exchange with unknown natives: hawks' bells, for example, knives, mirrors, quicksilver, and scissors. Over 2,000 kilos of ships' biscuits were carried, as well as dried fish, bacon, beans, lentils, flour, garlic, cheeses, honey, almonds, anchovies, white sardines, figs, sugar, and rice. Six cows (one on each ship except for the *Trinidad*, which had two) traveled, and there were three pigs. It was always said in Sanlúcar de Barrameda that Magellan spent more on the dry light fortified wine of the place, manzanilla, than on gunpowder.[16] The medicine chest traveled on the *Trinidad*.[17]

The fleet cost 8.78 million maravedís, of which the King produced 6.4 million and a merchant from Burgos, Cristóbal de Haro, who had always been especially interested in finding a western route to the Spice Islands, being a leading spice trader, contributed most of the rest. So the expedition was primarily a royal enterprise. (The only two other such had been Columbus's second voyage and that of Pedrarias.) Much of the royal contribution must have derived from the gold imported from the Caribbean.[18]

Magellan and his ships sailed first to Cape Verde and then to Sierra Leone, where it rained without ceasing. Some sharks followed the ships. The expedition harpooned several but, except for the smaller ones, did not find them good to eat. Often, men reported seeing Santo Elmo's fire;[19] sometimes the body of the saint himself seemed to appear, sometimes birds materialized without tails, sometimes birds of paradise hovered, and sometimes there were flying fish. Magellan set off southeast for "Verzin," the Italian word for redwood, that is, Brazil.

He reached that coast after sixty days of sailing, the longest maritime journey made without a stop until then. Pigafetta found the new land most abundant but was shocked to find that its indigenous people did not seem to worship anything. Yet they lived, he reported imaginatively, from 125 to 140 years. Both men and women went about naked, and they slept in cotton hammocks, slung in large dormitory houses where there might be a hundred people. They had canoes made of one piece of wood. They ate their enemies, not, apparently, because human beings tasted good, but because it was the custom to try to acquire the qualities of others. There were pretty parrots. For a hatchet or a knife, the indigenous people were prepared to give almost anything: one or two daughters as slaves, or five or six fowls; for a comb, two geese; and for a small mirror or a pair of scissors, so much fish that "ten men could not have eaten it." For a hawk's bell, they gave a fruit called a *battate*. For a pack of cards, they gave five chickens.

A pretty girl came on board, found a clove in a junior officer's cabin, and put it "with great gallantry between the lips of her 'natura,' as he put it." A clove was, of course, what Magellan would be seeking in the Moluccas above all. The girl's action seemed to augur well.

The indigenous people of Brazil certainly repay attention, for they provided the original "noble savage" of whom Dryden first wrote and in whom later European writers, above all Rousseau, exulted. Dryden's play *The Conquest of Granada* speaks of one who considers himself:

> . . . as free as nature first made man,
> Ere the base laws of servitude began,
> When wild in woods the noble savage ran.

Those generous men of the Enlightenment took their ideas from the intelligent observers of the sixteenth century. Peter Martyr, for example, told the Pope that "people coming back from Brazil had assured him that the people lived there in a golden age . . . and they naturally follow goodness." Erasmus's *In Praise of Folly* was inspired by Brazil, while Thomas More's *Utopia* must have been near—for the place was described as "south of the Equator" yet in the New World. Rabelais would similarly be influenced in *Pantagruel* by what he heard of Brazil. The first European visitors, such as Vespucci, described these Indians as living in benign if primitive socialism, owning everything in common, with neither money nor trade. Pigafetta recalled how naked Indian girls climbed aboard the Spanish ships and gave themselves to the Europeans with natural innocence—an impression confirmed a little later by the astounding French sailor Parmentier, who in the 1520s described those girls as "colts who had never experienced a rein."[20]

In his famous essay "On the Cannibals," the French writer Montaigne recalled how he had met people who had been to Brazil and how, forty years after Magellan, in the 1560s, some indigenous people were brought to France and presented to King Charles IX. By that time the French had reasonable interpreters. Montaigne asked one of these men what the natives had been saying. They were saying, it turned out, that they thought it extraordinary that so obviously splendid a country as France should have as their leader such a small man.[21]

Great differences existed among the Indians of Brazil at the time of the coming of the Portuguese, and these differences survive. The original population of the vast territory that now constitutes Brazil may have been 2.5 million. The Indian population is now 100,000.[22] So over the centuries a demographic catastrophe occurred.

Magellan and his men stayed thirteen days in Brazil and then sailed on past the Rio Plate without entering it, and in what is now Argentina, Pigafetta said that they met giants, of whom he gave a vivid description. By then they were far beyond any coast seen by any European.

Due to severe difficulties with the ships, the expedition stopped for five months in the bay and port of San Julián, five hundred miles north of Cape Horn. Magellan did not want to sail into icy waters without his ships being in perfect condition. The crews, left idle for so long, despaired of finding the mysterious strait; their food was rationed, and they were bored by both the sterility and cold of the land. Magellan thought that he should stay there till the spring. Many of his followers, though, desired to go home. They considered that they were involved in a pointless undertaking. There were also serious difficulties between the Portuguese and the Spaniards among the crews. It seemed odd to Spaniards, such as the Basque Elcano, the master of the *Concepción*, to hear Captain-General Magellan, a Portuguese, talking "in the name of the King." A not surprising dispute developed between Magellan and his Spanish captains—especially Quesada and Cartagena. The quarrel had begun earlier when there had been an altercation as to whether—and if so, how—to salute Magellan. On such trivial matters, the fates of empires have always depended.

On Palm Sunday, April 1, 1520, Magellan ordered his crews to go on shore to hear Mass. He invited the officers and pilots to lunch with him afterwards on the *Trinidad*. But only two men, Coca and Álvaro de la Mezquita (who had taken over command of the *San Antonio*), went to Mass and only Mezquita went to lunch. That night Quesada and Cartagena went to the *San Antonio* and, having seized Mezquita, told the crew of that vessel that it was under their orders, not those of Magellan. Juan de Elorriaga, from Guipuzcoa, the master, backed Magellan and was struck so hard by Quesada that he died two months later.

No one at first dared to take over command of the *San Antonio*. In the end, Elcano did, with Quesada to help. Cartagena went to the *Concepción*. Luis de Mendoza went to the *Victoria*.

The rebels had now captured most of the ships, and they sent word to Magellan that he should henceforth carry out the royal orders according to their interpretation. They added various irreverent statements. Magellan was furious. He ordered all the captains to come to the *Trinidad*, but the rebels asked him to go to the *San Antonio*. He dispatched Gonzalo Gómez de Espinosa, his constable, with six men, to the *Victoria*, with a letter to Luis de Mendoza. Mendoza read the letter and allowed himself a malign smile; seeing it, Gómez de Espinosa stabbed him in the throat and another sailor gave him a blow in the side. He fell dead. The constable and his armed men then seized the ship.

Much the same happened on the *Santiago*. The rebels on the *San Antonio* and the *Concepción* wished to flee, but Quesada sent Mezquita to Magel-

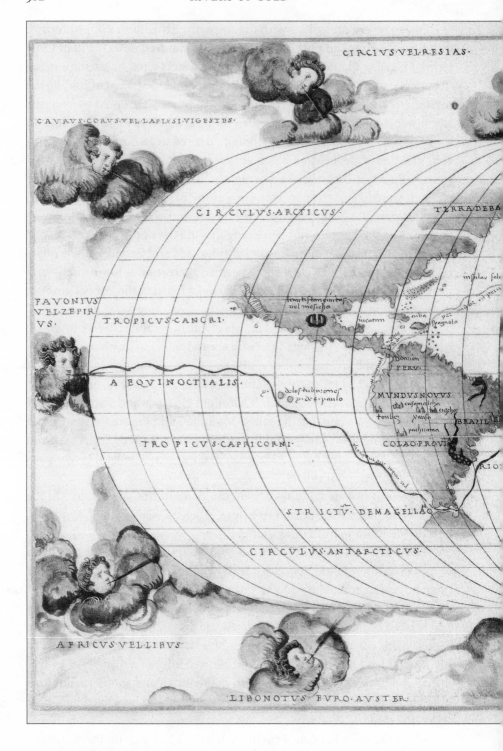

The voyage of Magellan and Elcano, 1519–22

SEPTEMTRIO·VELA·PARCTIAS·

AQVILO·VEL·BOREAS·

CECIAS·APELIOTES·

ASIA

fertilis terra maiuni montem

volga sine iha flumus quem tartari edul nocant

citracan emporium

 sacarum regio

Iaxar flunus far hia expo mari montem

catalo prouincia

fencha

SINARVM REGIO

SVBSOLA·NVS·

caspium mare

bactiana

fogdiana

media

parthia

carmonia

cathain

aracosta

cathaia ciuitas

ARABIA

FOELIX

PROVINCIÆ INSVLÆ·MOLOC

HÆ

gingui calicut cochin

ferlan rsula

malacha

Taprobana i fula nuns famatra

castello de tina de re de portugal

INDICVM·MARE·

INSVLA·S·LAVRETII·

C·DE·BONA·SPERANZA:

VVLTVRNVS·EVRVS·

AVSTER·VEL·NOTVS·

EVRO·NOTVS·

lan to seek an accommodation. Magellan said that it was useless. Elcano hesitated. Magellan bombarded the *San Antonio* with some of his artillery; later,
his men boarded it, and Elcano, Coca, and Quesada were arrested. Cartagena, on the *Concepción,* gave up without a fight.

At dawn, Magellan sent the body of Mendoza on shore, cut him into
four, and publicly denounced him as a traitor. Quesada was hanged and then
quartered. Others met only slightly less horrible ends; Cartagena was left behind, marooned, with a priest (apparently French, named Calmette). Peter
Martyr later wrote that he thought Magellan "had been within his rights in
so acting, but others said that he was not."[23] Magellan then pardoned forty
others who had compromised themselves in the rebellion, including Elcano.[24] At the same time, Esteban and Gómez fled with the *San Antonio,* intending to sail back to Spain, taking with them "a giant" they had captured.
Jerónimo Guerra made himself the captain, and they took Álvaro de la
Mezquita with them as a prisoner. They reached Spain in May 1521.

The *Santiago* was also lost, but all its crew were saved. The mutiny over,
the ships surviving eventually continued, past a so-called Cape of the Eleven
Thousand Virgins, into the narrows leading to the "strait" of Magellan.

The discovery of this strait, the goal of so much Spanish effort and the
target of so many expeditions in previous years, was a triumph. It was, Pigafetta said, 110 leagues long, say 350 miles, and was surrounded on both sides
by snowy mountains. The expedition at first assumed that it was a mere bay.
But Magellan believed that he knew better, perhaps because of prior information gathered in Lisbon, and he insisted on sailing on. The winds were
complicated. But Magellan persisted, weeping with happiness when they
passed Cabo Deseado and entered the calm of the Southern Sea, the "Pacific,"
as he would henceforth think of it. The nights at that time of the year were
only three hours long, for it was October. They called the strait the Estrecho
Patagónico after the territory of Patagonia, which received its name from the
mythical country in the novel *Sergás de Esplandián,* written by Garcí Montalvo, the author, or re-creator, of *Amadís de Gaula,* and published in Seville
by Cromberger in 1510.[25]

Magellan and his party remained in the Pacific for three months and
twenty days, meeting no storms and traveling, as Pigafetta says, four thousand leagues (about twelve thousand miles). At first he sailed north, along
the coast of Chile, then afterwards in a northwesterly direction. But nineteen
men died at this stage, as did "the giant." They then set out across the ocean,
turning west near what is now Valdivia, in Chile.

Magellan seemed to have an instinctive sense of which winds to seize
upon. No doubt he had learned something of their likely pattern when in

the East Indies. Food, on the other hand, ran short; the members of the expedition had to eat rats and moldy ships' biscuits and the water was foul. Many fell ill from scurvy, which at that time no one knew was best treated by eating lemons. One on the expedition wrote: "Had not God and His blessed mother given us good weather, we should all have died of hunger in that exceedingly vast sea. I truly believe that no such voyage will ever be made again."[26]

Magellan eventually reached the Marianas, the chain of islands that runs north to Japan, in March 1521. They called these the Islas de Ladrones, because the natives, who, of course, had never seen anything like a European, robbed them of whatever they could. For a time, Europeans thought of them also as the Islas de Velas Latinas, "of the Lateen Sails," because of the shape of the sails that the natives used for their fishing expeditions. (The islands did not receive their name of "Marianas" until the late seventeenth century when the Spanish queen María Ana sent a Jesuit mission there.)

Pigafetta described the natives with loving detail, saying that they lived in liberty, worshipped no deities, were naked (except that most women wore a thin piece of bark over their private parts); some wore their beards to their waists and hats of palm leaves "as if they were Albanians." They had houses of wood covered with planks and fig leaves, and slept on palm mats and palm straw. There were numerous formal exchanges of gifts between them and Magellan; fish, palm wine, and figs or bananas, later rice and coconuts, were the most important indigenous offerings. A little gold followed. Later still came sweet oranges and chickens. The expedition's fortunes varied. Magellan spent some time with a people whose monarch lived off rice on china plates, and drank pig's broth, as well as a rather superior palm wine.

So they continued. On the island of Satighan they found a bird as large as an eagle, and in Zzubu, in what is now Cebu in the Philippines, they heard news for the first time of the Portuguese voyages that had arrived ahead of them. Magellan's interpreter explained to the indigenous people, firmly, that their master, the King of Spain, was more powerful than the King of Portugal. Always there were exchanges of presents: Pigafetta gave the King of Zzubu a robe of yellow and violet silk, a red cap, certain pieces of glass, and two gilt drinking glasses. That monarch probably appreciated such attentions, for when the crews of Magellan first saw him, he was wearing only a cloth around his middle, a loose wrapper around his head, a heavy chain around his neck, and two large gold earrings. His face was painted. He was eating tortoise eggs. His subjects played music on strange instruments, and the Europeans danced with them.

In addition to presents, Pigafetta recalls fourteen pounds of iron being exchanged for ten weights of gold, and for other minor goods they obtained goats, pigs, and rice.

Magellan tried to ensure the conversion to Christianity of the rulers whom he met. He acted on the principle that if one captured the soul of the ruler, the people would be sure to follow. Thus he told the King of Zzubu that if he wished to become a Christian, he must burn his idols and raise a cross. Everyone should worship the Christian god on their knees and make the sign of the cross. The King agreed, and when he was baptized, he became known as "Don Carlos," and his brother, "Don Fernando"; and the same happened with the Queen and her ladies, who were much drawn to the image of Our Lady holding the baby Jesus. The Queen, who was heavily painted, with her lips and nails as red as those of a modern lady of fashion, became "Juana," her sister "Isabel," and her daughter "Catalina." At various stages, Magellan fired his artillery to celebrate these developments.

Often the descriptions by Pigafetta read as if they were passages in *Tirant lo Blanc* or some other chivalrous novel:

> One day, the Queen came in all her state. She was preceded by three damsels, who carried in their hands three of her hats. She was dressed in black and white, with a large silk veil with gold stripes that covered her head and shoulders. Many women followed her with their heads covered by a small veil, and a hat above that. The rest of their bodies were naked, except for a small wrapper of palm cloth that covered their private parts. Their hair fell flowing over their shoulders. The Queen, after making a bow to the altar, sat upon a cushion of embroidered silk, and the captain sprinkled over her and her ladies rosewater and musk, a perfume that pleased them . . . very much.[27]

Later, the King and his family swore fealty to the King of Spain. The Europeans, for their part, watched a ceremony in which a pig was blessed, and they also saw a Zzubu funeral.

Magellan agreed to fight the people of nearby Matan for the benefit of pleasing the King of Zzubu. It was a gratuitous adventure that deserved to end badly; and this battle on the island of Cebu, in the southern part of the archipelago, on April 27, 1521, concluded disastrously. Magellan entered the thick of the fighting, the ferocity of which he had underestimated. Almost immediately he was wounded by what Pigafetta calls "a scimitar," and lying on the ground, "there fell on him many lances of iron and cane, so much so that they deprived of life our mirror, our light, our comfort, and our guide."[28]

Duarte Barbosa, a cousin of Magellan's, also a Portuguese, now became captain. Pigafetta says that he was elected to that place, presumably by a show of hands. Juan Serrano, who had been chief pilot, also played a part in the new command, but he was soon left to be killed by the "Christian king" whom Magellan had believed an ally.[29]

Magellan's character was well described by Pigafetta: "One of his principal virtues was his constancy in the most adverse fortune. In the midst of the sea, he was able to endure hunger better than the rest of us. Versed in nautical charts, he also was better informed than any of us about the true art of navigation. It is certain that he knew, by his genius and by his intrepidity, without anyone having given him the example, how to attempt the circuit of the globe. . . ."[30] Las Casas, who knew Magellan slightly, described him as "a man of spirit, brave in his thoughts and capable of undertaking great things," even though as a person he had little authority, "being small of build."[31] Magellan's achievement was incomplete, but it was his voyage that led to the circumnavigation of the world, his vision that made him contemplate it, and his courage that led his ships through the strait that bears his name and across the biggest sea on earth.

The members of the expedition thought that they could now man only two ships, so they burned the *Concepción* and, after further curious meetings in the Philippines (also worthy, in the account of Pigafetta, to be incidents from *Amadís* or *Tirant lo Blanc*), returned to Spain across the Indian Ocean with the *Victoria* and the *Trinidad*. On their return journey, it was Borneo that most impressed Pigafetta, perhaps because he and some of his comrades were constrained to ride out from the royal presence on elephants. Here, there were some desertions among the remaining crew. Here, too, Christians for the first time on this journey encountered Islam, whose eastern transmogrification did not much remind them of old Granada.

They also found small and squat cinnamon trees, the lemon tree, and the sugarcane (apparently indigenous there) that had been the goal of Magellan in the first place. They found metal coins with a hole in the middle, heard stories of pearls as big as chicken's eggs, discovered white porcelain from China, and gum. Some of these were exchanged for bronze, iron, knives, and, in particular, spectacles.

Then the expedition reached the Moluccas, Tadore, and Ternate, "where the cloves grow," and there, Pigafetta says with pleasure, they found access nothing like as difficult as the Portuguese had made out. These Spice Islands had been captured by Muslims fifty years before, but all the same, the forty-five-year-old Muslim king of Tadore (Rajah Sultan Manzor) quickly agreed to be a vassal of the King of Spain. He even agreed to change the name of his island to Castile. These Muslims, the Spaniards thought, were far more amenable than those of the Mediterranean.

Despite the length of their journey, Magellan's successors had plenty to give away as presents: a robe of Turkish yellow velvet and one of brocade, a chair of red velvet, four ells of scarlet cloth, some yellow damask, white cambaye linen, caps, glass beads, knives, and some large mirrors. Europe was presented to the East rather than just Spain or Portugal, even if that linen had been made in India. The beads must have been Venetian. Perhaps the scarlet cloth was from the Cotswolds in England. Northleach may thus have played its part in this early "globalization."

The members of the expedition showed the Rajah how to shoot with a crossbow and a swivel gun, a weapon larger than an arquebus. This monarch was delighted to negotiate with Spaniards, for he had earlier quarreled with Francisco Serrano, the Portuguese captain-general, a friend of Magellan's, and had even tried to poison him with betel leaves.

The expedition bartered their merchandise successfully for cloves; for 10 ells of red cloth of good quality they obtained a *bahar* (over 4 kilos) of cloves. Another *bahar* was similarly gained by 15 hatchets—the great prized object of European civilization in the East, as in Brazil—15 ells of cloth of middling quality, 35 glass cups, 26 ells of linen, 17 ells of cinnabar, 17 ells of quicksilver, 125 knives, 50 pairs of scissors, and a kilo of bronze! When the expedition was ready to leave, each member of it did what he could to obtain as many cloves as possible, some of them selling their shirt, cloak, and coat to obtain some of the magic product that they knew they could sell prodigiously well in Europe. The Europeans observed, too, how cloves grew on high, thick bushes and how there were every year two harvests. They saw how the trees survived in the mountains, not in the plains. Mist apparently made the growth of cloves perfect. They also saw nutmeg trees and shrubs whose roots were ginger. They were in the Paradise for which they and so many Europeans had so long searched. The Spice Islands! They were there!

The Spaniards also learned some more disquieting news: a Portuguese captain, Diego López de Siqueiros, was sending a fleet of six ships against them, not knowing that Magellan was dead. But now with only one ship, the *Victoria*—the *Trinidad* had been left for repair in the care of the King of Tadore, with some fifty-three of the men—the remaining forty-seven men sought to avoid his attentions and abandoned Tadore on December 21, 1521.

The expedition, on its westward return to Spain, passed Java and Malacca, and sailed straight across the Indian Ocean before heading north, along the West African coast. These feats were described rather briefly by the Italian Pigafetta. He never much mentions Juan Sebastián de Elcano, the forty-five-year-old Basque of Guetaria, Guipúzcoa, who had become the new captain-general before they had reached Africa.[32] Pigafetta talks instead of the stories of China that reached his expedition: how musk was obtained by placing leeches on special cats; how the Emperor never met anyone; and how, if he wished to go anywhere, he would be accompanied by six ladies dressed exactly as he was, in order to create confusion among possible assassins. He also spoke of how the royal palace had seven walls around it, each guarded by men with whips and dogs. Again, when reading these descriptions, we feel that we are in the grip of a chivalrous novel. Pigafetta says that a Muslim who had lived in Peking told him of these strange things.

The *Victoria* eventually reached the Cape of Good Hope, "the most dangerous cape in the world," and from there some of the surviving Portuguese sailed north in canoes to Mozambique. But the "greater number of us, prizing honor more than life itself, decided on attempting at any risk to return to Spain." They sailed northwest to the Cape Verde Islands, where they obtained some rice and took on water for the final stretch home. All the way up the African coast they had to throw dead men into the sea, and, Pigafetta noted drily, "We made then a curious observation: that the Christians floated with their faces turned to the sea, but the Indians [presumably they had seized some in the Philippines] with their faces turned to the sky."[33] They discovered that since they had constantly sailed to the west, they had gained a day; it was a Wednesday, not a Thursday. They encountered some difficulties with the authorities, since of course the Cape Verde Islands were Portuguese, but eventually they left without hindrance.

On Saturday, September 6, 1522, the *Victoria* at last reached Sanlúcar de Barrameda, with a mere eighteen men on board (out of the 276 who had set out), mostly sick. It has always been said in Sanlúcar de Barrameda that Elcano requested a glass of manzanilla, the exquisite local light sherry, as his first demand.[34] The list of those who returned on the *Victoria* can be seen, proud if forgotten, on the wall of the old town hall in the Plaza del Cabildo in that town.

Two days later, on September 8, the eighteen survivors arrived at Seville and triumphantly discharged artillery from their ship. They subsequently went to Valladolid and were received by the King, who had returned to Spain from Germany earlier in the year and to whom Pigafetta, the persistent citizen of Vicenza, then gave his vivid account of the first journey around the world. The King rewarded Sebastián de Elcano with five hundred gold crowns, and he was authorized to take for his coat of arms a globe, with the motto *"Primus me circumdedisti."* Pigafetta's account of his circumnavigation was published in Italian in Venice in 1524.

The men of the *Trinidad* who had been left behind in Tadore by Elcano in March 1522 eventually sailed their ship, after it had been repaired, back across the Pacific, making for Panama. But the ship foundered, they fell in with hostile peoples, most were killed, and only a few of them were eventually able to return to India. Some of them died in Goa, but a handful reached Lisbon, where, characteristically, they were immediately imprisoned. Four of the fifty-seven managed to reach Spain, including the pilot, Ginés de Mafra.

The world had all the same been proved to be one planet. Thirty years after the first expedition of Columbus, Magellan—or rather, Elcano—showed that a route to the East could indeed be found by sailing west. The sphericity of the earth was demonstrated. No greater achievement has been performed. It has been claimed rightly as a great Spanish triumph, and so it was. All the same, the captain on whom all depended was a Portuguese, and the best chronicler was an Italian, as so often in the case of adventures of the sixteenth century. Most of the crew were Andalusians, but the captain who led the return was a Basque. It is not clear what happened to the English "constable," Master Andrés of Bristol, who was among those who set out; we must assume, though, that he died in the Philippines. But we are therefore once again before a European triumph appropriate for one approved by the greatest of the European rulers, the Emperor Charles V, a European more than he was a Spaniard, a Fleming, a German, or a Burgundian. Magellan and Elcano had directed a voyage to the end of the world, which, of course, turned out to be the same port from which they had embarked, and Sanlúcar de Barrameda, the racy city where the River Guadalquivir flows into the Ocean Sea, in the shade of the palace of the Duke of Medina Sidonia and on the edge of the sherry country, remains a place worthy to be considered the epicenter of the world.

Book Ten

THE NEW EMPIRE

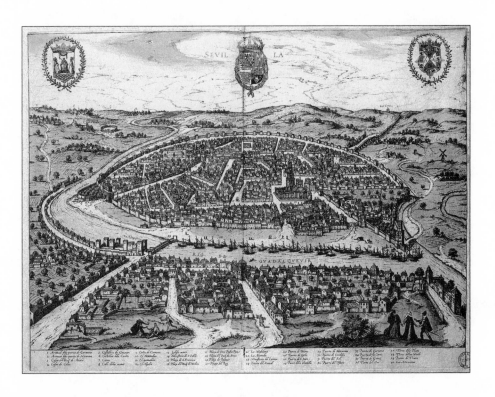

In the sixteenth century, Seville became the "capital" of the New World.

37

"The new emperor"

All the things of this land . . . are so many and of such a kind that
one might call oneself the new emperor of this kingdom with no
less glory than of Germany which by the grace of God your Sacred
Majesty already possesses.

Hernán Cortés to King Charles V,
October 30, 1520

In April 1520, Pedro Ruiz de la Mota, Bishop of Badajoz, preceptor, and
friend and adviser of Charles V, made a remarkable speech at Santiago de
Compostela, at a meeting of the Castilian Cortes in the Convent of San
Francisco. The Emperor at that time had not been crowned as such, but he
had been elected. He was planning to go to Germany in about a month for
his imperial coronation. In attendance in Galicia there was the court, the
disgruntled *procuradores* of Castile, as well as Francisco de Montejo and
Alonso Hernández Portocarrero, the representatives of Cortés. The last-
named had come, it will be remembered, with glittering prizes: gold and
silver, turquoise and feather mosaics, wooden carvings and weapons, musical instruments and even amazing people. These friends of Cortés were the
sensations of the time.

The Bishop declared that Charles was "more a king than all other kings."
The King was not like other kings, because Spain only represented "a third of
our power" (*un tercio de nuestro pan*). He was a king of kings, having descended from seventy kings. The people of Spain seemed sad because the
King was leaving for Germany. But why should they be sad? Charles had accepted the charge of being emperor and had to go to Germany to be
crowned. Why? For ambition? On the contrary, for the glory of Spain! The
King was not going to be only the king of the Romans and Roman emperor.
He was going to be Emperor of the World. That world, of course, also included that "other world of gold made for him," New Spain, "since before our
days it had not been born."[1]

What caused Ruiz de la Mota to talk in this way, using the word "emperor"? It was not one common to Spanish usage. True, the linguist Nebrija had said that language was also the companion of empire.[2] The author of the "Requirement" of 1513, Palacios Rubios, had said that the kings of Spain never recognized any superior: *"Rex es emperator in regno suo."* The courtier and historian Galíndez de Carvajal had written that "Spain never recognized the [Holy Roman] Empire, nor did the universal empire ever apply to her."[3] Spanish medieval monarchs had never formed part of the Holy Roman Empire, though King Alfonso X had contemplated being a candidate for that throne.

It is true that once or twice the Catholic Kings had considered themselves as emperors in their own land. The thirteenth-century Archbishop of Toledo, Rodrigo Ximénez de Rada, had also developed the idea of empire to describe the kingdoms then accumulated by the King of Castile. For him, the word "emperor" quite properly signified a ruler who dominated other monarchies. Perhaps Bishop Ruiz de la Mota had read the chapter in *Amadís de Gaula* in which the hero Apolidón is offered "the empire of Greece"?[4] It is equally true that Las Casas wrote, in respect of the second voyage of Columbus, that the Catholic Kings might style themselves emperors and sovereigns over all the kings and princes of the Indies.[5] In similarly chivalrous style, the hero of the war against Granada, Rodrigo Ponce de León, claimed to have been personally assured "by a very knowledgeable man and catholic Christian" that Fernando would not only drive the Muslims from Spain, "but conquer all Africa, too, destroy Islam, reconquer Jerusalem, and become emperor of Rome, of the Turks, and of the Spains."[6] (Fernando had for a long time thought that he would not die until he had liberated Jerusalem.)

Nebrija wrote: "And now who cannot see that although the title of 'empire' is in Germany, its reality lies with the Spanish monarchs who, masters of a large part of Italy and the isles of the Mediterranean, carry the war to Africa and send out their fleet, following the course of the stars, to the isles of the Indies and the New World, linking the Orient to the western frontiers of Spain and Africa."[7]

The speech of Bishop Ruiz de la Mota in Santiago also harked back to the romantic visions of the abbot and prophet Joachim de Fiore, who about the year 1300 had talked dreamily of "a world emperor"; and some admirers of Fernando the Catholic had talked of him in that context. But Charles, Prince of Burgundy and the new Holy Roman Emperor, ruler of realms beyond the sea with names he scarcely knew, was more entitled to the designation.[8] Columbus had not been alone at the court of Fernando and Isabel in envisaging just such a last emperor who would come to set the world to rights before its final days.

A cousin of Ruiz de la Mota, Gerónimo, also a citizen of Burgos but younger, set off for the Indies in August 1520. He was the son of a councillor of Burgos, García Ruiz de la Mota, had been for a time a steward of Diego Colón's, and had perhaps accompanied Colón to court. García Ruiz de la Mota was a *procurador* at the Cortes in 1520, as he had been on previous occasions. Gerónimo might even have heard his cousin's speech.[9]

After a short stay in Santo Domingo, Gerónimo left for New Spain in March 1521, in a vessel financed by the then veteran merchant Rodrigo de Bastidas, accompanying Julián de Alderete of Tordesillas, who would become royal treasurer in Mexico. There were several interesting fellow passengers, among them a cousin of Cortés's: Licenciado Juan Altamirano, who would be the judge in the *residencia* of Diego Velázquez; Alonso Cano, from Seville, who would be a pioneer in the use of mules in New Spain; Jerónimo López, who would later write a famous letter to the King (Emperor) about misgovernment in New Spain; and Diego de Marmolejo, a veteran of the wars in Africa. They would obviously have told Cortés the latest news as they knew it from Castile. Probably they arrived in time to talk to him before he sent to Spain his second letter to Charles V, through the safekeeping of his friend Alonso de Mendoza. That letter was long and vividly described how Cortés had been well received in Tenochtitlan by Moctezuma and how matters had gone wrong after the arrival of Narváez. It was dated October 30, 1520, the very month that Charles was crowned in Aix-la-Chapelle, though Cortés would not have known that; but because of difficulties in communication, the letter did not leave until the end of March 1521. The fact that Cortés addresses Charles as "Your Majesty," not "Your Highness," shows, though, that he was adequately informed about recent thinking at court.

Cortés explains that, unfortunately, he had not written regularly to describe his activities: "God knows how this has troubled me," he wrote, "for I wished your Majesty to know all the things of this land which, as I have already written in another report, are so many and of such a kind that one might call oneself the new emperor of this kingdom with no less glory than of Germany which by the grace of God your Sacred Majesty already possesses."[10]

These words of Cortés's come at the beginning of the letter, where perhaps they were slipped in as part of a revision after the rest of the document had been completed. So perhaps the idea of the Spanish Empire in those words was something conceived of by Bishop Ruíz de la Mota and then seized upon by Cortés, having had the very idea passed on to him by Gerónimo, the Bishop's cousin and his own new recruit, or by some of the other experienced men who accompanied him to New Spain.

There could have been an even more interesting source—not, as might be supposed, one of the characters with that title in a chivalrous novel. Despite the references to the empire of Greece, the emperors in *Tirant lo Blanc* or *Amadís* are on much the same level as other kings. But Cortés had defeated "the great Moctezuma," to whom he had referred in his first letter to Charles V as *"un grandísimo senõr."*[11] Usually those who wrote of Moctezuma in the sixteenth century spoke of him as "lord." But he was an emperor by Archbishop Ximénez de Rada's definition: a ruler of other kings, in Moctezuma's case the kings of Tacuba and Texcoco, not to speak of those of the Chalca, the Otomi, and the Totonacs. Then, as will be remembered, Cortés reported that Moctezuma had agreed to be a vassal of the Spanish Emperor. The example of the conquered Moctezuma could thus have influenced Cortés's expression.[12]

The notion of the Spanish Empire was thus launched by Cortés. For a long time the word was not generally used, and it certainly had no legal meaning. New Spain was a "monarchy" (*reino*). There would soon be other Indian monarchies (*reinos indianos*). But empire the Spaniards had, and eventually the lands became known as such, even if the king of Spain never assumed the title of emperor. These territories in the Indies were ones where the king of Castile had not only sovereign rights but rights of property, too. He was the absolute owner of all the American dominions.[13] The Crown was careful to exclude any possibility that the complicated arguments that existed in Aragon/Catalonia and Valencia might be transferred to the New World, even though, after the death of Queen Isabel in 1504, numerous individuals from those regions traveled to the Indies and though Aragon had had something close to an "imperial" experience in the Mediterranean.[14] Those educated men who grew up in the first twenty years of the sixteenth century may have been "Renaissance men," and all had a vision of ancient Rome that inspired them, even if that old empire was deemed by all wise men unsurpassable.[15]

In 1522, Spain's right to this New World was already being contested. King François I of France had declared that he would like to see the clause in the will of Adam that excluded France from the division of the world.[16] Certainly, corsairs from that country had captured two Spanish caravels bound for Spain from the Indies in 1521, and a fleet under Pedro Manrique, financed by a special tax (*avería*), was formed to face the danger. The next year, three armed caravels were sent out under Domingo Alonso de Amilivia, financed by the Casa de Contratación, to convoy eleven ships to

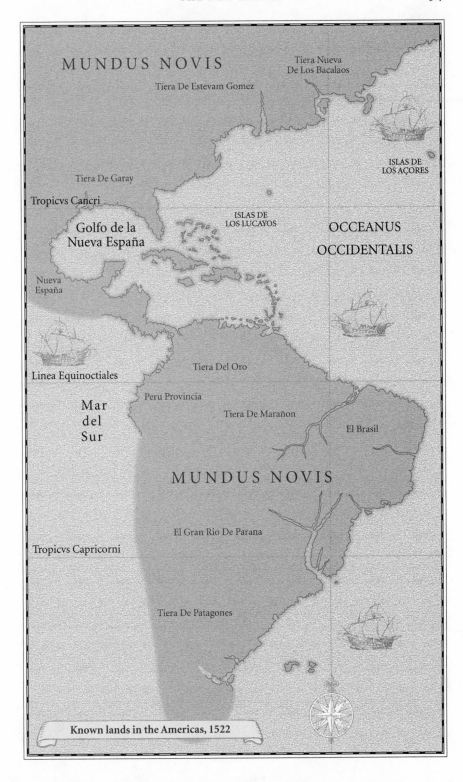

MUNDUS NOVIS

Tiera Nueva
De Los Bacalaos

Tiera De Estevam Gomez

ISLAS DE
LOS AÇORES

Tiera De Garay

Tropicvs Cancri

ISLAS DE
LOS LUCAYOS

OCCEANUS

OCCIDENTALIS

Golfo de la
Nueva España

Nueva
España

Linea Equinoctiales

Tiera Del Oro

Peru Provincia

Mar
del
Sur

Tiera De Marañon

El Brasil

MUNDUS NOVIS

El Gran Rio De Parana

Tropicvs Capricorni

Tiera De Patagones

Known lands in the Americas, 1522

the Canaries on their way to the Indies. A few months later, two ships of Cortés's coming from Vera Cruz were seized by the French captain Jean Florin off the Azores with a considerable quantity of booty, much of it feather mosaics, from Mexico.[17] The new empire was thus beginning to need bulwarks. It would soon have them—for example, Seville, a city where, as a modern historian once said, "the world's heartbeat" could be felt.[18]

38

"From the poplars I come, mama"

From the poplars I come, mama,
To see how the breeze moves the leaves;
From the poplars of Seville,
I've come to see my pretty friend,
From the poplars I come, mama,
To see how the breeze moves the leaves.

Carol, c. 1500[1]

The city that by 1522 had become the unofficial capital of this new empire of Spain in the New World was Seville. A generation later, Fernando de Herrera, the so-called divine poet of the place, remarked, "You are no city, you are a universe."[2] Of Seville, it was bravely stated on its Gate of Jerez: "Hercules built me, Caesar gave me walls and towers, and the Saint-King won me, with García Pérez de Vargas."[3] The city had indeed been conquered, "liberated," as the Christians thought, from the Muslims in 1248 by King (afterwards Saint) Fernando III. Yet memories of the old Islamic dominance were still everywhere to be seen—for example, the old court of oranges next to the cathedral and, towering above it, the Giralda, whence the muezzin had once called the faithful to prayer and which was now an elegant bell tower. Other memories of Islam were to be found everywhere: there were churches, such as the one in the newly named Plaza del Salvador, that had once been mosques. There were many houses within the city that had been built by Muslims, and those walls themselves were the work not of Caesar, but of the Almohades, a fanatical sect, the al-Qaida of the Middle Ages, that had conquered half of Spain in the twelfth century. In Islamic Seville there had been many bathhouses, and they were only slowly abandoned: the Baths of Queen Juana and those of San Juan de la Palma remained fashionable in the 1520s, even among the Christians.

The most important edifice that the Christians inherited from Islam was, however, the aqueduct from the springs of Carmona, which brought water to Seville and which entered the city at the Carmona Gate, to the east.

There was still everywhere in Seville an Oriental atmosphere, but the Renaissance was evidently on its way: the change was marked by the coming of wider roads, bigger squares in front of the palaces, and more obviously sumptuous buildings. Hitherto the streets had been narrow and labyrinthine, though mostly paved, but soon there would come the new "broad and happy" ones that so impressed Navagero, the Venetian ambassador, and also fine squares, though they were often full of rubbish.[4]

With few exceptions, the Muslims had abandoned Seville after its conquest by the Christians, mostly for North Africa, and their properties had been handed out by the King to followers of his and to other soldiers, the decisions as to who would have which section being decided by lot. Most of the new inhabitants, "mothers of the new Castile that is Andalusia,"[5] came indeed from Old Castile.[6]

In the fifteenth century two great families came to dominate and dispute power in the city: the Guzmáns and the Ponces de León. The former had developed their interest in the land on either side of the lower Guadalquivir after the late thirteenth century, being lords of Sanlúcar de Barrameda, the port where the river enters the Atlantic. They were the dukes of Medina Sidonia after 1445. The Ponces de León derived from Fernán Pérez Ponce, who became lord of Marchena, to the west of Seville, in the early fourteenth century, and his descendants became counts of Arcos de la Frontera in 1440, being afterwards marquises and dukes of Cadiz. The modern traveler may detect in Seville some remains of the old palaces of these families behind the Corte Inglés, in the Plaza del Duque de la Vitoria, and behind the Church of Los Terceros, in the Plaza de Ponce de Léon. But his imagination must be strong.

A third family that began to rival the other two in the fifteenth century were the de la Cerdas, royal counts and then dukes of Medinaceli, lords of El Puerto de Santa María. A palace of the Medinacelis, the Casa de Pilatos, remains a center of both attention and affection. Other families who played a great part in Seville despite connections elsewhere were the Portocarreros, the Zúñigas, the Dávalos, the Saavedras, and, increasingly, the Afans de Riberas.[7]

With much new commerce under way, the old aristocratic feud between the two most important families, the Ponces de León and the Guzmáns, had diminished in force. We should not forget a soothing intervention in the 1470s of Queen Isabel with Rodrigo Ponce de León, Marquis of Arcos, though the enmity between the two families was rekindled at the time of the rebellion of the *comuneros*. People with their surnames, younger sons of younger sons, no doubt, or perhaps bastards, had often gone to the Indies as emigrants in the first years of settlement.[8] Francisca Ponce de León, daughter of Rodrigo, the redhaired hero of the war against Granada, financed one of the ships in the fleet of Diego Colón in 1509, and Mencía, the Duchess of Medinaceli, another. The multifarious role of Juan Ponce de León in the Caribbean has been much noticed in earlier chapters, and a member of the Guzmán family played a great part in the early history of both La Española and Cuba.

Power in Seville, as elsewhere in cities in Castile, was vested in the town council. The *cabildo*, as this was known in Andalusia and soon in the Indies, had many privileges that disappeared during the course of the sixteenth century, but in 1522 these were still considerable, despite the increasing power of the *asistente*, by which title the centralizing official, elsewhere known as the *corregidor*, was known in Seville. This official was at the same time a mayor, a chief magistrate, the chief of the urban militia, and the local governor—in effect, the supreme local authority.

The *cabildo* had judicial duties till 1553. The chief magistrates and their deputies administered justice alongside the judge of the Gradas (in theory appointed to decide disputes about marketing on the steps of the cathedral, but he acquired wider powers). The center of judicial authority was the Casa Quadra, in the Plaza de San Francisco, and the *cabildo* itself met in those days in the Corral de los Olmos ("Elm Tree Yard" might be a literal, though inappropriate, translation) in the Plaza del Arzobispado, next to the court of oranges.

The *asistente* had as a rule a title of nobility, as did most of the forty or so senior councillors (known in Seville as the *"Veinticuatros"* because there had once been twenty-four of them), while the *jurados* ("the representatives of the people" in the phrase of King Enrique III, men popularly elected in the parishes) had to be of good family—which meant hidalgos. The six chief magistrates were great nobles named by the Crown (though soon the offices would be saleable): in 1522 they were the Dukes of Medina Sidonia and Béjar, the Marquises of Arcos, Tarifa, and Villanueva, and Martín Cerón, a commoner who conducted himself more ducally than most dukes. The chief constable (*alguacil mayor*) was the most important of the city's executive officials, being named by the monarch for life, with lodgings in the *cabildo*. He was the executor of justice and presided at meetings if the chief magistrates were not there. He also organized nocturnal watches and was the commander of the prison.

These noblemen of Seville controlled all municipal appointments, so it is not surprising that the chief notaries had been for several generations members of the Piñeda family; that the deputy to the chief constable, the *alférez mayor,* was always the Marquis of La Algaba; while the commander of the Alcázar was usually a Guzmán (the Count of Olivares). The commander of the castle of Triana was as a rule the Duke of Medina de las Torres. The officials carried out decisions of the *cabildo* (the *fieles ejecutores*), including two named by the councillors, two by the *jurados,* and two directly by the citizens. They controlled weights and measures, and such things as fishing rights. They visited the prisons and checked that the five hundred or more inmates were being fed, and were supposed to observe the enactment of punishments such as public beatings and executions to ensure that there was no untoward cruelty. They were never alone in such observations: the public liked to watch all such scenes, as well as the burnings inspired by the Inquisition just outside the city in the meadow of San Sebastián.

These municipal activities were financed by the proceeds of local taxes: for example, the *almojarifazgo,* the *alcabala,* and the *tercia.* The first was levied on imports and exports, the second was a purchase tax on imports into the city, and the last was the Crown's third share in the tithes offered to the Church.

The Moorish walls of Seville, part Almoravid, mostly Almohad, surrounding the city, stretched almost four miles, with two hundred or so towers and twelve gates,[9] as well as three or four small doors (*postigos*). Some stretches of the walls remain, for example near the Macarena Gate, though these are now scarred by bullet holes on the inside, a reminder that the executions carried out in Spain during the Civil War in the twentieth century were on a scale never seen in the days of Charles V. The most important of the towers in the sixteenth century were the Torre del Oro on the quay near the river and those of the Gate of Jerez, which housed the prison of San Hermenegildo. But each gate had towers, and most were lived in by relations or friends of officials on a wide variety of rents or other understandings.[10] The Torre del Oro had been built by the Almohades as a watchtower and then used as a treasure chest. In 1522, it was employed by the Casa de Contratación to store the precious metals brought back from the New World. Cortés's treasures sent back by his *procuradores* had been there for some months, to the fury of his father and friends. Seville, it was said, lay at the mouth of "a river of the Americas" that brought it gold and silver.[11] Next to this tower there was always in the early sixteenth century an improvised crane that had been used to unload stone and other material needed for the cathedral.[12]

From the walls to the east one could see the skillfully contrived three-hundred-yard bridge, also Muslim in origin, consisting of seventeen boats lying across the river, tied together by thick chains of iron; they linked the city with Triana, a dependent town, already really a suburb, important for the manufacture of porcelain and soap. It was the home of many of the sailors who went to the New World, as it was of shipping, while its gloomy, half-ruined Moorish castle of St. George had become the local headquarters of the Inquisition—a prison as well as a secret magistracy.

This bridge needed constant repair, the wood used being often obtained from the slopes of the Sierra Morena at Constantina. From time to time a stone bridge would be suggested to the *cabildo* or the Crown, but the idea always foundered, since it was thought that such a bridge would itself collapse because of the nature of the riverbed. Forward-looking citizens hoped that one day the River Guadalquivir would again be navigable up to Córdoba, as it had been in Roman days.

The commander of the walls, and so the chief defender of the city in any emergency, was Fernando Enríquez de Ribera, Marquis of Tarifa. He had in 1522 been to Jerusalem on a pilgrimage—via Italy—and, bringing back a little holy soil from that doomed territory, would soon build the Casa de Pilatos in remembrance of the journey. He was accompanied by the poet Juan del Encina, whose imagination must have been put to good use when his patron suggested a reconstruction of the house of Pilate in Seville.

From these walls one could see several monasteries outside the city: Las Cuevas, whose gardens delighted the Venetian Navagiero; the beautiful San Isidoro; and Los Remedios. Numerous orchards could also be seen: the Huerta del Corso, where the poet Baltasar del Alcázar would one day live, and the Huerta de la Flor in Triana, "the key to Aljarafe." Beyond the walls to the north lay the remains of Roman Itálica and, closer to the southeast, the execution ground in the meadow of San Sebastián, as well as the Jewish cemetery, just beyond the Puerta de la Carne. One could also see how Fernando Colón, the learned and bibliophilous bastard son of the first Admiral, was building a garden near his house outside the Puerta de Goles. Then there was the beautiful Huerta del Rey opening onto the Campana countryside, where the Marquis of Tarifa had a lovely country house, surrounded by orange trees and with a lake.

But the main sight to be seen lay to the east: the River Guadalquivir, the golden link with the Atlantic and the New World and, indeed, with the Old

World as well. There were still innumerable fish in this river, from lampreys to perch. On the banks there was the Arenal, a word that literally signified a place of sand, but here it had been dignified to indicate a world. One could observe each year ever greater maritime activity, for here Seville's commerce with the New World was organized. It was an activity already too extensive for the Arenal: there were not enough quays (and only one was of stone), too few moorings, and little space for expansion. Every year new shipbuilders would seek to break into the old circle of competitors, some being on the brink of great fortunes.[13] Merchants and sailors, captains and galley slaves, sellers of the goods needed for a journey to the Americas and notaries listing them, beggars and pilgrims, criminals hoping to arrange an escape, and adventurers dreaming of fortunes, all met on the Arenal. Poets were to be found there as well as prostitutes; the wives of galley slaves and of sailors could all be easily observed.

By 1522 the principal interest of the merchants was already the Indies. The ships being built for that trade were not large in comparison with the galleys that plied the Mediterranean, being rarely over one hundred tons' burden, but there were many of them: between 1506 and 1515, 289 ships sailed for the Indies; and between 1516 and 1525, 499.[14] The shipping register for Seville shows that the main destinations of vessels in these years were the Canaries and the New World.[15]

The ships that sailed to the New World were of many types, but the food carried on them was usually what it had been on the expedition of Pedrarias: chickens and horses, but no cows or other large animals. The average sailor could expect a liter of wine a day and perhaps a half kilo of ship's biscuits. To these might be added oil, vinegar, chickpeas, beans, dried or salted meat, and fish.[16] Every day an observer on the walls would see packing of one sort or another.

The merchants were beginning to bring back a diversity of American products: "brazil" dyewood and slaves, as well as gold and pearls. Soon there would be sugar from Caribbean cane, pineapples, potatoes, and tomatoes. These last three products were still scarcely known, but King Fernando had eaten potatoes and had tasted a pineapple and a few of both would soon be seen on the Arenal.

Within the walls of Seville the main buildings were connected with religion. Christianity dominated life. Men built churches to inspire, to overpower, and also to impress, for they were works of propaganda as well as of spiritual comfort. Private houses and palaces, however noble, seemed by comparison modest edifices in Seville, hiding in the Arab manner in *impasses* rather than facing avenues, though a few were just beginning to have a square in front of them, as was the case of the palace of the Duke of Medina Sidonia in what is now the Plaza de la Victoria. The exception to this was the magical palace of the Alcázar, a Moorish building enlarged and improved by the Christian King, Pedro the Cruel.

The biggest square was probably that of La Laguna, now the Alameda de Hercules, where bulls were regularly fought. But there was also the arcaded Plaza de San Francisco, already with pretty *miradores* and a fine fountain at one end, bordered by the town hall, the supreme court, the monastery of San Francisco, and the prison. A market in the square sold bread, fish, meat, and fruit and vegetables. Nearby there was the Plaza de San Salvador, in front of the old mosque, where rope sellers, candlemakers, and greengrocers plied their wares with zest.

The city was full of fountains: some public, many private in the patios of large houses. Perhaps they numbered three hundred in all,[17] the water coming by the aqueduct from Carmona.

The great building of Seville was the cathedral. Still today an object of awe with its seven aisles and its great height (145 feet in the nave, 170 in the dome), in the early sixteenth century it was for a time the largest building in Europe. Completed in 1506, and opened for services the following year, it had been begun in 1402 when the Almohad mosque, built by Al-Mansur but used as a church since 1248, had been at last pulled down. The archbishop responsible had determined to build on a large scale. The chapter is supposed to have said: "Let posterity when it admires it completed say that those who dared to devise such a work must have been mad." The cathedral was then bigger than the old St. Peter's in Rome, though Pope Julius II's new version would overtake it.

The cathedral was built on the basilicalike site of the old mosque and influenced by it: 430 feet long by over 300 wide. The first architect was probably Charles Galter of Rouen, on whose cathedral he had also worked. The detail indeed owed a great deal to French models. The chapter planned one hundred windows, of which the finest had been finished by 1522, including those by the master craftsman Cristóbal Alemán. There were numerous side chapels, some incomplete, though the legend was that the pretty Virgin of La Antigua—in the chapel of her name, with a rose in her hand and so admired by Columbus—had been painted by St. Luke himself and had remained miraculously hidden throughout the five hundred years of Muslim domination. (She had then played her part, so romantics said, in the liberation of the city by St. Ferdinand.) Columbus called a Carib island in the Leeward Islands after this Virgin, and Balboa's capital at Darien had been named for her, too.

Another picture in the cathedral was that of the Virgin of the Remedios on the main screen, painted about 1400 by a follower of the Sienese school. That Virgin had been a favorite of Hernán Cortés, and a friend of his from Medellín, Juan Rodríguez Villafuerte, had carried an image of her to Tenochtitlan and placed her in the temple of Huitzilopochtli in 1519.[18] Cortés had prayed to her near Tacuba on the west bank of the lake of Tenochtitlan, the day after the *noche triste.* Already in 1522 there were plans for the building of a sanctuary there, which would become in time the favorite church of Mexico's *criollos.*

The cathedral in Seville, like the commerce to the New World, was an international undertaking, for the golden reredos behind the high altar was a collaboration between the Castilian Jorge Fernández and the Fleming Pieter Dancart. Nearby stood the rich tomb, finished in 1510, of Archbishop Diego Hurtado de Mendoza, who died in 1504. This was the work of the Italian known as Miguel Florentino, while some of the external sculpture was the work of a Frenchman, Michel Perrin.

Beside the cathedral stood the Giralda, the Muslim tower built in the twilight of Almohad rule, whence, for 250 years, bells had summoned Christians to Mass on behalf of St. Justina and St. Rufina, the two patrons of Seville, Christian daughters of a potter of Triana who had insulted the goddess Salambo and had been put to death in the days of Diocletian.[19] The cathedral probably employed three hundred people, not counting servants. These included archdeacons of nearby towns as well as the priors of the local hermitages. There were 40 canons, 20 prebendaries, 230 assistant prebendaries, 29 clerks, and many choirboys. The chapter of the cathedral owned a substantial number of towns outside Seville.[20]

On the steps, *las gradas,* that surrounded this vast building and next to stone pillars that had served both the Roman temple and the Muslim mosque were to be found traders, sellers of trinkets as of jewels, big merchants and small shopkeepers, and, above all, money changers, the majority Jewish in the fifteenth century, many Genoese in the early sixteenth. The observant Venetian Navagero would write of how the merchants lingered all day in this, "the most attractive corner of Seville."[21] If it rained, the merchants would go into the cathedral itself, their horses and other animals accompanying them.

In the shadow of the cathedral (metaphorically speaking) lay nearly thirty parish churches and forty monasteries or convents. The most important was surely that of the Carthusians in Cuevas, founded in 1400. (Columbus's bones were there, with those of his brothers,[22] and Columbus's great friend at the end of his life, Fray Gaspar Gorricio, had lived his last years in that retreat.)[23] Navagero wrote that the gardens were so pretty that they constituted the best stepping-stone possible on the way up to Heaven. Then there were the Franciscans, three hundred brothers in two houses, the most significant one being just outside the old walls (on the site of the modern Plaza de San Francisco); and the Dominicans at their four sites of San Pablo, La Magdalena, Santo Tomás, and Nuestra Señora del Valle (refounded in 1507), with about 250 brothers all told. Both these orders had already made an impact on the islands of the empire in the Caribbean. The Dominican monastery of Santo Tomás was much associated with the Inquisition, for the first two Inquisitors of Seville in the 1480s had been friars there.

Also in La Magdalena were the Mercedarians, formally dedicated to the recovery of Christian captives in Muslim prisons, of which order Cortés's friend Fray Bartolomé de Olmedo was a shining example; while the Carmelite brothers were at Remedios, to the south on the edge of the river, toward Jerez. Two important monasteries of the fourteenth century were those of San Isidoro del Campo and San Agustín, established in an old nunnery near the Carmona Gate. San Isidoro was founded as a Cistercian stronghold in 1301 by Alonso Pérez de Guzmán, ancestor of the dukes of Medina Sidonia, and his wife, María Alonso Coronel, at Santiponce, a village that the order owned. After 1431, the Cistercians were substituted by Jeronymites. The second great foundation of that era, San Agustín, was created by the family of Ponce de León, whose town palace was nearby. The Ponces de León were the chief benefactors of these Augustinians, and many of the family were buried there. Probably there were 1,500 friars.

Half the religious houses of Seville were for women, of which the most important were those of the Carmelites, in two houses, San Clemente and Santa María, as well as the Poor Clares in Santa Inés, another house founded by María Fernández Coronel. In Santa Inés, the body of the founder was said to remain ever perfect even though it had been said that she had poured boiling oil over her face to protect herself from the lecherous King Pedro the Cruel. We should remember, too, Madre de Díos, founded in 1486 in the modern Calle San José, a building seized from its old owners by the Inquisition. It would eventually have among its sepulchres descendants of both Columbus and of Cortés.

These foundations dominated the skyline of Seville and took up half the space of the city. They were large employers of labor, and like noblemen, the monks lived on produce from farms established in the nearby countryside. A little wine from Cazalla, a ham from Aracena? Certainly.

The Inquisition in 1522 was a powerful religious institution. Its staff in the castle of Triana was ample, its local officers being the Inquisitor-General, three or four assistant inquisitors, a prosecutor, a judge who dealt with goods confiscated from those punished, like the owners of the site of the Madre de Dios, several lawyers, a magistrate concerned with "the secret prison," and another concerned with those who would never leave prison. There was a notary responsible for recording secret interrogations, an accountant, a porter, two chaplains, six theologians, and about fifty *familiares* (informants). Between 1481 and 1522 more than one thousand people had probably been burned to death in Seville, while another two thousand had been condemned and abjured (*reconciliados*). This was about half the total of those who died in this way in all Spain. The fear caused in consequence naturally was already poisoning the intellectual life of the city.

Some religious brotherhoods (*cofradías*) still in being in 2001 had been founded before 1500,[24] but most of those important today were creatures of the mid-sixteenth century, as was the regularization of the processions: a Virgin and Christ inspired by a professional group, such as bakers or stevedores, carried on floats (*pasos*), attended by scenes re-creating the Last Supper or the Crucifixion. They would be followed by penitents, usually whipping themselves in expiation of sins. The celebration of Corpus Christi in August was then more significant than Holy Week. Another festival of importance was the so-called feast of the little bishop (*obispillo*), celebrated on St. Nicholas's Day.[25] There were also frequent irregular processions, such as that of 1,500 half-naked evangelical Christians who made their way from Carmona to the Chapel of the Antigua in the cathedral.[26] Nor should we forget the procession of giants and wildly dressed children known as the *mojarillas*. Such manifestations passed to the New World. Thus Cortés and his men celebrated Palm Sunday in 1519, after a victory over the Maya at Potonchan, on the Gulf of Mexico, by holding a solemn Mass, and there was a procession and a cross put up in the square.[27]

The *cabildo* wanted a university, and in 1502 they gained a royal provision that authorized them to mount just such an institution for the study of theology, canon law, law, medicine, and some other liberal arts. Given the times, there had to be a religious justification for this: a papal bull of 1505 recognized that Seville lacked and needed a university, and a rich *converso*, Maese Rodrigo Fernández de Santaella, bought some houses, where he began to build the proposed structure. He had earlier shown his learning by translating Marco Polo's travels into Spanish. In 1515, Archbishop Deza, whose Jewish ancestry was often hinted at, founded his College of St. Thomas of Aquinas.

Similarly, hospitals had to have a religious sanction. There were many of these, some tiny; for example, the Hospital del Rey had only twelve beds. Perhaps there were in Seville seventy-six hospitals in all. Some specialized, and there was one that concentrated on the new disease of syphilis, the New World's chief contribution to European discomfort, still only partially relieved by pomade of mercury.

Seville had increased in size in recent years. In 1475, its population had probably numbered forty thousand.[28] But in 1520, there were perhaps sixty thousand inhabitants or even more. So many people came and went that it is hard to establish a reliable figure. Plague, hurricanes, droughts, famines, floods, all brought illness and death.[29] Plague in particular hit Seville hard between 1505 and 1510. The historian Bernáldez estimated that it killed twenty-eight thousand people.[30] A flood was equally damaging in 1507, while the famine of 1503 was a catastrophe, to be followed by another severe one in 1522. Syphilis was prevalent among the upper class and the prostitutes of the district near the river, the Mancebía. The cabildo's brothels seem to have been healthier.[31]

Then there was emigration: one out of three emigrants to the New World between 1492 and 1519 was Andalusian, and about two-thirds of those were from Seville. But these could not have totaled more than two thousand at most.

On the other hand, the population had been increased and enhanced by Genoese and Florentine merchants and their families, as well as by other foreigners, many of whom were by now fully hispanized. In municipal documents, between 1472 and 1480, sixteen Genoese merchants figure as having been active in Seville, but between 1489 and 1515, there were over four hundred.[32] Many took Castilian names: Marini became Marín; Castiglione, Castellón. The Genoese had had rights in Seville since the thirteenth century. For their help against the siege of Algeciras, so well remembered by Chaucer, Alfonso XI granted them freedom from paying the usual taxes. Many Castilians also came down to Seville in the hope of finding fame and fortune in the New World but sometimes remained in the capital of Andalusia. There were many Basques and Gallegos, too, most becoming sailors, while immigrants from Burgos were often traders, attracted similarly by new prospects beckoning in the Caribbean.

There were still many slaves in Seville, more than there had been in the 1490s. A city of southern Europe at this time might reckon its riches in terms of the size of its slave population. Several thousand black or Berber slaves, many bought in Lisbon or from merchants established there, such as Bartolomeo Marchionni, or their representatives, such as Piero Rondinelli, worked in Seville alongside some Muslim slaves, survivors of the old kingdom of Granada. There were, too, a few hundred captives from the Canary Islands, some native Americans, and still a few eastern Europeans, who, as we have seen, had formed the main source of slaves in the Middle Ages in both Italy and Spain.[33] Most were sold in the Patio de las Naranjas or on the steps, *las gradas,* of the cathedral, usually tattooed on their cheeks with a nail: a fleur-de-lis, a star, the cross of St. Andrew, or just the name of their master. They continued to act in all kinds of capacities: domestic servants, cooks, porters, wet nurses, founders of precious metals, tanners, potters, builders, messengers, and prostitutes. Slaves were not just the possessions of the rich; artisans, artists, and sea captains owned them, too. If the slaves from the Americas had proved better workers—rivals, say, to the blacks from Guinea—they would have been imported in large numbers to Spain. But they were too weak to seem competitive.

A small number of free ex-Muslims (*moriscos*) lived in their district, which had been theirs from the fourteenth century—the Adarvejo, near the Church of San Pedro. They were usually endogamous. In the early sixteenth century, their most common profession was that of builder. But others were greengrocers, grocers, spice merchants, tavern keepers, bakers, or just shopkeepers.

The situation was very different with the Jewish *conversos.* They were in danger, but they remained influential. They were often rich, usually well connected. An arrangement had been made for them in 1511 to go to the New World. If they could afford to pay the large sum of 3 million maravedís, they could join the great adventure of emigration. Others maintained excellent positions in public life—for example, Francisco de Alcázar, who had the confidence of the ducal house of Medina Sidonia and became Treasurer of Seville, even if he had been *reconciliado* in 1493. Alcázar, like the Duchess of Medinaceli and Francisca Ponce de León, owned a ship that traded with the Indies, the *San Salvador,* and had also bought the lordship of La Palma, higher up the Guadalquivir, from Diego Colón. Both he and the banker Alonso Gutiérrez de Madrid, also a *converso,* were councillors in Seville.[34]

Numerous such *conversos* were by now to be found in the New World. Most prominent were the Santa Clara family, one of whom, Cristóbal, had been treasurer in Santo Domingo, while his brother Bernardino had helped Cortés, as had Pedro de Maluenda, a well-connected merchant from Burgos who was commissary during the second part of Cortés's campaign and died in Tenochtitlan of an unidentified fever soon after the conquest. Another *converso* from Sanlúcar de Barrameda, Alonso Caballero, whose portrait with that of his brother Diego, painted by Pedro de Campaña, would soon be seen in the chapel of "El Mariscal" in Seville Cathedral, was Cortés's admiral after 1520. *Conversos* such as Juan Fernández de Varas and Rodrigo de Bastidas were among the richest entrepreneurs in Santo Domingo, and Las Casas, the indefatigable friend of the Indians, was also *converso.*

In his last years, King Fernando had hardened his policies on the *conversos.* For example, Lucero, the hated prosecutor of Córdoba, returned in triumph in June 1511 with all the charges about the practices of the Inquisition that tolerant men had mounted against him wiped away. In February 1515, the clerical council of Seville, under the chairmanship of Archbishop Deza, had demanded a statute that would prevent the children of those condemned by the Holy Office from entering the Church as priests. That unchristian statement was signed by many who seem themselves to have been *conversos,* perhaps hoping thereby to escape attention to their own persons.[35] Then a dispute between the town council of Seville and the Inquisition's receiver of goods, Pedro de Villacís, was decided by the King in the latter's favor.[36]

A crisis also occurred with the arrest for "Jewish practices" of Gutierre de Prado, a merchant who had been collector of ecclesiastical rents. This was a shock, since not only was Prado related to many prominent families, but also, worse, it turned out that he owed money to many more.[37] The alarm outshadowed the greatest previous Jewish scandal in the city, that of the arrest in 1494 of Álvaro del Río, a notary who had been secretary to Archbishop Hurtado de Mendoza and who had been burned in Segovia.[38]

Many of the majordomos of great noblemen in Seville were *conversos,* and men such as Francisco de las Casas, who served the Medina Sidonia, or Gómez de Córdoba, who had that post with the Marquis of Montemayor, must have felt far from secure, even if some of them who acted for the Duke of Cadiz, such as Diego García, became out of self-defense denouncers of Jews.

Seville had been known since Roman days for olive oil, wine, and wheat. The first was still not much used for cooking in the sixteenth century, yet it constituted the most important export, as it had in Muslim days, being carried then to Flanders, London, Genoa, Chios, and Messina. But now it was to be sold, and on a large scale, to the New World as well. "Seville owes everything to olives," wrote a modern historian, and the simple statement cannot be contradicted.[39] In the mid-fifteenth century, some 6.5 million kilos of olive oil were produced a year; in the sixteenth, that figure had risen by a quarter.[40] The best region for olives was the Aljarafe, the fertile country to the west, between Seville and Huelva, where small proprietors mixed as farmers with noblemen and religious orders. The harvest was mostly carried out by women from all over Andalusia, beginning on All Saints' Day, and lasted two months; the harvesters would live in special barracks (*cortijos*). They would be paid 5 or 6 maravedís a basketful, resulting in perhaps 300 maravedís per laborer.

The Genoese were as usual the leading merchants. Thus, in respect of anticipated purchases, more than half the quantity was bought by them, the biggest dealer being Jacopo Sopranís.[41] There were large warehouses for oil (*almacenes*) in most districts of Seville, especially in that of El Mar, the then neglected zone between the cathedral and the Arenal. The oil was held in oak vats, made elsewhere, and especially in Coria del Río, on the way to Sanlúcar de Barrameda, on the Guadalquivir. The list of those involved in olive oil is a social register of Old Seville, all the famous names from Genoa being included, but also local Spanish aristocrats—among them the Duke of Medina Sidonia, the Marquis of Arcos, the Count of Feria, and the Marquis of Priego.[42]

What was oil used for if not for cooking? For eating with bread, certainly, but above all for soap; and thanks to this, Seville had become the most important place in Castile for this product. Traditional soap was dark, made from oil mixed with potash, the main factory standing near the mosque in the Plaza of San Salvador. The monarchs had made of it a monopoly that they had let to the Marquis of Tarifa, who had the largest share of it. Another share was in the hands of Luis Ponce de León, Marquis of Cadiz. They sublet, as was the custom, usually to Genoese.

But by 1520 another type of soap was also enjoying successes. Francesco Sopranís Ripparolo, who hired a warehouse from the owners of the monopoly, had by then introduced a hard white version, made with oil and soda. His factories were in Triana, rented from the Almonte family, and at Santiponce, just outside Seville near the Jeronymite monastery of San Isidoro del Campo, from which he rented a warehouse. With his fellow Genoese Marco Castiglione, who had a third share, he controlled the market for soap until 1514 when he died. After 1517, Jacopo Sopranís, a cousin of Francesco, played the decisive part. The sales to the New World of this important product were considerable, these same Genoese traders soon having a foothold there. Clean hands, clean clothes, even clean feet were soon to be found everywhere in Spanish America. It may be recalled that Columbus allowed a monopoly to sell soap in La Española to a friend of his, Pedro de Salcedo.

After oil came cereals. Seville obtained its wheat from the fields of Carmona and from Écija. The harvests, of course, fluctuated. The richest wheat magnate was the Marquis of Priego, whose bankers were the inevitable Gaspare Centurione and Giuliano Calvo, himself a partner of Stefano Centurione. By 1516, wheat was available on a larger scale than it had been in the fifteenth century, and the Centuriones were the beneficiaries. The demand for flour in the Indies was greater every year, and the merchants knew that whatever else the settlers could not afford, this was essential. Until the conquest of Mexico and the consequent colonization of a temperate zone, Castilian wheat could not be replaced by local production (the first to grow wheat in the New World was the free black Portuguese Juan Garrido, who had fought in so many campaigns and who had his farm at Coyoacan).[43]

Seville and its surroundings were also then the main wine-producing region of Spain, though in the previous generation or so there had been new developments to meet local needs in the north, on the Rioja, the Duero, and the banks of the beautiful Miño, in Galicia. Demand for wine was greatly stimulated by commerce with the Indies. The travelers needed a product that lasted. Hence the attraction of the fortified wines of the Sierra de Morena, of Constantina, Cazalla, and Guadalcanal; that of Cazalla was the most sought after, for it made a great impression on the indigenous peoples.[44] The great sherries of Jerez and the manzanillas of Sanlúcar de Barrameda, the Duke of Medina Sidonia's port at the mouth of the Guadalquivir, were easy to ship on the fleets leaving from there.

Much of the wine was traded by Genoese (Bernardo Grimaldi, Benedetto Doria, and Antonio Piñelo) or Florentines (Piero Rondinelli), but Juan de Burgos, a merchant who brought supplies to, and then fought alongside, Cortés and remained in New Spain, perhaps because of his anxieties about being a *converso*, was also important. The biggest buyers were García de Jaén and Fernando de Sevilla, both *conversos*, the latter having been *reconciliado* in 1494.[45]

Spices, sugar, and rice were also easy to buy in Seville. The capital of the European spice trade was Lisbon, but the traders in Andalusia were very interested. Piero Rondinelli was prominent in buying pepper from merchants of Cremona who had established themselves in Lisbon.[46] This sale of spices was another near-monopoly of the Genoese.[47] Sugar obtained from cane in the Portuguese Atlantic islands was also a significant item in the markets in Seville. The same product from the Canaries began to appear after 1485. Again, the Genoese had a quasi-monopoly of the sales. Of course, this industry, which had employed Columbus in his youth, was also one for the future in the Caribbean.[48]

Cloth was made in Seville on some three thousand looms. But what was produced came nowhere near satisfying the demand, so the citizens of Seville, like those of the Indies, sought northern European imports. English woolens, for example, had been sold in the city since the fourteenth century, the powerful merchant Prato Francesco Datini being concerned as a middleman.[49] By 1500, most of the sellers of English textiles in Seville were in fact Englishmen, such as Thomas Maillard and John Day. Black cloth from the rich Flemish center of Courtrai was also popular. Small supplies of cloth derived from Rouen, Milan, and Florence, as well as some from Valencia, Segovia, and Baeza. These commercial connections with northern Europe make it understandable that one or two men from there would appear from time to time on expeditions bound for the Indies: "Master Andrés," for example, from Bristol, whom we have met with Magellan.

Another product of Seville was cochineal for coloring, arriving especially from the lands of the Medina Sidonia, such as, for example, Chiclana and Chipiona, near Sanlúcar, though it was inferior to that of Crete and Corinth. Mexican versions would soon make their mark. Other dyes, as we have seen earlier, derived from the Azores and the Canaries (orchil). In marketing these, adventurous merchants from Burgos now mixed happily with those of the south.

Seville was also full of small workshops producing for the local markets. Thus, there was an important leather factory, using not only Andalusian material but some from the Barbary coast. Boots and leather clothes were in demand in the Indies, as were light leather shields. The Genoese had a monopoly of the import of goatskins, their warehouse being in Cadiz. There were some craftsmen who were also merchants, such as Pedro López Gavilán. Piero Rondinelli of Florence was active in this business. The most sought-after fabric was probably camlet, an elegant mixture of camel's hair and silk. It came from Egypt, being made with the hair of goat as well as camel. Cyprus had long been a center of production, and Genoese families interested in cotton had sold it in Chios. In Seville, sellers of camlet were again almost all Genoese, Luca Battista Adorno being the most prominent.[50] Velvet was also a product where the Genoese were dominant. A workshop that was almost a factory, that in Triana producing gunpowder, was evidently another linked to the needs of the New World.

Triana had been a center of ceramics and pottery since Roman days, as it is today. There were in the early sixteenth century fifty ovens there, producing glazed earthenware, bricks, tiles, and dishes. But there were also clay plants in San Pedro, San Vicente, and Tablada. The techniques were ancient, but a new impulse had been given to them by a brilliant Tuscan, Francesco

Niculoso. As with soap, gunpowder, and cloth, the Indies soon became a big market for earthenware; the exports to the early settlement of Caparra, near San Juan, in La Española, for example, were especially impressive.

After clay, gold: Seville, because of its long connection with Islam, had been the Castilian capital of the gold trade in the fifteenth century. Its importance was Europe-wide: much of the gold of that time, all originally from West Africa (Bambuk, Bure, Lobi, Akan), came in bars or dust via Seville.

The book trade had its importance, too. Many of the famous romances, many of which have been discussed earlier, had been printed by the skillful Jacob Cromberger, a native of Nuremberg who had been living in Seville since 1500. His fine volumes could be bought on the Arenal in Seville or in the Calle del Mar (today, the Calle García de Vinuesa), leading to the Arenal from the cathedral. Customers included many adventurers before they set out for the Indies; for them the printed romance was often a cargo more intoxicating than manzanilla, almost as delicious as brandy.[51] Another literary success was the collection of ballads compiled by Hernando del Castillo and published in 1511, known as the *Cancionero General.* From this, Bernal Díaz could have learned of the significance of the River Rubicon, and Cortés would have been reminded of Sulla and Marius—references that, as their writings show, meant much to them: Bernal Díaz wrote that Cortés "crossed the Rubicon" when he entered the Mexican interior, and Cortés said in a lordly manner that the rivalry between Gonzalo de Sandoval and García Holguín as to who really captured the Mexican emperor Cuauhtémoc reminded him of a similar dispute between the Romans Sulla and Marius as to who captured Jugurtha, King of Numidia.

As important in the Atlantic trade, perhaps, was the demand for holy pictures and portable altars, reredoses and altar screens, depictions of the Virgin or of St. Martin, Christ, and St. Christopher—on such a scale that many indigenous people, on coming into contact with the Castilians, supposed that Christianity worshipped a positive pantheon of deities.

There were already many shops in Seville in the early sixteenth century. The sellers, from leather dressers to silk dealers, hatters to tailors, usually associated in guilds, half trade union, half religious brotherhood, which were established in certain "workshop streets" (*calles talleres*). Many did not have a special association and were, like the powerful sellers of gypsum, tied in with others (in this case, the builders and stonemasons). Still, walking through the city, one would have found breeches and doublets on display in the Calle Genova, hats and crossbows in the Calle de la Mar, horseshoes in the Calle de Castro, caps and shoes on *las gradas,* perfumes, haberdashery, and adornments for women in the Calle Francos, underwear in the Calle Escobar, and wooden, iron, steel, and golden objects, as well as light arms, in the Calle Sierpes. The consequence was that by 1526 the Venetian Navagero could say that Seville was sending to the Indies not only all the cereals and wines that they needed, but also all the necessary clothes.[52]

We are talking still of an age of wood. Timber was used for houses in Seville, for carts, for boats, for bolstering the strange bridge across the river, for barrels, and also for fires in ovens. Wood was thus the basis of many undertakings. But the local oak was almost used up—even the oak groves of Constantina were depleted. Pine was thought to be inferior, and so wood was imported from England, Galicia, Germany, and even Scandinavia. Another change had been the great increase in the production of hemp for rope-making, mostly along the banks of the River Guadalquivir.

So it was that in the early 1520s, Spain had not only a language ready for empire, as the philologist Nebrija had insisted was desirable, and not only a large number of people ready for the adventure of emigration, but also in Seville a city ready to be the capital of a New World. Here Columbus had returned after his great journey in 1493, here Elcano came back after his circumnavigation of the earth. Here Cortés's representatives—and, later, Cortés himself—would arrive after conquering the extraordinary monarchy of the Mexica. Pedrarias set off from Seville, as did Bobadilla, Ovando, and the poor Jeronymite priors. From here would leave for the Indies, and to here would come back, countless viceroys, governors and captains-general, commanders, explorers, missionaries, and settlers, on thousands of ships over the next few hundred years. They would bring with them gold and silver, chocolate and turquoise mosaics, sugar and coffee and, even more, astounding memories of conquests and improbable adventures that could scarcely have been dreamed of a generation before—except perhaps by assiduous readers of that great romanticist "Sir John Mandeville."

But the conquistadors did not seek only glory and gold. Most of them believed that the long-term benefit of their discoveries would be the acceptance by the natives of Christianity, with all the cultural consequences that that implied. They believed, as the Spanish Crown put the matter in 1504, that they were "ennobling" the new lands with Christians. They made their conquests with a clear conscience, certain that they were taking with them civilization, believing that they would in the end permit these new people to leave behind their backward conditions. Who can doubt now that they were right to denounce the idea of religion based on human sacrifice or the simple worship of the sun or the rain? As a twentieth-century French general wrote in the wake of his country's retreat from North Africa, "Every epoch has a way of looking at things that differs profoundly from what came before or comes afterward. Fashion in this domain is fickle and usually influences us more than we suppose. We believe ourselves free and reasonable beings. But we are all of us, whether we like it or not, the playthings of great waves of ideas that carry us forward."[53]

So it was with the generation of 1500 in Spain. They knew that their mission was to seek new Christian souls. Gold and glory were the supporters of their coat of arms, on which Christianity dominated the face of the shield.

One cannot read much of any work written in the sixteenth century without realizing that the wheel of fortune was a constant preoccupation. Dürer designed a handsome wheel in an engraving in about 1515. "Oh, with what affronts and buffetings is our time tormented by Fortuna," reflected the erudite Peter Martyr in a letter to the chancellor Mercurino Gattinara in January 1521.[54] The previous summer, in 1520, to commemorate the forthcoming coronation of the then so promising young hero of Europe, Charles V, as emperor, tapestries entitled "Honors" were ordered on the basis of cartoons designed by van Orley, then the best-known painter in the supremely civilized court of the Netherlands. One of these tapestries, now in the Spanish palace of La Granja, outside Segovia, represents the wheel of fortune. The goddess Fortune is to be seen throwing stones to one side, roses to the other; and among those to whom she is throwing roses we see Caesar in a boat; he might easily have been Hernán Cortés, the most remarkable of the conquistadors. Fortune had now begun to throw roses to Spain and would do so for several more generations, during which time the Spaniards—from Castile and Aragon, Galicia and Asturias, the Basque country as well as Granada—would establish themselves throughout the New World and, at home, make of their newly united country a great nation second to none.[55]

Appendix A: Family Trees

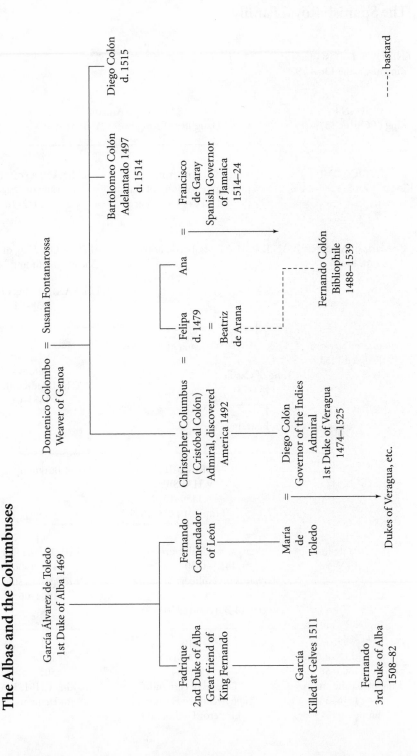

The Albas and the Columbuses

García Álvarez de Toledo
1st Duke of Alba 1469

Domenico Colombo   =   Susana Fontanarossa
Weaver of Genoa

Fernando
Comendador
of León

Christopher Columbus   =   Felipa
(Cristóbal Colón)   d. 1479
Admiral, discovered   =
America 1492   Beatriz
                          de Arana

Bartolomeo Colón
Adelantado 1497
d. 1514

Diego Colón
d. 1515

Ana   =   Francisco
          de Garay
          Spanish Governor
          of Jamaica
          1514–24

Fernando Colón
Bibliophile
1488–1539

Fadrique
2nd Duke of Alba
Great friend of
King Fernando

María
de
Toledo

Diego Colón
Governor of the Indies
Admiral
1st Duke of Veragua
1474–1525

García
Killed at Gelves 1511

Fernando
3rd Duke of Alba
1508–82

Dukes of Veragua, etc.

- - - - : bastard

The Spanish Royal Family

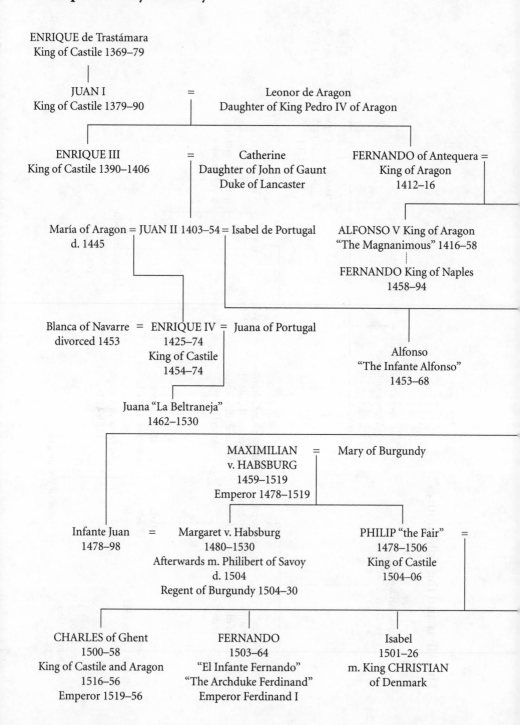

ENRIQUE de Trastámara
King of Castile 1369–79

JUAN I   =   Leonor de Aragon
King of Castile 1379–90   Daughter of King Pedro IV of Aragon

ENRIQUE III   =   Catherine   FERNANDO of Antequera =
King of Castile 1390–1406   Daughter of John of Gaunt   King of Aragon
                            Duke of Lancaster   1412–16

María of Aragon = JUAN II 1403–54 = Isabel de Portugal   ALFONSO V King of Aragon
      d. 1445   "The Magnanimous" 1416–58

                                                         FERNANDO King of Naples
                                                                1458–94

Blanca of Navarre = ENRIQUE IV = Juana of Portugal
   divorced 1453   1425–74
                   King of Castile   Alfonso
                      1454–74   "The Infante Alfonso"
                                                          1453–68

              Juana "La Beltraneja"
                   1462–1530

                          MAXIMILIAN   =   Mary of Burgundy
                          v. HABSBURG
                           1459–1519
                       Emperor 1478–1519

Infante Juan   =   Margaret v. Habsburg   PHILIP "the Fair"   =
  1478–98   1480–1530   1478–1506
                    Afterwards m. Philibert of Savoy   King of Castile
                            d. 1504   1504–06
                     Regent of Burgundy 1504–30

CHARLES of Ghent   FERNANDO   Isabel
    1500–58   1503–64   1501–26
King of Castile and Aragon "El Infante Fernando"   m. King CHRISTIAN
    1516–56   "The Archduke Ferdinand"   of Denmark
  Emperor 1519–56   Emperor Ferdinand I

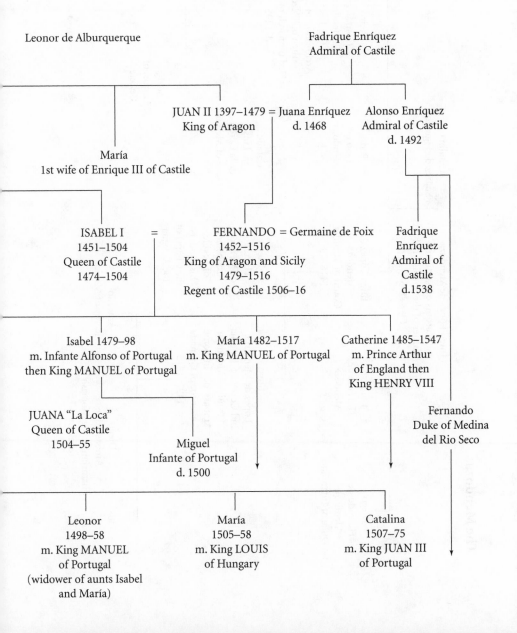

Leonor de Alburquerque

Fadrique Enríquez
Admiral of Castile

JUAN II 1397–1479 = Juana Enríquez   Alonso Enríquez
King of Aragon   d. 1468   Admiral of Castile
                                              d. 1492

María
1st wife of Enrique III of Castile

ISABEL I   =   FERNANDO = Germaine de Foix   Fadrique
1451–1504   1452–1516   Enríquez
Queen of Castile   King of Aragon and Sicily   Admiral of
1474–1504   1479–1516   Castile
                       Regent of Castile 1506–16   d.1538

Isabel 1479–98   María 1482–1517   Catherine 1485–1547
m. Infante Alfonso of Portugal   m. King MANUEL of Portugal   m. Prince Arthur
then King MANUEL of Portugal   of England then
                                                           King HENRY VIII

JUANA "La Loca"   Fernando
Queen of Castile   Duke of Medina
1504–55   Miguel   del Rio Seco
                     Infante of Portugal
                          d. 1500

Leonor   María   Catalina
1498–58   1505–58   1507–75
m. King MANUEL   m. King LOUIS   m. King JUAN III
of Portugal   of Hungary   of Portugal
(widower of aunts Isabel
and María)

The Mendozas

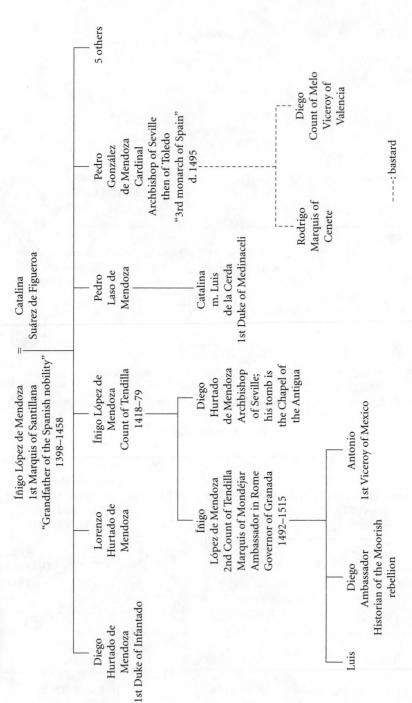

The Ponces de León

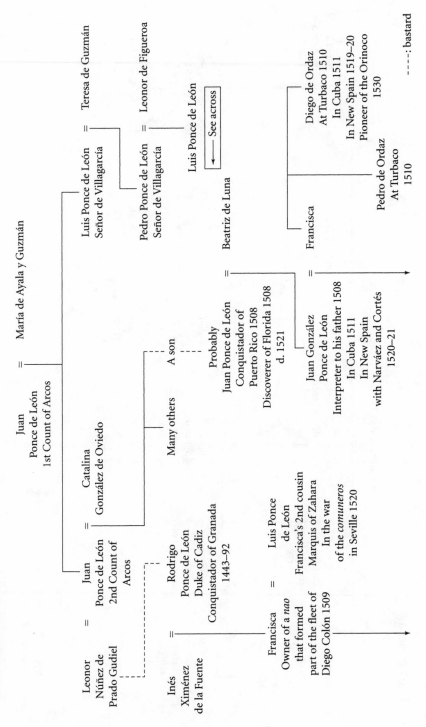

The Fonsecas

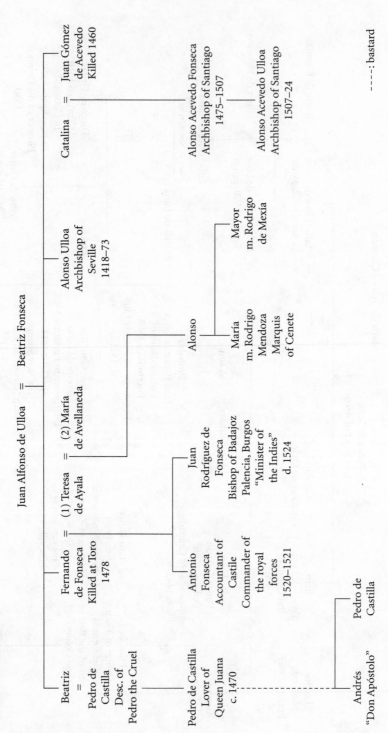

Juan Alfonso de Ulloa = Beatriz Fonseca

Beatriz = Pedro de Castilla Desc. of Pedro the Cruel

Fernando de Fonseca Killed at Toro 1478 = (1) Teresa de Ayala (2) María de Avellaneda

Alonso Ulloa Archbishop of Seville 1418–73

Catalina = Juan Gómez de Acevedo Killed 1460

Pedro de Castilla Lover of Queen Juana c. 1470

Antonio Fonseca Accountant of Castile Commander of the royal forces 1520–1521

Juan Rodríguez de Fonseca Bishop of Badajoz Palencia, Burgos "Minister of the Indies" d. 1524

Alonso

María m. Rodrigo Mendoza Marquis of Cenete

Mayor m. Rodrigo de Mexia

Alonso Acevedo Fonseca Archbishop of Santiago 1475–1507

Alonso Acevedo Ulloa Archbishop of Santiago 1507–24

Andrés "Don Apóstolo"

Pedro de Castilla

- - - -: bastard

Appendix B:
The Costs of Becoming Emperor, 1519

The balance was:	Rhine Florins
Gifts to the Archbishop of Mainz	103,000.00
his councillors	10,200.00
Gifts to the Archbishop of Cologne	40,000.00
his councillors	12,800.00
Gifts to the Archbishop of Trèves	22,000.00
his councillors	18,700.00
Gifts to the Elector of Saxony	32,000.00
his councillors	8,000.00
Gifts to the Elector of Palatine	139,000.00
his councillors	8,000.00
Gifts to the ambassadors of Poland, Bohemia, and Hungary	41,031.18
Expenses of Chancellery (Brandenburg)	100.00
Gift to Count Frederick of the Palatine (negotiator)	31,108.00
Gift to Margrave Casimir of Brandenburg	25,843.28
Gifts to counts, barons, chevaliers, nobles, and representatives of the cities	31,029.00
Costs for commissioners, councillors, secretaries	39,965.00
Costs for couriers, messengers, etc.	3,542.11
Costs for councillors of Emperor Maximilian	5,600.21
Costs in Switzerland	29,160.00
Costs for the purchase of Württemberg	171,359.47
Diverse costs	55,760.52
Bank charges	17,493.24

These sums were raised thus:

Jacob Fugger (Augsburg)	543,585.34
Bartolomé Welser (Augsburg)	143,333.00
Filippo Gualterotti (Florence)	55,000.00
Benedetto Fornari (Genoa)	55,000.00
Lorenzo de Vivaldi (Genoa)	55,000.00
TOTAL	851,918.34

Source: Léon Schick, UN GRAND HOMME D'AFFAIRES AU DEBUT DU XVIÈME SIÈCLE: JACOB FUGGER, *Paris 1957.*

Appendix C:
Registered Vessels
Sailing to and from the Indies, 1504–22

Year	Outgoing	Returning
1504 (from Aug. 14)	3	—
1506	22	12
1507	32	19
1508	46	21
1509	21	26
1510	17	10
1511	21	13
1512	33	21
1513	31	30
1514	30	46
1515	33	30
1516	42	10
1517	63	31
1518	51	47
1519	51	41
1520	71	37
1521	33	31
1522	18	25

Suggested Reading

Book One. Spain at the Crossroads

Several admirable books in English need to be mentioned. First there is John Elliott's *Imperial Spain* (London 1963), still as fresh and interesting as when it was first published. The last chapters of Angus Mackay's *Spain in the Middle Ages* (London 1977) and of Jocelyn Hillgarth's *The Spanish Kingdoms, 1250–1516* (2 vols., Oxford 1976–78) are excellent introductions. I much enjoyed John Edwards's more recent *The Spain of the Catholic Monarchs, 1474–1520* (Oxford 2000).

The main work in Spanish is that of two immensely learned historians, Manuel Fernández Álvarez and Luis Suárez Fernández, *La España de los Reyes Católicos*, in the series *Historia de España*, edited by Ramón Menéndez Pidal (Madrid 1978). There is also the excellent *La España de los Reyes Católicos* (Madrid 1999), of Miguel Ladero Quesada. Edward Cooper's *Castillos señoriales de la Corona de Castilla* (4 vols., Salamanca 1991) is of great value to all seeking the relationships between the masters of Spain in the late fifteenth and early sixteenth centuries.

Among biographies, it is hard to decide between Luis Suárez's *Isabel I, Reina* (Barcelona 2000) and Tarsicio de Azcona's *Isabel la Católica* (Madrid 2002). I also enjoyed Alfredo Alvar Ezquerra's very different *Isabel la Católica* (Madrid 2002). I have now had the benefit of Manuel Fernández Álvarez's *Isabel la Católica* (Madrid 2003). Peggy Liss's *Isabel the Queen* (Oxford 1992) is the best biography in English and particularly good on the influences on Isabel. King Fernando is less well served, and the only works from which I derived any benefit were Ernest Belenguer's *Fernando el Católico* (Barcelona 1999) and the essays in *Fernando el católico, pensamiento político, V Congreso de Historia de la Corona de Aragón* (Saragossa 1956). There is, though, also José María Doussinague, *El testamento político de Fernando el Católico* (Madrid 1950). The war in Granada is well analyzed in Ladero Quesada's *Castilla y la Conquista del reino de Granada* (Valladolid 1967). Prescott's description of this war, *The Art of War in Spain: The Conquest of Granada, 1481–1492* (London 1995) is still most readable. The best book about the last days of the Moorish emirate is that of L. P. Harvey, *Islamic Spain, 1250 to 1500* (Chicago 1990). The works of Felipe Fernández-Armesto on the Canary Islands are excellent: *Before Columbus* (London 1987) and *The Canary Islands After the Conquest* (Oxford 1982).

I avoid bibliographical recollections of the many works that I have read about the expulsion of the Jews. But the best seems to be Luis Suárez's *Documentos acerca de la expulsión de los judíos de España* (Madrid 1991). I found B. Netanyahu's *The Origins of the Inquisition in Fifteenth-Century Spain* (New York 1995) rewarding. I greatly benefited also from Juan Gil's *Los Conversos y la Inquisición Sevillana* (8 vols., Seville 2000–03).

Book Two. *Columbus*

The collection of Columbus's writings edited by Consuelo Varela and Juan Gil, *Textos y documentos completos* (Madrid 1992), is essential. Lives of Columbus from which I derived benefit include those by Consuelo Varela, *Cristóbal Colón, retrato de un hombre* (Madrid 1992), Jacques Heers's Franco-Genoese interpretation, *Christopher Colomb* (Paris 1981), and Felipe Fernández-Armesto's elegant *Columbus* (Oxford 1991). Samuel Eliot Morison's *Admiral of the Ocean Sea* (2 vols., Boston 1942) shows its age. In the vast literature on Columbus, who does not recall with pleasure the heroic Alice ("Miss Alice") of B. Gould's *Nueva lista documentada de los tripulantes de Colón en 1492* (Madrid 1984)? Antonio Sánchez González's *Medinaceli y Colón* (Madrid 1995) was useful, and Juan Manzano's *Colón y su secreto* (3rd ed., Madrid 1989) absorbing. I enjoyed my dear friend Mauricio Obregón's excellent *Colón en el Mar de los Caribes* (Bogotá 1990). See, too, Consuelo Varela's fascinating *Colón y los florentinos* (Madrid 1988) and Manuel Serrano y Sanz's *Los amigos y protectores aragones de Cristóbal Colón* (Barcelona 1991).

On the first stage of Spanish rule in La Española, there is Demetrio Ramos's *El conflicto de las lanzas jinetes* (Santo Domingo 1992). For a negative if interesting study, there is Kirkpatrick Sale's *The Conquest of Paradise* (London 1991). On the expansion of Spanish rule, there is Carl Ortwin Sauer, *The Early Spanish Main* (Cambridge 1966). On the later voyages of Columbus, there are Samuel Eliot Morison's *The European Discovery of America: The Northern Voyages* (Oxford 1971) and *The European Discovery of America: The Southern Voyages, 1491–1616* (New York 1974).

On the Tainos, the best introduction is Irving Rouse, *The Tainos* (New Haven 1992). Sven Lovén's *Origins of the Tainan Culture* (Göteborg 1935) still has much to commend it.

Book Three. *Bobadilla and Ovando*

Juan Pérez de Tudela's *Las Armadas de Indias* (Madrid 1958) is the best general introduction to this period. On Ovando, Ursula Lamb's *Frey Nicolás de Ovando* (Madrid 1956) holds the field.

Book Four. *Diego Colón*

On the slave trade in indigenous Indians, see Carlos Deive's remarkable *La Española y la Escalavitud del Indio* (Santo Domingo 1995); Enrique Otte's *Las Perlas del Caribe* (Caracas 1977) is very interesting. See also Luis Arranz's unfortunately unfinished life of Diego Colón, *Don Diego Colón*, vol. 1 (Madrid 1982) and the same's *Repartimientos y encomiendas en la Isla Española* (Madrid 1991). With Diego, we approach the question of the Spanish treatment of the Indians, and here the *Historia de las Indias* (3 vols., Mexico 1986), the great work of Bartolomé de las Casas, is the best beginning. Nothing written by Las Casas is irrelevant. But see also the works of Lewis Hanke, *All Mankind Is One* (De Kalb, Illinois 1974), *Aristotle and the American Indians* (London 1959), and, above all, *The Spanish Struggle for Justice in the Conquest of America* (Philadelphia 1949). The best life of Vespucci is that by Frederick J. Pohl, *Amerigo Vespucci* (London 1966).

Book Five. *Balboa and Pedrarias*

Here the best original source is that of the enemy of Las Casas, Gonzalo Fernández de Oviedo's *Historia general y natural de las Indias* (5 vols., vols. 117–21 in BAE, ed. Juan Pérez de Tudela, Madrid 1959, 2nd ed. 1992). Balboa needs a new biography. On Pedrarias, this field has now been illuminated richly by Carmen Mena, on whose books everyone writing of this era on Darien must now rely. See her *Pedrarias Dávila* (Seville 1992) and her excellent *Sevilla y las flotas de Indias* (Seville 1998).

Book Six. *Cisneros*

On Cisneros there is J. García Oro, *El cardenal Cisneros, Vida y Empresas* (2 vols., Madrid 1992–93). Here again Las Casas's history is essential; the life of the same by Manuel Giménez Fernández (*Bartolomé de las Casas*, 2 vols., Seville 1953, 1961) is an extraordinary achievement even though it essentially deals only with a few years (1516–21) of Las Casas's long life. It guided me through the work of Las Casas himself and also pointed me to relevant *legajos* in the Archivo de Indias. I have quoted a great deal from Las Casas because the conversations that he reports seem so vivid.

Book Seven. *Charles, King and Emperor*

On Charles V, the best life still seems to me to be that of Carl Brandi, *Carlos V, Vida y Fortuna de una Personalidad y un Imperio* (Madrid 1937). On Spain of the intellect of these years, see Marcel Bataillon, *Erasmo y España* (new ed., Mexico 1998). On the election of Charles V, see Hermann Kellenbenz, *Los Fugger en España y Portugal hasta 1560* (Salamanca 1999). On the economic life of Spain, see Ramón Carande, *Carlos V y sus banqueros* (3 vols., 3rd ed., Barcelona 1987). On bureaucracy, see Hayward Keniston, *Francisco de los Cobos* (Pittsburgh 1959). On literary life, see Irving Leonard, *Books of the Brave* (New York 1949). (Eschew the edition of 1992.) Few will escape being moved by Earl Hamilton's statement in the preface to his *American Treasure and the Price Revolution in Spain, 1501–1650* (Cambridge, Massachusetts 1934) that the author and his wife worked jointly for 30,750 hours on the book, carrying out 3 million computations. The book still has its uses.

Book Eight. *New Spain*

On Old Mexico, the bibliography is enormous. I recommend as a start the catalog to the Royal Academy's excellent exhibition on the subject in 2002–03. On the Spanish conquest, I venture to recommend my own *The Conquest of Mexico* (London 1993). See also my *Who's Who in the Conquest of Mexico* (London 2000). There are now also several modern lives of Cortés, of which José Luis Martínez's *Hernán Cortés* (Mexico 1990), with its four volumes of documents, is the most thorough. Bartolomé Bennassar's *Hernán Cortés* (Madrid 2002) has many merits.

Book Nine. *Magellan and Elcano*

There is no alternative to Pigafetta's account, *Primer Viaje alrededor del mundo*, which can be most easily read in the Spanish edition of Leocio Cabrero (Madrid 1985), but the Hakluyt translation edited by Lord Stanley of Alderley is also excellent. I have a weakness for any book by Stefan Zweig. See his *Magellan* (Barcelona 1955).

Book Ten. *The New Empire*

For Chapter 38, on Seville in 1522: the main books I consulted on this little piece of microhistory were Miguel Ladero Quesada's *La Ciudad Medieval, Historia de Sevilla* (Valladolid 1980); Francisco Morales Padrón's *Historia de Sevilla, La Ciudad del Quinientos* (Seville 1989); Ramón Carande's *Estudios de Historia, 2; Sevilla, fortaleza y otras temas sevillanos* (Barcelona 1990); Carlos Martínez Shaw's *Sevilla, siglo XVI* (Madrid 1993), which includes some excellent essays; Eduardo Trueba, *Sevilla marítima* (Seville 1990); and Enrique Otte, *Sevilla y sus mercaderes a fines de la Edad Media* (Seville 1996).

Glossary

adelantado: an official who, like a Roman proconsul, had both military and political functions.

alcaide: commander of a fortress.

alcalde: mayor or judge who presided over a town council.

alcalde mayor: chief justice.

alguacil: constable.

alhama, aljama: district of a town allocated to either Jews or Moors.

arroba: weight equal to 11 kilograms and 502 grams.

asiento: contract.

asistente: the equivalent of a *corregidor* in Seville.

audiencia: high court.

bergantín/brigantín: a low, small vessel, usually with two masts, capable of taking a sail or being rowed; easily maneuvered along coasts.

bozales: black slaves straight from Africa.

brazilwood: hard red wood (Caesalpina echinata) used for red dye.

caballero: knight.

cabildo: cathedral chapter; also town council.

cacique/cacicazgo: chief/chieftaincy, in Taino, often used in Spain for a political boss.

camarera mayor: lady of the bedchamber.

camarero: steward.

capitulación: agreement of a serious kind between two parties.

caravel: light round ship with three masts, usually carrying lateen sails.

castellano: a gold coin worth 485 maravedís.

cédula: decree.

comendador: commander, but used to indicate a senior official of a knightly order.

comitre: a captain who serves under an admiral; sometimes a royal captain.

comunero: rebel councillor.

contador mayor: chief treasurer/accountant.

contador mayor del reino: treasurer of the kingdom.

continuo: courtier.

contramaestre: boatswain.

converso: Jew or Muslim who converted willingly to Christianity.

corregidor: co-councillor appointed by the Crown in municipalities to control spending, etc.

criado: member of the household, royal or otherwise.

ducado/ducat: gold coin worth 375 maravedís. Cortés paid Alfaro 11 ducats for his passage to the Indies in 1506. Also used as a weight.

encomienda: In the Indies a number of Indians were allocated to a settler (the *encomendero*) who would use their services and their land in return for looking after them and teaching them Christianity. In Spain an *encomienda* was more to do with land than with people.

entrada: an expedition into the interior.

escribano: notary.

escudero: infantryman.

fanega: a dry measure equal to 55 liters.

fundador: foundry worker.

fundición: melting down.

galeón: a large ship with three masts.

hermandad: police.

hidalgo: a man of good birth but not a nobleman.

judería: a Jewish ghetto.

justicia: magistrate.

lateen: a triangular sail often used on the mizzenmast of a vessel, allowing the ship to tack more easily.

letrado: educated man.

libra de oro: ancient Castilian weight divided into 16 ounces and equal to 460 grams. Other parts of Spain had their own equivalents.

maestresala: steward.

maravedí: a copper coin that was the smallest measure of Castilian money and the most used. Ovando, the Governor of La Española in 1502, was paid 360,000 maravedís a year; Piñelo, the factor of the Casa de Contratación, 100,000 in 1503; and Vespucci, a chief pilot, received 75,000 in 1508. About 1492, the Charterhouse of (Cartuja de) las Cuevas had an annual income of about 1,111,000 maravedís.

marrano: a converted Jew who secretly practiced Judaism (vulgarism).

mayorazgo: entailed grant.

mestizaje: mixed-race group.

montañés: native of Cantabria.

monteros de Espinosa: royal bodyguards.

morería: Muslim ghetto.

morisco: A Muslim who has become Christian.

mozárabe: a Christian who survived in Muslim territory.

mudéjar: a Muslim who stayed in Christian territory; also the work he might carry out there, especially building.

naboría: an Indian recruited as a servant in the Caribbean, but not a slave.

peso: a silver coin supposed to be worth 450 maravedís.

procurador: a representative, as in a parliament.

reconciliado: anyone castigated or fined by the Inquisition.

regidor: a council member.

relación: report.

repartimiento: a division of territory.

repostero: chamberlain; one who looked after the royal plate and linen.

residencia: an inquiry into the actions of a departing magistrate or governor, so called because that official had to remain in residence for thirty days after his successor had arrived for the inquiry to be carried through.

tierra firme: mainland.

veedor: supervisor.

vega: cultivated valley.

veinticuatro: one of the twenty-four *regidors* of Seville and one or two other places in Andalusia.

vihuela: an early version of the guitar.

Spanish currency c. 1500:

The Spaniards at the time of the conquest of the New World employed many denominations with no clear rules of practice. *Pesos, castellanos, ducats,* and *maravedís* were all used. The usual coin was a *maravedí,* a copper coin equal to a ninety-sixth part of a Spanish gold mark, which in turn was equivalent to 230.045 grams.

1 real = 34 maravedís
1 ducat = 375 maravedís
1 peso = 450 maravedís
1 castellano = 485 maravedís

A *sueldo* (from *solidus*) was a tiny sum (*sou*), perhaps no more than a way of saying that.

A *marco* was a measure of about 11 ounces used for weighing both pearls and gold.

Bibliography

For a list of abbreviations, see page 575.

Manuscript Sources

Archivo Ceramelli Papiani (for Berardi, Rondinelli)
Archivo General de Indias
  I used the following sections:
    Contratación
    Indiferente General
    Justicia
    México
    Panamá
    Patronato
  The documents concerned are indicated in the references.
Archivo Histórico Nacional (Madrid)
Archivo de Protocolos de Sevilla
Archivo del Stato, Florence
Archivio Mediceo avanti il principe Fondo Guerra de Piccolomini de Aragona, Rondinelli papers

Other Primary Sources
Printed documents, firsthand accounts, sixteenth-century books

Aguilar, Fr. Francisco, *Relación breve de la Conquista,* written c. 1565, 1st ed. Mexico 1892; new ed. Germán Vázquez in *La Conquista de Tenochtitlan, Historia 16, Crónicas de América,* 41, Madrid 1988. Eng. tr. Patricia de Fuentes, intr. Ross Hassig, Norman, OK, 1993.

Alfonso X, *Las Siete Partidas,* ed. Francisco López Estrada, Madrid 1992.

Anales de Tlatelolco, Mexico 1948.

Andagoya, Pascal de, *Relación de documentos,* ed. Adrián Blázquez, *Crónica de Américas,* Madrid 1986.

Baeza, Gonzalo de, *Tesorero de Isabel la Católica,* 2 vols., ed. Antonio and E. A. de la Torre, Madrid 1956.

Bergenroth, Gustav Adolf, *Calendar of Letters . . . Relating to the Negotiations Between England and Spain,* London 1862.

Bernáldez, Andrés, *Cura de Los Palacios,* ed. Manuel Gómez-Moreno and Juan de M. Carriazo, *Historia del Reinado de los Reyes Católicos,* 2 vols., Seville 1969.

Catálogo de los fondos americanos del Archivo de Protocolos de Sevilla, ed. Fundación Rafael G. Abreu, 8 vols., Madrid and Seville 1930–2000, most reprinted recently.

Chacón y Calvo, José María, *Cédulario Cubano, 1493–1512* (*Los origenes de la colonización*), Madrid 1929 (Colección de documentos inéditos para la historia de Hispano-América, vol. 6).

Colección de documentos inéditos relativos al descubrimiento, conquista, y organización de las antiguas posesiones españolas de ultramar [*CDIU*], 25 vols., Madrid 1880–1932.

Colección de documentos inéditos relativos al descubrimiento, conquista, y organización de las posesiones españolas en américa y oceania [*CDI*], ed. Joaquín Pacheco and Francisco Cárdenas, 42 vols., Madrid 1864–89.

Collection des voyages des souverains de Pays-Bas, ed. M. Gachard, 4 vols., Brussels 1876 onward (vol. 1 covers the journeys of Philip the Fair and vol. 2 those of Charles V).

Colón, Cristóbal, *Autógrafos de Cristóbal Colón y papeles de América,* Madrid 1892 (papers from the Palacio de Liria).

——, *Diario de libro de la primera navegación,* ed. Francisco Morales Padrón, Seville 1992.

——, *The Four Voyages of Columbus,* tr. J. M. Cohen, Harmondsworth 1969. Includes extra material such as the will of Diego Méndez.

——, *Libro de las profecías,* Madrid 1992.

——, *Textos y documentos completos,* ed. Juan Gil and Consuelo Varela, 2nd enl. ed., Madrid 1992.

Colón, Fernando, *Historia del Almirante,* ed. Luis Arranz, Madrid 2000. There is a translation by Benjamin Keen, *The Life of the Admiral Christopher Columbus by His Son Ferdinand,* New Brunswick, N.J. 1959.

Córdoba, Fray Martín de, *Jardín de las nobles mujeres,* Valladolid 1500; also ed. H. Goldberg, Chapel Hill, NC, 1974.

Cortés, Hernán, *Cartas de relación,* ed. Angel Delgado Gómez, Madrid 1993. Eng. tr. Anthony Pagden, New Haven, CT, 1986, with introduction by Sir John Elliott.

Cortes de los Antiguos Reinos de León y Castilla, vol. 4: *1476–1537,* Real Academia de la Historia, Madrid 1882.

Cota, Sancho, *Memorias,* ed. Hayward Keniston, London 1964.

Cuevas, Mariano, S. J. *Documentos Inéditos del Siglo XVI para la Historia de México,* Mexico 1914.

D'Ailly, Pierre, *Ymago Mundi,* ed. Antonio Ramírez de Verger, Madrid 1992.

Díaz, Fr. Juan, *Itinerario de la armada del Rey Católico a la Isla de Yucatán, en la India, en el año 1518.* (See Aguilar, above.)

Díaz del Castillo, Bernal, *Historia Verdadera de la Nueva España,* 2 vols., Madrid 1982; *The True History of the Conquest of New Spain,* tr. A. P. Maudslay, 5 vols., Hakluyt Society, 2nd series, 23–25, 30, 40, London 1908–16. Abbreviated ed. for the twentieth century, tr. J. M. Cohen.

Documentos de los Reyes Católicos, 1492–1504, ed. Antonio Gomáriz Marín, Murcia 2000.

Fernández Álvarez, Manuel, *Corpus documental de Carlos V,* vol. 1: *1516–39,* 5 vols., Salamanca, 1973.

Fernández de Navarrete, Martín, *Colección de viajes y descubrimientos que hicieron por mar los españoles*, Carlos Seco Serrano, 4 vols., Madrid 1954.

Fernández de Oviedo, Gonzalo [Oviedo], *Libro de la Cámara Real del Príncipe Don Juan*, Madrid 1870.

——, *Las Quinquagenas de la nobleza de España*, Real Academia de la Historia, Madrid 1880, vol. 1 (the only one published).

——, *Historia general y natural de las Indias*, 5 vols.; 117–21 in *BAE*, ed. Juan Pérez de Tudela, Madrid 1959, 2nd ed. Madrid 1992.

Fita, Fidel, Fray Bernardo Boyl, and Cristóbal Colón, *Nueva colección de cartas reales*, *BRAH*, vols. 19–20, 1891, 1892.

Gachard, M., *Correspondance de Charles V et d'Adrien VI*, Brussels 1859.

Galíndez de Carvajal, Lorenzo, *Anales Breves de los Reyes Católicos*, in *Colección de documentos inéditos para la historia de España*, vol. 18, Madrid 1851, 237ff.

García Icazbalceta, Joaquín, *Colección de documentos para la historia de México*, new ed., 2 vols., Mexico 1980.

García Mercadal, J., *Viajes de extranjeros por España y Portugal*, 3 vols., Madrid 1952–59.

Gil, Juan, and Consuelo Varela, *Cartas de particulares a Colón*, Madrid 1984.

Gómez de Castro, Alvar, *De las hazañas de Francisco Jiménez de Cisneros*, Madrid 1984.

Guevara, Antonio de, *Epistolares Familiares*, *BAE*, Madrid 1850.

Guicciardini, Francesco, *The History of Italy*, tr. Sidney Alexander, New York 1969.

Lalaing, Antoine de, *Relation du premier voyage de Philippe le Beau en Espagne, en 1501*, Brussels 1876. (See, too, García Mercadal above.)

La Marche, Olivier de, *Le Chevalier Délibéré*, new ed. Paris 1946.

Landa, Fray Diego de, *Relación de las Cosas de Yucatán*, ed. Miguel Rivera, Madrid 1985.

Las Casas, Bartolomé de, *Apologética Historia Sumaria*, ed. Juan Pérez de Tudela, 2 vols., Madrid, *BAE*, vols. 95, 96, Madrid 1957.

——, *Historia de las Indias* [Las Casas], 3 vols., ed. Agustín Millares Carlo, intr. Lewis Hanke, Mexico 1986.

——, *Brevísima relación de la destrucción de las Indias*, ed. Consuelo Varela, Madrid 1999.

La Torre, Antonio de, *Documentos sobre relaciones internacionales de los Reyes Católicos*, 3 vols., Barcelona 1949.

León-Portilla, Miguel, *La Visión de los Vencidos*, Madrid 1985. Eng. tr. *The Broken Spears*, New York 1992.

López de Gómara, Francisco, *Hispania Victrix, Historia General de las Indias*, in *BAE*, 22, Madrid 1852.

——, *Anales de Carlos*, Spanish with Eng. tr. and intr. by R. B. Merriman, London 1912.

——*La conquista de México*, Saragossa 1552, new ed. José Luis Rojas, Madrid 1987. Eng. tr. L. B. Simpson, Berkeley, CA, 1964.

López de Mendoza, Íñigo, Count of Tendilla, *Correspondencia del Conde de Tendilla*, vol. 1, Madrid 1974.

Macchiavelli, Niccoló, *The Prince*, tr. and ed. George Bull, London 1961.

Mandeville, Sir John, *The Travels of Sir John Mandeville*, ed. A. W. Pollard, London 1900.

Marco Polo, *El Libro de*, ed. Juan Gil, Madrid 1992.

Marineo Siculo, Lucio, "Don Hernán Cortés," in *De Rebus Hispaniae memorabilibus libri*, vol. 25, Alcalá de Henares, 1530, new ed. Miguel León-Portilla, *Historia*, 16, April 1985.

Martorell, Joanot, and Martí Joan de Galba, *Tirant lo Blanc*, first pub. in Catalan 1490, first pub. in Castilian 1511; Eng. tr. David H. Rosenthal, London 1984.

Martyr, Peter, *Epistolario, Documentos inéditos para la historia de España*, vols. 9–12, Madrid 1953.

——, *De Orbe Novo*, tr. Francis MacNutt, New York 1912. There is a good new Spanish ed. by Ramón Alba, *Décadas del Nuevo Mundo*, Madrid 1989.

——, *Cartas sobre el Nuevo Mundo*, Madrid 1990.

Montaigne, Michel de, *The Essays of Michel de Montaigne*, tr. M. A. Screech, London 1981.

Morales Padrón, Francisco (ed.), *Primeras Cartas sobre América*, Seville 1990.

Morel-Fatio, Alfred, *Historiographie de Charles Quint;* includes a French translation of the autobiography of Charles (as well as the 1620 ed. in Portuguese), Paris 1913.

Muñoz, *Catálogos de la Colección*, ed. Real Academia de la Historia, 2 vols., Madrid 1955.

Murga Sanz, Mgr. Vicente, *Cedulario puertorriqueño*, vols. 1 and 2, Río Piedras 1964.

——, *Puerto Rico en los manuscritos de Don Juan Bautista Muñoz*, San Juan 1960.

Palencia, Alfonso de, *Crónica de Enrique IV, Historia de la Guerra de Granada*, tr. A. Paz y Melia, *BAE*, vols. 257, 258, Madrid 1973–75.

Paso, Francisco del, *Epistolario de Nueva España, 1505–1818*, 16 vols., Mexico City 1939 onward.

Paz y Mélia, A., *Nobilario de Conquistadores de Indias*, Madrid 1982.

Pérez de Guzmán, Fernán, *Generaciones y Semblanzas*, London 1965.

Pigafetta, Antonio, *Primer viaje alrededor del mundo*, ed. Leoncio Cabrero, Madrid 1985. See also the Hakluyt Society's translation, ed. Lord Stanley of Alderley, London 1874.

Popol Vuh: The Mayan Book of the Dawn of Life, tr. Dennis Tedlock, New York 1985.

Pulgar, Hernando del, *Crónica de los Reyes Católicos*, Madrid 1770.

Quiroga, Vasco de, *Utopia en América*, ed. Paz Serrano Gassent, Madrid 1992.

Rodríguez de Montalvo, Garcí, *Amadís de Gaula*, 2 vols., ed. Juan Bautista Avalle-Arce, Madrid 1991. There is a fine English translation by Edwin B. Place and Herbert C. Behm, Lexington, KY, 1964.

Rodríguez Valencia, Vicente, *Opinión de Españoles y extranjeros, Isabel la Católica*, 3 vols., Valladolid 1970.

Rodríguez Villa, Antonio, *El emperador Carlos V y su corte, según las cartas de don Martín de Salinas*, Madrid 1903.

Saco, José Antonio, *Historia de la esclavitud de la raza africana en el nuevo mundo*, 4 vols., Havana 1938.

Sahagún, Fr. Bernardino de, *Florentine Codex: General History of the Things of New Spain*, tr. Charles Dibble and Arthur J. Anderson, 12 vols., 1952 onward. Spanish ed. tr. Fr. Angel Garibay, 4 vols., Mexico 1956.

——, *Historia General de las Cosas de la Nueva España*, ed. Angel María Garibay, Mexico 1981.

Sandoval, Fray Prudencio de, *Historia de la vida y hechos del Emperador Carlos V*, 2 vols., Valladolid 1604–6.

Santa Cruz, Alonso de, *Crónica del Emperador, Carlos V*, 5 vols., Madrid 1920–25.

——, *Crónica de los Reyes Católicos*, ed. Juan de Mata Carriazo, Seville 1951.

Santa Teresa, *Vida, BAE*, 53–54, Madrid 1861.

Sanuto, Marino, *Diarii*, 55 vols., Venice 1887.

Serrano y Piñeda, Luciano, *Correspondencia de los Reyes Católicos con el Gran Capitán durante las campañas de Italia* in *Revista de Archivos, Bibliotecas y Museos*, vols. 20–29, 1909–13.

Splendeurs de la Cour de Bourgogne, Récits et Chroniques, Paris 1995.

Tapia, Andrés de, *Relación de algunas cosas de la que acaecieron al muy ilustre señor Hernando Cortés*, 1st ed., in Joaquín García Icazbalceta above. Eng. tr. in Patricia de Fuentes, *The Conquistadors*, Norman, OK, 1993.

Tlaxcala, Relación de, Mexico 1876.

Valera, Diego de, *Crónica de los Reyes Católicos*, Madrid 1927.

Vázquez de Tapia, Bernardino, *Información de Servicios y Méritos*, in Aguilar, Fr. Francisco, *Relación breve de la Conquista* (see above).

Warren, J. Benedict (ed.), *La Conquista de Michoacan, 1521–30*, tr. Agustín García Alcaraz, Morelia 1979.

Weiditz, Christoph, *Trachtenbuch*, 1529, facsimile ed. by Dr. Theodore Hampfe, Berlin 1927.

Zúñiga, Francescillo de, *Crónica, 1504–1527*, and *Epistolario*, in *BAE*, 36.

Zurita, Gerónimo, *Historia del rey Don Fernando el Cathólico* [sic], Saragossa 1610.

Secondary Sources, Books, and Articles

Acosta Saignes, Miguel, *Los Caribes de la Costa Venezolana*, Mexico 1946.

Addy, George M., *The Enlightenment in the University of Salamanca*, Durham, NC, 1966.

Aguado Bleye, P., " 'Tanto Monta': la Empresa de Fernando el Católico," *Revista Santa Cruz*, vol. 8, Valladolid 1949.

Aguedo Méndez, María, "Política y discurso en la conquista de México," *AEA*, 45, 1986, 67–82.

Alcalá, Ángel et al., *Inquisición Española y Mentalidad Inquisitorial*, Barcelona 1984.

Alegría, Ricardo E., "El uso de la terminología etno-histórica para designar las culturas aborígenes de las Antillas," *Cuadernos prehistóricos*, Valladolid, 1981.

Alonso, Pilar, and Alberto Gil, *La memoria de las Aljamas*, Madrid 1994.

Altman, Ida, "Spanish Hidalgos and America: The Ovandos of Cáceres," *The Americas*, 43, 3 (1957).

Altolaguirre, Angel de, *Vasco Núñez de Balboa*, Madrid 1914.

Alvar Ezquerra, Alfredo, *Isabel la Católica*, Madrid 2002.

Álvarez Rubiano, Pablo, *Pedrarias Dávila*, Madrid 1914.

Andalucía Americana: edificios vinculados con el descubrimiento y la carrera de indias, Consejería de Cultura, Junta de Andalucia, Seville 1989.

Angulo Íñiguez, Diego, "La Ciudad de Granada, visto por un pintor flamenco," *Al-Andalus*, 5, 1940.

——, *Pedro de Campaña*, Seville 1951.

Arcienegas, Germán, *Amerigo and the New World*, tr. Harriet de Onis, New York 1955.

Argenti, P., *The Occupation of Chios by the Genoese, 1346–1566*, 3 vols., Cambridge, England, 1958.

Arostegui, Cruz, *Piratas en el Caribe*, Madrid 2000.

Arranz, Luis, *Don Diego Colón*, Madrid 1982.

——, *Repartimientos y encomiendas en la isla española*, Madrid 1991.

Arrom, Juan José, *Fray Ramón Pané: Relación acerca de las antigüedades de los Indios*, Mexico 1988.

Auke, Pieter Jacobs, *Pasajeros y polizones sobre la emigración española en el siglo 16*, 1983.

Ávila, Carlos Lázaro, "Un freno a la conquista: la resistencia de los cacizagos indígenas," *R de I*, 1992.

Avilés Moreno, Guadalupe, "El arte mudéjar en Nueva España, en el siglo XVI," *AEA*, 37, 1980.

Azcona, Tarsicio, *Isabel la Católica, vida y reinado*, Madrid 2002.

Baer, Yitzak, *History of the Jews in Christian Spain*, New York 1961–66.

Ballesteros Gaibrois, Manuel, *La fundación de Buenos Aires y los indígenas*, Buenos Aires 1980.

Bataillon, Marcel, *Estudios sobre Bartolomé de las Casas*, Barcelona 1976.

——, *Erasmo y España, estudios sobre la historia espiritual del siglo XVI*, Mexico 1998 (original French ed. *Erasme et l'Espagne*, Paris 1937).

Batllori, Miguel, *La familia de los Borjas*, Madrid 1999.

Belenguer, Ernest, *El Imperio Hispánico, 1479–1665*, Barcelona 1994.

——, *Fernando el Católico*, Barcelona 1999.

——, *La corona de Aragón en la monarquía hispánica*, Barcelona 2001.

Beltrán, Juan, "Bojeo de Cuba por Sebastián de Ocampo," *Revista Bimestre Cubana*, 3, vol. 19, May–June 1924.

Benito Ruano, Eloy, *Los Orígenes del problema converso*, Barcelona 1976.

——, "La participación en la guerra de Granada," *I Congreso de la Historia de Andalucía*, Córdoba 1978.

——, *Un cruzado inglés en la guerra de Granada*, *AEM*, 9, 1979.

Bennassar, Bartolomé and Lucile, *Valladolid au siècle d'or*, Paris 1964.

——, *Inquisición Española*, Barcelona 1981.

——, *Le Voyage en Espagne*, Paris 1998.

——, *Hernán Cortés*, Madrid 2002.

Bermúdez Plata, C., *Catálogo de pasajeros a indias*, 3 vols., Seville 1946.

Bernal, Antonio-Miguel, *La Financiación de la Carrera de Indias, 1492–1824*, Seville 1992.

Bernal, Ignacio, *The Olmec World*, Berkeley, CA, 1969.

Bernand, Carmen, and Serge Gruzinski, *Histoire du nouveau monde*, Paris 1991.

Bernís, Carmen, *Trajes y modas en la España de los Reyes Católicos*, vol. 1: *Las Mujeres;* vol. 2: *Los Hombres*, Madrid 1979.

Borah, Woodrow, and Sherburne F. Cook, *Essays in Population History*, 3 vols., Berkeley, CA, 1979.

Bordejé y Morencos, Fernando de, *Tráfico de Indias y Política Oceánica*, Madrid 1991.

Bosch García, Carlos, *La esclavitud prehispánica entre los Aztecas*, Mexico 1944.

Boyd-Bowman, Peter, *Índice geobiográfico de más de 56 mil pobladores de la América Hispánica*, vol. 1: *1493–1519*, Mexico 1985.

Brading, David, *The First America: The Spanish Monarchy, Creole Patriots, and the Liberal State, 1492–1867*, Cambridge, MA, 1991.

Brandi, Carl, *Carlos V, Vida y fortuna de una personalidad y un imperio*, Madrid 1937.

Bullón y Fernández, Eloy, *Un colaborador de los reyes católicos. El doctor Palacios Rubios y sus obras*, Madrid 1927.

Cadenas y Vicent, Vicente, *Carlos I de Castilla, Señor de las Indias*, Madrid 1988.

Calderón Quijano, José Antonio, "Colón, sus cronistas e historiadores en Menéndez Pelayo," Seville, *AUH*, XVIII, 1956.

———, *Toponimia Española en el Nuevo Mundo*, Seville 1988.

Cantera Burgos, F., *Alvar García de Santa María y su familia de conversos, Historia de la judería de Burgos y de sus conversos más egregios*, Madrid 1952.

Carande, Ramón, *Homenaje a*, Madrid 1963.

———, *Galería de raros*, Madrid 1982.

———, *Carlos V y sus banqueros*, 3 vols., 3rd ed., Barcelona 1987.

———, *Estudios de Historia*, vol. 2: *Sevilla, fortaleza y otros temas sevillanos*, Barcelona 1990.

Cardaillac, Louis, *L'Espagne des Rois Catholiques, Le Prince Don Juan, symbole de l'apogée d'un règne, 1474–1500*, Paris 2000.

Caro Baroja, Julio, *Los Judeos en la España moderna*, 3 vols., Madrid 1961.

Carolus (Charles Quint), 1500–1558, Ghent 2000.

Carolus V, Imperator, Madrid 1999.

Carretero Zamora, Juan Manuel, *Cortes, monarquía, cuidades: Las Cortes de Castilla a comienzos de la época moderna, 1476–1515*, Madrid 1988.

Carril, Bonifacio del, *Los Mendoza*, Buenos Aires 1954.

Castillo Utrilla, María José del, "Temas iconográficos en las fundaciones Franciscanos en América y Filipinas en el siglo XVI," *AEA*, 38, 1981.

Castro, Americo, *La realidad histórica de España*, Mexico 1962.

———, *The Structure of Spanish History*, tr. Edmund L. King, Princeton, NJ, 1954.

Cedillo, Count of, *El Cardenal Cisneros, gobernador del reino*, 2 vols., Madrid 1921 (vol. 2 contains documents).

Cerezo Martínez, Ricardo, *La Cartografía náutica Española en los siglos XIV, XV, y XVI*, Madrid 1994.

Chabod, Federico, *Carlos Quinto y su imperio (Carlos V e il suo imperio)*, Spanish tr. from the Italian by Rodrigo Ruza, Madrid 1992.

Chacón y Calvo, José María, *Cédulario Cubano,* in *Colección de documentos inéditas para la historia de Hispano-America,* Madrid 1929.

Chagny, André, *Correspondance politique et administrative de Laurent de Gorrevod, 1517–1520,* 2 vols., Lyons 1913.

Chamberlain, Robert S., *Castilian Backgrounds of the Repartimiento-Encomienda,* Washington, DC, 1939.

Chaunu, Pierre and Huguette, *Séville et l'Atlantique, 1504–1650,* 7 vols., Paris 1955–59.

Collantes de Tirán, A., *Sevilla en la alta baja edad media,* Seville 1977.

Colón y Carvajal, Anunciada, and Guadelupe Chocano, *Cristóbal Colón, Incógnitas de su muerte, 1506–1902,* 2 vols., Madrid 1992.

Congreso de Historia de Andalucía, Córdoba 1978.

Congreso de Historia del Descubrimiento, Actas, 4 vols., Madrid 1992.

Congreso la Historia de la Corona de Aragón, Saragossa 1955.

Cooper, Edward, *Castillos señoriales de la Corona de Castilla,* 4 vols., Salamanca 1991.

Cortés Alonso, Vicenta, "La conquista de Canarias a través de las ventas de esclavos," *AEA,* 1, 1955.

——, "La producción documental en España y América en el siglo XVI," *AEA,* 41, 1984.

——, "La imagen del otro, blancos, indios, negros," *R de I,* 51, 1991.

Cotarelo y Valledor, A., *Fray Diego de Deza,* Madrid 1902.

Coury, Charles, *La médecine de l'Amérique précolombienne,* Paris 1969.

Crane, Nicholas, *Mercator: The Man Who Mapped the Planet,* London 2002.

Crosby, Alfred, W., *The Columbian Exchange,* Westport, CT, 1972.

——, *Ecological Imperialism: The Biological Expansion of Europe, 900–1900,* Cambridge, MA, 1986.

Curso de Conferencias sobre la Política Africana de los Reyes Católicos, Madrid 1953.

Deagan, Kathleen, "El impacto de la presencia europea en la Navidad (la Española)," *R de I,* 47, 1987, 713–87.

Defourneaux, Marcelin, *La vie quotidienne en Espagne au siècle d'Or,* Paris 1964.

Deive, Carlos Esteban, *La Española y la esclavitud del Indio,* Santo Domingo 1995.

Delgado Barrado, José Miguel, "Las relaciones comerciales entre España e Indias durante el siglo XVI," *R de I,* 50, 1990.

Delmarcel, Guy, *Los Honores: Flemish Tapestries for the Emperor Charles V,* Mechelen (Malines), Belgium 2000.

Diccionario de historia eclesiástica de España, ed. Quintín Aldea Vaquero et al., 4 vols., Madrid 1972.

Domínguez, L. L. (ed.), *The Conquest of the River Plate,* London 1891.

Domínguez Ortiz, Antonio, *La clase social de los conversos en la edad moderna,* Madrid 1955.

——, *Los judeo-conversos en la España moderna,* Madrid 1992.

Doussinague, José María, *Fernando el católico y el cisma de Pisa,* Madrid 1946.

——, *El testamento político de Fernando el Católico,* Madrid 1950.

Durán, Fr. Diego, *Historia de las Indias de la Nueva España,* new ed., 2 vols., Mexico 1867–80.

Duviols, J. Paul, *L'Amérique espagnole vue et revée*, Paris 1985.

Edwards, John, *The Spain of the Catholic Monarchs, 1474–1520*, Oxford 2000.

Eisenstein, Elizabeth L., *The Printing Revolution in Early Modern Europe*, Cambridge, MA, 1983.

Elliott, J. H., *Imperial Spain*, London 1963.

Enríquez de Guzmán, Alonso, *Libro de la Vida de*, ed. H. Keniston, *BAE*, 126, Madrid 1960.

Evans, Mark, *The Sforza Hours*, London 1992.

Ezquerra, Ramón, "El viaje de Pinzón y Solís al Yucatán," *R de I*, 30, 1970, 217–38.

Fernández Álvarez, Manuel, *Carlos V, el César y el Hombre*, Madrid 1999.

——, *Juana la Loca, La Cautiva de Tordesillas*, Madrid 2000.

Fernández Álvarez, Manuel, and Luis Suárez Fernández, *La España de los Reyes Católicos*, vol. 17 in the series *Historia de España*, ed. Ramón Menéndez Pidal, Madrid 1978.

Fernández-Armesto, Felipe, *The Canary Islands After the Conquest*, Oxford 1982.

——, *Before Columbus: Exploration and Colonisation from the Mediterranean to the Atlantic, 1229–1492*, London 1987.

——, *Columbus*, Oxford 1991.

Fernández Duro, Cesáreo, *Nebulosidades de Cristóbal Colón*, Madrid 1900.

Fernando el católico, pensamiento político, V Congreso de Historia de la Corona de Aragón, Saragossa 1956.

Fletcher, Richard, *Moorish Spain*, London 1992.

Ford, Richard, *A Handbook for Travellers in Spain*, 3rd ed., London 1855.

Foronda, Manuel de, *Estancias y viajes de Carlos V*, Madrid 1910.

Freyre, Gilberto, *The Mansions and the Shanties: The Making of Modern Brazil*, tr. Harriet de Onis, New York 1963.

——, *The Masters and the Slaves*, tr. Harriet de Onis, New York 1968.

García de Prodián, Lucía, *Los Judios en América*, Madrid 1966.

García de la Riega, Celso, *¿Colón español?*, Madrid 1914.

García Genaro, *Documentos inéditos o muy raros para la historia de México*, Mexico 1907, esp. vol. 15.

García Oro, J., *Galicia en los siglos XIV y XV*, 2 vols., Ponteverda 1987.

——, *El cardenal Cisneros, vida y empresas*, 2 vols., Madrid 1992–93.

——, *Cisneros, el cardenal de España*, Barcelona 2002.

García Sánchez, Francisco, *El Medellín Estremeño en América*, Medellín 1992.

García Valdecasas, Alfonso, *El Hidalgo y el honor*, Madrid 1948.

Garibay, Fr. Angel, *Historia de la literatura nahuatl*, 2 vols., Mexico 1953.

Gerbert, Marie-Claude, *Les noblesses espagnoles au Moyen Age*, Paris 1994.

Gerhard, Peter, *Geografía histórica de la Nueva España, 1519–1821*, tr. Stella Maestrangelo, Mexico 1986.

Gibson, Charles, *The Aztecs Under Spanish Rule*, Stanford, CA, 1964.

Gil, Juan, "Marinos y mercaderes en Indias, 1499–1504," *AEA*, 42, 1985, 297ff.

——, "Historiografía Española sobre el descubrimiento y los descubrimientos," *R de I*, 49, no. 187, Sept.–Dec. 1989.

——, *Mitos y utopías del descubrimiento*, 3 vols., Madrid 1989.

——, "Una familia de mercaderes sevillanos: los Cisbón," *Studi Storici in Memoria de Alberto Boscolo*, 3, Rome 1993.

——, "Las Cuentas de Cristóbal Colón," *AEA*, 41, 425ff.

——, *Los conversos y la Inquisición Sevillana*, 5 vols., Seville 2000–02.

Gilman, Stephen, *The Spain of Fernando de Rojas*, Princeton 1972.

Gil Munilla, Ladislao, "Diego de Lepe, descubridor del Marañón," *AEA*, 9, 1952, 73–99.

Giménez Fernández, Manuel, "Las bulas alejandrinas de 1493 sobre la historia y el sentido de las letras referentes a las Indias," *AEA*, 1, 1944.

——, "Hernán Cortés y su revolución comunera en la Nueva España," *AEA*, 5, 1948.

——, "El alzamiento de Fernando Cortés," *Revista de la Historia de América*, 31, Mexico, June 1951.

——, *Bartolomé de las Casas, Bibliografía crítica*, Santiago de Chile 1954.

——, *Bartolomé de las Casas*, 2 vols., Seville 1953, 1961.

——, *Breve biografía de Fray Bartolomé de las Casas*, Sevilla 1966.

Gómez, Thomas, *L'Invention de l'Amérique*, Paris 1992.

González, Julio, *Repartimiento de Sevilla*, Madrid 1951, new ed. Seville 1993.

González Jiménez, M., "Genoveses en Sevilla (siglos XIII–XV)" in *Presencia Italiana en Andalucía, siglos XIV–XVII*, Seville 1985.

González Olmedo, Félix, *Vida de Fray Fernando de Talavera, primer arzobispo de Granada*, Madrid 1931.

——, *Nebrija, debelador de la barbarie, 1441–1522*, Madrid 1942.

Gould, Alice B., *Nueva lista documentada de los tripulantes de Colón en 1492*, Madrid 1984.

Gounon-Loubens, J., *Essais sur l'administration de la Castile au XVIe siècle*, Paris 1860.

Greenblatt, Stephen, *Marvelous Possessions*, Chicago 1991.

Griffin, Clive, *Los Cromberger, la historia de una imprenta de siglo XVI en Sevilla y México*, Madrid 1991.

Grunberg, Bertrand, *L'univers des conquistadores*, Paris 1993.

Guerra, Francisco, "La epidemia americana de influenza en 1493," *AEA*, 45, 1985.

Guillén, Claude, "Un padrón de conversos sevillanos," *Bulletin Hispanique*, 65 (1965).

Gutiérrez de Santa Clara, Pedro, *Historia de las guerras civiles del Perú*, 6 vols., Madrid 1904–29.

Hamilton, Earl J., *American Treasure and the Price Revolution in Spain, 1501–1650*, Cambridge, MA, 1934.

Hanke, Lewis, *The Spanish Struggle for Justice in the Conquest of America*, Philadelphia 1949.

——, *Aristotle and the American Indians*, London 1959.

——, *All Mankind Is One*, De Kalb, IL, 1974.

Haring, C. H., *Trade and Navigation Between Spain and the Indies in the Time of the Habsburgs*, Cambridge, MA, 1918.

——, *The Spanish Empire in America*, New York 1947.

Harrisse, Henry, *The Discovery of North America*, London 1892.

Harvey, L. P., *Islamic Spain, 1250 to 1500*, Chicago 1990.

Hazañas y la Rua, Joaquín, *Maese Rodrigo Fernández de Santaella*, Seville 1909.

——, *La Imprenta en Sevilla*, Seville 1945.

Headley, John M., *The Emperor and His Chancellor*, Cambridge 1983.

Heers, Jacques, *Gènes au XVème siècle*, Paris 1961.

——, *Christophe Colomb*, Paris 1981.

Hemming, John, *Red Gold*, London 1978.

Henige, David, *Numbers from Nowhere*, unpublished, Madison, WI, c. 1996.

Heredia, Beltrán de Vicente, "Un precursor del maestro Vitoria," in *La Ciencia Tomista*, 40, 1929.

Hill, R. R., "The Office of Adelantado," *Political Science Quarterly*, 28, 1913.

Hillgarth, Jocelyn, *The Spanish Kingdoms, 1250–1516*, 2 vols., Oxford 1976–78.

Hinojosa, R., *Los despachos de la diplomacia pontificia en España*, 2 vols., Madrid 1896 (up till 1603).

Huizinga, J., *Erasmus of Rotterdam*, London 1952.

——, *The Autumn of the Middle Ages*, new tr. Rodney J. Payton and Ulrich Mammitzsch, Chicago 1996.

Hulme, Peter, *Colonial Encounters: Europe and the Native Caribbean, 1492–1797*, London 1986.

Hume, David, *History of England*, 8 vols., Dublin 1775.

Ibarra, Eduardo, "Los precendentes de la Casa de Contratación," *R de I*, 3, 4, 5, 1945.

Infessura, Stephanus, *Diario della città de Roma*, ed. Oreste Tommasini, Rome 1890.

Jacquot, Jean (ed.), *Les Fêtes de la Renaissance*, vol. 2: *Fêtes et cérémonies au temps de Charles Quint*, Paris 1960. This includes Bataillon's essay "Plus Outre: La Cour découvre le Nouveau Monde," 13–27.

Jones, R. O., *The Golden Age: Prose and Poetry*, London 1971.

Jongh, Jane de, *Margaret of Austria*, tr. from the Dutch by M. D. Herter Norton, London 1954.

Kagan, Richard (ed.), *Students and Society in Early Modern Spain*, Baltimore 1974.

——, *Ciudades del siglo de oro, las vistas Españolas de Antón van den Wyngaerde*, Madrid 1986.

Kamen, Henry, *The Spanish Inquisition: A Historical Revision*, New Haven, CT, 1997.

Kedourie, Elie (ed.), *Spain and the Jews*, London 1992.

Kellenbenz, Hermann, *Los Fugger en España y Portugal hasta 1560, Junta de Castilla y León*, Salamanca 1999.

Kendrick, T. D., *St James in Spain*, London 1960.

Keniston, Hayward, *Garcilaso de la Vega*, New York 1922.

——, *Francisco de los Cobos*, Pittsburgh 1959.

Khaldun, Ibn, *Histoire des Berbères et des dynasties musulmanes de l'Afrique septentrionale*, tr. and repr. Paris 1969.

Klein, Julius, *The Mesta: A Study in Spanish Economic History*, Cambridge, MA, 1920.

Kobayashi, José María, *La educación como conquista, empresa franciscana en México*, Mexico 1974.

Konetzke, Richard, *El Imperio Español: Origenes y Fundamentos,* tr. from the German, Madrid 1946.

——, "La emigración española al Río de la Plata," in vol. 3 of *Miscelánea Americanista,* CSIC, Madrid 1953.

——, *The Americas,* vol. 14, 1958.

Kriegel, Maurice, "La prise d'une décision, l'exclusion des juifs de l'Espagne en 1492," *Revue Historique,* 260, 1978.

Kubler, George, *Arquitectura Mexicana del siglo XVI,* Mexico 1983.

Kubler, George, and Martin Soria, *Art and Architecture in Spain and Portugal and Their American Dominions, 1500 to 1800,* Harmondsworth 1959.

Ladero Quesada, Miguel Angel, *Castilla y la conquista del reino de Granada,* Valladolid 1967.

——, "Les finances royales de Castille à le vieille des temps modernes," *Annales,* May–June 1970, 775–88.

——, *Los señores de Andalucía,* Seville 1973, Cadiz 1998.

——, *La Ciudad Medieval, historia de Sevilla,* Valladolid 1980.

——, *España Colombina,* Barcelona 1990.

——, *Andalucía en torno a 1492,* Madrid 1992.

——, *La Incorporación de Granada en la corona de Castilla, actas de symposium,* Granada 1993.

——, *La paz y la guerra en la época del Tratado de Tordesillas,* Valladolid 1994.

——, *La España de los Reyes Católicos,* Madrid 1999.

——, *Isabel la Católica y la política,* Instituto de Historia, Simancas, Valladolid 2001.

——, *El primer oro de América,* Madrid 2002.

——, *Grandes batallas: Las guerras de Granada en el siglo XV,* Barcelona 2002.

Ladero Quesada, Miguel Angel, with Manuel González Jiménez, *Diezmos eclesiásticos y producción de cereales en el reino de Sevilla, 1408–1503,* Seville 1979.

Lafaye, Jacques, *Los albores de la imprenta: el libro en España y Portugal, y sus posesiones de ultramar,* Mexico 2002.

Lamb, Ursula, "Una biografía contemporánea y una carta de frey Nicolás de Ovando . . . [November 1509]," *Revista de Estudios Extremeños,* vols. 3–4, Badajoz 1951, 693–707.

——, "Cristóbal de Tapia vs. Nicolás de Ovando", in *HAHR,* 33, Aug. 1953, 427–42.

——, *Frey Nicolás de Ovando,* introduction by Miguel Muñoz de San Pedro, Madrid 1956.

La Peña y de la Camera, José María de, "A list of Spanish *residencias* in the Archivo de Indias, 1516–1775," Library of Congress reference dept., Washington, DC, 1955.

La Torre, A. de, *Documentos sobre las relaciones internacionales de los Reyes Católicos,* 6 vols., Madrid 1949–51.

Lawson, Edward W., *The Discovery of Florida and Its Discoverer Juan Ponce de León,* St. Augustine 1946.

Lea, H. C., *A History of the Inquisition of Spain,* 3 vols., New York 1906.

Leonard, Irving, *Books of the Brave,* New York 1949.

Levene, Richard, "Introducción a la historia del derecho indiano," *BRAH,* 1924, 56–57.

Levenson, Jay A. (ed.), *Circa 1492: Art in the Age of Exploration*, New Haven 1991.

Lewis, C. S., *Studies in Mediaeval and Renaissance Literature*, Cambridge 1998.

Liss, Peggy, *Isabel the Queen*, Oxford 1992.

Llorente, Juan Antonio, *Historia crítica de la inquisición de España*, 10 vols., Madrid 1822.

Lobo Cabrera, Manuel, *La Esclavitud en las Canarias orientales en el siglo XVI*, Santa Cruz de Tenerife 1982.

——, "Esclavos negros a Indias a través de Gran Canaria," *AEA*, 45, 1985.

Lockhart, James M., *The Men of Cajamarca*, Austin 1972.

Lohmann, Guillermo, *Les Espinosa: une famille d'hommes d'affaires en Espagne et aux Indes à l'époque de la colonisation*, Paris 1968.

López, Lorenzo E., and Justo del Río Moreno, "Commercio y azúcar en la economía del azúcar antillano durante el siglo XVI," *AEA*, 49, 55–87.

Lorenzo, Eufemio Sanz, *Historia de Medina del Campo y su tierra*, 2 vols., esp. vol. 2: *Auge de las Ferias*, Valladolid 1986.

Los Franciscanos y el Nuevo Mundo, La Rábida 1992.

Lovén, Sven, *Origins of the Taino Culture*, Göteborg 1935.

Lynn, Caro, *A College Professor of the Renaissance*, Chicago 1937.

Mackay, Angus, *Spain in the Middle Ages, from Frontier to Empire, 1000–1500*, London 1977.

——, *Society, Economy and Religion in Late Mediaeval Castile*, London 1987.

Magnaghi, Alberto, *Americo Vespucci*, Studio Crítico, Rome 1926.

Mahn-Lot, Marianne, *Bartolomé de las Casas*, Paris 1982.

Mallett, Michael, *The Borgias: The Rise and Fall of a Renaissance Dynasty*, London 1969.

Manareu, Mahn, *Bartolomé de las Casas*, Paris 1966.

Manzano y Manzano, Juan, *La incorporación de las Indias a la corona de Castilla*, Madrid 1948.

——, *Cristóbal Colón, siete años decisivos de su vida, 1485–1492*, Madrid 1964.

——, *Colón y su secreto: el predescubrimiento*, Madrid 1976, 3rd ed. 1989.

——, *Los Pinzones y el descubrimiento de América*, 3 vols., Madrid 1988.

Maravall, José Antonio, *Carlos V y el pensamiento político del Renacimiento*, Madrid 1960.

Marcus, Raymond, *El primer decenio de las Casas en el Nuevo Mundo*, Ibero-American Archives, 1977.

Mariejol, J. H., *The Spain of Ferdinand and Isabella*, tr. Benjamin Keene, New Brunswick 1961.

Marrero, Levi, *Cuba: economía y sociedad*, vol. 1, Barcelona 1972.

Martínez, José Luis, *Hernán Cortés*, with 4 vols. of *Documentos cortesianos*, Mexico 1990.

Martínez del Peral Fortón, Rafael, *Las armas blancas en España e Indias*, Madrid 1992.

Martínez del Río de Redo, Marita, *La Fuerza y el Viento: La piratería en los mares de la Nueva España*, Mexico 2002.

Martínez-Hidalgo, José María, *Las naves del descubrimiento y sus hombres*, Madrid 1992.

Martínez Shaw, Carlos (ed.), *Sevilla, siglo XVI,* Madrid 1993.

Mattingly, Garrett, *Renaissance Diplomacy,* London 1973.

Maura Gamazo, Gabriel, *El Príncipe que murió de amor,* Madrid 1944.

Mayr-Harting, Henry, and R. I. Moore (eds.), *Studies in Medieval History Presented to R. H. C. Davis,* London 1985.

McNeill, W. H., *Plagues and Peoples,* Oxford 1977.

Méchoulan, Henri, *Les juifs d'Espagne, histoire d'une diaspora, 1492–1992,* Paris 1992.

Melis, F., *I mercanti italiani nell' Europa medievale e rinascimentale,* introduction by Hermann Kellenbenz, Florence 1990.

Mena García, Carmen, "El traslado de la Ciudad de Nombre de Dios a Portobelo," *AEA,* 40, 71–102.

——, *Pedrarias Dávila,* Seville 1992.

——, *Sevilla y las flotas de Indias,* Seville 1998.

Méndez Bejarano, M., *Histoire de la juiverie de Séville,* Madrid 1922.

Menéndez Pidal, Ramón (ed.), *La Idea Imperial de Carlos V,* Buenos Aires 1941.

——, *La Lengua de Cristóbal Colón,* Madrid 1958.

——, *Historia de España,* vol. 18: *La España de los Reyes Católicos,* Madrid 1978, pt. 1 by Luis Suárez Fernández and Juan de la Mata Carriazo; pt. 2 by Luis Suárez Fernández and Manuel Fernández Álvarez.

Mercado Sousa, Elsa, *El hombre y la tierra en Panamá (siglo XVI) según las primeras fuentes,* Madrid 1959.

Merriman, R. B., *The Rise of the Spanish Empire in the Old World and in the New,* 4 vols., New York 1918–38.

Milhou, Alain, *Colón y su mentalidad mesiánica,* Valladolid 1903.

Mira Caballos, Esteban, "Las licencias de esclavos negros a Hispanoamérica, 1544–50," *R de I,* 44, 1994.

Modica, Anne-Marie, *Discussions actuelles sur l'origine de syphilis,* Marseilles 1970.

Molina Martínez, Miguel, "El soldado cronista y su impresión del mundo indígeno," *AEA,* 41, 1984.

Moorhead, Max, "Hernán Cortés and the Tehuantepec Passage," *HAHR,* vol. 29, 321–80, 1949.

Morales Padrón, Francisco, *Jamaica Española,* Seville 1952.

——, "Descubrimiento y toma de posesión," *AEA,* 12, 1955.

——, *Historia de Sevilla, La ciudad del quinientos,* Seville 1989.

Morell Peguero, B., *Mercaderes y artesanos en la Sevilla del descubrimiento,* Seville 1986.

Morison, Samuel Eliot, *Admiral of the Ocean Sea,* 2 vols., Boston 1942.

——, *The European Discovery of America: The Northern Voyages,* Oxford 1971.

——, *The European Discovery of America: The Southern Voyages, 1491–1616,* New York 1974.

Mörner, Magnus, *La mezcla de razas en la historia de América Latina,* Buenos Aires 1969.

Moulin, Anne-Marie, and Robert Delort, "Syphilis: le mal américain," *L'Histoire,* 63, 1984, 87.

Muñoz de San Pedro, Miguel, *Francisco de Lizaur, hidalgo indiano de principios del siglo XVI*, Madrid 1948.

——, *Extremadura del siglo XV en tres de sus paladines*, Madrid 1964.

Murga Sanz, Vicente, *Juan Ponce de León*, San Juan 1971.

Muro Orejón, Antonio, "El problema de los reinos Indianos," *AEA*, 28, 45–56.

——, *Ordenanzes Reales sobre las Indias. Las leyes de Burgos, 1512–1513*, Seville 1956.

Nader, Helen, *The Mendoza Family in the Spanish Renaissance, 1350–1550*, New Brunswick, NJ, 1979.

Netanyahu, Benzion, *The Marranos of Spain*, New York 1966.

——, *Isaac Abravanel*, Philadelphia 1972.

——, *The Origins of the Inquisition in Fifteenth-Century Spain*, New York 1995.

——, *Toward the Inquisition*, Ithaca 1997.

Nordenskjöld, E., "The Guaraní Invasion of the Inca Empire in the Sixteenth Century," *Geographical Review*, New York 1917.

Núñez Jiménez, Antonio, *El Almirante en la tierra más hermosa. Los viajes de Colón a Cuba*, Cadiz 1989.

Obregón, Mauricio, *Colón en el Mar de los Caribes*, Bogota 1990.

——, *The Columbus Papers*, New York 1991.

O'Connor, John J., *Amadís de Gaula and Its Influence on Elizabethan Literature*, New Brunswick, NJ, 1970.

O'Gorman, Edmundo, *La idea del descubrimiento de América*, Mexico 1951.

Olmedo, Félix González, *Nebrija, 1441–1522*, Madrid 1942.

Olschki, Leonardo, "Ponce de León's Fountain of Youth," *HAHR*, 21, August 1941.

——, "Hernán Pérez de Oliva's 'Ystoria de Colón,' " *HAHR*, 23, May 1943, 165–96.

El Oro y la Plata de las Indias en la Época de los Austrias, Fundación ICO, Madrid 1999.

Orti Belmonte, Miguel A., *Ovando y Solís de Cáceres*, Badajoz 1932.

——, *La vida de Cáceres en los siglos XIII y XXVII*, Cáceres 1949.

Ortiz, Fernando, "La 'leyenda negra' contra Bartolomé de las Casas," *Cuadernos Americanos*, 45, 5, 1952, 146–84.

Otero Enríquez, Santiago, *Noticias genealógicas de la familia Velázquez Gaztelu*, Madrid 1996.

Otte, Enrique, "Documentos inéditos sobre la estancia de Gonzalo Fernández de Oviedo en Nicaragua," *R de I*, 74–75, 1958.

——, "Aspiraciones y actividades heterogéneas de Gonzalo Fernández de Oviedo, cronista," *R de I*, 71, 1958.

——, "El joven Carlos y América," in *Homenaje a Don Ramón Caranda*, Madrid 1963.

——, "La flota de Diego Colón," *Españoles y Genoveses en el comercio transatlántico, 1509; R de I*, 95–96, 1964, 475ff.

——, "Die Negersklavenlizenz des Laurent de Gorrevod," in *Spanische Forschungen der Görregesellschaft*, Erste Reihe, 22, 283–320, Münster 1965.

——, *Las Perlas del Caribe*, Caracas 1977.

——, "Cartas de Diego de Ordaz," in *Historia Mexicana, Cartas privadas de emigrantes a Indias*, Seville 1988.

——, "Los mercaderes transatlánticos bajo Carlos V," *AEA*, 47, 1990.

——, *Sevilla y sus mercaderes a fines de la Edad Media*, Seville 1996.

Pagden, Anthony, *The Fall of Natural Man: The American Indian and the Origins of Comparative Ethnology*, Cambridge 1982.

——, *European Encounters with the New World*, New Haven 1993.

Parish, Helen, with Harold Weideman, S. J., "The Correct Birthdate of Bartolomé de las Casas," *HAHR*, 56.

Parker, John (ed.), *Merchants and Scholars: Essays on the History of Exploration and Trade, Collected in Memory of James Ford Bell*, Minneapolis 1965.

Parry, John H., *The Establishment of the European Hegemony*, London 1961.

——, *The Spanish Seaborne Empire*, London 1966.

Pastor, Ludwig von, *History of the Popes*, tr. by Frederick Ignatius Antrobus, London 1898.

Paz y Melia, A., *El Cronista Alonso de Palencia*, Madrid 1914.

Pérez, Joseph, *Carlos V*, Madrid 1999.

——, *Los comuneros*, Madrid 2001.

Pérez de Tudela, Juan, "Política de contratación," *R de I*, 15, 1955.

——, *Las armadas de Indias, y los orígenes de la política de la colonización*, CSIC, Instituto Jerónimo Zurita, Madrid 1956.

——, *Mirabilis in altis*, Madrid 1983.

Phillips, Carla Rahn, *Ciudad Real, 1500–1750*, Cambridge, MA, 1979.

——, *Six Galleons for the King of Spain*, Baltimore 1986.

Pike, Ruth, *Enterprise and Adventure: The Genoese in Seville*, Ithaca, 1966.

——, *Aristocrats and Traders: Sevillean Society in the Sixteenth Century*, Ithaca 1966.

——, *Linajudos and Conversos in Seville*, New York 2000.

Pohl, Frederick J., *Amerigo Vespucci*, London 1966.

Poiret, Marie Françoise, *Le Monastère de Brou*, Paris 2001.

Porrás Muñoz, Guillermo, "Un capitán de Cortés, Bernardino Vázquez de Tapia," *AEA*, 5, 1948, 325–62.

Prescott, William H., *The Art of War in Spain: The Conquest of Granada, 1481–1492*, ed. Alfred D. McJoynt, London 1995 (and the chapters dealing with war in Prescott's *History of the Reign of Ferdinand and Isabella*, 3 vols., 1838).

Pulido Rubio, José, *El piloto mayor de la Casa de la Contratación de Sevilla*, Seville 1950.

Ramos Gómez, Luis, "Castillo del Oro," *AEA*, 37, 1980, 45–67.

——, "Los Lucayos guías náuticas," *R de I*, 49, 1986.

——, *El conflicto de las lanzas jinetes*, Santo Domingo 1992.

——, "El Repudio al Tratado de Tordesillas," Congreso Nacional de la Historia, Salamanca 1992.

——, (ed.), *La carta de Colón sobre el descubrimiento*, Granada 1983.

Ranke, L. von, *The Ottoman and the Spanish Empires in the Sixteenth and Seventeenth Centuries*, London 1843.

Real Díaz, José J., *El sevillano Rodrigo de Bastidas*, Archivo Hispalense, 2nd epoch, 36, 1962, 63ff.

Reitz, Elizabeth J., "Dieta y alimentación hispano-americana en el caribe . . . en el siglo XVI," *R de I*, 51, 1991.

Remesal, Agustín, *1494, La Raya de Tordesillas*, Valladolid 1994.

Resplendence of the Spanish Monarchy, New York 1991.

Reverte, Javier (ed.), *Exploradores españoles olvidados de los siglos XVI y XVII*, Madrid 2000.

Reyes y Mecenas, Madrid 1992.

Ricard, Robert, *The Spiritual Conquest of Mexico*, tr. Lesley Byrd Simpson, Berkeley 1974.

Rodríguez Demorizi, Emilio, *Los dominicos y las encomiendas en la Isla Española*, Santo Domingo 1971.

Rodríguez González, Ricardo, *Mercaderes castellanos del siglo de Oro*, Valladolid 1995.

Rodríguez Moñino, A., *Los pintores badajoceños del siglo* XVI, Badajoz 1956.

Rodríguez Prampolini, A., *Amadises de America. La hazaña de Indias como empresa caballeresca*, Mexico 1948.

Rodríguez Sánchez, Angel, *La población cacereña en el siglo* XVI, Salamanca 1976.

Rodríguez Villa, Antonio, *Bosquejo biográfico de la reina Juana*, Madrid 1874.

Romoli, Kathleen, *Balboa of Darien*, New York 1953.

Rosa Olivera, L. de la, "Francisco de Riberol y la colonia genovesa en Canarias," *AEA*, 18, 1972, 61–198.

Rosenblat, Angel, *La población indígena y el mestizaje en América*, 2 vols., Buenos Aires 1954.

——, *La población de América en 1492*, Mexico 1967.

Rouse, Irving, *The Tainos: Rise and Decline of the People Who Greeted Columbus*, New Haven 1992.

Ruiz-Domènec, José Enrique, *El Gran Capitán*, Barcelona 2002.

Ruiz Rivera y Manuela, Julián, and Cristina García Bernal, *Cargadores a Indias*, Madrid 1992.

Rumeu de Armas, Antonio, "Colón en Barcelona," *AEA*, 1944, 437–511.

——, *Piraterías y ataques navales contra las Islas Canarias*, vol. 1, CSIC, Instituto Jerónimo Zurita, Madrid 1947.

——, "Cristóbal Colón y doña Beatriz de Bobadilla," *AEA*, 28, 343–78.

——, *Alonso de Lugo en la corte de los Reyes Católicos, 1496–1497*, Madrid 1952.

——, *Itinerario de los Reyes Católicos, 1474–1516*, Madrid 1974.

Rummel, Erika, *Jiménez de Cisneros*, Tempe 1999.

Russell, Peter, *Prince Henry the Navigator*, New Haven, CT, 2000.

Saco, José Antonio, *Historia de la Esclavitud de la Raza Africana en el Nuevo Mundo*, 4 vols., Havana 1938.

Sáenz de Santa María, Carmelo, "La hueste de Alvarado en Perú," *AEA*, 43, 1983.

Salas, Alberto, *Tres Cronistas de Indias*, Mexico 1986.

Sale, Kirkpatrick, *The Conquest of Paradise*, London 1991.

Sánchez Blanco, Francisco, "Descubrimiento de la variedad humana . . . el impacto del nuevo mundo," *AEA*, 45, 1985.

Sánchez Gonzalez, António, *Medinaceli y Colón,* Madrid 1995.

Santillana, el Marqués de, *Los albores de la España Moderna,* 4 vols., Hondarribia 2001.

Sauer, Carl Ortwin, *The Early Spanish Main,* Berkeley, CA, 1966.

Sayous, A. E., "Les débuts du commerce de l'Espagne avec l'Amérique d'aprés de minutes inédites des archives notariales de Seville," *Revue Historique,* 1934.

Scelle, Georges, *La Traite négrière aux Indes de Castille,* 2 vols., Paris 1906.

Schäfer, Erns, *El Consejo Real y supremo de las Indias,* 2 vols., Seville 1935.

Schick, Léon, *Un grand homme d'affaires au début du XVIème siècle: Jacob Fugger,* Paris 1957.

Schwaller, John, "Tres familias mexicanas del siglo XVI," *Historia Mexicana,* 122, 1981.

Serrano, F. Luciano, *Los conversos D. Pablo de Santa María y D. Alfonso de Cartagena,* Madrid 1942.

Serrano y Sanz, Manuel, *Los amigos y protectores aragoneses de Cristóbal Colón,* Madrid 1918, reissued Barcelona 1991.

——, *Las orígenes de la dominación española en las Indias,* Madrid 1918, reissued Barcelona 1991.

Sicroff, Albert A., *Les Controverses des statuts de pureté de sang en Espagne du XVe au XVIIè siècle,* Paris 1960.

Simpson, L. B., *The Encomienda in New Spain, 1492–1550,* Berkeley, CA, 1934.

Skinner, Quentin, *Visions of Politics,* vol. 2: *Renaissance Virtues,* Cambridge 2002.

Soisson, Jean-Pierre, *Marguerite, Princesse de Bourgogne,* Paris 2002.

Spivakovsky, Erika, *Son of the Alhambra: Don Diego Hurtado de Mendoza, 1504–1575,* Austin 1970.

Suárez Fernández, Luis, *Historia de España: La España de los Reyes Católicos,* Edad Media, Madrid 1969.

——, *Documentos acerca de la expulsión de los judíos de España,* Madrid 1991.

——, *La expulsión de los judios de España,* Madrid 1991.

——, *Homenaje* (essays), Valladolid 1991.

——, *Isabel I, Reina,* Barcelona 2000.

——, *Enrique IV de Castilla,* Barcelona 2001.

——, *Nobleza y Monarquía,* Madrid 2002.

Subirats, Eduardo, *El Continente Vacío,* Mexico 1994.

Super, John C., *Food, Conquest, and Civilization in Sixteenth-Century Spanish America,* Albuquerque, NM, 1988.

Sweet, D. G., and Gary B. Nash (eds.), *Struggle and Survival in Colonial America,* Berkeley 1981.

Tate, Robert B., *Joan Margarit i Pau, Cardinal-Bishop of Gerona,* Manchester 1955.

Thomas, Henry, *Spanish and Portuguese Romances of Chivalry,* Cambridge 1920.

Thomas, Hugh, *The Conquest of Mexico,* London 1993.

——, *Quién es quién en la conquista de México,* Barcelona 2001.

Tibesaar, Fr. Antonino, "The Franciscan Order of the Holy Cross of Española, 1505–1559," *The Americas,* vol. 43, 3, 1957.

Tío, Aurelio, *Nuevas Fuentes para la historia de Puerto Rico,* San Germán 1961.

Todorov, Tzvetan, *La conquête de l'Amérique*, Paris 1982.

Tordesillas 1494, Madrid 1994.

Touissant, Manuel, *La conquista de Pánuco*, Mexico 1948.

Tra siviglia e Genova: notaio, documento e commercio nell'eta colombina, Milan 1994.

Trueba, Eduardo, *Sevilla Maritima*, Seville 1990.

Trueta Raspall, J., *The Spirit of Catalonia*, London 1946.

Valdeón Baruque, Julio, *España y el sacro imperio*, Valladolid 2001.

——, (ed.), *Isabel la Católica y la Política*, Instituto de Historia Simancas, Valladolid 2001.

Valdivieso, María, *Isabel la Católica, Princesa*, Valladolid 1974.

Vaquero Serrano, María Carmen, *Garcilaso, poeta de amor, caballero de la guerra*, Madrid 2002.

Varela, Consuelo, "El rol del cuarto viaje colombino," *AEA*, 42, 1985.

——, "El testamento de Amerigo Vespucci," *Historiografía y Bibliografía Americanistas*, 30, 2, Seville 1986.

——, "La Isabela," *R de I*, 47, 3, 1987, 733ff.

——, *Colón y los florentinos*, Madrid 1988.

——, *Cristóbal Colón, retrato de un hombre*, Madrid 1992.

Vasari, *Lives of the Painters*, Everyman ed., London 1927.

Velasco Bayón, Balbino, "El conquistador de Nicaragua, Gabriel de Rojas," *AEA*, 1985.

——, *Historia de Cuéllar*, 4th ed., Segovia 1996.

Verlinden, Charles, *L'esclavage dans l'Europe mediévale*, vol. 1, Bruges 1955.

——, "La population de l'Amérique précolombienne: Une question de méthode," in *Mélanges Fernand Braudel*, Toulouse 1973.

Vicens Vives, J., *Política del rey Católico en Cataluña*, Barcelona 1940.

——, *Historia Social*, Barcelona 1959.

——, *Historia crítica de la vida y reinado de Fernando II de Aragón*, Saragossa 1962.

Vincent, Bernard, *1492, "L'Année admirable,"* Aubier 1991.

Voche, Henri de, *John Dantiscus and His Netherlandish Friends as Revealed by the Correspondence*, Louvain 1961.

Walls y Merino, Manuel, *Primer viaje alrededor del mundo*, Madrid 1899.

Washburn, Wilcomb, "The Meaning of 'Discovery' in the Fifteenth and Sixteenth Centuries," *AHR*, Oct. 1962.

Wauchope, Robert (ed.), *Handbook of Middle American Indians*, 16 vols., Austin 1964–1976.

Weber, David J., *The Spanish Frontier in North America*, New Haven 1992.

Weckman, Luis, "Las bulas alejandrinas de 1493 y la teoría política del papado medieval," *Publicaciones del Instituto de Historia*, 2, Mexico 1949.

——, *La Herencia medieval de México*, Mexico 1984.

Wilson, Edward M., and Duncan Noir, *A Literary History of Spain: The Golden Age of Drama*, London 1971.

Wright, I. A., "The Commencement of the Cane Sugar Industry in America," *AHR*, 21, 1916.

——, *The Early History of Cuba,* New York 1916.

Zavala, Silvio, *Sir Thomas More in New Spain,* New York 1955.

——, *Recuerdo de Vasco de Quiroga,* Mexico 1965.

——, *Las instituciones jurídicas en la conquista de América,* 3rd ed., Mexico 1988.

Zweig, Stefan, *Magellan,* Barcelona 1955.

Notes

Sources cited often are referred to by abbreviations. Otherwise, the reference is indicated as follows: the full title of a work is given at its first mention; thereafter, the book, article, or other source is shown by citing in square brackets, after the author's name, the chapter in which the work was first mentioned, then the note number. Thus Azcona [1:21] means that the full title, etc., of the work by Azcona will be found in chapter 1, note 21. The abbreviations below refer to the editions of the work used, not necessarily the best.

Note: Many footnotes in Spanish have been included because so often the language of the golden age in Spain has a fascination all its own.

Abbreviations

AEA: Anuario de Estudios Americanos
AEM: Anuario de Estudios Medievales
AGI: Archivo General de las Indias
AGS: Archivo General de Simancas
AHR: American Historical Review
APS: Archivo de Protocolos, Seville
BAE: Biblioteca de Autores Españoles
BAGN: Boletín del Archivo General de la Nación, Mexico
BRAH: Boletín de la Real Academia de la Historia, Madrid
CDI: Colección de documentos inéditos relativos al descubrimiento, conquista, y organización de las posesiones españolas en América y Oceania, 42 vols., Madrid 1864–89, ed. Joaquín Pacheco and Francisco Cárdenas
CDIU: Colección de documentos inéditos relativos al descubrimiento, conquista, y organización de las antiguas posesiones españolas de ultramar, 25 vols., Madrid 1880–1932
cit: cited
Cu: Cuadernos Americanos
ed: edition; edited by
f: folio
fn: footnote
Fr: Father, sometimes Fray
HAHR: Hispanic American Historical Review
intr: introduced by
Las Casas: Bartolomé de las Casas, *Historia de las Indias,* ed. M. Aguilar, 3 vols., Madrid 1927
leg: *legajo*
lib: *libro*

Lic.: licenciado

mgr.: monsignor

ms.: maravedís

NF: Neue Folge

Oviedo: Gonzalo Fernández de Oviedo, *Historia general y natural de las Indias,* 5 vols., ed. Juan Pérez de Tudela, Madrid 1959

p: *pieza,* i.e., piece (in archives)

qu.: quoted by

r.: *ramo,* i.e., section (in archives)

r: recto, i.e., right side (in folio pages)

R de I: Revista de Indias

repr.: reprinted by

res.: *residencia* of

tr.: translation; translated by

v: verso, the other side (in folio pages)

vol.: volume

Chapter 1

1. Tr. L. P. Harvey, *Islamic Spain, 1250–1500,* Chicago 1990, 219.

2. In a town once known to the Muslims as Atqua and, to the Christians, as Ojos de Huéscar. Peter Martyr reported that the fire had been caused by a piece of "candlewood," a resinous tree used to give light, dropped in the Queen's tent (*Epistolario,* in *Documentos inéditos para la historia de España,* Madrid 1953 [hereafter Martyr], 9, 160).

3. In 1483, he had led 350 lances against the Moors and had been named commander (*alcaide*) of the fortress in the city of Jaén, when the Moors had withdrawn. He was also cousin of a famous royal minister of another generation, Álvaro de Luna. For his subsequent actions, see ch. 9 below.

4. Martyr [1:2], 91.

5. "el de las hazañas." It would be interesting to know if this Pulgar, like the historian of the same name, was a *converso.*

6. Martyr [1:2], 91.

7. Ludwig von Pastor, *History of the Popes,* tr. Frederick Ignatius Antrobus, London 1898, 5, 338.

8. See Petrus Christus II's *Our Lady of Granada,* usually dated "c. 1500," now in the Museo del Castillo, in Peretallada. See illustration in this book, at end of first plate section, and Diego Angulo Íñiguez, "La Ciudad de Granada, vista por un pintor flamenco," in *Al-Andalus,* 5, 1940, 460–70.

9. Antoine de Lalaing, *Rélation du premier voyage de Philippe le Beau en Espagne, en 1501,* Brussels 1876, 204–8.

10. Those who had fled from Antequera had in Granada their own quartier, La Antequerela.

11. See Ibn Khaldun, *Histoire des Berbères et des dynasties musulmanes de l'Afrique septentrionale,* tr. and repr., Paris 1969, 4, 74.

12. Circular letter of King Yusuf III of Granada, c. 1415, found in Aragon and published by J. Ribera and M. Asín, *Manuscritos árabes y aljamiados de la Biblioteca de la Junta,* Madrid 1912, 259, cit. L. P. Harvey [1:1], 59.

13. These figures come from Ladero Quesada in "Isabel y los musulmanes," in *Isabel la Católica y la política,* Instituto de Historia de Simancas, Valladolid 2001.

14. The more popular designation *moros* was often used, too, and the place where they lived, *morerías.* Muslims who became Christians were known as *moriscos. Mudéjares* were known as *sarracenos* in Aragon.

15. Abu' l'-Abbas Ahmad al-Wanshari, c. 1510, qu. Harvey [1:1], 58.

16. *Las Siete Partidas,* ed. Francisco López Estrada and María Teresa López García-Berdoy, Madrid 1992, 420: "deben vivir los moros entre los cristianos en aquella misma manera que . . . lo deben hacer los judios; guardando su ley y no denostando la nuestra . . . en seguridad de ellos no les deben tomar ni robar lo suyo por fuerza."

17. *Historia del Abencerraje y la hermosa Jarifa,* perhaps Antonio Villegas, Madrid 1551–65.

18. Six hundred eighty-three slaves were given to prelates or knights, seventy to Cardinal Mendoza. A few were sent to the Pope.

19. Alfonso de Palencia, *Crónica de Enrique IV, Historia de la guerra de Granada,* ed. A. Paz y Melia, *Biblioteca de Autores Españoles* (hereafter *BAE*), vols. 257, 258, Madrid 1973–75, 57. Merlo was the Crown's man in Seville, the *asistente.*

20. Luis Suárez, *Isabel I, Reina,* Barcelona 2000, 221.

21. Tarsicio Azcona, *Isabel la Católica, Vida y Reinado,* Madrid 2002, 184.

22. J. Masía Vilanova, "Una política de defensa mediterránea en la España del siglo XVI," in *Fernando el Católico, pensamiento político, V Congreso de Historia de la Corona de Aragón,* Saragossa 1956, 99ff. See also W. H. Prescott, *The Art of War in Spain: The Conquest of Granada, 1481–92,* London 1995 (a reprinted version of his chapters on the war in his life of Fernando and Isabel), 181.

23. L. P. Harvey [1:1], 228, 256.

24. Hernando del Pulgar, *Crónica de los Reyes Católicos,* Madrid 1770, 177–79.

25. Macchiavelli, *The Prince,* tr. and ed. by George Bull, London 1961, 119. Macchiavelli said: "In our own time we have Fernando of Aragón the present king of Spain. He can be regarded as a new prince because, from being a weak monarch, he has risen to being, for fame and glory, the first king of Christendom. If you study his achievements, you will find that they were all magnificent and some of them unparalleled. At the start of his reign, he attacked Granada and that campaign laid the foundation of his power." Sir John Elliott (*Imperial Spain,* London 1963, 34) similarly wrote: "A vigorous renewal of the war against Granada would do more than anything else to rally the country behind its new rulers."

Chapter 2

1. In the twentieth century, Don Juan told his son Don Juan Carlos that he, too, "had to be nomadic" (*El País,* November 20, 2000, 29).

2. Antonio Rumeu de Armas, *Itinerario de los Reyes Católicos, 1474–1516,* Madrid 1974, 157–64; 179–83.

3. See the list of such journeys in Rumeu de Armas [2:2], 14–15, and fns 3–18.

4. The point is made by Azcona [1:21], 371.

5. The tradition is that the Flemish fifteenth-century tapestries near the tombs of these monarchs in the cathedral at Granada were among those carried around by them. But Isabel had 370 tapestries, it is said.

6. Suárez, [1:20], 120, uses the word "theatrical" for these.

7. The imperial chancellor of Charles V, Gattinara, thought that the peripatetic court had a Roman precedent. See A. H. M. Jones, *The Later Roman Empire,* Oxford 1964, 1, 366–67. The "comitatus," the combination of ministries attached to the Emperor, constituted "in fact a migratory body." The dukes of Burgundy were equally nomadic, and so was the Emperor Maximilian. For their remarkable travels, see *Collection des voyages des souverains des Pays-Bas,* ed. M. Gachard, vol. 1, Brussels 1876, 9–104.

8. This order had been founded in the fourteenth century and had by 1490 about thirty-five priories.

9. The sense of a lost past is powerfully experienced today if one visits La Mejorada, where the once splendid patios are covered by mallows, and wild dogs roam the cells: "Corn is where Troy was."

10. According to Lorenzo Galíndez de Carvajal (*Anales Breves de los Reyes Católicos,* in *Colección de documentos inéditos para la historia de España,* Madrid 1851, vol. 18, 229–30), "Los reyes tenían un libro y en él memoria de los hombres de más habilidad y méritos para los cargos que vacasen, y lo mismo para la provisión de los obispados y dignidades eclesiásticas."

11. It survives as the famous Parador there.

12. The only king to return to Asturias before Charles V went there involuntarily in 1517 was Pedro the Cruel.

13. See Luis Suárez, *Nobleza y Monarquía,* Madrid 2002, 145.

14. Richard Kagan (ed.), *Cuidades del Siglo de Oro: Las vistas españolas de Anton van den Wyngaerde,* Madrid 1986, 70.

15. Christoph Weiditz, *Trachtenbuch,* 1529, in Deutsches Museum, Nuremberg, and facsimile edition of Dr. Theodore Hampe, Berlin 1928. Weiditz came to Spain in the train of the Polish ambassador Dantiscus. The relation is a happy reminder that there have been times when rich Poles have helped poor Germans.

16. Otherwise Philippe de Bigarn of Langres in Burgundy, the great master of sculpture in the cathedral of Burgos. Perhaps he was from Burgos. His life was long, his production varied.

17. Most people would say that the best portrait is the anonymous one given by her to the Cartuja de Miraflores, now in the Palacio Real in Madrid. Other good portraits of Isabel are to be seen in the Real Academia de la Historia, the Museo del Prado, with Fernando and alone, and in the Royal Collection, Windsor, England. There is also, but not from life, the fine sculpture on her tomb in Granada by Domenico Fancelli (c. 1514). See Azcona [1:21], 18–19, for a discussion.

18. Queen Isabel the mother only died in 1496, already far removed from sanity for many years.

19. Azcona [1:21], 89, comments that she was "de espléndida belleza pero sin dote."

20. See the case for him skillfully made by Luis Suárez, *Enrique IV de Castilla*, Barcelona 2001.

21. By this arrangement, Afonso after the wedding would be styled "Prince of Castile and León" and "Prince of Asturias." He could keep those titles even if the two had children. The children would be brought up in Castile, and their household would be Castilians. When Enrique died, the two would reign in Castile. If, afterwards, Isabel died first, Afonso would continue as king of Castile. If the plan was not carried through, Afonso would marry Juana.

22. See Azcona [1:21], 68ff and 75. He points out that "el hecho incontrovertible es que Juana fue jurada princesa heredera y [en los 1460] que ninguna duda surgió entonces sobre su nacimiento legítimo." In his life of Isabel, Luis Suárez insists that Isabel herself could have had no doubts about Juana's illegitimacy: Juana's mother had lovers and other illegitimate children (the Castillas). Also, and surely more important, Enrique admitted that his marriage to Juana had taken place with a cousin without papal approval, so that, by canon law, "La Beltraneja" was not legitimate. See Luis Suárez [2:20], 235–36. Alfonso de Palencia, the historian who was soon to be Isabel's secretary, reported rumors, too, that Enrique was not the son of his supposed father.

23. Gutierre de Cárdenas, nephew of Alonso de Cárdenas, the Grand Master of the Order of Santiago, was for a long time in the household of Archbishop Carrillo; he joined Pacheco, often followed the Infante Alfonso, and then became *maestresala* of the household of Isabel in 1468, after Toros de Guisando, and went with Palencia to Saragossa in 1469 to bring back to Valladolid the Prince of Aragon, Fernando. At the proclamation in Segovia in 1474, he rode before Isabel with a naked sword, promising punishment to criminals. From 1475 he was second *contador del reino* (treasurer of the kingdom). He took a lead in the latter stages of the war in Granada; he was repulsed at first at Málaga, but led the Spanish troops into the Alhambra in January 1492. By that time he "always lived in the palace," was Commander of León, *contador mayor* (chief treasurer), and rich. He led the delegation to England for the marriage of Catherine of Aragon. He was a negotiator at Tordesillas and was no good. He died c. 1502.

24. Alfonso de Palencia (1423–92) studied first with Alfonso de Cartagena, Latin secretary and chronicler to the Castilian monarchs in 1456–74. His history of the reign of Enrique IV (*Crónica de Enrique cuarto, BAE*, vols. 257, 258) is among the most influential works of Spanish history. He attacked Enrique for giving some of his power to favorites, argued that he had brought civil war, and alleged that he had made treaties too favorable to Muslims. He then became secretary to Isabel and, with Gutierre de Cárdenas, went to bring Fernando to Valladolid in 1469. He was a principal source for such historians as Bernáldez, Pulgar, Valera, etc., as for Prescott in his *History of the Reign of Ferdinand and Isabel*, 3 vols., 1938.

25. John Edwards, *The Spain of the Catholic Monarchs, 1474–1520,* Oxford 2000, 266.

26. See María Isabel del Valdivieso, "La Infanta Isabel, Señora de Medina del Campo," *Estudios de Historia Medieval,* in *Homenaje a Luis Suárez,* Valladolid 1991. See also *Historia de Medina del Campo y su tierra,* ed. Eufemio Lorenzo Sanz, 2 vols., Valladolid 1986.

27. Azcona [1:21], 115, emphasizes the Aragonese initiative. The bull that was presented by Mgr. Veneris purported to say that Pius II had issued a similar bull in 1464.

28. See Ernest Belenguer, *La Corona de Aragón en la monarquía hispánica,* Barcelona 2001, chs. 2–3.

29. "La hermandad de las marismas."

30. Since, in the early stages, Aragon played less of a part in the Spanish Empire in the Indies than Castile, the kingdom is not considered in detail here.

31. See Juan Manuel Carretero Zamora, *Cortes, monarquía ciudades: Las cortes de Castilla a comienzos de la época moderna, 1476–1515,* Madrid 1988.

32. Palencia [1:19], 287–96, vividly describes the journey.

33. Juana, her daughter, told an English diplomat in May 1505, after Isabel's death, that it was not only in her that that passion reigned, but it did so, too, in her mother (cit. Azcona [1:21], 25). "Notorio es que no fue otra cosa que los celos y no sólo se halla en mí esta pasión, más la Reyna, mi señora . . . fue asímisma celosa. . . ."

34. "Suplico a vuestra señoría que más a menudo vengan las cartas que, por mi vida, muy tardías vienen" (Vicente Rodríguez Valencia, *Isabel la Católica en la Opinión de Españoles y Extranjeros,* 3 vols., Valladolid 1970, 3, 108).

35. Alfonso became Archbishop of Saragossa and himself had illegitimate descendants. Juana married Bernardino Fernández de Velasco, Constable of Castile.

36. Probably in 1500 the whole population of the peninsula was a little over 6 million, of which Portugal constituted a million. See Azcona [1:21], 323.

37. This is insisted upon by Azcona [1:21], 115.

38. Pulgar [1:24], 36: "É habia una gracia singular, que cualquier que con él fablase, luego le amaba é le deseaba servir."

39. Manuel Giménez Fernández, *Bartolomé de las Casas,* vol. 1, Seville 1953.

40. Fernando as "un mujeriego sin freno" is discussed in Manuel Fernández Álvarez, *Juana la Loca: La Cautiva de Tordesillas,* Madrid 2000, 57ff.

41. Other pictures are in the Musée des Beaux-Arts, Poitiers, and in the British Royal Collection (unknown painter) at Windsor. See also the *Virgen de la Merced* of Diego de la Cruz and his workshop, with his family and Cardinal González de Mendoza, in the Real Monasterio de las Huelgas, Burgos.

42. Peggy Liss, *Isabel the Queen,* Oxford 1992, 76.

43. Alonso de Quintanilla was the official who later floated the idea of a national police, or Hermandad, in 1476, before the Cortes at Madrigal. He organized the Genoese help (the Ribarolo, Pinelli) for the conquest of the Canaries in the 1480s. The Duke of Medinaceli, in his letter to Cardinal Mendoza of 1493, says Quintanilla had added his support to the idea of Columbus's voyage. Columbus would often go to Quintanilla's house to dine, thanks to Cardinal Mendoza.

(Gonzalo Fernández de Oviedo, *Historia general y natural de las Indias*, BAE, 2nd ed., Madrid 1992, 1, 22.)

44. Andrés de Cabrera, *mayordomo* of Enrique IV's, c. 1472, was *alcaide* of Segovia and also leader of Segovia's *conversos*. He was named Marquis of Moya and then married Beatriz de Bobadilla, Isabel's *camarera*. Suárez [1:20] speaks of him as "el de las gestiones decisivas" (162). He was continually used by Isabel and by 1492 was rich.

45. Mendoza's cardinalate was probably arranged by Rodrigo Borgia as a quid pro quo for his change of politics. Borgia was in Spain from June 18, 1472, to September 12, 1473, entering and leaving by Valencia, of which city he had been bishop since 1458. See Miguel Batllori, *La familia de los Borjas*, Madrid 1999, 92.

46. Palencia [1:19], 156–57: "la señora Princesa dançó allí e el señor Rey cantó delante de ella e estovieron en su gajasa do gran parte de la noche. . . ."

47. In Castile, monarchs are not crowned as in France and England.

48. Palencia [1:19], 154.

49. Bishop Mendoza would become Chancellor of the Secret Seal, Chacón chief accountant, Cárdenas his deputy, while Rodrigo de Ulloa, who had worked with King Enrique, would be third in command. Gabriel Sánchez, an Aragonese and a *converso*, would take charge of the royal household's finances.

50. Bartolomé de las Casas, *Historia de las Indias*, 3 vols. (hereafter Las Casas), Mexico 1986, 1, 156: "Su gran virtud, prudencia, fidelidad a los reyes y generosidad de linaje y de ánimo."

51. Richard Ford, *A Handbook for Travellers in Spain*, 3rd ed., London 1855, 1, 320.

52. See also Mendoza's tomb in Toledo Cathedral, which his will specified should be "transparent and open, sculptured on both sides." It was probably by Sansovino. There is a portrait of the cardinal, in red with a red hat, in the *Virgen de la Merced* and with the family of the Catholic Kings in Las Huelgas, Burgos. Another portrait of him, bald, is in the Retablo del Cardenal in San Ginés, Guadalajara, apparently by Juan Rodríguez de Segovia, "el maestro de los Luna." He founded the Colegio de Santa Cruz, the first Renaissance building in Spain, in Valladolid. Here *letrados* would be trained for the royal service. They were to have *limpieza*, that is, be free from accusations of Jewish blood. The cardinal appears on the tympanum.

53. Suárez [1:20], 115.

54. Liss [2:42], 122–23.

55. Isabel's books included Landulfo de Saxonia's *Life of Christ, el Jardín de las nobles doncellas*, by Fray Martín de Córdoba, the *Soliloquies* of Fray Pedro de Guadalajara, and Fray García Ximénez de Cisneros's *Exercitorio de la vida espiritual*, as well as numerous (early) chivalric romances.

56. Juan del Encina worked for the Duke of Alba, and we should imagine how one of his musical plays was performed in the castle of the Duke at Alba de Tormes on Christmas Eve 1492. Encina was a master of both music and poetry.

57. Thus she told her confessor, Talavera: "No reprehendo las dádivas y las mercedes. . . . No el gasto de las ropas y nuevas vestiduras, aunque no carezca de culpa en lo que en ello ovo de demasiado." (See Rodríguez Valencia [2:34], 3, 5 for a dis-

cussion.) The German traveler Munzer saw her always dressed in black, "Viaje por España," in J. García Mercadal, *Viajes de Extranjeros por España y Portugal,* Madrid 1952, 404. Antoine de Lalaing made a similar point in 1501: "No hablo de los vestidos del rey y de la reina, porque no llevan más que paños de lana."

58. Martyr [1:2], letter 150.

59. For example, Sir Peter Russell, cit. Edwards [2:25], 1.

60. An excellent account of this war is given by Edwards [2:25], 23ff.

61. For another prophecy, see ch. 37.

62. As Fernando showed, for example, in his benign settlement of the social problems of Cataluña (he secured the end of the chronic political crisis between peasants and landlords).

63. Luciano Serrano y Piñeda, *Correspondencia de los Reyes Católicos con el Gran Capitán durante las campañas de Italia,* in *Revista de Archivos,* Bibliotecas y Museos, vols. 20–29, 1909–13, dated July 10, 1505.

64. "De semblante entre grave y risueño," Munzer in García Mercadal [2:57], 406. Of biographies of Fernando, the most recent is that of Ernest Belenguer, *Fernando el Católico,* Barcelona 1999.

65. Martyr [1:2], 50.

Chapter 3

1. Alexander the Great arriving at Gordium found a yoke to which a knot had been tied so badly that no one could undo it. He who did so was assured of world conquest. Alexander cut the knot with his sword, saying "Tanto Monta," which in Spanish of the fifteenth century came to mean "It's the same thing (da lo mismo)." In other words, Fernando was invited to assert his rights by taking the direct route. See P. Aguado Bleye, " 'Tanto Monta': la Empresa de Fernando el Católico," *Revista de Santa Cruz,* 8, Valladolid 1949.

2. For example, Bernáldez talked of Castile being full of "mucha soberbia, é de mucha herejía, é de mucha blasfemía é avarica, é rapina, é de muchas guerra é bandos, é parcialidades, é de muchos ladrones é salteadores, é rufianes é matadores, é tahures, é tableros públicos. . . ." (Andrés Bernáldez, *Historia del Reinado de los Reyes Católicos,* 2 vols., Seville 1869, 25.)

3. Azcona [1:21], 214–15, who points out that the social standing of the Council was humble, being often composed of clever men on the make.

4. The development of the *corregidor,* appointed by the Crown in all large cities, meant that in Castile the danger of municipalities seeking independence in an Italian style was much reduced (the *corregidor* had existed since the fourteenth century, but was only in general use from the 1480s).

5. A nephew, Jorge Manrique, was a far more famous poet. In 1494 there were fifty-four cities of Spain that had a *corregidor.*

6. Francesco Guicciardini, *The History of Italy,* tr. Sidney Alexander, New York 1969.

7. Klein's figure (Julius Klein, *The Mesta,* Cambridge 1920, 27). Klein estimated 2.6 million in 1477 and 1512. The royal income came from "servicio y montazgo" of

the flocks, whose travels along the "cañadas reales," eighty-five yards wide, were absolutely guaranteed.

8. Earl Hamilton, *American Treasure and the Price Revolution in Spain, 1501–1650,* Cambridge 1934, 157.

9. Granada would be added after 1492. The towns were Ávila, Burgos, Córdoba, Cuenca, Guadalajara, Jaén, León, Madrid, Murcia, Salamanca, Segovia, Seville, Soria, Toledo, Toro, Valladolid, and Zamora. Zamora claimed to speak for Galicia!

10. For a summary of the medieval background, see Edwards [2:25], 42.

11. The best summary is that in chs. 7–8 and 11 of Azcona's biography [1:21], 87.

12. Perhaps the numbers had been nearly twice that in 1486–87, at the time of the fall of Málaga. See Ladero Quesada, in *La Paz y la guerra en la época del Tratado de Tordesillas,* Valladolid 1994, 270.

13. "La bien cercada, tú que estás en par del río."

14. Figures in Ladero Quesada [1:13], 271–72.

15. David Hume, *History of England,* 8 vols., Dublin 1775, vol. 3, 278.

16. See Ladero Quesada [1:13], 266.

17. For example, once Mendoza offered a dinner to the Curia on the banks of the Tiber, at which—echoes of Petronius—each course was served on different silver, which was afterwards thrown into the river. Unknown to his guests, Tendilla had set nets in the river so that all except one spoon and two forks were retrieved. When the Vatican cut off his supply of firewood, he bought some old houses and had them ransacked for their timber. For a portrait, see a medal dedicated to him of 1486.

18. For faces of the sixteenth century, see John Pope-Hennessy, *The Portrait of the Renaissance,* New York 1963. For dress, see Carmen Bernís, *Trajes y modas en la España de los Reyes Católicos,* vol. 1: *Las Mujeres,* vol. 2: *Los Hombres,* Madrid 1979.

19. I have accepted Martyr's figure ([1:2] 1, 113), but see Ladero Quesada [1:13], 266.

20. See the fine new biography by José Enrique Ruiz-Domènec, *El Gran Capitán,* Barcelona 2002. The campaign in Andalusia would be for "El Gran Capitán" a rehearsal for that in Italy.

21. In the tenth century, a huntsman (*montero*) of Espinosa saved the life of Count Sancho García of Castile. Thereafter, the *monteros* became the royal bodyguards.

22. A. de la Torre, *Documentos sobre las relaciones internacionales de los Reyes Católicos,* 6 vols., Madrid 1949–51.

23. Miguel Angel Ladero Quesada, *Los señores de Andalucía,* Cadiz 1998, 247–48.

24. On the subject of medieval Spanish (and Italian) slavery, see Charles Verlinden's *L'Esclavage dans l'Europe médiévale,* vol. 1, Bruges 1955. See also my own *The Slave Trade* (London 1977), especially ch. 4. For the status of slaves in Christian Spain, see *Las Siete Partidas* [1:16], pt. 4, Título 21, "De los siervos" [*sic*].

25. Martyr [1:2], 2, 120.

26. Oviedo [2:43], 1, 52: "Cuanto más que han acá pasado diferentes maneras de gentes; porque, aunque eran los que venían, vasallos de los reyes de España, ¿quién concertá al vizcaíno con el catalán, que son de diferentes provincias y lenguas? Cómo se avernán el andaluz con el valenciano, y el de Perpiñan con el

cordobés, y el aragonés con el guipuzcoano, y el gallego con el castellano . . . y el asturiano e montanés con el navarro?"

27. Lord Scales is called "Count of Escala," by Martyr [1:2], 1, 93, from "Britain."

28. Ladero Quesada [3:15], 270.

29. The word derives from the German *Hakenbühse*, hookgun.

30. Perhaps a corruption of "bombard."

31. Variants included the *cerbatana*, the falconet, and the *ribadoquín*.

32. See Hermann Kellenbenz, *Los Fugger en España y Portugal hasta 1560*, Junta de Castilla y León, Salamanca 1999, 8. The Spanish contribution to this commerce was coral, cotton, rabbit skins, aromatic fruit, and, above all, saffron.

33. The first Catalan edition was the work of a German printer, Nicolas Spindeler, summoned to Valencia to publish the book by Juan Rix de Cura. Dedicated to the Infante Fernando of Portugal, it would be published in Castilian in 1511. It was written in Valencian between 1460 and 1466. See *Don Quixote*, 1, ch. 6.

34. See Irving Leonard's *Books of the Brave*, New York 1949, 115.

35. Born in Settignano in 1469, Fancelli came to Spain young and remained till his death in Saragossa in 1519.

36. Francisco Sevillano Colom, "La Cancillería de Fernando el Católico," *V Congreso de Historia de la Corona de Aragón*, Saragossa 1956, 215–53.

37. Juan Gil, *Los conversos y la Inquisición Sevillana*, 5 vols., Seville 2000–2, 2, 11. Among the *converso* secretaries of the Catholic Kings were Fernando Álvarez de Toledo, son of the *corregidor* of Toledo; Andrés de Cabrera; Juan Díaz de Alcocer; Juan de la Parra; and Hernando del Pulgar. We should not forget Fray Hernando de Talavera or Diego de Valera.

38. See Palencia [1:19], 15.

39. See John Edwards, "The 'Massacre' of Jewish Christians in Córdoba, 1473–74," in Mark Levene and Penny Roberts, *The Massacre in History*, New York 1999.

40. Luis Suárez, "La Salida de los Judíos," in *Isabel la Católica y la Política*, ed. Julio Valdeón Baruque, Valladolid 2001, 86. Elsewhere he explains the principal charges formulated against the *conversos*. Netanyahu thinks that the aim of the Inquisition was to "destroy the *marrano* community. The advocates of the Inquisition, of course, knew this and the *conversos* knew it well." The *conversos* were those who converted willingly; *marranos* those whose conversion was forced.

41. See Suárez's *Isabel I* [1:20], 299.

42. Netanyahu, *Toward the Inquisition*, New York 1997, 198–99.

43. Although 2,000 is quoted by many, these figures are debated. For example, Alfredo Alvar Ezquerra, *Isabel la Católica*, Madrid 2002, 98, suggests that for the reign of the two monarchs, the number was 9,000—out of a total of 10,000 *conversos*.

44. A tax farmer was a man who collected taxes on behalf of a higher authority.

45. J. Vicens Vives, *Historia crítica de la vida y reinado de Fernando II de Aragón*, Saragossa 1962, 654. Isabel had previously had Salomon Byton as her doctor.

46. Sixteen in Aragon, thirty-one in Castile, one in Navarre.

47. Edwards [2:25], 197.

48. Altogether there were about two hundred monasteries in Spain, of which fifty were Cistercian, six Praemonasterian, and most of the rest Benedictine, some dependent on the foundation at Cluny. There were about two hundred Franciscan *conventos,* a few Dominican, and thirty-four Jeronymite.

49. See Louis Cardaillac, *L'Espagne des Rois Catholiques, Le Prince Don Juan, symbole de l'apogée d'un règne 1474–1500,* Paris 2000, 113–223.

50. Helen Nader, *The Mendoza Family in the Spanish Renaissance,* New Brunswick, NJ 1979, 109.

51. Manuel Fernández Álvarez, *Corpus documental de Carlos V,* Salamanca 1973, 5 vols., 1, 167fn, 62.

52. Suárez Fernández [1:20], 28.

53. Pulgar [1:24], 313–14.

54. See Miguel Angel Ladero Quesada, "Les finances royales de Castille a la vieille des temps modernes," *Annales,* May–June 1970.

55. Martyr [1:2], 3.

56. The best portrait would seem to be that in the Museo Naval, Madrid. See also the impression in Alejo Fernández's *La Virgen de los Mareantes* in the Alcázar, in Seville, which may reflect Fernández's recollection of Columbus from the time he was living in Córdoba. My description derives from several sources: for example, Las Casas [2:50], 1, 29. Oviedo [2:43], 1, 8, who saw him in 1493, says that Columbus was "de buena estatura e aspecto, más alto que mediano y de recios miembros; los ojos vivos e las otras partes del rostro de buena proporción; el cabello muy bermejo, y la cara algo encendida e pecoso; bien hablado, cauto, e de gran ingenio, e gentil latino ... gracioso cuando quería, iracundo cuando se enojaba." There is a fine portrait by Sebastián del Piombo in the Metropolitan Museum, New York, but is it of Columbus?

Chapter 4

1. Las Casas [2:50], 1, 163: "tal empresa como aquella no era sino para reyes."

2. *Anon in Poesie,* ed. L. Cocito, 1970, 566, cit. Felipe Fernández-Armesto, *Before Columbus,* London 1987, 106.

3. Guicciardini [3:6], 9.

4. Pastor [1:7], 5, 241.

5. Joanot Martorell and Martí Joan de Galba, *Tirant lo Blanc,* tr. David H. Rosenthal, London 1984, 198.

6. Fernández-Armesto [4:2], 119.

7. For the Genoese in Chios, see Philip Argenti, *The Occupation of Chios by the Genoese, 1346–1566,* 3 vols., Cambridge 1958.

8. Jacques Heers, *Gènes au XVème siècle,* Paris 1961, 68–71.

9. Sir Peter Russell, *Prince Henry the Navigator,* New Haven 2000, 249, illuminates this side of Genoese commerce.

10. Argenti [4:7], 333, warns us against thinking that those called Centurione, Grimaldi, Pinelli, etc., were all descendants of persons bearing these surnames.

They were sometimes merely associates united in an "albergo" under such a name.

11. Suárez [1:20], 121.

12. The cardinal appears on the tympanum—more banker than bishop, says Peggy Liss [2:42], 260.

13. Gonzalo Fernández de Oviedo, *Las Quinquagenas de la Nobleza de España,* Royal Academy of History, 1, Madrid 1880.

14. Qu. Consuelo Varela, *Cristóbal Colón, retrato de un hombre,* Madrid 1992, 124. See Etoy de Benito Ruano, "La participación en la guerra de Granada" (*I Congreso de Historia de Andalucia,* 2, Córdoba 1978).

15. See, for example, Celso García de la Riega, *¿Colón español?,* Madrid 1914; Henri Vignaud was the inventor of the Jewish legend, taken up by Madariaga.

16. Cristóbal Colón, *Textos y documentos completos,* ed. Juan Gil and Consuelo Varela, Madrid 1992, 423.

17. The best biography in Spanish is that of Consuelo Varela [4:14]; in English by Felipe Fernández-Armesto (*Columbus,* Oxford 1992), and in French by J. Heers, the historian of Genoa (*Christophe Colomb,* Paris 1981). Juan Gil's essay "Historiografía Española sobre el descubrimiento y descubrimientos" in *Revista de Indias* (hereafter *R de I*), 49, 187, Sept.–Dec. 1989, is a fine introduction to the writing about Columbus.

18. Colón [4:16], 356, "siendo yo nacido en Génova."

19. Colón [4:16], 356.

20. Las Casas [2:50]. Las Casas saw and probably listened to Columbus in 1493 on his return from the first voyage. Whether he saw him again in, for example, 1497–98 or in 1500–2 is quite uncertain.

21. "De muy pequeña edad," Colón [4:16], 444.

22. Colón [4:16], 89–91; also Las Casas [2:50], 1, 31.

23. Las Casas [2:50], 1, 31.

24. Bernáldez [3:2], 1, 357: "hombre de alto ingenio sin saber muchas letras."

25. Columbus described going to Ireland in a letter to the King and Queen in 1495; see Colón [4:16], 285.

26. See Peter Russell's admirable *Prince Henry the Navigator* [4:9]. Perhaps it was really Cape Juby.

27. This was Willem Bosman, *A New and Accurate Description of the Coast of Guinea,* Eng. tr. London 1705.

28. Strabo (64 B.C.–A.D. 21) was a geographer of Greek descent, though he had Asiatic blood. He was a Stoic, who believed that there was one landmass. His work was a storehouse of knowledge, much of it interesting, some of it true.

29. Samuel Eliot Morison, *The European Discovery of America: The Northern Voyages,* Oxford 1971, 61–62.

30. Las Casas says so [2:50], 1, 144.

31. A "lateen" (*latin*) sail was a triangular one, suspended by a long yard at an angle of about 45 degrees to the mast.

32. Morison [4:29], 8.

33. See *El libro de Marco Polo,* ed. Juan Gil, Madrid 1992.

34. "No hay que creer que el océano cubra la mitad de la tierra": see Pierre d'Ailly, *Ymago Mundi*, ed. Antonio Ramírez de Verger, Madrid 1992, 150. For d'Ailly, see J. Huizinga, *The Autumn of the Middle Ages*, Chicago 1996, 124.

35. See Stephen Greenblatt, *Marvelous Possessions*, Chicago 1991, 26ff.

36. Russell [4:9], 99.

37. Henry Harrisse, *The Discovery of North America*, London 1892, 378, 381. The letter was reprinted in Spanish by Las Casas [2:50], 1, 63.

38. Martín Fernández de Navarrete, *Colección de viajes y descubrimientos que hicieron por mar los españoles*, 4 vols., Madrid 1954, 1, 299, 300. See Heers [4:17] for the date, 88. Others think the letter was only sent in 1492. In fact, it is 12,000 miles to China from the Canary Islands.

39. Navarrete [4:38], 1, 300: Toscanelli was especially interested in comets and held open court in Florence to intelligent young men in his day, who included Leonardo da Vinci and, probably, Amerigo Vespucci.

40. Fernando Colón, *Historia del Almirante*, ed. Luis Arranz, Madrid 2000, 66.

41. Fernando Colón [4:40], 62.

42. Discussion of the mistake can be seen in Morison's *The European Discovery of America: The Southern Voyages, 1491–1616*, New York 1974, 30–31.

43. See Edmundo O'Gorman, *La Idea del descubrimiento de América*, Mexico City 1951, and, in particular, Juan Manzano y Manzano, *Colón y su secreto: el predescubrimiento*, Madrid 1976, 1989. Oviedo [2:43] rejected the idea, 1, 16.

44. See Manzano [4:43], 21.

45. For Bishop Ortiz, see Las Casas [2:50], 1, 151. Fernando Colón [4:40], 64–67, called Ortiz "Calzadilla."

46. João de Barros qu. Heers [4:17], 101.

47. Alfred W. Crosby, *Ecological Imperialism*, Cambridge 1986, 79, thought that slaves were brought from the Canaries and Majorca as early as 1342.

48. The Spanish Canary Islands were then governed by Diego García de Herrera and his wife in Peraza; his grandfather had added La Gomera to the Spanish Canarian collection. They were succeeded by their son, Fernando Herrera, and his wife, Beatriz de Bobadilla.

49. Felipe Fernández-Armesto, *The Canary Islands After the Conquest*, Oxford 1982; Vicenta Cortés Alonso, "La conquista de Canarias a través de las ventas de esclavos," *Anuario de estudios Americanos* (hereafter *AEA*), 1, 1955, 498.

50. Fernández-Armesto summarizes the evidence [4:49], 10.

51. See Fernández-Armesto [4:2].

52. Manzano says that Marchena was supportive of Columbus because he had been told about the secret of the "unknown pilot." See [4:43], 22. For Velasco, see Las Casas [2:50], 1, 68.

53. A friend wrote so to me: "ya que una neblina caprichosa todo la tapa y muchas veces se confunden con unas nubes bajas que parecen formar montañas, colinas y valles."

54. Evidence of García Hernández, doctor of Palos, in Navarrete [4:38], 2, 330–31.

55. They were attached to the household of Álvaro de Portugal, one of the children of the executed Duke of Braganza who had fled to Spain recently.

56. This dating derives from Rumeu [2:2], 419.

57. Oviedo [2:43], 1, 22, gives the credit to Mendoza and Quintanilla that Columbus saw the monarchs.

58. The great pile of the Archbishop's Palace in Alcalá can still be seen, covering with its park territory an area large enough for any modern bishop to hide from the world.

59. Alfonso de Palencia [1:19], 205.

60. Bernáldez [3:2], 1, 359: "los mostró el mapa-mundi, de manera que puso en deseo de saber de aquellas tierras."

61. "E les fizo relación de su imaginación," Bernáldez [3:2], 1, 358.

62. Las Casas [2:50], 1, 149.

63. They had the right to load the third part of all cargoes on all ships that left Castilian ports. They also received a third part of the profits of the royal ships on their journeys, as well as the third part of the *quinto real* of all enterprises. See Privilegio of Aug. 17, 1416, cited in Navarrete [4:38], 1, 262–93, where the full rights, etc., of the old admirals are explained. These papers were in the Columbus archives in the possession of the dukes of Vergara. The rights of Fadrique in 1512 are explained in a document of 1512, in ibid., 293–95:

    1. Each ship that left Seville would have to pay to the admiral 20 maravedís per ton, though with a maximum of 3,000 ms.;

    2. Each ton of merchandise taken from Seville would pay a tax to the admiral of 8 ms. per ton;

    3. The admiral should be paid 5 *reales de plata* per every 100 tons of ballast;

    4. Every bottle of wine or oil taken from Seville should pay 5 *blancas* to the admiral;

    5. Every ship of 100 tons would pay 1,450 *reales* for anchorage;

    6. Each quintal of ropes, etc., and hemp would pay 25 ms;

    7–19. Wheat, iron, biscuit, grain, sardines, wool, oysters, clams, etc., should all pay various taxes to the Admiral.

64. Las Casas [2:50], 1, 156.

65. Archivo General de Simancas (hereafter AGS), *Patronato real,* 28–31, quoted in Azcona [1:21], 491.

66. Manzano [4:43], 24.

67. A full list of the members does not seem to survive. Among them there was Rodrigo Maldonado de Talavera, a professor of law at Salamanca, who had negotiated with Portugal and came to know it well, and was a member of the Consejo Real.

68. Las Casas [2:50], 1, 157–58.

69. Manzano [4:43], xvii, 104, suggested that Columbus told Deza his secret deriving from the "unknown pilot."

70. Bernáldez [3:2]. Juana was the sister of Pedro Velázquez who at the time of her appointment in 1479 had been secretary of the queen, and of Antonio de Torre, who went to the Americas with Columbus on his second voyage. Later, she married Juan Dávila.

71. Navarrete [4:38], 2, 348. Las Casas thought that Talavera was the chief negative

influence, Peter Martyr the contrary. Consuelo Varela sides with Martyr in this debate. See Las Casas [2:50], 1, 167.

72. Las Casas [2:50], 1, 145, 155.
73. Rumeu [2:2], 426.
74. Colón [4:16], 92; Antonio Sánchez González, *Medinaceli y Colón*, Madrid 1995, 172.
75. See Las Casas [2:50], 1, 153, for Bartolomeo: "de menos simplicidad—que Cristóbal . . . no mucho menos docto en cosmografía."
76. Las Casas [2:50], 1, 161.
77. Navarrete [4:38], 1, 302: "algunas cosas cumplideras a nuestro servicio."
78. Letter of 1505.
79. Sánchez González [4:74], 133. The last de la Cerda, Isabel, married Bernardo de Foix, first Count of Medinaceli, the bastard of Béarne, son of Gaston Phoebus, who had come down into Spain in one of the "white companies" to assist the Trastámara. The Estado de Medinaceli had been created by King Enrique II in 1368 with the title of count, being raised to a dukedom in 1479.
80. As qu. Prescott [1:22], 182.
81. Las Casas [2:50], 1, 164.
82. See John Edwards, *War and Peace in Fifteenth-Century Spain*, in *Studies in Medieval History Presented to R. H. C. Davis*, Henry Mayr-Harting and R. I. Moore, eds, London 1985, 65f.
83. Ibid., 60.
84. Las Casas [2:50], 1, 162–63.
85. "Tal empresa como aquella no era sino para reyes," Las Casas [2:50], 1, 163. These letters are lost. Sánchez González, the archivist of the Medinaceli Foundation, suggests that they were stolen.
86. They were *consuegros*, for his daughter, Leonor, married Rodrigo, the Marquis of Cenete, the Cardinal's son.
87. AGS, Estado, leg. 1–2, in Navarrete [4:38], 1, 310.
88. "Protesté a vuestras altezas que toda la ganancia d'esta mi empresa se gastase en la conquista de Hierusalem, y vuestras altezas se rieron, y dixeron que les plazía y que sin esto tenían aquella gana. . . ." (Diary of first voyage, December 26, 1492, in Colón [4:16].)

Chapter 5

1. Harvey [1:1], 310.
2. *Nubdha-Kitah nubdhat al-asr fi Akhabar mulūk Baní Nasr,* ed. and tr. Carlos Quirós and Alfredo Bustani, "Fragmentos de la época sobre noticias de los reyes nazaritas," *BAE*, 1905–29, qu. Harvey [1:1], 310–11.
3. The part of the Gran Capitán can be followed in the excellent new biography by Ruiz-Domènec [3:20], 200ff.
4. A *capitulación* was normally a document that would reserve rights to the Crown in the territories concerned but that also guaranteed rewards to the leader of the expedition.

5. "Aquella santa conquista que el nuestro muy esforçado rey hizo del reino de Granada. . . ." Prologue to *Amadís de Gaula* by Garcí Rodríguez de Montalvo, ed. Juan Bautista Avalle-Arce, Madrid 1991, 128.

6. Bernáldez [3:2], 1, 302.

7. Alonso de Santa Cruz, *Crónica de los Reyes Católicos,* ed. Juan de Mata Carriazo, 2 vols., Seville 1951, 1, 47.

8. Observe it at the "point" of the coat of arms in the Isabella Breviary, p. 6. It was not a Muslim sign.

9. Rumeu [2:2], 190.

10. Martyr [1:2], 172.

11. Borgia had on his coat of arms a fighting bull.

12. Pastor [1:7], 4, 334.

13. Harvey [1:1], 326.

14. The first marquis was the legitimatized son of Cardinal Mendoza.

15. "con determinada voluntad de pasarse a Francia. . . ." Las Casas [2:50], 1, 167. Manuel Serrano y Sanz, *Los amigos y protectores Aragoneses de Cristóbal Colón,* Madrid 1918, reissued Barcelona 1991, dates this Jan. 1492. Las Casas [2:50], 1, 167.

16. Letter from Ayala to the Catholic Kings, July 25, 1498, in Bergenroth, *Calendar of Letters . . . Relating to the Negotiations Between England and Spain,* London 1862, 1, 176, qu. Harrisse [4:37], 2.

17. Fernando Colón [4:40], 93.

18. Sánchez González [4:74], 229.

19. Las Casas [2:50], 1, 168–70: "haber intentado saber las grandezas y secretos del universo."

20. "las reglas o límites de su oficio." But he had "ánimo notificarle lo que en mi corazón siento." Las Casas [2:50] 1, 168.

21. Varela [4:14], 7.

22. Fernando Colón [4:40], 93.

23. Serrano y Sanz [5:15], 136–38.

24. Serrano y Sanz [5:15], 117. Harrisse in his life of Columbus argued that the idea of Santangel's intervention was a fantasy. Varela says Santangel's Florentine partner, Juanotto Berardi, was involved in loans.

25. It still stands, a reminder that a bridge can lead two ways.

26. Navarrete [4:38] 1, 303.

27. Fernando Colón [4:40], 94. See Ricardo Zorraquín Becú, "El gobierno superior de las Indias," in *Congreso de Historia del Descubrimiento, Actas,* 4 vols., Madrid 1992, 3, 165ff., for an analysis of the curious wording of the grants to Columbus.

28. "las dichas mares oceanas."

29. "aquellas islas e tierra firmes."

30. "ha descubierto."

31. Text in Las Casas [2:50], 1, 172–73.

32. Sánchez González [4:74], 230.

33. Bernáldez [3:2], 1, 280.

34. An indulgence was a remission of a punishment for sin.

35. Frederick Pohl, *Amerigo Vespucci,* London 1966, 31, quotes an interesting letter of 1489 from Lorenzo Pier Francesco de' Medici to Vespucci about Berardi.

36. Dr. Rodericous, Sebastián de Olano, and Francisco de Madrid, of whom the last named was chancellor to the Crown, a *converso,* his mother being Jewish. See Gil [3:37], 3; Navarrete [4:38], 1, 305.

37. Navarrete [4:38], 1, 307.

38. Qu. Varela, *Retrato* [4:14], 104: "Sobre el maravilloso descubrimiento del nuevo mundo."

39. Las Casas [2:50], 1, 343.

40. When exactly Nebrija presented this book to the Queen seems unclear. It is said that it occurred when the court was at Salamanca, but the court was not in Salamanca in 1492, and would not go there again till 1497. It is also said that Talavera, when still Bishop of Ávila, introduced Nebrija to the Queen, though preoccupied by calming (*allanar*) matters to prepare for Columbus's first voyage. But Talavera became Archbishop of Granada in 1491. Probably the presentation was in Valladolid in August 1492, the court being there for two months, not in Salamanca. This first grammar of a Romance language was written, according to Menéndez Pidal, "en esperanza cierta del Nuevo Mundo, aunque aún no se había navegado para descubrirlo." Asked what the point of the book was, Nebrija replied: "Después que vuestra Alteza meta debajo de su yugo muchos pueblos bárbaros y naciones de peregrinas lenguas, y con el vencimiento aquellos tengan necesidad de recibir las leyes que el vencidor pone al vencido, y con ellas nuestra lengua, entonces por esta arte gramatical podrían venir en conocimiento de ella, como agora nosotros deprendemos el arte de la lengua latín para desprender el latín" (Ramón Menéndez Pidal, *La Lengua de Cristóbal Colón;* Madrid 1958, 49). See Félix González Olmedo, *Nebrija, Debelador de la barbarie,* Madrid 1942.

41. Maurice Kriegel, "La prise d'une décision: l'expulsion des Juifs d'Espagne en 1492," *Revue Historique,* 260, 1978. Kriegel stresses the complete surprise of the Spanish Jews in 1492. Had not Fernando, as late as Feb. 28, 1492, guaranteed the loans of the *alhama* in Saragossa?

42. The monarchs wrote to many cities and noblemen with a copy of the decree, including to the Duke of Medinaceli (Bernáldez [3:2], 332–40). The edict is printed by Fidel Fita in *Boletín de la Real Academia de la Historia* (hereafter *BRAH*), 11, 512–28.

43. Martyr [1:2], 173. He considered the Jews a "bogus race" (*raza falaz*) (op. cit., 177).

44. Luis Suárez Fernández, *Documentos acerca de la expulsión de los judíos de España,* Valladolid 1964, doc. 177. This was a letter directed to the see of Burgos.

45. For a good summary, see Edwards [2:25], 226.

46. As summarized in Suárez, *Isabel I* [1:20], 292.

47. See F. Cantera, "Fernando del Pulgar y los conversos," *Sefarad,* 4, 1944, 296–99.

48. Martyr [1:2], 1, 101.

49. Martyr [1:2], 1, 201.

50. The thought is that of Suárez [1:20], 354.
51. Martyr [1:2], 1, 201.
52. Two recent Lives are Erika Rummel, *Jiménez de Cisneros*, Tempe 1999, and Juan J. García Oro, *El cardenal Cisneros: vida y empresas*, 2 vols., Madrid 1992–93, of which there is a shorter version, Barcelona 2002.
53. *Cortes de los Antiguos Reinos de León y Castilla*, vol. 4: *1476-1537*, Real Academia de la Historia (Madrid 1882), 149–51.
54. Benzion Netanyahu, *The Origins of the Inquisition in Fifteenth-Century Spain*, New York 1995, 842.
55. Gil [3:37], 2, 12.
56. "¿Creéis que esto proviene de mí? El Señor ha puesto este pensamiento en el corazón del rey." Y luego prosiguió: "El corazón del rey está en las manos del Señor, como los ríos de agua. Él los dirige donde quiere" (Suárez [1:20]). See also B. Netanyahu, *Isaac Abravanel*, Philadelphia 1972, 55, and *The Jewish Quarterly Review* 20 (1908), 254. I am grateful to Professor Netanyahu for his help in this matter.
57. Julio Caro Baroja, *Los Judíos en la España Moderna*, 3 vols., Madrid 1961, 1, 178; *Spain and the Jews*, Eli Kedourie (ed.), London 1992, 14. Kriegel [5:41] discusses the role of Señor before 1492, suggesting that his actions had lost him the support of the Jewish community as a whole.
58. Kamen in Kedourie [5:57], 85. Ladero Quesada thought in terms of 95,000 Jews in Castile, perhaps 12,000 in Aragon. Suárez [1:20] suggested a total of 70,000–100,000. Azcona ([1:21], 446) accepted 200,000. Alvar Ezquerra suggested 200,000, with 100,000 converted ([3:43], 99). Netanyahu [5:56] thought that there were 600,000 Jews in 1391, 300,000 in 1490.
59. Haim Bernart, also in Kedourie [5:57], 114. See Elliott [1:25], 98.
60. See Pilar Alonso and Alberto Gil, *La Memoria de las Aljamas*, Madrid 1994, and above all Henri Méchoulan, *Les Juifs d'Espagne, histoire d'une diaspora, 1492–1992*, Paris 1992.

Chapter 6

1. For the population, see Miguel Angel Ladero Quesada, *La Ciudad Medieval, Historia de Sevilla*, Valladolid 1980, 73.
2. Navarrete [4:38], 1, 309.
3. Navarrete [4:38], 1, 307.
4. Las Casas [2:50], 1, 176. For them, see Juan Manzano y Manzano, *Los Pinzones y el descubrimiento de América*, 3 vols., Madrid 1988.
5. Celebrated now since it was the birthplace of Juan Ramón Jiménez, whose poems are today to be seen on all street corners. For the population, see Ladero Quesada [6:1], 73.
6. Also known as *La Gallega*, having been built in Galicia.
7. Isabel the Queen had substituted the *alcaide*, Juan de Cepeda, for Juan de Porres on the ground that, as Porres wrote to the Queen, "Ay dos o tres bocas de infierno donde se adora el diablo" (Azcona [1:21], 255).

8. The suggestion that there were on board an Irishman, William Ines, and an Englishman, Talarte de Lajes, now seems, alas, to be a mistake. See Alice B. Gould, *Nueva lista documentada de los tripulantes de Colón en 1493*, Madrid 1984, 364.

9. For an analysis of the crews, see ibid. Also, see Serrano y Sanz [5:15]; Navarrete [4:38], 1, 310.

10. Navarrete [4:38], 2, 329. Umbría may have been a brother of the Gonzalo de Umbría who created difficulties on Cortés's expedition in 1519 and had his heel cut in consequence.

11. R. Ramírez de Arellano, "Datos nuevos referentes a Beatriz Enríquez de Arana y los Arana de Córdoba," *BRAH*, 37 (1900), 461f.; and 40 (1902), 41–50.

12. AGI, Contratación, cit. Hamilton [3:8], 45.

13. The first brandies were devised in medieval Cataluña by Arnau de Vilanova. Searching as he was for the philosopher's stone, he found something more important: he began to distill alcohol first for treatment of wounds, then, mixed with aromatic herbs, as a drink. The matter is discussed in J. Trueta, *Cataluña (The Spirit of Catalonia)*, London 1946, 63. See E. Nicaise, *La grande Chirurgie de Guy de Chauliac,* Paris 1890, 45, which suggests that instead the Arab physician Rathes may (ironically, as a Muslim) have been decisive.

14. Known in Spain as *ampolletas* or *relojes de arena.*

15. Las Casas mentions the astrolabe [2:50], 1, 189, in respect of a planned mutiny: the crew thought that they might throw Colombus overboard and "publicar que había él caido, tomando el estrella con su cuadrante o astrolabio." Behaim's globe influenced a generation of mariners.

16. Kirkpatrick Sale, *The Conquest of Paradise,* London 1991, 19. The diary that we possess is that which is printed by Las Casas in his chs. 35–77 ([2:50], 1, 179ff.). This is a summary with quotations, perhaps done in the 1540s, using a copy of Columbus's original made by a scribe of whom nothing is known.

17. Heers [4:8], 184.

18. Beatriz was the daughter of Juan Fernández de Bobadilla, *alcaide* de los Alcázares de Madrid and *corregidor* of that city, by Leonor Ortiz. Juan Fernández was the first cousin of the Marquesa of Moya. See Antonio Rumeu de Armas, *Cristóbal Colón y Doña Beatriz de Bobadilla,* El Museo Canario, *AEA,* 28, 343–78.

19. All that is known of the friendship with Columbus of "La Cazadora" is what was reported by Miguel Cuneo, who wrote, in a letter to Geronimo Annari, of "la señora del lugar de la cual nuestro almirante estuvo una vez prendado" (*Primeras Cartas sobre America,* Seville 1990, ed. Francisco Morales Padrón, 141).

20. The word is that of John Elliott [1:25], 46.

21. Las Casas [2:50], 1, 191; Harrisse [4:37], 401.

22. Las Casas [2:50], 1, 189.

23. "Así que muy necesario me fue la mar alta que no pareció salvo el tiempo de los judios cuando salieron de Egipto contra Mosen que las sacava del cautiverio."

24. Navarrete [4:38], 2, 333.

25. Navarrete [4:38], 2, 334. The questionnaire in the *probanza* of 1513 says that Martín Alonso said: "Adelante, adelante, que esta es armada e embajada de tan altos principes como los Reyes nuestros señores de España, e fasta hoy nunca ha

venido a menos, nunca plegue a Dios que por nosotros vengan estas a menos; que si vos, señor, quisieres tornaros, yo determino de andar fasta hallar la tierra o nunca volver a España; e que por su industria e parecer, pasaron adelante. . . ." Various sailors who heard this told the story to some witnesses such as Rodríguez de la Calva, Martín Núñez, and Juan de Ungría, etc., but none of them testified.

26. Colón [4:16], 108.

27. Manzano [4:43], 355ff.

28. One or two examples can be seen in the Museo del Ejército, Madrid.

29. Triana is said to have been distressed by the lack of attention paid to him and to have abandoned the Christian religion in a sulk and gone to live in Africa (Oviedo [2:43], 26). Triana and Rodríguez Bermejo are still sometimes supposed to be separate people, but Alice Gould seems to have settled the matter.

30. For the identification of San Salvador with Watling Island, see Mauricio Obregón's *Colón en el Mar de los Caribes*, Bogotá 1990, 87ff.

31. For a study of the Tainos, see ch. 8. Others have suggested different islands: for example, Samaná Cay and even Egg Island, at the entrance to New Providence Channel.

32. Francisco Morales Padrón, "Descubrimiento y toma de posesión," in *AEA*, 12, 1955, 333. Morales Padrón points out that Columbus never claimed to "discover" a new world. The claim was only made in 1526 by Oviedo.

33. "ligeramente se harían cristianos."

34. Peter Martyr, *De Orbe Novo,* tr. Francis MacNutt, New York 1912; see also *Décadas del Nuevo Mundo,* ed. Ramón Alba, Madrid 1989, 34, 37.

35. Colón [4:16], 113.

36. "buenos servidores" qu. Carlos Esteban Deive, *La Española y la esclavitud del Indio,* Santo Domingo 1995, 43. Las Casas ([2:50], 1, 208) wrote of this enslavement: "Yo no dudo que si el almirante creyera que había de suceder tan perniciosa jactura y supiera tanto de las conclusiones primeras y segundas del derecho natural y divino como supo de cosmografía y de otra doctrinas humanas, que nunca el osara introducir ni principiar cosa que había de acarrear tan calamitosos daños porque nadie podrá negar de ser hombre bueno y cristiano; pero los juicios de Dios son profundísimos y ninguno de los hombres los puede ni debe querer penetrar."

37. Colón [4:16], 114: "tomada de una, se puede decir de todas."

38. Colón [4:16], 121.

39. Letter to Santangel, in Colón [4:16], 223.

40. Colón [4:16], 124.

41. Colón [4:16], 125–26.

42. See Gil [3:37], 4, 273f., for the Jerez (Xerez) family.

43. Fernando Colón [4:40], 119, and Colón [4:16], 132.

44. Colón [4:16], 151.

45. Las Casas [2:50], 1, 240.

46. Fernando Colón [4:40], 125; Colón [4:16], 157.

47. Colón [4:16], 163.

48. "El Almirante . . . cree que esta gente de Caniba no ser otra cosa sino la gente del Gran Khan. . . ." Las Casas [2:50], 1, 257.

49. Greenblatt [4:35], 63, argues that this was a "horrible misfortune" and without it "the destructive forces would have come more slowly and there might have been time for a defense."

50. Colón [4:16], 180–99: see list in Navarrete [4:38]. On this day, Columbus recorded that he had said to their *altezas* (Highnesses) that "toda la ganancia d'esta mi empresa se gastase en la conquista de Hierusalem." "Vuestras altezas se rieron y dixeron que les plazía. . . ."

51. Fernando Colón [4:40], 120.

52. Ibid.

53. Las Casas [2:50], 1, 288.

54. Fernando Colón [4:40], 82; Peter Martyr and Andrés Bernáldez [3:2], 1, 367, say forty.

55. But it is not obvious whether Columbus merely showed the *cacique* the coin or left it with him.

Chapter 7

1. Martín Núñez, Juan de Ungría, Pedro Ramírez, Juan Calvo, Hernando Esteban, García Hernández, Cristóbal García, Diego Fernández Colmenero, and Francisco García Vallejo, as well as Pinzón's son Arias Pérez, of whom only García Vallejo had been on the voyage.

2. Navarrete [4:38], 2, 338.

3. Martyr [6:34], 14; Colón [4:16], 198ff.

4. See commentary by Manzano [4:43], 427.

5. Colón [4:16], 194–95.

6. Martyr [6:34], 12.

7. Serrano y Sanz [5:15], 146–48.

8. Las Casas [2:50], 1, 313.

9. Las Casas [2:50], 1, 316–18.

10. Heers [4:8], 200, calculates thus.

11. Fernando Colón [4:40], 226.

12. The contents of the letter suggest that March 4 not 14 was the correct date. Surely otherwise Columbus would have told the King and Queen that he had seen their Portuguese cousins.

13. Colón [4:16], 233: "suplico que en la carta que escriva d'esta victoria, que le demanden un cardenalato para mi hijo y que, puesto que no sean en hedad idónea, se le dé, que de poca diferencia ay en el tiempo d'él y del hijo del Oficio de Medizis de Florencia a quien se dió el capelo sin que aya servido ni tenga propósito de tanta honra de la cristianidad."

14. The addressee was of course the right person for Columbus to write to.

15. Colón [4:16], 148; Las Casas [2:50], 1, 323ff.

16. Agustín Remesal, *1494, La Raya de Tordesillas*, Valladolid 1994, 85.

17. Colón [4:40], 216fn, 172.

18. Zennaro's letter is in the Archivo di Stato in Modena. The version printed by Morales Padrón [6:19], 105–7, is in M. Vannini's *El mar de los descubridores,* Caracas 1974. A copy was sent by Jacopo Trotti to Hercules I, Duke of Ferrara, ambassador of Ferrara. He had not only seen but heard discussion about the letter. The letter may be falsely dated.

19. "porque siendo el mundo redondo devia forzosamente dar la vuelta y encontrar la parte oriental."

20. AGS, Estado, leg. 1–11, f342, published by Navarrete [4:38], 1, 310.

21. Varela [4:14], 169.

22. Rumeu [2:2], 200.

23. Martyr to Tendilla and Talavera, Martyr [1:2], 226–27.

24. On Dec. 12, on a high platform in Barcelona, the would-be assassin's right hand, which had carried the dagger, was cut off, as were the feet that had carried him to the council chamber; the eyes that had guided him were cut out and then the heart that prompted him was extracted and burned. Pincers tore the flesh from his body, which then was turned over to the people to be stoned and burned. For Isabel's ignorance, see Suárez [1:20], 123.

25. "Pues vemos cómo los reyes pueden morir en cualquier desastre. Razón es aparejar a bien morir" (Suárez [1:20], 119).

26. Lorenzo Galíndez de Carvajal spoke of Columbus in his *Anales Breves de los Reyes Católicos* [2:10], 277, but in respect of 1491.

27. Guicciardini [3:6], 91. An account of the election of Alexander can be seen in a letter to Lope de Ocampo, published in Batllori [2:45], 251.

28. Martyr [1:2], 1, 210.

29. Martyr [1:2], 1, 218.

30. See Batllori [2:45], 149ff.

31. Guicciardini [3:6], 10; for a summary of his life, see Batllori [2:45, 91ff.]. I cannot resist recalling here the splendid life by that great survivor, and my friend in Rome of the 1960s, Orestes Ferrara, *Il Papa Borgia,* Milan 1953.

32. Stephanus Infessura, *Diario della città di Roma,* ed. Oreste Tommasini, Rome 1890; *Fonti per la storia d'Italia,* 5, 288; qu. Pastor [1:7], 5, 389.

33. Navarrete [4:38], 1, 311. The letter was of March 30, 1493.

34. Las Casas [2:50], 1, 332.

35. Las Casas [2:50], 1, 333. Antonio Rumeu de Armas "Colón en Barcelona," *AEA,* 1, 1944, reminds us that Las Casas was not there, however. Those who were included the historian Fernández de Oviedo, probably Columbus's son Fernando, and the King's cousin, "the Infante Fortuna."

36. Martyr [6:34].

37. Navarrete [4:38], 1, 316.

38. Las Casas [2:50], 1, 334.

39. Francisco López de Gómara, "Hispania Vitrix, Historia General de las Indias," in BAE, 22, Madrid 1852, 167.

40. Rumeu [7:35], 43.

41. Varela [4:14], 168; Heers [4:8], 202.

42. The only copy of the letter printed in April 1493 is in the New York Public Library and was shown to me in 1995 by Paul Leclerc. *La carta de Colón sobre el descubrimiento,* ed. Demetrio Ramos, Granada 1983, discusses it. Was it perhaps a pious fraud by the Crown? See also Fernando Colón [4:40], 219fn, where no doubt is mentioned.

43. Fernando Colón [4:40], 222–23.

44. Fernando Colón [4:40], 224.

45. Fernando Colón [4:40], 226.

46. Qu. Felipe Fernández-Armesto [4:2], 97.

47. Martyr [1:2], 1, 236–37. Letter of May 14, 1493, to Juan Borromeo.

48. Martyr [1:2], 1, 242.

49. Martyr to the Archbishop of Braga, Oct. 1, 1493, in *Cartas Sobre el Nuevo Mundo,* Madrid 1990.

50. Martyr [7:49], 33–34.

51. Letter to Santangel in Colón [4:16], 220: "Cómo en treinta y tres dias pasé a las Indias con la armada que los ilustrísimos Rey e Reina Nuestros Señores me dieron. . . ."

52. Wilcomb Washburn, "The Meaning of Discovery in the Fifteenth and Sixteenth Centuries," *American Historical Review* (hereafter AHR), Oct. 1962.

53. Fernando Colón [4:40], 63–65.

Chapter 8

1. A 13,000-year-old female skeleton was apparently found near Mexico City by Silvia González of Liverpool in 2002. There are some who believe that some human beings reached what are now the Americas about 40000 or 25000 B.C.

2. Ricardo E. Alegría, "El uso de la terminologia etno-histórica para designar las culturas aborigenes de las Antillas," *Cuadernos Prehistóricos,* Valladolid 1981.

3. *Colección de documentos inéditos relativos al descubrimiento, conquista y organización de las posesiones españoles en América y Oceania,* 42 vols., Madrid 1864–82 (hereafter *CDI*), 11, 413.

4. She may have indicated in some way how the Spaniards were conducting themselves in the Caribbean.

5. Carl Ortwin Sauer, *The Early Spanish Main,* Berkeley, CA, 1966, 24.

6. *CDI,* 11, 417.

7. *CDI,* 11, 428.

8. Woodrow Borah and Sherburne F. Cook, *Essays in Population History,* vol. 3, Berkeley, CA, 1979.

9. Verlinden, Rosenblatt, Arranz.

10. *CDI,* 7, 400.

11. See for a discussion Silvio Zavala, *Las instituciones jurídicas en la conquista de América,* 3rd ed., Mexico 1988, 667; see also Las Casas [2:50], 2, 558.

12. See David Henige, *Numbers from Nowhere,* unpublished MS, Madison WI, 1996. Charles Verlinden thought 40,000 in La Española in 1492 (see his article "La

population de l'Amérique précolombienne. Une question de méthode," in *Mélanges Fernand Braudel,* Toulouse 1973, 2, 453–52).
13. Irving Rouse, *The Tainos,* New Haven, CT, 1992, 9.
14. Las Casas, *Apologética Historia Sumaria,* ed. Pérez de Tudela, 2 vols., *BAE,* 95, 96, Madrid 1957, 44.
15. Columbus's diary of Dec. 13, 1492.
16. Miguel Cuneo, in Morales Padrón (ed.) [6:19], 143.
17. Colón [4:40], 183.
18. Sven Lovén, *Origins of the Taino Culture,* Göteborg 1935. Carl Sauer concluded a chapter in his *The Early Spanish Main* [8:5] by saying, "The tropical idyll in the accounts of Columbus and Peter Martyr is largely true. The people suffered no want. They took care of their plantings, were dexterous at fishing and bold canoeists and swimmers. They designed attractive houses and kept them clean. They found aesthetic expression in woodworking. They had leisure to enjoy diversion in ballgames, dances and music. This judgement quite ignores the threat from the Caribs."
19. Sauer [8:5], 56.

Chapter 9

1. Fernández-Armesto [4:2], 221. Allegretti was Sienese *commissario* in Bagni di Petriolo and later *podestà.*
2. López de Gómara [7:39], 242; Gerónimo Zurita, *Historia del Rey Don Fernando el Cathólico* [*sic*], Saragossa 1610, 30–32.
3. Remesal [7:16], 61.
4. Lope de Herrera was a minor official, thought of by the monarchs as their *"mensajero."* See *CDI,* 21, 372, and also *CDI,* 38, 201.
5. Remesal [7:16], 85.
6. Navarrete [4:38], 1, 312.
7. Remesal [7:16], 86.
8. Instructions and costs of this fleet are in Navarrete [4:38], 1, 346ff.
9. See García de Resenda, *Cronica dos feitos del Rey Dom João,* 2, Lisbon 1622.
10. That is three hundred miles. For Carvajal's life, see Batllori [2:45], 263ff. He became a cardinal in September 1493.
11. According to Infessura [7:32]. Pastor doubted that that was so.
12. Colón [4:16], 1, 466.
13. Las Casas [2:50], 1, 336.
14. Pastor [1:7], 6, 177, says so, but on what evidence? See M. Giménez Fernández, "Las bulas alejandrinas de 1493 sobre la historia y el sentido de las letras referentes a las Indias," AEA, 1, 1944, 171–429, and also L. Weckman, "Las bulas alejandrinas de 1493 y la teoría política del papado medieval," *Publicaciones del Instituto de Historia,* 2, Mexico 1949.
15. Text in Latin in Navarrete [4:38], 1, 312ff.; tr. 1, 315.
16. *CDI,* 16, 356–62.

17. Pastor [1:7], 6, 162.
18. See Manuel Giménez Fernández, *Bartolomé de las Casas*, Madrid 1953, 1961, 2, 142.
19. Navarrete [4:38], 1, 329–30. See Adelaida Sagarra Gamazo, "La formación política de Juan Rodríguez de Fonseca," in *Congreso* [5:27], 1, 611. For this remarkable family, see Edward Cooper, *Castillos señoriales de la corona de Castilla,* 4 vols., Valladolid 1991, 1, 176ff.; Ernst Schäfer, *El Consejo Real y Supremo de las Indias,* 2 vols., Seville 1935, 1, 2; and *Reyes y Mecenas,* Madrid 1992, 324. A portrait of Fonseca can be seen on the reredos of the cathedral in Palencia and also, younger, in the cathedral of Badajoz.
20. It is easy to make Fonseca a villain for everything that went wrong in the Spanish Indies, but of course the fact was that Fonseca could have had no idea what the Caribbean was really like.
21. Navarrete [4:38], 1, 320.
22. Navarrete [4:38], 1, 326.
23. "visoreyes y gobernadores que han sido e son de los dichos nuestros reynos de Castilla y León."
24. Cit. Remesal [7:16], 72: "por una linea o raya que hemos hecho marcar qua pasa desde las islas de los Azores a las islas Cabo Verde, de septentrión al austro, de polo a polo."
25. Navarrate [4:38], 1, 336.
26. Rumeu de Armas [7:35], 38.
27. Navarrete [4:38], 1, 327–28. It would not be surprising to find that he was connected with the Sorias, who were condemned by the Inquisition, for which tragedy see Gil [3:37], 3, 339.
28. *CDHR*, 30, 68: also Navarrete [4:38], 1, 323. For the Hermandad, see Luis Suárez Fernández and Manuel Fernández Álvarez, *La España de los Reyes Católicos,* that is, vol. 17 of *Historia de España,* ed. Ramón Menéndez Pidal, Madrid 1978, 232–50.
29. Navarrete [4:38], 1, 321, 324. Zafra was typical of the new *letrados,* or civil servants, of his epoch—a man without a past or even as it would seem a family. The fact that his surname is a place-name suggests a possible *converso* connection and indeed a Fernando de Zafra, a tailor of Seville, figures in the "padrón de los habilitados" in Seville in 1510 (Gil [3:37], 5, 493).
30. Navarrete [4:38], 1, 329.
31. Navarrete [4:38], 1, 352.
32. Navarrete [4:38], 1, 321. Villareal would seem to be the family of Villareal of Toledo, for whom see Gil [3:37], 5, 482ff.
33. Gil [3:37], 1, 386.
34. Navarrete [4:38], 1, 322.
35. Navarrete [4:38], 1, 339.
36. Ibid.
37. Las Casas [2:50], 1, 338.
38. Pastor [1:7], 6, 163.

39. C. H. Haring, *Trade and Navigation Between Spain and the Indies in the Time of the Habsburgs,* Cambridge 1918, 4; Juan Pérez de Tudela, *Las armadas de Indias, y los orígenes de la política de la colonización,* CSIC, Madrid 1956, 31.

40. Navarrete [4:38], 1, 342; cf. *CDI,* 39, 165.

41. Navarrete [4:38], 1, 344.

42. Remesal [7:16], 74: "Plugo a Nuestro señor Jesús Cristo sujetar al imperio de los reyes de España las Islas Afortunadas cuya admirable fertilidad es tan notoria. Y hasta ahora mismo les ha dado otras muchas hacia la India hasta aquí desconocidas, que se juzga no las hay más preciosas y ricas en todo lo que del mundo se conoce."

43. *CDI,* 30, 164–65.

44. *CDI,* 30, 183, 184–86.

45. *BRAH,* 1891, 19, 187 et seq., qu. Pastor [1:7], 6, 163.

46. Pastor [1:7], 5, 410.

47. Varela [4:14], 155.

48. Navarrete [4:38], 1, 345.

49. Remesal [7:16], 93.

50. Navarrete [4:38], 1, 356–57.

51. Navarrete [4:38], 1, 363–64. The letter is also in Las Casas [8:16], 1, 350–51.

52. Navarrete [4:38], 1, 362.

53. Navarrete [4:38], 1, 354.

Chapter 10

1. Consuelo Varela [4:14], 109. Las Casas [2:50], 1, 346, suggests 1,500. Fernando Colón says that he and his brother, Diego, watched their father's fleet leave.

2. Las Casas [2:50], 1, 347, says that Diego, whom he knew, was "una persona virtuosa, muy cuerda, pacífica, y más simple y bien acondicionada que recatada ni maliciosa."

3. Heers [4:17], 200.

4. The comment of Consuelo Varela [4:14], in *Retrato.* Las Casas [2:50], 1, 347, says he was named captain-general of the fleet.

5. Fernando Colón [4:40].

6. Las Casas [2:50], 1, 347. Altogether, Columbus wrote later (to Juana de la Torre, Colón [4:16], 265) that there were two hundred people "sin sueldo." See, for the *converso* origin of these brothers, see Gil [3:37], 3, 120ff. Pedro was the father of Fray Bartolomé. See Las Casas [2:50], *Historia,* 30.

7. See Robert B. Tate, *Joan Margarit i Pau, Cardinal-Bishop of Gerona,* Manchester 1955.

8. See Gil [3:37], 1, 33, Demetrio Ramos, *El conflicto de lanzas jinetes,* Santo Domingo 1992, 16fn, 7, and Serrano y Sanz [5:15], 227.

9. Fernando Colón [4:40], "habían acudido tantos caballeros e hidalgos y otra gente noble, que fue necesario dismunir el número. . . ."

10. Las Casas [2:50], 1, 348. "Todas las perfecciones que un hombre podía tener corporales."

11. The list in Demetrio Ramos is Francisco de Olmedo, Diego de Sepúlveda, Antonio Quintela, Antonio de Peñalosa, Diego de Leyva, Arias Gonzalo, Francisco de Estrada, Rodrigo Vázquez, Lope de Cáceres, Gonzalo Pacheco, Diego Osorio, Antonio Román, Rodrigo de Arévalo, Alonso Serrano, Cristóbal de León, Pedro Coronado, and Diego Cano, with a certain Villalba (*veedor*). There were seven whose names Ramos could not establish.

12. See Juan Gil and Consuelo Varela, *Cartas de particulares a Colón*, Madrid 1984.

13. Fidel Fita, Fray Bernardo Boyl, and Cristóbal Colón, "Nueva Colección de cartas reales," *BRAH*, 19, 20, 1891–92, 173ff., 184.

14. The phrase is from Consuelo Varela [4:14], 113.

15. Boil's inspiration, Francisco de Paola, was canonized in 1519, a little more than a century after his birth in 1416.

16. Pastor [1:7], 6, 163.

17. Ibid.

18. Las Casas [2:50].

19. First published in Venice in 1571 and later in Brasseur de Bourbourg's *Relation des Choses de Yucatan*, of Diego de Landa. See also the edition of Juan José Arrom, Mexico 1988; Martyr [6:34], 80.

20. The reformed Franciscans, the Observants, had met at Florence on May 26 and became excited at the prospect of vast new territories to convert to their version of Christianity. Fr. Antonino Tibesar, OFM, "The Franciscan Order of the Holy Cross of Española, 1505–1559," *The Americas*, vol. 43, 3, 1957.

21. "Castilla y le mandé dar a una muger que de Castilla acá benía. . . ."

22. Martyr [6:34], 22.

23. Giménez Fernández [9:18], 2, 551, wrote that "parece cierta la especie, no documentalmente comprobada, de que ya en el segundo viaje de Colón fueron algunos negros o loros esclavos. . . ." For Marchionni, the most interesting Florentine businessman of Lisbon, see my *The Slave Trade* [3:24], 83–85.

24. Bernáldez [3:2], 301.

25. Navarrete [4:38], 1, 321.

26. Colón [4:16], 236.

27. Las Casas [2:50].

28. Morales Padrón [6:19], 183.

29. Fernández-Armesto [4:49], 42.

30. Álvarez Chanca in Morales Padrón [6:19], 111; Cuneo, in the same, 141.

31. Cuneo in Morales Padrón [6:19], 141.

32. Álvarez Chanca in Morales Padrón [6:19], 113.

33. Cuneo in Morales Padrón [6:19], 142. For La Deseada, see Oviedo [2:43], 1, 34. See also the evidence of Juan de Rojas, discussed by Manzano [4:43], 480–81.

34. Martyr [6:34], 20.

35. Álvarez Chanca in Morales Padrón [6:19], 114–16.

36. Martyr [6:34], 19.

37. "Al final, nos encontramos de acuerdo de tan manera, que os digo que eso parecía amaestrada en una escuela de rameras": Cuneo in Morales Padrón [6:19], 144.

38. Colón [4:16], 239.

39. It was in the tenth century that the number became fixed at 11,000, thanks to a misreading of a text that spoke of "eleven virgins."

40. Álvarez Chanca in Morales Padrón [6:19], 121.

41. Fernando Colón [4:40], 241.

42. Martyr [6:34], 22.

43. Fernando Colón [4:40], 167, and Las Casas [2:50], 1, 355.

44. Álvarez Chanca in Morales Padrón [6:19], 130.

45. Martyr (perhaps using Antonio de Torres's reports) [6:34], 23.

46. Álvarez Chanca in Morales Padrón [6:19], 132. Note that Consuelo Varela and Juan Gil show (Colón [4:16], 243fn, 16) that the pensions to the heirs of those killed were paid after 1508.

47. Fernando Colón [4:40] and Las Casas [2:50], 1, 362, say the seventh, Cuneo the eighth.

48. Chanca in Morales Padrón [6:19], 130.

49. Las Casas [2:50], 1, 362.

50. Ramos [10:8], 70.

51. Bernáldez [3:2], 2, 21. It is not at all easy to decide when this was. Álvarez Chanca says that on Jan. 1, 1494, he decided to land in order to sleep. Morison said that it was on Jan. 2 that the fleet arrived at Isabela.

52. Morales Padrón [6:20], 134–35.

53. Las Casas [2:50], 1, 363.

54. Colón [4:16], 248.

55. "Memorial que para los reyes dió el almirante don Cristóbal Colón en la ciudad de la Isabela," Jan. 30, 1494, Antonio Torres, in Navarrete [4:38], 195–202, 262. See also Las Casas [2:50], 1, 365.

56. Álvarez Chanca in Morales Padrón [6:19], 137.

57. Cuneo in Morales Padrón [6:19], 146: "la búsqueda de oro" was "por lo que, principalmente, había emprendido un viaje tan largo."

58. Ibid., 147: "por la codicia de oro, todos no mantuvimos fuertes y gallardos."

59. Oviedo [2:43], 2, 123.

60. Américo Castro, *The Structure of Spanish History,* Princeton, NJ, 1954, 130.

61. Las Casas [2:50], 1, 366; Sale [6:16], 145fn. See Samuel Eliot Morison, *Admiral of the Ocean Sea,* 2 vols., Boston 1942, Appendix 1, for a detailed discussion.

62. Navarrete [4:38], 1, 196–205.

Chapter 11

1. Colón [4:16], 291. See, for this journey, Antonio Núñez Jiménez, *El Almirante en la tierra más hermosa. Los viajes de Colón a Cuba,* Cadiz 1985: "yo tenía esta tierra por firme, no isla."

2. Cuneo in Morales Padrón, [6:19], 146.

3. Ibid., 147.

4. Fernando Colón [4:40], 122.

5. *CDI,* 21, 365–66; Las Casas [8:14], 1, 367.

6. Ramos [10:8], 209.
7. Navarrete [4:38], 1, 196.
8. Cuneo in Morales Padrón [6:19], 147; "y también, mientras España sea España, no faltarán traidores; asi el uno denunció el otro, de manera que casi todos fueron descubiertos, y a los culpables muy fuertemente azotados: a unos les cortaron las orejas, a otros la nariz, y daba compasión verlos."
9. Fernando Colón [4:40], 176.
10. Ramos [10:8], 95; Navarrete [4:38], 1, 365ff.
11. Colón [4:16], 270.
12. "la justicia sea mucho temida."
13. Colón [4:16], 281.
14. Las Casas [2:50], 1, 408.
15. Deive [6:36], 15.
16. Las Casas [2:50], 1, 383.
17. Colón [4:16], 254ff.
18. Isabel is supposed to have said that if she had had three sons, she would have liked one of them to have been King of Castile, the second the Archbishop of Toledo, and the third a notary of Medina del Campo.
19. Liss [2:42], 277.
20. Gil [3:37], 1, 188.
21. Gil [3:37], 1, 107.
22. Liss [2:42], 297.
23. Martyr [6:34], 41. Melchor had been the royal ambassador at the court of the pope the year that Málaga fell.
24. Navarrete [4:38], 1, 368; *CDI*, 16, 560.
25. Navarrete [4:38], 3, 485.
26. *CDI*, 36, 178.
27. "en lo de las carnes, vea cómo las que se enviaren sean buenas."
28. *Consuegro*, Spanish for co-father-in-law, is a word that ought to be launched into English usage. The letter, dated May 21, 1494, was published by Batllori [2:45], 222–24.
29. Rumeu [2:2], 210–11.
30. Navarrete [4:38], 1, 369.
31. "una raya, o linea derecha de polo a polo del polo arctico al polo antartico que es del norte al sur, la cual raya o linea e señal se haya de dar y de derecha como dicha es, a 370 leguas de las islas de cabo verde para la parte de poniente por grados o por otra manera. . . ." Navarrete [4:38], 1, 378ff.
32. Demetrio Ramos, *El Repudio al Tratado de Tordesillas*, Congreso Nacional de la Historia, Salamanca 1992.
33. John Parry, *The Spanish Seaborne Empire*, London 1966, 46.
34. Other names are in Navarrete [4:38], 1, 387ff.
35. Cuneo, letter in Morales Padrón [6:19].
36. Colón [4:16], 291.
37. Bernáldez [3:2], 49.
38. I. A. Wright, *The Early History of Cuba*, New York 1916, 18.

39. A. Núñez Jiménez [11:1] says so.

40. The incident does not figure in Las Casas, ch. 96; but see Heers [4:17], 219.

41. Morales Padrón [6:19], 217; Navarrete [4:38], 1, 387ff.

42. Las Casas [2:50], 1, 345.

43. Martyr [6:34], 92. See, for this journey, Francisco Morales Padrón, *Jamaica Española*, Seville 1952, 5–10, and Bernáldez [3:2], 2, 71ff.

44. Fernando Colón [4:40], 191. Sale [6:16] suggests "Reiter's syndrome," following dysentery.

45. Fernando Colón [4:40], 198.

46. Oviedo [2:43], 1, 49–50.

47. Las Casas [2:50], 1, 378.

48. Oviedo [2:43], 1, 49.

49. Ibid.

50. AGI, Contratación, 5089, 1, f.106r, qu. in Fernando Colón [4:40], 284 fn20.

51. For Bartolomeo Colón, see Las Casas [2:50], 1, 153.

52. Oviedo [2:43], 1, 51, and see Serrano y Sanz [5:15], 233; Las Casas [2:50], 1, 427.

53. "todos sus principales males eran de hambre."

54. Las Casas [2:50], 1, 425: "Así Dios me lleve a Castilla."

55. Fernando Colón [4:40], 194.

56. Ibid.

57. Fernando Colón [4:40], 200.

58. See Arrom [10:19], passim.

59. Pérez de Tudela [9:39], 89, esp. fn 37.

60. Navarrete [4:38], 1, 394.

61. Las Casas [2:50], 1, 411: "Una de las principales cosas porque esto nos ha placido tanto es por ser inventada, principiada y habida por vuestra mano, trabajo e industria y parécenos que todo lo que al principio nos dixistes que se podía alcanzar por la mayor parte, todo ha salido como si lo hubiérades visto antes. . . ."

62. Navarrete [4:38], 1, 392: "quiere que se le envien todos los mas halcones que se pudiese."

63. Heers [4:17], 317.

64. Rumeu [2:2], 212ff.

65. Navarrete [4:38], 3, 501.

66. "que era burla . . . no era nada el oro que había en esta isla y que los gastos que sus altezas hacían eran grandes, nunca recompensables" (Las Casas [2:50], 1, 421).

67. Charles's claim to the throne of Naples derived from his grandmother María, a sister of the "Bon Roi René" of Naples who for years lived royally in France even if he never reigned in Italy.

68. Delaborde, 324, qu. Pastor [1:7], 5, 432.

69. Guicciardini [3:6], 44.

70. Guicciardini [3:6], 72.

71. Sagarra Gamazo, in *Congreso* [5:27], 636.

72. For the American origin of syphilis, see Morison [10:61], App. 1. There may have

been, however, a European or Old World variety. See Alfred W. Crosby, *The Columbian Exchange*, Westport, CT, 1972, 122–56, and W. H. McNeill, *Plagues and Peoples*, Oxford 1977; the similarities between the spirochetes that cause yaws and syphilis are well discussed.

Chapter 12

1. Cardinal Mendoza died in Alcalá in Jan. 1495.
2. R. O. Jones, *The Golden Age, Prose and Poetry*, London 1971, 7.
3. Las Casas [2:50], 3, 277: "era mucho más experimentado el señor obispo en hacer armadas que en decir misas de pontifical. . . ."
4. Las Casas [2:50], 2, 90.
5. "abrigó continuamente mortal odio al almirante y sus empresas y estuvo a la cabeza de quienes le malquistaron con el rey."
6. Antonio de Guevara, in *Epistolares Familiares, BAE,* Madrid 1850, 36. Francescillo de Zúñiga, the fool of Charles V, said of him that he was "herrero de Tordelones y vasija llena de polvora."
7. See *Reyes y Mecenas* [9:20], 234ff.
8. Las Casas [2:50], 1, 416–17; Oviedo [2:43], 1, 64–68.
9. Cuneo, in Morales Padrón [6:20], 160: "creo por el aire más frío el cual no estaban acostumbrados."
10. Cuneo, *ibid.*
11. See Deive [6:36], 58, for this theory.
12. Rouse [8:13], 14.
13. Ramos [10:8], 130.
14. Las Casas [2:50], 1, 378.
15. See Pérez de Tudela, who develops this idea in *Las Armadas* [9:39], 259. For Pérez de Tudela, Columbus was a typical Italian mercantilist, deriving his thoughts from the Mediterranean and translated to the Caribbean. For Columbus, the "empresa de las Indias" had for its goal the establishment of an exploitation of Oriental riches, by means of a monarchical monopoly with which he would be associated. All ideas of colonization would be inferior to this. But there would be necessarily a *factoria-fortaleza* that would be served by a *hueste asalariada*. In contrast, there was the Castilian tradition, whose civil servants were thinking in terms of the settlement of new lands, according to ideas worked out during the *reconquista* in Spain itself, characterized by a *repartimiento* so that the conquerors could share the risks and benefits.
16. Fernando Colón [4:40], 535.
17. Pérez de Tudela found an anonymous report saying this; cit. Luis Arranz, *Repartimientos y Encomiendas en la Isla Española*, Madrid 1991, 34.
18. Pérez de Tudela [9:39], 101.
19. Letter of the Reyes Católicos, April 12, 1495, to Fonseca in Archivo General de Indias (AGI), Patronato, leg. 9, r.1. Navarrete [4:38], 1, 401.
20. "cerca de lo que nos escribisteis de los indios que vienen en las carabelas, parécenos que se podrán vender mejor en esa Andalucía que en otra parte, debeislo

facer vender como mejor os paresciere. . . ." Navarrete [4:38], 1, 402. See also Consuelo Varela [4:14], 128, and Pérez de Tudela [9:39], 107, fn 80.

21. Navarrete [4:38], 1, 404.

22. Deive [6:36], 69.

23. Morales Padrón [6:19], 151: "hay en todas las islas tanto de caníbales como de indios." Quite an admission!

24. Navarrete [4:38], 1, 399–401.

25. Pérez de Tudela [9:39], 103.

26. Navarrete [4:38], 1, 397. Pérez de Tudela [9:39], 107.

27. For commentary, see Haring [9:39], 5.

28. *BRAH*, 19, 199, qu. Pérez de Tudela [9:39], 93.

29. Navarrete [4:38], 1, 394.

30. Gil [3:37], 1, 387.

31. Antonio-Miguel Bernal, *La financiación de la carrera de Indias, 1492–1824*, Seville 1992, 152.

32. *Colección de documentos relativos al descubrimiento, conquista y organización de las antiguas posesiones españolas en América y Oceanía*, 25 vols., 1880–1932 (hereafter *CDIU*), 1, 241. Not 1512 but 1495, qu. Pérez de Tudela [9:39], 95.

33. Navarrete [4:38], 1, 406.

34. Pérez de Tudela [9:39], 110.

35. "By command of the *inquisidors* during the whole of this year *el aguacil* Pedro de Mata and the fiscal Francisco de Simancas paid large sums not only to Bishop Fonseca (896,880 ms.) but also to the main stewards of the bishop such as the Genovese Bernardo and Luco Piñelo (1 million ms. and 1,293,9040 ms.); as to the *converso* Jimeno de Briviesca (606,000 ms.), this last sum being given in Sanlúcar so that García de Campo, *criado de* Bernardo Piñelo, would take it to Puerto de Santa María"; Gil [3:37], 1, 387.

36. The pilots included Juan de Moguer, Bartolomé Roldán, Ruy Pérez de la Mora, and Francisco del Castillo (Pérez de Tudela [9:39], 114).

37. There were also the usual cargoes: wheat, barley, wine, olive oil, vinegar, and also three hundred rabbits, in large baskets filled with lettuce. On the way, in Gomera, in the Canary Islands, they also bought a hundred sheep and goats.

38. Fernández-Armesto [4:2], 114.

39. Colón [4:16], 316–30: "algunos frailes devotos y fuera de codicia de cosas del mundo."

40. Carvajal became a cardinal on Sept. 20, 1493, remaining, though, Bishop of Cartagena in Spain, a see that he later exchanged for Sigüenza.

41. *Cancionero*, qu. Jones [12:2], 29: "porque según dice el maestro Antonio de Lebrija, aquel que desterró de nuestra España los barbarismos que en la lengua latina se habían criado, una de las causas que le movieron a hacer arte de romance fue que creía nuestra lengua estar agora más empinada y polida que jamás estuvo, de donde más se podía temer el decendimiento que la subida; y así yo por esta misma razón creyendo nunca haber estado tan puesta en la cumbre nuestra poesía y manera de trobar, parecióme ser cosa muy provechosa poner en

el arte y encerrarla debaxo de ciertas leyes y reglas, porque ninguna antigüedad de tiempos le pueda traer olvido. . . ."

42. Las Casas [2:50], 1, 431; AGI, Contratación, leg. 3249, r., qu. Pérez de Tudela [9:39], 116.

43. Colón [4:16], 368.

Chapter 13

1. Martyr [1:2], 1, 330.

2. Morison thought that Columbus dressed as a monk because of a desire for anonymity. Sale [6:16] suggests some kind of penitence was being expressed. But surely there was a connection with the monastery of La Rábida, where he had been so encouraged. Gil [3:37], 3, 94, implies that Bernáldez may have been a *converso*: like every other intelligent person in Spain at the time, it would seem!

3. The masters were García Álvarez de Moguer, San Juan de Ajanguis, and Fernando de Palomares for the Breton boat, the owner being Juan Fernández de Alcoba. The pilots were Niño, Juan de Humbría, and Pero Sanz de la Puebla.

4. Antonio Rumeu de Armas, *Alonso de Lugo en la Corte de los Reyes Católicos*, Madrid 1952. The prince established himself in Almazán after the departure of the court in July 1496. The palace was a house belonging to Pedro Mendoza, the lord of the town. For this little court, see Cardaillac [3:49], 136ff., and Gonzalo Fernández de Oviedo, *Libro de la Cámara Real del Príncipe Don Juan*, Madrid 1870, *passim*.

5. Navarrete [4:38], 1, 408.

6. Las Casas [2:50], 1, 435: "Hizoles un buen presente de oro por fundir . . . muchas guaycas o car´tulas . . . con sus ojos y orejas de oro y muchos papagayos."

7. Bernáldez [3:2], 2, 78: "Traía un collar de oro el dicho D. Diego, hermano del dicho Caonaboa, que le facia el almirante poner cuando entraba por las ciudades ó lugares, hecho de eslabones de cadena, que pesaba seicientos castellanos, el cual vi y tuve en mis manos. . . ."

8. Martyr [1:2], 1, 316.

9. Fernández-Armesto [4:17], 25. The work of Marco Polo was translated into Spanish only in 1502, by Rodrigo Fernández de Santaella, founder of the University of Seville.

10. Harrisse [4:37], 3. Henry VII had granted Cabot's petition to cross the Atlantic on March 5, 1496. Cabot crossed in a small vessel of fifty tons, with eighteen men, leaving Bristol in the summer, reaching the "New Found Land," where he found much cod. The Spanish ambassadors to the court of England, Pedro de Ayala and Ruy González de Puebla, told Henry VII that those territories belonged to Spain: "he did not like it," they reported to Spain.

11. The bull *Si convenit* was the document that gave the monarchs this title. The Pope did not forget to mention in his citation Fernando and Isabel's expulsion of the Jews.

12. Martyr [1:2], 1, 332; see Cardaillac [3:49], 170ff.

13. Margaret had been formally married on Nov. 5, 1496, when the Infante Juan was represented at Saint Pierre, Malines, by Francisco de Rojas, ambassador to Flanders and a cousin of the King. For the death of Juan, see Cardaillac [3:49], 206.

14. Cisneros laid the first stone of the University of Alcalá (to be built by Pedro de Gumiel) in March 1498. The Catholic Kings were still in the town. It would be ten years before the university would begin work. "Complutense" is the Latin word for Alcalá.

15.
> . . . papas y emperadores
> y prelados
> Así los trata la muerte
> Como a los pobres pastores
> De ganados.

Or:
> Nuestras vidas son los ríos
> Que van a dar en la mar,
> Que es el morir:
> Allí van los señoríos.

("Coplas a la muerte de su padre," xiv.) These are among the most famous lines in Spanish poetry.

16. Margaret would eventually return to Flanders, in order to marry the Duke of Savoy and then act as the Regent of the Low Countries after his death. What a tragedy that so clever a princess should die without children! Her many portraits, as a child by Jean Hey, by Bernard van Orley, and, above all, in stained glass as well as in marble in the church at Brou, in Bourg-en-Bresse, to honor herself as well as her Savoyard husband, show her charm to later generations.

17. Las Casas [2:50], 2, 531: "daría dos o tres tumbos en el infierno." Cuéllar, who perhaps owed his job to Juan Velázquez de Cuéllar, his cousin who was *contador mayor* of the prince, was said by Oviedo to have been a "persona de bien e ataviado e zeloso e avisado en lo tocava a la limpieza e lealtad de su oficio" (Oviedo [13:4], 86).

18. Las Casas [2:50], 1, 439, says that there were three hundred.

19. Las Casas [2:50], 1, 445.

20. Oviedo [2:43], 1, 49: "cuando tornaban a España algunos de los que venían en esta demanda del oro, si allá volvían, era con la misma color del; pero no con aquel lustre. . . ."

21. Navarrete [4:38], 1, 408–9.

22. Navarrete [4:38], 1, 410.

23. Navarrete [4:38], 1, 423.

24. Las Casas [2:50], 1, 480: "pidió tantas condiciones y preeminencias, si había de tener aquel cargo, se enojaron los reyes y lo aborrescieron."

25. "Paresceme se deva dar licencia a todos los que quisieren yr" (Morales Padrón [6:19], 5).

26. Bernáldez [3:2], 334: "se dió licencia a otros muchos capitanes . . . e fueron e descubrieron diversas islas."

27. Navarrete [4:38], 1, 430: "facultad a vos, don Cristóbal Colón, nuestro almirante del mar Oceano, e nuestro visorrey e gobernador en la dicha isla para en todos los terminos della podades dar e repartir, e dades e repartades a las tales personas e a cada uno de los que agora viven e moran en la dicha isla e a los que de aqui adelante fueren a vivir e morar en ella. . . ."

28. The comment of Juan Pérez de Tudela.

29. Navarrete [4:38], 1, 409.

30. Rumeu [2:2], 235–36.

31. "pasó a las dichas islas y tierras firmes de India."

32. "se movió con muchas prisa a enbiar una armada suya estas islas y tierras firmes . . . [with the help of] pilotos y marineros y gentes que venían con el dicho almirante."

33. Published by Antonio Rumeu de Armas, *Un escrito desconocido de Cristóbal Colón,* Madrid 1972, and see also Colón [4:16], 333ff. It was Rumeu who thought that there might be a connection with Tordesillas.

34. Liss [2:42], 295.

35. Henceforward there would be
    (a) a *blanca,* of vellon (a mixture of copper and silver), to be worth ½ maravedí;
    (b) a *real,* of silver, worth 34 maravedís;
    (c) a *ducat* (or *excelente*) of gold, worth 375 maravedís. This was a copy of the Venetian ducat.
    A separate currency obtained in Valencia and Catalonia; they, too, had an *excelente* and also a *principal.*
    See Hamilton [3:8], 51. For the money in Valencia, see the same, 104ff.

36. Fernando Colón [4:40], 186.

37. Colón [4:16], 430.

38. See his marginal note on Pierre d'Ailly, quoted in Colón [4:16], 90.

39. Pierre d'Ailly [4:34], 43.

40. Colón [4:16], 351.

41. Colón [4:16], 353ff.

42. "ciudad noble y poderosa por el mar."

43. "me hicieron su almirante en la mar con todas las preheminecias que tiene el almirante don Enrique en el almirantazgo de Castilla . . ."

44. Colón [4:16], 353ff. Also Navarrete [4:38], 1, 436.

45. Fernando Colón [4:40], 363–64. "Tu padre que te ama más que a sí."

46. Ibid.

47. Ibid., 365.

48. The costs were originally to be 6 million maravedís, of which 4 million were to be employed in provisions and 2 million in wages.

49. See M. González Jiménez, "Genoveses en Sevilla (siglos XIII–XV)," in *Presencia Italiana en Andalucia, siglos XIV–XVII,* Seville 1985.

50. Navarrete [4:38], 1, 498.

51. Ibid.

52. Las Casas [2:50], 1, 497, says that he was "hombre muy capaz y prudente y de autoridad."

53. Martyr [6:34], 55. Martyr said that another purpose was that he also wanted to avoid "certain French pirates."

54. Fernández-Armesto [4:49], 14.

55. Colón [4:16], 408.

56. Fernando Colón [4:40], 371.

57. *CDI*, 39, 413: "e allí en nombre del Rey e de la Reina nuestros Señores, tomamos la posesión de la dicha provincia, la que tomó el dicho Pedro de Terreros. . . ."

58. Navarrete [4:38], 2, 344.

59. Navarrete [4:38], 2, 344.

60. Colón [4:16], 373.

61. Ibid., 380–81.

62. For this section I relied on Paul Kirchhoff's chapter in *The Handbook of the Middle American Indians,* ed. Robert Wauchope, 16 vols., 1964–76, 4, 481–93.

63. Colón [4:16], 383. *Margarita* is, of course, Spanish for "pearl."

64. A point well made by Bernal [12:31], 101.

65. Colón [4:16], 403, from Las Casas [2:50], 2, 33.

66. Martyr [6:34], 50.

67. Bartolomeo may have used the name of Domingo after his and the Admiral's father, Domenico Colombo of Genoa, but more likely because the city was founded on the day of Santo Domingo, Aug. 8.

68. Pérez de Tudela [9:39], 163.

69. Oviedo [2:43], 1, 72.

70. Las Casas [2:50], 1, 449.

71. Pérez de Tudela [9:39], 161. Pedro de Valdivieso, a Burgalés, Adrián de Muxica, a Basque, and Diego de Escobar, a Sevillano, all participated.

72. Martyr [6:34], 54.

73. Fernando Colón [4:40], 246, 195.

74. Ursula Lamb, *Frey Nicolás de Ovando,* Madrid 1956, 126, wrote that "it is superfluous to say that the *encomenderos* so invested with land were rebels and, for the same reason, were not the type of persons whom the Crown would have considered worthy of being concerned with the well-being of the Indians."

75. Pérez de Tudela [9:39], 157.

76. Las Casas [2:50], 2, 70.

77. Las Casas [2:50], 2, 173: "¿Qué poder tiene el Almirante para dar a nadie mis vasallos?"

78. Letter to the monarchs sent in the ship, Fernando Colón [4:40], 407.

79. Colón [4:16], 407–8.

80. "mugeres atan hermosas que es maravilla."

81. Colón [4:16], 409.

82. Colón [4:16], 408.

83. Cesáreo Fernández Duro, *Nebulosidades de Cristóbal Colón,* Madrid 1900, 182.

84. Text in Las Casas [2:50], 1, 1151.

85. Colón [4:16], 412: "cada uno pudiese venir a mi y dezir lo que les plazía."

86. Robert S. Chamberlain, *Castilian Backgrounds of the Repartimiento-Encomienda*, Washington, DC, 1939. Richard Konetzke pointed out that it is a mistake to "suppose the Christianization of the infidels was a moving factor in the antecedent history of the discovery of America—an interpretation that springs from confusing the Reconquista . . . with a crusade" (Konetzke, *The Americas*, 14, 1958, 182).

87. See C. H. Haring, *The Spanish Empire in America*, New York 1947, 43, and Fernández-Armesto [4:17], 139.

88. Navarrete [4:38], 1, 44.

Chapter 14

1. As heads of the bedchamber to Kings Enrique III and Juan II; or, as *alcaides* of fortresses.

2. A poem written by Alvar Gómez de Ciudad Real, then attached to the household of Cardinal Mendoza, "On the Marvellous Description of the New World," was much circulated among Beatriz's descendants—to recall that, though one Bobadilla may have dispossessed the Admiral (Francisco, in 1500), another had helped him win his opportunity.

3. Navarrete [4:38], 443. Las Casas [2:50], 2, 176. The instruction was signed by both the Catholic Kings and by Miguel Pérez de Almazán, the secretary who no doubt drafted the document, and by Gómez Juárez, another *letrado* who was now the chancellor of Castile.

4. Navarrete [4:38], 1, 444, 445.

5. Navarrete [4:38], 1, 446.

6. Martyr [6:34], 67.

7. Las Casas [2:50], 1, 465.

8. Las Casas [2:50], 2, 173.

9. Colón [4:16], 409.

10. Qu. Fernández-Armesto [4:2], 25.

11. Bernáldez [3:2], 2, 80.

12. Fray Juan de Trassiera, his own steward; Fray Francisco Ruiz and Fray Juan Robles; and two Fleming lay brothers, Fray Juan de Leudelle (or de la Duela), known as "El Bermejo," and Fray Juan de Tisín, who had been with Columbus on his second voyage in 1493, in company with the mysterious Boil. See Tibesaar, *The Franciscan Promise*, 378. The Franciscan Observants were keen to go to the New World and had received encouragement from their vicar-general, Olivier Maillard, to go.

13. There is a portrait of Ruiz in the Museo de Valencia de San Juan, Madrid.

14. Martyr [1:2], 1, 200.

15. Zurita [9:2], qu. Liss [2:42], 318. Zurita was for a time gentleman of the chamber to Charles V; afterwards he was secretary of the Inquisition and author of *Anales de la Corona de Aragón*.

16. Konetzke [14:86].

17. Las Casas [2:50], 1, 469.

18. Deive [6:36], 70.

19. Navarrete [4:38], 1, 318; Las Casas [2:50], 2, 146; Morison [4:42], 104–8.

20. Martyr [6:34], 70.

21. Martyr [6:34], 71: "tierra continente."

22. *Cédula* of Dec. 2, 1501, from Écija, in *CDI*, 31, 104–7.

23. See Serrano, "El Viaje de Alonso de Hojeda en 1499, *Congreso*" [5:15], 2, 11–136.

24. Important documentation of this voyage is in *Autógrafos de Cristóbal Colón y papeles de América*, Madrid 1892, papers from the Palacio de Liria.

25. For the life and background of this extraordinary individual, see ch. 20.

26. Las Casas [2:50], 2, 115, gives the departure date as May 20. This account contains an extensive defense of the reputation of Columbus against the presumed (but false) assertions of Vespucci. Ch. 20 discusses Vespucci in detail. For this voyage, see Morison [4:42], 186ff.

27. Pohl [5:35] discusses. There remain some unanswered questions about Vespucci's travels.

28. Ibid., 46.

29. Morales Padrón [6:19], 213.

30. For a consideration of the Brazilian Indian, see ch. 36.

31. Morales Padrón [6:19], 218.

32. "dad la cara a vuestros enemigos que Dios os dará la victoria." See Pohl [5:35], 60–61.

33. "tentar el mar y la fortuna."

34. Ramos, *Audacia*, 74.

35. Manzano [6:4], 1, 268.

36. Morales Padrón [6:19], 223.

37. This letter to Lorenzo, incidentally, does not read as if Vespucci had been to the Americas before. His admirers (for example, Harrisse [4:37], 355) argue he had been there in 1496 or 1497.

38. Morales Padrón [6:19], 224.

39. Pohl [5:35], 137.

40. Las Casas [2:50], 2, 154. See Morison [4:42], 211ff.

41. Martyr [6:34], 75–78.

42. Las Casas [2:50], 2, 156; Marañón is a small town in the province of Logroño, whence no conquistador of that time came. The word means "pimp" in Gallego. Could that be relevant?

43. Navarrete [4:38], 2, 328: "todo lo que hoy esta ganado desde la isla de Guanaja hacia el norte, e que estas tierras se llaman Chabaca e Pintigrón e que llegaron por la vía del norte fasta 23 grados e medio e que en esto no andubo el dicho don Cristóbal Colón ni lo descubrió ni lo vido" (Evidence of Ledesma).

44. Navarrete [4:38], 2, 325. Las Casas [2:50], 2, 159, 208. There was later controversy. In 1513, Lepe claimed to have discovered "la vuelta de levante," being acompañied by Juan González, a Portuguese of Palos, Juan Rodríguez, *piloto*, Alonso Rodríguez de Calco, García de la Monja, Fernando Esteban, Cristóbal García, Pedro Medel, and Luis del Valle. See L. Gil Munilla, "Diego de Lepe, descubridor

64. Las Casas [2:50], 2, 203–4.

65. Colón [4:16], 440.

66. Las Casas [2:50], 2, 199.

67. "Si me quexa del mundo es nueva, su usar de maltratar es de antiguo."

68. "Llegué yo y estoy que no ay nadie tan vil que no piense de ultrajarme" (Colón [4:16], 430).

69. Las Casas [2:50], 2, 190.

70. *CDI*, 24, 22–25. A Spanish translation of the original Latin.

71. Francisco (Francesco) Riberol (Ripparolo, Rivarolo) was the son of Pietro Giovanni Sopranis Riparolo and Bianchina, daughter of Pietro Grimaldi. The Riparolos hispanized their name as Riberol. They came from Rivarolo, a village on the mountain behind Genoa. Francesco, one of four sons, was a Genoese merchant in Seville, with a fortune from banking, cloths, dyestuffs, and sugar. He bought part of the rights for the sale of cloth from Pedro de Ribadeneira, and became the chief producer of soap in Seville, with Mario Castiglione. Two years later Castiglione sold him half his soap factory in Triana. Riberol had established sugar plantations in the Canaries in return for his help in the conquests there, where he seems to have been the richest merchant in the 1490s. He and his brothers Cosmo and Gianotto succeeded the Lugos as the main dealers in orchil from the islands, in collaboration, to begin with, in Gomera with Inés de Peraza and later Gutierre de Cárdenas in Tenerife. He and Cosmo married sisters, Giacometta and Benedetina Sopranis de Andora, while his sisters Salvaggina and Mariola married Nicoló and Gregorio Cassana. Riberol was a financier of Columbus's fourth voyage and is mentioned in a letter from Columbus to Gorricio in May 1501 (Colón [4:16], 456), and to Diego (May 1502, Colón [4:16], 478). He probably sold to Cortés the pearl that that captain would in 1519 give to the Mexican emperor Moctezuma's nephew. He, and later his son Bartolomeo, dominated the soap industry of Seville until Francisco's death in 1514. His nephew, Pietro Giovanni Ripparolo, and his son-in-law, Bernardo Castiglione's nephew, Pietro Benedetto Basigniana, and later Jacopo Sopranis continued the monopoly till 1521.

72. The family of Sanchís was involved in the famous murder by *conversos* of the Inquisitor of Saragossa, Pedro Arbués, in 1485, while he prayed in the cathedral. Gabriel was accused of having proposed the murder. After a long inquiry, many *conversos* were executed, including the father-in-law of Gabriel, Luis de Santangel, a relation of his namesake who financed Columbus.

73. Bernal [12:31], 178.

74. Harrisse [4:37], 60.

75. Las Casas [2:50].

76. Harrisse [4:37], 59–76. Miguel Corte-Real returned on Oct. 11, 1502, from Newfoundland with indigenous people and some goods. Alberto Cantino, ambassador of Ferrara in Lisbon, wrote on Oct. 18 to his master, Duke Hercules, about the journey and described how they had found a great territory and kidnapped people, bringing them back to the King of Portugal, while Gaspar Corte-Real had turned south and was never heard of again (Morales Padrón [6:19], 253–65).

77. *Chronology of Voyages*, 72, qu. Harrisse [4:37], 128.

del Marañón," *AEA*, 9 (1952), 73ff., and J. Gil, "Marinos y mercaderes en Indias, 1499–1504," *AEA*, 42 (1985), 313ff.

45. Gil [3:37], 4, 336, discusses his genealogy. He was the son of Alonso Fernández Ojos and Ana Bastidas. He married Isabel Rodríguez de la Romera—all of Triana.

46. Navarrete [4:38], 1, 447. See J. J. Real, "El sevillano Rodrigo de Bastidas," *Archivo Hispalense*, 111–12, 1961, and J. Gil [14:44], 317, 387.

47. Las Casas [2:50], 2, 302.

48. For which see ch. 15.

49. Oviedo ([2:43], 1, 63) has a rather inaccurate description of this journey. Bastidas had an "información de servicios y méritos" that did not mention any detail of the expedition.

50. Some of the best-known explorers were with Mendoza—Nicolau de Coelho, Bartolomeu Díaz, Duarte Pacheco, and Pero de Ataideo. *CDI*, 38, 441–50; Navarrete [4:38], 1, 449. Las Casas does not mention this journey.

51. See Gil [14:44], 304ff., also 433ff.

52. The fleet also had on board Bartolomeu Díaz, the hero of the expedition of 1487, Nicolau de Coelho, Sancho de Tovar, Diego Díaz, the brother of Bartolomeu, Alfonso Ribeiro, Simão de Miranda, Aure Gomes, and Gaspar de Lemus.

54. Nothing suggests that Cabral's journey to Brazil could have been other than an accident. Yet Portugal was full of rumors to the contrary. An adventurer from the Azores, Gasper Corte-Real, received a letter patent from King Manuel of May 12, 1500, in which there figures the following: "Whereas Gaspar Corte Real . . . formerly did make great efforts of his own free will and at his own cost with vessels and men, spending his fortune and at the peril of his life to discover islands and a continent. . . ." See also Morison [4:42], 217–29.

54. The situation was rendered the more complex by the arrival of Alonso de Hojeda near Jaragua in September 1499. But he made it evident that he was against both the Admiral and Roldán, and he eventually withdrew to Spain. The arrival of Vicente Yáñez Pinzón at the end of his voyage further complicated matters for some days before Yáñez also withdrew.

55. Azcona [1:21] discusses, 511.

56. Navarrete [4:38], 1, 447. This was one of the last documents on which Columbus signed himself Viceroy and Captain-General of the Indies, and it was counter-signed by his secretary, an Extremeño who had come with him on the second voyage, Diego de Alvarado.

57. Colón [4:16], 420.

58. Fernando Colón [4:40], 428.

59. A good account is that of Harvey [1:1], last chapter.

60. Las Casas [2:50], 2, 183.

61. Las Casas [2:50], 2, 185.

62. Las Casas [2:50], 2, 188.

63. Guillermo Céspedes del Castillo, in *Historia Social*, ed. J. Vicens Vives (Barcelona 1959), 2, 532.

Chapter 15

1. "Mediano de cuerpo y la barba muy rubia y bermeja. . . . De codicia y avaricia muy grande enemigo" (Las Casas [2:50], 2, 214).
2. Ursula Lamb [13:74], 23.
3. *CDI*, 31, 13–25.
4. "oficios de justicia e juridición civil e criminal, alcaldías e alguacildalgos dellas de las Indias, Islas, y Tierra Firme del Mar Oceano."
5. Esteban Cavallo, Juan and Álvaro Rodríguez, Juan Fraba, and García Osorio. AGI, Indif. 418, lib. 1, f. 77, qu. Pérez de Tudela [9:39], 196.
6. "otros esclavos que hayan nacido en poder de cristianos nuestros súbditos y naturales."
7. For example, on Columbus's third voyage when he stopped in the Cape Verde Islands.
8. *CDI*, 30, 523.
9. Haring [9:39], 26.
10. *CDI*, 31, 13ff., and 50ff.
11. Navarrete [4:38], 1, 546. The royal share, eventually "the royal fifth," tied the Spanish Crown into the success of the mining enterprises in the New World.
12. "de manera que ellos conozcan que no se les hace injusticia."
13. These inquiries, known as *residencias*, might be reintroduced to face modern ministers, ambassadors, and commissioners in Brussels.
14. Giménez Fernández [2:39], 196, 236; see also Las Casas [2:50], 2, 452, 557–58, 562.
15. Navarrete [4:38], 1, 456–58.
16. Las Casas [2:50], 2, 227.
17. *CDI*, 30, 527. There is a list of thirty-seven people who accompanied Arriaga in Giménez Fernández [2:39], 2, 594. They included Diego de Nicuesa, afterwards famous; Diego Ramírez, the only man who was a laborer and who was probably with Narváez in Mexico; Gonzalo de Ocampo; and Rodrigo de Mexía.
18. *CDI*, 30, 526. Giménez Fernández [2:39], 2, 590–91. See also Pérez de Tudela [9:39], 194.
19. Navarrete [4:38], 2, 349, 351. Hojeda himself said that his second expedition was in 1501, but the documents in AGS (Simancas) studied by Navarrete show that it must have been 1502.
20. Colón [4:16], 473–76.
21. Colón [4:16], 473–76: "plazer y holgura: pesadumbre y hastío."
22. Fernando Colón [4:40], 277. But this did not prevent Isabel and Fernando from making a new contract with Yáñez Pinzón on Sept. 5, 1501, whereby Yáñez would pay only a sixth of what he found to the Crown. His journey would be one of settlement, not of discovery. He would also be governor of "the lands newly discovered." Then, a week or so later, on Sept. 14, the monarchs concluded a *capitulación*, this time with Diego de Lepe, the discoverer of the River Marañón, with a new variant: in contrast to what had just been agreed with Yáñez Pinzón, the aim now would be to stimulate discovery. On goods and treasure found on land previously visited by Spaniards, one-half would be payable to the Crown, but

only a sixth on what was obtained from new territories. Much the same arrangement was made with Juan de Escalante on Oct. 5. *CDI*, 31, 5–12.

23. Navarrete [4:38], 1, 548.

24. Colón [4:16], 479–80; Navarrete [4:38], 1, 471–72.

25. Pérez de Tudela [9:39], passim.

26. *CDI*, 31, 121.

27. See Pedro Mexía de Ovando, *Libro o memorial* . . . in Biblioteca Nacional MS no. 3183, f. 2, cit. Miguel Muñoz de San Pedro, "Francisco de Lizaur," in *BRAH*, c. 23, 1948.

28. *CDI*, 39, 13–14.

29. For the family, see Gil [3:37], 1, 247, and Giménez Fernández [2:39], 2, 953. A kinsman was Bartolomé de Alcázar, a poet known for such lines as "A uno muy gordo de vientre y muy resumido de valiente."

30. Giménez Fernández [2:39], 2, 696. The relationship of Ovando and Monroy was remote, and I have not found how Francisco fitted into the main line of the Monroys. A bastard?

31. Colón [4:16], 268.

32. Las Casas [2:50], 2, 214 and 368.

33. AGI, Indif. gen., leg. 418, f. 64, discussed in Pérez de Tudela [9:39], 200.

34. There were with Ovando others who later traveled with Cortés: Francisco Dávila, Juan Suárez (his future brother-in-law), Cristóbal Martín Millán de Gamboa, Juan Pérez de Arteaga, Lorenzo Suárez of Portugal, Francisco Ramírez el Viejo (and his wife, Juana de Godoy), Benito de Cuenca, Domingo Díaz (an Italian who could not remember who his parents were), Juan de Gamarra, Diego Sánchez de Sopuerta, Bernardino and Antonio de Santa Clara, and Juan de Cáceres. There were also Gonzalo Velázquez de Lara and Gutierre de Badajoz, whose sons Francisco and Gutierre were both with Cortés.

35. Fray Alonso de Espinar, Fray Bartolomé de Turégano, Fray Antonio de Carrión, Fray Francisco de Portugal, Fray Antonio de los Mártires, Fray Mases de Zafra, Fray Pedro de Hornachuelos, Fray Bartolomé de Sevilla, Fray Juan de Hinojosa, Fray Alonso de Hornachuelos, Fray Juan de Escalante, Fray Juan Francés, Fray Pierre Francés, and four lay brothers, Juan, Martín, Luis Sánchez, and Pedro Martínez.

36. Pedro Díaz de la Costona, Alonso de Illescas, Fernando Guiral, and Alonso Fernández.

37. Muniz qu. Pérez de Tudela [9:39], 201; Lamb [13:74], 73, fn 43.

38. The charm of Sanlúcar remains, as does the palace of the Medina Sidonia.

39. Las Casas [2:50], 2, 215.

40. The monarchs introduced on Feb. 12 a royal ordinance (*pragmática*) that sought to complete the Christianization of Castile: all *mudéjares* over fourteen (over twelve for women) were given two and a half months to choose either baptism or emigration.

41. Liss [2:42], 335.

42. This was the usual title of an adult heir to the throne of Castile, like the Prince of Wales.

43. Liss [2:42], 336.
44. Fernández-Armesto [4:49], 14.
45. Garay had been a friend of Hernán Cortés, according to Díaz del Castillo (*Historia Verdadera de la Nueva España*, 2 vols., Madrid 1982), between about 1506 and 1510 when both were relatively young men in La Española.
46. The *residencia* was an import from old days in Spain.
47. Fernández-Armesto [4:49], 26. Other members of the family such as Batista were well established in Tenerife.
48. Colón [4:16], 482–83.
49. The family had been involved in all Genoese trading, from the Crimean outpost in Caffa to that in England, and they would be the first Genoese to establish a branch of their business in Santo Domingo.
50. Colón [4:16], 476–78.
51. Navarrete [4:38], 1, 223.
52. Navarrete [4:38], 2, 328. In 1520, he would carry home to the New World the surviving slaves whom Hernán Cortés took to Spain in 1519 with Francisco de Montejo and Alonso Hernández Portocarrero. Juan Sánchez, *piloto mayor,* and Antón Donato, *contramaestre,* were both on the *Santo.*
53. Nicknamed the "Bermuda."
54. See Gil [3:37], 3, 84.
55. Colón [4:16], 487.
56. See Jesús Varela Marcos, "Antón de Alaminos, 'El piloto del Caribe,' " in *Congreso* [5:27], 2, 49ff. We hear of Alaminos as a *"grumete"* in 1502 from Las Casas [2:50], 3, 157.
57. Navarrete [4:38], 2, 328.
58. Their stores, etc., are mentioned in Navarrete [4:38], 1, 229–31. Consuelo Varela has done much better with her "El rol del cuarto viaje colombino," *AEA,* 42, 1985, 243ff.
59. Rafael Donoso Anes speaks of this slave receiving a wage. All the same, he was a *"negro esclavo."*
60. Las Casas [2:50], 2, 209–10.
61. Colón [4:16], 485–86.
62. Colón [4:16], 494.
63. Fernando Colón [4:40], 279.
64. Colón [4:16], 485.
65. Las Casas [2:50], 2, 220–24.
66. Giménez Fernández [2:39], 1, 224.
67. Ursula Lamb, "Cristóbal de Tapia versus Nicolás de Ovando," *Hispanic American Historical Review* (hereafter *HAHR*), 33, Aug. 1953.
68. Las Casas [2:50], 2, 226: "el oro no era el fruto de árboles para que llegando lo cogiesen."
69. Qu. Pérez de Tudela [9:39], 218.
70. Las Casas [2:50], 2, 226.
71. Ibid.
72. Earl Hamilton [3:8], 123.

73. Pérez de Tudela [9:39], 219.

74. Las Casas [2:50], 2, 231–32.

75. Gil [3:37], 1, 155, and also 4, 28. Esquivel came to La Española, I assume, with Ovando, but possibly with Colón, on the second voyage.

76. We soon find that one of the slaves, baptized as Juan, was sold to Francisco Velázquez in the Castilian city of Olmedo. He fled aged thirty but was recovered.

77. Lamb [13:74], 128.

78. Las Casas [2:50], 2, 213.

79. Cf. Alvarado in Tenochtitlan, Cortés in Cholula.

80. This tragedy appears to have been witnessed by Diego Méndez, back on the island looking for help for Columbus, who was marooned in Jamaica; Lamb [13:74], 130.

81. Las Casas [2:50], 238–39; Oviedo [2:43], 1, 83.

82. See María Luisa Laviana and Antonio Gutiérrez Escudero, "Las primeras obras públicas en el nuevo mundo y su financiación: Santo Domingo 1494–1572," in *Congreso* [5:27], 551, 523ff.

83. Enrique Otte, *Las Perlas del Caribe,* Caracas 1977, 251; Las Casas [2:50], 2, 235.

Chapter 16

1. "Azúa" would seem to have been an indigenous word to which the Spaniards added the golden suffix "de Compostela" because of the presence there of a Gallego.

2. That claim is discussed skeptically by Navarrete [4:38], 2, 350. But he admits that Columbus may have seen a report that showed that there was no strait in the continuation of the southern American coast.

3. Colón [4:16], 487.

4. It seems certain that these Indian merchants would have talked of meeting Columbus and that the rumor of these bearded Spaniards would have reached Mexico/Tenochtitlan. See below, ch. 33.

5. Colón [4:16], 488.

6. These paragraphs derive from Paul Kirchhoff, in *Handbook* [13:62], 4, 219–29.

7. *CDI,* 39, 416.

8. Fernando Colón [4:40], 284.

9. Fernando Colón [4:40], 285.

10. The Mayan Indians are discussed in ch. 33.

11. Fernando Colón [4:40], 286. Columbus does not seem to mention this in his own *relación,* unless he was speaking of it when he spoke of Ciguare. Perhaps some of these Maya would be caught up in Cortés's conquests in Mexico.

12. Fernando Colón [4:40], 288.

13. A recent duke of Veragua was pointlessly murdered by terrorists in El Salvador c. 1985 when serving with the Spanish embassy there.

14. Cit. Lewis Hanke, *The Spanish Struggle for Justice in the Conquest of America,* Philadelphia 1949, 25.

15. See Méndez's will in Navarrete [4:38], 1, 240–47, tr. by J. M. Cohen in his *The Four Voyages of Columbus,* Harmondsworth 1969, 305ff.

16. Colón [4:16], 491.
17. Colón [4:16], 492.
18. In his will, in Navarrete [4:38], 1, 245.
19. Fernando Colón said that Méndez and Fieschi left with two canoes, each with six Christians and ten Indian paddlers from Jamaica to Santo Domingo.
20. Colón [4:16], 501.
21. Fernando Colón [4:40], 328; Méndez's account, 315.
22. "During which time he burned or hanged eighty-four ruling caciques, among them the lady Anacoana, the greatest chieftain in the island."
23. Fernando Colón [4:40], 328.
24. Méndez refers to this [16:15], 316.
25. Colón [4:16], 504–5. Fernando said that he took no letters.
26. Colón [4:16], 18, fn 4.
27. Qu. Fernández-Armesto [4:49], 98. On Nov. 4, 1504, there was received in Spain the bull *Illius fulciti presidio,* which accepted the Spanish petition for an archbishop of the Indies and two bishops. The site of the metropolitan see was to be "Hyaguatensis," which has never been identified. Maguacensis (Concepción de la Vega) and Bayunensis (near Lares de Guanaba in the northeast) were the names of the two bishoprics. Anyway, these were not carried through. There were endless delays in establishing the bishoprics, and it was not till 1511 that Alonso Manso, García de Padilla, and Pedro de Deza were named for the three seats (Colón [4:16], 516).
28. Pierre and Huguette Chaunu, *Séville et l'Atlantique,* 7 vols., Paris 1956, 1, 116, propose 3 for 1501, 23 for 1506 (12 returning), 33 for 1507 (19 returning), and 45 for 1508 (21 returning).
29. Gil [3:37], 3, 384.
30. Pérez de Tudela [9:39], 239, citing Muñoz Collection, Real Academia de la Historia, Madrid A-102, f. 210r; see also Fernando Ortiz, "La 'leyenda negra' contra Bartolomé de las Casas," *Cuadernos Americanos,* 65, 5, Mexico 1952, 155.
31. Miguel Ladero Quesada and Gonzalo Jiménez, *Diezmo eclesiástico y producción de cereales en el reino de Sevilla, 1408–1503,* Seville 1979, 91.
32. Heers [4:8], 20; Liss [2:42], 327.
33. Gil [3:37], 2, 12.
34. Gil [3:37], 1, 211.
35. Navarrete [4:38], 1, 321.
36. For Gutiérrez, see Ramón Carande, *Carlos V y sus banqueros,* 3 vols., 3rd ed., Barcelona 1987, 2, 85ff., and Kellenbenz [3:32], 41.
37. The guarantors included Martín Centurione, Alfonso de la Torre, and Diego de la Fuente.
38. Enrique Otte, *Sevilla y sus mercaderes a fines de la Edad Media,* Seville 1996, 169.
39. "Lo que parece se debe proveer, para poner en orden el negocio y contratación de las Indias," in AGS (Simancas), published by the great scholar Ernst Schäfer, in *Investigación y Progreso,* year 8, no. 2.
40. AGI, Indif., Gen., leg. 120, lib. 3, f. 4f; Navarrete [4:38], 1, 472 ff., and *CDIU,* 5, 29–42.

41. Earl Hamilton [3:8], 13, fn 1.
42. Schäfer [9:19], 1, 12, and Miguel Angel Ladero Quesada, *El primer oro de América*, Madrid 2002, 10.
43. The Casa was reorganized in 1507 in order to prevent fraud and to ensure that the Crown received its share of the profits (see *CDI*, 39, 159–62, of Nov. 29, 1507).
44. *CDI*, 31, 139ff. (from Alcalá de Henares); see Eduardo Ibarra, "Los precendentes de la Casa de la Contratación," *R de I*, 3, 4, 5, 1941.
45. Qu. Schäfer [9:19], 1, 13, fn 1.
46. *CDI*, 31, 212, dated January 8, 1504, from Medina del Campo.
47. It moved to Cadiz in the eighteenth century.
48. Pérez de Tudela, "Política de Contratación," *R de I*, 15, 1955, 380.
49. *CDI*, 31, 174–79.
50. *CDI*, 31, 156–74.
51. AGI, Indif., Gen., 418, 1, f. 95v. The last-named is one of the oldest Marian antiphons; and Ave María remains the most popular of prayers.
52. *CDI*, 31, 176.
53. That year, 1503, Cisneros had convoked a group of scholars to work on his planned Bible in seven languages: Nebrija, the great Latinist and philologist, would do the Vulgate; Demetrio Ducas of Crete, Diego López de Stúñiga, and Hernán Núñez would do the Greek text; and three *conversos*, Alfonso de Alcalá, Pablo Coronel, and Alfonso de Zamora, would do the Hebrew text.
54. It was signed by a number of secretaries: Gricio, Zapata, Lic. Johannes, Lic. Tello, Lic. de la Fuente, Lic. Santiago, and Lic. Polanco. See Navarrete [4:38], 2, 414.
55. "donde estaba una gente que se dice caníbales."
56. "prendiendose para los comer como de fecho les comen."
57. "los dichos caníbales sean castigados por los delitos que han cometido contra mis súbditos."
58. "los pueden cautivar e cautiven para los llevar a las tierras e islas donde fueron e para que los pueden traer e traigan a estos mis reinos e señoríos." Navarrete [4:38], 1, 550–51.
59. Summarized in Hanke [16:14], 26.
60. *CDI*, 31, 209–12. See Arranz [12:17], 92. Also in Navarrete [4:38], 1, 481.
61. So at least says the Real Academia's dictionary.
62. Las Casas [2:50], 3, 28.
63. Otte [16:38], 140.
64. Sannazaro was of Spanish origin but lived in Naples.
65. Rumeu [2:2], 300–8.
66. See Ruiz-Domènec [3:20], 341ff. Pastor [1:7], 6, 241.
67. Martyr has a very exciting account of the death of Alexander: poison intended for other cardinals but drunk by mistake by the Pope and his son Cesare (Martyr [1:2], 2, 69).
68. Martyr [1:2], 2, 86.
69. Ballesteros Gabrois, in *Fernando el Católico, pensamiento* [1:22], 133.
70. See Suárez [1:20].

71. L. B. Simpson, *The Encomienda in New Spain, 1492–1550,* Berkeley, CA, 1934, 32. The list of the Queen's executors contained no surprises. They were Fernando, the King; inevitably, Cisneros; Antonio de Fonseca, the chief accountant of the realm (*contador mayor*) and brother of the "Minister for the Indies," Bishop Fonseca; Juan Velázquez de Cuéllar, the Queen's chief accountant and a member of the famous family of public servants, being a cousin of that Diego Velázquez who was at the time deputy of Ovando, in western La Española; Fray Diego de Deza, the Infante Juan's chief preceptor, just appointed to the archbishopric of Seville in succession to Cardinal Hurtado de Mendoza and Columbus's friend; and Juan López de Lazarraga, a secretary to the monarchs since 1503.

72. Oviedo [2:43], 3, 130–37; Navarrete [4:38], 2, 39.

73. Colón [4:16]: "con tanta diligencia y amor como y más que por ganar el Paraíso."

74. Azcona [1:21], 48.

75. Martyr [1:2], 2, 91.

Chapter 17

1. Martyr [1:2], 2, 213. "A ti hija mía como la señora del reino, corresponde elegir el lugar donde prefieres que vayamos." La reina le replicaba "los hijos deben obedecer constantemente a sus padres."

2. Clause 26 of Isabel's will provided that Fernando should exercise the government of Castile in three circumstances.

3. The great courtier Juan Manuel, ex-ambassador of Fernando and Isabel to Maximilian, a Spanish aristocrat of royal blood, was the organizer in Flanders of a party favorable to Philip; while the Duke of Alba and the Count of Tendilla seemed firmly for Fernando. Fernando also had the support of his cousin, the Marquis of Denia, the Count of Cifuentes, as well as Pedro de Farjardo, the *adelantado* of Murcia. But Philip soon had backing from the Count of Benavente, the Marquis of Villena, and the Dukes of Nájera and Medina Sidonia, all of whom feared Fernando ("the Bat" or the "old Catalán," as they called him) as a potentially strong king who would, if he could, diminish their power still further. The Constable, Velasco; the Admiral, Enríquez; and the Duke of Infantado, the head of the Mendozas, were all studiously neutral, allying with one another in the name of Isabel.

4. Elliott [1:25], 127.

5. Otte [16:38], 140. This was the year when, in order to improve the postal service of Castile, a *correo mayor* was appointed, the task being given to the celebrated family the Taxis. Aragon had always had a good postal service. Now Castile was going to be bullied into ensuring better arrangements. Within a generation the Taxis could guarantee deliveries of letters from Rome to Madrid in twenty-four days in summer, twenty-six in winter.

6. Rumeu [2:2], 321.

7. Gil [3:37], 1, 231.

8. Rumeu [2:2], 318.

9. Gil [3:37], 1, 232: "este negocio de la santa inquisición; lo cual, placiendo a Dios, se hará en breve tiempo."

10. Gil [3:37], 1, 232.

11. Martyr [1:2], 3, 22: "Su puerto no conoce igual. Tiene capacidad para todas las naves que surcan por los mares." This journey of Philip's can be studied in A. Lalaing's voyage in *Collection des Voyages des Souverains des Pays-Bas*, ed. M. Gachard, Brussels 1876, 389–451.

12. Colón [4:16], 531.

13. Martyr [1:2], 2, 35; "es más duro que el diamante."

14. Martyr [1:2], 2, 103.

15. This is well described in Liss [2:42], 355.

16. Martyr [1:2], 2, 1.

17. Santa Marina del Rey, Astorga, Ponferrada, Villafranca de Valcarcel (May 21–June 4), Ponferrada again, Matilla de Arzón, Santa Marta, Rionegro, and Asturianos.

18. See Martyr for a firsthand account [1:2], 2, 139–40. There is a dramatic picture of the meeting painted by an anonymous artist, now in the possession of a descendant of a cupbearer to Philip, in the Château de la Follie, Ecaussines d'enghien, Belgium. See the illustration to this book in the first plate section.

19. See Manuel Fernández Álvarez, *Carlos V, el César y el Hombre*, Madrid 1999, 81 and fn 20.

20. Rumeu [2:2], 325.

21. Pastor [1:7], 8, 9.

22. Martyr [1:2], 2, 100. For his imprisonment, see the same, 106.

23. Gil [3:37], 1, 232.

24. See Ruiz-Domènec [3:20], 401–16; John M. Headley, *The Emperor and His Chancellor*, Cambridge 1983, 74. There was also a secretary and, in the reign of Charles V, a third regent was found, the Neapolitan jurist Sigismundo Loffredo.

25. Fernández Álvarez [2:42], 139.

26. Martyr [1:2], 2, 83–84.

27. Fernández Álvarez [2:42], 210.

28. As usual, a vivid description can be found in Martyr [1:2], 2, 163 and 173.

29. Hamilton [3:8], 320. The figures were precisely 247.6 instead of 87.9. Olive oil prices doubled in those six years also: 155 ms. in 1501, 310 in 1507.

30. Otte [16:38], 142. Prominent among the importers was a Florentine, Pietro Bartolini, on behalf of his compatriot, Piero Rondinelli.

31. Other names included Luca Battista Adorno, Silvestre de Brine, Manuel Cisbón, Bernardo Pinello, Simone Fornari, Gaspare and Francesco Sauli, Stefano Gustiniano, Donatino Marini, and Ambrosio Spinola.

32. Otte [16:38], 176.

33. Rumeu [2:2], 340.

34. Martyr [1:2], 2, 202.

35. Pastor [1:7], 6, 291.

36. Rumeu [2:2], 336.

37. Martyr [1:2], 2, 213.

38. In the interim, Margaret briefly married Philibert of Savoy, who died young in much the same way that Philip had died, drinking too much water after exercise.

39. Schäfer [9:19], 1, 29–30.

40. "*Supplico*," with two p's, interestingly, *à l'italien.*

41. Colón [4:16], 528.

42. Fernando Colón [4:40], 284.

43. Colón [4:16], 532.

44. At the time of writing, it seems possible that a DNA test will be carried out to give precise knowledge of where the body is. For Columbus's finances, see Juan Gil, "Las Cuentas de Cristóbal Colón," *AEA*, 41, 1984, 425ff.

45. Cristóbal Colón, *Libro de las Profecías,* Madrid 1992, 7.

46. Navarrete [4:38], 1, 492.

47. Navarrete [4:38], 1, 494.

Chapter 18

1. Serrano y Sanz [5:15], 48fn, 11.

2. *CDI*, 31, 233–37.

3. "islas inútiles de las que ningun provecho se espera."

4. Pérez de Tudela [9:39], 227.

5. Pérez de Tudela [9:39], 228.

6. Las Casas [2:50], 2, 340.

7. *CDI*, 31, 214–15.

8. *CDI*, 31, 216, and April 30, 1508, in *CDIU*, 5, 138.

9. For the birth of Ponce de León, see Vicente Murga Sanz, *Juan Ponce de León,* San Juan 1971.

10. For this campaign, see Las Casas [2:50], 2, 266–68.

11. See Elliott [1:25], 67–68.

12. AGI, Indif. Gen, leg. 418, f. 142 sig. Toro, Dec. 27, 1504, qu. Lamb [13:74], 184.

13. Otte [16:38], 251.

14. Oviedo [2:43], 1, 78.

15. AGI, Contratación, leg. 4674, lib. manual de Sancho de Matienzo, 1, f. 59r, cit. Juan Gil (ed.), *El libro Greco-Latino en su influencia en las Indias.*

16. The only copy of this first edition is in the British Library in London—appropriately, since many of the scenes are played out in a mysterious kingdom that did not then exist: "Great Britain."

17. See Henry Thomas, *Spanish and Portuguese Romances of Chivalry,* Cambridge 1920, and Irving Leonard, *Books of the Brave* [3:34]. The introduction by Rolena Adorno to the latter edition is a model of political correctness. But that of Juan Bautista Avalle-Arce to his edition of *Amadís* [5:5] is excellent.

18. Leonard [3:34], 25.

19. Qu. Leonard [3:34], 44.

20. Leonard [3:34], 24.

21. *La Vida de Santa Teresa de Jesús,* BAE, Madrid, 2 vols., 1861, vol. 1, 24. The passage is deservedly famous: "Era aficionado á libros de caballerías y no tan malo

tomaba este pasatiempo, como yo lo tomé para mi; porque no perdía su labor, sin desenvoliémonos para leer en ellos. . . ."

22. Bernal [12:31], 178.

23. Ibid.

24. Qu. Lamb [13:74], 156.

25. AGI, Contratación, leg. 4674, f. 75.

26. AGI, Indif. Gen., leg. 418, tomo I, f. 180v (Segovia, Sept. 15, 1505), qu. Lamb [13:74], 178.

27. AGI, Indif. Gen., leg. 418, ff, 181v–183, r., qu. Pérez de Tudela [9:39], 229: "Paresceme que se deben enviar a conplimiento de cien esclavos negros."

28. Ironically that was also the year when the *Laocoön*, the sculpture of the strangling by serpents of the priest of Troy by a first-century sculptor from Rhodes, was found in a Roman vineyard belonging to Felice di' Freddi, in what had been the Baths of Titus. Pope Julius sent his favorite architect, the Florentine Giuliano Sangallo, to look at it, which he did, accompanied by Michelangelo, and by Sangallo's son, aged nine. The son recalled that his father immediately said: "This is the Laocoön mentioned by Pliny. . . ." The Pope bought it and installed it in the Belvedere. It was felt to be "the most perfect embodiment of the life and spirit of the ancient world that had yet been seen" (Pastor [1:7], 6, 489). It influenced Raphael, Michelangelo, and Bramante. Lessing made it the theme of his essay that discussed the difference between poetry and the fine arts (1766). Thus two worlds would change in the same year, but only the Roman one was noticed.

29. AGI, Contratación 4674, f. 91, r., qu. Pérez de Tudela [9:39], 229; Martyr [6:34], 109.

30. Earl Hamilton [3:8], 42.

31. See the *Residencia vs. Ovando,* where there were many questions such as question 14: "Si saben que en traerse muchos ganados a esta ysla ansy vacas como ovejas rescibe gran bien la ysla e mucho servicio Dios y su Alteza . . . ," which received such answers as "Es notorio en esta ysla . . . los ganados se multiplan mucho en ella. . . ."

32. Lamb [13:74], 172–73.

33. The King's letter was of Sept. 15, 1505. See Pérez de Tudela [9:39], 334, and Lewis Hanke, *All Mankind Is One,* De Kalb, IL, 1974, 10.

34. In *Residencia vs. Ovando:* "No cumplía las cartas que sus Altezas enviaban para que se diesen indios a algunas personas e que no trataban bien a los buenos. Los moços de los moços de los cocineros tienen indios en muchas cantidad."

35. See the entry on Cortés in my *Quién es quién en la conquista de México,* Barcelona 2001.

36. Pasamonte had been named to his post by Conchillos, who always tried to look after the interests of fellow Aragonese. But he had worked for the King, whom he had accompanied to Naples, whence he was called back in 1506. He was a controversial individual. But Las Casas, no friend of mendacity, wrote of him that he was "a man of wisdom, prudence, experience and authority, honest and had the reputation of having been chaste [*casto*] all his life" ([2:50], 2, 345–46).

37. *CDI,* 26, 248.

38. Navarrete [4:38], 1, 495: "he mandado al almirante de las Indias que vaya con poder a residir y estar en las dichas Indias a entender en la gobernacion dellas, segun el dicho poder sera contenido hase de entender que el dicho cargo y poder ha de ser sin perjuicio del derecho de ninguna de las partes."

39. Navarrete [4:38], 1, 495–97; see also Ida Altman, "Spanish Hidalgos and America: The Ovandos of Cáceres," *The Americas,* 43, 3, 1957, 323ff. The King addressed "los concejos, justicias, y regidores, caballeros, escuderos, oficiales e homes buenos de todas las islas, Indias [sic] e tierra firme del mar oceano e a cada uno de vos salud e gracia."

40. García Gallo, in *Fernando el Católico, pensamiento político* [1:22], 154.

41. Consuelo Varela [4:14], 116.

Chapter 19

1. Rouse [8:13], 17.

2. *CDI,* 31, 309ff.; Navarrete [4:38], 2, 78. For Puerto Rico, see two volumes of documents ed. by Mgr. Vicente Murga Sanz: first, *Puerto Rico en los manuscritos de Don Juan Bautista Muñoz,* San Juan 1960, and second, *Cédulario Puertorriqueño,* Río Piedras 1961. Also see Aurelio Tío, *Nuevas Fuentes para la historia de Puerto Rico,* San Germán 1961, and Murga Sanz [18:9], 3–5.

3. *CDIU,* 5, 148–55.

4. Francisca, daughter of Rodrigo Ponce de León, the victor in the war in Granada, referred in a document of April 18, 1518, Archivo de Protocolos de Sevilla (hereafter APS), oficio 10, escribanía de Diego López, qu. Murga Sanz [19:1], 22, to Juan Ponce de León, the conqueror of Puerto Rico, as her cousin.

5. Ramos [10:8], 109; Oviedo ([2:43], 2, 90), who knew him, says that he was on Columbus's second voyage.

6. Las Casas [2:50], 2, 504. It is now some way from the sea.

7. Oficio 15, lib. I, escribanía de Bernal González Valdesillo, f. 3rd tercio del legajo, May 20, 1508 (APS, 1, 381).

8. Las Casas [2:50], 2, 373: "hombre muy hábil y que le había servido en las guerras mucho."

9. Qu. Morison [4:42], 386.

10. Morison [4:42], 504.

11. See Garrido's *Información de Servicios y Méritos* in AGI, Mexico, leg. 203, no. 3. He later fought in Cuba, Florida, and Mexico with Cortés. The others who accompanied Ponce de León are discussed in Murga Sanz [19:1], 35.

12. R. R. Hill, "The Office of Adelantado," *Political Science Quarterly,* 28, 1913, 654. See also Haring [13:87], 23–25. Hill points out that there was probably an *adelantado* in Old Castile in the tenth century, certainly in the twelfth.

13. See Juan González Ponce de León's *Información de Servicios y Méritos,* AGI, Mexico, leg. 203, no. 19. Oviedo speaks well of him as *la lengua,* "an interpreter," but seems not to have known his relation with the commander.

14. *CDI,* 34, 480. This is Ponce de León's own account. See Las Casas [2:50], 356, and Oviedo [2:43], 2, 90.

15. AGI, Mexico, leg. 203, p. 27 of my transcription, "por guanines colgando de las orejas y de las naryzes."

16. Oviedo [2:43], 2, 100.

17. Juan González Ponce de León was also a witness in Juan Garrido's *Información de Servicios y Méritos,* AGI, Mexico, leg. 204, no. 1.

18. This was a *hacienda grande,* to the east of what is now San Juan. The Indians there were put to work by Ponce de León looking for gold in the Toa valley. See Rouse [8:13], 158.

19. Murga Sanz [19:1], 21, 34.

20. Deive [6:36], 83.

21. Las Casas [2:50], 2, 386–90.

22. Oviedo [2:43], 2, 102.

23. Ibid. See also Murga Sanz [19:1], 75, for comment.

24. *Cédula* of Sept. 27, 1514, at Valladolid in AGI, Indif. Gen., leg. 419, lib. V. For the other adventures, see ch. 20. For this phase in Ponce's career, see Murga Sanz [19:1], 160.

25. Oviedo [2:43], 2, 107.

26. "La más hermosa de todas cuantas había visto en las Indias," qu. Morales Padrón [6:19], 25.

27. Morales Padrón, *Jamaica* [11:43], 88.

28. Díaz del Castillo [15:45], 1, 395.

29. For the conquest of Jamaica, there is *CDI,* 32, 240ff.; *CDU,* 1, 1; *CDIU,* 4, 312; and Las Casas [2:50], 2, ch. 56.

30. Oviedo [2:43], 2, 184.

31. Deive [6:36], 95 and ref.

32. Morales Padrón [6:19], 94; for Garay, see *CDI,* 2, 420, 558.

33. Martyr [1:2], 402.

34. AGI, Mexico, leg. 204, no. 3.

35. Morison thought that there were two men of this name.

36. See Morison [4:42], 198.

37. Oviedo [2:43], 3, 133.

38. Ibid.

Chapter 20

1. Pohl [5:35], 35.

2. Pohl [5:35], 137.

3. Professor Morison says that Soderini had been at school with Amerigo Vespucci.

4. It had been to his son John, Duke of Calabria, that Antoine de la Salle dedicated his strange, historical-geographical work *La Salade,* which contained a map of the world that did not show Britain. Queen Margaret of "Anjou," married to King Henry VI of England, had been another child of the "Bon Roi René."

5. Saint-Dié and the neighboring towns had been part of the Duchy of Lorraine, actually "Upper Lorraine," which itself was part of the Holy Roman Empire. It was razed by retreating Germans in 1945. The dukes of Lorraine were French in

origin, coming from an ancient family named Vaudémond. Duke René II was a successful ruler: he had expanded the territory of Lorraine and interested himself greatly in everything new. He had also helped to defeat the last independent Duke of Burgundy, Charles the Rash, at Nancy in 1477.

6. One well-preserved copy of the "planisphere" was found in Wolfegg Castle in 1901 and was apparently bought by the Library of Congress in 2001 for $10 million.

7. See, for an interesting discussion, Heers [4:17], 220.

8. Had someone already been to the Pacific from Europe? A Portuguese? Mr. Peter Dickson thinks so. See *The Times* (London), Oct. 8, 2002, p. 15. Magellan was so sure he would find the strait that now has his name that one can only speculate why that was so (see ch. 36). I myself think that guesses play a large part in geography, as in history.

9. Martyr [6:34], letter to Leo X, 163.

10. Pohl [5:35], 174.

11. See Nicholas Crane, *Mercator*, London 2002, 97ff.

12. Alberto Magnaghi, *Amerigo Vespucci, Studio Crítico*, Rome 1926. Cit. Pohl [5:35], 72.

13. As Pohl says, "A successful name is a work of art."

14. The first page of text in all editions of that letter of Vespucci runs: "Quando apud maiores nostros nulla de ipsis fuerit habita cognitio et auditibus omnibus soit nouvissima res."

15. Pohl [5:35], 176. "Ut ad perquirendas novas regiones versus meridiem a latere orientis me accingam per ventum qui Africa diciter."

16. "Dead reckoning" was the estimate of a ship's position from the distance traveled as recorded in the log and the courses steered by the compass, with corrections for current, etc., but without taking into account any astronomical observations.

17. See comment in Haring [9:39], 285.

18. *CDI*, 36, 251ff. The first *padrón real* is reproduced on pp. 197 and 287.

19. Martyr [1:2], 1, 271.

20. Unless he went to Florence for a time. Vasari says that Leonardo da Vinci drew the head of Vespucci as "a fine old man." That must have been between 1508 and 1512 unless he was making a mistake—or unless Leonardo made an unrecorded visit to Seville! (Vasari, *Lives*, Everyman, London 1927, 2, 16.)

21. Consuelo Varela, "El testamento de Amerigo Vespucci," *Historiografía y Bibliografía Americanistas* 30, 2, Seville 1986, 5. The will is in the APS; see Oficio 1, lib. 1, escribanía Mateo de la Cuadra, f.367, April 9, 1511 (APS 8, 711).

22. Las Casas [2:50], 2, 335. Their instructions are in *CDI*, 22, 1–13. They are dated March 23, 1508. The journey cost 1,700,863 ms., as is shown in the accounts of the Casa de Contratación, published by Ladero Quesada [16:42], 52. The only study of this journey is Ramón Ezquerra, "El viaje de Pinzón y Solís al Yucatán," *R de I*, 30 (1970), 217ff.

23. See Las Casas [2:50], 2, 374, and Oviedo [2:43], 2, 37. The instructions are in *CDI*, 22, 13.

24. Martyr [6:34], 98.
25. Martyr [1:2], 1, 195. See, for Talavera, *CDI*, 1, 212; 22, 158, and 284ff.
26. Las Casas [2:50], 406.
27. Las Casas [2:50], 2, 504.
28. Having sailed first with Bastidas in 1501, Balboa had remained in Santo Domingo after 1502.
29. Oviedo [2:43], 3, 143.
30. Martyr [6:34], 1, 211.
31. For Aguilar, see the *Información de Servicios y Méritos,* in Patronato, leg. 150, n.2, r.1, of which a transcription was kindly given to me by Francisco Morales Padrón.
32. Martyr [6:34], 214.
33. *CDIU,* 17, 265.
34. Martyr [6:34], 234–35.
35. Martyr [6:34], 235–36.
36. Rouse [8:13], 20–21.
37. *CDI,* 22, 26–32, has the *capitulación* with Ponce de León dated Sept. 26, 1512. For a brief modern investigation, see Edward W. Lawson, *The Discovery of Florida and Its Discoverer Juan Ponce de León,* St. Augustine, FL, 1946. A more helpful study is in Murga Sanz [19:1], 100ff, where there is a list of the ships' companies.
38. See Jesús Varela Marcos, "Antón de Alaminos: el piloto del Caribe" in *Congreso* [5:27], 2, 49ff.
39. See Garrido's *Información de Servicios y Méritos* in AGI, Patronato, leg. 204, no. 3. All of the eight witnesses seem to have been with Garrido in Florida. They did not say much, but they were survivors of that journey.
40. Martyr [6:34], 294. Oviedo [2:43], 2, 105, was scornful: he said that the search for the fountain made old men like children. Legend had it that fifty-six aged companions of Alexander the Great recovered their complexions of forty years earlier by bathing in a river near the Tigris and the Euphrates that flowed out of the Garden of Eden. See Leonardo Olschki, "Ponce de León's Fountain of Youth," *HAHR,* 21, August 1941, 362–85.
41. Morison [4:42], 507.
42. Ibid., 511. This was the third Spanish contact with the Mayan world. The first was Columbus's meeting off Honduras in 1502 (see ch. 11) followed by Díaz de Solís's and Pinzón's in 1508 (see ch. 14).
43. Murga Sanz [19:1], 117.

Chapter 21

1. "con mucha casa."
2. The only study of Diego is Luis Arranz, *Don Diego Colón,* Madrid 1982, of which the first volume only has been published. It takes the life to 1511. These ships were owned by all of the most prominent shipowners of Seville: both Gaspare and Bartolomé Centurión, Mencía Manuel, Duchess of Medinaceli, Francisca Ponce de León, daughter of the famous Rodrigo, Jacome Grimaldi (a part share),

Manuel Cansino, Francisco Garay, and Miguel Díaz de Aux (a half share), and Tomás de Castellón (Castiglione) were among the investors in this expedition. See AGS, Consejo Real, leg. 43, f. 5, for the register of the fleet, analyzed in Enrique Otte, "La flota de Diego Colón, Españoles y Genoveses en el comercio trasatlántico de 1509," *R de I,* 95–96 (1964), 475ff.

3. See Emelina Martín Acosta, "García de Lerma en la inicial penetración del capitalismo mercantil en América," in *Congreso* [5:27], 2, 429ff.

4. Las Casas [2:50], 371: "más fué heredero de las angustias e trabajos e disfavores de su padre, que del estado, honras y preeminencias que con tantos sudores y, afliciones ganó."

5. Navarrete [4:38], 1, 498–504. See also Arranz [21:2], 184.

6. "un memorial muy largo y muy particular . . . de la manera que ha tendido en la buena gobernación de la dicha isla . . ."

7. "muy larga y particularmente todas las cosas de alli."

8. Instructions are printed in *CDI,* 32, 55ff.

9. Qu. Juan Gil, *El libro Greco-Latino* [18:15]. At that time books were listed by number, not name. That only became necessary in 1550.

10. For all matters related to population, see the splendid work of investigation by David Henige, *Numbers from Nowhere* [8:12], kindly given to me by the author.

11. *CDIU,* 5, 197ff.

12. See, for example, Carlos Bosch García, *La esclavitud prehispánica entre los Aztecas,* Mexico 1944.

13. Letter from Fernando el Católico to Pasamonte, Valladolid, May 3, 1509, in AGI, Indif. Gen, 418, lib. iii.

14. *CDI,* 36, 288–89.

15. Las Casas [2:50], 2, 345. Lamb, "Cristóbal de Tapia," *HAHR,* 33, Aug. 1953.

16. Ursula Lamb [15:67]: "las haciendas desta tierra no son nada sin indios."

17. Muñoz Collection, Real Academia de la Historia, Madrid, vol. 90, f. 58.

18. See the accounts of Sancho de Matienzo, as published by Ladero Quesada [16:42], 27.

19. See Earl Hamilton's figures [3:8], 123.

20. Schäfer [9:19], 1, 19.

21. Navarrete [4:38], 1, 505–9; see Haring [9:39], 29; Schäfer [9:19], 1, 178: "no consintáis o dejéis pasar a las Indias a ninguna persona de las prohibidas."

22. Giménez Fernández [2:39], 2, 673. The friars were Fr. Pedro de Córdoba, Fr. Antonio Montesinos, Fr. Bernardo de Santo Domingo, and Fr. Domingo de Mendoza. They would be reinforced before the end of the year by Fr. Thomás de Fuentes, Fr. Francisco de Molina, Fr. Pedro de Medina, Fr. Pablo de Trujillo, and Fr. Tomás de Berlanga.

23. Las Casas [2:50], 2, 381–82.

24. AGI, Patronato, leg. 11, r. 5; *CDI,* 7, 43.

25. García Gallo in *Fernando el Católico, pensamiento político* [1:22], 154.

26. Navarrete [4:38], 2, 83–85.

27. "Testimonio de reclamación y protesta de D. Diego Colón," etc., December 29, 1512, summarized in *CDHI,* 7, 232, qu. Haring [13:87], 19.

28. These were Fr. Lope de Paibol, Fr. Hernando de Villena, Fr. Domingo Velázquez, Fr. Pablo de Carvajal, Fr. Juan de Corpus Cristi, and, a little earlier, Fr. Tomás de Toro.
29. Las Casas [2:50] 2, 441. This, of course, is Las Casas's version of events, and Fray Antonino S. Tibesar criticizes it. "Montesinos" was often rendered "Montesino."
30. "la cabeza no muy baja." This could have been the motto of the Dominican order in the New World.
31. Las Casas [2:50], 2, 446–47.

Chapter 22

1. Deive [6:36], 95.
2. Vicente Cadenas, *Carlos I de Castilla, Señor de las Indias,* Madrid 1988, 123.
3. *CDI,* 32, 304–18.
4. Deive [6:36], 96.
5. Otte [15:83], 116.
6. José María Chacón y Calvo, ed., *Cédulario Cubano, 1493–1512,* in *Colección de documentos inéditos para la historia de Hispano-América,* Madrid 1929, 429.
7. Chacón y Calvo [22:6], 445ff.
8. Las Casas [2:50], 2, 449.
9. Fernández-Armesto [4:49].
10. Las Casas [2:50], 2, 450.
11. John Major, 1470–1540, spent half his life in Paris, the rest in Haddington.
12. Martyr [1:2], 2, 142.
13. Las Casas [2:50], 2, 459–62, gives the speech. Mesa was subsequently named bishop of Cuba, which island he never visited, and he died as bishop of Elna, in Cataluña.
14. Perhaps he was related to Cortés, whose mother's half-sister was Inés de Paz, precisely of Salamanca. Cortés stayed with her when at the university about 1490.
15. Beltrán de Heredia, "Un precursor del maestro Vitoria," in *La Ciencia Tomista,* 40, 1929, 173–90.
16. See the study of Eloy Bullón y Fernández, *Un colaborador de los reyes católicos. El doctor Palacios Rubios y sus obras,* Madrid 1927. Bullón's title (Marquís of la Selva Alegre) appears to be a justification of the peerage. Palacios Rubios entered the Consejo Real in 1504.
17. *CDI,* 7, 24–25, Las Casas [2:50], 1, 442. Las Casas recommended Cardinal Cisneros to read Palacios and to have his and Paz's works published.
18. Gregorio's speech is given in Las Casas [2:50], 1, 471–75.
19. Antonio Muro Orejón, *Ordenanzas Reales sobre los Indios. Las Leyes de Burgos, 1512–1513 (AEA),* Seville 1956. For a list of seven preliminary conclusions of eight members of the committee, see Las Casas [2:50], 2, 456–570.
20. This followed a different stratagem. In 1504, the son of a *cacique* was sent back to Spain in a vessel of Luis Fernández's to learn Spanish. His death, and that of several others, led the Spaniards to later reverse the idea implicit in this: in-

stead of sending the Indians to be educated in Spain, Spaniards would go to the Indies; and Suárez was asked to go out to Santo Domingo to teach grammar to the sons of *caciques*. His teaching was based on Nebrija's *Gramática*, though Latin had also to be taught to enable pupils to understand jurisprudence and theology. A certain "Diego Indio" was taken back to Seville to be "industriado en las cosas de la fe o en otras cosas de buena crianza e conversación para cuando hobiere de tornar a la dicha isla pueda aprovechar a los vecinos e moradores della en la salud de sus animas e conciencias." He was to be lodged by Luis de Castillo, a chaplain of the chapel of Santa María de Antigua en Sevilla, for an annual fee of 8,000 ms. But he died before he could return home.

21. Hanke [16:14], 25; the laws are in Las Casas [2:50], 2, 482–89.
22. The first of these was at the time the King's confessor.
23. Antonio Rodríguez Villa, *Bosquejo biográfico de la reina Juana*, Madrid 1874, 33.
24. These amendments are summarized in Las Casas [2:50], 2, 492ff.
25. Fernández de Enciso, *Memorial,* in *CDI,* 1, 441–50.
26. Qu. Hanke [18:33], 35. This would eventually seem to give the Crown of Castile another title, beyond that of the initial grants of the Pope, to the territories in the New World.
27. Arranz [12:17], 196.
28. *CDI,* 1, 50ff.
29. *CDI,* 11, 216–17.
30. Otte [15:83], 118.
31. Otte [15:83], 119.
32. See Helen Parish, with Harold Weideman S. J., "The Correct Birth Date of Bartolomé de las Casas," *HAHR,* 56, 385.
33. According to Claude Guillen in "Un padrón de conversos sevillanos," *Bulletin Hispanique* 65 (1965). Marianne Mahn-Lot, *Bartolomé de las Casas,* Paris 1982, 12, also suggested that the Peñalosas of Segovia were a *converso* family. See now Gil [3:37], 3, 121 and 460, whose study seems decisive. Bartolomé was not related to the noble Sevillano family of Las Casaus.
34. Arranz [12:17], 540, 564.
35. Giménez Fernández [2:39], 2, 89, 385.
36. Las Casas [2:50], 1, 332.
37. See Raymond Marcus, *El primer decenio de Las Casas en el Nuevo Mundo,* Ibero-American Archives, 1977, 87ff. Mahn-Lot [22:33], 19, however, thinks he was involved.
38. Las Casas [2:50], 1, 466.
39. Las Casas [2:50], 3, 26, 87.
40. Las Casas [2:50], 2, 17, 53.
41. Las Casas [8:14], 164, 528: "de las flautas, este se celebraba en el treceno día de enero con gran licencia de lascivia ... andando los hombres vestidos de vestiduras de mujeres por toda la ciudad, enmascarados, haciendo bailes y danzas, y la memoria y vestigio de ellos yo lo he visto los días que estuve el año de siete, digo quinientos y siete, que de estas Indias fui a Roma."

42. Las Casas [2:50], 2, 385–86. "La cual fue la primera que se cantó nueva en todas estas Indias; y por ser la primera, fué muy celebrada y festejada del almirante [Diego Colón] . . . porque fué tiempo de la fundición. . . ."

43. Fernando had been in Lerma on July 22, Aranda de Duero July 27–Aug. 9, Gumiel de Hizan Aug. 11–23—though going back to Aranda Aug. 15–20—San Esteban de Cuéllar Aug. 24, Segovia Aug. 25–Sept. 15, Sotos Albos, Fresno de Cantespino, Piquera de San Esteban, Burgo de Osma, Almazán, Monteagudo, and, finally, Calatayud, for the Cortes of Aragon Sept. 29–Oct. 18, then Sigüenza, Cogulludo, Buitrago, La Pedrezuela, Alocobendas, and Madrid, where he arrived on Oct. 29. Afterwards he was at Móstoles, Casarrubios, Cazalegas, Talavera, Oropesa, Mesillas, and Castejada. To find a less rigorous climate for the winter than Castile, the King stayed at Plasencia off and on till the end of year, with short visits to La Abadía, Dec. 6 to 11, to go hunting, and to Galisteo, Dec. 13–18. See also Giménez Fernández [2:39], 2, 673, and David Brading, *The First America*, Cambridge 1991, 74.

44. Las Casas [2:50], 3, 108–10.

45. AGI, Contratación, 4675, lib. 1, cit. Manuel Giménez Fernández, "Hernán Cortés y su revolución comunera en la Nueva España," *AEA*, 5, 1948.

46. Marcel Bataillon, *Erasmo y España*, Mexico 1998, 56.

47. Álvar Gómez de Castro, *De las hazañas de Francisco Jiménez de Cisneros*, Madrid 1984.

48. Gil [3:37], 1, 251.

49. *CDIU*, 5, 197–200, 5, 191ff.

50. Chacón y Calvo [22:6], 467.

51. Navarrete [4:38], 1, 516.

52. Gil [3:37], 1, 255.

53. Navarrete [4:38], 1, 514: "universal patriarca de toda ella."

54. Rumeu [2:2], 411.

55. Navarre, in Spain, retained its Cortes, its other institutions and customs, and even its coinage. But it was to become part of Castile. In June 1512, Pope Julius, now Fernando's ally, had finally triumphed in Italy, securing the withdrawal of all French troops and the loss of all French possessions there.

56. Otte [15:83], 123.

57. Otte [15:83], 123 and fn 601.

58. Garcés had been a conquistador but had apparently killed his wife, a *cacica* of La Vega in La Española, on suspicion of adultery, after which he wandered in the hills for four years before being received and pardoned by the Dominicans.

59. Giménez Fernández [2:39], 2, 681. See also AGI, Justicia, 47, no. 3.

Chapter 23

1. AGI, Justicia, leg. 49, *Residencia* taken of Diego Velázquez de Cuéllar. For this chapter see also Chacón y Calvo (ed.) [22:6], Cedulario cubano 1493–1512.

2. Las Casas [2:50], 2, 486.

3. Las Casas [2:50], 2, 339.

4. *CDI*, 39, 11–12. He had killed a certain Juan de Velázquez in Jerez.

5. Martyr [6:34]. Others probably included Sancho Camacho and his brother.

6. *CDI*, 11, 414. See Juan Beltrán, "Bojeo de Cuba por Sebastián de Ocampo" in *Revista Bimestre Cubana*, 3, 19, May–June 1924.

7. Las Casas [2:50], 2, 510.

8. See Santiago Otero Enríquez, *Noticias genealógicas de la familia Velázquez Gaztelu*, Madrid 1916.

9. For the life of this conquistador, see Balbino Velasco Bayón, *Historia de Cuéllar*, 4th ed., Segovia 1996, 326ff.

10. Most of these are being revived thanks to the efforts of a clever mayor.

11. Gonzalo de la Torre de Trassierra, *Cuéllar*, Madrid 1896, 2, 213; Levi Marrero, *Cuba: Economía y Sociedad*, Barcelona 1972, 1, 117, says he was in Italy with the Gran Capitán: the dates do not fit the suggestion.

12. AGI, Indif. Gen., leg. 419, lib. 5, 94v, qu. Arranz [12:17], 306–7.

13. I. A. Wright [11:38], 24, 45: See also Marrero [23:11], 1, 163.

14. Others with Diego Velázquez included Cristóbal de Cuéllar, who had been *contador* in La Española and had once been with the Infante Juan; Antonio Gutiérrez de Santa Clara, as *fundidor,* one of an emigrant family of *conversos;* Andrés de Duero, who is said to have been with the Gran Capitán in Naples; and others such as Diego and Pedro de Ordaz, who had already been in the Caribbean for several years, together with several members of the Velázquez family, such as Baltasar Bermúdez, Bernardino Velázquez, Francisco de Verdugo, another Diego Velázquez, a nephew of the "Governor," and Pedro Velázquez de León, who would play a part in the conquest of Mexico. For a partial list of *vecinos* of Cuba in 1510–16, see Marrero [23:11], 1, 138. Another who went with Velázquez was Juan Garrido, who had fought in Puerto Rico. See AGI, Mexico, 204, no. 3.

15. Las Casas [2:50], 2, 524.

16. It is worthwhile recalling the comments of Irene Wright, who spent so many years seeking material in the Archive of the Indies on the early history of Cuba, that "the descriptions of Las Casas do not differ from documents which I have seen . . . except when one comes to figures" [11:38], 15–16.

17. Oviedo [2:43], 2, 113; Las Casas [2:50], 2, 524. There is no memory of Narváez in Navalmanzano.

18. Wright [11:38], 28.

19. Las Casas [2:50], 2, 536–37.

20. Las Casas [2:50], 2, 539.

21. Las Casas [2:50], 3, 95.

22. Las Casas [2:50], 2, 542. Again, Las Casas is curiously silent about the identities.

23. See Marrero [23:11], 110–15.

24. Wright [11:38], 40.

25. *CDI*, 32, 369, of March 20, 1512.

26. See Muñoz Collection, Real Academia de la Historia, Madrid, f.90, 120r, 119v, 120r.

27. *CDIU*, 1, 32.

28. *CDIU*, 6, 4ff.

29. Velázquez himself received good allocations; and so did allies of his such as Manuel de Rojas, Juan Escribano, and his brother Juan de Soria, at Bayamo; Juan de Alia at Havana; Juan Rodríguez de Córdoba at Sancti-Spiritus; and Alonso Rodríguez at Guaniguanico. Wright [11:38], 49.

30. The artist's mother, Jerónima, was a Velázquez; her father was Juan Velázquez, that is with a Christian name often found, like Diego, among the Velázquez de Cuéllars. Several Velázquezes left Cuéllar for Seville in search of fame and fortune in the sixteenth century, and it would not be altogether surprising to discover that one of the Governor's brothers—Anton, Ruy, or Gutierre—had a son, Juan, the painter's grandfather—though, since the painter was particularly concerned with his ancestry (as the inquiry carried out in respect of him in the 1650s made evident), it must be improbable.

31. See list in *CDI*, 11, 412–29.

32. There were Fray Gutierre de Ampudia, Fray Bernando de Santo Domingo, Fray Pedro de San Martín, and Fray Diego de Albeca (Las Casas [2:50], 3, 99–103).

33. *CDI*, 11, 428. The report was mentioned without comment by Carl Sauer in his *The Early Spanish Main* [8:5]. See also Marrero [23:11], 1, 107.

Chapter 24

1. *CDI*, 39, 238–63. Note: Henceforward I refer to Núñez de Balboa as "Balboa" for ease of understanding. He added that they had more gold than health ("más oro que salud") and also that "nos ha faltado más la comida que el oro." And there were these "rios de oro mui ricos." Angel de Altolaguirre, *Vasco Núñez de Balboa*, Madrid 1914, 13–25.

2. "se resolvió de elegir algún procurador . . .": Martyr [6:34], 131.

3. *CDI*, 39, 241.

4. "para conquistar mucha parte del mundo."

5. Martyr [6:34], 137: "sus caras atestiguan lo malo que es el aire de Darien, pues están amarillos como los que tienen ictericia, e hinchados, si bien ellos lo atribuyen a la necesidad que han pasado."

6. Martyr [6:34], 150: "Cavan tambien de la tierra unas raices que nacen naturalmente y los indigenas las llaman batatas; cuando yo las vi, las juzgué nabos de Lombardia o gruesas criadillas de tierra. De cualquier modo que se aderecen asadas o cocidas no hay pasteles ni ningun otro manjar de mas suavidad y dulzura. La piel es algo mas fuerte que en las patatas y los nabos y tienen color de tierra, pero la carne es muy blanca. . . ."

7. Oviedo [1:2], 3, 206.

8. Las Casas [2:50], 3, 15: "la fama de que se pescaba el oro en tierra firme con redes . . . para ir a pescarlo casi toda Castilla se movió."

9. Martyr [6:34], 1, 314.

10. "así por mar como por tierra, a la Tierra firme, que se solía llamar e ahora la mandamos llamar Castilla aurífera."

11. Instructions, in *CDI*, 39, 280, and in Navarette [4:38], 205–41; see also Álvarez

Rubiano, *Pedrarias Dávila,* Madrid 1914, 49, and Carmen Mena García, *Pedrarias Dávila,* Seville 1992, 211.

12. Martyr [6:34], 138.

13. *CDI,* 39, 123.

14. Martyr [6:34], 1, 282.

15. Martyr [6:34], 1, 284–85.

16. See Elsa Mercado Sousa, *El hombre y la tierra en Panamá (siglo XVI) según las primeras fuentes,* Madrid 1959.

17. Martyr [6:34], 166; Oviedo [2:43], 3, 210ff; Las Casas [2:50], 594.

18. Martyr [6:34], 167.

19. Martyr [6:34], 1, 288. See Morales Padrón [6:33], 342.

20. Martyr [6:34], 1, 292.

21. Martyr [6:34], 1, 307.

22. See Samuel Lothrop, in Wauchope, ed. [13:62], 253–56.

23. Carmen Mena García, *Sevilla y las flotas de Indias,* Seville 1998, 259.

24. Ibid., 67; see also Ladero Quesada [16:42], 62.

25. Las Casas [2:50], 3, 14, "de mucha edad porque pasaba de sesenta años."

26. "la santa conquista de Granada e Africa . . . en la toma de Oran donde os señalistes muy honoradamente . . . en la toma de Bugía . . ."

27. Oficio 15, escribanía Bernal González Vallesillo, f.151, last tercio del legajo, Jan. 13, 1514 (APS, 1, 1017). This indicates the collaboration between Gaspar Centurión and Juan de Córdoba; see also Oficio 15, lib. único, escribanía Bernal González Vallesillo, f., first tercio del legajo, Jan. 30, 1514 (APS, I, 1026). This shows that Pedrarias received 10,599 ms. from Augustín and Bernardo Grimaldi.

28. AGI, Panama, leg. 233, Sept. 1513, qu. Mena [24:23], 82: "como si de subditos españoles se tratase."

29. APS, 9, 118, Sevilla, Jan. 30, 1514, qu. Mena [24:23], 82fn, 34.

30. APS, 9, 107, Sevilla, also qu. Mena [24:23], 83.

31. Mena [24:23], 83.

32. "todos escogidos entre hidalgos y personas distinguidas."

33. "la más lucida gente de España que ha salido." Pascal de Andagoya, *Relación de documentos,* ed. Adrián Blázquez, *Crónica de Américas,* Madrid, 1986, 83.

34. See Mena [24:23], 73ff. for a discussion.

35. According to Mena, there were 278 seamen, and she gives a roll call of 226 of them—saying that among them there were 107 men from Andalusia, 28 from the Basque country, 8 foreigners, 18 from Galicia, 7 from Asturias, 12 from Castilla la Vieja (Mena [24:23], Sevilla, 133).

36. Andagoya [24:33], 10.

37. "tiene alguna experienca de las cosas de Tierra Firme y también para cosas de armada."

38. Other captains were Luis Carrillo, Gonzalo Fernández de Lago, Contreras, Francisco Vázquez Coronado (not the discoverer of Colorado), and Diego de Bustamante y Atienza. Among future conquistadors of New Spain were Francisco de Montejo, Bernal Díaz del Castillo, Juan Pinzón, Ortiz de Zúñiga, Martín

Vázquez, Antonio de Villarroel, Alonso García Brabo, the replanner of the city of Mexico, Pedro de Aragón, probably Juan de Arcos, Vasco de Porcallo, Angel de Villafaña, and his father, Juan de Villafaña. Hidalgos were Sancho Gómez de Córdoba, courtiers Francisco de Soto and Diego de Lodueña of Madrid; royal guards, such as Pedro de Vergara and Francisco de Lugones; servants of Queen Juana, such as Cristóbal Romero, Juan Ruiz de Cabrera, or children of servants of the King, such as Juan de la Parra, son of a secretary of the King of the same name, Juan de Beyzama, Pedro de Gómez, Salvador Girón, and Miguel Juan de Rivas, and Gaspar de Espinosa, all of whom had been personally recommended to Pedrarias by the King himself. See Mena [24:23], 778.

39. For Oviedo, see the introduction to the *Historia* by Pérez de Tudela, "Vida y escritos de Gonzalo Fernández de Oviedo," Madrid, *BAE,* 175, and also his prologue to *Batallas y Quincuagenas,* Real Academia de la Historia, 1983. See also María Dolores Pérez Baltasar, "Fernández de Oviedo, Hito innovador en la historiografía," in *Congreso* [5:27], 4, 309ff.

40. In the Muñoz Collection, Real Academia de la Historia, Madrid, there figure the names of others: Toribio Contado, García Rivero, Miguel or Martín Fernández, Juan de León, Diego Osorio, Gonzalo Alonso, Juan Ruiz de Guevara, Antonio de Aranda, Juan de la Puente, Pedro de Rozas, the bachiller Villadiego, and Juan de Buendía.

41. Mena [24:23], 46.

42. "sayo de seda e muchos de brocado": the expression of Judge Zuazo in a letter to Chièvres.

43. *CDI,* 39, 280–316, "muy malos vicios y malas costumbres."

44. Valladolid, June 18, 1513, in AGI, Panama, 233, lib. 1, qu. Mena [24:23], 42.

45. Deive [6:36], 105.

46. "es uno de los más grandes que hoy hay en el mundo."

47. The other pilots were Pedro de Ledesma, Andrés de San Martín, Antonio Mariano (an especially recommended Italian), and Andrés García Niño. Ledesma had been on the third and fourth voyages of Columbus. In the last of these, he had sided with the rebels against the Admiral and his brothers, and he had been wounded by Bartolomeo Colón. Then he had been to the coast of Central America with Yáñez Pinzón and Díaz de Solís in 1508.

48. Mena [24:23], 79.

49. "que no consintáis que ninguno pueda abogar asi como clerigo o como lego."

50. Mena [24:23], Seville, 333.

51. Mena [24:23], 334.

52. Martyr [6:34], 140.

Chapter 25

1. AGI, Panama, leg. 233, lib. 1, 49–50, qu. Cadenas [22:2], 147–49.

2. "un honbre y una mujer de quien nosostros y vosotros y todos los honbres nosotros vinieren."

3. "entraré poderosamente contra vosotros y vos haré guerra por todas las partes y maneras que pudiera y vos subjetaré al yugo y obedencia de la iglesia y sus altezas y tomaré vuestras personas de vuestras mugeres e hijos y los haré esclavos y como tales los venderé y dispondré dellos como su Alteza mandare y vos tomaré vuestros bienes y vos haré todos los males e daños que pudiere como a vassallos que no obedecen ni quieren recibir a su señor. . . ."

4. Oviedo [2:43], 3, 230.

5. Las Casas [2:50], 3, 31: "y cosa es de reír o de llorar."

6. Oviedo [2:43], 230: "Más parésceme que se reía muchas vesces . . ."

7. Instructions of Fray Juan de Quevedo (1515) to *maestrescuela* Toribio Cintado, in Altolaguirre [24:1], 104.

8. "mansos como ovejas."

9. "Señor, Pedrarias ha llegado a esta hora al puerto que viene por gobernador de esta tierra."

10. Martyr [6:34], 209.

11. Mena [24:11], 50–53. The exact nature of Pedrarias's infirmity is impossible to ascertain. Balboa's letter to the King of Oct. 16, 1515, summarizes these events. It is in Navarrete [4:38], 2, 225ff.

12. Martyr [6:34], 261.

13. Andagoya [24:33], 85–86.

14. AGI, Patronato, leg. 26, r. 5, Jan. 18, 1516, qu. Pedro Álvarez Rubiano, *Pedrarias Dávila*, Madrid 1944, 439–45. The appendices to this old book contain invaluable unpublished documents.

15. Martyr [6:34], 1, 403.

16. Mena [24:11], 59.

17. Martyr [6:34], 351.

18. Martyr [6:34], 405.

19. "estaban como ovejas se han tornado leones bravos."

20. "es hombre muy acelerado en demasia."

21. The pearl, which was painted by Titian, was stolen by José Bonaparte.

22. Martyr [6:34], 1, 404.

23. Cit. Mena [24:11], 98.

24. Las Casas [2:50], 3, 182: "ya yo le he dicho que será bien que echemos aquel hombre de allí."

25. Las Casas [2:50], 3, 85.

26. Las Casas [2:50], 84–86.

27. Espinosa, Diego Márquez, Alonso de la Puente, Pizarro, Juan de Castañeda, and Pascal de Andagoya, for example. Cit. Mena [24:23], 135.

28. Martyr [1:2], 3, 176, 203.

Chapter 26

1. Pulgar [1:24], 124: "de la fortaleza de Madrigalejo se habían fecho mayores crimenes e robos, mandola derribar."

2. Lorenzo Vivaldi and Flerigo Centurione, Vincencio Spinola and Pietro Nigrone, Giuliano Calvo and Benedetto Castiglione, as well as Giovanni Matosta de Moneglia and Pietro Giovanni Salvago, and the brothers Jacopo and Gerónimo Grimaldi.

3. Giménez Fernández [2:39], 1, 117, and Headley [17:24], 44.

4. The investors in an expedition of 1514 included judges Villalobos (in whose house in Santo Domingo the thing was planned) and Ortiz Matienzo, the *contador real* Gil González Dávila, and Pedro de Ledesma, the secretary of the *Audiencia*, while Rodrigo de Alburquerque was responsible for the last *reparto* of territory, and the *contador* Juan García Caballero invested later. These were all officials. Merchants who were investors in 1514 included Juan Fernández de Varas and Diego Caballero ("El Mozo").

5. Prices were certainly unsteady in Castile in the early sixteenth century. Taking 1521–30 as a basis, Earl Hamilton [3:8], 189, thought that prices stood at 68.5 maravedís in 1501, rose to 110.6 in 1506 and were down to 72.8 per *fanega* in 1512, rising to 80.73 in 1516. The big rises did not occur till after 1545.

6. For speculation, see Fernández Álvarez [17:19], 67 fn 5.

7. For commentary, see Haring [9:39], 35.

8. The will was signed in the presence of the Aragonese protonotary Velázquez Climent. A protonotary was a member of the Vatican's College of Notaries. Again, see Fernández Álvarez [17:19], 69.

9. Martyr called the house "desguarnecida e indecorosa."

10. Fernández Álvarez [3:51], 48–49.

11. Harvey [1:1], 139, 150.

12. Giménez Fernández [2:39], 1, 72.

13. *Sancho Cota, Memorias,* ed. Hayward Keniston, London 1964, 77. See also Keniston's *Francisco de los Cobos,* Pittsburgh, PA, 1959, 32.

14. Alonso de Santa Cruz, *Crónica de los Reyes Católicos* [5:7], 215, says that, on hearing of the birth of Charles in 1500, Queen Isabel said to Fernando: "Tened por cierto, señor, que éste ha de ser nuestro heredero, y que la suerte ha caydo al reino, como en santo Matías para el apostolado."

15. An exception was Charles de Valera, son of Diego de Valera the historian.

16. Huizinga [4:34], 75.

17. The news of Pavia in 1525 reached Charles in Madrid, where he had just written an autobiographical note: he wished "lesser quelque bonne memorye de moy . . ." for "jusques icy n'ay fait chose qui rendonde a l'honneur de ma personne. . . ." For Burgundy and its impact, see Bertrand Schnerb, *L'État Bourguignon, 1363–1477,* Paris 1999, and his delightful *Splendeurs de la cour de Bourgogne,* Paris 1995.

18. John of Saxony, the young Señor de Balançon, the Elector Frederick V of the Palatine, Fürstenberg, Max Sforza.

19. Letters from Manrique and Lanuza as qu. Giménez Fernández [2:39], 1, 58.

20. The most famous remark of Maximilian to Charles was "Mon fils, vous allez tromper les Français, et moi, je vais tromper les Anglais."

21. "en lo cual se capta la fuerte tendencia 'caballeresca.' " Qu. in Federico Chabod, *Carlos Quinto y su imperio,* Spanish tr. from the Italian by Rodrigo Riza, Madrid 1992, 56.

22. Marino Sanuto, *Diarii,* 55 vols., Venice 1887, 20, 422, 324. This is a description by Lorenzo Pasqualigo in a letter: "de mediocre estatura delgado hasta lo imposible, pálido, muy melancólico . . . con la boca siempre . . . abierta."

23. The best portrait of Charles at this time is by Conrad Moit, c. 1517, in the Gruuthuse Museum, in Bruges. See also the fine portrait of the same time in the Fitzwilliam Museum, Cambridge.

24. A recent life is that by Jean-Pierre Soisson, *Marguerite, Princesse de Bourgogne,* Paris 2002.

25. Giménez Fernández [2:39] 1, 16. Contarini was later famous for his study of the Venetian constitution, *De Magistralibus Venetorum.*

26. The best study of the influence of Chièvres is in Chabod [26:21], 55–61.

27. "selon la raison en manière qu'ils devront raisonablemente contenter."

28. There is an anonymous picture of Croÿ in the Musée des Beaux-Arts, in Brussels.

29. Martyr discusses this [1:2] 1, 211, also 213.

30. Count of Cedillo, *El Cardenal Cisneros, gobernador del reino,* Madrid 1921, 2 vols., 2, 30–31: "my muy caro e muy amado amigo señor."

31. Cedillo [26:30], 2, 87; Alonso de Santa Cruz, *Crónica del Emperador, Carlos V,* Madrid 1920–25, 5 vols., 1, 106–10: "no hay necesidad en vida de la reina, nuestra señora, su madre, de se intitular Rey, pues lo es; porque aquello sería disminuir el honor y reverencia que se debe por ley divina y humana a la reina nuestra señora, vuestra madre. . . . Y porque por el fallecimiento del rey católico, vuestro abuelo, no ha adquirido más derecho de lo que antes tenía, pues estos reinos no eran suyos."

32. Cedillo [26:30], 2, 99.

33. Keniston [26:13], 26.

34. Joseph Pérez, *Carlos V,* Madrid 1999, proposes the word.

35. Chabod [26:21], 64.

36. Fray Prudencio de Sandoval, *Historia de la vida y hechos del Emperador Carlos V,* Valladolid 1604–06, vol. 1, 73–74.

37. Cedillo [26:30], 2, 136–7.

38. Fernández Álvarez [3:51], 171.

39. Several of the men who would have led the "gente de ordenanza" would later be leaders of the *comuneros:* for example, Bravo in Toledo.

40. AGI, Patronato, leg. 252, r. 1, doc. 1.

41. Las Casas [2:50], 3, 112: "los remedios que parezcan ser necesarios."

42. Marcel Bataillon, *Estudios sobre Bartolomé de las Casas,* Barcelona 1976.

43. Giménez Fernández [2:39], 1, 128.

44. *CDI,* 7, 14–65. This memorandum in the Archive of the Indies is written in Las Casas's hand. See discussion in Hanke [16:14], 57.

45. *CDI,* 10, 114ff.

46. *CDI,* 1, 253ff.

47. "que Dios le dé buen paradiso."
48. *CDI*, 7, 428.
49. *CDI*, 10, 549–55.
50. AGI, Patronato, leg. 252, r. 12, p. 2.

Chapter 27

1. "por evitar lo que podía en disfavor de la una o de la otra sentirse o decirse."
2. Las Casas [2:50], 3, 115.
3. See their accomplished reports in *CDI*, 1, 247–411; also Las Casas [2:50], 3, 119.
4. Bartolomeo Colón, as cit. in Henige [8:12].
5. AGI, Patronato 252, r. 2, in *CDI*, 14–65.
6. *CDI*, 23, 310–31.
7. Las Casas [2:50], 3, 123: "vivir, estar y conversar los unos con los otros." The word "Republic" had no antimonarchical connotations.
8. Las Casas [2:50], 3, 138: "De quién nos hemos de fiar? Allá, vais, mirad por todo."
9. Dated Sept. 16, 1516, to be seen in Las Casas [2:50], 3, 1, 36.
10. Giménez Fernández [2:39], 1, 220.
11. Las Casas [2:50], 3, 138.
12. Ibid.
13. Gil [3:37], 3, 226.
14. Oficio 4, lib. 1, escribanía Francisco Segura, f. 33, January 3, 1506 (APS, 7, 237).
15. Probably on Aug. 29, 1506 (see document in oficio 4, libro 2, escribanía Francisco Segura, f. 102–3, sin fecha, but "las escrituras anterior y posterior estan fechadas en 29 de agosto" [APS, 7, 379], cited, and, in the Spanish ed., reproduced in facsimile in my book *The Conquest of Mexico*, London 1993).
16. Oficio 4, lib. 3, escribanía Francisco Segura, f. 286 (1506) (APS, 7, 388).
17. Oficio 4, lib. 4, escribanía Francisco Segura, f. 201, Oct. 20, 1506 (APS, 7, 432).
18. See, for example, in the records of the Casa de Contratación, Ladero Quesada [16:42], 34, 35, 36.
19. Oficio 4, lib. 1, escribanía Mateo de la Cuadra, f. 176v, Feb. 14, 1511 (APS, 7, 703).
20. Oficio 4, lib. 3, escribanía Manuel Segura. f. end of the leg., Sept. 23, 1506 (APS, 1/177).
21. Oficio 4, lib. 1, escribanía Manuel Segura, f. 493, 496, 499 (1516) (APS, 7, 793).
22. Otte [15:83], 134.
23. Las Casas [2:50], 3, 144–45.
24. Otte [15:83], 133.
25. Las Casas [2:50], 3, 141. "A la mi fé, padre, porque así me lo dieron por destruición, conviene saber que si no los pudiese captivar por paz que los captivase por guerra."
26. Giménez Fernández [2:39], 1, 373.
27. Population statistics are discussed to great effect in Henige [8:12], especially 81.
28. Antonio de Villasante, Andrés de Montemarta, and Diego de Alvarado, who had come with Colón in 1493; Pedro Romero, who seems to have come in 1499; Gonzalo de Ocampo and Juan Mosquera, who had come with Ovando in 1502; Jerónimo de Agüero, Miguel Pasamonte, Lucas Vázquez de Ayllón, and Marcos

de Aguilar, who had all come in Diego Colón's day, as well as merchants, such as Antonio Serrano and Juan de Ampiés, and a few churchmen (Fray Bernardo de Santo Domingo, a Dominican who had come in 1510 with Pedro de Córdoba; and Fray Pedro Mexía, provincial of the Franciscans).

29. Giménez Fernández [2:39], 1, 326ff., 331.
30. Las Casas [2:50], 3, 152.
31. "Desde esta ysla, se arme para ir por ellos a la ysla de cabo verde y tierra de guinea o que esto se pueda hazer por otra cualquiera persona desde esos reinos para los traher acá."
32. Las Casas [2:50], 3, 79.
33. José Antonio Saco, *Historia de la Esclavitud de la Raza Africana en el nuevo mundo,* 4 vols., Havana 1938, 1, 75–78.
34. Giménez Fernández [2:39], 2, 555.
35. AGI, Indif., Gen., leg. 419, lib. 7.
36. Ibid. For Portugal, see Giménez Fernández [2:39], 2, 35, fn 103.
37. Las Casas [2:50], 3, 154.
38. AGI, Justicia, leg. 43, no. 4. See testimony of Antonio Cansino in the *residencia* vs. Zuazo.
39. Las Casas [2:50], 3, 166.
40. It seems that Charles was helped to embark on this journey thanks to a loan of 100,000 florins from King Henry VIII, who was, of course, married to Charles's aunt, Catherine. See Fernández Álvarez [3:51], 1, 50.
41. Summarized in Giménez Fernández [2:39], 1, 359–64.
42. "respecto a la importación de esclavos negros a las Indias y dar licencia para llevarlos a los nuevos pobladores no es conveniente abrir la puerta para ello, y habrá que esperar a la llegada de su alteza."
43. The printing was complete in 1517, but the Pope only gave approval for it to be made available in 1520. The printer was Arnao Guillén de Brocar, publisher of the work of Nebrija who became concerned with the Bible but quarreled with everyone. Cisneros had paid heavily for Hebrew manuscripts. The Latin text was by Juan de Vergara and Diego López de Zúñiga; the Greek by a Cretan, Demetrius Ducas, and Hernán Núñez de Guzmán; the Hebrew was the work of two *conversos,* Pablo Coronel and Alfonso de Zamora.
44. Fernández Álvarez [3:51], 1, 71–78.
45. Zuazo to Cisneros in Muñoz Collection, Real Academia de la Historia, Madrid, qu. Giménez Fernández [2:39], 2, 121, fn 394.
46. This motto had been adopted by Charles as his, striking out the "ne" in front that limited his domain to the world this side of the Pillars of Hercules.
47. Kellenbenz [3:32], 234. Wolf Haller von Hallerstein (1492–1559), after 1531 became treasurer-general to Queen Mary of Hungary. His house in Brussels was at the corner of the modern Place Royale and the Rue de la Régence, the site of the Musée des Beaux-Arts.
48. Laurent Vital, "Relación del primer viaje de Carlos V a España," in J. García Mercadal [2:57], 1, 675–77.
49. Vital [27:48], 678.

50. "Se hacian muy soberbios y entraban por la fuerza en las huertas y en las posadas y maltrataban a los huéspedes, mataban a los hombres por las calles sin tener temor alguno de la justicia y finalmente intentaban todo lo que querían y se salían con ello."
51. Santa Cruz [5:7], 1, 165–7: "inconversable y enemigo de la nación española." The word *inconversable* surely should have a future.
52. Fernández Álvarez, [3:51], 80.
53. Vital [27:48], 699.
54. Giménez Fernández [2:39], 1, 405.

Chapter 28

1. See Bartolomé and Lucile Bennassar, *Valladolid au Siècle d'Or*, Paris 1964, 474–77. For the javelins, see Marcelin Defourneaux, *La vie quotidienne au Siècle d'Or*, Paris 1964, 152.
2. Las Casas [2:50], 3, 167.
3. AGI, Patronato, leg. 170, r. 22, qu. extensively by Giménez Fernández [2:39], 2, 398ff.; he considered the marginalia by Fonseca, etc.
4. The first Spanish edition of *Utopia* was not until 1627.
5. *Utopia*, published in 1516, was published in Basle in 1518.
6. ". . . como el rey era tan nuevo . . . y había cometido todo el gobierno de aquellos reinos a los flamencos sudidichos . . . y ellos no cognosciesen las personas grandes ni chicas y muchas más las cosas tocantes las Indias, como más distantes y menos conocidas."
7. A portrait of Le Sauvage in the Musée des Beaux-Arts, in Brussels, by Bernard van Orley, the court painter to the Archduchess Margaret, shows him considerate, if elderly.
8. Giménez Fernández [2:39], 2, 34.
9. Las Casas [2:50], 3, 168.
10. These included Pánfilo de Narváez, Velázquez's second in command in Cuba; Gonzalo de Guzmán, who had also gone to Cuba, though he still had an *encomienda* in La Española; Gonzalo de Badajoz, who had been in Darien with Nicuesa and then Pedrarias; Cristóbal de Tapia, the ex-*alcaide* of the fortress in Santo Domingo and enemy of Ovando, who was among the earliest settlers in La Española to found a sugar mill, in Vega Real; as well as Sancho de Arango, a *procurador* of Puerto Rico.
11. "los indios no tienen capacidad natural para estar por sí."
12. AGI, Patronato, leg. 173, no. 2, r. 2, doc. 3, f. 5: "sería más la costa que el provecho."
13. "de Castilla vayan o dejen llevar negros a los vecinos."
14. "Si las yslas que oy están pobladas, vuestra alteza permitiesse que se despoblasen de los vezinos sería muy grand pérdida, porque por aventuras están otras yslas y tierras mucho más ricas e mejores que las descubiertas, por descubrir."
15. Bernal Díaz del Castillo [15:45], 86ff. The route home was chosen by the pilot Alaminos, a great specialist in the Gulf of Mexico. Las Casas [2:50], 3, 156.
16. See ch. 34.

17. These ships were the flagship, the *San Sebastián,* another caravel also called the *San Sebastián,* a third called the *Trinidad,* and a brigantine called the *Santiago.* Later the brigantine dropped out and was replaced by the *Santa María de los Remedios.*

18. The detail in the description of Grijalva's journey in Oviedo [2:43], 2, 132 ff., is such that it seems possible he had access to a private account.

19. Las Casas [2:50], 3, 173.

20. And last bishop, too! See Father Raphaël de la Vierge Marie, *Description de la belle église et du couvent royal de Brou, manuscrit* between 1692 and 1696, and between 1711 and 1715, Bibliothèque de la Société d'émulation de l'Ain, Bourg-en-Bresse. Marie Françoise Poiret prints, in her excellent *Le Monastère de Brou,* Paris 2001, 10, a letter of Jan. 1512 from the chief accountant, Étienne Chivillaird, to Gorrevod about his difficulties in satisfying everyone.

21. André Chagny, *Correspondence politique et administrative de Laurent de Gorrevod, 1517–1520,* 2 vols., Lyons 1913, 1, 361.

22. "... ninguna cosa los mata sino la tristeza de spiritu de verse en tanta servidumbre y cautiverio y del mal tratamiento que les hazen, tomando las mujeres y las hijas que lo sienten mucho, y hazerles trabajar demasiado y el comer no en tanta abundancia como fuera menester."

23. "... ytem han dar sus altezas largamente licencia para poder llevar esclavos negros, cada uno quantos quisiere ..."

24. Giménez Fernández [2:39], 2, 424ff.

25. "sea quitar los yndios a Vuestra alteza, y al almirante, y a mí, y a las otras personas que no los han de tener, y a los jueces ..."

26. *CDI,* 34, 279–86, the accuracy of which transcription is discussed by Giménez Fernández [2:39], 2, 139, fn 443.

27. "la mejor tierra del mundo donde nunca hay frio ni calor demasiado, ni que de pena. Siempre verde ... todo se crea; ninguna se muere ... cañaverales de azúcar de grandísimo tamaño."

28. Zuazo's letter is in *CDI,* 1, 292–98.

29. It had also been an Aragonese tradition to discuss business at dinner—as King James I the Conqueror regularly did (see Fernández-Armesto [4:49], 15).

30. Las Casas [2:50], 3, 174.

31. Keniston [26:13], 47; Las Casas [2:50], 3, 170. Conchillos had been dismissed.

32. Keniston [26:13], 33.

33. Las Casas [2:50], 170–71.

34. Francisco López de Gómara, *Anales de Carlos V,* English and Spanish texts intr. by R. B. Merriman, London 1912, 256. "Codicioso y escaso ... holgaría mucho de jugar a la primera y conversación de mugeres."

35. Santa Cruz [26:31], 1, 170; see also *Cortes* [5:53], 4, 260ff.

36. See Fernández Álvarez [17:19], 58.

37. Chabod [26:21], 85.

38. Santa Cruz [26:31], 1, 169.

39. Qu. Giménez Fernández [2:39], 2, 434–45.

40. Las Casas [2:50], 3, 181–82.

41. Las Casas [2:50], 3, 172.

42. This was March 22, 1518.

43. At Calatayud, Charles had had a disconcerting experience. Walking in the street, a laborer had called out: "Shut your mouth, your Highness! The flies around here are very naughty!"

44. For example, the Codex Vindobonensis, an early copy of Cortés's letters to King Charles V.

45. See Antonio Rodríguez Villa, *El emperador Carlos V y su corte, según las cartas de don Martín de Salinas,* Madrid 1903.

46. Chabod [26:21], 86.

47. This was published by Fabié in Appendix 4 of his life of Las Casas. See also Bataillon [22:46], 326–31.

48. Qu. Giménez Fernández [2:39], 2, 444.

49. "Para facilitar el aumento de la mano de obra esclava se preconizaba la libertad para la importación de esclavos negros bozales por mercaderes o por vecinos e incluso la organización de la trata de negros por la corona; y que concede igualmente libertad de importación de esclavos indios de las islas lucayos y de tierra firme, se organizen por la Corona la captura y venta de indios caribes."

50. Giménez Fernández [2:39], 2, 156–59, summarizes.

51. Gil [3:37], 1, 184. A *marco* was a measure of eight ounces.

52. Elliott [1:25], 137.

53. This is the argument of Giménez Fernández [2:39], 2, 209.

54. Charles de Poupet (Popeto) (Laxao), Lord of "Poligni," who had been with Charles VIII at Naples, then moved to support Felipe el Hermoso; he was afterwards with Maximilian and was preceptor of the Archduke Ferdinand. He was one of Charles V's instructors, later in his inner council. He recommended in 1523 that people other than Spaniards should be encouraged to go to the Indies. He became protector of Las Casas by 1520, and "Cavallero de nuestro consejo," supporter of Hernando Cortés's, c. 1522, then ambassador of Charles to Portugal for the wedding with Isabel in 1525.

55. Las Casas [2:50], 3, 187.

56. Las Casas [2:50], 185.

57. Las Casas [2:50], 3, 177.

58. For Gorrevod's ambition, see Giménez Fernández [2:39], 1, 284, and 2, 613ff.; also Georges Scelle, *La Traite négrière aux Indes de Castille,* 2 vols., Paris 1906, 1, 149–50.

59. The grant is in AGI, Indif. Gen., leg. 419, lib. 7, 121; Scelle [28:58], 1, 755, publishes the grant: see Deive [6:36], 235.

60. AGI, Indif. Gen., 419 1.7 of Oct. 21, 1518. In addition to the signatures indicated in the text, there is, following the "*Yo el Rey,*" the sentence "*Señaladas* [signed by] *de Obispo y de Don García de Padilla. . . .*" The *obispo* (bishop) was Fonseca. The most serious study of this contract is by Enrique Otte, "Die Negersklavenlizenz des Laurent de Gorrevod" in *Spanisches Forschungen der Görresgesellschaft, Erste Reihe,* 22, Munster 1965.

61. Chagny [28:21], 1, 123: "je ne sache autre chose digne d'écrire."

62. See Carande [16:36], 2, 85ff.

63. AGI, 46, 6, I, f. 58, qu. Scelle [28:58], 1.

64. Scelle [28:58], 1, 154–56.

65. The complicated affair of the resale of the contract is masterfully handled in Otte's article [28:60].

66. Rozendo Sampaio Garcia, *Aprovisionamiento de esclavos negros na América*, São Paulo 1962, 8–10. The name sometimes appears as Forne, Fornes, sometimes as Fornis.

67. Oficio 15, lib. 2, escribanía Bernal González Vallesillo, f. 507, June 18, 1515. Here we hear how Pedro de Aguilar received from Francisco de Grimaldi and Gaspar Centurión eight pipes of wine from Guadalcanal and four empty skins consigned in the name of Juan de Córdoba to be taken in the *nao Santa María de la Antigua* (APS, 1/1206). In Oficio 15, lib. único, escribanía Bernal González Vallesillo, f. 134, Feb. 7, 1516, Luis de Covarrubias, master of the *San Antón*, and the biscuit maker Luis Fernández obliged themselves to pay Francisco de Grimaldi and Gaspar Centurión 72.5 ducats for what they had provided for the ship to take them to Cuba (APS, 1, 1245).

68. Oficio 15, lib. 2, escribanía Bernal González Valdesillo, f. 230, Aug. 17, 1517. Here Juan and Sebastián de Torres undertake to pay Juan Rodríguez of the vessel *Santa María* 13 ducats to take them to Santo Domingo (APS, 1,144).

69. Las Casas [2:50], 3, 274.

70. AGI, 46, 6, I, doc. 95, doc. 5, qu. Scelle [28:58], 1, 190.

71. *CDI*, 7, 423fn, speaking of the concession.

Chapter 29

1. Manuel Serrano y Sanz, *Las orígenes de la dominación española en las Indias*, Madrid 1918, reissued Barcelona 1991, 580–82. This work includes the author's *Los amigos y protectores aragoneses de Cristóbal Colón* [5:15], which has recently been separately published.

2. As qu. Hanke [16:14], 60.

3. Las Casas [2:50], 3, 189–90.

4. Las Casas [2:50], 3, 191–92. "¿Vos, padre, a qué queréis ir a las Indias siendo tan viejo y tan cansado?" Respondio el buen viejo, "A la mi fe, señor, a morirme luego, y dejar mis hijos en tierra libre y buenaventurada. . . ."

5. Las Casas [2:50], 3, 190.

6. Las Casas [2:50], 3, 191: "por falta que tenga acá, porque cada uno tenemos 100,000 maravedís de hacienda y aún más . . . sino que vamos por dejar nuestros hijos en tierra libre y real." A most surprising statement for the sixteenth century!

7. Las Casas [2:50], 3, 193: "Por Dios," Fonseca said, "que es gran cosa, gran cosa es."

8. Scheurl, *Briefbuch*, Aalen 1562, 2, 109, qu. Headley [17:24], 80. See also Carl Brandi, *Carlos V, vida y fortuna de una personalidad y un Imperio*, Madrid 1937, 47.

9. Cf. Richard Haas's book on the United States in the 1990s, *The Reluctant Sheriff*, New York 1997.

10. *CDI,* 32, 332–53; "not without errors," commented Giménez Fernández [2:39]!

11. Hanke [16:14], 46.

12. Cadenas [22:2], 198.

13. Otte [15:83], 162.

14. *CDI,* 31, 366–68; Las Casas [2:50], 2, 272.

15. Deive [6:36], 157.

16. Sauer [8:5], 203.

17. See Kellenbenz [3:32], 505. The bankers of Augsburg, the Fuggers, helped to procure and market this. Ulrich von Hutten would say that he had been cured, thanks first to Christ, then to the Fuggers.

18. Giménez Fernández [2:39], 2, 638.

19. Giménez Fernández [2:39], 2, 375.

20. Molins lies a few miles west of Barcelona. The modern visitor is hard-pressed to find any sign of a royal presence.

21. These were Fernández de Velasco, the Constable; Fadrique Enríquez, the Admiral; and the dukes of Alba, Béjar, Cardona, Nájera, Escalona, Infantado, and the Marquis of Astorga. The Count of Benavente refused the invitation, saying that "he was very Castilian and so could not be honored by foreign orders."

22. AGI, Patronato 252, r. 3, doc. 1, summarized in Giménez Fernández [2:39], 2, 730.

23. Léon Schick, *Un grand homme d'affaires au début du xvième siècle: Jacob Fugger,* Paris 1957, 170–74.

24. Letter from Valladolid dated April 24, 1523, quoted by Schick [29:23], 161.

25. For confirmation of the role of Margaret, see Kellenbenz [3:32], 77.

26. This elector had returned to him also the manor of Haguenau, which Frederick of Saxony had appropriated during the war of the Bavarian succession.

27. Brandi [29:8], 95; Chabod [26:21], 96.

28. These figures are all rounded. See appended table on p. 484 for details.

29. Elliott [1:25], 137.

30. Giménez Fernández [2:39], 2, 259. Actually, it was not Charlemagne who had divided the empire, but his son, Louis le Débonair.

31. "Porque, señor, tan grandes reinos, y provincias tan diversas, con la monarquía imperial, no se pueden conducir ni gobernar bien sin buen orden y buen consejo, que consisten en la elección de las personas, pues se tiene frecuentemente más carestía de gente que de dinero. Es necesario que Vuestra Majestad [*sic*] tenga más ciudado en proveer que los oficios y beneficios sean honorados con personas virtuosas dignas y suficientes que en querer decorar personas indignas e inhabiles mediante oficios, beneficios y dignidades."

Chapter 30

1. Richard Levene, "Introducción a la historia del derecho indiano," *BRAH,* 1924, 56–57.

2. Juan Manzano y Manzano, *La incorporación de las Indias a la corona de Castilla,* Madrid 1948.

3. Earl Hamilton [3:8], 42. The figure given by Hamilton was 9,153,220 grams.

4. I. A. Wright, "The Commencement of the Cane Sugar Industry in America," *AHR*, 21, 1916, 757–58.

5. Hanke [16:14], 46.

6. Las Casas [2:50], 3, 312.

7. Schäfer [9:19], 1, 35–36, discusses.

8. "¿Cómo, señor, estuvieron ellos tres meses forjándolos y haciéndolos . . . y tengo yo que responder agora en un credo? Demelos . . . cinco horas. . . ."

9. Summarized in Deive [6:36], 173.

10. Otte [15:83], 162.

11. Deive [6:36], 123.

12. Such as the merchants Diego Caballero, Juan Fernández de las Varas, Rodrigo de Bastidas, and Juan Mosquera.

13. Deive [6:36], 17ff.

14. Santo Tomás and San Juan Bautista, on the coast near Higuey; Mejorada, near Cotui, named of course after Prior Figueroa's monastery so loved by the Catholic Kings, and another, unnamed, in La Vega.

15. San Juan de Ortega, in Bonao; Villaviciosa, in La Vega; Santiago, on the River Yaque; Verapaz, in Jaragua—the names as usual echoing well-remembered places in Old Spain.

16. AGI, Justicia, leg. 47, no. 3. Jacome de Castellón was the illegitimate son of Bernardo Castiglione, a merchant of Genoa, and Inés Suárez of Toledo (Otte [15:83], 109, 239; Giménez Fernández [2:39], 2, 1199). He was born in 1492, a *mercader* of Santo Domingo, where he went in 1510, and a brother of Tomás. He was involved with trade in indigenous Indians. He was also involved with *ganaderías* (cattle ranching) and *haciendas*. In 1513, Castellón had been a partner of Diego Caballero, "El Mozo," and Jerónimo Grimaldi, in trading Indian slaves. In 1518 he was still active on the Pearl Coast, mixing evangelization, trade (wine, arms, including swords and even *lombardas*), and forced labor. See Deive [6:36], 157, 374. In 1522, he was captain of an armada of his own to the coast of Cumaná, where he was asked to build a fortress, of which he was named *alcaide* in 1524 and paid 900 pesos. But he continued to live in Santo Domingo and had Andrés de Villacorta as his lieutenant. He carried out numerous journeys for indigenous slaves, so it was appropriate that in 1527, when he obtained a coat of arms, it should have had on it a fortress and four Indians' heads.

17. Antonio Flores, the Governor of La Vega, became chief magistrate of Cubagua, off the Pearl Coast, to prevent breaches of these rules. He was Figueroa's trusted friend. But he turned out to be a brute, appointing friends of his own to important places under him: for example, Juan Martín de Trebejo, a Portuguese muleteer, as *alguacil*, and García González Muriel, *veedor* of a recent armada, as notary (*escribano del juzgado*). Flores's aim was to increase the quantity of both pearls and slaves, not to improve the way that the latter were obtained. But becoming "the determining power in Cubagua" (*papa y rey y alcalde mayor de Cubagua*), and himself benefiting from both businesses, as well as establishing the happy principle that "his lies are worth more than other people's truths," he eventually fled in 1520, being succeeded by Francisco de Vallejo, at a higher salary.

18. Deive [6:36], 235.
19. "No hay mercader que tenga consciencia ni verdad."
20. "Señor, por lo que me toca de las Indias, soy obligado a besar las manos de vuestra señoría."
21. "¿Que sermón os traigo para predicarnos?"
22. "Por cierto señor, días ha que yo deseo oír predicar a vuestra señoría, pero también a vuestra señoría certifico que le tengo aparejados un par de sermones, que si los quisiere oír y bien considerar, que valgan más que los dineros que trae de las Indias. . . ."
23. Las Casas [2:50], 3, 337.
24. Juan de Zúñiga y Avellaneda, born Jan. 17, 1488, son of Pedro de Zúñiga y Velasco, second Count Miranda, to begin with a supporter of Philip I, was in Flanders 1506–17 with a minor post in the royal household. He became *camalengo* to Charles V in 1511, then *camarero*, then Caballero de Santiago, and from 1535 was Philip II's godfather and adviser: *ayo del príncipe*. Always in the confidence of Charles V, who made him ambassador to Portugal after the *comuneros'* war of 1520–21, since many of the leaders of the rebellion took refuge in that country. He was in Portugal (with Laxao) to work on the wedding of the King with Isabel. He was majordomo of Philip II's from 1539. He seemed to be a great friend and supporter of Cobos, but Charles V said he was as jealous of that statesman as he was of the Duke of Alba. Cobos once wrote that "don Juan de Zúñiga is working hard for himself. I do not mean against me, lest I myself become suspect by that comment. He wants complete control, without regard for the loyalty and service of the rest and, to gain that, he does everything he can to make him his only privy councillor, to such a point that his ambition is known. . . . The sternness and rigor with which he brought up the Prince has been turned into sweetness and gentleness, all of it arising from flattery to help him attain his goal" (Cobos to Charles V, Keniston [26:13], 271).
25. Las Casas [2:50], 3, 337–38.
26. Las Casas [2:50], 3, 339.
27. See Fernández Álvarez [17:19], 97–99.
28. "Su majestad manda que habléis si algunas cosas tenéis de las Indias que hablar." Las Casas [2:50], 3, 340.
29. Keniston [26:13], 57.
30. Las Casas [2:50], 3, 242.
31. Las Casas [2:50], 3, 244.
32. Bataillon [26:42], 232.

Chapter 31

1. Qu. Chabod [26:21], 103.
2. There were two Barbarossas: Arudj, assassinated by the Spanish governor of Oran, the Marquis of Gomera, in 1518; and Khayr al-Din, who converted Algiers into the main Turkish pirate base of the Mediterranean. He became Bey of Algiers in 1536.

3. Chabod [26:21], 92.

4. Qu. Headley [17:24], 27.

5. The mother of Louis XIV was Anne of Austria, daughter of Philip III of Spain.

6. Santa Cruz [5:7], 1, 255.

7. We can still see this fine room.

8. See list in Giménez Fernández [2:39], 2, 341.

9. "más rey que otro, porque tiene más y mayores reynos que otro."

10. "el imperio vino a busca a la España . . . Rey de Romanos y emperador."

11. "el fundamento, el amparo y la fuerza de todos los otros" . . . "el huerto de sus placeres, la fortaleza para su defensa, la fuerza para atacar, su tesoro y su espada han de ser los reinos de España." Diario de las sesiones de las Cortes Españolas.

12. Martyr [1:2], 3, 306.

13. This speech was published in Rome by Jacobus Mazochius of Augsburg, and there was a German edition by Martin Landsberg of Leipzig.

14. Ramón Menéndez-Pidal, La Idea Imperial de Carlos V, Buenos Aires 1941, 10.

15. Discussed by Haring [13:87], 20.

16. "Dios creó los indios libres e no subjetos ni obligados a ninguna servidumbre que de aquí adelante se guarde lo que sobre ello está acordado y definido."

17. Las Casas [2:50], 3, 361: "Los Indios generalmente debían ser libres y tractados como libres y traídos a la fe por la vía que Cristo dejó establecida."

18. "la via mahomética." Las Casas [2:50], 3, 361.

19. Las Casas [2:50], 3, 363. Las Casas was probably thinking of people such as Pedro de Rentería, his ex-partner in Arimao, Cuba, but also such persons as Gabriel de Peñalosa, his uncle, Gonzalo de Ocampo, and Juan de Villoria, all of whom had respectable records of humane conduct in the New World.

20. Hanke [16:14], 46.

21. See Genealogy 2 in my Conquest of Mexico [27:15].

22. Ibid.

23. Text of discussions in CDI, 18, 27, also CDI, 12, 458. This is discussed in Silvio Zavala, Las instituciones jurídicas en la conquista de América [8:11], 524ff.

24. Sandoval [26:36], 1, 219.

25. Martyr [1:2], 3, 335.

Chapter 32

1. So says Brandi [29:8], 169, but there is no English source that backs this statement. Where Brandi derived his information about the treasure is unknown. As Professor Scarisbruch, the biographer of Henry VIII, pointed out, he could not have invented the story.

2. Perhaps the picture by Lucas van Leyden known as The Card Players is an impression of Charles negotiating with Wolsey and with his aunt, Margaret, in the center telling her nephew to eschew France? The picture is in the Thyssen Collection, Madrid.

3. There is an account by Alonso de Valdés to Peter Martyr in Martyr [1:2], 3, 93.

4. This account is discussed in my *Conquest of Mexico* [27:15], 536–37. Dürer later made an engraving, *The Reformation in the City,* printed by Poel. Rather remarkably, Dürer does not seem to have made any drawing of what he saw.

5. See Chabod [26:21], 111.

6. Chabod [26:21], 110.

7. Chabod [26:21], 113.

8. Menéndez-Pidal [31:14], 17.

9. Headley [17:24], 35.

10. Sandoval, 2, 123.

11. Pérez [26:34], 53.

12. As Charles Péguy put it: "Tout commence en mystique et se termine en politique."

13. Gil [3:37], 1, 286.

14. See Gil [3:37], 3, 195ff. for Alcázar's life and descendants.

15. Giménez Fernández [2:39], 2, 967, publishes a facsimile of the letter.

16. Gil [3:37], 1, 289.

17. See Cooper [9:19], 2, 1109.

18. See Fernández Álvarez [3:51], chs. 14, 15.

19. The old regime continued on at least one level: thus, on March 23, 1521, after a moment of anxiety lest some mutineers might seek to seize the castle of Triana in Seville, and another such moment lest there might have to be an interruption in the plans of the Inquisition, there was an *auto-de-fe* "in which three men and two women were burned, among whom was Alonso Tello, once an *alcalde ordinario* of the city, as well as Beatriz de Albornoz, "La cochina," a butcher. Two absent men were burned in effigy: Jacques de Valera, once a *continuo real,* and his father, Álvaro Pérez de Rosales, both of whom had gone to Fez, in Morocco, and become Jews (Gil [3:37], 1, 291).

20. Las Casas remarked: "Ad plura teneitur, reverendísima dominatio sua Deo et proximis quia unicuique mandavit Deus de proximo suo"; and Adrian replied, also in Latin, "Ad minus debetis mihi vestras orationes." He added, "Ego iam dicavi me prorsus obsequio et obedientiae vestre, reverendísima dominationis in quo proposito usque ad mortem inclusive perseverabo. . . ."

21. Haring [13:87], 20.

22. Among whom were Blas Fernández, Francisco de Soto, Juan de Vagrumen, Alonso Sánchez, Guillermo de la Rocha, Fernán Martín, Pedro Hernández, Gonzalo Escribano, and Antonio Blas.

23. Pedro Gutiérrez de Santa Clara, *Historia de las Guerras Civiles del Perú,* 6 vols., Madrid 1904–29, 1, 36–40.

24. Las Casas [2:50], 3, 384.

25. Arranz [12:17], 543.

26. George Kubler and Martin Soria, *Art and Architecture in Spain and Portugal and Their American Dominions, 1500–1800,* Harmondsworth 1959, 63; Peter Boyd-Bowman, *Indice geobiográfico de más de 56 mil pobladores de la América Hispánica, 1493–1519,* Mexico 1985, 1, 127. It is a hall church, the north door being

essentially Gothic, the west portal plateresque. Rodrigo Gil de Liendo of Santander was the architect.

27. Las Casas [2:50], 3, 369.
28. *CDI*, 10, 32–9.
29. Las Casas [2:50], 3: "la más preciosa moneda que los indios amaban."
30. Las Casas [2:50], 3, 379.
31. Las Casas [2:50], 3, 386.
32. Oviedo [2:43], 36, ch. 1.
33. Santa Cruz [26:31], 5, 15. Charles would on this occasion remain in Spain for seven years, the longest period he ever spent in the kingdom or anywhere else.
34. Joseph Pérez, *Los comuneros*, Madrid 2001, 137.
35. See Francisco Morales Padrón, *Historia de Sevilla, la ciudad del quinientos*, Seville 1989, 131.

Chapter 33

1. This chapter and the two following ones were difficult for me to write since some time ago I wrote a history of the conquest [27:15]. The present treatment of the civilization of the Mexica depends on the first five chapters of my earlier book, suitably amended to take new discoveries into account.
2. Fr. Angel Garibay, *Historia de la literatura Nahuatl*, 2 vols., Mexico 1953, 1, 90.
3. There are now about fifty such languages in Mexico. For the vexed question of the size of the pre-Columbian population, see Appendix 1 to my *Conquest* ([27:15], 609).
4. I use the word "Mexica" to describe the people of ancient Mexico, not "Aztecs." "Mexica" is how the people concerned spoke of themselves. They may have called themselves "Aztec" at an early stage in their history since they were said to have come from Aztlán, but in the sixteenth century, the usage "Aztec" was unknown and figures in no memoir or chronicle of the era. None of the Spanish conquistadors or chroniclers used the word. "Aztec" was a nineteenth-century usage popularized by the Jesuit Clavijero in his *Historia Antigua de México* and by North Americans, such as Prescott and Bancroft.
5. Ignacio Bernal, *The Olmec World*, Berkeley 1969, 187.
6. Mary Pohl et al., "Olmec Origins of Mesoamerican Writing," *Science*, December 6, 2002.
7. The Olmecs only received their name in 1929 from Marshall Saville, then director of the Museum of the American Indian; they themselves may not have known it.
8. *Scientific American*, March 1977.
9. They had the corbeled vaulting by which two legs of a vault are held together until the space between can be bridged by capstones.
10. The so-called *códices* gained that name from the Spanish conquerors, who thought that the cloth folded together between wooden covers resembled pharmacists' lists of medicines.

11. Perhaps for Mexicans it foreshadowed the dual worship by modern Mexicans of the Virgin of Guadalupe and of Christ.

12. The main square in Salamanca in the sixteenth century was smaller than it is today. Nor is it clear whether any of the conquistadors had been to Venice.

13. "Las dádivas desmedidas, los edificos reales,
Llenos de oro, las vaxillas tan fabridas,
Los enriques y reales del tesoro,
Los jaeces, los cavallos de su gente y atavíos tan sobrados,
¿dónde iremos a buscallos?
¿qué fueron sino rocíos
de los prados?"

                                        Jorge Manrique

14. The fact that maize was known in Italy and in England as "Indian corn" or *gran turco* is an indication as to how confused the men of the European Renaissance were about geography.

15. See above, pages 220–21.

16. There are some in the Museum of Mankind in Vienna.

17. Of which the British Museum has the best collection.

18. Gilberto Freyre, *The Masters and the Slaves,* tr. Harriet de Onis, New York 1968, 183, claims this beneficent product for Brazil.

19. By far the best short account of religion in ancient Mexico is Henry Nicholson, "Religion in Prehispanic Central Mexico," in the *Handbook of Middle American Indians,* vol. 10, Austin 1971.

20. En todas partes está
Tu casa, Dador de la vida,
La estera de flores,
Tejada de flores por mí
Sobre ella te invocan los príncipes.

21. Fr. Diego Durán, *Historia de las indias de la Nueva España,* new ed., 2 vols., Mexico 1867–80, 2, 128.

22. *CDI,* 39, 415: a certain Benito González, a Valencian, said in 1515: "Que el dicho almirante el postrimero viaje que fizo descobrió una tierra dicha Maya. . . ."

23. Fr. Toribio de Motolinía in Joaquín García Icazbalceta, *Colección de documentos para la historia de México,* new ed., 2 vols., Mexico City 1980, 1, 65.

24. Oviedo [2:43], 1, 124.

25. Jorge Klor de Alva, "Martín Ocelotl," in D. G. Sweet and Gary B. Nash (eds.), *Struggle and Survival in Colonial America,* Berkeley, CA, 1981.

26. Martyr [6:34], 241, in a letter to Pope Leo X: "¿Eh, tambien vosotros tenéis libros? ¡Cómo! También vosotros usáis de caracteres con los cuales os entendéis estando ausentes." Possibly this Corrales was Rodrigo de Corrales, from Medina del Campo.

27. Fernando Alvarado Tezozomoc, *Crónica Mexicayotl,* Mexico 1949, 1987, 684ff.

28. Tezozomoc [33:27], 685.

29. Las Casas [2:50], 3, 165.

Chapter 34

1. "Harto amigo mío," says Las Casas [2:50], 3, 156. A fuller description of this voyage can be read in my *Conquest of Mexico,* [27:15], ch. 7.
2. The *Enciclopedia de México,* 7, 3859, says he was born in 1475.
3. Probanza of 1522, 189, in *BAGN,* Mexico 1937, 9, ed. E. O'Gorman.
4. "que viniese con la dicha armada en busca de nueva tierra" (Alaminos in Probanza of 1522).
5. "con tiempo contrario que les dio no pudieron tomar las islas de los Lucayos, do daban, e aportaron en la costa que dicen que es de Yucatán" (Probanza of 1522, 189).
6. For the whole question of "taking possession," see again Morales Padrón [6:19], passim.
7. "Otras tierras en el mundo no se habían descubierto mejores," in Díaz del Castillo [15:45], 1984.
8. Andrés de Monjaraz said in 1522 that "él quería ir a Castilla para hacer saber a sus altezas cómo el habia descubierto la dicha tierra de Yucatán" (Probanza of 1522, 208).
9. A memorial to Antonio Velázquez de Bazán, the heir of Velázquez, shows that Grijalva was indeed his nephew (*CDI,* 10, 82). Again, see ch. 7 of *The Conquest of Mexico* [27:15] for a fuller account.
10. "No traía licencia para poblar, sino para bojar e recatar en la dicha tierra" (Probanza of 1522, 191).
11. Oviedo [2:43], 2, 118–48.
12. I have not yet found Angel Bozal, *El Descubrimiento de Méjico. Una gloria ignorada: Juan de Grijalva,* Madrid 1927.
13. Alaminos recalled "aún delante de este testigo el dicho Diego Velásquez riñó con el dicho Juan de Grijalva" (Probanza of 1522, 232).
14. Martyr [1:2], 3, 325.

Chapter 35

1. "Señor nuestro: te has fatigado, te has dado cansancio: ya a la tierra tú has llegado. Has arribado a tu ciudad: México. . . ." Bernardino de Sahagún, *Historia General de las Cosas de la Nueva España,* vol. 4, ed. Angel María Garibay, Mexico 1981, 108.
2. This countess was a daughter of King Enrique IV's chief minister, Pacheco, and was described by Palencia ([1:19], 38) as *"cruel y corrumpida,"* cruel and corrupt, who kept her son for a time in a narrow well. For these dates, see my *Conquest of Mexico* [27:15]. These connections are explored in a genealogical table on p. 627.
3. Membership was about 3,000, of whom 10 percent usually attended. In 1519, sheep numbered over 3 million. See Klein [3:7].
4. Among those who had been at Salamanca with Cortés was Fray Diego López of Medellín, who said that "había estudiado alguno tiempo en el estudio donde es-

tudiado el dicho don Hernando" ("Audiencia en Truijillo," *BRAH*, 1992, 199). Las Casas testified to his skill in Latin: "Hacia ventaja en ser latino, porque había estudiado leyes en Salamanca y era de ellos bachiller" (Las Casas [2:50], 2, 475). Lucio Marineo Siculo commented: "Deleitaba mucho en la lengua latina" (*De los memorables de España*, Alcalá de Henares, 1530, ff. 208 211 r.).

5. Inés de Paz was an aunt of Cortés's, and he stayed in her house in Salamanca.

6. Cortés shared the mayoralty of Santiago in 1516 with Alonso de Macuelo, in 1517 with Gonzalo de Guzmán, who would become his enemy, and in 1518 with Alonso de Mendoza, who was later his ally (*Residencia vs. Andrés de Duero*, AGI, Justicia, leg. 49, f. 204).

7. See, for a discussion, my *Quién es quién en la conquista de México* [18:35], 77–79. The best edition of Cortés's letters is that of Angel Delgado Gómez, *Cartas de Relación*, Madrid 1993, though the English edition of Anthony Pagden (*Letters from Mexico*, with an introduction by Sir John Elliott, New Haven, CT, 1986) is admirable, too.

8. Instructions to Cortés from Diego Velázquez in José Luís Martínez, *Documentos Cortesianos*, Mexico 1990, 45–57.

9. See my own *Quién es quién en la conquista de México* [18:35].

10. In the *Residencia vs. Velázquez,* several witnesses testified to this effect: for example, Rodrigo de Tamayo, who said: "Este testigo oyó decir al capitán Hernando Cortés cuando yva a conquistar a la Nueva España quel adelantado le avia dado licencia para llevar de esta isla ciertos yndios" (in answer to question 23).

11. See the *Información of Servicios y Méritos* of this individual carried out in Écija on Jan. 7, 1520 (AGI, Patronato, leg. 150, no. 2 r.1). I owe my knowledge of this document to Francisco Morales Padrón.

12. "Y en parte donde el susdicho los mató era casi dos leguas de donde estaba el dicho marqués y su gente, a como el dicho Angel Tinterero vido al dicho Gerónimo Aguilar aun que estaba muy desconocido de ser cristiano según el traje que traya, le conosció en la habla porque le habló" (declaración de Martín López in *Información de Andrés de Rozas*, 1572).

13. For Aguilar's companion, Gonzalo Guerrero, see Bibiano Torres Ramírez, "La odisea de Gonzalo Guerrero en México," in *Congreso* [1:22], 369ff.

14. Sahagún [35:1], 44.

15. See above, ch. 31.

16. "Por el mes de noviembre pasado halló en Sevilla un Portocarrero e Montejo que venían de la tierra nueva que se ha descubierto e que dixeron a este testigo como el dicho Gerónimo de Aguilar hera bibo . . ." (AGI, Patronato, leg. 150, no. 2, r.1).

17. Díaz del Castillo [15:45], 2, 21.

18. Sahagún [35:1], 44.

19. The conversation seems to have occurred in January 1520.

20. See my *Conquest of Mexico* [27:15], 328.

21. See the testimony of witnesses discussed in my *Conquest of Mexico*, 324ff.

22. His grandson said so. See Zavala [8:11], 745.

23. Sir John Elliott so argues in his Introduction to Anthony Pagden's edition of the *Cartas de Relación* of Cortés to Charles V [35:7].

24. Evidence of Jerónimo de Sepúlveda in the *Residencia vs. Velázquez:* "quando fue Pánfilo de Narváez a Yucatán . . . llevaba muchos yndios d'esta ysla las personas que con el yvan que unos dezian que los llevaba con licencia del adelantado e otros syn ella" (question 23).

25. *CDI*, 27, 10: "los que venían, que heran mala xente, vizcaynos . . ."

26. In J. Díaz et al., "La Conquista de Tenochtitlan," *Historia*, 16, ed. Germán Vázquez, Madrid 1988, 191. Aguilar became a Jeronymite in the Escorial after the war and wrote this account to inform his fellow brothers.

27. Cortés's concessions were that Tlaxcala should always have a garrison in Tenochtitlan; that Tlaxcala should be given Cholula; that Tlaxcala should never have to pay tribute to anyone who ruled in Tenochtitlan, including Spain; and that they should share whatever booty there was after the fall of Tenochtitlan. The evidence for this derives from the *Información de Tlaxcala*, 1565, and is discussed by me in *Conquest* [27:15], 737, fn 57. The treaty with the Tlaxcalteca was usually neglected in all histories before my own.

28. See Charles Gibson, *Tlaxcala in the Sixteenth Century,* New Haven, CT, 1952.

29. There were nine separate expeditions to Vera Cruz to assist Cortés after that of Narváez: they were directed by Hernando de Medel, Rodrigo Morejón de Lobera, Juan de Nájera, Francisco de Rosales, Antonio de Carmona, Francisco de Saavedra, Juan Suárez, Julián de Alderete, and Juan de Burgos, as well as some men left over from Ponce de León's last expedition to Florida. For details, see my *Quién es quién* [18:35], passim.

30. For the lives of these individuals, see *Quién es quién* [18:35], 291–94. Córdoba was referred to by both Giménez Fernández [2:39], 2, 963, and Morales Padrón [32:35], 111, as the financier or *financiador* of Cortés, but neither gave evidence to support this. I searched Giménez Fernández's papers in the archive of the Ayuntamiento de Sevilla for evidence of this without success. See also Giménez Fernández's "El Alzamiento de Fernando Cortés según los libros del tesorero de la Casa de la Contración," in *Revista de la Historia de América*, 31, Mexico, 1–58.

31. See, for example, Thomas J. Riedlinger (ed.), *The Sacred Mushroom Seeker*, Portland, OR, 1990, 96.

32. For a discussion of the losses in this war, see my *Conquest* [27:15], 528.

33. Díaz del Castillo [15:45] 1, 97.

34. Díaz del Castillo [15:45] 2, 515.

35. Samuel Purchas, *A Discourse of the Diversity of Letters Used by the Divers Nations of the World,* Hakluyt Posthumous, 20 vols., Glasgow 1905, 1, 486; and Tzvetan Todorov, *La Conquête d'Amérique,* Paris 1982. Greenblatt [4:35], 9, who drew attention to Purchas's comment, talks of "a complex, well-developed and above all mobile technology of power, writing, navigational instruments, ships, warhorses, attack dogs, effective armour, and highly lethal weapons."

36. For a description, see the *Información de Servicios y Méritos of Francisco de Montano* in AGI, Patronato, leg. 54, no. 7, r.1.

37. See my *Conquest* [27:15], 561. See also George Kubler's fine study, *Arquitectura mexicana del siglo XVI*, Mexico 1983, ch. 1.
38. Hernando Cortés [35:7], 450.
39. Martyr wrote on March 7, 1521 [1:2], 4, 143–45.
40. These Investigaciones de Servicios y Méritos were the basis for my *Who's Who in the Conquest of Mexico*, London 2000.

Chapter 36

1. Aranda had married Ana Pérez Cisbón, of a well-known *converso* family. Aranda's daughter Juana married another merchant from Burgos, Fernando de Castro. See Gil [3:37], 3, 518.
2. "¿Y si no halláis estrecho por donde habíes de pasar a la otra mar?" Las Casas [2:50], 3, 175.
3. See Oviedo [2:43], 2, 229; and Antonio Pigafetta, *Primer Viaje Alrededor del Mundo*, ed. Leoncio Carbrero, Madrid 1985, 58, 27. An English tr. is in the Hakluyt Society, no. 52, reprinted 1992. Pigafetta, an Italian from Vicenza but from a Tuscan family, was born between 1480 and 1491. One can see his family's house in Vicenza behind the Basilica, and on it there is the phrase "Il n'est rose sans épine." There is also a villa belonging to the Pigafettas in Agugliaro, near the Villa Saraceno, which is now dilapidated though attractive. The history of that small town shows a large family tree of the Pigafettas. Antonio's father was probably Marco Pigafetta, a cultivated Renaissance man. Antonio himself served in the galleys of the Order of Rhodes against the Turks. He went to Spain in the suite of the nuncio Francesco Chieragati, going first to Barcelona. He applied to join Magellan, "prompted by a craving for experience and glory." Perhaps Magellan, a Knight of Santiago, welcomed Pigafetta as a passenger because he was a Knight of Rhodes.
4. Morison [4:42], 302, suggests that another map had been made by Johannes Schöner of Nuremberg.
5. Solís's instructions are in *CDI*, 39, 325, 327.
6. Las Casas [2:50], 3, 105.
7. Cadenas [22:2], 107–8.
8. See *CDI*, 22, 46–52, 65.
9. See Oviedo [2:43], 2, 229; and Pigafetta [36:3], xxix. Also Oviedo [2:43], 2, 217.
10. Letter of Sept. 28, 1518, cit. in Pigafetta [36:3].
11. Navarrete [4:38], 421ff.
12. See a collective work, *A viagem de Fernão de Magalhães e a questão das Molucas*, Lisbon 1975. But much of the material can be found in Navarrete [4:38], 2, 417ff.
13. Morison implies he was illegitimate: [4:42], 338.
14. Pigafetta [36:3], iii.
15. Oviedo [2:43], 2, 237, said that he was chief pilot.
16. 594,790 ms. on wine, 564,188 ms. on armaments including gunpowder. I am grateful to Mauricio González for these figures.
17. Navarrete [4:38], 2, 415f.

18. Navarrete [4:38], 2, 502f. Earl Hamilton [3:8], 45. Haro was later a factor of the Fuggers in Spain, for which see Kellenbenz [3:32] 43, 59, etc.
19. Electric light sometimes seen on the masts of ships before or after a storm.
20. Paul Gaffarel, *Histoire du Brésil français au seizième siècle,* Paris 1878, cit. John Hemming, *Red Gold,* London 1978, 17.
21. *The Essays of Michel de Montaigne,* tr. M. A. Screech, London 1987, "On the Cannibals," 240.
22. See Hemming [36:20], 487.
23. Martyr [6:34], 2, 353.
24. This story of the rebellion of San Julián derives from Navarrete, *Historia de Juan Sebastián Elcano,* in Manuel Walls y Merino, *Primer Viaje Alrededor del Mundo . . . ,* Madrid 1899. Elcano's own account can be seen in Navarrete [4:38], 2, 520f., 580f.
25. The best secondary description is that of Morison [4:42], 380ff.
26. The journey was similar to that taken by Bougainville in 1767–68.
27. Pigafetta [36:3], 94.
28. Pigafetta [36:3], 111; Navarrete [4:38], 2, 447.
29. Oviedo [2:43], 2, 223.
30. Pigafetta [36:3], 102.
31. Las Casas [2:50], 3, 175.
32. Elcano gave replies to a detailed questionnaire about the journey that can be seen in Navarrete [4:38], 2, 581ff.
33. Pigafetta [36:3], 161.
34. This is also from the records of Mauricio González.

Chapter 37

1. "Otro nuevo mundo de oro fecho para él, pues antes de nuestras días nunca fue nascido." The speech is to be seen in the record of the Cortes, *Cortes de los Antiguos Reinos de León y Castilla* [5:53], 4, 285ff. Fernández Álvarez [17:19], 19, discusses.
2. See ch. 4.
3. Galíndez de Carvajal [2:10].
4. *Amadís de Gaula* [5:5], 1, 506.
5. Las Casas [2:50], 1, 338: the phrase was ". . . constituyó y cría los dichos Católicos Reyes y a sus sucesores de Castilla y León, príncipes y reinos de todas estas Indias, islas y tierras firmes, descubiertas y por descubrir . . ."
6. Qu. Edwards [2:25], 223.
7. Qu. Liss [2:42], 308.
8. See Menéndez Pidal [5:40].
9. For Ruiz de la Mota, see John Schwaller, "Tres familias mexicanas del siglo XVI," in *Historia Mexicana* 122 (1981), 178. He does not mention any *converso* blood in the family.
10. Cortés [35:7], 161: "porque he deseado que Vuestra Alteza supiese las cosas desta tierra, que son tantas y tales que como ya en la otra relación escribí, se puede in-

titular de nuevo emperador della y con título y no menos mérito que el de Alemaña que por la gracia de Dios Vuestra Sacra Majestad posee. . . ."

11. Cortés [35:7], 160.

12. Cortés added the following, in his fourth letter [35:7], to show that he had not forgotten his proposal: "Creo que con hacer yo esto, no le quedará a vuestra excelsitud más que hacer para ser monarca del mundo." In his fifth letter, Cortés speaks of Charles V as the Emperor "en la tierra esta . . . a quien el universo por providencia divina obedesce y sirve" (Ibid., 143).

13. For a discussion, see Antonio Muro Orejón, "El Problema de los Reinos Indianos," in *AEA,* 27, 45–56.

14. This was stressed by R. B. Merriman in *The Rise of the Spanish Empire,* 4 vols., New York 1918–38, 2, 221.

15. See, for example, Quentin Skinner, *Visions of Politics,* vol. 2: *Renaissance Virtues,* Cambridge 2002.

16. E. G. Thomazi, *Les flottes d'or,* Paris 1956.

17. See my *Conquest* [27:15], 569.

18. Fernand Braudel cit. *Sevilla, Siglo XVI,* ed. Carlos Martínez Shaw, Madrid 1993, 115.

Chapter 38

1.   "De los álamos vengo, madre,
        De ver cómo los menea el aire.
        De los álamos de Sevilla,
        De ver mi linda amiga,
        De los álamos vengo, madre,
        De ver cómo los menea el aire."
                        Villancico, c. 1500

2. Cit. Martínez Shaw [37:18], 14.

3. "Hércules me edificó / Julio Cesar me cercó de muros y torres altas / y el rey santo me ganó con Garci Pérez de Vargas."

4. Cit. Morales Padrón [32:35], 42. Antoine de Lalaing noted when he was in Seville with the Archduke Philip in 1501 that the streets were "all bricked" (García Mercadal [2:57], 1, 473).

5. For the resettlement, see Julio González, *Repartimiento de Sevilla,* Madrid 1951, new ed., Seville 1993.

6. "madres de la nueva Castilla que era Andalucia."

7. See Ladero Quesada [3:23], chs. 1 and 2.

8. In 1516, Dr. Juan Calvete, then *juez de residencia,* wrote to Cisneros saying that "en este cabildo . . . los unos siguían en todo lo que ofrecía la voluntad del Duque e Duquesa de Medina Cidonia y del asistente Juan de Silva . . . y la otra parte de regidores y veintecuatros . . . estauan en favor del Duque de Arcos. . . ."

9. See Lalaing in García Mercadal [2:57], *loc. cit.,* for an impression.

10. The gates were De la Carne (previously De Minoar, near which there was a *matadero* outside); Jerez; Carbón; Postigo de Azacanes; Puerta del Aceite; Arenal

(near which was the *almacén de sal*); Triana (one of the three gates through which wheat and barley could enter); Puerta de Goles (the word is a derivation of "Hercules"), afterward Puerto Real; Puerta de San Juan (or del Ingenio); Bib-Ragel (Barqueta or Almenilla); Macarena (Bab Maquarana, a wheat gate); Córdoba; Puerto del Sol (Bib Afar); Puerta Osario; and Carmona (a wheat gate; but also where the water from Los Caños de Carmona entered).

11. Jaime Esclava Galán in Martínez Shaw [37:18], 29.

12. Mena [24:23], 236.

13. See Julián B. Ruiz Rivera y Manuela and Cristina García Bernal, *Cargadores a Indias*, Madrid 1992, ch. 1.

14. These are the figures of Huguette and Pierre Chaunu [16:28], 6 (1).

15. Otte [16:38], 124.

16. Mena [24:23] published how the chaplain to Dr. Matienzo, together with Benito de Villoria and Juan Ponce, went to Villaba del Alcor on the way to Huelva and spent thirty-eight days there buying five hundred casks of wine from the *vinateros* of the place, coming back to Seville partly by *carretas*, partly by river.

17. Morales Padrón [32:35], 41.

18. AGI, Mexico, e.g. 203, no. 2. He was "un amigo e persona muy piadosa del dicho don Hernando."

19. A belfry of another one hundred feet was added by Fernando Ruiz in 1568.

20. See the map in M. González Jiménez, *Propriedades y rentas territoriales*, reproduced in Miguel Ángel Ladero Quesada, *Andalucía en torno a 1492*, Madrid 1992, 44.

21. Navagero, in García Mercadal [2:57], 1, 849.

22. See the beautiful volume *Historia de la Cartuja de Sevilla*, Madrid 1992.

23. See Consuelo Varela's essay in [38:22]. Gorricio was from a family from Novara, in northern Italy, and died in 1515.

24. For example, Los Negritos, studied so successfully by Isidoro Moreno. See his *La Antigua Hermandad de los Negros de Sevilla*, Seville 1997. The Cofradía de los Negros was founded in the 1390s by Archbishop Gonzalo Mena y Roelas.

25. See Martínez Shaw's description in his essay "Que la fête commence!" in his *Sevilla* [37:18], 179–80.

26. Zúñiga cit. Carlos Álvarez Santaló, *Le diable au corps*, in Martínez Shaw [37:18], 149.

27. *CDI*, 27, 333, and other evidence cited in Thomas [27:15], 680, n. 80.

28. Ladero Quesada [6:1] thinks 40,000 "at the end of the Middle Ages," cf. Gil [3:37], 1, 21.

29. See María Teresa López Díaz, *Famines, pestes et inondations*, in Martínez Shaw [37:18], 131.

30. Bernáldez [3:2].

31. See Michel Cavillac, in Martínez Shaw [37:18], 124.

32. Four hundred thirty-seven to be precise. There were among them 11 Centuriones, 12 Gentiles, 14 Gustinianis, 14 Sopranises, 16 Salvagos, 17 Piñelos, 19 Dorias, 26 Cattaneos, and no less than 28 Spinolas. But don't forget that these were trade surnames, not necessarily family names. Rice and sugar were among the prod-

ucts in which they had a quasi-monopoly; in respect to the former, for example, it was imported from Valencia, and of forty-two sales recorded, only two were not managed by Genoese.

33. See Verlinden's *L'Esclavage dans l'Europe médiévale,* vol. 1, Bruges 1955.

34. For the Alcázar family, see Ruth Pike, *Linajudos and Conversos in Seville,* New York 2000, 122.

35. Gil [3:37], 2, 104–5.

36. Gil [3:37], 1, 258.

37. Gil [3:37], 1, 261; and 4, 104.

38. Had the sin of Álvaro been purged by the contribution to the church of his son, Bartolomé del Río, who had been a success at the Vatican under both Julius II and Leo X and who had become Bishop of Scala in Rome? Not perhaps as yet— though he later undertook the building of the Capilla de Scala in the cathedral in Seville to make amends.

39. Otte [16:38], 29.

40. Otte [16:38] 30. An *arroba* was, as far as olive oil was concerned, twenty-six liters.

41. Otte [16:38], 35.

42. Otte [16:38], 38–39.

43. See Garrido's *Información de Servicios y Méritos.*

44. Oviedo [2:43] has a good description of the effect on the *naturales* of Yucatan.

45. Otte [16:38], 43; Gil [3:37], 4, 258 and 301.

46. Along with other well-known Genovese such as Giovanni Tomasso Spinola, Bartolomeo Negroni, Gerónimo Salvago, and, above all, Melchor Centurione.

47. Marco Cattaneo, Francesco Pinello, Jacopo Grimaldi, and Tomasso de Morteo, alongside Rondinelli.

48. Those mostly concerned were Antonio Sopranis, Silvestre Vento, Leonardo Cattaneo, Lorenzo Pinello, Luca Battista Adorno, Franco Leardo, Jacopo and Gerónimo Grimaldi, Gerónimo Brignole, Niccolo Grimaldi, Melchor Grimaldi, and Gaspar Imperiale. But there were also the Sienese Gerónimo Buonseni and the Burgalés Alonso de Briones and Francisco de Lugo (Otte [16:38], 155–56).

49. See Iris Origo, *The Merchant of Prato,* London 1957, 85, 91.

50. The list of those who dealt in camlet can be seen in Otte [16:38], 160.

51. See Irving Leonard [3:34], 96 and passim.

52. Navagero, in García Mercadal [2:57], 1, 851.

53. General André Beaufre, *Le drame de 1940,* Paris 1970, 48.

54. "¡Oh! con qué afrentas y bofetadas atormenta nuestros tiempos la Fortuna!" wrote Martyr [1:2], 4, 121.

55. *Fortuna* is no. 5 in the series and can easily be seen in the *Catálogo de Tapices del Patrimonio Nacional,* Madrid 1986, 40.

Index

About the Author

HUGH THOMAS studied history at Cambridge and Paris. His career has encompassed both America and Europe, and history and politics, as a professor at New York and Boston Universities and as chairman of the Centre for Policy Studies in London. He was awarded a peerage in 1981. Hugh Thomas is the author of *The Spanish Civil War*, which won the Somerset Maugham Prize; *Cuba: The Pursuit of Freedom; An Unfinished History of the World*, which won the National Book Award for History; *Armed Truce: The Beginnings of the Cold War; The Conquest of Mexico;* and *The Slave Trade.*

About the Type

This book was set in Minion, a 1990 Adobe Originals typeface by Robert Slimbach. Minion is inspired by classic old-style typefaces of the late Renaissance, a period of elegant, beautiful, and highly readable type designs. Created primarily for text setting, Minion combines the aesthetic and functional qualities that make text type highly readable with the versatility of digital technology.